W. W. COTTERMAN

Information Processing Management

To Ruth, Eric, and Dad
for making this project a reality

Information Processing Management

Ralph A. Szweda, CDE

**PROFESSOR,
DATA PROCESSING SCIENCES,
MONROE COMMUNITY COLLEGE**

AUERBACH® publishers

princeton
philadelphia
new york
london

Library of Congress Catalog Card Number: 71-171055
International Standard Book Number: 0-87769-102-9

First Printing

Printed in the United States of America

Contents

Introduction

Research studies clearly indicate the perpetually demanding nature of the data processing manager's job. He must integrate management principles and practices with his tools to prevent or minimize such problems as poor utilization of manpower and hardware, ineffective or nonexistent documentation, and lack of management controls. He must be a combination administrator and technician, with administrative proficiency outranking technical ability, for he cannot allow himself to become overly enamored of the technological side of his job. Instead, he must develop and direct the technological skills of his subordinates in order to harness the power and potential of data processing and respond to the needs of the entire organization. To cope with these requirements, the data processing manager must successfully apply management functions to the available resources.

This book is designed to provide the reader with a knowledge of management principles and their application to the activities of the data processing organization. It is not intended to cover all management principles, nor does it pretend to offer answers to all problems encountered by the data processing administrator or manager.

The first three chapters provide the foundation of the book. They are concerned with those management principles that most directly affect the data processing function. Subsequently, the interaction of these principles may be viewed in the various tasks and functions performed by the data processing administrator or manager. These chapters stress the interaction required between the executive committee and other functional activities that are affected.

Chapters 4 to 9 begin the discussion of the tools and practices used by the data processing manager in managing his function. The principles discussed in the first three chapters are interrelated with the subjects discussed in these chapters.

Chapter 1 discusses the management process as it affects the data processing function. The chapter considers the role of objectives in the management process—their determination, definition, measurement, and attainment—then concentrates on what a manager must do to keep his function working purposefully and harmoniously to achieve the best possible results. The concluding portion of the chapter is concerned with the manager's role in problem-solving, in which he must establish a feedback apparatus for the detection, identification, and correction of problems.

Chapter 2 is concerned with the development of a structural organization for the data processing function. The manager must develop, direct, and control an operating environment that will make optimal use of the available resources and interact properly with other functions affecting data processing activity. Discussed in this chapter are such subjects as mono-functional and multifunctional servicing, business and scientific structures, line-staff relationships, closed- and open-shop programming structures, and project management.

Chapter 3 concentrates on the human resources aspect of data processing. Such topics as job descriptions, analyses, and factors; personnel recruitment, selection, and training; and performance appraisal are discussed.

Chapter 4 discusses the use of standards in the management process. This subject is given considerable attention because the availability or lack of standards can improve or minimize the operational effectiveness of data processing. The extensiveness of the subject requires dividing the standards topic into two chapters. Chapter 4 is concerned primarily with documentation standards, whereas Chapter 6 discusses performance standards. In Chapter 4 we discuss such topics as documentation guidelines, standards for the various data processing functions, documentation control, and record management.

Chapter 5 is concerned with the physical environment in which the data processing activity must operate. The manager must select an operating environment that enhances the productivity as well as the well-being and efficiency of his personnel. Included in this chapter are such topics as the objectives of layout planning, site evaluation, and planning considerations.

Chapter 6 is concerned with scheduling a major problem for the data processing manager. To meet the varied requirements of scheduling, the manager must develop a plan that will enable him to make the best use of his resources. The plan will be based on a number of performance standards, which are discussed in this chapter. Included are scheduling factors, factors affecting each specific functional activity, and the development of a schedule.

Chapter 7 is concerned with the qualitative aspects of the management process. Quality controls are necessary to ensure procedural and mathematical accuracy during the information-processing cycle. This chapter provides an in-depth discussion of the various types of controls available to the data processing manager.

A data processing manager is constantly being called on to give a cost/benefit justification for a new system, program, or approach. To facilitate this justification, he uses a survey and initiates feasibility studies. In addition to discussing these two topics, Chapter 8 also considers how the executive committee should evaluate the recommendations of the feasibility study.

The approved system, program, or approach must subsequently be implemented. For instance, the manager must decide if the project will be developed and implemented by his own staff or by an external vendor. If it is to be done by a vendor, vendor specifications must be developed to meet the organization's requirements. Chapter 9 discusses the methods for validating a vendor's proposal, the negotiation of the contract, and the approaches to conversion and implementation.

Each chapter includes a case study and review questions.

1

The Management Process

INTRODUCTION

Management is an activity that is evident in all organizations, irrespective of whether they are industrial, commercial, governmental, educational, professional, or religious. Its existence becomes more meaningful to us when we consider that it is management that is responsible for the efforts and achievements of each organization.

As an activity, management within any one organization may be strongly influenced by the organization's stockholders (or members), employees, competitors, and public. To maintain an effective level of harmony among all of these groups ranks as a most difficult management task.

Management Defined

Management is an activity that strives to accomplish a single goal or series of goals through the effective application of available manpower, machines, money, and materials. The term "management" should be regarded as an activity rather than as the managerial personnel within an organization. Such personnel should be described by the general term "managers." Managers are the people who are responsible for operation of the organization.

1

What Does a Manager Do?

A manager is responsible for the application of the five management functions—planning, organizing, coordinating, directing, and controlling—to an operation or activity. In this role he formulates the proper mix of managerial efforts by raising certain basic questions regarding the meaning and purpose of his activity (see Figure 1.1). As he develops the answers to these questions he begins to execute the management process. Managers are the administrators and supervisors, at all levels of an organization, who make things happen through the efforts of their subordinates. A manager can be the chief administrator, manager of data processing, director of information services, systems and procedures manager, supervisor of EAM operations, data control section supervisor, and so on.

The first two of the six basic questions involve knowing *what* is to be done and *why* it is to be done; these questions must be answered before starting on any planning of objectives or defining of specific goals. The third question is concerned with the *how* of the operation; this means determining the optimal application of the available resources—of manpower, materials, money, and machines. The fourth question is *who* will actually do the work; here the personnel requirements must be determined. Logically we now move on to the fifth question, of *when* will the work be done; this implies the necessity of a schedule for all related events. The final and most important basic question is *where*. (It should be realized that this deals with the setting of an operation or activity in the organizational environment, not with the room location in which the goal must be accomplished.) To answer this basic question involving where, the manager must determine how other organizational activities effect and relate to his own objective. For example, he has to gauge the contribution, to be made by these activities, the type of communications that needs to be established and maintained, and their demands on the services of the activity?

In order for the manager to successfully answer each of the six basic questions in management, he must be capable of envisioning the total operation and its interrelated activities. It is not enough for him simply to display professional technical competence in the management of an information processing activity. The information processing manager also has to have the ability to apply the management functions to the development and maintenance of an operationally effective activity.

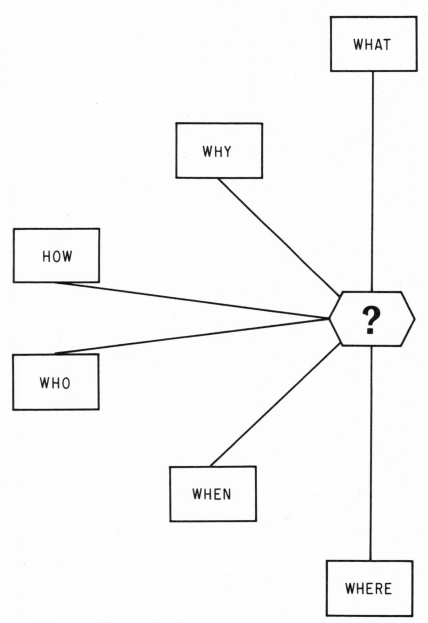

Figure 1.1. Basic Questions in Management

Approaches to Management Activity

There are two approaches to management activity within an organization. These are the dynamic approach and the static approach.

Using the dynamic approach, the manager evaluates each problem or situation in its own setting to develop a relevant goal-attainment plan. He applies a realistic attitude to the existing situation, to the resources available, and to his possible courses of action. This enables him to design, develop, and direct an operationally effective activity. Such an approach provides for the evaluation of results and their comparison with the desired goals, as well as for the realignment or adjustment of activities as needed in order to achieve the objective.

This approach lacks standard solutions and patterns applicable to a situation or problem, so that many managers tend to shy away from the dynamic approach. Another reason why a manager may be unenthusiastic about this approach is based on the fact that progress must be repeatedly evaluated in terms of the desired end result, time schedule, and output quality. And this, in turn, means that the manager must have preestablished some schedule of expected results against which he can compare the actual progress of the activity. It is this need for constant monitoring that can dampen a manager's enthusiasm for the dynamic approach. Nevertheless, any criticism of the dynamic approach is valid only if a manager is unable to apply the management functions that are an integral part of this approach. The manager willing and able to deal with change is the manager who applies the dynamic approach to managerial activity.

Figure 1.2 illustrates the dynamic approach. It is clear that after the objective has been defined and the plan of action implemented, the progress of the operation is monitored and evaluated. The monitoring process is a continuous one. The evaluation process involves comparing the actual results with the planned ones at preestablished points, so that some measurement of progress can be made. If a deviation is found at any such point, the manager must then select the best course of action to ensure that the operation will continue to move toward the desired end result.

The static approach is simpler than the dynamic approach because it places each situation in an ideal environment. This doctrinal approach to management is based on the belief that all situations and problems are similar in nature, and that all work either flows logically in a straight

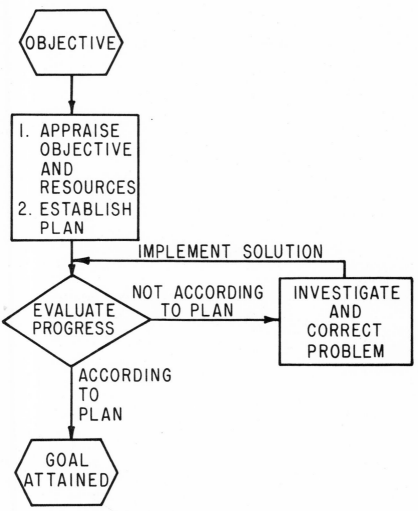

Figure 1.2. Dynamic Approach to Management

line or can be arranged to operate in such a pattern. Consequently, it utilizes solutions that have already been developed in other situations and in response to other problems.

The static approach includes no provision for monitoring progress because no acceptable norms or deviation parameters are established during the planning stage of the management process. This lack of monitoring simplifies the controlling function because goal attainment

Figure 1.3. Static Approach to Management

in the static approach is dependent upon a set of rules or procedures. In some cases, as a consequence of the absence of any norms or parameters, the end result produced may turn out to be a forced happening rather than the desired objective. This is because rules and procedures that ignore the question of "where"—the setting in which the actual operation will be executed—tend to produce an end result unaffected by the implementation of the original plan. Unfortunately, this may not be detected until the process has been terminated.

The static approach is a very orderly one. It is good to use if the manager is unable to develop a capability for realistic judgment in evaluating a situation or problem. It is also the better technique to use if the manager is unable to react quickly to any unexpected condition that may arise during the process.

Figure 1.3 illustrates the static approach. The objective is defined, and then the plan is implemented according to a set of standardized rules and procedures believed to be applicable to all situations. It is clear that, in the process, there is no monitoring or evaluation of progress or interim results.

A manager's decision to apply either the static or the dynamic approach will be influenced by his educational background, training, and outlook. An immediate superior's attitude may also temper the decision. Managing an operation or activity requires a positive approach to a problem or situation, as well as to the resources available, in order to achieve a desired goal. Therefore, an operationally effective manager must know what is happening, be willing to evaluate his operation, and be able to interrupt it at any point or step to implement necessary corrections.

The Role of Objectives in Management

Every managerial action should be geared to the achievement of a desired goal. However, before any effort is expended on goal attainment, the manager should know and understand the specific purpose of the objective and why he is striving to achieve it. Subsequently he must determine the scope of the objective not only in relation to the total concept of his responsibility, but also in terms of its relative importance to the overall organization. Consequently, if it seems that the proposed objective will have an unfavorable effect on the organization's current policies and plans, the manager will have to either restate the original objective or find an alternative objective. An information-processing organization is frequently concerned with evaluating the effects of objectives on such projects as feasibility studies, operating schedules, and new or existing systems and programs.

Having completed his preliminary determinations, the manager is in a position to substantively and effectively define the general or broad objective. What happens when he does that is illustrated in Figure 1.4. The broad objective in this example is to establish a statistical quality control system. In order to develop such a system, the manager has to identify and define the major steps leading to this goal. These major steps thereby become the specific objectives, each of which then has to be broken down into the required detailed steps (as indicated in the example). The specific objectives, then, are the interim goals that have to be met in order to achieve fulfillment of the broad objective.

In situations requiring such specific objectives, the manager must determine the interdependence of these steps and must assign a priority to each of them. These actions enable him to establish a hierarchy of objectives, which is based on the supposition that achievement of some specific goals depends on the successful attainment of others. In addition, the manager must be able to integrate all of these specific objectives so as to achieve a basic level of effectiveness in each and every one of them.

There are no hard and fast rules that can be routinely followed in order to define an objective or to determine the completeness of such a definition. Each manager has to decide for himself about the accuracy of his definition. He should not expect to follow a pattern that had been used for some other situation, problem, or organization. Rather, he must develop his own skills, through being able to realistically and thoroughly appraise, identify, and interpret both the broad and specific objectives. He should not be discouraged if, as a beginner, he has some difficulty in defining an objective, for accuracy comes with a manager's growth in experience, especially in applying the management functions.

The Broad Objective	The Specific Objectives
	1. Initiate development of System
	a. Analyze requirements
	b. Design system
	2. Establish Equipment Requirements
	a. Evaluate existing equipment
	b. Determine equipment requirements
	c. Prepare vendor specifications
	d. Evaluate vendor proposals
	3. Design Forms
	a. Prepare form layouts
	b. Place orders with vendors
	4. Select and Train Personnel
	a. Evaluate personnel resources
	b. Recruit personnel
	c. Select personnel
	d. Train personnel
TO	5. Implement Conversion
ESTABLISH	a. Convert files
A STATISTICAL	b. Convert data records
QUALITY CONTROL	c. Establish controls
SYSTEM	
	6. Perform Systems Test
	a. Debug computer programs
	b. Conduct parallel test
	c. Evaluate results
	d. Modify plan, if necessary
	7. Implement New System
	a. Conduct orientation seminars
	b. Train users
	c. Complete documentation
	d. Cutover to new system
	8. Perform Follow-up Evaluation
	a. Compare actual versus planned results
	b. Modify system if and as necessary

Figure 1.4   Example of Broad and Specific Objectives

Review Questions: Group 1A

1. Define the term "management."
2. How would you describe the role of a manager?
3. If you were the manager of an information-processing activity, why would you choose the dynamic approach to management and not the static approach?
4. Under what conditions would you, as a manager, decide against using the dynamic approach in management activity?
5. Why is a complete understanding of an objective regarded as an important part of the management process?

THE PHASES AND FUNCTIONS OF MANAGEMENT

Management activity in every operation is divided into two distinct phases. These are the pre-executory phase and the executory phase.

The pre-executory phase is activated after the manager has clearly defined the objective. It is during this phase of management activity that the manager initiates the preliminary proceedings necessary to implement the steps toward achievement of the desired goal. These proceedings are three of the five basic management functions: planning, organizing, and coordinating.

One of the manager's first steps in the pre-executory phase is to communicate the broad and specific objectives to his subordinates, as well as to any other people who may be affected by the operation. In addition, he is responsible for selecting the best course of action and establishing a network of interdependent procedures. The results of the manager's preparatory planning, organizing, and coordinating efforts will be made operational during the executory phase of management.

In the second phase of management activity, the executory phase, the manager oversees the implementation of the prepared plan of action in order to achieve the desired objective. In doing this, he performs the remaining two basic management functions: directing and controlling. With the assistance and cooperation of his subordinates, he activates all resources, and guides them and keeps them flowing into the goal-attainment pattern.

Although there is an imaginary boundary between the pre-executory and the executory phases of management activity, the manager should be ready at all times to re-plan, reorganize, and re-coordinate in order to maintain the operation on course.

Figure 1.5 illustrates the pre-executory and executory phases of management activity. It also shows how these phases relate to the five basic management functions.

The Pre-Executory Phase

After the objective has been defined, the manager turns his attention to the steps that will enable him to accomplish the objective. Although it is conceivable that some objectives can be attained with little or no pre-planning effort by the manager, it is unlikely that he would receive many if any such assignments. Therefore, the manager responsible for achieving a certain objective can expect to use the basic management functions of planning, organizing, and coordinating.

The Planning Function

Planning may be defined as the technique used by the manager to design and develop a functional operation. It is the foundation from which all future management activity will be generated. During the planning process, the manager defines the broad objectives, formulates the specific objectives, visualizes how the operation will function and how the operation will affect the entire organization.

UNDERSTANDING THE OBJECTIVE. The manager's first step in any planning activity is to successfully interpret his assignment. In addition to defining the broad objective, he has to determine the specific objectives and their relationship to one another. This knowledge will enable the manager to ascertain the resources he will require and to decide whether or not the broad objective is indeed attainable. Having formulated the specific objectives, the manager must identify the necessary task to be performed and the interdependency required of each to achieve the desired goals.

1. *Evaluating the Situation.* In evaluating the situation, the manager resolves or answers three basic questions. These are:
   a) What is currently being done?
   b) What is the span of time involved?
   c) What is the objective's relationship to the organization?
   a) What is Currently Being Done? It is necessary for the manager to

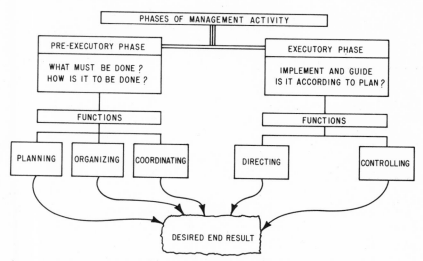

Figure 1.5. The Phases and Functions of Management Activity

study what is currently being done because the existing situation or operation is already accomplishing certain objectives. These objectives must be compared with the proposed ones to determine whether the effect of realizing the new goals will result in the same problem-riddled situation or whether it will alleviate the condition. This is a most difficult task for the manager because very often the effect is not evident until a planned activity has been initiated or completed. A manager must have the foresight to analyze the past, present, and future and consequently ascertain the probable effectiveness of the objective.

The manager also faces a dilemma when he evaluates an objective for a proposed operation. The proposal has been made to either alleviate an existing problem or to avoid any possible future problems.

Every objective affects the overall organizational structure in which a manager must operate. Therefore, the manager has to determine the extent to which other elements of the organization will be involved. After he ascertains which organizational groups will have an influence on the end result, he determines the degree and extent of their contribution to accomplishment of that desired result. The difficult aspect of the manager's task here is that he must communicate with all levels of the organization as fairly and objectively as possible.

Company policies and procedures also affect the setting of a situation. Consequently, the manager needs to establish how they relate to his operation because they are responsible for the conduct of all operations within the organization.

The manager's appraisal of the current situation makes him aware of the existing organizational structure, the role of the groups within it, the existing policies and procedures, and the organizational resources that are available to him. This knowledge gives the manager an understanding of the kind of system he must design and develop in order to achieve the desired goal.

b) What Is the Span of Time Involved? In planning, a manager becomes involved in a span of time which may range from a short-term period to a relatively long-term period. He has to consider the time element because he has the responsibility for developing an overall schedule for the proposed plan, as well as a detailed one for the sequence of operations.

Plans for the immediate future or for a period of time within two years of the present are regarded as short-term plans. Many data processing activities fall within this time interval. Such activities as processing one-time reports or preparing holiday or summer-vacation schedules are typical examples of short-term planning.

In contrast, such important activities as the design and development of a new system or the conversion to new computer hardware systems require long-term planning. This kind of planning is concerned with a time interval that begins about two years from the present and extends to an indeterminable date in the future. However, the manager has to deal with immediate as well as future goals within this framework. This is why he needs to have the capability to execute short-term objectives within the context of a long-term plan. To do this successfully, he has to learn to adjust the schedule in response to changes that may occur in any of the immediate, intermediate, or future objectives. The manager quickly discovers that it is easier to consider short-term planning than long-range planning. This is because although all kinds of planning can be influenced by changes in hardware, software, organizational goals, or business conditions, the effects of such changes can be measured and anticipated much more accurately on a short-term basis. Consequently there is a tendency for the manager to overemphasize immediate goals at the expense of the development of adequate long-range objectives. The manager must integrate the short-term and long-term goals into a plan in which the former will blend and contribute to attaining the long-range objectives.

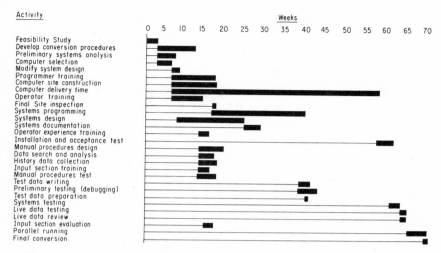

Figure 1.6. Sample of Modified Gantt Chart Used in Computer Installation Project

Whether he is dealing with short-term or long-term plans, the data processing manager finds it useful, when considering the time element in planning, to make use of a Gantt chart, modified Gantt chart (see Figure 1.6), or a PERT network diagram (see Figure 6.38).

c) What Is the Objective's Relationship to the Organization? The manager establishes the objective according to the degree of its importance within the overall organizational structure. When the priority or level of importance has been determined, the manager then integrates the objective into the entire organizational system. This can be a difficult task because the data processing manager is not always aware of the executive committee's long-term plans. However, knowledge of organizational objectives, which are generally well defined, enable him to develop a plan that will fit into the existing or proposed organizational structure.

The plan that is developed will be affected by the priority and relative significance attributed to the specific objectives and the time span involved.

2. Selecting the Best Course of Action. After the manager has acquired a thorough understanding of the objective and has evaluated the situation so that he knows what resources he has available, the time span involved, and the setting in which he must function, he is ready to move on to the next stage of planning. Drawing on his knowledge of the strengths and weaknesses of a given situation, he formulates several courses of action for investigation and consideration.

After the manager has developed several such alternatives, he then tests each hypothesis to select a course of action that will produce either the best results or the most appropriate solution to a problem. Each possible course of action is tested for:

a) Ease of operation
b) Acceptability
c) Flexibility
d) Resource specifications

a) Ease of Operations. When testing his hypothesis for ease of operation, the manager is examining the plan to determine if it is simple or complex. The degree of simplicity or complexity will influence operational effectiveness. An operation that is too simple may not accomplish all of the desired objectives, whereas a complex operation may either require too much time to implement or may exceed the capability of the manager's manpower, money, or machine resources.

b) Acceptability. To be effective, a plan of action must be acceptable to the upper-echelon managers, as well as to the manager's own subordinates. The manager may well find a common attitude of resistance to change; or he may find that the top-level executives are much more concerned about the present than the future. To avoid rejection of, or resentment to, his proposal, the manager should employ the techniques of education and persuasion. For example, he can offset or eliminate much of the resistance by communicating the reasons for the proposed change and by disseminating a general description of the plan. In addition, it may be useful for the manager to solicit opinions and suggestions from any or all of the people who may be affected by his plan. This method sometimes reveals considerations that have been overlooked in the investigative phase but that now merit review and evaluation.

The manager must also be careful to consider less obvious matters that may have some bearing on the acceptability of his proposed course of action. For example, he needs to determine whether or not his plan has a payroll provision that may affect a contractual agreement with a labor union. If such a provision violates the agreement in any way, it could well result in an unnecessary and potentially harmful labor grievance. The manager has to give the same care and consideration to local, state, and federal laws in order to make sure that implementation of his plan will not infringe upon them and thereby cause unnecessary embarrassment or loss to the organization.

c) Flexibility. All planning efforts need to be flexible because they are subject to change in the earlier as well as in later stages. Therefore, the manager must be capable of reacting promptly and accurately to any adverse conditions, problems, or deviations that may occur in an operation and of adjusting the plan in response to this reaction. Very often, as part of the plan, the manager makes provision for contingency and reference plans to allow for greater facility in modifying an original proposal (see Chapters 4, 6, and 7). In the dynamic approach to management, every plan that has been formulated and implemented must be monitored and the results evaluated as the operation passes through the pre-executory and executory phases. Whether or not such monitoring makes it necessary to revise or modify the plan, any changes can be achieved only if the original plan is flexible.

d) Resource Specifications. The manager needs to determine the basic resource specifications for his plan, because formulation of the details of implementation is impossible without knowledge of what manpower, materials, machines, and money are necessary and available to initiate and maintain the operation. If the manager needs to find additional resources or to strengthen existing ones, then he must be fully aware of these factors as early as possible so that the goal will be attained within the allocated time span.

Operational effectiveness of a plan is measured by the results obtained; therefore, it cannot be rigid because data processing operations are performed within a dynamic framework. In essence, each plan is tentative and subject to modification and to implementation of alternative actions. The manager needs to visualize the total operative system and the relationship of interdependent activities, as well as the effect of change on the organization. It is a desirable quality for a manager to have the ability to see ahead and plan within the long-term context.

Many of the actions performed by the manager as part of the planning function are also an inherent part of a feasibility study (see Chapter 8). These activities will be conducted by information processing specialists under the direction and control of the manager.

The Organizing Function

After the manager has selected his plan of action, he then establishes the framework within which the objective is to be attained. Setting up such a framework represents the organizing function, which is basically concerned with the establishment of an organizational structure, development of procedures, determination of resources, and the allocation of resources.

It is important to note that organizing is a dynamic activity. Good results cannot be guaranteed simply as a result of applying a well-ordered pattern. Therefore, a manager must employ periodic monitoring to determine whether his organizational concept is meeting present and future needs. The concept must be designed to reflect proper balance among all functions, for an improper balance in the design of the organizational structure can result in a disproportionate weighting of elements. This, in turn, may give the lesser elements more consideration than they should be given; or it may mean that some major elements are overlooked or incorrectly analyzed. Either way, an improper balance invariably results in the creation of problems.

It must be emphasized and noted that, in most instances, the manager is not able to develop an organizational concept rapidly. This lack of speed is useful, because to rush into a pattern without approaching the situation realistically could well result in a disastrous predicament for the manager (see Chapter 2).

1. INTERRELATING THE VARIOUS RESPONSIBILITIES. The primary function of an organization structure is to establish a framework through which decisions can be made and initiated. It is through this structure that the scope and extent of responsibilities are defined, and the functional interrelationships are identified. Within the organizational framework there are two patterns of relationship that the manager needs to develop and recognize. These patterns are identified as the formal and informal structures.

The formal structure delineates the various organizational positions, together with their responsibilities, functions, and lines of authority. An informal structure develops within the framework of the formal one as a result of close relationships among certain personnel in the group. These informal groups can have a marked effect on the formal structure because they involve human emotions, interests, and personal feelings.

It is obvious, therefore, that the manager needs to consider the effects of such informal groups while he is developing his organizational structure. These groups exist in every organization where people are banded together for attainment of a common goal. Their influence stems largely from the data bits and pieces they derive from the operation and the manner in which they disseminate the information throughout the organization. For example, data on a pending computer conversion or system innovation may be freely exchanged at the luncheon table in the company cafeteria or at a social affair; the circulation of such information could have a positive or negative effect on the organization. The significant influence that these informal groups can bring to bear, directly and indirectly, on the activity of the entire group must be given consideration in the formulation of the organizational concept.

Within the structural aspects of organization underlying the formal structure, there are four basic points to consider. These are:

a) Unity of Command
b) Span of Control
c) Assignment of Effective Personnel
d) Delegation of Authority

a) *Unity of Command.* The unity of command means that authority and responsibility for directing and controlling the actions aimed at are vested in a single manager at each supervisory level in an organization. The chief administrator at the top of the managerial hierarchy retains overall authority and responsibility for the objective. It is important, however, that he delegate authority and responsibility throughout the organization from one manager to another, so that each may accomplish his assigned tasks. The amount of authority and responsibility decreases with each successively lower level.

As a result of the delegation of authority and responsibility, there is a need for a network of clearly defined supervisory channels. Each such channel provides for the effective flow of communications from the top to the bottom, and back. The two-way flow of information through the network allows for instructions and orders to move downward and for information on progress and problems to flow upward.

The downward communications should be simple and direct, so that there is little or no demand for interpretation and clarification from the subordinate levels. Any such call for interpretation and clarification implies the possibility of distortion of meaning and intent, which could delay or hamper goal attainment. Thus, in preparing communications, the manager not only must strive for clarity, but must also remember that his subordinates have a variety of backgrounds and experiences. Handled effectively, downward communications can also help to create a satisfying and cooperative attitude among the manager's subordinates.

The upward communications provide a flow of information from the subordinate levels concerning the status of the progress being made on the operation, as well as any problems that may have arisen. This reverse flow of information, frequently referred to as feedback, is evaluated and utilized by the upper echelon in directing and controlling the activity. The manager must not at any cost block the flow of data and ideas from those involved in the operation, because such an action hampers the decision-making process and could result in failure to achieve the objective.

b) *Span of Control.* The concept of span of control is concerned with the number of subordinates who can be effectively supervised at given levels within an organizational structure. In many organizations, this is determined by applying a mathematical figure to the number of individuals each manager should control. Such ratios generally vary from 14:1 to 18:1. In some organizations, though, the number of subordinates reporting to a manager is increased, in an effort to reduce operating costs. The number of subordinates reporting to any one manager may fluctuate above or below the ratio during a given time span. A particular manager may control 14, 5, or 18 subordinates, for the 14:1 ratio is simply a corporate average that can be used as a basis of comparison for cost purposes.

There is no predetermined formula that can be applied to every organizational level and manager. Each level of activity has to be analyzed independently to determine the number of subordinates needed. It is important to note that each manager can be limited in the number of subordinates he can effectively manage with his own personal experience, the time available to give subordinates, and the ability of his subordinates to carry out their assignments.

Simply stated, there is a point of diminishing returns which is reached if the organizational unit is expanded to a size that will dilute the operational effectiveness of the manager. A major factor in determining that point has to do with the fact that as people are added to an organizational unit, the number of organizational relationships increases. Consider, for example, a manager who supervises two subordinates, A and B. He is directly involved in two relationships—himself and A and himself and B. But he is also concerned with the relationship between A and B. If another person is added to the unit, the relationships increase from three to six, even though there has been only one personnel addition.

Often, as part of the feasibility study, a manager and his staff will be called on to make recommendations to the chief administrator regarding the span of control for a particular organizational unit (see Chapter 8). The proposals should be made only after an evaluation of the operational effectiveness of such a unit has been made. The impact of suggested personnel changes on the organization has to be made known to the chief administrator.

c) Effective Assignment of Personnel. In order for an organizational unit to attain maximum operational effectiveness, its manager must evaluate and select the proper personnel; in each case he must assign the right man to the right job (see also Chapter 3). Making such assignments is a difficult task for the manager, because neither jobs nor people are the same. Each job requires particular skills or abilities of the person performing it. And each individual has his own hopes, ambitions, capabilities, likes, and dislikes. Therefore, in addition to having full knowledge of each job, the manager must learn about and assess each member of his organization and then effectively match each person with the right job.

The most dynamic aspect of any organization is its human element, so the manager most willing to focus on his working relationship with his subordinates is the manager who stands to reap the greatest rewards. An interactive manager encourages his subordinates to assist him in the detection, identification, and solution of problems. To secure such cooperation, the manager needs to carefully appraise the capabilities, desires, and motivations of his personnel. Furthermore, he finds it important to help develop the capacities of the subordinates and to stimulate their levels of performance. At the same time, he treats his personnel as people, not machines, for he recognizes that they are all different and that they do not pursue their own interests with the same degrees of determination, motivation, or consistency. Therefore, it is important psychologically as well as operationally for the manager to express a continued willingness to know his subordinates and take an interest in their well-being.

d) Delegation of Authority. After being assigned a position of responsibility in an organizational unit, the manager then begins to delegate authority to his own subordinates in the hierarchical structure. This is no simple matter, for it involves a great deal more than merely drawing blocks on the organization chart or completing generalized job descriptions.

The delegation of authority is a very necessary and important part of the organizing function because it can have either a positive or negative effect on the manager's operational effectiveness. If a typical manager appraises his position realistically, he finds that nearly one-half of his time is devoted to routine work. Delegation of some or all of such work would enable him to devote more time to the active direction and control of his operation. A manager can also improve the morale of his subordinates and provide training and experience by giving them certain managerial responsibilities. It has been estimated that a manager who spends 75 percent of his time in applying the management functions to an activity can lead his organizational unit to high productivity. In contrast, a manager who spends two-thirds of his time in helping to do the routine work and only one-third in management activity finds that the unit is low in productivity. To offset this negative effect, such a manager will spend many hours beyond his normal workday helping to do the work. This condition is really acceptable only for short-term emergency periods, for any prolonged activity of this type results in a state of fatigue that will greatly reduce the mental and physical effectiveness of the manager.

There are many people outside of the profession who wonder why there are data processing managers who pursue such a suicidal course. There are at least three common reasons—or excuses—and not one of them is really defensible or logical.

The most common excuse is phrased in various ways, such as: "It is easier for me to do it than to have to tell somebody and wait for him to give me what I want," or "I don't have time to explain this to somebody or write it out for him." This type of thinking obviously stems from the fact that the manager is confident of his ability as a technician, but uncertain of himself as a leader.

A second excuse is: "It will be my head that rolls if he goofs!" Here the manager feels that he knows the technical side of the job and is capable of achieving the objective, but that he is uncertain about his personnel's reliability. If a manager is unable to determine the capabilities of his personnel, he will never be able to effectively assign any responsibility to anyone. And this, in turn can lead to disastrous results and weaken the organization. The dynamic aspects of the data processing field make it impossible for anyone to become an autocratic individualist and also be successful in operating an organizational unit.

A third common excuse is that the manager lacks the manpower or the qualified manpower. Although it is true that the industry is currently suffering from a shortage of qualified technicians, managers are at least partly responsible for this condition because many of them are reluctant or unwilling to train people to alleviate the shortage. The *training* of personnel, no less than the supervision of subordinates, ranks as an essential part of the management process. (The training function is discussed in detail in Chapter 3.)

The manager's willingness to delegate responsibility is only the first step toward putting the principle into practice. He soon discovers that some subordinates are unwilling to accept authority, that some are leaners or followers, and that some simply cannot supervise. That is why the manager very often has to train people to accept responsibility.

It is also important for the manager to realize at the very beginning that some of his subordinates may be able to perform certain functions as well if not better than he can. Accepting the fact that every person has certain strengths and weaknesses, the manager should strive to delegate authority in a way that capitalizes on the strengths of his subordinates. He may have to settle for an output or a job performance of slightly lower quality than if he had personally accomplished the task. However, this is a compromise he must be willing to make. It gets him away from the routine work. At the same time, the subordinate will gain experience in accomplishing the task—experience that will be reflected in his future performance.

Before actually delegating authority, the manager makes certain that the subordinate has the capability and the personality to accept such responsibility. After this has been determined, the manager then decides upon the limits to be set on the delegated authority. In establishing such limits, the manager must clearly stipulate the following:

1. The Goal or Objective
2. The Chain of Command
3. The Progress Reports Required
4. The Time Span
5. The Span of Control
6. Budget Limitations

1. The Goal or Objective. The manager must be explicit and exact about the goal or objective that the subordinate is expected to achieve. Such a specification will enable the subordinate to plan and organize his own operation or assignment to achieve the desired end.

2. The Chain of Command. Who will be the immediate superior to

whom the subordinate will report his progress and from whom he will seek assistance if required? It is vital that an open communications channel be maintained in order to report subordinate's progress and to prevent his overextending the scope of his authority and responsibility.

Looking at this matter from the subordinate's point of view, it can be stated that the subordinate wants and needs to receive clear and understandable instructions so that he knows what is expected of him and what the manager will and will not permit him to do.

3. The Progress Reports Required. The managers should state clearly the type and frequency of progress reports to be made by the subordinate. To determine the progress being made, the manager may require statistical, oral, or written reports.

Statistical reports are generally in the form of charts, graphs, or numerical tabulations. Figure 1.7 is an example of the kind of statistical report used to indicate the progress being made by the programming group in preparing for installation of new computing equipment. Such a report form provides statistical information on the manning strength of an activity, the number of programs written in different languages, and the stages of completion. This type of presentation may or may not be adequate to indicate the results achieved. If the manager requires additional information, he must contact the project leader or programming manager. Brevity may prove to be an advantage, because only specific information will be collected and there will be no need to filter the feedback. Also, the specific data categories facilitate the updating of existing status information. Depending on the length and importance of the project, the statistical reports may be required on a daily or weekly basis.

Oral reports tend to be biased or may be inaccurate because of the subordinate's inability to communicate with his immediate supervisor. Yet they can be effective if the manager is able to perceive and understand any such bias or to recognize any communications difficulties. Not only are oral reports personal and immediate, but they also help to give the subordinate the feeling that he is not merely an errand boy. In addition, the manager can directly query the subordinate individual to determine if any problems have arisen. What is more, the two men may be able to resolve any such difficulties at the time the report is being made. If oral reports are made frequently, they can serve as an excellent monitoring device through which evaluation and adjustments can be made.

PERSONNEL ASSIGNED				PROGRAMS BY LANGUAGES					PERCENT OF PROGRAMS					
SENIOR PROGRAM ANALYST	PROGRAM ANALYST	PROGRAMMER	PROGRAMMER TRAINEE	RPG	BAL	COBOL	FORTRAN IV	PL/I	DEFINED	CODED	DESK CHECKED	TESTED	COMPLETED	DOCUMENTED

Figure 1.7. Sample of Statistical Report

Written reports may be used to provide information on the progress or status of an activity or operation. Such reports are generally used to provide some feedback on special or extended projects. For example, daily written reports may be prepared to give the status of a data conversion project; preliminary reports may be prepared on the status of construction of a data processing facility; and interim reports may be prepared and issued from time to time on the progress in a long-term conversion from one type of computing hardware to another. Written reports are also used to convey the results of problem-solving or other investigative work. Figure 1.8, for example, is a written report prepared by a systems analyst as a result of an investigation to determine the reasons for preparation of erroneous reports by a functional activity.

Written reports represent, in most cases, an after-the-fact type of reporting, so that they can be only of limited value in quickly changing situations; too much time may be spent in their preparation and too little gained from the time and energy expended.

On the other hand, there is also the danger that written reports may be prepared too quickly; hastily prepared reports may lack valid or complete data and consequently be of little or no value in decision-making.

4. Time Span. The subordinate must be aware of the time period involved or available so that he may plan and schedule his own operation accordingly.

5. Span of Control. Just as the manager knows his span of control, so it is important for the subordinate to know the number and caliber of

A major problem, which has caused the delay in the maintenance of records, especially for mechanized systems, is the lack of understanding by the personnel involved with the use of data processing techniques. Personnel are not aware of how data processing systems function or what can be obtained from such systems. Therefore, more training for clerical personnel is needed. The role of clerical personnel in input preparation and providing accurate source data for the system is not clearly understood. The outgrowth of this has been that the transcription of information has been performed on a "when the time is available" basis. Consequently there has been a lack of continuity, and a high incidence of error in the processing of data. The lack of personnel partially attributes to the error rate and lack of continuity. However, the lack of importance accorded to data processing within the department is also a significant factor.

Figure 1.8   Sample of Written Report

persons who will come under his supervision during the assignment.

6. Budget Limitations. When a budget is allocated to a particular project the subordinate should be made aware of this fact to assist him in deciding when and what action to initiate. The subordinate should be told the actual dollar value involved, what resources may be funded, and who must authorize the expenditures.

2. THE DEVELOPMENT OF PROCEDURES. The other major component of the organizing function (after interrelating the various responsibilities) is the development of procedures that will prescribe the manner or techniques to be used in achieving the objective. These procedures will become the focal point of the operation during the executory phase, for the manager will use them to direct and coordinate the effort of the organization unit.

Each procedure is developed as a result of breaking down an operation into its component steps. These are then carefully analyzed to determine the most efficient and effective way of accomplishing the desired task. The details are documented to provide for uniformity and standardization in the operation (see Chapter 4).

Figure 1.9 illustrates a typical data processing procedure. It is a procedure for the preparation of either a machine listing or a reproducing of a set of cards for the personnel manager. The procedure directs the most effective use of the manpower, machine, and material resources. Following this procedure will ensure that each time the personnel manager requests this report, the desired end result will be produced for him. Also, the data processing manager can use the same procedure to establish his machine-loading schedule and make personnel assignments (see Chapter 6).

The Coordinating Function

This is the third and last management function in the pre-executory phase of the management process.

The coordinating function cannot be initiated until the manager has gained a clear understanding of the overall setting. The setting must be understood because no operation can be executed in a vacuum; data processing activity cuts across all organizational lines, so that it influences other activities or is influenced by them.

Coordination is the process of establishing communications with those elements not under the direct control of the manager, but which influence or are influenced by the manager's operation. It necessitates the smooth blending of all the integral parts to provide for maximum output.

To help understand the coordination required in an operation, it is useful to examine a situation in which the data processing manager is responsible for the production of remittance advices and drafts for an accounts payable application. For this type of application the network of coordination would have to include the accounts payable section of the accounting department, together with the treasury, inspection, receiving, and purchasing departments. Together, these groups are responsible for the order entry, receival of the goods, verification of quantity and condition, verification of payment amounts and discounts, authorization of payment, and the transmittal of the drafts to the vendors. Furthermore, there may also be by-products of the application, such as various journal entry reports, billing to subsidiaries or other plants, and input for an inventory control application; this would necessitate coordination between the financial, results accounting, and inventory control functions.

In this example, the data processing manager must employ measures to ensure that the inputs from the purchasing, accounts payable, inspection, and receiving groups are correct, and that any adjustments made to any purchase or invoice order are correct and properly applied (see also

MACHINE OPERATION #1

SORT, ALTERNATE METHODS

A. Sort the Employee Master Card File (keeping the Hourly and Monthly separated) on the name field, card columns 1–4 alpha. The cards will then either be prepared for a listing or reproduced as per the requirements specified by the personnel manager.

B1. (ALTERNATE METHOD) *List* the above sorted cards on the accounting machine utilizing control panel #B42, on 3 part stock paper ($8\frac{1}{2} \times 11$). No alteration switches are required. After completing the listing proceed to step D. Forward the listing to the personnel manager. Return the cards to cabinet A-11.

B2. (ALTERNATE METHOD) *Reproduce* the sorted cards from step A into the following format:

Field Identification	From c.c.	To c.c.
Name	1–18	1–18
Employee Number	19–24	30–35
Occupation Code	29–32	50–53
Organization Number	47–49	47–49
Card Code (Emit "5")		80

Hold the reproduced cards for step C, return the original cards to the Employee Master File Cabinet A-11.

C. Interpret the reproduced cards from step B2 as follows:

Field Identification	Punch Positions	Print Positions
Name	1–18	10–27
Employee Number	30–35	1–6
Occupation Code	50–53	40–43
Organization Number	47–49	58–60

Hold the interpreted cards for step D.

D. Sort the Employee Master Card from step C (keeping the Hourly and Monthly separated) on organization number, card columns 47–49. Forward the sorted cards to the personnel manager.

NEXT OPERATION: *End*

Figure 1.9   Sample of Machine Operating Procedure

Chapter 7). In addition, the manager must abide by the rulings of the treasury department on draft amount limits and national contract payments. And where the output becomes input for by-product reports, the manager must ensure that it is correct and properly entered into the system. The data processing manager is dependent upon all of these other organizations for meeting his time schedules, for corrections and adjustments, and for relevant output for decision-making. Therefore, it becomes imperative that he establish close coordination between his operation and those activities which affect it.

1. PROBLEMS. The problems of coordination can be eased by the application of several techniques. Among these are:

a) The Reduction of Specialization

b) The Use of Committees

c) The Use of Effective Channels of Communication

a) *The Reduction of Specialization.* The reduction of specialization can reduce or eliminate the communications problems between specialized units. When an organization becomes overspecialized, it is increasingly difficult for the manager to obtain the required maximum contribution of interaction from all units. Reducing the amount of specialization thereby makes it easier for him to get that contribution, which always requires a high degree of interaction between time and events.

b) *The Use of Committees.* Committees can be very effective in suggesting ideas; in disseminating information; in establishing contacts for securing approvals or agreements, or for initiating new systems; and in providing advice on how a project should be accomplished. To be effective, a committee must have a clear understanding of its functions and objectives. Generally, a manager will provide the committee chairman with a written memorandum expressing the purpose and scope of the committee, its authority, and its responsibility. Committees are said to be more effective when they are limited in size to between three and seven members, and when all members are of equal rank or position.

Many managers are opposed to the use of committees because they feel such collective work is time-consuming and totally ineffective; these managers are obviously strong believers in the axiom that if you don't wish for something to be accomplished, simply place it in the hands of a committee for action. Some managers even approve of this dubious quality, for they like to utilize committees either to stymie progress or as an excuse for inaction. Nevertheless, it must be pointed out that, despite these abuses, committees have been useful in performing objective evaluations and in suggesting broad means of attaining desired goals.

c) The Use of Effective Channels of Communication. The channels of communication can be used effectively in disseminating data that is vital to the performance of an operation or in providing informational data to interested persons. The channels can also be effective in the process of securing information regarding an operation or activity. However, there are instances when channels become ineffective and thereby either contribute to or create difficulties. For example, users of an output may become dissatisfied because of results that are inaccurate, incomplete, or lacking clarity, but they fail to communicate their dissatisfaction to the data processing manager. In this case, the key to initiating a solution is to establish a clear line of communication from the users to the manager. Consider another example: the output falls into disuse, but the data processing personnel continue to produce the report because they have not been informed otherwise. If this is a relatively new report, they will find out as a result of the follow-up conducted soon after a report has been implemented. However, if there is no follow-up and there are no reports control studies being conducted by the organization, such ineffective output may go undetected for some period of time. Again, the solution has to begin with the effective use of channels of communication.

2. THE CATEGORIES OF COORDINATION. The operational category of coordination involves coordinating the various activities of a manager's function and the activities of persons in other functions involved in a system or project. This form of coordination is necessary in order to implement and maintain a multi-functional approach to the use of data processing services. Coordinating the activities of a manager's own function is not difficult, because much of it can be achieved through the delegation of authority. Coordination with those external functions involved in a manager's operations, however, is more challenging but necessary. It is necessary for the development of systems which will enjoy both utility and durability.

The informational category of coordination provides for a broad band of communications efforts—keeping the executive committee, managers, subordinates, and other personnel fully informed. It is not intended that this form of coordination be used to pay lip service to other functions. Informational coordination provides a means of resolving conflicts, securing clearances, disseminating ideas, and for developing and maintaining organizational contacts. For data processors, informational coordination can be a highly effective mechanism for disseminating ideas and information about the capabilities and uses of data processing techniques. Subsequently this may facilitate the development and/or maintenance of inter-system cooperation.

The two patterns of coordination are interwoven to help provide for a smooth functioning of operations, facilitate development of broader systems, and rectify any problems which may arise. The patterns provide the ways and means for maximizing the operational effectiveness of the data processing organization.

Review Questions: Group 1B

1. Why should a manager have to concern himself with the pre-executory phase in the management process?
2. What would happen (if anything) if a manager chose to ignore evaluating a situation?
3. It is important for a manager to clearly define the supervisory channels in an organizational structure. Explain why.
4. One of the difficulties encountered in many organizations is the inability of a manager to effectively supervise all of his subordinates. Why is this a problem? How does this type of problem occur?
5. Why are some managers unwilling or hesitant about delegating authority to their subordinates?
6. If you, as a manager, were assigned a particular goal to achieve, what would you want to know initially?
7. Why must a data processing manager be concerned with the coordination of activities?

The Executory Phase

It is during the execution phase that the manager implements and oversees the prepared plan of action that has been developed during the pre-executory phase by application of the planning, directing, and coordinating functions. At this stage, the manager is concerned with utilizing the directing and controlling functions of management in order to bring the plan to fruition. However, the pre-executory functions do not cease so that the new management functions can be initiated. Rather, all five functions are incorporated into the executory phase of management, for the manager has to be ready at all times to replan, reorganize, and re-coordinate as needed. Nevertheless, his principal emphasis is on giving direction and control.

The Directing Function

The directing function is sometimes referred to as the execution, or action, function. In the broadest sense, direction is the manipulation of the available resources according to the formulated plan in order to achieve the objective. This requires that the manager make the day-to-day decisions that will make the operation effective and keep it moving according to plan.

This management function consists of three major elements. The first of these is the communications element, which involves the transmission of the policies, objectives, and procedures to all those persons who are connected with the operation. The second element is the training of personnel, which involves the development and education of personnel so that they can carry out their assigned responsibilities related to goal achievement. The third element is the establishment of a patter of operations; this requires the development of ways and means to guide the operation.

Traditionally, the term "directing" has been limited by various writers on the subject to mean the "direction of people." In a dynamic environment, however, directing involves the total operation. This means that the manager has to be concerned with directing both people and procedures. In an actual operation, the manpower resource is concerned with the utilization of the other available resources—materials, machines, and money. For the manager to put all of these resources into action, in definite relation to one another, requires the use of procedures, which provide the linkage in a series of interrelated steps to produce the desired end result. Personnel and procedures are not independent of each other; rather, they are interdependent, for it is only through the combined interaction of them that the manager can be fairly certain that the desired end result will actually be achieved.

1. THE DIRECTION OF PERSONNEL. People, the most dynamic element in any operation, must be given careful consideration because they are unlike any other resource at the disposal of the manager. And the manager has to carefully integrate this unique resource into his operating plan.

The success of the manager in achieving teamwork among his subordinates depends on the degree of understanding and interest which he has in his people. The following statements are some valid generalizations that apply directly to this issue of teamwork. It can be said of the people in an organizational unit that:

—They work best when they know that the manager is interested in them and recognizes their wishes.

—They make every attempt to fulfill the complete expectations of the manager.

—They work more effectively when they know that the manager is attempting to make good use of their talents, abilities, and suggestions.

—They work best for a manager whom they can trust and respect, and who lets each subordinate know how he fits into the total spectrum.

—They work best when kept informed about all matters that concern or affect them.

Undoubtedly, there are many other generalizations that could be added to this list; these, though, are probably the most important ones.

2. THE DIRECTION OF PROCEDURES. As important as the directing of people is the directing of procedures. The procedures oral or written for a particular operation, will, in answer to five of the six basic questions in management, specify: what is to be done, how it is to be done, who will do it, where will it be done, and when it is to be done.

The procedures are aimed at putting into motion the plan that has been developed in the pre-executory phase. They cover the general and interdepartmental policies, departmental matters, and technical instructions. In addition to being focussed on the main objective, they are designed to achieve several other specific purposes:

—To provide the performance standards against which the output can be effectively measured with application of the control function.

—To assist in the training of personnel.

—To ensure uniform application of company policies and administrative rules.

—To ensure that each operation will be performed uniformly.

—To ensure a smooth operation and provide for a control of progress.

a) *Auditing Procedures.* Procedures are essential to every operation for the maintainance of its effectiveness. Consequently, the procedures need to be periodically reviewed for removal, revision, or replacement, and for their retaining as much simplicity as possible. Furthermore, whenever changes are made to a procedure the information about these changes need to be conveyed to all affected parties. Unfortunately, this very important procedural procedure is all too often overlooked within a data processing activity, with the ultimate result of chaos or mismanagement of an operation, project, or installation. To deal with this mistake, many firms implement an annual procedural audit. The data processing procedure illustrated in Figure 1.9 is the kind of procedure that should be audited annually.

The reviewer-auditor determines if the procedures are current, relevant, clear, and compatible. If a procedure is current, it reflects all changes that had been effected since the previous audit. If it is relevant, it contributes to the effectiveness of the current operation. If it is clear, it is easy to read and understand. If it is compatible, it is comparable with other procedures within the system, which, in turn, reduces the chances of conflict in the goal-attainment process.

Controlling

The controlling function is a monitoring activity. It is used to compare the current output from an ongoing operation with the planned results that had been formulated during the pre-executory phase and that had been implemented with the directing function. The controlling function also makes provision for problem detection, identification, and correction if necessary.

The ability to monitor an activity requires that the manager understand clearly the objective to be reached and the setting in which the operation is to be performed. It also requires that he be aware of the acceptable standard of performance and the allowable parameters for deviation from that standard. In monitoring an activity, the manager can gain a clear and graphic understanding of progress-versus-plan by making use of PERT network diagrams, Gantt charts, or modified Gantt charts (see also Chapter 6).

1. THE FEEDBACK CONCEPT. The feedback concept is a technique applied repeatedly during the controlling function to evaluate the performance of an operation. The operation's progress is monitored to determine if current performance conforms with planned performance. This comparison provides a status indicator (deviation or normal), which is then evaluated by the manager to determine if corrective action is necessary or potentially beneficial. Any corrective input is fed into the

operation, where once again it will be monitored and evaluated. This monitor-evaluate-correct process has become universally known as the feedback concept.

Figure 1.10 provides the diagrammatic basis for a fuller understanding of the feedback control mechanism in operation within an organization. This mechanism is often referred to simply as the feedback loop.

The function of the feedback loop begins after the initiation of the operation being directed toward the attainment of a desired goal. Current performance or output is compared with the plan at point A on the diagram. If the actual progress and the planned result are the same at this point, then the status of the operation is registered as normal and the operation continues until monitored again at point F. However, if, at point B, the actual progress is above or below the planned result, the status of the operation is indicated as a deviation. It is at this point and time that the feedback of information becomes extremely important and that the series of steps beginning at point B are initiated.

It is important to note that in a real operation (rather than an idealized sample such as this), several checkpoints are included at which the actual-versus-planned comparison is made. Should a deviation be detected at any of these points, then the alternate path is immediately taken so that the problem analysis can begin at point B.

At point B, the actual feedback loop is initiated with the analysis of the problem. The deviation must be investigated to recognize the problem and to specify the deviation. The analysis of the deviation, or variance, should reveal: what the deviation is, where the deviation actually occurred, and when the deviation occurred. *What* the deviation is must be known to determine the deviations seriousness and its possible effects on succeeding phases of the operation. If the manager does not understand the problem, he can hardly hope to correct the cause and remedy the effect. If there are several problems involved, the manager must be able to recognize and identify them individually and to assign a priority for analysis and solution. *Where* the deviation actually occurred must be known in order to help isolate the event and to provide critical information for the problem-solving phase. *When* the deviation occurred must be known in order to pinpoint the occurrence and to reduce the amount of probing time required for problem analysis.

When each of these three factors is known, the manager's task is to uncover the possible causes of the deviation. The difficulty here is to recognize how the various events or activities in a total operation are

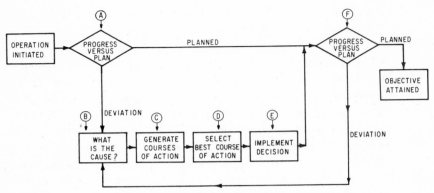

Figure 1.10. Feedback Control Concept

interrelated and how the process of change affects this interrelationship. It is imperative that the manager fully understand the setting and the objective, because this understanding will enable him to envision this interrelationship of factors, which, in turn, will help him to isolate the most important cause or causes.

Because the significant cause or causes is sometimes difficult to find, the manager has to be prepared to initiate some careful probing and analysis. He must, at the same time, recognize the possible dangers inherent in hasty judgments or conclusions about the cause. His best approach, therefore, is to use the facts uncovered to develop a hypothesis and then test it.

The best way for the manager to test his hypothesis is to tear apart the explanation. This is not a very simple task because the manager may have to explode his own theory in order to avoid reaching a false conclusion—an activity that is not very flattering to his ego. However, it is a useful method for recalling the hard-to-find reasons for a deviation in an operation.

When the manager has determined the significant cause or causes, he is ready to move on to the next stage of the feedback control mechanism, marked by point C in the illustration. At this point in the loop, the manager determines whether or not he needs to take corrective action. If he does need to, he then considers the possible courses of action that will enable him to correct or modify the situation.

At point D in the loop, the manager selects the best course of action. He assesses each course of action for acceptability, flexibility, ease of operation, and resource specifications (the same basic tests that the manager applies in the planning function of the pre-executory phase).

It is at this stage in the feedback control mechanism that the manager usually begins to feel pressed for time. His difficulty is that, while still committed to completing the objective within a specified time period, he has much less allowable time for re-planning than he had for the initial planning. This time limitation may well force him to select the most expedient course of action rather than the best one. Furthermore, he has to be more specific in assessing his revised course of action so that he will be able to determine very quickly any actual or potential problems that may arise from its implementation. This means he needs to initiate controls to serve as an early warning system. Such a system requires dependable feedback so that the manager can begin to cope as soon as possible with the problem. In addition, he also needs to set up some contingency plans for dealing with the problem once it has been identified by the early warning system. Without these various forms of preplanning, the manager cannot hope to operate successfully within a dynamic environment.

Having selected the best or most expedient course of action, the manager then implements this plan in order to modify or correct the operation in which the deviation occurred. Implementation takes place at point E in the diagram.

Again, at point F, the manager monitors the activity to determine that the operation is proceeding according to the original or modified plan. If the actual results meet the planned results, then the operation will terminate successfully. If, however, another deviation is found to exist, the feedback control mechanism is reactivated by branching back to point B where the problem-solving process must be reinstituted.

To see how the feedback concept works in reality, it is useful to examine the following practical example. A data processing activity involved in preparing a payroll on unit-record (EAM) equipment is making a series of control checks to determine if the payroll taxes had been computed correctly on the calculator. The first such check, on federal taxes, is made by multiplying the total number of exemptions by the legal exemption amount. The result of the multiplication (the total value of the exemptions) is then subtracted from the gross amount to arrive at the taxable gross. The taxable gross is then multiplied by the federal tax percentage to arrive at the total amount of federal tax that should have been deducted. At the end of this control check, the control total and the original EAM total are compared. The comparison should result in one of two conditions:

—The totals match, therefore there is no problem and the next step in the normal processing cycle may be executed.

—The totals do not match, therefore the manager has to determine *what* the deviation is, as well as *where* and *when* it occurred.

In this example, the manager directs the data control clerk to compare the totals on the control sheet against each of the EAM totals (number of exemptions, total value of exemptions, gross amount, taxable gross amount, and federal tax amount). This procedure should isolate a point at which an error may have occurred. If there is disagreement on all of the totals, then the data control clerk must go back to the first step in the development of the control totals. This procedure would require the following:

a) Verifying the accuracy of the number of exemptions total. The control sheet total must agree with the total generated at the time the master payroll file was updated. The EAM totals must also agree with the starting control total. If there is agreement, then the data control clerk should proceed to the next step, that of calculating the total value of the exemptions. A variance in the control clerk's totals may be the result of a transposition or posting error. When the total is corrected the control clerk may proceed to the next step. If there is a variance in the EAM totals the cause of the error may be more difficult to locate. Investigation may indicate that the cause of the variance is the result of machine error, keypunch error when a card was made over, missing master card, or an error in control panel wiring. When the cause is determined and corrected it may be necessary to reprocess all or part of this phase of the payroll procedure.

b) Recalculate the total value of exemptions. Either manually or by using a calculating device, the control clerk must recalculate the total value. The newly calculated result is matched against the control clerk's totals and the EAM totals. If no variance is found, the taxable gross is calculated. A variance in the control clerk's sheet total may indicate a calculation error or one of the previously mentioned error possibilities— transposition or posting. An error in the EAM total may indicate a machine error, or an error in control panel wiring. Again, all or part of the payroll may have to be reprocessed.

c) Calculate the taxable gross amount. The procedure followed in the previous step would be executed here. The same conditions could again be responsible for a variance. If no variance is found, the federal tax-amount will then be calculated.

d) *Calculate the federal tax amount.* Again, the same procedures are executed. The same conditions could again be responsible for any variance. In our example this is the last point at which an error should have occurred.

The feedback control concept is a very important part of the controlling function because it provides the means of checking on the overall effectiveness of the operation. As a monitoring activity, feedback control is an integral part of the dynamic approach to management activity. It cannot function in a static environment because it requires that the manager constantly evaluate the results being achieved, remove any existing or potential problems, and replan, reorganize, recoordinate, and redirect the elements in order to keep the operation flowing smoothly within the defined parameters. It is obvious that the static approach makes no provision for any such activities.

Review Questions: Group 1C

1. Discuss the comment, "He is a good manager because he rolls up his sleeves and pitches right in to get the job done."
2. The direction of procedures is considered to be as important in the management process as the direction of personnel. Why?
3. Explain the controlling function as it is used in the management process.
4. Explain the feedback concept as it is applied to the dynamic approach in management.
5. In what ways does the feedback concept affect all of the managerial functions?

SUMMARY

In this chapter we have discussed the basic concepts of the management process. This material provides a fundamental understanding of the framework within which a data processing manager must act. In addition, it defines and describes the various major aspects of the management process that affect the manager.

Management is an activity that provides for the interactive application of available resources to achieve a desired goal. This activity is defined and guided by a manager, who strives to develop an optimal mix of his manpower, machine, material, and money resources in order to attain the stated objective. The manager conducts his activity utilizing either the static or dynamic approach to management. The static approach deals with the activity in terms of an ideal environment in which the application of pre-defined rules and procedures will produce the desired end result. The dynamic approach recognizes that conditions relating to an operation can and do change. Therefore, it requires that a manager evaluate the setting first and then formulate his plan of action. It also requires that the manager constantly monitor and evaluate the progress of his activity to determine how the actual results compare with the planned ones. Any deviation from the plan must be identified, evaluated, and promptly corrected if necessary. Whether a manager selects the static approach or the dynamic approach depends on his own training, background, and experience, as well as on the approach preferred by his supervisor.

Before a manager activates the management process, he begins by resolving a broad objective into specific objective, and subsequently into the detailed steps that must be accomplished to achieve the desired end result. Having properly defined his objective and its components, the manager implements the basic management functions of planning, organizing, and coordinating. These three functions constitute the pre-executory phase of the management process, during which the manager decides what and how the objective is to be accomplished and with what human and material resources he will be working.

Having formulated his procedures and assembled his resources, the manager moves into the executory phase of the management process. During this phase, he implements the procedures and guides the resources in the goal-attainment process, using the basic management functions of directing and controlling. In the directing function, the manager is responsible for activating the operation, which involves directing both people and procedures. During the controlling function, he compares and evaluates the actual results of the operation with those established during the pre-executory phase. This activity involves the feedback concept, which is an integral part of the dynamic approach to management. Feedback control provides the manager with an excellent technique for problem detection, identification, and correction, which enables him to maintain progress as planned and to achieve the desired goal.

CASE STUDY

Case Study 1.1: The Raleric Manufacturing Company

Eric Anthony, the president of the Raleric Manufacturing Company, announced at the staff luncheon that he was delegating to the vice-president for data processing services the task of developing a production control system for the company. He was hopeful that such a system would reduce the number of machine setups—a step that would increase productivity and significantly lower scrap-loss due to changeovers. These improvements, in turn, should reduce the company's operating costs and increase its profits. Mr. Anthony expressed his desire that, as part of the proposed production control system, all existing manufacturing layouts be replaced by bill of materials and master piece parts catalogs.

The vice-president for data processing services, Mr. Edwards, remarked that the engineering organization was currently in the process of centralizing and standardizing the manufacturing layouts and this would delay the start of the project. So Mr. Anthony ordered the engineering organization to place this project on a high-priority status and to assign additional personnel to the project to assure its prompt completion within the very near future. Mr. Cardwell, the vice-president for financial affairs, then advised the group that the engineering organization would have to assign piece part numbers, where lacking, for those part numbers which presently did not change from one process to the next. He also asked if the proposed system could include a master cost bulletin magnetic tape for the cost accounting system.

Mr. Anthony then appointed a four-man committee consisting of the vice-presidents for engineering, financial affairs, production control, and data processing services. He asked the committee to prepare a preliminary report that would specify the steps that would have to be undertaken to initiate the development of the proposed system. He also told the committee to determine the time span to be required for implementation of the system, as well as to estimate the resources that would be needed. He named Mr. Edwards chairman of the committee.

Discussion Questions

1. Did Mr. Anthony stipulate any broad or specific objectives? If so, what were they?

2. Was Mr. Anthony correct in delegating responsibility for the development of the production control system to Mr. Edwards? Explain your answer.
3. Would implementation of the proposed system mean that any patterns of coordination would have to be developed? If so, what would they be?
4. Was Mr. Anthony correct in delegating the responsibility for the preparation of the preliminary reports to the committee?
5. Were the instructions given by Mr. Anthony to the committee correct?
6. Would it have been better if Mr. Anthony had delegated the responsibility for the preparation of the preliminary reports to lower ranking subordinates? Explain your answer.

2

The Structural Organization of Data Processing

INTRODUCTION

It is evident today that many organizations still view data processing simply as a means of reducing clerical activity, as providing a record-keeping capability for vast amounts of historical data, or as a tool for the accounting department.

This widespread attitude is not new. It began in the 1920s, in the early days of punched card equipment, and it remained essentially unchanged thereafter, passing unscathed through the mid-1950s, when computers were first utilized in business data processing activities.

Responsibility for this now traditional attitude lies with both the vendors and users of data processing equipment. The vendors, for example, originally marketed their equipment as laborsaving and record-keeping devices.

Among the users, the financial managers were quick to recognize the capability of the equipment for processing and calculating vast amounts of data in order to provide faster billing, incentive records, payrolls, and other accounting reports. The financial managers in control of the equipment serviced their own needs first and they made any surplus machine or personnel time available to other functional activities. As a result, financial managers tended to monopolize the equipment to the extent that no other organizational groups were able to effectively utilize the services of the data processing function.

As time went by, more and more organizations decided to obtain a data processing capability, but they did so mostly for the financial function, giving little or no consideration to the overall needs of the organization. As a consequence, such functional activities as manufacturing, purchasing, marketing, traffic, personnel, and research had very limited access to data processing equipment, unless they were fortunate enough to have their own installations—which was rarely the case.

This attitude about data processing has limited the full-scale use of the hardware, as well as the development of multi-functional or sophisticated systems. It has also served to discourage many potential users. Small wonder, then, that there are now still only a few organizations that have effectively realized data processing's full potential as a management tool.

Any data processing function can be successful if the upper-echelon executives recognize that the hardware can and must be utilized by the entire organization. There is an ever-increasing interrelationship between the various functional activities, and it is these activities that provide the data elements used by the upper echelon in the decision-making process.

THE ROLE OF TOP MANAGEMENT

In one way or another, the present-day data processing activity can cross all functional lines within an organizational structure in one horizontal sweep. Consequently, as a result of the overall approach, data processing can provide the managers with a great variety of information that will assist them in planning, organizing, coordinating, directing, and controlling an operation or organization.

To move from a traditional mono-functional to this modern multi-functional approach requires the total involvement of upper-echelon management. This means that, to begin with, the executive committee must establish broad and specific objectives. For a data processing activity, the broad objective should be to set up a management information system for effective decision-making. And the specific objectives should provide for setting up subsystems to support the management information system. It is important to note, however, that a management information system is not necessarily a total systems concept approach.

The definition of objectives requires that the upper echelon determines the setting of this activity so that the activity will contribute to the overall effectiveness of the organization. This necessitates the establishment of short-term and long-term plans. The short-term plans may require the initiation of interim or corrective actions that will de-emphasize the mono-functional approach and initiate conversion to the multifunctional concept. The long-term plans need to be aimed at making the data processing activity operationally effective. These plans, as well as long-term policies, should be established by the executive committee, because this is the only group that has a comprehensive view of the needs and goals of the organization.

A deep and continuing involvement on the part of the executive committee, in the direction and control of the information-processing function, will give impetus to the development of multi-functional systems. This commitment is made more effective by placing the data-processing function at a higher level in the organizational structure. Such a hierarchical arrangement enables the top echelon to maintain close control on the data processing activity, as well as to determine the activity's effectiveness and its compatibility with stated objectives. The upper echelon must at all times evaluate the contribution of the data processing function to ensure that quality and quantity are maintained, that time schedules are met, and that the cost-versus-gain ratio is kept reasonable.

Close control by the upper echelon is one aspect of management that is all too often overlooked or disregarded. Consequently, when an installation begins to falter, the upper echelon tends to try remedying the problem by acquiring additional equipment—an action that, in most cases, only compounds the problem. When such an installation runs into trouble, the best solution is for the upper echelon to become directly involved and to undertake a reappraisal of the installation's objectives.

This upper-echelon role requires that the executive committee be educated regarding the potentialities of data processing as a decision-making tool. Furthermore, to provide for the effective interaction of the upper echelon and the data processing facility, it is also important to teach the data processing managers the techniques of management, as well as to provide them with knowledge of the organization's overall structure and its long-term goals.

Traditionally, the idea of upper-echelon involvement in data processing has not been popular in the typical executive committee, principally because most of the executives in this group have not been very knowledgeable about data processing. This situation is changing, however, because increasing numbers of top executives are now attending sessions on the subject of data processing being presented by the American Management Association and other professional groups. In addition, many organizations are having management consulting firms and academic institutions develop specialized seminars for the training of top and middle managers (see Chapter 3).

Very little, however, is being done to train data processing managers in the management functions. This is a major drawback, for if a data processing manager is to manage effectively, it is essential that he have a full knowledge of these managerial tools and skills.

In an effort to minimize the managerial problems, many organizations have added to the ranks of their data processing management by promoting personnel from management training programs who have demonstrated their managerial capability. The tangible benefits from this alternative may prove to be only temporary. The nondata-processing-oriented manager may find that his background, training, and experience keep him from properly defining and measuring his objectives. Consequently he will be unable to communicate his objectives to his people and his managers. He may also lack the ability to determine if a goal is attainable. In addition, the manager must understand and know how to apply the basic tools such as management controls, documentation and performance standards, and scheduling in the role of a data processing manager. Ultimately most organizations recognize the need for providing the nondata-processing-oriented manager with training in information-processing technology. The training is not intended to make them experts but to deal effectively with the problems, power, and potential of information processing.

Summing up, it needs to be reiterated that the executive committee must accept the basic idea that the investment made in data processing equipment and related support elements can be recovered only through total upper-echelon involvement.

RESPONSIBILITY FOR ADMINISTRATION AND CONTROL

Because data processing is a management tool of great depth and breadth, its capability should not and cannot be limited to one functional activity within the organization. This is why the overall responsibility for the administration and control of a data processing function lies with the top echelon of the organization.

The authority and responsibility for the data processing function should be delegated by the executive committee to an upper echelon executive who is capable of determining total organizational requirements. In a large business or corporate structure, this executive should be the vice-president for data processing or the director of data processing; in a religious, governmental, or professional organization, he should be a high official of comparable standing. In cases where such authority has to be delegated to a financial executive, it should be made clear that the organizational structure developed for data processing will meet the information processing needs of the overall organization. This expansion of objectives may necessitate either the acquisition of additional equipment or the development of an additional processing facility to service the needs of the nonfinancial, functional activities.

The Chief Administrator

The chief administrator for a data processing function, generally an upper echelon executive, has a number of important responsibilities, all of which are an inherent part of the management process. These responsibilities require him to:

—Define the broad objectives and develop the specific objectives for the function.

—Develop the procedures and policies.

—Delineate the structural aspects of the data processing function.

—Develop the lines of authority and responsibility.

—Establish criteria for the recruitment, selection, and training of personnel.

—Establish the proper liaison channels with those functions directly and indirectly involved with the data processing function.

—Assist in the procurement of the necessary resources.

—Develop the means for evaluating the progress and effectiveness of the data processing function.

—Guide the activity toward the goals established by the executive committee.

—Define the feedback control system to be used.

These responsibilities are the ones delegated to the chief administrator by the top echelon of the organizational hierarchy.

The Data Processing Manager

The data processing manager may be responsible to the executive committee; he may be the chief administrative officer of the organization, the chief administrator of the data-processing function, or the administrator or manager of some other functional activity such as accounting, engineering, marketing, or production control. The placement of the data processing manager's position in the overall organizational structure will determine the depth and breadth of his responsibilities. The responsibilities are also affected by the objectives stipulated for the data-processing function by the upper echelon. Therefore the data processing manager may have to assume the responsibility for defining broad and specific objectives for the function, the development of policies for the activity, the delineation of the data processing organizational structure, and so forth, in addition to his regular duties and responsibilities.

Generally, the data processing manager is expected to:

—Develop the sequence of steps, operations, and procedures to accomplish the stated objectives.

—Balance the available resources to maintain a proper productive mix.

—Establish the priorities and schedules that will maintain operational effectiveness.

—Develop the necessary controls for accuracy, quality, and costs.

—Establish utilization data on manpower, equipment, and materials.

—Develop a budget and a system of cost accounting for services rendered.

—Provide for recruitment, selection, and training of personnel.

—Establish a system for appraisal and evaluation of personnel.

—Maintain proper channels of communication.

—Guide the data processing activity in accordance with the plan.

—Evaluate procedures to determine their effectiveness.

—Establish a feedback control system for evaluation of operational results.

—Advise the chief administrator on equipment utilization and needs.

—Advise the chief administrator about failure as well as success.

These responsibilities are major aspects of the management process and must be implemented to provide for the operational effectiveness of the data processing function. They are discussed further in succeeding chapters of this book.

Review Questions: Group 2A

1. Why must a multi-functional approach to the use of data processing services be developed in each organization?
2. Why should the executive committee become involved in the direction of the data processing activity?
3. One of the primary responsibilities of a data processing administrator is to define the feedback control system. Explain why this is an important responsibility.

BUSINESS AND SCIENTIFIC ACTIVITIES

A data processing function can be subdivided into two major categories. These are the business activity and the scientific activity.

Business data processing is concerned with the manipulation of large data files to assist in the day-to-day operation of the organization. This element of the data processing activity provides information for the financial, marketing, personnel, inventory control, production control, purchasing, and other nontechnical functional activities. Scientific data processing, also referred to as computational data processing, is involved with the application of mathematical programming techniques to the solution of technical and scientific problems.

Some organizations maintain this division into two elements, but give major emphasis to the scientific category. Very often, in such cases where there has been a major organizational shift toward a scientific emphasis, the scientific element is equipped with a computer while the business element is limited to punched card equipment or smaller computing systems. In other organizations, the scientific category is given prime utilization of the equipment, with any excess time being provided for business applications. Some organizations maintain equal but separate hardware and support facilities for the business and scientific elements of their data processing activities.

The particular arrangement of the functional structure selected by an organization depends on the overall purposes or objectives of the organization, the type of organization, and the strengths and weaknesses of its key personnel. The best judge of whether the business and scientific activities should be maintained separately or combined is the top echelon, because this is the managerial group that has a panoramic view of the organization's requirements.

Separate Activities

There are two major reasons why many organizations favor the maintenance of separate data processing activities for the business and scientific elements. First, each element is a different kind of activity that involves different objectives, support, and equipment. Second, the development of systems and subsystems for each element will be neither inhibited nor compromised.

The accompanying illustrations of organization charts show three variations on the theme of maintaining separate data processing facilities for business and scientific data processing.

Figure 2.1 is a chart for an organization with two distinct facilities. The business data processing facility reports to the superintendent of business data processing, who in turn reports to the vice-president of administration. The scientific data processing facility reports to the superintendent of engineering and ultimately to the vice-president of manufacturing. The lines of authority, the objectives, and the activities are in each case totally independent of each other. However, the scientific function is mono-functional in that it serves only the engineering needs, whereas the business function is multi-functional because it services various activities in the organization.

In Figure 2.2 the two data processing facilities are separated, but they both report to the controller. This approach to organization may be immediately unacceptable to some executives because they cannot envision a scientific data processing manager reporting to a controller. They fear that such an arrangement creates a difficult situation because the controller is basically business-oriented and does not understand the needs of the scientific group. This attitude stems largely from their fear that the business element will, if given the opportunity, dominate data processing objectives and budgets.

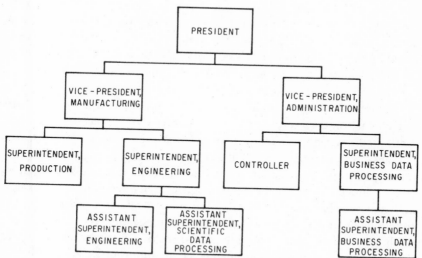

Figure 2.1. Separate Facilities: Example A

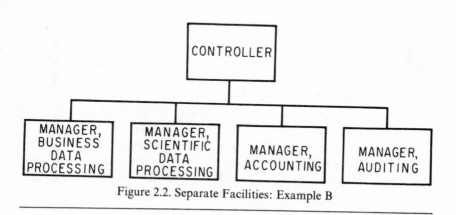

Figure 2.2. Separate Facilities: Example B

49

Nevertheless, it must be recognized that the controller is generally a member of the executive committee and that he is very much concerned with the operation of the organization. He is responsible for determining the cost of the products produced or services rendered. He considers the cost in terms of organizational effectiveness, so he is in the best position to evaluate tangible and intangible costs and savings. As a result, he is able to effectively assign the necessary cost objectives to both the scientific and business data processing functions.

Figure 2.3 illustrates what is probably the best organizational arrangement for the establishment of separate data processing facilities. Both facilities report to the director of data processing operations, who is placed on an upper level of the organizational hierarchy and reports directly to the vice-president of operations. The data processing function is also independent of the manufacturing, engineering, and business activities, so that it is in a better position to offer service in a multifunctional manner. There is also the advantage that the business and scientific functions are reporting to a director who is oriented toward data processing needs and problems. (It is important to add here that many data processing personnel resign and seek employment in another organization because the director was *not* oriented toward data processing.)

Combined Activities

Some organizations feel that the business and scientific activities can best work hand-in-hand, thereby reducing the number of organizational relationships and simplifying the chain of command. Their principal reasons for combining the activities are that:

—It reduces operating costs through more effective utilization of personnel and equipment.

—It provides for the development of an effective management information system because it integrates the various interacting and interrelating functional activities into a cohesive unit for data processing purposes.

—An integrated system permits the introduction of control features into the feedback process.

—With the advent of third-generation computing systems it may now be economically feasible to integrate the hardware and software for

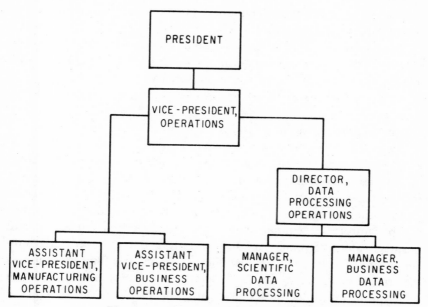

Figure 2.3. Separate Facilities: Example C

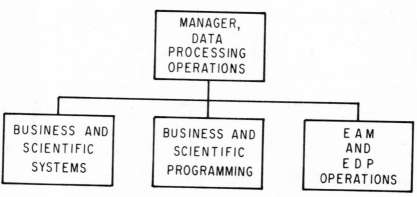

Figure 2.4. Integrated Facilities: Example A

51

both activities, thereby reducing operating costs through more effective utilization of resources.

The current and future technological advances in the data processing industry will move more organizations toward using a combined data processing facility. The decision, however, can only be made by the executive committee after it has considered the organization's overall requirements.

The accompanying illustrations show three examples of combined, or integrated, data processing.

Figure 2.4 shows an arrangement in which the systems personnel for the business and scientific functions are integrated under the direction of one manager. Similarly, the programmers for both elements are placed under a single programming manager. And the EAM and EDP operations group controls the equipment utilization for both the scientific and business applications. Such an arrangement facilitates the effective utilization of the personnel, because they work on scientific and business material without making any distinction. The hardware configuration in this type of integrated structure is adequate to service both elements, which thereby makes it possible to avoid the investment and operating cost involved in having duplicated processing facilities and personnel. Combining the applications of the two elements ensures effective utilization of the processing equipment, because in scientific installations the volume of input, output, and processing is very often low.

In Figure 2.5 the systems and programming personnel are integrated into one group under the direction of a single manager. However, there is a separation of equipment facilities for both elements. The equipment facilities are separated because the scientific installation is maintained for research experimentation, and has to be available when needed by the research personnel. In many organizations, such a research facility is equipped with analog or special-purpose computing devices, which cannot readily be used for business processing applications.

Some organizations prefer to use the format illustrated in Figure 2.6, in which the business and scientific elements are maintained as separate sections or groups under the direction of a programming manager and systems manager respectively. Under this type of structural arrangement, the business systems and programming personnel service all nontechnical systems and applications. And the technical systems and programming personnel service the technical function or activities. Use of this arrangement implies that there is an adequate work load to support

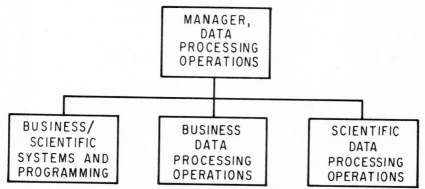

Figure 2.5. Integrated Facilities: Example B

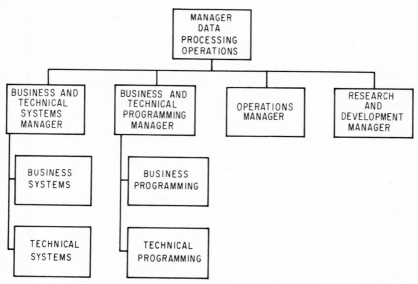

Figure 2.6. Integrated Facilities: Example C

53

separate functions. But during dips in the work load, some organizations use their technical systems and programming personnel to assist the business subject-matter specialists. Therefore, although this type of arrangement provides for integrated activities, it also maintains a separation of objectives for the business and technical functions. However, the operations group and the research and development group are fully integrated, with no separation of personnel or objectives.

LINE AND STAFF ACTIVITIES

In most organizations, the people can be classified in terms of two basic structural types or activities. These are the line activity and the staff activity.

The line activity, the one most closely connected with the actual operation, is very often referred to as the "doer" or operating activity because it is instrumental in attaining the objective. It is at the line level in the hierarchical structure that the basic management functions of directing and controlling are applied to any plan developed at the staff level.

The staff activity provides advice and support for strengthening the line activity. This level is manned by people who are specialists with a breadth of knowledge, skills, and experience. The abilities of the staff specialists relieve the line manager of detailed technical chores, which he himself either may not be capable of dealing with or may not have the time to do so. A staff specialist cannot generally direct outside of his own realm, so his plans, suggestions, or recommendations must be carried out through the line activity. This lack of authority to direct others sometimes creates problems, because staff specialists may exceed their delegated authority. However, in many organizations, they produce tangible output rather than mere talk—an output that a line activity can implement.

Figures 2.7 and 2.8 illustrate two different line-staff relationships. In Figure 2.7 the research and development group and the systems group are placed on a staff level to serve in an advisory and planning capacity for the director of data processing. The research and development group is placed at the staff level because one of its primary functions is to evaluate the overall effectiveness of the various data processing functions. At this level, it is not competing with any other functional group,

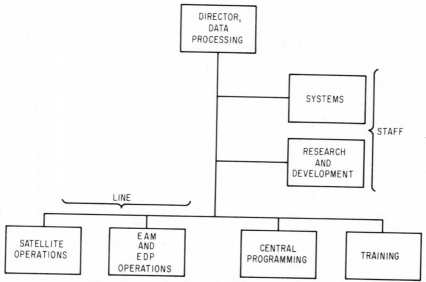

Figure 2.7. Line-Staff Relationships: Example A

so it will be more objective in its appraisal. The systems group is placed at the staff level to add objectivity to its operations. At this level, it has the additional leverage to ensure that the systems that are designed and developed will be implemented by the functional groups at the line level.

In Figure 2.8 the systems and programming personnel are placed at the staff level to produce the technical documentation for the training, EDP operations, and EAM operations groups. The tangible output produced at the staff level is implemented by the operating services at the line level. Generally, in this type of a structural arrangement, the systems and programming group is small and the personnel often perform both systems and programming functions.

Conflict Between Line and Staff

Some problems inevitably arise in every organizational structure that has line and staff activities. The most common problems are associated with the following five points of conflict:

1. The delegation of authority to the staff group may not have been clarified or made explicit.

2. In data processing, the line supervisors very often resent the

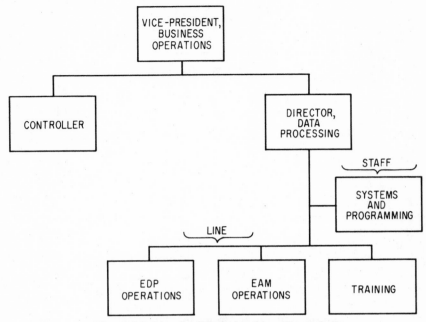

Figure 2.8. Line-Staff Relationships: Example B

additional training given to staff personnel and/or the importance overtly or implicitly attributed to the staff group.

3. The staff personnel resent their lack of authority to implement their own ideas.

4. Line personnel tend to develop empires and will resist any changes that they feel may threaten their position or control.

5. Line personnel resent the disparity between their own budget and the operating budgets provided for a staff group.

Easing the Conflict

Conflict between line and staff activities can hamper any organization. Therefore, the data processing administrator must work diligently to resolve or reduce the conflict and to gain maximum output from each organizational level. Much of the conflict can be resolved by establishing a two-way communications channel, which will allow an even flow of information and resources between the two levels. Another effective tactic is to establish a liaison committee for the exchange of information on new or pending projects, as well as for the discussion of problems. These are just two general suggestions. It is also valuable to examine each of the five most common points of conflict (mentioned above), together with some tentative solutions.

1. THE DELEGATION OF AUTHORITY. The delegation of authority to the staff group must be made explicit. Very often the executive committee fails to be explicit in communicating the parameters of the assignment. Most of the associated problems are generated by failure to communicate the time span, span of control, budget limitations, as well as failure to clarify the objectives or goal. To overcome these problems, more definitive specifications from the executive committee are necessary. However, when this information is not volunteered by the upper echelon, the manager of the staff group must request it. As stated in the previous chapter, a manager cannot begin to function effectively until he understands the role of the objective. When the staff group has formulated a preliminary plan, it should discuss the plan, particularly the portions that affect the operating level, with the line level activity. Communicating this information will help to remove the barriers of misunderstanding, resolve problems, and answer questions posed by either level.

2. ADDITIONAL TRAINING. Many organizations provide the staff group with more educational and training opportunities because of the nature of its work. The staff group is usually involved in feasibility studies, evaluation of new hardware and/or software, and developing new techniques or functions that require additional knowledge or information. However, there are occasions when key line personnel could also be included, as, for example, during presentations by the vendors of new hardware and/or software. This would provide the line people with some understanding of the material, and it would also improve communications on the subject in any subsequent discussions. Furthermore, training for line personnel should be provided periodically to maintain their effectiveness. It must never be neglected on the invalid if all too common grounds of "lack of time." (See also the detailed discussion of training in Chapter 3.)

3. STAFF LEVEL RESENTMENT. Line activities consider themselves the lifeblood of the organization. They believe they can get the job done if the staff activity would only leave them alone. Consequently they label all staff activity ideas as too costly, advice as ineffectual, and help as

being of the wrong kind. The attitudes and criticisms are strongly re-
sented by the staff activity.

To minimize the waste that results from such conflicts requires
involvement by the upper echelon. This group must recognize the fact
that they established a staff level activity manned by high-salaried experts because the need for advice and assistance was evident. They
cannot afford to have the staff activity efforts subject to rejection at the
pleasure of a line manager.

One approach to minimizing the frustrations and resentment is for
the executive committee to declare that the staff group has the exclusive
right to advise and service the line function. This should put an end to
situations in which the operations manager agrees at his own discretion
to develop a system or program for a user.

The executive committee may also become directly involved by
acting as a disseminator of the staff activity outputs to the line activity.
As a result, the line activity becomes directly accountable to the executive committee for the implementation of an idea, standard, documentation, schedule, or plan. There is little likelihood that the line manager
will be very critical of the information communicated to him in this
manner. Also, it will insure that the advice is followed, because the line
manager will be unwilling to enter into direct conflict with his superior.
Though this approach may appear to be coercive to the line level, it does
force the staff activity to produce the kinds of advice and service needed
by the line manager.

4. LINE LEVEL EMPIRES. Empire builders can only be eliminated
through the executive committee becoming involved in the data processing activities. The empire builders—"Joe Zero's" as they are sometimes
called—outwardly give every appearance of cooperating with others,
but, in reality they impede progress or implementation. This may be
because they may have authoritarian personalities and want to keep
their thumb on everything. Or they may be insecure and consequently
act to impede implementation because they do not fully understand the
project, system, procedure, or application. Very often, however, the staff
group can improve and secure the cooperation of the line level managers
through the use of liaison committees and conferences.

5. BUDGET DISPARITIES. Arguments regarding budget disparities
generally tend to be overinflated. The disparities appear in personnel

costs because salaries are higher at the staff level owing to the required skills and competence of people in the staff group. In situations where the line manager or staff manager feels that his budget is inadequate, he should make his case known to his immediate superior. The case must not be a blanket request, but rather a well-supported documentation including such figures as development expenses for systems and/or programs, equipment operating expenses, construction costs for new or enlarged installation, program and system maintenance costs, number of personnel in a breakdown by occupational grouping, average hourly utilization of equipment per week, average hourly utilization of equipment per peak week, etc. The availability of such information will expedite the presentation, eliminate many unnecessary questions, and increase the chances of acceptance.

Review Questions: Group 2B

1. What are the advantages of maintaining separate data processing facilities for the business and scientific functions?
2. Why would it be beneficial for an organization to combine the data processing facilities for the business and scientific functions?
3. Traditionally, the operations group has been placed at the line level on the organization chart. Why?
4. What are the causes of conflict between the staff and line level activities within the data processing function? Can the problems be resolved? If so, briefly explain how.

THE FUNCTIONAL ORGANIZATION

As the organizational structure expands, it becomes more complex. To simplify this structure, many organizations employ the process of divisionalization in order to break down a major function into its component parts or activities. This process is frequently applied to the data processing function.

The five component activity groups of the data processing function are the:
—Systems Design and Implementation Group
—Programming Group
—Advanced Planning and Development Group
—Operations Group
—Training Group
This divisionalization is illustrated in Figure 2.9.

The Systems Design and Implementation Group

A system can be described as the detailed plan or arrangement for the interrelationship and interaction of available resources to accomplish a given task. To develop a rationalization of the interdependence of these activities involves analysis and design. The analysis phase is concerned with determining the following factors:
—The source of the data elements
—The process required to maintain the development and flow of these data elements
—The steps and operations required to produce a useful output
—The type of output required
The design phase is concerned with the development of a procedure or system that will include the above-mentioned requirements and accomplish a given task or objective. The system needs to provide for the collection, classification, and manipulation of data, to utilize the available resources and to lead to meaningful reports. It is such systems that represent the foundation of the data processing activity.

The systems design and implementation group, commonly referred to simply as the systems group, is very often maintained as a staff level agency. This means that the group has to implement its ideas, concepts, and designs through the operations group and/or the programming group. The structural and functional arrangements vary from organization to organization. The detailed organizational format of the data processing function is developed by upper-echelon executives who base their decision on organizational objectives, as well as on the function's relationship to the existing structure and its contribution to the overall effectiveness of the organization.

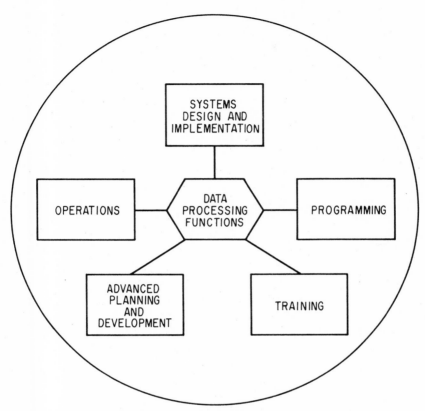

Figure 2.9. Divisionalization of the Data Processing Function

After a problem has been defined, requirements established, and the solution developed, the systems group must implement the approach. For the systems personnel, the implementation process is primarily one of coordination. Prior to the actual implementation the analyst must conduct a readiness review to ensure that all of the interacting elements and factors are ready for cut-over. The analyst must evaluate the status of user and operation's documentation, physical facilities for installation of new equipment, computer programs, personnel training, and so forth. When actual implementation occurs, the analyst must monitor the effected activities to ensure that all operations are proceeding according to plan. If any problems are detected, the analyst must coordinate with the personnel responsible for that segment to initiate remedial action.

Within a reasonable period of time after implementation, the analyst must conduct a follow-up, which is made to determine that all problems have been resolved, that the implemented plan is achieving the stated objectives, and that the previously stated savings and benefits have been achieved.

Responsibilities

In most data-processing activities, a systems group has six major responsibilities. These are:
1. The analysis of existing manual systems
2. The analysis of existing punched card systems
3. The analysis of computerized systems
4. The analysis of proposed systems
5. The analysis and design of changes in existing (operational, manual, punched card, and computerized) systems
6. The design of systems for manual, punched card equipment, and computerized operations

1. EXISTING MANUAL SYSTEMS. In any organization, manual systems must be investigated to determine whether or not it is feasible to convert them to an automated process. All manual systems do not readily lend themselves to automation, so it is useful to use the following three good tests, which should be applied to the evaluation of any manual system:

a) Can It Be Done Better Mechanically? This first test implies that the information can be provided more readily and more accurately than it can under the manual system.

b) Can It Be Done More Economically? Economic feasibility should be based primarily on tangible savings and only secondarily on the intangibles. Automated systems are very often justified on the basis that the information will be made available more readily, thereby enabling the manager to make decisions more quickly. This is a loaded statement because it implies that the manager must have quick access to the information at any cost. It may be very nice to have the information sooner, but is it really necessary and does it warrant the extra cost involved?

c) Can the Same Type of Information Be Provided? This third test is one that must be thoroughly applied to any manual system. It is made to ensure that the user can receive the information he needs to do the job with and in the format that will increase and not impede his productivity.

A common complaint among many users of data processing services is that they do not now receive all of the pertinent information that was formerly available to them. Another complaint is that they now have to use two different reports to assemble the desired information. Maintaining an open communications channel between the systems group and the user during the analysis phase can reduce or eliminate such conditions. If such a condition becomes unbearable, it will eventually have to be changed, thereby incurring additional development expenses.

2. EXISTING PUNCHED CARD SYSTEMS. An analysis of punched card systems will most generally be made when an organization is either converting to or considering computerized operations. This is a necessary step in order to take full advantage of computer equipment. Converting from a punched card system to a computerized system without making significant changes will result in uneconomical runs and the need to develop additional controls.

Some organizations attempt to reduce their initial development cost for systems and programming by converting from unit-record applications to computerized unit-record applications. The computerized unit-record applications are direct conversions of EAM control panels to computer programs, written most generally in a report program generator (RPG) or assembler language. No real attempt is made to integrate or analyze the operations; rather, all that is done is to convert each control panel in its existing form to a computer run. Inevitably, this results in a multitude of programs, with each of them performing a separate function, such as listing, tabulating, calculating, etc.

The author has personally observed an organization equipped with a medium-scale computer with four tape drives using a computerized unit-record approach to processing. For three years the organization continued to process the hourly rated employees payroll by utilizing the computer only as a high-speed printer and calculator.

Formerly, the organization had used an IBM 407-519 accounting machine and reproducing punch combination to summarize the total regular and overtime hours worked and to punch the results in a card called the "gross card." The gross card was then merged with an employee master card for calculation of gross earnings on the IBM 604-521 calculator and punch combination; then the end results were punched into a new card called the "calculated gross." The calculated gross card was subsequently processed on the IBM 604-521 for calculation of the social security and federal income taxes and, in another pass, the state income tax. Anyone familiar with the design of systems would question the economic feasibility of such a disjointed unit-record application.

Then the calculator and punch were replaced by the installation of the computer system. Therefore, the organization had no choice but to write programs to perform the calculator functions. Initially, it converted the two calculator control panels into two separate tax calculation programs. After six months, someone decided that the two tax programs could be combined into one program. The organization did not take such a "large" step, though. Instead, it just combined the summarizing of hours and calculation of gross earnings into one program. Nevertheless, the data processing manager boasted that he had reduced payroll processing time from five to four days, which resulted in a saving for the organization. It is very questionable whether in fact the organization did actually derive any tangible savings in its conversion from the old unit-record payroll to a computerized system. Though the organization had at its disposal a powerful processing tool, it chose to computerize without optimizing the benefits of the hardware.

Such benefits could have been obtained fairly easily. In such a situation, the availability of magnetic tape can be utilized to incorporate the employee master card, year-to-date and quarter-to-date taxes and earnings, deductions, and other personnel information into master tape records, with one such record for each employee. This would expedite input and output functions by reducing or eliminating card handling and processing. Also, it would take only one program to process the entire payroll, from the calculation of gross earnings to net earnings, as well as the printing of pay details and drafts. Such a system would produce substantial and tangible savings for an organization. It is conceivable that the entire payroll for approximately five thousand employees could be processed in approximately ten hours. In this instance, the tangible savings would exceed the development costs incurred for systems and programming effort.

3. COMPUTERIZED SYSTEMS. Some experts estimate that no computerized system lasts more than two years without a major or significant change. This view is based primarily on the fact that changes in organizational objectives are bound to occur and that systems personnel be-

come more sophisticated in their approach to the computer. For example, when an organization initially converts to disk-oriented hardware from unit-record equipment or a card-oriented computer, the early applications continue to utilize serial rather than random access techniques and continue to lack good data management practices. As the personnel gain operating experience and confidence, they revise their applications to utilize the random access techniques.

In any conversion, the systems personnel apply the methods and the hardware and/or software that are most familiar to them, and they tend to continue doing so until they develop a sense of security and an adequate level of confidence about the new approach. Such conservatism cannot prevail for any prolonged period of time, because it tends to reduce or eliminate any tangible savings to be gained from the conversion.

In organizations that insist on a definite conversion or installation schedule, the personnel tend to choose the approach that will yield the fastest, though not necessarily the most efficient, results. This practice is undertaken with the stated understanding that the application will be modified at a later date, when more time is available. However, some organizations never reach the point when time is available. Consequently, optimal results are never achieved, tangible savings are never maximized, and the desired objectives are only partially attained. No computerized system, however good, is infinitely perfect; therefore, changes can and should be made as frequently as needed in order to improve the system's operational effectiveness.

4. PROPOSED SYSTEMS. A typical organization experiences change: new ideas evolve, changes in organizational objectives and needs arise, legal requirements are imposed that affect the existing operation, potential users are found, and numerous other situations develop. Such changes invariably give rise to proposals for new systems. In addition, the organization receives a stream of vendor announcements about new or improved hardware and software. These announcements must all be analyzed to determine their potential operational effectiveness and economic feasibility. The analyses may indicate that certain proposals lack economic or practical justification, or that advances in the state of the art are still not sufficiently developed to permit practical design and implementation. The analyses may also show that a current proposal is definitely valid, but that the organization would be wise to wait for further technological developments in the field before making any deci-

sion. For example, some current proposals for the use of data collection or data communications devices could well be affected by the progress being made in laser technology. Similarly, current proposals for expediting the input into a data processing system may change with the continuing development of optical character recognition (OCR) devices.

The OCR and other proposals may not be economically feasible because the cost of the hardware currently available may still be prohibitively expensive for the organization. Or they may be technically unsatisfactory; for example, the volume of source documents may be low, the quality of paper or impressions unacceptable, or the documents may be either too large for the equipment or incorrectly designed. Such economic and technical factors can weigh heavily in the evaluation of a proposal.

When a proposal is found to have merit, the systems group should initiate a feasibility study to determine the proposal's practical and economic justification. The feasibility study will critically investigate the impact of a proposal on the organization, its present and future objectives, the existing system, and its cost effectiveness. If there is justification for proceeding with development of the proposal, then the design of the system will be initiated. It is possible, however, that a change to an existing system may also facilitate the user's needs.

The analysis of proposed systems also includes comparative assessments. The current operation is studied and evaluated and then compared with the proposed approach in order to determine the advantages and disadvantages of each operation. This kind of comparison can be effectively made only by conducting a feasibility study. (The subject of feasibility studies is discussed in detail in Chapter 8.)

5. CHANGES IN EXISTING SYSTEMS. The need for new information, shifts in emphasis regarding objectives, and other organizational changes commonly give rise to the necessity of changing an existing system. In these cases, as in those relating to proposals for new systems, the systems group must analyze the situation, determine what should be done, and then implement the changes wherever possible. The systems group uses the same basic methods of analysis. It studies and evaluates the current operation, investigates the possible changes, examines the possibilities of using improvements in hardware and software, and initiates feasibility studies as needed.

The following is a good example of changing an existing system. An organization is currently receiving accounting data for the general ledger from its subsidiaries through the mail. The competition of business has forced the headquarters accounting organization to advance the closing of the books by two days. Consequently, the submission schedule of the subsidiary reporting units must be altered to reflect the new requirements. The first thought of the subsidiaries would be to advance their operating schedules. Investigation by the systems group may reveal that such a step may not be possible and that a revision in the mode of data transmission to the headquarters accounting organization may be required. The systems group would then initiate a feasibility study to decide upon an expeditious and economical mode of data transmission.

6. DESIGN OF SYSTEMS. The design of systems is one of the most important responsibilities of the systems group. In the previously mentioned responsibilities, there is a limited amount of design work performed by the analyst when considering possible alternatives. The preliminary design specifications must be subsequently detailed and finalized to produce a solution to the problem. The design of systems is concerned with development of procedures necessary for the processing of data and the establishment of management controls to ensure the attainment of a given objective. The specifications developed by the group must optimize the input, output, processing, storage, and communications characteristics to produce a well-designed data processing system. These specifications include such items as source document, form, card, and record layouts; system flowcharts; operating instructions; and other essential documentation for the programming, operations, and training groups of the data processing function. The accompanying illustration, Figure 2.10, is an example of a system flowchart included in the documentation package of a student dropout reporting application. (The subject of documentation is discussed in detail in Chapter 4.)

Review Questions: Group 2C

1. How may a data processing activity be structured by function?
2. Which tests should be applied in evaluating a manual system when it is being considered for conversion to an automated process?
3. Why must the systems group be concerned with existing manual, punched card, and computerized systems?

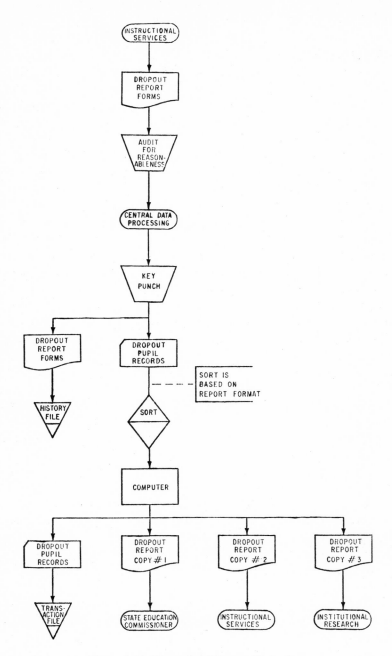

Figure 2.10. Example of System Flowchart

The Programming Group

The task of programming has now become one of program design rather than, as it used to be, merely a matter of either coding or control panel wiring. In only a few instances today does a programmer still write programs in actual machine or binary language code. Instead, he is concerned with designing a solution to the problem that will maximize the effective use of software operating systems and higher level language assemblers and compilers.

The programming group is found only in computerized data processing activities. In some small organizations, the systems personnel also serve as the programming personnel, which requires that the programming function be integrated with the systems function. In some large organizations, the programming activity is not only completely separate but may be subdivided into business and scientific elements. Programming personnel then become specialists in each of the respective elements. The programming group, like the systems group, is very often maintained as a staff level activity. However, in some instances, it is an independent line function.

Responsibilities

A programming group usually has the following six major responsibilities:

1. The design of programs for the development and implementation of computerized data systems
2. The development of modular and generalized programs
3. The writing of utility and conversion programs
4. Maintenance of existing programs
5. Maintenance of a program library
6. Wiring of control panels for computer, unit-record, or peripheral equipment

1. PROGRAMS FOR COMPUTERIZED DATA SYSTEMS. Generally, the primary responsibility of the programming group is the design of computer programs to facilitate the development and implementation of computerized data systems. The programmer must structure a solution enabling him to maximize the effectiveness of the available hardware

and software, and to reduce or eliminate the duplication of programming effort.

The programmer initiates his design task by analyzing the problem statement, input, output, and file specification, and user requirements in order to develop a tentative solution. The solution should be reviewed with the analyst to ensure that the preliminary logic and assumptions are correct. There is a danger, however, that the problem, specifications, and requirements may be in a state of flux and that any tentative planning may turn out to be useless. This is why the programmer needs to know precisely what the computer can be expected to do. Otherwise, he will find himself constantly adding, changing, and modifying the program; the end result will be an inefficient set of instructions with many hidden "bugs"; and, consequently, the developmental costs will increase, as will the recurring costs for maintenance. After the review has been made, the programmer may begin to detail his solution and prepare for program coding, testing, debugging, and documentation.

Well-designed programs are essential to the data processing function. A well-designed program reduces testing and debugging time, which represents a large part of development cost. Also, compared with an ill-prepared one, it is easier to use and maintain; it provides greater flexibility for expansion and/or modification; and it generally interacts more effectively when combined with other programs in a data system.

A program must be carefully designed so that it can interact effectively with other programs, and it should make efficient use of the hardware and the software resources so as to optimize the throughput. In addition, it should provide the user with ease of operation—an important factor too often overlooked by programmers. A complex program setup very often results in errors or problems, which necessitate reruns or supplementary processing. And if it is not only complex but also tricky, it may be even more difficult to debug, modify, and maintain.

In many programs, repetitive functions are duplicated in coding, a situation that unnecessarily increases the program size and the time needed for compilation and processing. The use of modular programs can reduce or eliminate such duplication of programmer effort, and it can also reduce developmental, operating, and recurring costs.

The programmer, therefore, needs to determine precisely how processing is to occur and how his program will interact and mesh with the other elements of the data system. In evaluating the situation and deciding upon the best course of action, the programmer must also take into consideration the available hardware, software, and manpower resources, as well as the desired objectives.

Past experience in many organizations shows that failure to undertake sufficient planning before developing a program results in much patching and rewriting of the program. The end result generally is a program that fails to meet the desired objective. This problem occurs so frequently that most people seem to have become conditioned to it and to believe that little or nothing can be done to correct it. But this does not have to be the case, especially if managers give serious and sufficient thought to the procedures of program design before any expenditure of time, money, and effort is made and wasted.

2. MODULAR AND GENERALIZED PROGRAMS. Modular and generalized programs are written and used in order to facilitate the work of the programming group, as well as the individual programmer. Modular programs are complete programs or program segments that have been designed to become an integral part of another program in order to perform repetitive or complex tasks. The previously designed, tested, and debugged modules are available for linkage and interface with a variety of programs.

Generalized programs are those programs that have been specially designed to facilitate the production of a variety of user requests based on different constraints and parameters.

Program modules are used to extend the number of operations, to eliminate duplicate coding of repetitive routines, and to increase the number of operations through a mainline program. The concept of program modules is not new. Since the early days of programming, subroutines and subprograms have been used to extend the capabilities of a program. Initially, the modules were developed as subroutines for scientific applications. However, with the advent of operating systems, modules became an important aspect of programming.

To be operationally effective, the modules must be standardized and have a considerable degree of uniformity. This is not a disadvantage, because standardization provides for better interaction between the module, the mainline program, and the operating system—thereby reducing programming cost and effort. Although some flexibility may be lost, this is overcome by program compatibility. The previously coded modules (that is, input-output control routines, subprograms, subroutines, and macros) can be linked in a hierarchical structure to the mainline program in order to reduce programming, testing, and debugging time and costs. Because of their general nature, certain modules, such as data handling and statistical analysis routines, may be linked to a variety of different programs; this eliminates the necessity of rewriting such routines each time they are needed.

In the early days of programming, generalized programs were used primarily for report generation and for sorting. Since then, however, the uses have declined as the equipment vendors have supplied report program generator and sorting packages as part of the software. Generalized programs now have a variety of other applications. Many present-day organizations, for example, have developed generalized file maintenance routines to update the source files of numerous operational systems and applications. In addition, they have developed generalized calculation packages for such functions as multiplication, division, etc.; in some cases, they have produced these packages as modules for linkage to a variety of programs.

Modular and generalized programs very often require increased memory, machine time, and development. Nevertheless, the extra costs resulting from these increases are offset by savings in the planning, writing, testing, and debugging of the individualized programs that would otherwise be needed to accomplish the same desired goal.

In some large data processing organizations, in addition to preparing modular and generalized programs, the programming group is responsible for the development of new computer languages, sorts, compilers, debugging aids, and/or the improvement of existing software systems. Organizations lacking this development capability in their programming staff compensate by purchasing or leasing a variety of software packages from consulting or software firms.

When the modular and generalized programs are effectively utilized, they can increase the group's productivity and reduce the probability of undetected program bugs or errors.

3. UTILITY AND CONVERSION PROGRAMS. Conversion programs are written to audit the input and to translate data, files, and tables from one format to another in the implementation of a computerized data system. Very often this programming group responsibility also includes writing the programs for computer-assisted audits. Conversion programs are particularly useful as a form of management control (see Chapter 7).

Utility programs are written to handle a great many repetitive computer operations requiring programs for such functions as tape-to-tape,

tape-to-card, and memory dump. They are written by the programming group to assist the operations group in its day-to-day productive processing. Although these programs are important for the operation of the computer and peripheral equipment, they are not utilized for normal productive processing.

4. PROGRAM MAINTENANCE. The maintenance of existing computer programs is an essential but time-consuming responsibility. Many data processing organizations estimate that from 15 to 20 percent of the programming group's budget is expended on the maintenance task.

The time required for maintenance can be reduced significantly through the application of sound design concepts during original planning and development. It can also be reduced further by the subsequent application of program and documentation standards.

As part of its maintenance responsibility, the programming group also has to deal with the modification and alteration of existing programs that result from changes made in a computerized system, tax factors, parameters, hardware, or software. These program changes must be analyzed and inserted; then the revised programs have to be thoroughly tested, debugged, and documented before they are operational for productive processing.

One of the most common difficulties at this stage is that the documentation of changes is very often overlooked by the maintenance programmer. Consequently, future maintenance activity is delayed until he becomes aware of the reason for, and the degree of change or modification in, prior maintenance operations. (The subject of program documentation is discussed further in Chapter 4.)

In some organizations, the responsibility for program maintenance is relegated to a relatively inexperienced programmer, such as a junior programmer or trainee, in the belief that performance of this task requires very little practical experience. This assumption may be somewhat valid in organizations where good programming design concepts and documentation standards are stressed. However, because of the differences in program logic, an inexperienced programmer may well expend more time and effort than a more experienced person would have in performing the maintenance function.

5. LIBRARY MAINTENANCE. A program library can be a very important part of a programming operation. Such a facility should contain a duplicate copy of each currently operational program written by the programming group. It may also contain special programs written by the

equipment manufacturer's staff, by other users, and by programmers within other divisions or subsidiaries of the organization. Programs acquired by the library from sources outside of immediate organization can very often be directly adopted or modified for productive operations, thereby saving valuable programming time and effort.

This responsibility for library maintenance also includes the updating of software packages (operating systems, program translators, utilities, special application programs, etc.) with the changes supplied by the equipment and software vendors, or by other users. As these changes are meant to improve or expand the software, it is essential that they be made and tested. It is equally important that the back-up card deck, tape reel, or disk pack for the software are also updated and tested. In many organizations, the primary medium is maintained, but the changes are not immediately reflected in the back-up. Therefore, if the primary source is altered or destroyed, valuable production time may be lost until the package can be reconstructed. For example, an organization using a disk-operating system needs to make sure that the back-up pack, as well as the main disk pack, is kept properly updated. Then, if the primary pack becomes accidentally altered or destroyed, it is simply a matter of removing the primary pack from the disk drive and replacing it with the back-up pack—an easy shift that means only a minimal loss of productive time. This is a form of external management control essential to the operation of a data processing organization. (Controls are discussed more fully in Chapter 7.)

6. CONTROL PANELS. The programming group exercises its responsibility for the wiring of control panels primarily in instances where an organization has satellite operations serving as feeder units for a centrally located computing operation. In this type of setting, the feeder units are generally not staffed with technically qualified personnel; consequently, all control panels have to be wired by the central organization. The programming personnel wire and test the control panels and then draw them on wiring diagrams. These diagrams become part of the documentation and are used by the operations personnel to physically wire the necessary control panels for an application.

In some organizations, the programming group performs all wiring of control panels for the operations group. In this type of arrangement, the actual wiring of the control panels is done with permanent wiring and/or with wiring protected by a cover mounted on the panel frame.

Subsequently, the operating personnel has only to select the desired control panel from the storage racks for productive operations. This mode of operation helps to reduce or eliminate any processing errors resulting from faulty or incomplete panel wiring.

Some computing systems require the use of control panels in order to carry out their operation. In such cases, the necessary control panels are wired and maintained by the programming personnel.

Review Questions: Group 2D

1. Why should a manager encourage and enforce good design practices in programming?
2. In what ways do program modules play an important part in increasing the productivity of the programming personnel?
3. Should the manager of a small data processing function be concerned with program maintenance? Explain your answer.

The Advanced Planning and Development Group

This is an essential group within the data processing activity, yet it is most frequently overlooked or ignored. It is primarily concerned with determining the present and future operational effectiveness of the data processing function. The group also provides advisory services to the other groups within the data processing activity and the executive committee. The advanced planning and development group is called upon to evaluate new hardware and software developments and the application of information-processing techniques.

The actual name used for the group and/or the group personnel may vary from organization to organization. The most common designations include internal management consultants, corporate systems planners, corporate systems specialists, planning and design, etc.

The advanced planning and development group is involved in a multitude of activities affecting data processing. Given the proper authority and responsibility, it can do much to make data processing an effective and versatile management tool. In instances where an organization is unable to establish an advanced planning and development group, it is definitely sound policy and economically feasible for the organization to utilize a consulting firm to perform all or some of the following responsibilities.

Responsibilities

The major responsibilities of an advanced planning and development group are:

1. The determinating of the overall functional effectiveness of the data processing function
2. The evaluation of the effectiveness of existing data processing systems
3. The investigation and analysis of data processing activities and systems within other organizations
4. The investigation and study of new hardware developments
5. The investigation and study of new software developments
6. The validation of standards

1. OVERALL FUNCTIONAL EFFECTIVENESS. This first responsibility requires that the group develop a means of evaluating and measuring the progress of the data processing function. Such a procedure is necessary for determinating the extent of the contribution being made to the overall effectiveness of the organization. As a consequence of this "profit-motivated" role, the advanced planning and development group is often referred to as a watchdog group.

When implemented effectively, the group's evaluation procedure monitors problem areas, the cause of any problem, the corrective action that should be implemented, and the correction's effect on the total operation. The evaluation procedure also requires the application of the feedback control concept (see Chapter 1) to help reduce or eliminate actual or potential trouble areas, as well as to initiate any re-planning, reorganizing, re-communicating, and redirecting that may be needed.

The evaluation is intended to highlight the strengths and weaknesses of all of the activities within the data processing function. So, for example, the advanced planning and development group may be asked to investigate the reasons for the delays being experienced by the operations group in meeting output deadlines. Such delays could significantly affect the decision-making process. In this case, it would be the responsibility of the advanced planning and development group to identify the problems and their causes, and then to make recommendations to the executive committee for implementation of corrective action.

2. EFFECTIVENESS OF EXISTING SYSTEMS. The evaluation of existing systems is essential in determining their necessity, relevancy, and contribution—that is, their effectiveness. The various tests involved in this evaluation process represent a thorough audit of existing systems that is intended to eliminate ineffective or useless procedures. Data processing is accurately regarded as a service, but it can be an inordinately expensive service unless such evaluative procedures are utilized. Periodic "weedouts" must be conducted to eliminate a waste or misuse of available resources and valuable production time. The guidelines for evaluation of reports and a reports control system audit are included in Chapter 7.

3. INVESTIGATION OF OTHER ORGANIZATIONS. The advanced planning and development group can play a very important role in the organization by establishing and maintaining a dialogue with other organizations. This facilitates the investigation and analysis of data processing activities and systems that may be more fully developed or sophisticated than those currently operational in the group's own organization. Much information can be gained from such an interchange, and it could result in a significant reduction in the cost of programming and systems development.

4. INVESTIGATION OF NEW HARDWARE. Most organizations tend to be inundated with announcements regarding new or improved equipment for data processing. Each organization faces the difficult task of evaluating these various devices to determine their potential applicability to the organization's existing or proposed applications. Previously this was a task generally undertaken by the systems personnel; however, it is now very time-consuming and requires some specialized knowledge, so that it tends to be delegated to the advanced planning and development group.

5. INVESTIGATION OF NEW SOFTWARE. Software announcements should also be carefully scrutinized by the advanced planning and development group. Improved software helps make possible the design and implementation of more systems that are either new or sophisticated. The software can also be used to simplify or expand existing productive processes in the operations group or programming group.

Not all software is routinely acceptable or applicable, so that each software package must be carefully investigated and analyzed to determine its potential effect on, and effectiveness in, existing and proposed systems.

6. VALIDATION OF STANDARDS. Evaluation of the data processing activity requires the utilization of methods and performance standards. The uniformity of operations is determined through application of the methods standards; actual progress is evaluated through application of the performance standards.

The advanced planning and development group usually has the responsibility for designing, developing, and implementing these standards, as well as for conducting a follow-up analysis of their functional effectiveness. In addition, the group also continues to audit existing standards to ensure their effectiveness as well. The group's own effectiveness is important because well-formulated standards help provide for optimal utilization of the organization's manpower, machine, money, and material resources. (The subject of standards is discussed more fully in Chapters 4 and 6.)

The Operations Group

The operations group is responsible for the production of decision-making information. As such, it is the focal point of data processing activity—the point where the output of the systems, programming, training, and advanced planning and development groups must be integrated in order to provide for an optimal productive process. The interaction of these functional resources must be carefully coordinated by the chief administrator and manager of the data processing function.

In many organizations, the operations group is harassed, maligned, and forced into the role of "goof-guilty" scapegoat. This negative attitude stems from the attribution of human characteristics to data processing equipment. Consequently, the equipment is deemed responsible for all human failings and all errors actually committed by data processing and non-data processing personnel. An operations group that is constantly under such stress will undoubtedly be failing to meet a large percentage of its objectives.

To provide for and maintain an effective activity the operations manager must be fully aware of the factors of time, quality, quantity, and cost, each of which forms an essential part of the responsibilities delegated to the operations group.

Responsibilities

The group's primary responsibilities are:

1. The establishment and maintenance of an effective production schedule
2. The establishment of controls and standards to maintain accuracy
3. To provide for conversion of source data
4. The establishment and maintenance of communications channels between the operations group and satellite operations
5. The establishment of a records control system

1. THE PRODUCTION SCHEDULE. Establishing a production schedule is a very difficult task. The schedule must be flexible enough to allow for production runs, special reports, reruns, preventive and unscheduled maintenance, program and system testing, and the compilation and assembly of programs. It must be constructed in such a manner as to give due consideration to each of the influencing factors and, at the same time, to provide for an optimal utilization of all available resources. The operations manager must monitor his schedule closely in order to ensure adherence to the stipulated times, as well as to detect, identify, and correct any scheduling problems that may occur. Failure to develop and maintain a realistic operating schedule will serve only to create a variety of problems, which may result in a waste of valuable manpower, machine, material, and money resources. (The subject of scheduling is covered in detail in Chapter 6.)

2. CONTROLS AND STANDARDS. Because information used in decision-making must be accurate, management controls must be developed and utilized to ensure high quality of input, processing, and output. In order to maintain accuracy and operational effectiveness, the operations manager generally concerns himself with the establishment of document, accounting, and procedure controls. In addition, he has to develop or adapt methods and performance standards to provide for more effective utilization of resources and for realistic scheduling. (Standards are discussed more fully in Chapter 4. Scheduling and management controls are discussed in Chapters 6 and 7, respectively.)

3. DATA CONVERSION. The operations manager must give a great deal of attention to the conversion of data from human-sensible to machine-sensible language. What is more, the volume of transactions and source document formats affects the conversion rate. Most of the conversion is performed through the process of key punching data elements into punched cards from the source documents; however, this process is comparatively slow and very often causes a production backlog. Some data conversion is performed through the use of data recorders or inscribers. These provide for the transcription of input to magnetic tape or magnetic disks, which, in turn, expedite the passage of input into the computing system. Figure 2.11 illustrates a typical data recorder used for recording data on magnetic tape. A third method of conversion now gaining in popularity involves data conversion through the use of optical scanning devices, which reduces the key punching effort.

Actual conversion is only one facet of conversion responsibility. In addition, the operations manager must also verify the translation through manual or automated means prior to data manipulation. (Verification is discussed more fully, as an aspect of management controls, in Chapter 7.)

4. COMMUNICATIONS WITH SATELLITE OPERATIONS. Satellite operations can be very important because often they supply the input for many of the reports processed by the operations group. In many instances, the operations manager does not have direct control of this unit, so he must establish and maintain a communications channel to permit a free flow of information and resources. The communications network may enable him to schedule satellite operations, at least to the extent that they affect his activity.

5. RECORDS CONTROL SYSTEM. In many organizations, the operations manager has acquired a new responsibility in recent years. This is the responsibility for retention and maintenance of the data elements stored on punched cards, paper tape, magnetic tape, magnetic disk packs, and other media used in the information-processing cycle. This activity has become necessary because preparation of many of the management reports now requires historical data ranging in age from a few months to several years for comparison purposes in decision-making. The maintenance of such data creates storage and processing problems for the operations manager. He must establish a file retention

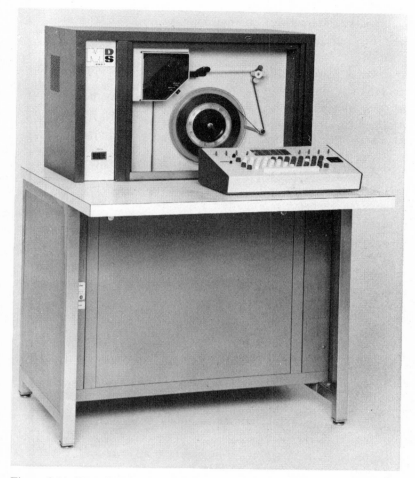

Figure 2.11. Data Recorder—MDS 6401. Courtesy Mohawk Data Sciences Corporation.

system to protect these records against accidental destruction or deliberate alteration, as well as to maintain their processing quality. (Retention safeguards are discussed as part of management controls in Chapter 7.)

The Training Group

Many organizations cling to the mistaken belief that training is a simple task, claiming that training involves no more than merely showing others how to perform a job or how a job is performed. Seeing this as a relatively simple task that requires very little time and no formal structure or plan, such organizations ignore the development and implementation of sound training programs. The function of training may sound simple in principle, but it never is in practice.

The effectiveness of any operation can be measured in part by the quality of the personnel assigned to the function responsible; such quality is developed by providing competent training and experience for the personnel involved in the process. Operational effectiveness can also be measured in part by the volume of requests for the function's services; such requests represent a gauge of how well the function is understood and valued by its present and potential users, and that in turn depends largely on how well the personnel are trained.

It is clear that an operationally effective organization is dependent on a well-structured training program. Because the training group serves such an essential function, its importance must not be minimized nor its responsibilities diluted. (Training is discussed more fully in Chapter 3.)

Responsibilities

A training group customarily has the responsibility to provide:
1. Technical training for data processing personnel
2. Technical and informational training for user organization personnel
3. Informational training for managers at all levels of the organization structure
4. Informational training for other members of the organization

1. TRAINING FOR DATA PROCESSING PERSONNEL. The training group will coordinate the use of training services offered by vendors, management consultants, colleges and universities, and professional educational services for the data processing personnel. Some of these sources may also be used to provide in-house training. If training is not available from these sources, is too limited, or is too costly, it is particularly important that a training capability be developed and maintained by the training group within the organization that will provide general orientation or detailed operating instructions. Software training programs teach

program language syntax of a given language, use of a programming language for problem-solving, and the application of software techniques or packages. Software training is generally very detailed and is provided primarily for programming personnel or subject-matter specialists.

However, a training group may be required to provide modified forms of software training. For example, the group may develop a special software course for systems and advanced planning personnel in order to provide a balance between orientation and detailed information.

The training group should also have the capability to provide data processing personnel with training in the simulation, direct access methods, programming for the use of inquiry units, and so on. Similarly, it should be able to teach the use of such applications as information retrieval, computer-assisted instruction, the bill of material processor, sort-merge, etc. (The bill of material processor is an important and popular IBM System/360 application program originally developed for production control application. Because of its linkage record capability, however, it is now also used in other areas.) The depth and breadth of knowledge provided by the training group for data processing personnel should lead to a handsome rate of return on investment through well-designed systems and programs that optimize the use of available resources.

2. TRAINING FOR USER PERSONNEL. Training is as essential for users as it is for data processing personnel, because the users in an organization operate equipment, write programs, and submit input and/or utilize the output. Engineering and technical personnel are often provided with software training that emphasizes problem-solving techniques. In educational organizations, teaching personnel are taught the use of programming languages such as FORTRAN as a tool for test item analysis, a form of computer-assisted instruction.

There is a general fallacy about hardware training that, to become an "expert," an operator simply needs to learn which buttons to push, to become aware of a few do's and don'ts (if the instructor is that generous), and to acquire some actual experience. Very often the end result of such informal training is faulty input data, equipment breakdown, excessive equipment downtime, the development of bad operating habits, and so on.

Vendors generally provide some limited on-hands or orientation-type training upon initial installation of the device. However, the operating manuals they provide are very general and include few if any examples. Therefore, to offset the possibility of any serious problems, the training group needs to develop practice workbooks that give detailed instructions—complete with proven examples—for dealing with various types of situations, conditions, and problems. Development of such workbooks must be a primary responsibility of the training group.

Users who write their own programs need to be provided some level of instruction regarding the various languages implemented for problem solving. This training program must cover the use of those computer instructions that facilitate the efficient use of computer storage, reduce translation and processing time, and simplify debugging. The user must also be made aware of any submission standards required by the operations group, such as job control card formats, priority or storage allocation codes, use of account numbers, etc. Figure 2.12, an excerpt from a user's manual published by an educational institution, details the job control card format required of all users submitting a program for translation or a production run. This type of training procedure enables the data processing function to provide high-quality service for the users and to make optimum use of its resources.

The training group is also responsible for making sure that any changes in the requirements are communicated to the users. Many organizations publish periodic newsletters to make the users aware of changes and modifications, or of the availability of any new software capabilities. Figure 2.13 consists of two extracts from such a newsletter intended for programming users.

Frequently neglected by data processing managers is training for users who are responsible for input preparation, utilization of output, data origination, coding or conversion. Some organizations have prepared documentation regarding completion of forms, types of forms to use, etc. Figure 2.14 consists of an excerpt from a standards manual detailing the standard procedure for completion of a form. Some organizations include within the documentation the procedure for interpreting the output and its manipulation.

Many organizations imprint frequently used codes on the reverse side of a punched card or printer form. Some incorporate explanations of the columnar data on the reverse side of a printer form to simplify

Columns	Content
1–2	**/ /**
3	Blank
4–6	"JOB"
7	Blank
8–12	Account number (assigned)
13	Blank
14–23	Name of user (last name first)
24	Blank
25–27	User's own program number
28	Blank
29–31	Department number (faculty and staff use only)
32	Blank
33–35	Course identification (alpha prefix)
36–39	Course identification number
40–41	Course/Section number
43	Blank
44–60	Name of instructor (student must include)
61	Blank
62–67	Date (mo., day, yr. sequence in numeric form only)

Figure 2.12   Example of User Job Control Card Format

interpretation of the output in view of the user. This can be an inexpensive and effective way of providing necessary data in a convenient form to the user. Figure 2.15 illustrates the front and reverse sides of a punched card used as input for an off-the-job injury reporting system. The codes on the reverse side are used to identify the physical location where the reported injury occurred, the contributing cause, and the anatomical part affected.

When a system or application is implemented or modified, the training group is responsible for providing the users with the training and orientation necessary to ensure operational effectiveness. This task also

> ### Loading Programs from Tape Files
>
> A number of users have experienced some difficulty because of the tape loading technique required by the RAS Operating System. To circumvent the problems until a new loader system is released, the following is recommended:
>
> Copy your files on disk utilizing the standard copy functions, and load from the disk file.
>
> ### New Feature for SNOBOL 4 Users
>
> 1. The reserved words ?ABEND, ?ANCHOR, ?DUMP, ?FTRACE, and ?TRACE only accept integers as values.
>
> 2. ?TRACE is automatically decremented by 1 after tracing action as an aid in eliminating endless trace loops. The trace should be initialized to the number of traces desired. When ?TRACE has been decremented to zero, the tracing option is turned-off.

Figure 2.13   Extracts from a Computer Services Newsletter

affords the group an opportunity to test the documentation for accuracy and effectiveness. It can also serve to expose any difficulties or problems inherent in the design or documentation.

3. TRAINING FOR MANAGERIAL PERSONNEL. A practical awareness of the subject matter on the part of managerial personnel greatly helps to promote total management involvement, as well as implementation of a multi-functional approach to data processing service. Several organizations have developed in-house programs to provide different types and levels of training for managerial personnel. Nevertheless, such instruction remains the one aspect of training most often overlooked in an organization.

4. TRAINING FOR OTHER MEMBERS OF THE ORGANIZATION. The data processing activity must be regarded as a service function. Its growth and increased effectiveness is dependent upon both existing and potential users. The potential users may be responsible for proposing the development of new systems or applications that eventually result in massive cost reduction and improved operating efficiency. However, potential users are very often unaware of the capabilities of data processing as a management tool, so that they fail to make any proposals or suggestions. This is the organization's loss. It is also the reason why

RALERIC FREIGHTWAYS	DATA PROCESSING MANUAL 10.1

December 15, 1971

STANDARD PROCEDURE

Subject INSTRUCTIONS FOR PREPARATION OF AIR SHIPPING LABEL	Application no.

Performed By	Action
Warehouseman	1. After the appropriate entries have been made on the shipping document, the warehouseman will prepare a shipping label for each piece. The following information must be entered on the shipping label. a. *Consignor:* Enter the name of the organization making the shipment. b. *Destination:* Enter the final destination of the shipment. The destination is derived from the shipping document. c. *Document Number:* Enter the document number from the shipping document. d. *Weight:* Enter the weight of this piece *only.* e. *Piece Count:* Indicate the number of this piece and the total number of pieces in the shipment. For example, Piece 1 of 10 pieces would be coded as 1 / 10. 2. Affix firmly each shipping label to each piece in the shipment. 3. Forward the shipping document to the traffic control clerk. 4. Place the cargo in the appropriate storage area.

Prepared by	Approved by	Approval date

Figure 2.14. Example of Standard Procedure for Completing a Form

DEPT.	E-NUMBER	NAME					OCCUP. CODE	SERVICE DATE	PERIOD ENDING

The form contains the following structured fields:

RECORD OF ATTENDANCE

	DAYS ABSENT	SICKNESS ABSENCE	PERSONAL ABSENCE	OTHER
PAID THIS YEAR				
NOT PAID THIS YEAR				
TO BE PAID THIS PERIOD				

APPROVALS

EMPLOYEE	MGR.	SUPT.	OTHER

APPROVALS PRESCRIBED IN M.D.I. 9.14.1.

HOURS WORKED

	DAY	STD.	O.T.	NIGHT BONUS
MON				
TUES				
WED				
THUR				
FRI				
SAT				
SUN				

NOTES

This card is for calendar reporting roll only.

If absence involves off-the-job injury, complete reverse side of this form.

Rules are prescribed in M.D.I. 9.14.2.

IF ABSENCE WAS CAUSED BY OFF-THE-JOB INJURY, CHECK ONE BOX IN EACH COLUMN BELOW:

LOCATION	CAUSE	PART AFFECTED
☐ 1. HOME	☐ 1 SLIP, FALL	☐ 1 HAND
☐ 2 PUBLIC	☐ 2 LIFTING	☐ 2 ARM
☐ 3 SPORTS	☐ 3 HAND TOOLS, SHARP OBJECTS	☐ 3 FOOT
☐ 4 PRIVATE CAR	☐ 4 STRUCK, STRUCK BY	☐ 4 ANKLE OR LEG
☐ 5 PUBLIC TRANSPORTATION	☐ 5 MACHINE (POWER EQPT. OR AUTO)	☐ 5 EYE
☐ 6 PEDESTRIAN	☐ 6 ELECTRICITY	☐ 6 HEAD
☐ 7 OTHER	☐ 7 HEAT, COLD, EXPLOSION	☐ 7 BODY (TRUNK)
	☐ 8 CHEMICALS, POISONING	☐ 8 INTERNAL
	☐ 9 ANIMALS, INSECTS, OR PLANTS	☐ 9 COMBINATION
	☐ 0 OTHER	☐ 0 OTHER

DATES OF ABSENCE
FROM _____
TO _____

If there are two or more occasions of absence within one pay period due to off-the-job injuries, complete and attach Form RAS 1819 for the second and subsequent absences.

Figure 2.15. User Instruction: Example of Off-the-Job Injury Reporting System Punched Card

training, even of a general kind, is needed for other members of the organization.

Some organizations are now making it a practice to conduct special orientation seminars for their personnel. These seminars, presented with the hope of stimulating employee thought and action, provide information about hardware, software, systems, and applications. The practice appears to be successful and gaining in popularity. For example, an executive of a blue-chip firm has advised the author that his organization has recorded substantial savings since implementing such seminar programs.

Review Questions: Group 2E

1. Explain why the advanced planning and development group of the data processing function is very often referred to as a watchdog group.
2. What factors must be considered by the advanced planning and development group in monitoring the progress and effectiveness of an operation?
3. What general elements must an operations manager consider when developing a production schedule?
4. What benefit, if any, would a data processing manager derive from recommending and implementing training for user personnel?

VARIATIONS IN PROGRAMMING STRUCTURES

Recent developments in software technology and application have given rise to variations in the formats of programming structures. Consequently, there are three generally accepted formats. They are the closed shop structure, the open shop structure, and the semi-open shop structure.

The Closed Shop Structure

The closed shop structure is, at present, the more popular format. In this type of arrangement, the programming effort is performed by a group of highly specialized personnel who write programs from detailed specifications prepared by systems personnel or subject-matter specialists. The programming personnel are directed and controlled by the data processing administrator.

The following is a brief example of how the closed shop structure operates. When a hospital automates its medical laboratory results reporting system, a laboratory technician provides the data processing personnel with the necessary specifications for calculation, adjustment, and conversion of test data. The specifications are then converted to the necessary programs by a programmer in the hospital's own data processing unit.

The method of establishing a closed shop varies from organization to organization. In some organizations, for instance, subject-matter specialists are selected for their knowledge, trained in data processing techniques, and then reassigned to the programming function. This gives the data processing administrator the flexibility of having programming personnel who are qualified to prepare their own detailed specifications and who are capable of communicating freely with their own functional area. Business data processing activities are dominated by this type of arrangement.

Another method, used by several educational institutions, is to select personnel from the admissions, bursar's, testing, planning, and other offices, and then permanently reassign these people to the data processing unit as subject-matter programming specialists. This provides for an excellent liaison and a proper priority perspective, and it also expedites the automation of those areas.

Industrial organizations tend to reassign personnel from the accounting, inventory control, and production control areas as subject-matter specialists in a programming structure.

The Open Shop Structure

In the open shop format, all programming is performed by subject-matter specialists who are subordinate to a manager outside the data processing realm, rather than to the data processing administrator. For these specialists, programming is only an auxiliary activity, in that their primary responsibility is the performance of tasks within their own subject-matter area. The open shop format is found most frequently in scientific and technical environments. Engineers in particular write their own programs, using a mathematical language, such as FORTRAN or ALGOL, to assist them in the solution of their problems.

Most of the open shop programs are of a one-time or short-term nature, undertaken to fulfill an immediate or temporary need. For instance, an engineer who is experiencing wire breaks on a copper rod wire-drawing machine may write a program to determine the tension adjustments required for a continuous productive process. Although there is some possibility that this program would be reused in the future, the factors affecting the reuse situation could vary, so that a new mathematical model would have to be designed and a new program written to perform the calculation formula. On the other hand, a construction or architectural engineer may write an analysis program to determine the amount of stress than can be applied to a selected building material; a program of this type has more universal application and could subsequently be utilized for tests on various building materials.

The Semi-open Shop Structure

The semi-open shop structure is a hybrid form of the open and closed structures. In this type of format, a staff of programming specialists is maintained to support major subject-matter area users. The programming specialists are assigned to subject-matter areas to write programs from specially prepared specifications. The assignments carry the advantage of enabling a programmer to become oriented in the subject-matter area.

In one optical engineering organization, for example, a programming specialist has been assigned to the group for writing, testing, and debugging of the necessary programs. The availability of this resource person permits the engineers to devote their time to research functions, with only minor concern for problem manipulation and calculation. The programmer also serves as a liaison man between the data processing operations group and the engineering personnel in order to secure the necessary machine time for compilation and processing of the programs.

The Popularity of Open Shop Structures

In recent years there has been a trend toward the formation of open shop structures. There are several reasons for this increasing popularity:

—It eliminates the communications impediment, which occurs when a subject-matter specialist attempts to convey his problem to the computer programming specialist. Crossing the jargon barrier between the two specialties is very often the principal difficulty eliminated by the open shop format.

—The availability of time-shared computer networks provides users with direct access to a computational facility. This capability enables people having a limited knowledge of computers but a working knowledge of a computer language to utilize the remote equipment for problem solving.

—The developments in software have simplified the task of programming to some degree. Programming languages such as FORTRAN, BASIC, and APL, do not require that the user have extensive knowledge of computers before attempting to write and execute a program. These languages are included in the curricula of many colleges and universities, thereby greatly increasing the number of people having a potential to write programs for problem solving.

—There is a belief that it is cheaper to train a subject-matter specialist in programming than to attempt to train a programmer in the subject-matter areas.

—Many people are convinced that a program can be written, tested, debugged, and implemented more quickly because there is no need to either allocate data processing manpower for the project or negotiate a priority in the data processing projects schedule.

There are many pros and cons that can be leveled at each type of organizational structure. However, it does appear that the open shop format will be most popular in the future, particularly since many colleges and universities are including programming courses in their curricula. With some additional training, the people taking these courses will be able to write their own programs to solve their job-related problems. Also, the increased use of interactive terminals linked to computing facilities will tend to encourage "do-it-yourself" programming by non-data processing personnel.

Among the disadvantages to the open shop is the lack of programming standardization and proper documentation, which could lead to a duplication of effort and waste of resources. Also, the lack of programming expertise on the part of most users, coupled with their limited knowledge of computer capability, will result in an increased workload for the computer—a situation that may tend to disrupt the normal production process. There is also some question about the efficient utilization of terminals linked to the computer. Improper utilization will increase the operating cost and limit the terminals' effectiveness in decision-making. At present, remote or local conversational-mode processing can be regarded as a luxury item for many organizations. In a multi-programmed operations environment, it will be necessary to provide additional management controls to prevent the accidental or deliberate alteration or destruction of data and programs. (The subject of standards and documentation is discussed more fully in Chapter 4. Management controls are covered in Chapter 7.)

THE PROJECT MANAGEMENT CONCEPT

Project management is a structural arrangement that is specifically designed to achieve a one-time objective, such as development of an on-line student registration system. The complexity of a project may require a selected manpower concentration from a number of interrelated functional activities, acting under the leadership of a project manager. When the concept is applied to data processing projects, the manpower concentration consists of a select team or task force of data processing and nondata-processing personnel. The data people, primarily systems and programming personnel, may be from both within and outside the organization; the latter should be key personnel in the functional activities affected by the project. Upon completion of the project, these non-data people should be reassigned to their functional areas to assist in the administration of the new system. During the life of the project, they provide the necessary liaison between the project teams and the functional area. This facilitates definition of the primary and secondary goals, determination of system and subsystem requirements, development of a workable system, effective documentation, smoother conversion and cutover, more effective follow-up, and on-schedule implementation.

The concept of project management offers some unique opportunities for an organization. At the same time, because it is such a dynamic approach to management, it makes considerable demands upon the organization. To be effective, project management requires an effective project manager, a definable goal, adequate resources, and good controls. The project manager must be a manager who can make things happen. He does not have to be a good technician but he does have to be a good controller. Throughout the life of the project, he must closely monitor the operation and ensure that all resources are being effectively applied. The goal must be a definable one, because it cannot be in a state of flux, for that would lead only to a waste of valuable resources. Adequate resources must be available because there must be a full-time commitment to the project; a halfhearted commitment will result in an inadequate system and/or the failure to cutover on a scheduled date. Good controls—including good feedback controls—are necessary to ensure that the project proceeds according to plan and schedule; deviations may result in a project overrun and a waste of valuable resources.

The project management concept is generally utilized only in larger organizations. Some of these firms prefer to utilize a variant form of these basic approach, a form known as the multiple project concept. The multiple-project concept is applied when an organization has more than one project under development at a time, a situation not unlikely in a large organization where as many as 12 to 15 teams may be organized for a variety of projects. Some of these organizations have organized their staff-level data processing groups into project teams, under which each system or problem is treated as a single project (see Figure 2.16). The resources are then allocated to achieve each project's objectives. Furthermore, either the data processing administrator or the manager must act as a coordinator in order to ensure that the budget, hardware, software, and material resources are being used effectively.

The project management concept is utilized by small- and medium-sized organizations for individual projects. The concept is applied to projects considered major innovations, which usually require new techniques and advances in the state of the art. Although projects may be critical, complex, costly, or long-term, they may still be designated project management status. The development of a total management information system in most small- and medium-sized organizations would be designed, developed, and implemented using the project management concept. Depending on the actual type of project, the project manager may report to the chief executive officer or to an executive committee member; most often, though, he will report to either the data processing administrator or the manager.

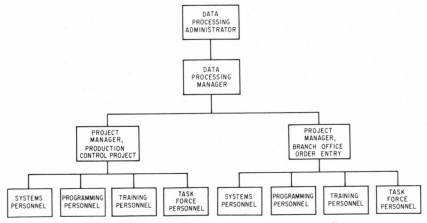

Figure 2.16. Project Management: Multiple Projects Concept

Review Questions: Group 2F

1. Why is it advantageous for a programming manager to have subject-matter specialists on the programming staff?
2. There is a current trend toward the use of open shop programming structures. Give the reasons for this trend.
3. How does the project management concept differ for individual projects and multiple projects?
4. What specific factors are important to the successful execution of a project management approach? Discuss these factors.

SUMMARY

In this chapter we have discussed the structural organization of data processing, together with the role of data processing in the overall organizational framework. If the data processing function is to be successful, it must be guided by the executive committee. It must also have a specific set of objectives and a particular setting within the organization. The interest in the data processing activity cannot be temporary; rather it should be a continuing, active, and meaningful involvement because data processing sweeps vertically and horizontally across all functional activities.

Despite the importance of data processing, there is no clear-cut or magical way of structuring the function. Consequently, the structural format of each individual data processing function can vary; however, it should include the basic divisionalization into the systems design and implementation, programming, advanced planning and development, operations, and training groups.

The decision to adopt or implement a particular structural format involves consideration of organizational objectives, budgets, available hardware, software, and personnel expertise.

Of the three types of programming structures, the open shop structure is gaining in popularity. The subject-matter specialists who have been trained in programming are able to write, test, and debug their own programs to assist them in problem-solving and decision-making processes. The availability of time-sharing networks and user-oriented programming languages such as BASIC and APL have enabled nondata-processing personnel to use the computer directly as a tool.

Project management may also be used to help achieve a desired goal. However, the concept requires involvement by the executive committee, a dynamic project manager, adequate resources, a definable goal, and good controls. All projects do not readily lend themselves to this approach. It would not be feasible for an organization to concentrate its resources on a simple, relatively short-term project.

Large organizations may apply the concept to individual or multiple projects. The concept may be readily applied to individual projects because they are generally of a complex nature, requiring a variety of skills, and involve many other functional activities. The application of the concept to multiple projects may not necessarily be based on the criteria mentioned above. Many organizations structure their staff personnel into a multiple-project arrangement and treat each individual system or program as a project. This type of arrangement requires a significant amount of coordination to ensure proper utilization of resources.

CASE STUDY

Case Study 2.1: The Raleric Manufacturing Company

You have been employed by the Raleric Manufacturing Company as the data processing manager. In this capacity, you will report directly to the controller who is a member of the executive committee. The executive committee has delegated to you the responsibility for developing a structural format that will contribute to the overall effectiveness of the Raleric organization.

At present, the data processing operations group is a line activity directed and controlled by the manager of payroll services. The manager of payroll services reports directly to the superintendent of accounting, whose position places him at the staff level but not on the executive committee. The superintendent reports to the controller through the assistant controller.

The systems and procedures group, consisting of a systems analyst and three programmers, reports to the manager of industrial engineering. The manager, in a line level position, reports directly to the director of engineering and manufacturing operations. The director's position is on the same level as that of the controller and is also an executive committee position.

There is also a satellite unit-record equipment operation, which is primarily concerned with the printing of merchandise shipping tickets, shipping notifications, and shipping releases. Data from these applications becomes input for the daily sales analysis report and for the weekly billing produced by the operations group. The operations manager is responsible for the satellite operation's personnel and equipment, but not for its operating schedule. That schedule is controlled by the manager of merchandise operations.

Training is presently limited to implementation of new systems and modifications. It is conducted by the systems analyst in conjuction with a personnel department member, who is concerned primarily with recruitment of personnel and only secondarily with organizational training.

A clerk in the payroll group is responsible for preparing and maintaining attendance reporting statistics. She key punches her own input cards and has these verified by the data processing operations group. The data is used for a variety of weekly, monthly, quarterly, and annual reports, which are processed by the operations group. The operations manager is also responsible for the key punch machine and for the storage of the source documents and input used in the absence-reporting application.

The engineering organization contracts with a local university for computer program writing, testing, debugging, and processing.

Discussion Questions

1. What structural format would you, as the data processing manager, recommend for the data processing activity? Be prepared to illustrate and defend your answer.
2. What type of structural format would you recommend for the programming function? Why?
3. Do you agree with the split-responsibility arrangement for the satellite operation? If so, what are the advantages and disadvantages of such an arrangement? If not, how and why would you alter the arrangement?

4. Would you recommend that the training function be wholly absorbed by the personnel department in order to free your systems analyst for other responsibilities?
5. Would you recommend terminating the contract with the university and having the data processing function take on all of the programming activity needed for the engineering and technical operations?
6. Would you recommend the reassignment of the attendance statistics clerk to the data processing operations group?
7. Do you feel that the functional activity title "systems and procedures" has any pronounced influence upon the type of organizational format established?

3

Personnel Selection, Training, and Appraisal

INTRODUCTION

Before any operation can be initiated, a careful analysis of the manpower resource requirements must be undertaken. This analysis is concerned with both the goals and the manpower resources that are required and available.

After the manager has completed his definition of the broad objective, he should have a complete understanding of his specific objectives and tasks and a reasonable estimate of the resources available within a given time-frame. He can then inventory the available human resources to determine their experience, educational background, and trainability. This manpower is then matched with the draft of the organizational structure in order to study the relationships of the various positions and the strengths and weaknesses of each employee. Any defects in the organizational plan will be exposed at this time. Correction of them may require the creation of new or additional positions, elimination of positions, and/or the recruitment of additional personnel. When the organizational format has been made reasonably firm, the manager devotes his attention to the preparation of detailed job descriptions and related matters, together with the selection of personnel, the training of personnel, and the appraisal of personnel performance.

JOBS: DESCRIPTIONS, ANALYSIS, FACTORS, AND CLASSIFICATION LEVELS

Job Descriptions

A job description is a written statement about an individual position. It delineates the tasks, duties, and responsibilities associated with the position. It is the manager who prepares a job description for each position within the data processing structure. These descriptions become the basis for recruitment, selection, training, and appraisal of personnel.

Most job descriptions cover the following ten basic topics:

1. Job title
2. Wage rate, salary, and salary range
3. Tasks and duties
4. Reporting to whom
5. Relationship to total structure
6. Number of subordinates
7. Equipment involved
8. Working conditions
9. Physical Demands
10. Specialized Qualifications

1. JOB TITLE. The job title is used to identify the position within the structure. It is relevant only to the organization in which this classification has been made; it cannot be used readily to identify a position in another organization because titles and their descriptions differ greatly from organization to organization. Therefore, any inter-organizational comparison must be coupled with a description of the position's tasks, duties, responsibilities, and other requirements.

2. WAGE RATE, SALARY, SALARY RANGE. The remuneration specification for the position indicates whether the employee is paid on an hourly, weekly, monthly, or annual basis. If a salary range is included, it indicates the lower and upper compensation values for the position. The description should also indicate whether the amount is incremented either on a progression scale (in which case the step structure should be included) or merit basis.

3. TASKS AND DUTIES. The listing of tasks and duties defines the specific responsibility for the position. These specifications give the employee a clear understanding of what is expected of him and provide a basis for managerial evaluation of performance. In addition, they are

particularly useful for indicating the training requirements for a given position.

4. REPORTING TO WHOM. There must be a clear designation of the supervisory position to which this position is subordinate. This identifies the immediate relationship to the chain of command. And it makes it clear to the employee as to whom he should notify or consult when problems or questions arise. It also indicates where instructions originate, as well, and the extent of the delegated authority.

5. RELATIONSHIP TO TOTAL STRUCTURE. The channels of communication that need to be established and/or maintained are delineated by indicating the relationship of the employee's position to the overall organizational structure.

6. NUMBER OF SUBORDINATES. The job description for a managerial position must indicate the number of subordinates included in the span of control. It must also specify the number and type or types of personnel to be directed and controlled by the manager.

7. EQUIPMENT INVOLVED. In data processing occupations, specialized equipment is involved in most job positions, particularly in the programming and operations areas. The equipment involved in these jobs should therefore be specified for all positions, especially for newly created ones. Such specifications are particularly important in the recruitment, selection, and training of personnel. The type of equipment also indicates the training, background, and experience required of an employee in order to successfully perform the tasks and duties associated with each position.

8. WORKING CONDITIONS. These are concerned with environmental factors, legal requirements, and schedules. Noise and temperature are two common environmental factors to which an employee may be subjected in data processing occupations. The number of hours in a work week, the shift work requirements, and frequency of overtime are affected by the operating schedule. An employee should be made aware of these schedule requirements before he agrees to accept the position.

There may also be certain contractual obligations with a labor union which may require working on a rotating shift basis. This specification should be included in the job description.

Some states have legal restrictions regarding the employment of females on certain shifts, or the number of hours worked in a day or week. These limitations must be included and clearly indicated particularly in positions which may be filled by male or female employees.

9. PHYSICAL DEMANDS. For most data processing occupations, the physical demands are the same as for typical office positions. In some installations, limited walking may be required, or perhaps the need to physically transport cards and other materials. In punched card installations, though, the positions may well involve a considerable amount of standing, moving, and lifting. It is obvious that the proper planning and layout of the equipment and traffic patterns in an installation or organization generally have a strong influence on the physical demands required of the employees. (Installation planning and layout are discussed further in Chapter 5.)

10. SPECIALIZED QUALIFICATIONS. Some positions require that an employee possess specialized training and experience in order to cope with the demands of particular jobs. In upper-level positions, such as those in the systems, programming, and advanced planning areas, these specialized requirements may be exacting. For example, such a position may require a university or college degree in a particular subject-matter field; an advanced degree plus managerial, planning, or programming experience in a subject-matter or functional area; or successful completion of specialized programming or subject-matter courses.

Figure 3.1 illustrates a job description used by one organization. Note that some of the previously discussed topics have not been included on the form. It is a practice of this organization to include only so-called necessary information on the form for managerial positions. The salary, for example, is deleted because it is considered confidential information. The job description forms for the subordinate personnel would include all of the previously discussed topics. (General job descriptions are also discussed in Appendix I.)

Job Analysis

The requirements and specifications for managerial or nonmanagerial positions are determined as the result of a job analysis. This process involves the collection of data elements regarding the position and integrating the elements into a narrative format that results in a job description.

For a newly created position, the manager must ascertain all of the mental, physical, and manual factors. These specifications and requirements will only be temporary, as should be clearly indicated on the job

JOB DESCRIPTION

Job Title: Manager of Data Processing
Department: Data Processing
Reporting to: Vice-President, Finance
Supervises: 5 Systems Analysts
2 Coding Clerks
1 Operations Research Analyst
5 Programmers—Business Applications
2 Programmers—Technical Applications
2 Computer Operators
5 Key Punch Operators
2 Peripheral Equipment Operators
1 Tape Librarian

Duties: Under general guidance of the Vice-President of Finance, is responsible for the overall direction and administration of all functions and activities of the Data Processing Department. He directs and coordinates through subordinate managers such activities as: the analyses and design of systems that will provide for the most effective utilization of the data processing equipment for scientific and business applications; the development of feasibility studies; the determination of equipment specifications and requirements; the development of programs to satisfy systems requirements; the establishment and maintenance of a program library; the scheduling and operation of the data processing equipment; the establishment of performance and quality standards.

He also determines the personnel requirements, plus selecting, training, and evaluation policies; prepares the overall budget requirements and the chargebacks for services rendered by his organization; establishes the policy for mechanization of applications within the company; establishes and maintains the channels of communication between his department and other departments within the organization.

Specialized Qualifications: A college education with a degree in Business Administration or Engineering or the equivalent in training and experience. A minimum of eight years experience in the various data processing functions in business and/or scientific applications, with at least two years of managerial experience.

Figure 3.1   Sample Job Description

description form. When the position has been filled, it must then be restudied to determine the adequacy or inadequacy of the original requirements and specifications. Initially, then, the job description offers a set of guidelines to assist in the recruitment and selection of personnel, and in the direction and control of an activity.

A position currently authorized and manned must be studied in detail by the manager or a trained job analyst. This audit will determine the tasks and duties being performed, as well as the accuracy and relevancy of the job requirements and specifications.

There are various ways of undertaking the analysis of a job, but it is important to emphasize that each way requires that the employee be advised of the purpose and extent of the study. This is essential for maintenance of good employee relations because job analyses are conducted for purposes of promotion, training, and performance evaluation, as well as for establishment of new positions and the development or evaluation of current job descriptions.

Approaches to Job Analysis

There are three basic approaches used in performing a job analysis. These approaches, or methods, are:
1. The questionnaire method
2. The direct observation method
3. The conference method

1. THE QUESTIONNAIRE METHOD. In this approach, the employee is asked to complete a specially prepared detailed questionnaire. His responses provide the data elements indicating this particular position's mental, physical, and skill requirements; duties and responsibilities; and working conditions. The questionnaire responses are frequently verified by a brief observation of, or an interview with, the employee that is conducted by his manager or a job analyst. The interview provides an opportunity to secure supplementary data not gathered in the questionnaire, as well as to resolve any questions arising from the responses given.

The questionnaire method can be somewhat of a disadvantage in the process of job analysis. For example, it is difficult to develop a questionnaire of a universal nature, applicable to all positions. Furthermore, the preparation of a collection instrument for each position can become a very time-consuming task.

Nevertheless, the questionnaire is very suitable for analyzing positions in data processing, because the personnel are accustomed to dealing with paper work. Also, it is particularly useful when analyzing positions that are scattered geographically. There is also an important ancillary benefit: direct employee participation in job analysis, as in the questionnaire approach, is an excellent technique for developing good employee relations.

2. THE DIRECT OBSERVATION METHOD. In this approach, the employee is closely observed in the performance of a particular operation or series of operations. The observations, made within a predetermined time period or on a given day, are recorded on a scratch pad or on a specially prepared observation form.

This method enables the observer (the manager or job analyst) to prepare a detailed description of the work performed. The description is based on breaking down the work into units called elements. Each element is observed and recorded on the form together with a time notation. Fine timings are generally not required for analysis of data processing occupations, so that a wristwatch or wall clock suffices for any timings required. In addition to operation times, the timings indicate time allowances required for personal needs; the effects of fatigue factors resulting from visual, physical, or mental activities; and the occurrence and frequency of any delays. The end result is that the job is described in terms of the operations performed by the employee and the amount of time required for each particular operation. The observer's write-up can then be compared with the job description for evaluation of the position.

There are certain difficulties and drawbacks inherent in the direct observation method. For example, there is the danger that the elements may be defined too precisely, thereby becoming unmanageable. Also, there is a psychological handicap in the use of a watch in direct observations: people tend to dislike being timed at their work, so that several timings may be required to establish standardized times relatively free from distortion. There is also the implication that the use of timing requires the services of a trained job analyst and that the evaluation of the end result may be a very complicated process. This, however, depends upon the actual amount of detail required and developed. In addition, there is some question as to whether or not the direct observation method can adequately cover the diversity of functions performed in most data processing occupations.

The principal advantage of the method is that it can provide detailed data useful for planning, scheduling, evaluating performance, and job costing. It can also provide excellent feedback on problems and bottlenecks in an operation.

3. THE CONFERENCE METHOD. Under this approach, the manager or job analyst holds a series of conferences or meetings with an employee. During these sessions, the employee is questioned in detail about the activities relating to his position. Notes are made and then analyzed to filter out any unnecessary or inaccurate information. Subsequently, they are compared with the existing job description, which, as a result, may have to be modified or revised.

This is the most time-consuming method of job analysis. However, because of its thoroughness, it is the best one for analyzing positions that require specialized skills.

Job Factors

In each job analysis method previously discussed, selected job factors must be given consideration. These factors represent certain basic requirements in a position and are subsequently used as a basis of wage rate or salary determination and job classification level assignment. The factors are arbitrarily established by each organization and depend on the activity requirements for a given position.

The factors most frequently considered in connection with data processing occupations are:
—Education
—Experience
—Training
—Physical demands
—Working conditions
—Equipment
—Mental attitude
—Ability to work with others

Varying degrees of importance or worth are accorded to each of these factors, based on job requirements. The education factor in a job analysis is used to determine the level of mental development needed to understand and perform the related tasks. In performing the job analysis, the manager or job analyst determines the level of mental development required for the position. This determination is compared against a previously established scale. The scale indicates the mental requirement for a given level on the scale and the worth of that level. For example, the lowest level for mental development on the scale may require the ability to read and write, add, and subtract numbers. The upper end of the scale may require the technical knowledge to deal with much more complex problems. Subsequently a value or worth must be assigned to each of these levels on the scale, for wage and salary determination and job level classification assignment. (Examples of the use of these factors and their varying degrees of applicability are given in the position descriptions included in Appendix I.)

Job Classification Levels

Jobs can be graded or classified with respect to levels of relative importance. At present, nearly every position in the data processing field falls into one of the three following categories:
1. The specialist level
2. The semiskilled level
3. The trainee level

1. THE SPECIALIST LEVEL. This level applies to positions normally regarded as key technical positions in the organization. Each such position requires that the job holder has full technical knowledge, plus the competency to operate effectively at the highest level. People qualify for specialist rating by virtue of training and experience in one or more subject-matter areas and by demonstrating their ability to coordinate, direct, and control others, with minimal supervision of their own activities. Such people include project coordinators, directors and leaders, together with senior systems, senior programming, senior planning, and senior operations personnel.

2. THE SEMISKILLED LEVEL. Positions at this level require average knowledge of a subject-matter specialty, plus the ability to perform under an average-to-minimal amount of supervision. Generally, people in this category are capable of working on several phases or projects with enough self-direction so that they need only general direction. In some instances, semiskilled personnel are delegated minor direction and control responsibility. Included in this category are systems analysts, systems associates, junior systems analysts, programmers, junior programmers, and operating technicians.

3. THE TRAINEE LEVEL. Included in this category are people employed at the base or entry level, as well as those being trained or

developed in a particular skill or subject-matter specialty for ultimate progression to the semiskilled level. The trainees perform routine functions requiring constant direction and control. Among the people in this category are trainees for management, programming, systems, research, and operations, together with program coders, coding clerks, assistant console operators, and tape handlers.

Figure 3.2 illustrates the application of the classification method to the programming activity, as well as the possible progression paths through the three levels within that occupational grouping. (Of course, the actual position titles and progression paths vary from organization to organization.)

The effect of classification levels on salary ranges is illustrated in Figure 3.3. Each level has a normal range with a stated upper and lower salary parameter. The job factors and the classification levels are used to establish the monetary worth of each position.

Review Questions: Group 3A

1. What are the ten basic topics included in a job description?
2. Name and briefly describe the approaches to job analysis.
3. Discuss one of the job classification levels particularly relevant to data processing personnel. What job titles may be included at that level?

OCCUPATIONAL GROUPINGS

There are six major occupational groupings in the data processing activity. These are:
1. Systems analysts and designers
2. Programmers
3. Time-sharing systems monitors
4. Console operators
5. Peripheral equipment operators
6. Tape and disk librarians

Within each of these occupational groupings are included the manager, specialist, semiskilled, and trainee levels. As to specific positions, there are a variety of titles based upon individual or organizational preferences, as well as external influences.

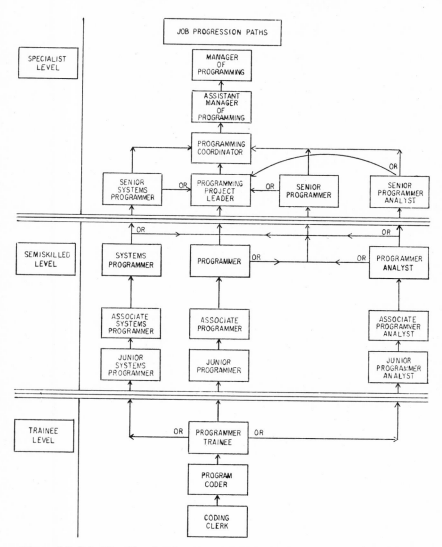

Figure 3.2. Job Classification Levels and Job Progression Paths in Programming Activity

Systems Analysts

Those in this grouping are involved with the analysis of tasks and the formulation of job specifications. Their work is utilized as plans or

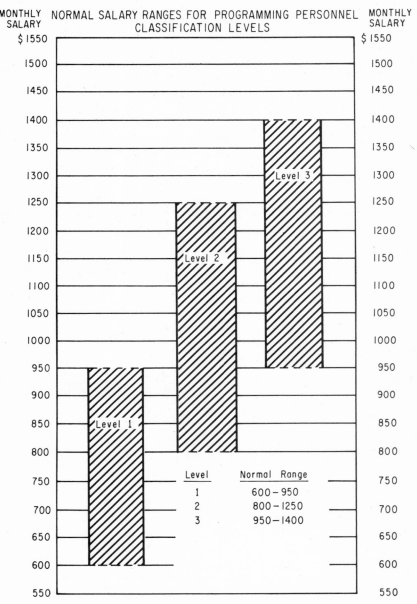

MONTHLY SALARY — NORMAL SALARY RANGES FOR PROGRAMMING PERSONNEL — MONTHLY SALARY
CLASSIFICATION LEVELS

Level	Normal Range
1	600 – 950
2	800 – 1250
3	950 – 1400

Figure 3.3. Sample Chart of Classification Levels and Salary Ranges

guides by user organization, operations, or programming personnel employed in the development and implementation of a system.

Initially, the systems analyst conducts a detailed survey to gather preliminary data about the setting. During the survey, he collects and documents data about the organizational structure and its policies, equipment installed and on order, and systems operational and planned. The systems analyst must determine and understand how these various elements affect the current operation and any proposed changes. Also, he must evaluate the extent and value of contributions made by the affected functional activities to the system under consideration. (The survey process is discussed more fully in Chapter 8.)

After reviewing the documented survey data and completing the definition of his objectives, the systems analyst conducts the feasibility study. (See Chapter 8.) He begins with the collection and documentation of data about the existing system. This data, together with information on the overall requirements, is needed for him to determine: the effectiveness of the current system; the conditions and criteria required to achieve the objectives; the potential effect of a proposed system or modification of objectives on the organization; a comparison of the tangible and intangible benefits, costs and savings, number and types of records, and files and documents that are involved in the project; and the development of new approaches and general equipment specifications. After the systems analyst has synthesized and evaluated this data, he prepares a report of findings and recommendations for the data processing manager or administrator.

After the report has been accepted and approved by the data processing manager, the requirements of the system are finalized. The systems analyst will then—either by himself or in association with other systems personnel and subject-matter specialists—formulate the detailed development and implementation specifications for the proposed system. These specifications consist of a system flowchart; system interface requirements; data base, file, input, and output specifications; management control requirements; mathematical models or formulae; algorithms; decision tables; codes; and preliminary user procedures. In some organizations, the specifications also include a program flowchart in macro-diagram format.

In a computerized operation, the specifications are forwarded to the programming group for development of the necessary computer programs. In addition, the specifications are used by the systems analyst to prepare a set of procedures for manual, unit-record, or satellite operations.

The systems analyst is a key person in a data processing activity. In the performance of his duties, he very often executes the management functions of planning, organizing, coordinating, directing, and controlling. The typical systems analyst has the capacity to undertake such duties because the people employed in this occupational grouping are generally experienced data processing specialists with sound business or applications experience.

In many small organizations, the systems analyst is responsible not only for his own systems work but also for the design and development of computer programs. Some of these organizations elect to classify an individual in this combined occupational position as a programmer analyst.

Most organizations include the operations research positions within the systems occupation grouping. This is simply for convenience, in that most such firms employ only a limited number of operations research or management-operations analysts. Several large organizations have established this as a separate occupational and organizational grouping within their facilities.

(Descriptions for the various positions in the systems group are included in Appendix I.)

Programmers

A programmer designs, develops, and implements the instructions and programs needed to solve various business, technical, and scientific problems. He begins the design function by studying the job specifications and the flowcharts developed by a systems analyst or subject-matter specialist. If there is no program flowchart, the programmer prepares a macro-diagram representing his generalized solution to the problem. He then develops a micro-diagram illustrating each step required in the solution of the problem. To verify the logical validity of his design, he desk checks the micro-diagram. After that, he codes the logic in the syntax of a selected programming language.

The completed instructions prepared by the programmer represent the source program, which is then converted to a predetermined format in punched cards, magnetic tape, or paper tape. In a time-sharing or remote job entry environment, the programmer may enter his source statements directly to the computer via a keyboard terminal device. The source program must then be assembled or compiled through a translation process into an object program containing the computer-sensible code. Following translation, the programmer develops sample data and a plan in order to test the accuracy and validity of every condition and instruction in the object program. This process, commonly known as testing and debugging, may require correction or alteration of some program steps. After having resolved the accuracy of the program and its compatibility with planned objectives, the programmer prepares program documentation. The program documentation must be included in the documentation folder for a given system, so as to simplify any subsequent maintenance or modification. The documentation will be used by the systems group, operations group, and user organization to implement the new system. (The subjects of testing and documentation are discussed more fully in Chapters 6 and 4, respectively.)

In addition to designing and developing new programs, the programmer is also expected to modify and maintain existing programs. (This activity is covered in Chapter 6.)

The programmer may also be expected to develop programmer's programs—macros, modules, subroutines, subprograms, input-output control systems, etc.—to improve programmer productivity and reduce programming time and cost. In some organizations, programmers who are capable of performing such tasks are designated as systems programmers or software programmers.

In larger installations, the programmer may have responsibility for the direction and control of the coding of instructions performed by a coding clerk or programmer trainee. In addition, the programmer's work on testing and debugging may be performed in conjunction with junior programmers, associates, or trainees.

(Position descriptions for the various occupations in the programming group are included in Appendix I.)

Time-sharing Systems Monitor

This is a relatively new occupational grouping. It is currently gaining in prominence as a result of the increasing installation of third-generation computing systems equipped with a time-sharing capability. Furthermore, there is speculation that this occupation will become an integral and vital part of fourth-generation computing system operations.

Working under the supervision of the operations manager, the time-sharing systems monitor directs and controls the time-shared computer, the users, and the operating personnel connected with the hardware. The monitor establishes the schedule of operations, which is based on a predetermined operations priority status. From his console, he directs the stacking, batching, and input of programs, data, and files according to priority, aiming for optimal operating efficiency. He directs the computer operators to mount and ready the data communications terminals, tape transports, data cells, disk drives, input, output, and storage devices. In addition, he services all interrupts indicated by the operating system that require manual intervention.

In some organizations the monitor has the authority to change quantum time and storage allocations for users, depending upon priority needs and operating efficiency; at the same time, though, he has to ensure that no valid user is denied access to the system. The monitor may also assist in the assembly, compilation, testing, and debugging of programs.

The monitor records all problems occurring in the operation of the time-sharing system. He makes special notation of any software bugs detected and the action taken to bypass or correct an error. In addition, he will initiate diagnostic procedures according to a predetermined plan in order to locate and identify the source and cause of an error.

No position description for a time-sharing systems monitor has been included in Appendix I because there is little agreement at present among organizations concerning the job requirements and salary range for this position. Many people have chosen to regard this position as that of a console operator or senior console operator. Others are of the opinion that this position should be filled by a senior systems analyst with a great deal of programming expertise; they contend that the need to change priorities, and time and storage allocations, requires a highly talented individual. Still others contend that a highly qualified software programmer is needed to reduce the impact of "crashes" and to expedite restarts when required; they believe that these capabilities are more important than the ability to change priorities, and time and storage allocations.

Console Operators

The console operator functions under the direction and control of

Figure 3.4 Console Operator. Courtesy IBM Corporation.

the operations manager. (See Figure 3.4.) The operator, at the console, supervises the operation of the computing system in order to maintain optimum operating efficiency. In addition, he mounts and makes ready for operation such devices as tape transports, disk drives, card readers and punches, paper tape readers and punches, data cells, printers, and other input, output, and storage units.

When a program halt, indicator, or interrupt is detected on the console, it is the operator's responsibility to service the computer as required. In addition, he has the duty of maintaining machine utilization records.

The console operator is generally responsible for the assembly and compilation of programs. In some organizations, he assists the programmer in the testing and debugging of programs; in others, he conducts the testing and debugging according to the test plan provided.

(Descriptions of positions in this occupational grouping are given in Appendix I.)

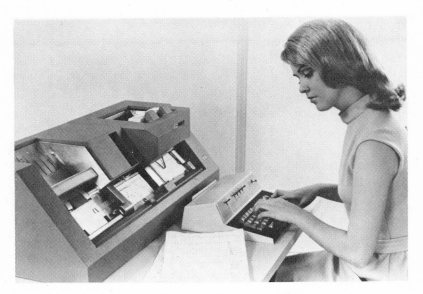

Figure 3.5. Key Punch Operator. Courtesy IBM Corporation.

Peripheral Equipment Operators

The typical peripheral equipment operator is responsible for the operation of punched card and auxiliary information processing machines that are not under the direct control of the central processing unit.

He is also responsible for the handling and storage of all inputs and outputs. In some organizations, he is also required to wire the control panels for the various machines. In addition, he may have to assist the console operator or the time-sharing systems monitor.

The title "peripheral equipment operator" is a broad one because it is used to cover a number of occupational activities. Among the most common positions within this grouping are key punch operator (see Figure 3.5), verifier operator, card-tape-converter operator, data typist, high-speed-printer operator, sorter-machine operator, unit-record equipment operator, tabulating-machine operator, etc.

Tape and Disk Librarians

The tape and disk librarian is responsible for maintaining all control records on reels of magnetic and paper tape, magnetic and punched cards, tape cartridges, and disk packs. The librarian records such information as media identification number, contents of each medium, retention dates, security, and other data (see also Chapter 7). In addition, the librarian is responsible for issuing and refiling the media in specially designed vaults or cabinets. The librarian is also responsible for the scraping, cleaning, and cutting of magnetic tapes, as well as the splicing of paper tapes, in order to increase their effective utilization. This occupational grouping is found in medium and large-scale installations. In smaller installations, such functions are performed by a peripheral equipment operator.

In some organizations, the librarian is given the additional responsibility of control of the documentation and technical manuals. The librarian controls the withdrawal of documentation folders, plus the updating of their contents when modifications or changes are made. The librarian also controls the dissemination of manufacturers' manuals and the updating of those manuals.

SELECTION OF PERSONNEL

The effectiveness of any organization is determined by the personnel employed rather than by the power of the computing equipment, the utility of the software package, or the sophistication of the systems designed. The manager must staff his organization with personnel who are technically competent and personable. Technical competency is essential because in most organizations the manager will have little or no time to train the people. Personality is important because data processing personnel are required to interact with a variety of people in different occupations. They must be able to operate under pressure or adverse conditions, maintain emotional stability, and be willing to accept criticism.

Desirable Attitudes and Characteristics

There are a number of important attitudes and characteristics that are generally considered to be desirable in applicants for the various data processing occupations. An applicant should be able to:

—Work well with and through other people

—Sell ideas to users, colleagues, and all levels of the managerial hierarchy

—Think creatively, logically, and objectively
—Analyze and review problems and situations in their own settings and contexts
—Work well under pressure
—Persevere despite frustrations and adverse conditions
—Make sound evaluations and decisions
—Communicate well in speech and writing
—Give constant attention to details and accuracy
—Analyze written and graphic specifications
—Work with thoroughness and dependability
—Apply good judgment in determining the relative importance of operations
—Accept responsibility
—Stand for most of the day, if necessary
—Accept criticism from others
—Understand written and verbal instructions
—Work competently with his hands
—Adapt easily to changes

The specific attitudes, characteristics, education, and background desired in an applicant vary from employer to employer. The background and educational requirements for the systems analyst and programming occupations are more demanding than for other nonmanagerial data processing occupations. Scientific programmers and analysts must have a backgound in the sciences, mathematics, or engineering. Analysts and programmers working in a commercial environment are expected to have a general business and accounting background. Operations research personnel must have a strong background in statistics and advanced mathematics, because their work will involve them in mathematical modeling, simulation, and linear programming.

Educational Levels

Most employers in the data processing field consider a high school diploma to be the basic educational minimum for employees in all occupations (although there are exceptions to this rule, as indicated below). There are also many jobs available to people who have had some post-high school education but not enough college to earn a bachelor's degree. These people are generally graduates of a data processing, computer science or systems program at a two-year college. They have received concentrated training in data processing subjects, as well as in mathematics and accounting.

Many organizations require a university or college degree for positions within systems and programming. Some require either education beyond the bachelor level or advanced degrees for positions in the operations research and the scientific computing area. Degree holders are regarded by most organizations as the best candidates for managerial positions.

A manager has to recognize that, in general, the increasing complexity and sophistication of new systems and programs require the use of personnel with increasingly higher educational qualifications. However, it is also important that he realistically appraise the educational requirements for each position and comprehend the interrelationship of various personnel factors. For example, when a manager raises the educational requirements for a position, he must increase the salary correspondingly. In doing so, though, he may cause budgetary and morale problems in his organization. The budgetary problems may arise when the executive committee feels that the salary levels are disproportionately high relative to productivity and tangible dollar savings. And morale problems may occur when it becomes impossible to advance or promote all of the personnel. Another problem that can arise is related to task assignment. All data processing tasks do not require a high level of proficiency or intelligence. Consequently they fail to challenge the zeal and interest of a programmer or analyst. The end result in these situations may be a high rate of personnel turnover.

Despite the growing complexity of the data processing industry and the corresponding rise in educational requirements, there has also been a selective downgrading of educational demands. Owing to a continuing shortage of qualified personnel, some organizations are now recruiting not only high school graduates but also high school dropouts for trainee positions in operations occupations. These may not be the most glamorous positions, but they are essential to an organization and they do give many people a start in a promising professional field.

It must also be added that there have been many successful people in data processing who have had very little or no formal education beyond the high school level. Some did not even get that far. They all qualified instead by virtue of their experience, interest, and ability. Nevertheless, a sound education is still a great asset.

Sources of Supply

Today, demand far exceeds supply in terms of competently trained data processing personnel. Various estimates made by government and professional sources indicate that this condition will not improve before at least the mid-1970s. Potential and/or productive sources of personnel, therefore, are of great interest to almost every data processing organization and manager.

There is no one single source that is best for recruitment for all purposes. This factor, plus the limited supply, means that organizations utilize all available sources as much and as best as they can.

Personnel recruitment and selection is a very costly activity. An organization may spend between $1500 and $5000 to hire an employee. Included in this cost are such items as advertising, interviewing, testing, travel, agency fees, and telephone charges. Although the high cost may result largely or exclusively from the use of outside placement services, the cost of using an in-house personnel-seeking group may well be comparable. So it behooves an organization to investigate each available source and to gain access to the best possible candidates available. This may help to reduce personnel turnover and the associated costs.

There are several basic kinds of sources from which to recruit candidates for the various occupational groupings. These include:

1. Other organizations
2. Colleges and universities
3. Hardware vendors
4. Professional associations
5. Specialized employment agencies
6. Management consultants
7. Other units within organization

1. OTHER ORGANIZATIONS. These constitute the most common source for recruiting experienced personnel, particularly when a specialized skill or a specific experience background is required. Personnel in data processing are nomadic by reputation and willing to move for a promotion, increase in salary, new challenge, or a chance to acquire new or more experience. These wanderers are generally recruited as a result of personal contact by the manager, one of his colleagues, or a subordinate. Sometimes they are found through advertising.

2. COLLEGES AND UNIVERSITIES. There are a number of community and junior colleges as well as some four-year colleges offering two- and

four-year degree programs in machine operation, programming, systems, computer sciences, and related subjects. They provide personnel for entry at the trainee and semiskilled levels. Graduates of four-year institutions who show an aptitude for programming may be employed and trained at the equipment vendor's school, or in the organization's own facility. They may then be assigned to programming at the trainee or semiskilled level. Many business administration majors are accepted as systems trainees. Mathematics majors are generally accepted as programmer trainees; experience has proven that other majors can also qualify for this position.

Many organizations send professional recruiters or members of their personnel department to the campuses to screen potential employees. Or they notify the college placement centers about positions available. Students who have registered with the placement centers are then notified about these availabilities.

In some communities, college students preparing to graduate are interviewed during the Christmas vacation period at a centralized location established either by the local chamber of commerce or a professional business group. Such an arrangement gives an organization an excellent opportunity to screen a large number of potential candidates.

3. HARDWARE VENDORS. The vendors are very often aware of data processing people who are job hunting. They can be an excellent source for recommendations because they have an opportunity to observe the work and habits of potential candidates. In many instances, vendors are also aware of performance evaluations made by a prospective candidate's present employer. Some hardware vendors do not wish to become involved because any recommendation may serve to weaken the operational effectiveness of one of their own accounts. Some, however, are willing to check with and advise their colleagues.

4. PROFESSIONAL ASSOCIATIONS. Professional associations such as the Data Processing Management Association have formal or informal placement committees at the chapter level. These committees are able to provide organizations leads or résumés on potential candidates. Generally, a manager must be a member of such an association in order to participate in the placement service and thereby gain access to potential candidates.

5. SPECIALIZED EMPLOYMENT AGENCIES. There are a number of specialized employment agencies, sometimes called personnel consultants, that recruit potential candidates on a fee basis paid by the em-

ployers. The fees for most data processing positions range from 10 percent to 22 percent of the annual salary. The effectiveness of such an agency is very dependent upon the skill of the recruiter and the reputation of the agency. The difficulty with utilizing many of these agencies is that they only direct or refer candidates to the employer; it becomes the employer's task to do the actual screening. However, some agencies do effectively screen out candidates within a given set of parameters.

6. MANAGEMENT CONSULTANTS. Like hardware vendors, management consultants also have an opportunity to observe potential candidates. In addition, they may also serve as screening agencies for the employer; in fact, some of them will actively recruit personnel for clients.

7. OTHER UNITS WITHIN ORGANIZATION. An organization—especially a large organization—can turn out to be an excellent but frequently overlooked source of personnel for itself. It provides an opportunity for employees to move up from within—a form of promotion that can be used to reward an employee for being conscientious, aggressive, and loyal. Non-data processing employees who are subject-matter-oriented can be trained in data processing techniques. What is more, as a result of their familiarity with company policies and practices, they can require less training time and can become productive sooner.

Very often the personnel department within an organization will maintain a skills inventory file. This inventory can be an excellent source for locating personnel with some experience and background in data processing. Many large organizations maintain an organization-wide skills inventory system.

Interviews

The interview offers the manager an opportunity to meet face-to-face with a prospective employee. This occasion enables the manager to become personally acquainted with the candidate, to observe the candidate's motivation, appearance, attitudes, ideas, reactions, and ability to express himself; and to discuss and explore the candidate's background, education, experience, and training. In turn, the candidate has an opportunity to learn more about the position in detail, as well as about working conditions, the organization and its objectives, wage and salary policies, and appraisal practices. Consequently, a properly conducted interview can prove to be beneficial for both parties, for it is a two-way communications channel enabling each party to obtain important information.

As a prelude to the actual interview, the manager formulates generalizations about the candidate's personality and ability based on his reputation, application, and/or résumé.

A reputation develops from speaking engagements, participation in seminars, presentations of technical papers to professional societies, and publication of papers or other work. Or it may be carried and maintained orally, as a result of work on a particular project or technique.

The completed application form provides basic data about the prospective employee. It generally includes such information as age, marital status, number of dependents, other personal data, educational institutions attended and degrees or certificates attained, occupational goals, and references. The data on the application form should be explored in detail during the interview.

The résumé provides a detailed description of a candidate's background, education, specialized training, employers, duties and responsibilities at each position, salary history, publications, and professional association activities. This information is generally well prepared by an applicant and provides an excellent basis for questions at the interview.

The manager should prepare for the interview by familiarizing himself with this data. Therefore, he may prepare a summary sheet or card of important items. In addition, he may either list particular questions to ask or important information he wants to convey.

Most interviewers prefer to begin the session by discussing an applicant's interests. It is important to determine that the applicant's interests are consistent with the position under discussion and organizational objectives. Having ascertained the proper interest, most managers then prefer to discuss the applicant's background and experience. Generally it is during this segment that the manager poses his questions to the candidate. From this point, the discussion moves toward an explanation of the position. Here the manager should explain the duties and responsibilities of the position, as well as the salary and performance appraisal policies, advancement opportunities, incentive plans, travel requirements, expense policy, fringe benefits, and so forth.

Providing a prospective employee with this information enables him to evaluate a job offer as fairly as possible. Very often a candidate refuses to accept a position because he has not been given the "big picture"—because he has not been given enough information by the interviewer. There is also the possibility that a candidate may accept a position only to leave an organization within a relatively short period of time because, during the interview, he made certain invalid assumptions about the position, organization, or its policies.

Actual interviewing methods vary from organization to organization. Interviews for low-level positions are generally conducted by the manager in his office. For more important positions, interviews may be conducted off-the-premises at a private club or restaurant during a luncheon or dinner with several different managers. Or the interview may be conducted at the organization's offices, with the prospective candidate talking to different managers in their own offices throughout the day. This committee approach to interviewing and evaluation is becoming more popular because it allows for applicant appraisal by several persons. Their evaluations are then discussed by the group to determine if the prospective candidate would fit into the organizational structure. If they think he would, then the selection process will generally continue with testing of the candidate.

For many managerial positions, the candidate's wife is also invited to participate in the interview. In this type of interview, the candidate is appraised for his social bearing as well as personality and technical ability. A prospective employer uses this meeting as an opportunity to view the reaction of the wife to travel by the husband, the couple's willingness to relocate geographically, the wife's general appearance and manners. Needless to say, many a candidate who may have otherwise qualified has failed to meet the social appraisal criteria deemed important for a particular position.

References

References are still included in the selection process, but their value is questionable. It appears that references from friends are generally unreliable and that the same may be true of references from former employers.

References tend to have what is termed either a positive halo effect or a negative halo effect. The positive halo effect occurs when the candidate is rated much too high in his references. Most people have a tendency to overrate an individual because they would not like to see the man fail to secure a position because they gave an unenthusiastic reference. At the other extreme, a former employer, upset because the employee either has left the organization or is contemplating such a move, may deliberately downgrade the person, thereby creating a negative halo effect. There are many authoritarian managers who like to utilize this particular technique, feeling that it is this "human relations" approach that keeps the organization together. Perhaps it does serve to keep the organization together; it certainly does serve to disrupt the organization's operational effectiveness.

Many organizations ask a former employer to provide information about a candidate's dates of employment, starting and ending wage or salary rate, job title or a job statement briefly describing the tasks and duties, and in some instances a forced choice answer to the question, "Would you employ this person again?"—"Yes" or "No." However, in the author's view, a candidate's progress can be better ascertained from the salary history, detailed résumé, and interview.

Testing

Tests are included in the selection process because they can either furnish information that cannot be obtained any other way or validate information secured by some other method. The tests are not in themselves used as a selection determinant, but rather as a supplementary device utilized as objectively as possible. Consequently, test scores are combined with other factors to help the manager formulate a balanced judgment about a prospective employee. (A listing of tests used in a battery for selection of data processing personnel is given in Appendix II.)

The tests, which are principally psychological, are grouped together in the following five categories:
1. General intelligence tests
2. Aptitude tests
3. Proficiency tests
4. Tests relating to occupational interests
5. Personality tests

1. GENERAL INTELLIGENCE TESTS. These are designed to indicate a person's capacity to understand and learn. They cannot be used to indicate his ability to apply his learning and understanding in his work. General intelligence tests measure such traits as verbal and numerical ability, word fluency, abstract and logical reasoning, space perception,

judgment, and memory. The results of such a test may be given either as a total score, called a global score, or as separate scores for each element of the test (such as verbal, numerical, or abstract reasoning).

2. APTITUDE TESTS. These are designed to predict success in an occupation or future assignment by measuring the traits or abilities necessary for success in a specialty. The tests measure logical thinking and reasoning, instruction comprehension, coding ability, numerical ability, memory, verbal ability, and other required traits or abilities.

3. PROFICIENCY TESTS. These are constructed to measure either a person's ability to perform a task or his practical knowledge of a specialty. In essence, they measure the mental and physical capability of an applicant. The applicant is required to perform a given task that simulates a real job setting, such as writing a program, drawing a system or program flowchart, wiring a control panel, or key punching a deck of cards.

4. TESTS RELATING TO OCCUPATIONAL INTERESTS. These are designed to measure an applicant's occupational interests through numerous, rather indirect questions concerning his own characteristics. The tests do not provide an indicator of ability or success, but they should reflect the general scope and strength of an individual's interests. In evaluating this type of test, the applicant's likes and dislikes for various activities, persons, and things are compared with those of persons who have become a success in a given field. It must be remembered, though, that the results provide no proof that the applicant himself may be qualified for achievement in the occupational grouping or that his interests will remain unchanged.

5. PERSONALITY TESTS. These constitute an attempt to determine the general psychological makeup of an individual in terms of traits that cannot readily be determined by direct observation or interviewing. The traits investigated include emotions, confidence, stability, aggressiveness, sociability, extroversion, objectivity, and impulsiveness. Such tests attempt to determine an individual's attitudes toward himself, toward others, and toward various aspects of life, as well as how he thinks others regard him. If he has not been properly trained in testing procedures, the user of this type of testing device should be very cautious in how he interprets the results. However, he does not necessarily have to rely upon himself for qualified interpretation. Many colleges and universities maintain centers for test administration and interpretation. Fur-

thermore, there are psychologists in private practice who also provide such services.

Nevertheless, personality tests are still highly controversial. They have their supporters, of course, but there are also many people who are convinced that the tests should be scrapped and that other means should be used to secure the same information. Without weighing all of the arguments, it may be appropriate to refer here to a colleague of the author's, who strongly advocates the use of this type of test in personnel selection. He supports his argument by stating that in those instances where the organization executives have overridden a negative recommendation by their psychologist, they have subsequently been proven wrong.

Before leaving the subject of personality tests, it may be interesting to briefly discuss a recent and perhaps somewhat unorthodox innovation in personality testing. This is the now-increasing use of handwriting analysis as a tool for personality assessment. Graphologists contend that handwriting is a spontaneous expression of a person's feelings, thoughts, and attitudes.

In most instances, the sample used is the handwritten application or other documents used in the recruitment process. The applicant may also be asked to write a brief statement about his interests, or some other subject, on an 8 1/2″ × 11″ sheet of unlined paper. A trained graphologist takes the handwriting sample and analyzes it in terms of the strokes, slants, spaces, and signs, as well as the size of the margins. The results of the analysis are then interpreted by the graphologist to arrive at a personality profile of the applicant.

Though this testing technique has been assailed or ridiculed by many people, it does appear to be gaining in industrial acceptance, as indicated by the fact that some of the prestigious "Fortune 500" companies are now using it as part of the selection process. Such users apparently accept the idea that a valid correlation exists between the graphologist's assessments and the applicant's actual characteristics.

One of the major problems with handwriting analysis is the exactness of the method of analysis. The analysis is based on a graphologist's judgment because there are no measurable or ratable scales available for evaluation purposes. Also, empirical studies conducted by testing experts have shown that attempts to relate the handwriting elements to personality traits rarely yield positive results. Physical handicaps (such as a vision defect) may affect the validity of the test results.

Validation of Tests

The practical value of a test is determined by its validity and reliability. A test is considered valid if and when it measures a characteristic it is supposed to measure with reasonably high reliability. The characteristic being tested must be representative of the actual operations or tasks performed. The measure indicates how well the person does it and the quality and quantity of the end product. We can observe a person reading a programming problem specification, but we cannot observe his comprehension of what he is reading. The best possible estimate of the person's reading comprehension is one based on a test performance. Therefore, when a manager selects a test for inclusion in the test battery (a group of tests used in the selection process), he must make certain that the test content or situations and materials are identical, or very similar, to the actual operations or tasks.

A test is considered reliable if and when the same person achieves approximately the same score each time he is tested, even after an interval of several years. In order to arrive at some practical judgment of an individual, there must be consistency in the test measurements. Otherwise any practical judgment or action based on the test becomes impossible. As in the case of validity, the manager must carefully examine the reliability data on a test. The lower the reliability of the score, the more tentative any judgment or decision.

Of course no test is perfectly valid or reliable. But a well-designed test can be conducted with a high degree of accuracy, which is beneficial to the overall selection process. Selecting well-designed tests for the test battery from the numerous psychological tests available on the market is not a big problem. However, when in-house tests are developed, the manager must make sure the tests have been experimentally and statistically proven valid and reliable. Internally developed proficiency tests can be highly suspect. Of course, no test is perfectly valid or reliable. But a well-designed test can be conducted with a high degree of accuracy, which is beneficial to the overall selection process.

The manager must also be concerned with test-score interpretation. In examining a score or scores, he needs to understand what the score really means. He also needs to understand the significance of the difference or similarity in test scores when two or more tests are used.

Scores are generally expressed as standard scores that indicate how much the individual's score varies from the arithmetic mean of all scores in the tested group. This enables the manager to compare all tests used in the test battery.

Review Questions: Group 3B

1. What personal attitudes or characteristics are desirable in a potential candidate for a data processing position?
2. Why is personnel selection such a costly item?
3. What are the sources of supply for potential employees needed in a data processing activity? Discuss briefly the merits of each source.
4. Why is the interview such an important tool in the selection of personnel?
5. What is a positive halo effect?
6. What is the purpose of a proficiency test?

TRAINING OF PERSONNEL

Training is a method of teaching theory and application to people in order to increase their operational effectiveness. Because it is essential to have personnel who are able to analyze problems and develop solutions for them, one important objective of any training program should be to encourage the development of the ability to think, rather than the learning of a set of techniques to be applied in accordance with a predefined set of rules.

There are several major advantages accruing to the organization that conducts an efficient personnel training program. Such a program:

—Increases personnel efficiency because the employees are informed about the organization's policies, practices, and procedures. Also, it reduces the "break in" time, thereby making a person fully productive sooner.

—Helps to reduce personnel turnover. People who are given training feel that the organization is interested in them and that it is willing to utilize their abilities.

—Instills a spirit of cooperation and teamwork in the employees. People work better when they feel that they are a part of the organization. Training gives them an opportunity for promotion, acquiring responsibility, and performing new functions or activities.

—Lowers the operating costs. A person functions more productively when he understands what must be done and what he is expected to do in accomplishing the goal.

—Eases the manager's work load. A properly trained person accomplishes the assigned tasks with less supervision, thereby enabling the manager to devote more time to other management activities.

Training Methods

There are many methods that can be used, but all of them customarily fall into one or another of two major categories. These categories are formal training and informal training.

Formal Training

Formal programs are concerned with specific techniques, such as those involved in management games and programmed learning, as well as seminars conducted by equipment vendors. Formal programs provide intensive training in problems of varying degrees of difficulty that an individual may or may not encounter in an on-the-job situation. The material presented is either generalized or specialized depending upon the training objectives and needs of the organization.

Much of the training utilizes a classroom situation. A typical formal program is generally concentrated into a brief time span—a day, several days, or a week—or it may be extended over a period of weeks or months. Some programs are conducted on the basis of one full day of classes per week. Others represent a type of work-study program, in which employees work in the morning or afternoon for several hours and then attend classes either before or after the work period.

One disadvantage to the formal method is that a person in training is at least partially nonproductive for some period of time. However, training costs are incurred with the anticipation that short-term losses will eventually become long-term gains.

The actual choice of formal training program depends upon the current and future objectives of an organization. A manager must realistically assess the skills and abilities of his own staff to select the best plan of action. He must also extend the assessment beyond his own activity to all functional activities within the organization, for the training of managerial and user personnel may help to increase the extent and effectiveness of current contributions to a system. Furthermore, arranging training for people not presently involved in data processing may well provide future benefits in the form of improved communications and tangible savings.

The most commonly used methods in a formal training program are:
1. Management games
2. College and university courses
3. Programs offered by professional associations
4. Programs offered by management consultants
5. Training supplied by equipment vendors
6. Professional education services
7. Programmed learning
8. Organizational training groups

1. MANAGEMENT GAMES. These constitute a teaching technique designed to develop the decision-making ability of an individual; experience in management functions; and effective utilization of manpower, materials, machines, and money.

Most management games are group-participation activities based on the use of competitive teams. In a typical game, each team is given a set of conditions to apply in order to produce quantitative results. Although the educational value and effectiveness of these games have been questioned by some authorities, management games have proven to be beneficial in providing employees with awareness of how interdependent activities affect both the management process and the steps involved in decision-making.

The games customarily considered most relevant to training in the data processing field are general management games and functional games.

General Management Games. General management games utilize abstract models of generalized companies in generalized industries, with emphasis on executive decision-making activities that can be affected by a number of interacting variables. Ordinarily the playing of these games involves the use of medium-scale or large-scale computer systems, although some games are handscored instead.

General management games are most commonly used for training upper-echelon managers. At present, though, they are also being used in the training of lower-level managers, management trainees, and high-potential employees. The games are usually administered and evaluated by the organization's own training group. However, some of the game sessions are conducted at a vendor's educational facility or at a college or university facility.

Functional Games. Functional games are aimed at developing specific skills or techniques through simulating one element or one aspect of the business structure, such as production control, inventory planning, or a job shop environment. There is also at least one functional game available for providing training in management of a programming activity. Developed by the System Development Corporation of Santa Monica, California, this game is known by the acronym STEPS (*S*taff *T*raining *E*xercise for *P*rogramming *S*upervisors). The design of the functional game may require the use of competing teams or the interaction of an individual within the parameters and constraints of the game. Most of the games are played in conjunction with a computer.

2. COLLEGE AND UNIVERSITY COURSES. Many colleges and universities are well-equipped with specialized equipment, facilities, and instructors to provide a variety of data processing programs, such as lectures, courses, workshops, institutes, and conferences. Some of these programs are specifically tailored to the needs of a particular organization or industry. Most, however, are general programs intended to provide training in a variety of subjects for many interested persons. In many cases, the educational institutions award credit hours, which may be applied toward degree-granting programs—thus enabling participants to continue their formal education after the training session has been completed.

Anyone desiring information about available courses should contact the registrar's office at local colleges and universities. It is also useful to check with the professional data processing associations, as well as to consult the *Computer Directory* published annually by *Computers and Automation Magazine.*

3. PROGRAMS OFFERED BY PROFESSIONAL ASSOCIATIONS. These organizations conduct specialized seminars and development programs for members and nonmembers. The American Management Association, for example, offers a variety of seminars for the development of personnel. And such organizations as the Systems and Procedures Association, the Data Processing Management Association, and the Association for Computing Machinery offer seminars on a local, regional, or national basis for interested persons. They also offer self-development programs through participation in study groups, informal discussions with other

members, and information made available through newsletters, journals, and other association publications.

(The names and addresses of professional associations are included in Appendix IV.)

4. PROGRAMS OFFERED BY MANAGEMENT CONSULTANTS. Using the programs provided by management consultant firms is becoming a popular way of providing training for an organization's personnel at all levels, so that these firms are now very much involved in the training of personnel. They have developed a variety of general and specialized seminars, which are available in all major U.S. cities. In addition, they also develop, on a contract basis, special seminars and programs designed to fit an organization's own needs and desires. These customized courses may be presented by either the consultant's staff or the organization's own training specialists.

The names and addresses of management consulting firms engaged in providing educational services may be secured from the local telephone book, the *Computer Directory*, or the *Business Automation Reference Guide*, which is published annually by Business Press International.

5. TRAINING SUPPLIED BY EQUIPMENT VENDORS. Equipment vendors are currently the major suppliers of training and media for managerial, user, and data processing personnel. However, the vendors' preeminence is diminishing, for there is now a discernible trend away from them and toward other sources.

One of the most frequently cited reasons for this trend is the increase in costs. Customers used to obtain training and media from the vendors at little or no cost. Since June 1969, however, most customers have had to pay for the service. What is more, the vendors' courses continue to be offered at geographical locations that are not readily and generally convenient for many organizations, so that customers have to pay travel and lodging expenses as well as the service fee.

Another reason—perhaps the most important one—for the move away from vendors' instruction programs is customer dissatisfaction with the subject matter offered. Many customers feel that if they must pay for a course, they would like to have the material tailored more closely to their own needs. Although the vendors have expressed an interest in customizing education services, some organizations have not been entirely pleased with the proposals. Furthermore, the vendors' courses continue to reflect the vested-interest viewpoint of the manufacturers, whereas many customers would prefer a more universal approach to such subjects as data communications, time-sharing, modular programming, and so forth.

Although vendors maintain a fairly standard range of available courses, their teaching methods have changed in recent years. Therefore it is useful to consider the overall topic under two separate headings: teaching methods and course offerings.

Teaching Methods. Teaching methods have changed since the inception of third-generation hardware and concepts. Consequently, the traditional classroom method of teaching and learning now supplements rather than dominates vendor education services. The new approach to vendor-provided training is based on the use—either singly or in combination—of such media as programmed instruction materials, student texts, reference manuals, audio-education packages, video tapes, and systems exercise card decks.

The programmed instruction materials, generally referred to as PI materials, utilize the basic concept of the student reading short, sequential explanations of the material and then answering questions on his reading as he goes. Only after demonstrating his comprehension of one segment of the material does the student advance to the next segment. The student is able to learn at his own pace while on the job. His progress is evaluated through a test administered by the vendor or the organization's training group. The PI materials are used to cover introductory, preliminary, or background data with a follow-up of a day or more in a classroom. This follow-up is sometimes referred to as the workshop session or simply as the wrap-up.

Student texts have also been developed by the vendors to augment the training process. The texts are limited to the presentation of an introductory or single data processing concept. Unlike the reference manuals, the student texts are written in a more descriptive manner, with examples and illustrations to facilitate understanding. This approach bridges the gap between classroom instruction and the use of reference manuals, which are generally written to provide information for people already possessing basic knowledge of the subject matter. The student texts are also very useful for self-teaching and self-development. Most of these texts are available only from vendors; some, however, may be obtained through publishers.

The reference manuals are written to provide either very specific data about a subject or generalized or introductory information. They have traditionally been used as textbooks in the vendor courses, although unlike most textbooks, they include very few teaching-type examples. Manuals currently play a supplementary classroom role, being used to amplify information taught by the instructor, as well as to provide reference aid in the solution of problems.

Audio education, a relatively new teaching concept, is also utilized by the vendors. The typical audio-education package consists of an audio tape and an illustration book or packet. The student concentrates on listening to the tape for the basic subject matter, referring to his illustration book or packet as specifics are noted on the tape. Audio-education packages are used for teaching various generalized and specialized topics. If an adequate number of illustration books or packets are available with an organization, a number of people can participate in one session. However, the vendor audio-education packages are intended primarily for use as individualized learning tools. After a user has completed his learning session, the materials may be passed on to another user in the organization. Depending on the subject matter involved, a test to assess comprehension may be administered by the vendor's organization or the organization's training group. Some audio packages have been established as prerequisites for entry into vendor classroom training sessions.

Video tapes represent another relatively new concept in teaching data processing. IBM, for example, offers a program that is based on the use of video tapes in what is referred to as a learner-paced format. This is an innovative method that attempts to involve the student more intently in the learning process. The instructor is a consultant rather than a lecturer, and the format stresses the use of learning objectives, video tapes, programmed instruction materials, and audio education and other self-study materials to convey the subject matter. The student must complete the exercises assigned by the instructor, and in many of the courses must pass a test given at the end of the session.

Systems exercise decks are used primarily for training operating personnel in computer operation. They teach an operator to initialize the processor, load jobs, and respond to interrupts.

Course Offerings. The course offerings cover executive orientation, and general data processing orientation, professional development, hardware operation, and applications.

The executive orientation courses are designed to familiarize the upper echelon with the components of a computer or unit-record system and with programming languages, systems design, and the role of data processing and its functional organization. Such courses are not intended to make the executive an expert, but rather to enable him to communicate more effectively and to understand his involvement in data processing.

The general data processing orientation courses provide introductory, background, or basic information about the hardware, programming languages, operating systems, etc. Some of these courses, taken by data processing personnel, serve as prerequisites for subsequent professional, applications, and hardware courses. And some courses provide general orientation for users and other people not directly involved in data processing.

Professional development courses, designed for people directly involved in data processing, deal with specifics in systems analysis and design, programming languages, operating systems, data management concepts, and other related subjects. In an attempt to increase the educational effectiveness of these courses, the vendors have recently integrated these offerings with the use of the various teaching media. The use of these media has reduced the amount of time spent away from an organization by employees receiving vendor-supplied training. (There are also other benefits, which are discussed under programmed learning, below.)

Hardware operation courses, which also utilize the various teaching media for instruction, are designed to teach the fundamentals, operation, and wiring of unit-record, computer, and peripheral equipment.

Applications courses are designed to provide students with the fundamental concepts of the subject matter, together with specific information on the application and also on the conversion and operational requirements. At present, most of these courses have the classroom-lecture setting as their mode of instruction; however, there are also a few that have been established as audio-education packages. Applications courses include general-concept courses, industry-oriented courses, and hardware-oriented courses. A typical general-concept offering would be an introduction to inventory management or shop scheduling. Industry-oriented courses include such topics as demand deposit accounting for financial institutions; another is management information system for hospitals. There are many hardware-oriented courses. One example is the bill of materials processor package for the IBM 360 computer.

6. PROFESSIONAL EDUCATION SERVICES. Within the last few years there has been an increase in the number of companies offering data processing educational services for presentation in major cities throughout the country. These companies have developed seminar packages for managerial and data processing personnel to cover such topics as programming techniques, controls, applications, and fundamental concepts. The subject matter is concentrated, in that the seminar sessions last only between one to five days, with the average being two or three days.

These company-supplied seminar sessions are considered to be less expensive than the courses offered by vendors. Furthermore, they tend to offer a broader viewpoint and/or more of an in-depth approach to a particular topic. Also, many of the topics covered in the seminars are not normally included in vendor-supplied training programs. One major reason for these last two differences is that the seminar leaders are people who come from diverse backgrounds and who have distinguished themselves in the subject matter.

(A list of some of the organizations offering such education services is included in Appendix V. Additional names and addresses can be found in the *Computer Directory* and in the *Business Automation Reference Guide*.)

7. PROGRAMMED LEARNING. Programmed learning techniques are designed and developed to train personnel quickly and more effectively at a lower cost per student. A number of different programmed learning media have evolved since the original concept was developed by Harvard University psychologist B. F. Skinner. However, their advantages are very similar. The principal advantages (which are not mutually exclusive) are:

—The user may learn at his own pace. He is not required to complete a unit within a given time period.

—The user actively interacts in the learning process because he is ready to learn and respond.

—The material is structured to cover large segments of information in a minimal amount of learning time.

—The student's advancement is based on his achievement; therefore, he is immediately and constantly aware of his progress.

However, there are also disadvantages that need to be understood. The principal ones are:

—The teaching and test materials are difficult to develop.

—The development process is very time-consuming. And the costs involved may not be offset by savings in training costs.

—Failure to design and develop the materials properly results in a user advancing to another segment before mastering the previous segment of information.

—Some of the subject matter may be affected by obsolescence or changes. Depending on the media form, it may be difficult to respond with a modification or revision.

Initially, programmed instruction materials were made available for the teaching of number systems, data processing concepts, and programming languages. Subsequently, though, the range of materials was expanded by the vendors and publishing companies to include a number of different topics such as programming of direct access storage devices and data communications concepts.

There are also various specialized forms of programmed learning, among which are computer assisted instruction materials, video tapes, single-concept films, and audio-education materials.

Computer assisted instruction (CAI) materials are intended to teach programming languages, the use of conversational time-sharing terminals, and data processing concepts. One disadvantage to the CAI approach is that it not only requires the use of conversational terminals but also preemption of the computer for educational purposes for a predetermined time period each day. The latter can be a significant problem, because only a limited number of courses are available from vendors, professional educational services, and colleges and universities. Also, course materials may not be operable on the organization's equipment configuration. Therefore the training group will prepare a course package that makes use of the organization's equipment. Furthermore, it can be both difficult and time-consuming to develop CAI materials.

Video tapes are used to teach programming languages, hardware operation, applications, and many other subjects. These tapes have been developed by vendors, consulting firms, and companies involved in education services, but they are used mostly by colleges, universities, and in-house training organizations.

Single-concept films are increasing in popularity as a form of programmed learning. At present they are being prepared by professional educational services, colleges and universities, and in-house training groups. Some of the popularity may be attributed to the fact that these films can be mounted in 8-mm cartridges and used in desk-top viewers by either individuals or groups. The films are used to teach hardware operation, programming languages and techniques, data processing concepts, systems analysis and design techniques, and many other topics. In some cases, the films are supplemented by textual materials that develop the film concepts and provide written problems for the students to solve.

Audio education is another popular form of programmed learning. The popularity may be due to the practical convenience of the tape cassettes and tape players. For example, material can be recorded on both sides of the tape cassette, which means that depending on the density of the tape surface, each cassette has a playing time ranging from 20 minutes to an hour per side. The cassettes are used to teach such topics as terminology, programming fundamentals, and application concepts. Some of the audio packages include textual materials, which illustrate or expand a particular topic. The available audio-education packages have been developed by vendors, management consultants, professional educational services, colleges and universities, and in-house training groups.

8. ORGANIZATIONAL TRAINING GROUPS. Being fully aware of the substantial investment of manpower, money, machine, and material resources required for every program or system developed and implemented, many organizations recognize that the operational effectiveness of data processing is dependent upon sound training practices. They also know that costs can be reduced and savings realized if the personnel concerned—managerial, user and data processing—are all trained effectively. This is why many organizations either are establishing or already have established in-house training groups to develop, implement, and coordinate training programs and resources. Such groups, although within the data processing activity, are intended to facilitate the training of executives and users, as well as data processing personnel. Used effectively, these in-house training groups can help remedy what has been a fairly common organizational deficiency—that of being very methodical in providing training for data processing personnel, but being lax about including users and managers. Adequate training for user personnel in particular must be arranged prior to conversion and implementation of a system or program; and the effect of that training must be evaluated following implementation.

The dynamic and innovative nature of data processing requires that continuing education be developed and implemented in every organization to update the professional skills of the data processing personnel.

This form of preventative maintenance maximizes the skills and abilities of the staff and helps to sustain their operational effectiveness. In addition, it reduces or minimizes turnover because it eliminates one of the major reasons why data processing personnel leave an organization: fear of becoming technically obsolescent. There is a risk, though, that some personnel will leave because this kind of training helps qualify them for other positions. Nevertheless, most organizations have found that employees given training in the state of the art and new techniques develop a broader viewpoint and greater proficiency—valuable qualities that are ultimately reflected in reduced development and maintenance costs, and perhaps even increase the level of tangible savings.

Because the development of training programs can be very expensive, many organizations utilize external sources to develop, implement, and provide training or training materials. The in-house training groups also attempt to develop some training materials and integrate existing innovative teaching media in their educational programs. This approach enables an organization to reduce the costs of providing quality education. The effective coordination of teaching media by the in-house group can reduce away-from-the-job time by eliminating or minimizing the need to send employees to off-premises facilities for training. Implied is the fact that effective use of teaching media can reduce away-from-the-job time. This, in turn, can help to increase productivity and possibly to reduce personnel costs. Many organizations employ additional personnel to cover for those engaged in some phase of training.

Informal Training

Informal training programs are designed to involve the participant in the learning process while in an actual on-the-job setting. This alleviates or eliminates some of the confusion that can occur in moving from the theoretical to the actual environment. There is also the advantage that the person is not only learning but also working to some extent, thereby providing some return on investment almost immediately. The disadvantage is that the training period must be somewhat lengthy to cover an adequate number of situations and experiences.

The three most popular forms of informal training are:
1. Job rotation
2. Special assignments
3. Committee assignments

The choice among these training methods varies according to either the position for which an individual is being trained or the background he should have. Job rotation is probably the most frequently used informal training method, especially for people entering a data processing occupation at the trainee level. Special assignments and committee assignments are more relevant to training personnel at the semiskilled and specialist levels.

1. JOB ROTATION. Job rotation involves training of personnel either in the various activities of one particular function or within the entire organizational structure. Effective use of this technique requires that the organization's training coordinator or functional manager develop a job rotation plan for each person that is based on both the organization's objectives and the person's skills and abilities. The plan must include the sequence of activities to be followed; the type, extent, and length of training to be given at each activity; and an evaluation technique that will indicate if the trainee is qualified to move to the next phase. To be beneficial to both the trainee and the organization, this method requires a great deal of coordination. The need is apparent when many employees are involved in job rotation.

2. SPECIAL ASSIGNMENTS. The special assignments approach to training is used primarily for employees in managerial or management training positions. The technique is also used for employees who are not in a formal management training program but who have demonstrated high potential for managerial responsibility. In this method, the trainee is assigned a specific task to perform or goal to attain. He is kept under observation during the performance of his duties in order to determine how well he defines an objective and plans the goal-attainment process. The special assignments should be used to maximize the individual's skills, abilities, and potential, rather than to correct his weaknesses to any large degree. Very often the employee is assigned to a position of supervisory responsibility so that he can be evaluated in terms of his ability to handle such an assignment and to work with others. If this is to be an effective form of training, the results of the assignment must be discussed with the trainee in order that he can learn from his experience. This discussion should be conducted immediately upon conclusion of the assignment. It should not be postponed until the periodic employee appraisal is conducted, for the delay would only defeat the purpose of training and minimize the learning experience.

3. COMMITTEE ASSIGNMENTS. The committee approach to training is used as a means of having an employee actively participate in the

workings of an organization through a committee, thereby broadening his knowledge and experience. Under this approach, a trainee is assigned to a committee position that will give him the chance to achieve an understanding and awareness of organizational interaction. In this setting, he becomes involved with the views of others, with the adjustments being worked out, and with the compromises that must be made—all of which give him the opportunity to gain insight into company policies and practices. Depending upon the type of committee and degree of responsibility involved, an individual can gain either vast or limited experience and understanding from participation in this training technique.

Who Should be Trained?

In many organizations, training is very much neglected, underestimated, or misunderstood. Some firms view it as an expensive luxury because it does not produce any direct revenue. Others see it as a necessary evil—one that, unfortunately, requires some attention. "Some attention" frequently turns out to be assigning the training responsibility on a part-time basis to some member of the organization. Very often the assignee is an individual who has no background or experience in training and who approaches his additional duty in a disgruntled or haphazard manner. Organizations with this attitude toward training, as well as those that ignore the matter completely, fail to understand that the success of any organization, no matter how small, depends on having effective personnel. And the best way of developing and maintaining such personnel is implementation of a well-planned and well-coordinated training program.

Personnel turnover has frequently been attributed to the lack of training. Failure to provide basic, developmental, or advanced training has resulted in turnover rates as high as 50 percent. Figures ranging from 15 to 30 percent have been quoted as average annual turnover rates. However, even an annual rate as low as 15 percent can be very costly to any organization. The loss of just one employee necessitates a recycling of the recruitment and selection process resulting in an expenditure of $1500 to $5000. Added to that cost is an additional sum that represents the loss in salary until a new employee becomes fully productive at the end of the familiarization, or break-in, period, which may last from two to twelve months.

The data processing activity crosses all functional activity boundary lines within the organization. Therefore, each member of the organization should be given some measure of training or orientation concerning data processing. The amount and type of training required varies in accordance with the employee's level and degree of involvement in the data processing function. The employees can be grouped as follows:

1. Managers
2. Data processing personnel
3. User personnel
4. Other personnel

1. MANAGERS. Managerial personnel at all levels should be given orientation and training in the use of data processing as a management tool. The degree and extent of such training varies from level to level within the hierarchical structure. At each level, training should include instruction about current and potential applications, as well as the problems and conditions involved in utilizing the tools.

Managerial personnel are generally trained through the use of materials and courses provided by vendors, professional associations, and colleges and universities, professional educational services, and in-house training groups. Also, some organizations have developed and implemented their own courses to teach data processing fundamentals to all levels of the managerial hierarchy.

2. DATA PROCESSING PERSONNEL. These people must be given continued training so that they can retain their qualitative and quantitative capability in a fast-changing technical field. This is particularly important for personnel in the advanced planning and development group, because continuing education plays a key role in maintaining their effectiveness.

At present most of the training is provided by vendors. However, additional training is supplied by in-house groups, management consultants, professional education services, colleges and universities, and professional associations, together with the use of programmed learning media from a variety of sources and the application of the informal training methods.

All employees in the data processing activity must be trained in the implementation of emergency operating procedures. This requires their familiarity with:

—Location of, and method by which to turn off, the electrical power supply

—Location of emergency telephones and/or signal boxes
—Responses to audible and/or visual alarms
—Location of master panic switches
—Location of fire extinguishers and their use in basic firefighting techniques
—Protection of hardware
—Protection of valuable records
—Location of emergency exits
—Evacuation procedures

Availability of this documentation simplifies the training of new personnel and provides reference material for long-term employees. However, simply providing this information is not enough, in terms of the effective response that may well be needed in an emergency. Therefore, the manager must develop an emergency readiness training program in order to achieve the maximum personnel effectiveness needed for such a response. A very important part of this training is to conduct drills under simulated realistic conditions. Developing the actual cases may be difficult, but it can be accomplished without endangering the personnel, materials, files, and equipment. The drills can be most beneficial, for they indicate the state of personnel readiness and the effectiveness of the documented emergency procedures.

3. USER PERSONNEL. User personnel are provided with training and orientation for several reasons. First, to facilitate their understanding, use, and processing of such outputs as management reports, exception reports, and production reports. Second, to provide training in the preparation of inputs and source documents. Third, to provide training in the operation of certain kinds of equipment, such as key punch machines, data recorders, sorters, and data communications terminals—devices that user organizations may have on hand to facilitate input preparation, file selection operations in their activity, and problem-solving. Furthermore, training is arranged for user personnel prior to the conversion and implementation of new or modified programs and systems.

User training may be provided by an in-house group, data processing personnel, vendors, management consultants, or professional educational services. Training in the operation of conversational terminals is generally facilitated through the use of a computer assisted instruction package. Training in hardware operation is accomplished through the use of programmed instruction materials, video tapes, on-the-job instruction, and vendor-supplied courses. In addition, management consultants, professional educational services, vendors, and in-house groups may be used to provide users with training in application concepts and packages.

4. OTHER PERSONNEL. Organizational personnel in general should be given relevant orientation to increase their awareness of the potential of data processing for their particular applications. This type of orientation also serves to remove doubts and fears from the minds of potential users, thereby increasing the possibility of their cooperation with and acceptance of the data processing function. Much of the training for interested non-data processing personnel is provided by in-house groups or data processing personnel. For specialized applications, it may be very beneficial to have these interested people attend seminars conducted by vendors, professional educational services, or professional associations.

Review Questions: Group 3C

1. Why should a personnel training program be developed in every organization?
2. Management games are included in many formal training programs. Why?
3. There is a growing trend toward including programmed learning methods in training programs. Why?
4. What steps must be taken by an operations manager to ensure the effectiveness of the job rotation method of informal training?
5. Should the manager of a small data processing organization concern himself with obsolescence training?
6. If your organization utilized an open shop programming structure, for whom would you recommend training in programming techniques?

APPRAISAL OF PERSONNEL PERFORMANCE

The appraisal, or merit-rating, process is implemented during the executory phase of management, when the goal-attainment plan has been initiated and is operative. The bases for judgment are the performance standards previously defined during the pre-executory phase. Primarily, the appraisal process is intended to provide periodic evaluation of an employee's actual and potential performance. Yet, directly and indirectly, much information can also be learned about an organization's policies and problems.

A well-executed personnel appraisal program has the following effects:

—It is an indicator of a person's performance and improvement. The manager rates the employee's performance for the appraisal period as unsatisfactory, fair, average, very good, or outstanding. The ratings provide the manager with a relative measure of the employee's performance compared with that of others in the same job. The appraisal also affords the manager an opportunity to recognize and commend employee self-development. Such an action very often provides a motivating stimulus for continued self-development and performance improvement.

—It identifies the strengths and weaknesses of an individual. This information enables a manager to conduct an effective counseling session with the employee. Furthermore, it enables the manager to recommend a development plan for improvement and acceleration of growth. This must be a tangible plan to benefit the employee and the organization, for the organization can ill-afford to have a manager expound some vague plan for maximizing the strengths and potential of an employee.

—The manager gains a new understanding of his employees, for the appraisal increases his awareness of their current efforts and contributions. Also, it may provide some indication of the type and level of assistance that may be anticipated in the future. In addition, it identifies continuing above-average or outstanding performances, which may subsequently be rewarded by salary increases, new assignments, or promotions.

—It identifies the skills and abilities possessed by an individual. This identification of capabilities provides the manager with an informal skills inventory file. The information is especially useful when the manager wishes to delegate additional responsibility to an employee, make assignments to special projects, or promote personnel.

—It provides an evaluation of the personnel selection and training techniques. The manager can check his decisions on personnel selection with the appraisal results. Also, he can determine whether or not the training programs are adequate.

—It can provide data on the adequacy or inadequacy of company policies and/or practices. Very often a manager learns that the lack of compatible or relevant policies or practices hinders an employee's efforts. For example, he may learn that an employee is being required to computerize a payroll application within the same parameters previously applied to the unit-record approach.

The Appraisal Process

Personnel appraisal requires an unbiased rating of an individual's current performance, in a number of preselected traits and characteristics, and his potential performance. The actual performance—for the various traits and characteristics, which may include such items as accuracy or appearance—is gauged in terms of a predefined standard established during the organizing function of the pre-executory phase. The standard must stipulate clearly what has to be accomplished or what is acceptable to meet current operating needs, policies, or practice. And it must cover a range of measurable levels, so as to provide for performance comparisons of employees. The standard then becomes the yardstick for determining whether an employee's actual performance is at, above, or below the planned level.

Actual performance should be determined only after the manager has had an opportunity to observe the employee for a reasonable amount of time. One brief observation is insufficient and can lead to ·inaccuracy in performance measurement and subsequently in the full appraisal. Repeated observation is also necessary to isolate any weak, unsatisfactory, or barely acceptable performances. When he observes such conditions, the appraiser should make a brief report of the fact, together with a tangible illustration. This information is needed because there is more involved here than simply determining work performance: the manager has to be concerned with correcting the situation. The information provides the basis for an effective counseling session. Furthermore, in addition to being prepared for discussion of the problem, the manager has to be ready to recommend action for improvement or fortification of a trait or characteristic. He needs to determine the type of training program that should be planned and implemented to expedite the employee's development.

An employee's potential performance has to be rated separately because of the subjective nature of the evaluation. Potential performance is an estimate or projection by the appraiser of an employee's capabilities. It often has little factual substance and tends to be biased. Nevertheless, potential must be rated because it becomes the basis for planning the employee's future course and development. To realize this performance potential, the manager must obviously develop and implement a meaningful training plan.

It is important to add that such a training plan must also be realistic, in that some employees will not rise beyond a certain level of competence or proficiency. In such instances, the manager has to be concerned with having the employee maintain a satisfactory performance level. This does not mean the employee should receive no more training after reaching that point, but that he should be given training appropriate to the maintenance of his level of proficiency.

Actual and potential performance are sometimes confused by the appraiser. For example, one data processing manager was dissatisfied with the "low" output of a programmer whom he had rated as a good "software type." The programmer, however, was not writing any software packages; instead, he was being utilized for performing modifications and maintenance to existing programs. Therefore, he had been rated for what he could possibly do and not for what he had actually been doing. Another manager once rated the output capability of one of his programmers by the man's size and weight. He held the opinion and the expectation that the programmer could "out-produce" anyone else because he was bigger. Eventually, the programmer's failure to produce in direct proportion to his anatomical structure resulted in a lower performance rating.

Although these two examples represent flagrant violations of the very purpose of performance appraisal, they are not isolated cases. Providing for an objective appraisal is easier said than done. It is very difficult to refrain from becoming subjective when evaluating the various traits and characteristics. Deliberately or accidentally, the appraisal process often becomes a reward or punishment mechanism rather than a management tool.

Appraisal Characteristics and Traits

The characteristics and traits most frequently evaluated during the appraisal process are:

1. Quantity and quality of work
2. Economy of time
3. Thoroughness
4. Attitude toward superiors
5. Attitude toward job
6. General knowledge
7. Accuracy
8. Versatility
9. Personal appearance
10. Other characteristics and traits

1. QUANTITY AND QUALITY OF WORK. The quantity and quality to be produced are measured against the performance standard established for each individual position or occupational grouping.

2. ECONOMY OF TIME. This characteristic is concerned with a person's ability to organize and use his time effectively. A person capable of properly organizing his project time will register high productivity. However, the appraiser needs to determine if the desired quality level was also achieved.

3. THOROUGHNESS. The appraiser must determine the degree of completeness that can be attributed to the task or tasks accomplished by the employee. He must also ascertain if the projects have truly been completed, in that some employees "complete" their projects quickly, but are found to be still adding, changing, or correcting something many weeks or months later. But if they are still unfinished after a reasonable time has elapsed, the manager should assign some other staff member the responsibility for satisfactory completion of the project. The manager should then make note of this fact for use in the subsequent appraisal and counseling session.

4. ATTITUDE TOWARD SUPERIORS. This indicates an employee's ability to accept and follow instructions under adverse as well as favorable working conditions. A person with an uncooperative or rebellious attitude will not be very dependable or reliable and certainly cannot be counted upon to accept responsibility.

5. ATTITUDE TOWARD JOB. This depends very much on whether or not the employee is in the right job. He may be unhappy or unsuccessful because he has been placed in the wrong position. It is also possible that the employee is bored with his present position because he has exhausted its challenge or because it may have become a kind of dead-end job with no place to go until someone else dies, retires, or is promoted. A

negative attitude may also be evident if the employee is not qualified for a position, if he has been inadequately trained, or if he has apparently misunderstood the duties and responsibilities of his position. Evaluating an employee's attitude toward his job is most difficult unless the manager has had an opportunity to steadily observe the employee and collect adequate data.

6. GENERAL KNOWLEDGE. In appraising this characteristic, the manager evaluates an employee's ability to utilize his knowledge of data processing, a subject-matter specialty, the organizational structure, and the workflow. There may be a tendency on the part of the manager to overestimate what the general requirements for a position should be. The appraisal should be based on the job knowledge criteria stipulated in the job description for that position. The general knowledge requirements for a junior programmer position, for example, will not be comparable to that of a senior programmer. It would be grossly unfair for a manager to apply the general requirements of the latter's position to all programmer positions in the organization.

7. ACCURACY. This trait may be appraised individually or as part of the thoroughness trait. It is concerned with an employee's ability to perform a task or series of tasks with exactness and precision. This implies that when the project is completed, it satisfies the desired objectives; will be useful in the future; will have relatively low maintenance requirements; and will be easy to change or modify.

8. VERSATILITY. This trait is generally used in appraising upper level positions in the data processing function, where the personnel are often required to work under adverse conditions or to take on a multiplicity of projects within a normal workday. In determining versatility, the manager evaluates the employee's ability to cope with stress and other environmental conditions. People who are potential managers must have the ability to operate in a dynamic environment that is characterized by ever-changing conditions and requirements.

9. PERSONAL APPEARANCE. This trait is used to evaluate such factors as neatness, grooming, general appearance, dress, and posture. What constitutes acceptable or presentable appearance will depend on existing organizational policy. There is a tendency to emphasize this trait in the appraisal of data processing personnel because a presentable personal appearance can help make the employee and/or his material acceptable to others and can remove some preliminary barriers in face-to-face contact. The reason for applying this emphasis is that many executives

believe that the appearance of a person is an excellent indicator of several characteristics, such as ability to organize, resourcefulness, attitude toward job and supervision, cooperation, and initiative. There is, however, no scientific support for such beliefs.

10. OTHER CHARACTERISTICS AND TRAITS. These include health, maturity, problem-solving ability, punctuality, ability to grasp instructions, judgment, and many others. The list can be very long indeed, depending on differences among organizations, occupational groupings, and the level of detail required in characteristic classifications.

Appraisal Techniques/Formats

There are a number of specialized formats available for recording the manager's appraisal of a subordinate. These can be used to provide a historical record for employee development and other decisions. Among the most frequently used appraisal techniques/formats are:

1. Graphic scales
2. Checklists
3. Narratives
4. Critical incidents
5. Man-to-man comparisons
6. Forced choices

1. GRAPHIC SCALES. These scales represent the more popular type of rating form in use today. As illustrated in Figure 3.6, the kind of scale known as the personnel rating form includes a listing of the desired traits or characteristics (plus a brief definition of acceptable performance) on the left side of the form. The rest of the form is usually occupied by a series of blocks for indicating the rating degrees possible for each trait or characteristic, ranging from unsatisfactory to outstanding. There is one block for each rating degree, so that the employee's attainment level for each trait can be clearly indicated.

The results on the rating form can then be plotted in a rating profile, as illustrated in Figure 3.7, and subsequently compared to that of another employee. Alternatively, the rating-form results can be used to develop a numerical rating comparison, as shown in Figure 3.8. In this, each segment of a degree block is assigned a numerical value to provide a final rating score for an employee.

Some graphic-scale forms include a comment block on the front or

Job classification _____
How long has employee been under your supervision?_____ mos.
How long in present classification?_____ mos.

Quartile Points / TRAIT	Unsatisfactory				Fair				Average				Very Good				Outstanding				Score
	1	2	3	4	1	2	3	4	1	2	3	4	1	2	3	4	1	2	3	4	
	Q	Q	Q	Q	Q	Q	Q	Q	Q	Q	Q	Q	Q	Q	Q	Q	Q	Q	Q	Q	
	1	2	3	4	5	6	7	8	9	10	11	12	13	14	15	16	17	18	19	20	
Quantity of Work — The amount of efficient and productive output achieved.																					
Quality of Work — The degree of accuracy, dependability, and thoroughness of the output achieved. Consideration should be given to degree of difficulty, but not to quantity.																					
Job Knowledge — The amount of knowledge and skill possessed to perform the tasks assigned.																					
Initiative — The sense of responsibility possessed by an individual to generate action when required, and the perseverance for completing an assigned task.																					
Cooperation — The ability to work with and for others. Consideration should be given to morale, tact ability to accept criticism, courtesy, and friendliness.																					
Judgment — The ability to analyze situations and available data to arrive at sound conclusions.																					
Adaptability — The ability to be involved successfully in activities at one time.																					
																	Total	score			

Rater_____ Date _____
Date rating discussed with employee_____
Employee reaction to rating_____

Figure 3.6. Graphic Scale: Sample Personnel Rating Form

PERSONNEL RATING PROFILE

Trait or Characteristic	Employee Value					Employee Value					Employee Value				
	unsat.	fair	avg.	v.good	outstand	unsat.	fair	avg.	v.good	outstand	unsat.	fair	avg.	v.good	outstand
	1 2 3 4 5 6 7 8 9 0 1 2 3 4 5 6 7 8 9 0					1 2 3 4 5 6 7 8 9 0 1 2 3 4 5 6 7 8 9 0					1 2 3 4 5 6 7 8 9 0 1 2 3 4 5 6 7 8 9 0				
Quantity of Work															
Quality of Work															
Job Knowledge															
Initiative															
Cooperation															
Judgment															
Adaptability															

INSTRUCTIONS: For each employee shade the center bar over to the equivalent numerical score rating for a given trait or characteristic.

Figure 3.7. Graphic Scale: Sample Personnel Rating Profile

153

NUMERICAL RATING COMPARISON

JOB CLASSIFICATION:

CHARACTERISTIC OR TRAIT	TOTAL POSSIBLE SCORE	EMPLOYEE NAMES							
QUANTITY OF WORK									
QUALITY OF WORK									
JOB KNOWLEDGE									
INITIATIVE									
COOPERATION									
JUDGMENT									
ADAPTABILITY									

Figure 3.8. Graphic Scale: Sample Numerical Rating Comparison

reverse side to provide additional information on a particular trait. Comments, though, may be somewhat biased. Furthermore, they are sometimes used to defend the rater's position rather than provide meaningful information useful in a planning session to indicate areas for employee improvement.

2. CHECKLIST. This technique is used either by itself or in conjunction with another method. It utilizes an extensive checklist of questions about the employee's behavior and traits. The rater simply marks a "yes" or "no" answer to each question. Some checklists list statements about behavior that are applicable to several positions in the organization. When performing his appraisal, the manager is asked to check only those statements that are applicable to an employee's position. This procedure is not very satisfactory because some confusion may occur over which statements are relevant to a given position.

The checklist technique does not require an evaluation of performance but rather a report of it by the rater. Each trait has a specific weighted value, which goes toward determining the final score. Evaluation of the score is then implemented.

3. NARRATIVES. This format utilizes a subjective evaluation technique to determine an employee's outstanding, above average, satisfactory, and unsatisfactory actions and contributions regarding job performance. The technique implies that the rating will be determined through utilization of predetermined standards for comparison, and that it will be made objectively and factually. Such an evaluation can be used to great advantage in the planning session that follows the appraisal.

4. CRITICAL INCIDENTS. The appraiser observes the employee's behavioral patterns while on the job and records any critical incidents as they occur. The behavioral aspects that constitute critical incidents are predetermined in order to provide for standardization of reporting and appraising. Furthermore, each of the incidents is assigned a weighted value for rating purposes. Then the score values are collected and tallied for purposes of comparison. The following represents the type of report that may be made based on an observation of a critical incident and used in the appraisal: The employee has personally developed the necessary systems and procedures required by the corporation's subsidiaries to implement engineering cost accounting and reporting. The employee indicated an outstanding proficiency in his specialty. In accomplishing his assigned duties he totally disregarded adverse working conditions,

long overtime hours, minimal availability of the computer, and the lack of machine operating assistance.

5. MAN-TO-MAN COMPARISONS. In this technique, certain traits are selected for inclusion in the appraisal process. The selected traits are then matched to the employees within the organization. The person who most closely personifies the trait is placed at the top of the scale; the person who least meets the qualification is placed at the bottom; and one person who is considered to be average for the trait is placed in the middle of the scale. Every employee is then rated against the three men on the scale and is awarded a score for the trait on the basis of the comparison. The evaluation and rating process is repeated for each trait. Then the scores for all traits are tallied to provide the basis for overall comparisons.

6. FORCED CHOICES. This rating technique makes an attempt at removing bias from the appraisal process. This is accomplished by forcing the rater to choose from among predetermined descriptive statements those that are applicable to the employee being appraised. The rater's choices are compared against the list prepared by a specially organized committee of managerial or senior personnel in the functional activity, or by a personnel specialist. The list of applicable statements is developed after a study of the existing manpower resources. Based on the relative importance of each statement in the listing, a numerical score is assigned to each statement. The responses made by the rater are compared and scored to arrive at a total score. The rater is then notified how the employees for a given position compare with each other in a quartile ranking. The forced-choice technique cannot be used for planning, counseling, or follow-ups purposes, because the rater is not made aware of the desired behavioral norm or standard established by the committee or personnel specialist. It may also be difficult to compare the results of a previous appraisal period because the norm or standard may have changed.

Communicating the Results

It can be said that the primary purpose of any appraisal program should be personnel development. It can also be said to be almost universally true that people want to know where they stand and that they appreciate a fair and constructive evaluation of their performance. Therefore, when an appraisal has been completed, the results should be communicated to the employee. Furthermore, if the manager handles the communication process correctly and does not dwell on minor weaknesses, the employee will not resent being criticized if the appraisal is based on objective fact and not on biased opinion.

The success of the counseling session that follows the appraisal depends not only on the appraisal itself but also on what happens during the session. This is why it is important for the manager to make careful preparations for the interview. In addition to trying to anticipate at least some of the questions the employee will raise during the session, the manager must be prepared to handle the inevitable employee reaction to the appraisal. A negative reaction badly handled can bring on an argument that can disrupt the session by creating an air of hostility and antagonism. Therefore, the manager must be ready to listen to the objections presented by the employee and to present tangible facts and situations. Lastly, the manager must consider the employee's strengths and weaknesses he plans to discuss, as well as the corrective action or improvement he will recommend. This type of preplanning helps to make the counseling session beneficial for both parties.

Having completed his planning, the manager is ready to discuss the rating results with the employee. This is a serious matter that should be conducted in a professional manner. Too often this aspect of the appraisal process is conducted in such a poor manner that it produces no tangible benefit for either party. Unfortunately, in these instances it may produce ill will that can have a long-lasting effect on the organization. The manager, therefore, must try to place the employee at ease as much as possible. He should then proceed to explain the purpose of the interview and the rating plan used. After that, he proceeds to convey the rating results to the employee. It is at this point that the manager can expect some of the reaction or questions, or both, which he had anticipated in the pre-counseling phase. This is why he should begin by emphasizing the employee's strong points, giving him a clear understanding of what he is doing well. Any praises that are extended should be sincere and not merely platitudes intended to soothe an employee, for insincerity can be readily detected and does more harm than good.

After giving the employee an opportunity to absorb the results relating to his strengths and self-improvement, the manager should advise the individual of his weaknesses or traits that require improvement. In this presentation, the manager should avoid comparative discussion of anyone else—including himself. Above all, the manager should not dwell unendingly upon errors. Nevertheless, he needs to be prepared to cite specific examples or incidents relating to the employee's problem areas. This is also a good time to clear up any misunderstandings about exactly what is expected from the employee. The manager should allow the employee to raise questions and discuss the problems.

It is important that the manager be aware of his own biases and prejudices. Very obviously there are traits a person favors and others that irritate him, and it is these kinds of likes and dislikes that can so easily lead the manager into a closed-mind attitude. Therefore, such biases and prejudices must be recognized, avoided, minimized, or masked. An open mind on the part of the manager is essential in order for a feeling of mutual confidence to develop between him and the employee.

The discussion should then move on to ways of improvement. Improvement must come in the form of corrective action that will involve some self-improvement plan and/or participation in a formal or informal training program. If there are any desirable traits or characteristics that need to be developed further, then these must also be discussed with the employee, because improvement in this area could lead to a promotion, new responsibilities, or a salary increase.

In the concluding phase of the counseling session, the manager should discuss the effect and meaning of the rating. He should also mention the follow-up appraisal that will be conducted within a reasonable time after this meeting. Each successive appraisal has some effect upon the growth status of an employee, for it shows whether he has progressed, stood still, or regressed. A manager must be willing to accept the fact that some members of his functional activity will be average performers. As such, they will remain at the same level throughout their period of employment. It is obvious that their appraisal ratings will be relatively the same for each appraisal period. However, this does not mean that they should be omitted from the regular appraisal process. It is important that *every* employee clearly understand his status because it may motivate him either to improve or at least to maintain an acceptable performance level.

The follow-up is an essential element of the appraisal and counseling process. Therefore, the manager should continue to exhibit interest in the employee's work and progress after the initial appraisal. Failure to do so and failure to conduct a significant follow-up will destroy any mutual confidence and trust established during the appraisal process.

During the initial counseling session the employee may have disagreed with the results and indicated constructively why his point of view should be supported and the rating changed. If so, the manager must investigate the assertion and communicate his findings to the employee during a meeting after the follow-up has been completed. If the manager decides the rating should be changed, he should make sure it is done promptly, because in many instances the rating form becomes a historical record that is used for a multiplicity of purposes. The follow-up also provides the manager with an opportunity to determine if, as a result of a promise of training made during the previous session, the employee is now involved in a meaningful, utilitarian training program.

Review Questions: Group 3D

1. Why must an organization develop a personnel appraisal program?
2. A manager must evaluate actual and potential performance separately during the appraisal of an employee. Why?
3. What is the most popular rating method in use today? Would you recommend using it or would you prefer to use some other method or methods?
4. Many organizations appraise their personnel, but do not communicate the results to the employees. Is this a good or bad policy? Why?
5. What is the purpose of the follow-up that is conducted after the appraisal and counseling session?

SUMMARY

The "information explosion" has created new employment opportunities in the data processing industry. The growth in the number of installations has increased the need for qualified personnel.

In this chapter we began by discussing the elements of job analysis and construction of job descriptions. The analyses confirm the requirements for a given position. These human resource requirements are stipulated in a job description for each position.

Due to the complexity of the manpower requirements, a variety of occupational groupings have evolved. Within each of the major occupational groupings there are a number of related occupational or job titles grouped in a hierarchy according to the three classification levels, specialist, semiskilled, and trainee.

When the personnel requirements have been defined, the manager must concern himself with the recruitment, selection, training, and appraisal of personnel. Recruitment and selection can be difficult because of the skills required in data processing occupations and the limited supply of qualified persons. Personnel selection may be accomplished through the use of tests and interviews. This is a very costly effort, and an organization must strive to select the best possible candidate for each position. Proper selection may also minimize the rate of employee turnover. A manager should never overlook the possibility of recruitment and selection from within. Utilizing personnel with the proper aptitude, background, and experience, from an internal source, will reduce hiring and job-orientation costs.

The effectiveness of any organization is dependent upon the quality of its personnel. Their quality and effectiveness can be developed and maintained through formal and informal training programs. An employee development program that includes both types of programs is advisable for most occupational groupings and organizations. It must be emphasized that organizations can no longer afford to approach training in a haphazard manner. Failure to provide training programs can result in high employee turnover and a waste of valuable resources.

To determine the effectiveness of any operation it is necessary to periodically appraise the organization's manpower resources. The appraisal process indicates an employee's actual performance, his potential, and—through use of a follow-up procedure—his development. The appraisal process may be conducted in a variety of ways; however, it is ineffectual unless the results are communicated to the employee. It is important that the technique be divorced from any direct or immediate salary increases. The appraisals should be used primarily for employee training and development.

CASE STUDIES

Case Study 3.1: The Porter-Cardwell Food Processing Company

The Porter-Cardwell Food Processing Company is upgrading its data processing installation from an IBM 1401 card computer. It has recently placed an equipment order for a new IBM 360/30 computer equipped with two disk drives and 65,000 positions of magnetic core. A disk operating system will be utilized for job control and software. Delivery of the new computer has been scheduled for two years from date of order.

Ray Cardwell, vice-president for financial affairs, has asked you, as manager of data processing, to prepare a detailed report indicating what impact the equipment upgrading will have on the manpower resources. He is particularly concerned about changes in structural format and in recruitment requirements.

Discussion Questions

1. What structural organization format do you propose for the data processing activity?
2. Would you consider evaluating the existing job titles? To what extent?
3. If you found it necessary to recruit additional personnel, what source or sources of supply would you consider?
4. Would you propose including tests in the selection process? If not, why not? If so, what test or tests would you recommend using for employee selection?
5. Should the organization consider training programs because of the impending conversion? Which, if any, employees would you recommend for training?

Case Study 3.2: The Raleric Manufacturing Company

The Raleric Manufacturing Company has a medium-sized computer installation with a staff of six programming and two systems personnel. The organization has had no standard programming language in the past. However, in an attempt to alleviate the problems caused by the lack of qualified personnel, the organization has now established a language standard. The decision has been made to utilize FORTRAN and COBOL. FORTRAN IV is the standard language for all scientific and technical applications; COBOL is used for programming commercial applications.

After the decision was made to standardize the languages, Richard Walters, Raleric's data processing director, surveyed the language skills of his programming staff. As a result, he found that only one program-

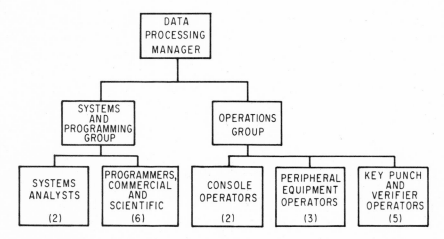

mer is familiar with COBOL but that all of them know FORTRAN. However, their knowledge of FORTRAN varies because of individual differences in experience with language levels, vendors, compilers, and operating systems.

Mr. Walters has named you to be the organizational training specialist. You are to present your training plan to him in one week.

Discussion Questions

1. What objectives would you propose for the training function?
2. What type of functional organization structure would you propose for
   the training activity?
3. What type of training program or plan would you propose for the
   data processing personnel?
4. Do you feel that, based on your appointment by and instructions
   from Mr. Walters, the scope of the training activity extends beyond
   the immediate data processing function?
5. Would you propose a training program for other organizational personnel? If so, what plan would you suggest?

Case Study 3.3: The Winston Wire Works

Charles Willis, the manager of programming and systems for the
Winston Wire Works, has just completed the quarterly employee appraisal. The company uses a graphic rating scale to evaluate each trait or
characteristic as very good, good, fair, or unacceptable. Each of these

rating degrees has a numerical score ranging in descending value from four to one. The traits or characteristics included in the form are: quality of work, appearance, technical ability, creativeness, initiative, and cooperation.

The company has a policy of granting merit increases on the basis of appraisal results. The percentage of increase is left to the discretion of the manager. There is an unwritten policy that an employee will not receive more than two consecutive merit increases in a year, an exception being made when an employee performs in an outstanding manner. Company policy requires that the manager communicate the appraisal results and amount of salary increase, if any, to the employee.

In carrying out the quarterly appraisal, Mr. Willis began by speaking first to the employees with the highest ratings. This decision was based on his belief—widely known by his subordinates—that the people with high ratings need very little counseling because they are professionals and know exactly what is required of them.

William Harris, a senior systems specialist for the company, was called into the office for his counseling session. At the outset, Mr. Willis announced rather apologetically that Mr. Harris would not receive a merit increase for the coming quarter. This was necessary because Mr. Harris had performed at an unsatisfactory level during the previous three months.

Mr. Harris had been somewhat prepared for some unfavorable news because he had not been among the first to be called in for a counseling session. Nevertheless, he was both shocked and angered by the manager's statement. Mr. Harris asked why his rating had dropped two rating degrees, reminding Mr. Willis that in the previous period his performance had been rated as "good." No merit compensation had been granted at that time because he had received increases in the two previous quarters. Mr. Willis replied by stating that the specialist was already the highest paid member of the department.

Mr. Harris then countered by noting that he had been in the department longer than any other person; also, that he had been assigned a disproportionate share of the departmental workload because of his background and experience. What was more, during the past quarter alone, he had completed the development and implementation of a project that netted the organization $100,000 in tangible savings.

The manager acknowledged these facts. Then he severely criticized what he said was Mr. Harris's inability to secure the cooperation of the data processing operations manager during recent parallel tests, a significant inability. Mr. Willis went on to say that this failure alone was serious enough to negate all other favorable aspects of the appraisal. The specialist replied by reminding Mr. Willis that they had previously discussed the matter at length and that, as a result of their conversation, Mr. Willis had determined that it was his own responsibility to discuss the matter with Arthur Carney, the operations manager. Mr. Willis had agreed with Mr. Harris that it was very important to have operations personnel involved in parallel testing.

Mr. Willis now stated that it was the responsibility of the systems analyst on the project to secure the cooperation of all parties concerned. The ability to work with and through others is a very essential trait in a systems analyst. He further added that if Mr. Harris was unable to improve this situation significantly, his performance rating would remain at its present lower level.

Mr. Harris asked about his past experience in dealing with people. Mr. Willis stated in a somewhat harsh tone, "I don't care about the past—it is the future I am concerned with." Mr. Harris replied, "Well, I guess I will have to start shopping around for a new job," and he walked out of the manager's office.

Discussion Questions

1. How would you rate Mr. Willis's conduct of the appraisal?
2. Do you feel that the graphic scale rating method is appropriate for this organization? Would you suggest that a new or additional form be used? If so, which one?
3. What additional characteristics or traits, if any, would you recommend for inclusion on the appraisal form?
4. How would you evaluate Mr. Willis's conduct of the counseling session following the appraisal?
5. Do you agree or disagree that a single characteristic or trait should affect the entire appraisal result?
6. Do you feel that Mr. Harris exhibited a bad attitude toward the job and his manager? On the basis of his last remark, would you ask for his resignation? Would you discharge him?
7. Did Mr. Harris offer any constructive criticism or tangible solution to the problem?
8. How should the appraisal and counseling session have been conducted?

4

Management Control Through the Use of Standards

INTRODUCTION

Standards are an important tool in the management process in that they directly affect the manpower, materials, machines, and money. They are essential to the planning of operations; the development of schedules; the determination of personnel, equipment, material, and budget requirements; evaluation of output or progress, and the comparing of fiscal expenditures with projected or budgeted allocations.

Standards may be placed in either of two major classifications: guides and yardsticks.

Guides are developed and implemented during the planning, organizing, and directing functions. They include policy manuals, standard operating procedures, systems documentation, codes, and so forth. Guides are generally referred to as documentation or methods standards. (This theme is developed more fully elsewhere in this chapter.)

Yardsticks are used to monitor an activity and to establish and maintain uniformity in operating procedures and processes. Yardsticks are commonly referred to as performance standards. Performance standards are an integral part of the controlling function in the management process because they are used to locate and identify problems, remove bottlenecks, and maintain qualitative and quantitative output. There are various kinds of performance standards applicable to specific situations.

Among these are key stroke standards for key punch operators, and program design and development standards for programming personnel. (Performance standards are discussed more fully in Chapter 6.)

Standards may also be developed for a product to provide for identification and comparison in production, purchasing, marketing, and industrial engineering activities.

THE DEVELOPMENT, IMPORTANCE, BENEFITS, AND DOCUMENTATION OF STANDARDS

Methods of Developing Standards

Standards are developed or established during the planning function for use in managing operations during both the pre-executory and executory phases. Some of them are developed by governmental agencies, technical societies, and trade, manufacturers', and industrial associations. However, most standards are developed by each organization for its own use.

There are four basic methods used in the development of standards. They are:

1. Estimating
2. Experience basis
3. Scientific techniques
4. Records basis

1. ESTIMATING. Standards set by estimation are often referred to as guesstimates, because they are simply reasonable approximations of what models should be. As there needs to be an element of flexibility within a standard, guesstimates can be adjusted in line with current needs and operating conditions.

2. EXPERIENCE BASIS. Using experience is a common standards-developing technique. The manager applies his prior training, experience, knowledge, and other factors to determine the requirements and methods to be applied. The danger in utilizing this approach is that the manager may not evaluate all of the necessary elements in an existing situation or setting for inclusion in a standard. However, based on his past experience, an effective manager can produce meaningful standards.

3. SCIENTIFIC TECHNIQUES. These techniques utilize various scientific

procedures, such as time study, mathematical models, measuring instruments, and specially designed software. In addition, provision is generally made for personal factors, fatigue, equipment, and delays. The application of some of these techniques may require specialized training or experience. As a result, the manager may need to secure the assistance of in-house or external activities in the development of a standard.

4. RECORDS BASIS. This method utilizes empirical data collected from payroll, accounting, budget, or other types of records. A standard developed from such data is reasonably accurate because it is based on available information about a past performance for personnel, equipment, funds, or materials.

Reformulation

In the development of a preliminary standard, the manager may utilize any one of the four methods or a combination of them. After he has formulated the standard, it is implemented and then evaluated to determine its effectiveness. The evaluation must include a feedback procedure aimed at locating problem areas. Subsequently, the manager may find it necessary to reformulate the standard, in which case he has to determine its probable effect on the operation before actuating it. The feedback procedure is reinitiated to ascertain whether the correction or modification provides a satisfactory answer or solution to the problem. The effective standard must then be established as one of the interacting control elements in the management process.

The Importance of Standards

Before any manager develops, implements, maintains, or enforces standards, he needs to fully understand their importance to the organization. The same applies to the upper echelon in the hierarchical structure, without whose support no standards program can be effective. It must be readily accepted that standards are an important tool in planning, as well as the means of simplifying the organizing, directing, and controlling functions of the management process.

Standards are important because they can:
1. Determine the effectiveness of the organization
2. Be a basis of communications
3. Minimize the impact of personnel changes
4. Ensure compliance with the policies and practices

5. Minimize the effect of changes
6. Be used to establish schedules
7. Be used to determine manpower requirements
8. Be an aid in cost estimating and budgeting

1. THE EFFECTIVENESS OF THE ORGANIZATION. In the dynamic process of management, the manager must constantly monitor output in order to determine his function's progress and effectiveness. This determination is made by comparing the results of the operation plus resource utilization with the level of desired quality and achievement. The specifications must be defined by the manager during planning, in that they become the standards for preparing schedules, determining resource requirements, and balancing resource utilization. For example, a manager who has established personnel performance standards in his programming activity will be able to determine if a programmer is discharging his duties and responsibilities at the desired level of performance. This is because the programmer's effectiveness is measured by his ability to function within or above that standard.

2. A BASIS FOR COMMUNICATIONS. A standard serves as a communications medium between the various functional activities that are directly and indirectly involved in data processing operation. It becomes a documented source of information on such items as design and testing practices for systems and programs, change procedures, acceptable documentation formats, standard charting symbols, authorized codes, and management controls. For example, the standardized charting symbols used in system and program flowcharting can be clearly understood by the systems, programming, operations and audit personnel. (See Appendix III for illustrated discussion of symbols.) Furthermore, standardized documentation of data processing applications enables the internal and external auditors to audit and review the operational systems and programs.

3. THE IMPACT OF PERSONNEL CHANGES. Personnel turnover can be very costly and disruptive to an organization, especially in terms of having to train new employees. To help cope with this problem, standards must be developed and implemented for symbols, labels, abbreviations, charting techniques, input-output specifications, macros, and other programming, analysis, and documentation techniques. These standards can be readily employed in training new personnel, thereby reducing the break-in period and maintaining the production schedule with only minimal disruption.

4. COMPLIANCE WITH POLICIES AND PRACTICES. Every organization needs to establish policies and practices that will serve as guides for managerial activity. These provide for uniform adaptation and enforcement of duties, responsibilities, and administrative and operating practices in the management process. Also, they relieve the manager of the responsibility for making repetitive decisions for similiar problems and situations. Record file retention policies, absence reporting, and supplies requisitioning procedures fall into this general classification. In addition, the availability of standardized practices and policies enables the manager to delegate authority to his subordinates. Each subordinate can avail himself of this standards information to complete any assigned task with a minimal amount of supervision.

5. THE EFFECT OF CHANGES. It is necessary in data processing operations to establish standards that will simplify the transition from one system into another, as well as from one type of hardware to another. To provide for a more orderly conversion, standardization must be developed for such items as charting symbols and techniques, tables, label conventions, and documentation of applications. Simplifying the conversion process reduces costs and errors, thereby expediting the return on investment in a new system, program, or hardware. Standards are also used effectively in feasibility studies to reduce cost and time expenditures incurred in the conduct of such a project. Through the application and utilization of established standards, much time can be saved in the preparation of cost and savings schedules, the determination of conversion and production schedules, and the initial design of proposed systems.

6. ESTABLISHING SCHEDULES. In both planning and directing, the manager needs performance standards in order to develop realistic project or operation schedules. These standards are applied to the allocation of resources and to the selection and evaluation of personnel and equipment. They effectively indicate the time required to perform an operation or task through application of the necessary resources.

7. MANPOWER REQUIREMENTS. Manpower requirements must be quantified. However, before this can be accomplished, the manager has to develop the measure of personnel performance required for an effective operational system. The established standard is then used to develop a production, conversion, or planning schedule based on projected results. For example, when a manager establishes a key stroke productivity standard for his key punch personnel, he defines the number of card

columns to be punched and the type of data. Then he evaluates the source documents to be processed in order to establish his projected productive capability. After that, the key stroke rate is applied to total production requirements to indicate the number of key punch personnel necessary for an effective operation.

8. COST ESTIMATING AND BUDGETING. It is essential in any organization to have standards available for indicating the cost of an operation or modification. Before any decision can be made, it is necessary that cost estimates be available and budget requirements be established. Failure to make a sound financial projection can cause rejection or reduction of an operation or project. Furthermore, it can prove to be a costly venture if the monetary requirements are overestimated or underestimated: underestimating costs may make it necessary to borrow money or reallocate additional funds; overestimating costs can be a wasteful practice in that more funds may have been borrowed or allocated than needed, or some other activities may have been curtailed or postponed to divert funds to this project.

Data processing personnel must constantly provide cost and savings data for existing or proposed projects. It is essential, therefore, that effective standards are developed to ensure that all cost evaluations are conducted on the same basis.

Benefits of Standardization

There are a number of tangible benefits to be derived from standardization. Some are obtained immediately and others are of a long-term nature. In both cases, the manager must weigh them carefully. An effective standardization program offers an organization the opportunity to avail itself of the following benefits:

—A firm control over the resources through providing a system of checks and balances

—A possible reduction in operating costs through more effective utilization of resources

—A means of evaluating the effectiveness of an operation or organization by applying a realistic performance standard to the feedback cycle

—Simplification of the process of training personnel

—A two-way communications medium that links the top echelon

with the subordinates, personnel on the same level with each other, and data processing personnel with other people in interrelated in-house or external activities

—Quality and accuracy in operations by clearly defining what output and/or results are desired

—Reduction of dependence upon individuals in an operation or organization

These are but a few of the measurable benefits derived from the development, establishment, maintenance, and enforcement of management standards. (Additional advantages will become evident in this and other chapters of the book.)

Documentation of Standards

To be effective, a standards program must provide for the documentation of all guides and yardsticks. The reasons for undertaking such documentation is that it:

1. Provides a permanent record
2. Establishes a basis for audit and review
3. Makes communicable information available

1. A PERMANENT RECORD. A documented standards program provides a permanent record of the policies, practices, procedures, and techniques to be enforced within an organization. These can be distributed in the form of what is called a policy or practices manual in order to ensure uniform application in all situations and problems. Included in such a manual are specific items such as attendance reporting, sick-leave policy, authorization limits on purchase requisitions, grievance procedures, safety guides, and many other topics.

Performance standards for data processing and other functional activities are properly recorded in data processing or industrial engineering standards manuals, which are intended for use in planning, organizing, scheduling, budgeting, and costing activities. The availability of such standardized data ensures that the necessary manpower, material, equipment, and fiscal requirements are ascertained and met. The documented performance standards include all of the relevant factors and variables in each calculation; this provides for uniformity of application, saves recalculation time, and reduces or eliminates errors.

Systems, programming, and operations documentation of procedures and techniques are made available in data processing manuals. Such documentation includes console operating instructions, descriptions of systems, program listings, standardized macros, and numerous other related items.

2. A BASIS FOR AUDIT AND REVIEW. To retain their effectiveness, standards must be reviewed periodically in terms of their currency, relevancy, clarity, and compatibility. Failure to maintain currency affects the validity of managerial decisions made on the basis of an existing standard. The relevancy must be questioned to determine its contribution to the effectiveness of the existing operation. If a standard has lost its value, it must be deleted or reconstructed to avoid any confusion or problems arising from its continued existence. Clarity is necessary to eliminate misinterpretation, which can result in the misuse of valuable resources. A standard must also be reviewed to determine its compatibility with other existing standards. If there is a conflict with such standards, then some modification or change must be made. This is not a simple task because the manager has to define, limit, analyze, and evaluate the problem. When the problem has been isolated, he determines the best approach and then implements it in the form of a revised standard.

3. AVAILABILITY OF COMMUNICABLE INFORMATION. Documentation facilitates an interchange of information between intra-functional and inter-functional activities, subsidiaries, satellite units, and other organizations. This capability is particularly important when a manager is responsible for a centralized data processing organization and must disseminate information to reporting units. It is also important in instances where large organizations, such as holding corporations, require an interchange of information between the subsidiary organizations and the corporate offices. The documentation on a unique program, for example, would be submitted to the holding corporation's administrator of data processing, who would arrange for copying and distribution of the documentation. Any subsidiary that could utilize the computer program would have the capability of implementing it, with little or no delay and at a fraction of the original development cost.

Review Questions: Group 4A

1. What are the differences between a performance standard and a

methods standard?

2. Name and briefly describe the techniques used to develop a standard.
3. How are standards applied to the management process?
4. What are some of the tangible benefits that may result from the application of standards to the management process?
5. Why is it important to document standards?

GUIDELINES AND ENFORCEMENT

Guidelines for Documentation

There are guidelines or rules that should be followed in the effective documentation of standards. These guidelines specify that:

1. All documentation must be identified
2. The standard must include a statement of purpose
3. Master set and copies must be given maximum protection
4. Revisions should be in the form of complete pages
5. Specialized symbols should be used to indicate new and/or revised materials
6. Specialized symbols should be used to indicate deletions
7. Effective dates of revision must be indicated

1. IDENTIFICATION OF DOCUMENTATION. A brief but self-explanatory title must be included on the first page of each standard in order to facilitate identification. In addition, the date the standard became effective should be given at the top of each page to indicate the currency status of a standard. Furthermore the manual should be identified, by code number or some other means, at the top of each page. This system of page and content identification simplifies the maintenance and filing procedures. Figure 4.1 shows two examples of identification headings used on documentation. The ones illustrated are for the first page of a standard; subsequent pages would include the same information except for the title.

2. STATEMENT OF PURPOSE. Each directive, policy, practice, or standard must carry a general statement of purpose as its first entry. The statement should be written in layman's terminology so as to make the document's purpose readily identifiable by any member of the organization. In Figure 4.2 are given two sample paragraphs, each of which could be a statement of purpose on a document.

```
R. S. COMPUTATIONS, INC.        Data Processing Manual
                                                   10.1
                                    September 22, 1971


                      Data Processing Glossary
```

```
R. S. COMPUTATIONS, INC.    Data Processing Manual 10.1
November 10, 1972           Part I
                            Chapter 5
                            Section 11


                      Data Processing Glossary
```

Figure 4.1   Samples of Identification of Documentation

```
1. GENERAL

   The purpose of this instruction is to prescribe the documentation
   format for data processing applications.
```

```
1. GENERAL

   This instruction prescribes the numbering systems which are to
   be used to facilitate the identification of computer programs, mag-
   netic tapes, and/or magnetic disk packs.
```

Figure 4.2   Samples of Statement of Purpose

3. Protection for Master Set and Copies. It is best to store the complete and updated master standards in a separate building with fire-resistant rooms, which should have a fire-resistance capacity of not less than two hours and be equipped with an automatic sprinkler system. The materials should be kept in noncombustible containers, such as metal files or cabinets. Safeguarding complete and updated master standards provides protection against loss, fraud, theft, destruction by fire or other disaster, access by unauthorized personnel, and illegal alteration of modification of their contents. (The subject of safeguards is also discussed in Chapter 7.)

Similarly, copies of the documentation must be maintained and kept in separate areas for reasons of security and internal audit control.

There is now an increasing trend toward the auditing of data processing procedures and programs by internal and/or external auditors. The auditors' review process includes a comparison of the master documentation with the copies. In addition, it involves detection of possible fraud and includes tests for currency, relevancy, clarity, and compatibility.

4. Complete Pages for Revisions. Changes in the manuals should be in the form of complete pages. This permits complete withdrawal of the old page and insertion of the new one. The new pages are identified by the effective date and the standard's identification at the top of each page.

Page substitution eliminates the necessity of entering or deleting materials by pen or pencil. Generally the responsibility for performing these alterations is delegated to a secretarial or clerical employee, who performs the task on a "when-time-is-available" basis. Consequently, changes are either made in an incomplete and inaccurate fashion or are not made at all. This haphazard approach destroys the accuracy, relevancy, and timeliness of a standard. In the experience of this author, the substitution of complete pages has proved to be the more popular and effective method for maintaining documentation.

5. Specialized Symbols and New and/or Revised Materials. Specialized symbols such as a single "*" or "@" should be used to identify the new and/or revised material added or inserted to a page since the last revision. This will readily indicate to the reader where a change has been made. Figure 4.3 illustrates the use of the "@" symbol to identify a revision of a paragraph that has been revised to clarify the instructions, data flow, process, and responsibilities. If the special sym-

---

(*Before Revision*)

4. The payroll clerk will forward the clock cards to the control clerk for posting to the Input Register before being submitted to the Key Punch Section.

(*After Revision*)

@ 4. The payroll clerk will forward the employee clock cards to the data control clerk. The data control clerk will post the batch control information to the Input Register. After the information has been posted, the batched clock cards are submitted to the Key Punch Section for conversion. @

Figure 4.3   Identification of Material Revisions

bol was not included at the beginning and end of the revised material, the user would have to read both the deleted page and the new page to learn what had been specifically revised in the paragraph.

6. SPECIALIZED SYMBOLS AND DELETIONS. Specialized symbols such as an "*" or "@" may also be utilized to indicate deletions. However, to clarify the difference between a revision and a deletion, it is recommended that a double "**" or "@@" symbol be used for deletions.

In Figure 4.4, a single asterisk symbol appears at the beginning and end of the revised paragraph. This alerts the user to the fact that a revision has been made. In continuing with the review, the user will note the double asterisk symbols within the paragraph. These symbols may indicate the deletion of one or more sentences at this point within the narrative. In the example given, only one sentence had been deleted. This was the sentence about charge code 3645. In addition, some changes were made in phraseology, as well as in clarification of form size.

Figure 4.5 illustrates the use of the double "@@" symbol to indicate deletion of the final paragraph of a procedure. In this example, it is unnecessary to utilize a single "@" symbol to indicate a revision. The

---

(*Before Revision*)

4. At the end of each month the data processing operations group will prepare a listing of all scrap loss transactions. The data cards will be sorted by accounting charge code. All items in charge code 3645 will be listed on 3-part, 10×13 form. Items in charge code 8966 will be listed on a 6-part, 8½×11 form. Other charge codes are listed on 2-part paper.

(*After Revisions*)

* 4. At the end of each month the data processing operations group will prepare a listing of all scrap loss transactions. The data cards will be sorted by the accounting charge code, card columns 44–47.** All items in charge code 8966 will be outputted on a 6-part, 8½×11 form. All other charge codes will be outputted on a 2-part, 8½×11 form.   *

Figure 4.4   Identification of Sentence Deletions

double "@@" symbol following the paragraph number immediately signals the deletion of the previous material.

The "@" and "*" symbols can also be used, in their appropriate single or double forms, to indicate that a major portion of the material has been added, revised, or deleted on a page. These should be positioned in the upper-left and lower-right corners of a page for prompt identification. Figure 4.6 illustrates the use of a single "*" symbol at the top and bottom of a page from a unit-record oriented procedure. In examining the before and after segments, it can be seen that changes have been made to the control levels, card columns, and file disposition.

---

b. As an aid preparation of the M-98B report.
8. @@

Figure 4.5   Identification of Paragraph Deletions

Consequently, each part of machine operation #5 has been affected. This is why it is more practical to simply begin and end the page with a special symbol rather than individually mark each change on the page.

7. EFFECTIVE DATES OF REVISION. To maintain and ensure currency, it is necessary to include the revision date at the top of each page. This indicates the effective date of the addition, deletion, or modification to

---

(*Before Revision*)

(Top of Page)

D. P. Operations Manual 10.2   October 15, 1970
Part I   Job Number RS-103
Chapter 5
Section 10

Machine Operation #5
Merge and Sequence Check

A. Select the previously reproduced property accounting summary cards, which are in sequence (Intermediate) property class (card columns 1–5) and (Minor) line number (card columns 6–7), and place these in the primary feed of the collator. Select the consolidated property accounting cards, which are also in sequence by property class and line number, from file cabinet 2-E and place these in the secondary feed of the collator. Wire the control panel to merge as follows:

Control Level	*Field Identification*	*Card Columns*
Minor	Line Number	6–7
Intermediate	Property Class	1–5

B. Sequence check the merged file using the same controls as indicated in step A.

1. Hold the file for Operation #7, Step B.

Page 15

(Bottom of Page)

Figure 4.6   Identification of

the standard. In addition, the date of previous issue for a given page should also be included at the top of each revised page.

Figure 4.7 illustrates a suggested date block to be included at the top of each page. The inclusion of the date simplifies filing of changes and auditing of the manual.

When revisions are received by a manager, he reviews them to

(After Revision)

(Top of Page)

* D. P. Operations Manual 10.2   December 1, 1971
Part I   Job Number RS-103
Chapter 5
Section 10

Machine Operation #5
Merge and Sequence Check

A. Select the previously reproduced property accounting summary cards, which are in sequence (Major) ledger code (card column 37), (Intermediate) property class (card columns 2–6), and (Minor) line number (card columns 7–8), and place these in the primary feed of the collator. Select the consolidated property accounting cards, which are also in sequence by ledger code, property class, and line number, from file cabinet 2-E and place these in the secondary feed of the collator. Merge the files, controlling as follows:

Control Level	Field Identification	Card Columns
Minor	Line Number	7–8
Intermediate	Property Class	2–6
Major	Ledger Code	37

B. Sequence check the merged file, using the same controls as indicated in step A.

1. Hold the sequence checked file for Operation #6, Step A.

Page 15*

(Bottom of Page)

Major Revisions on a Page

R. S. COMPUTATIONS, INC.   Data Processing Manual 10.1
                            Reissue *May 31, 1971*
                            Replaces issue of *Dec. 1, 1970*

Data Processing Glossary

Figure 4.7   Identification of Revision Date

determine their effect on his functional activity. Following the review, he communicates the revisions to the affected subordinates. If any clarification or orientation is required, the manager is in a position to take immediate action. Prompt action will eliminate or minimize any subsequent problems.

Enforcement of Standards

Behind each standard there must be some enforcement provision that has the backing of the executive committee. Every standard is in danger of falling victim to indifference and casualness if the upper echelon does not clearly state that it expects them to be followed as prescribed unless modified or deleted. Failure of the executive committee to assume this responsibility may result in subordinates assuming authority for policy-making and direction that has not been delegated to them. Lack of adherence to standards may result in problems, bottlenecks, implementation of faulty corrective procedures, unnecessary fiscal expenditures, and interruptions in the production schedule.

Enforcement is not only concerned with adherence. It also involves:
1. Audits and reviews
2. Temporary standards
3. Modification and revision
4. Distribution and follow-up

1. AUDITS AND REVIEWS. Standards have to be audited and reviewed periodically to maintain their effectiveness. Otherwise, they may fall into a state of disregard and misuse. Some persons will completely avoid using them due to a lack of confidence; others will apply them only selectively, for their own advantage. It is clear, therefore, that an out-

dated or obsolete standard can become the source of problems and result in ineffective decisions. It is also clear that every effort must be made to uncover any deficiencies and to correct them accurately and promptly. This can best be accomplished through regularly scheduled audits and reviews of existing standards. If the task is too massive, then the most frequently used standards should be examined regularly, with all others being reviewed on a sampling basis to ease the workload. However, an adequate number must be covered during each review to ensure that every standard receives at least one audit per year in terms of its currency, relevance, clarity, and compatibility.

2. TEMPORARY STANDARDS. Enforcement is also concerned with the temporary modification and/or revision of standards. One of the major problems is the unwarranted and illegal change or modification of a standard, which can affect the standards accuracy, compatibility, and relevance. In some instances, such as satellite operations, it may be necessary to deviate from an established standard. However, such departures must be approved by the controlling standards group. This procedure involves submitting a written request containing a complete explanation for any deviation. Because of its ultimate effect upon the overall organization, a deviation must be evaluated by the control group in terms of relevancy to a given standard and compatibility with others. Subsequently, the group will either grant its approval or reject the request. Approval, though, should be limited to a specified time period. Upon expiration of the dated approval, the original request must be reviewed before any extension is granted or revocation made. This procedure provides a form of management control to prevent a proliferation of deviations.

Many organizations facilitate identification of authorized deviations by printing them on nonwhite paper and filing them in front of the affected pages in the appropriate standards manual. The deviations are also identified by the words, TEMPORARY STANDARD, and placement of the effective duration period at the top of the first page. Figure 4.8 illustrates a page heading as it may appear on a temporary standard.

When a temporary standard is extended, a cover page with the new effective period indicated must be issued. This removes the necessity of any pen or pencil alterations, as well as any doubts or confusion regarding the effectiveness of the standard. When audits and reviews are made, the outdated standards must be removed from the manuals if this has not been done already.

```
┌─────────────────────────────────────────────────────────────────┐
│                    TEMPORARY STANDARD                             │
│                                                                   │
│   R. S. COMPUTATIONS, INC.     Data Processing Manual 10.1        │
│                                Effective Period:                  │
│                                Sept. 15, 1972 to                  │
│                                Oct. 15, 1972                      │
│                                                                   │
└──∿──────────────∿──────────────────────────∿────────────────∿────┘
```

Figure 4.8   Sample Page Heading for a Temporary Standard

If a standards deviation is authorized for only a selected group or function, this must be clearly indicated at the top of the first page. This point is illustrated in Figure 4.9.

3. MODIFICATION AND REVISION. Every organization needs to establish a procedure for the proper modification or revision of a standard. This activity can be performed only by the standards group, with the proper approval of the executive committee. In formulating a change, the standards group should consult the affected personnel and give them an opportunity to review the drafts and make suggestions. Occasionally one of the parties affected may become uncooperative or resentful and may provide some distorted information or deliberately omit some facts. This problem can be overcome by verifying the data through direct observation or by checking with an alternate source. Despite these hazards, the personal contact will help to "sell" the standard because people are generally averse to unexpected and impersonally presented changes.

The modified standard should then be prepared for approval by the chief administrative officer in the organization. He should be a member

```
┌─────────────────────────────────────────────────────────────────┐
│                    TEMPORARY STANDARD                             │
│                                                                   │
│   R. S. COMPUTATIONS, INC.     Data Processing Manual 10.1        │
│                                Effective Period:                  │
│                                Sept. 15, 1971 to                  │
│                                Oct. 15, 1971                      │
│                                                                   │
│   N.B. Temporary Standard for the Alexander Street Office Only.   │
│                                                                   │
└──∿──────────────∿──────────────────────────∿────────────────∿────┘
```

Figure 4.9   Example of a Temporary Standard for a Selected Group

of the executive committee and be at least two levels above the manager of the standards group. When the executive committee has approved the standard, it is then published.

4. DISTRIBUTION AND FOLLOW-UP. Following publication, the standard is distributed to all functional activities that maintain standards manuals. The master copy should be placed in the appropriate master manual and filed in a protective facility. A reference copy should also be maintained in the standards group for use by standards personnel and other members of the organization not having immediate access to the manuals.

The distribution pattern for all changes and/or additions is stipulated in the distributions paragraph of the foreword to each manual. A sample distributions paragraph is included in Figure 4.10. Following initial distribution of the manual, each subsequent distribution pattern is shown on a change sheet. A sample of a change sheet is illustrated in Figure 4.11. The change sheet is a multi-purpose document. Its primary purpose is to alert the user that his function's copy of the relevant manual must be updated and to identify the pages affected in the attachment paragraph. The change sheet also provides limited instructions for updating the manual in paragraph 1. The second paragraph provides a historical record of the previous page changes made to this standards manual. The change sheet also explains the use of the special symbols and identifies the distribution pattern for the standard.

The distributed copies are inserted in the appropriate manuals by the secretarial staff in the various receiving groups. To ensure proper updating by the users, the standards group conducts periodic audits to determine content currency and validity.

A follow-up should be conducted on each reissued standard within a reasonable period of time to determine its effectiveness. The determination is made by comparing the standard's functional effectiveness with planned objectives. If it fails to meet the desired objectives, the standards group must then continue with the application of the feedback concept (discussed in Chapter 1) to resolve the problem.

Review Questions: Group 4B

1. In the documentation of standards, certain guidelines must be established. What are these?

Data Processing Manual 10.1 R. S. COMPUTATIONS, INC.
Part II November 10, 1971

FOREWORD

1. *PURPOSE.* This part of DP Manual 10.1 contains the electronic data processing procedures necessary to the implementation and operation of the Inventory Control functional area.

2. *FORMAT.* This part of the manual is divided into sections; each section represents a specific report and/or output to be derived from the computerized process.

3. *CHANGES AND SUPPLEMENTS.* Changes and supplements to this manual will be distributed in the form of complete pages or sections. This will permit withdrawal of the old page and insertion of the new page. New pages will be distinguished from old pages by the date at the top of the page.

New and/or revised material that has been added to a page since the last revision will be indicated by a single "@" symbol preceding and following the material added. When a portion of the text has been deleted, double "@@" symbols will be inserted to denote the deleted material. In the event that a majority of the text on a page has been changed, a single "@" symbol will appear in the upper-left and lower-right corners of the page.

Recommended changes to this manual should be brought to the attention of the Corporate Standards Group.

4. *DISTRIBUTION.* Changes or supplements will be forwarded from the Corporate Standards Group direct to the functional activities concerned through normal channels, unless otherwise specified. However, to ensure that staff and operating activities maintaining basic manuals receive all changes, the user should advise the publications distribution section of the proper routing for all changes and/or additions to the manual.

Figure 4.10 Sample Foreword to Standards Manual

CHANGE *3*   R. S. COMPUTATIONS, INC.
Data Processing Manual 10.1   December 8, 1971
Part II

TO BE FILED IN FRONT OF *PART II*, DP MANUAL 10.1, JANUARY 2, 1971.

   1. Changes to this manual are made on a page basis. Upon receipt of each change, the user will insert the change into its respective place in the manual. The numbered change sheet will be filed as directed for reference purposes.

   2. Previously published changes are as follows:

      Change 1, April 9, 1970, Sections 1 and 14

      Change 2, May 12, 1970, Section 22

   3. The symbols "@" and "@@" are used throughout to indicate additions, deletions, and revisions.

                   E. A. Szweda

                   Vice-President

                   Administrative Services

Attachment:

   Change 3—Insert pages where indicated

   Section 9 (13.1, 13.6)

Distribution:

   To all holders of Part II, DP Manual 10.1

Figure 4.11   Sample Change Sheet

2. Why are special symbols used in the documentation of standards?
3. Behind each standard there must be some enforcement provision. Why?
4. In what ways must a standard be made effective?
5. How should temporary deviations to a standard be handled?

THE PRINCIPAL STANDARDS

Standards for Systems Groups

Through its many activities and responsibilities, the systems group has a more far-reaching effect than any other group within the data processing function. For example, it is the systems group that establishes data processing policies, practices, procedures, requirements, and preparatory actions for others to follow. This frequently involves the group in the preparation and enforcement of standards.

Benefits of Systems Documentation

One of the most important standards to be established and enforced by the systems group is the documentation of data processing systems.

Such a standard provides or may provide the following benefits:

—A content and format guide for documentation of all data processing procedures, policies, practices, and requirements

—A complete record of the evaluation of a system, from analysis to implementation

—A method for the generation, maintenance, and dissemination of technical and support data for a particular program, system, or project

—Instructions for preparation of input and interpretation of the output and/or reports

—Data for simplifying and facilitating either conversion to new or upgraded equipment or adoption of a new approach

—Data on system and performance requirements, codes, schedules, resources, budgets, and other related elements for use in equipment and system feasibility studies

—Data for efficient scheduling of operations and equipment

—A basis for audit and review procedures and updating that are required as a result of modification or change

—A communications medium for the transfer of information

Managerial Responsibility

Many data processing managers do not wish to become involved in documentation of systems because they consider it threatening to their own indispensability. Or they dismiss it on the grounds that it is too time-consuming and that it detracts from performance of normal daily activities and development of new systems. In addition, such managers often regard the expenditure of funds to be inadvisable for such a relatively nonessential item as documentation. This form of negative or ill-advised thinking either floats down generally from the upper echelons or results specifically from the executive committee's lack of awareness about the importance or significance of documentation.

Despite any absence of encouragement from above, a manager should assume a positive approach to documentation, the most economical and efficient way to do anything is to execute it correctly *the first time*. Prevention of problems is less costly in terms of both manpower and money.

Some managers prefer to excuse themselves from responsibility by using the timeworn phrase, "We are too busy at the moment; we will complete the documentation when things ease up." In the experience of this author, though, a data processing group never realistically reaches a point where "things ease up." The dynamic nature of data processing calls repeatedly for the development of new applications and for the maintenance and improvement of old ones. So the things-ease-up argument clearly indicates that a manager has failed to schedule time in the overall project for the documentation task. Nevertheless, no system is complete until it has been thoroughly documented. Therefore, a manager should realistically expect to allocate between 10 and 20 percent of project time to the generation and maintenance of documentation. The actual allocation of time depends upon the size and complexity of the system.

Elements of a Systems Standard

The established standard must require that complete documentation be developed to facilitate interaction by the functions involved in the development, implementation, maintenance, and operation of the system. Such a requirement directly affects the systems group, but, in addition, portions of it provide a primary information base for the programming, operations, and user functions.

The systems standard consists of a number of descriptive elements. The eight principal elements, and their components, are:
1. The system abstract
2. The system flowchart
3. The program flowchart
4. Layout information

5. User instructions

6. Operating instructions

7. Program listing

8. Glossary

For each application, the applicable descriptive elements on the above list are grouped together and incorporated into a system description manual, which provides the details needed in order to understand, develop, activate, and operate an application.

1. THE SYSTEM ABSTRACT. The system abstract is a general description of the total system—a summary of the various interacting elements. It describes the data manipulation and computational phases; the conditions and/or parameters required; the interfaces between input, output, and data base files; and information about the hardware and software. The abstract is written in layman's terminology, which facilitates understanding by managers, auditors, and other interested personnel.

A typical system abstract (as illustrated by the form shown in Figure 4.12) may contain the following information:

—A descriptive title that aptly identifies the system for the user.

—The functional area in which the system is operative. This may require the development of a functional-areas listing, such as Payroll, Accounting, Industrial Engineering, Production Control, etc. Some organizations prefer to use a numerical code for identification purposes. (The code may be inserted in the Application No. block shown in the illustration. Some organizations prefer to use a more elaborate scheme for identification and control purposes. Such a numbering scheme is subsequently discussed under control of documentation.) This can prove to be a disadvantage unless all the users have a working knowledge of the coding scheme.

—The effective date showing when the system was operative after testing and debugging. When a change or modification to the system is made, the revision date must be shown on the abstract. In some organizations, an "R" is appended to the date to provide a revision reference. In addition, some organizations include a copy of the previous abstract, along with correspondence and other relevant data, in the reference section of the system description manual.

—A clear and concise description of the system, written in layman's terminology. This description states the objectives of the system, required functions, performance parameters, interfaces between the various files, and the interrelationship of the various functional elements of the organization affected by the system. This segment is used by audit personnel to provide for verification of actual performance in terms of stated goals.

—Equipment configuration—that is, the type of data processing equipment used, including the peripheral equipment and special features, to achieve the objective. However, this segment should not include information about equipment or features that are part of the basic hardware complement but that are not utilized in the system being described.

—The maximum primary and auxiliary memory storage requirements needed to perform the computer-related operations. For the sake of clarity, each type must be identified separately.

—The programming language or languages used in the computer-related operations such as COBOL, FORTRAN, PL/I, AUTOCODER, RPG, etc.

—A description of the input, output, and data base files, given in layman's terminology. This should include form names and numbers, as well as assigned file names. (If an organization utilizes data base files, the input and/or output blocks could be subdivided to facilitate separate identification.)

—The date of approval by the manager of the systems group.

The actual form layout adopted by a data processing organization depends on its goals and needs. An alternative to the kind of form shown in Figure 4.12 is a very simple form on which can be stated the purpose, method of processing, restrictions, and storage and equipment requirements. A completed example of this type of form appears in Figure 4.13.

The original copy of the abstract should be maintained with the entire documentation package for a given system in a separate fire-resistant room. Reproduced copies should be placed in each documentation folder distributed to the systems, programming, operations, and user groups.

2. THE SYSTEM FLOWCHART. Included in every documentation folder must be a complete system flowchart. Such a chart is the basis for the development of an entire system. It provides an overall picture, which can be used to:

—Indicate the origination, flow, and disposition of data elements

—Indicate major operations and users

—Indicate the type and extent of management controls

—Implement forms, and reports control studies

SYSTEM ABSTRACT	APPLICATION NO.	EFFECTIVE DATE __ / __ / __	PAGE __ OF __
SYSTEM TITLE			

SYSTEM DESCRIPTION

EQUIPMENT CONFIGURATION	RELATED SYSTEMS
STORAGE REQUIREMENTS (PRI. & AUX.)	PROGRAMMING LANGUAGE(S)

INPUT DESCRIPTION	OUTPUT DESCRIPTION

APPROVED BY	APPROVAL DATE

Figure 4.12. System Abstract Form

190

R. S. COMPUTATIONS, INC.   Data Processing
                                                  Manual 10.1
Part II   May 17, 1971

Abstract of Hourly Payroll Program

Purpose: This system is designed to process the hourly rated employees payroll. It provides for computation of gross pay; social security, federal, state, and city taxes; and the application of deductions for determination of net amount. The system utilizes a single program written in Report Program Generator on an IBM 360 Model 20 computer.

The basic employee information and computations are printed on the Statement of Payroll Account issued to each employee. The program provides for punching of calculated current earnings cards for use in the Labor Distribution System; a year-to-date taxes and earnings record for use in various management reports; and a draft card used in printing the employee payroll draft.

In addition, the program utilizes several subroutines. These provide for: processing of cash advances and adjustments; processing of garnishments and other types of levies; determination of taxable earnings and limits under the social security law; determination of deductions that cannot be applied against the current payroll; and the accumulation of total earnings, taxes, and deductions for preparation of departmental controls.

Method: Sets of cards (one set per employee, with cards grouped by card code) are read into the computer in employee number sequence. For each employee there is a basic employee information and rate card; a second basic employee information and rate card if an employee carries a dual rate; current earnings cards; cash advances or adjustments; the year-to-date taxes and earnings record; priority deductions (deductions not applied in previous payroll processing), garnishments, or levies; and current payroll deductions.

Restrictions: The following represent processing restrictions within the computer program:

1. The cards must be within employee number sequence
2. The card set for each employee must be in a controlled order sequence, based on card code in card columns 79–80
3. Each employee card set must contain a tax and earnings card, card code 48 in card columns 79–80

Storage Requirements: 4000 positions of primary core storage.

Equipment Specifications: 4K, IBM 360 Model 20 computer equipped with a Basic Operating System.

Figure 4.13   Alternative System Abstract

—Give management an understanding of a system

—Identify any bottlenecks and duplications of effort

—Serve as a basis for audit and review

—Effect or investigate changes in an existing system

—Identify the entry, use of forms, and disposition of forms in a forms control study

—Identify the work flow in a reports control study

The symbols used on the flowchart should be the standard ones developed by the American National Standards Institute (ANSI). These are illustrated in Figure 4.14 (as well as being both defined and illustrated in Appendix III). They may be drawn on either a blocked or an unblocked flowcharting worksheet. The blocked form (see Figure 4.15) is generally preferred because it provides for a preprinted block, or coordinate, reference number. Some organizations utilize an unreferenced blocked worksheet; they prefer to use a notation appearing either to the right or left of the flowline bisector or in the striping. Generally, the name of the operation appears to the left of the flowline and the block or coordinate reference number appears to the right. Both are placed above the symbol. The inclusion of a block or coordinate reference number in the striping is contrary to general usage and violates the ANSI standard. The horizontal striping is generally used in a program flowchart to make reference to another part of the flowchart that provides a detailed explanation.

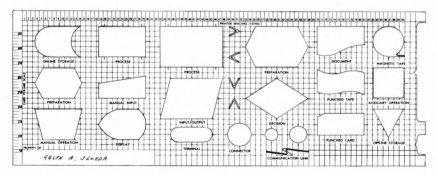

Figure 4.14. Flowchart Symbols

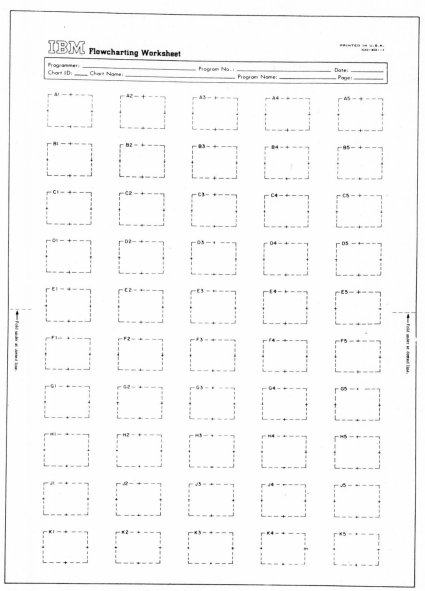

Figure 4.15. Sample Flowchart Worksheet. Courtesy IBM Corporation.

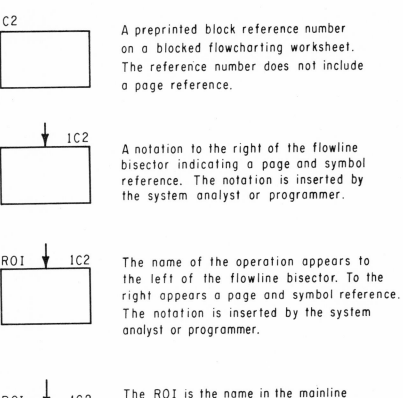

Figure 4.16. Flowchart Reference Notation

These points are illustrated in Figure 4.16.

3. THE PROGRAM FLOWCHART. The program flowchart, which is sometimes called the logic diagram or block diagram, is a graphic representation of the computer-related operations in a system. It provides a basis for program modification, maintenance, and audit.

There are two basic types of program flowchart. They are the (a) macro-diagram and the (b) micro-diagram.

a) *The Macro-diagram.* The macro-diagram illustrates the overall logic for each computer program; that is, it indicates the major decisions and alternate paths, the operations, and the linkage to subroutines and subprograms. These generalized operations have to be translated into detailed steps on a micro-diagram before any program coding can be initiated.

A macro-diagram should be machine- and software-independent, but applicable to any hardware configuration or programming language. It must be clear and complete, but brief so as not to duplicate the charting performed on the micro-diagram.

Figure 4.17 illustrates a simple macro-diagram. The logic indicates only the major operations and does not attempt to specify the many detailed steps required to accomplish each major task. For example, the card input operation identified as "A" calls for the inputting of a record, its storage, and definition of the data elements contained therein. This relationship is further illustrated in Figure 4.18, in which step "D" of the macro-diagram is translated into the required number of steps on the micro-diagram.

There are certain rules for the preparation of macro-diagrams that must be implemented in order to establish an effective documentation standard. These rules specify that:

—The symbols used should be the standard ones developed by the ANSI.

—The macro-diagrams should be drawn on paper that can be readily reproduced so as to simplify distribution of copies. In some organizations, the diagrams are drawn on 8 1/2″ × 11″ white bond paper, which can be quickly reproduced on most copying machines. Organizations with more sophisticated copying machines can use paper of larger sizes, as well as flowcharting worksheets.

—Copies of the diagrams should be placed in the various documentation folders.

—Each diagram should contain an identification block in the lower right corner of each page. A sample block is illustrated in Figure 4.19.

—Each symbol on the macro-diagram should be identified by an alphabetic character in sequence from A to Z. If more than 26 symbols are required, a double-letter identification mode can be used; that is, from AA to ZZ.

b) *The Micro-diagram.* The micro-diagram is a detailed translation of the operations shown on the macro-diagram and the input, output, and storage requirements included in the layout information. It illus-

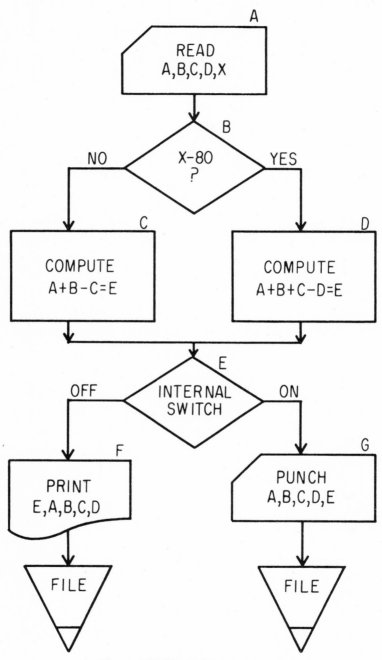

Figure 4.17. Simple Macro-Diagram

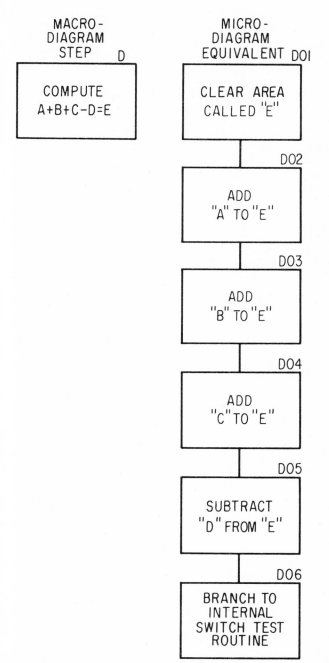

Figure 4.18. Comparison of Macro-Diagram and Micro-Diagram Steps

trates in logical sequence the data transfer, decision, calculation, exception, input, and output steps. Depending on the policies and practices of the data processing organization, the micro-diagrams may be generalized or detailed. In the latter form, each symbol drawn on the diagram is the equivalent of one source program language statement. In a generalized version of a micro-diagram the programmer depends on his memory and/or notes to code all of the necessary source program steps. (Micro-diagrams are discussed more fully in this chapter under standards for the programming group.)

In many installations the systems group prepares the macro-diagrams and, after a review of the requirements, submits them to the programming group for preparation of the micro-diagrams and coding of the computer instructions. In some installations, the micro-diagrams are prepared by the systems personnel, who will then submit them to the programming group for coding. In still other installations, the programming staff prepares its own macro- and micro-diagrams based on information obtained from the system abstract and from the systems personnel.

Program Name _____

Program # _____

Programmer(s) _____

_____

_____

Effective Date _____ / / Revision _____

Page _____ of _____

Figure 4.19   Program Flowchart Identification Block

4. LAYOUT INFORMATION. The documentation must include complete layout information because it affects each project. The principal items involved in layout information are:

a) Card input/output

b) Printer output

c) Optical scanning and/or MICR document input and output

d) Magnetic and/or paper tape input and output

e) Random access layouts

f) Primary and auxiliary memory layouts

g) Console typewriter/keyboard input and output

h) Visual data displays

a) *Card Input/Output.* The input and output formats for punch cards must be clearly specified. A very important part of the systems analysis and design activity is to develop and establish these formats to facilitate detailed programming and/or wiring.

The general rules for card layout standards are:

—Each card format used must be illustrated on a card layout form; to reduce the number of pages in a folder, a multiple-card layout form can be used (see Figure 4.20)

—Vertical lines should be drawn separating each field in order to identify field definitions

—Horizontal lines should be drawn over each field in order to identify field names

—Each layout form should be identified with the name of the application or system, the program name and number, and the effective date.

Sample copies of the card forms used should be included in the

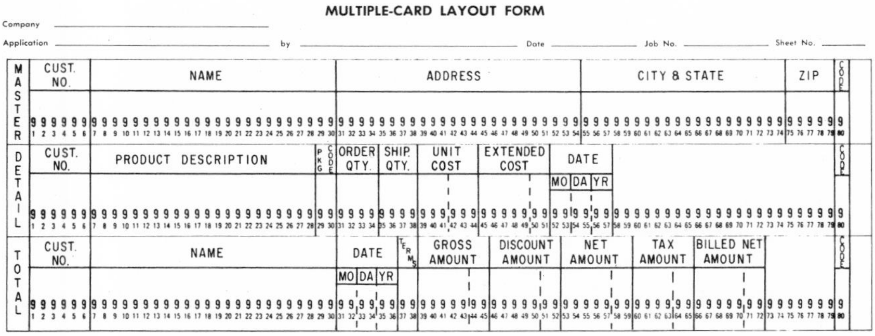

Figure 4.20. Sample Card Layout Form

system description manual. Provision should also be made for inclusion of a reference relationship to the application, the program names and numbers utilizing the cards, and effective dates. Generally this type of information is found on the back of the cards included in a manual. When this approach is undesirable or not feasible, the card may be attached to a sheet of bond paper and the relevant information listed below the card in the space remaining.

RECORD FORMAT FORM

FILE MNEMONIC _____ DATE ____ / ____ / ____

RECORD POSITION		FIELD	PROGRAM		DATA
FIRST	LAST	LABEL	MNEMONIC	LENGTH	CHARACTERISTICS

Figure 4.21. Sample Record Format Form

Some organizations prefer to use a record format, a form for which is illustrated in Figure 4.21. In addition to stipulating the physical location of the data elements, the form provides for entry of assigned program mnemonics, count, and data-type specification. These provisions enhance the value of the documentation for an organization. Preference for the record format is based on the fact that the format simplifies the replication process and ensures uniformity in layout form utilization.

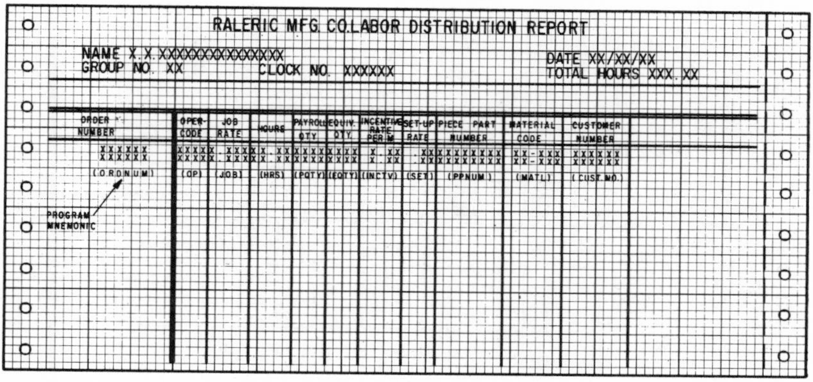

Figure 4.22. Printer Spacing Chart

b) *Printer Output.* The printer output specifications (see Figure 4.22) must be developed and illustrated on a printer spacing chart before any detailed programming or wiring is initiated. When the chart format is approved by the user, the chart becomes the basis of vendor form ordering and approval specifications. Under no circumstances should the data processing organization release its only copy of a printer spacing chart, which is to be produced as a preprinted form, to the vendor. This may well lead to misunderstandings, delays in shipment, and the need to re-draw the layout form to verify the accuracy of a vendor's form proof. An error or omission in preparing a new printer spacing chart for the vendor could prove very time-consuming and costly to the organization. The original copy must be photocopied to produce at least one copy of the printer spacing chart. The photocopy is used as a basis of verifying the accuracy of the vendor-produced report form. Also, the copy is included in the system description manual as part of the system's documentation.

Following the development and implementation of the desired out-

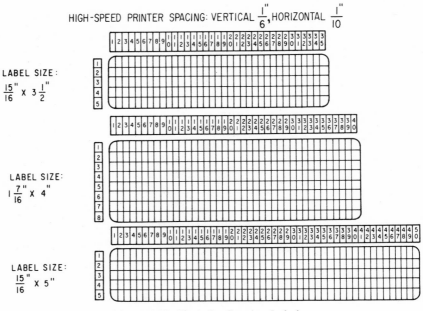

Figure 4.23. Chart for Spacing Labels

put format, the printer spacing chart becomes the basis of all subsequent report evaluations, modifications, and maintenance.

Though the printer planning chart may be used for designing continuous labels, the planning chart illustrated in Figure 4.23 is more suitable.

The physical specifications for a form vary for the different printer devices and vendors. They are included in the equipment manuals and should be checked before any detailed planning and design is initiated.

A completed printed sample of the output should be included in the system description manual. It will be used by the auditor for comparison purposes and by the executive committee as a source of information. A reproduction, or carbon copy, of this form should also be included in the user's manual (if applicable) and in the operator's manual.

Each planning chart and sample form should be identified with the application or system name, report title, program name and number, and effective date.

A record format form (see Figure 4.21) may be used to supplement the planning chart. This form provides for inclusion of the output record program mnemonics in the documentation.

c) *Optical Scanning and/or* MICR *Documents.* Samples of the optical

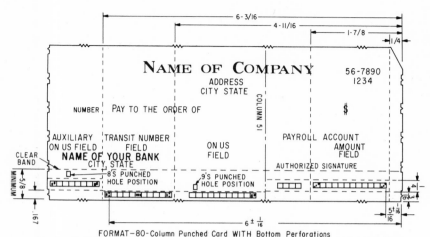

FORMAT—80-Column Punched Card WITH Bottom Perforations
The clear band extends from right edge to 1/4" beyond last or left character printed or in this case to left edge. Field boundaries are defined by dimensions shown. The number of digits, spaces, use of symbols, etc. in On Us Field(s) varies with banks and machine manufacturers.

Figure 4.24. MICR Planning Sample

scanning documents and the magnetic ink character documents (MICR) used for input and output, together with the document planning forms, must also be included in the system description manual. Each planning form and sample document should include the same identification specifications as previously indicated. The design specifications for OCR, OMR, and MICR documents are given in the vendors' equipment manuals. A sample of planning specifications for an 80-column punched card draft utilizing MICR is illustrated in Figure 4.24. A sample of a planning layout for an OMR document is illustrated in Figure 4.25.

Copies of the actual form samples should be included in the system description manual, user's manual, and operator's manual.

d) Magnetic and/or Paper Tape Input and Output. The format of magnetic and paper tape records used for input and/or output must be clearly specified. On each tape-layout form (see Figure 4.26), there must be a reference linkage to the application or system; program name(s) and number(s); assigned name for a tape; and input or output specification. Owing to the length of a tape record, there may be need for several record layouts in the manual.

The general rules for tape-layout standards are as follows:

—Vertical lines should be drawn to identify each field

—Field names should be printed over the horizontal lines in a given field

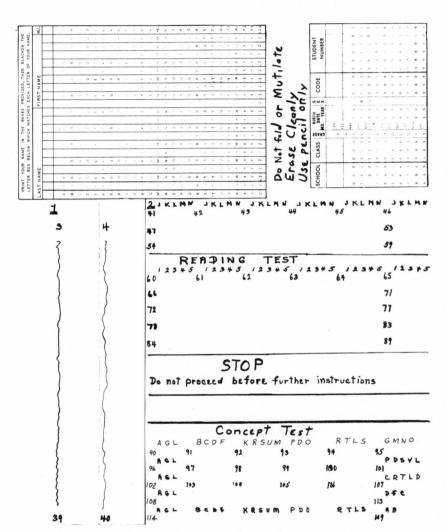

Figure 4.25. Sample Planning Layout for OMR Document

FILE MNEMONIC _____   RECORD MNEMONIC _____
    DENSITY _____   DATE _____

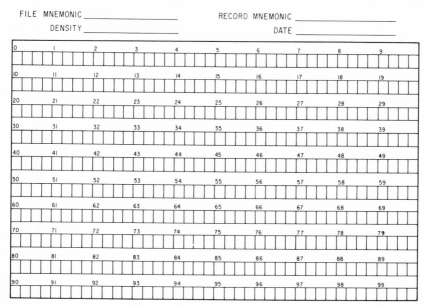

Figure 4.26. Tape Layout Form

—All special characters used for tape processing, such as record, block, end-of-tape, or end of transmission marks, should be illustrated

—The blocking factor for each magnetic tape should be specified, namely, fixed-fixed, fixed-variable, etc.

—If no blocking factors are used, the specification should be included to indicate the length of a record—fixed or variable.

An organization may prefer to utilize a record format form as previously illustrated in Figure 4.21. When coupled with a file specification (see form illustrated in Figure 4.27), the record format provides additional relevant planning, implementation, and documentation data not available on the tape layout form illustrated in Figure 4.26.

e) Random Access Layouts. The specifications for random access devices are very similar to those of tape devices, with the exception that the former include a record of assigned and unassigned memory locations, wherever applicable.

In the interest of file security, the unrelated storage assignments should be identified solely as reserved areas without any detailed data specifications. This information is generally shown on a record layout worksheet (see Figure 4.28).

The user may prefer to utilize record format and file specification forms instead of the vendor-recommended forms for a given storage medium.

f) *Primary and Auxiliary Memory Layouts.* Occasionally a program requires the allocation of special internal-storage areas for tables or record construction. These may be specified on a record layout worksheet (Figure 4.28) or a record format form (Figure 4.21).

Allocations on an auxiliary memory device, such as disk, drum, card random access or data cell, may also be specified on these forms, which are used to effectively indicate the assigned locations and their data characteristics.

g) *Console Typewriter/Keyboard Input and Output.* The console typewriter/keyboard can be used very effectively for such items as input data entry; specification of output medium and/or mode; definition of parameters; presentation of error messages; initiation of checkpoint, restart, and recovery procedures; and establishment of management controls. The information is documented on a console instruction sheet (see Figure 4.29). The console instruction sheet describes to the systems analyst, programmer, console operator, user, and auditor how to use the computer program. The documented functional data for this form must be developed by the systems and programming personnel.

h) *Visual Data Displays.* Despite the increased use of such devices as the cathode-ray tube display, many organizations fail to include a replication of the output in their documentation. Though most of the peripherals are installed at the same location as the main computer, a copy of the output should be included in the system description, user's manual, and operator's manual. The documented terminal display illustrates the output format as it should appear in response to a desired action. The terminal output format is supplemented by the operating instructions developed for the user and for the operations personnel.

Figure 4.30 illustrates a bed census display generated on an IBM 2260 for use in a hospital information system. The user-requested data will be displayed below the program-generated columnar descriptors.

5. USER INSTRUCTIONS. These provide the clerical and control procedures describing *who* does *what* and *when.* They describe input preparation and submission, interrelationships between data elements, priority designations, clerical processing, data element descriptions, authorizations required, accuracy and procedural controls, coding structures, and

FILE SPECIFICATION	APPLICATION NO.	PROGRAM NO.	PAGE __ of __

FILE MNEMONIC

STORAGE MEDIUM	STORAGE MODE

HEADER LABEL DATA

TRAILER LABEL DATA

RECORD TYPE	MAXIMUM LENGTH

BLOCK FACTOR	MAXIMUM SIZE

RECORD SEQUENCE

FILE SECURITY CLASSIFICATION	RETENTION PERIOD

REMARKS

APPROVED BY	DATE

Figure 4.27. File Specification Form

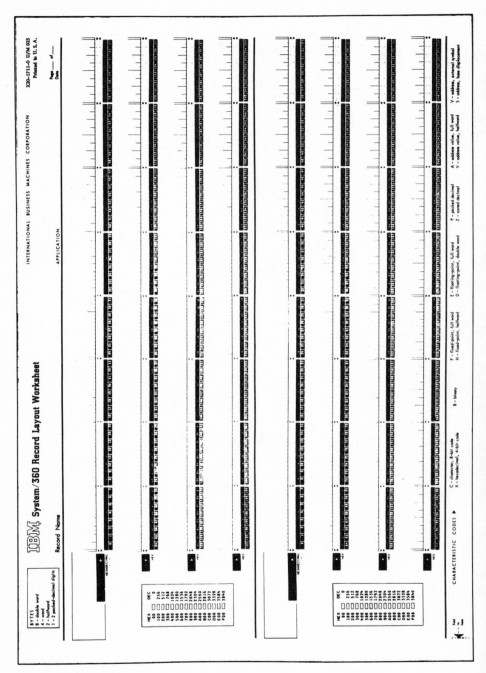

Figure 4.28. Record Layout Worksheet. Courtesy IBM Corporation

208

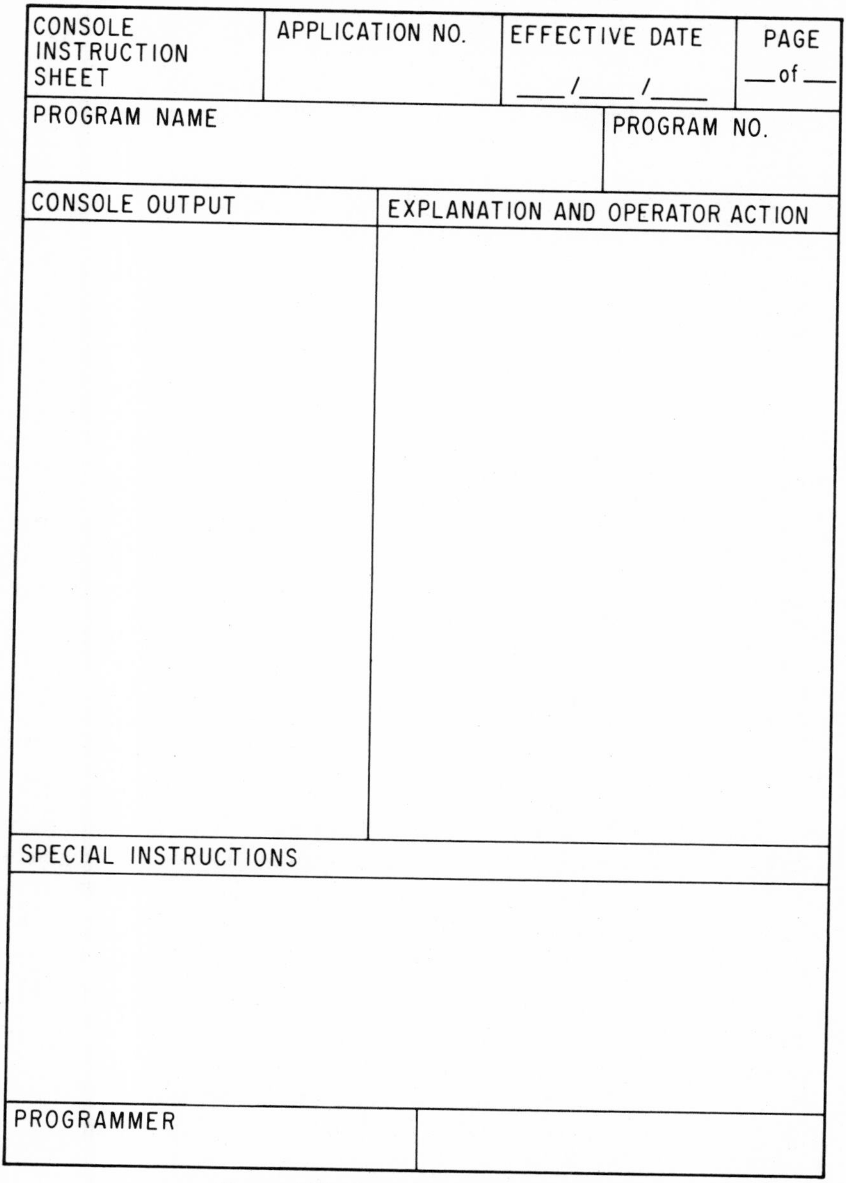

CONSOLE INSTRUCTION SHEET	APPLICATION NO.	EFFECTIVE DATE ___ / ___ / ___	PAGE ___ of ___
PROGRAM NAME		PROGRAM NO.	

CONSOLE OUTPUT	EXPLANATION AND OPERATOR ACTION

SPECIAL INSTRUCTIONS

PROGRAMMER

Figure 4.29. Console Instruction Sheet

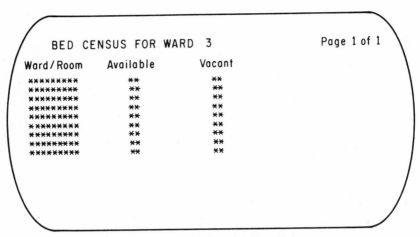

Figure 4.30. Visual Data Display Format

distribution patterns by functional title. This information is developed and implemented in a user's manual; it is also included in the system description manual. The user instructions should be established in two modes: the (*a*) normal mode and the (*b*) alternate mode.

a) The Normal Mode. The normal mode specifies the procedures to be followed in the regular operation of a given system. These procedures, sometimes referred to as job-preparation procedures, generally deal with the input, output, and update segments of a system.

The input segment specifies the input sources, purpose and functions served, contents, element descriptions, references required, editing instructions, samples, and document identification. The output segment specifications include the medium and mode, element descriptions, formats, query responses and requirements, validity checks, and samples. The update segment provides a complete description of all expected inputs to be entered or processed against existing files; it identifies the inputs, formats, sources, volumes, and retention, frequency, and error-correction procedures affecting the updating process.

An extract from a user's manual is illustrated in Figure 4.31. A code listing that may be part of the user instructions is illustrated in Figure 4.32.

b) The Alternate Mode. The alternate mode consists of a set of procedures—sometimes called contingency procedures—that facilitates processing of a system under other than normal conditions. "Other than normal conditions" may describe such situations as those resulting from fire, flooding, vandalism, hardware failure, power failure, or serious human error. An alternate mode procedure is developed only after the manager has carefully analyzed the effect and cost of a processing delay upon the overall organization. Processing of critical systems may require the development and testing of one or several alternate-mode operating procedures. Depending upon the level of importance, the manager may establish alternate procedures to facilitate processing under a revised operating schedule, reduced or limited scope of operations, or a revised processing mode. Or the alternate procedures may allow for processing at a back-up facility on a limited or relatively normal operating schedule.

The alternate procedures are generally maintained in a binder and indexed with tabs designating the condition covered—Destruction of Data File, Loss of Power, etc.

Some organizations prefer not to include the alternate-mode user instructions in their standard documentation package. Instead, they limit access to key individuals. Nevertheless, it does not in any way reduce an organization's security if the fact that alternate processing procedures are available is made known in the systems description, user's manual, and operator's manual. For it is essential that key operating personnel and key user personnel must have some form of access to the alternate procedures.

Limited-access provisions do not always work as well in practice as originally planned in theory. For example, an analyst taped a codified listing of alternate procedures to the slide tray of a desk. When he left the organization, his successor found the listing, but he disposed of it because he did not understand the codified jargon. Subsequently, when a question arose about a back-up procedure, a file-cabinet search had to be made in order to determine procedural availability. Another organization was even less fortunate in its handling of alternate procedures. A listing of the available alternate procedures was taped to the side of a bookcase; the procedures themselves were maintained in an unmarked binder in the bookcase. One day, the painters came along and removed the contents of the bookcase and stacked the material on the floor. They removed the listing and placed it with the temporarily displaced materials. After the paint had dried, a young secretary was asked to replace the materials in the bookcase. She refiled all of the materials except for the

RALERIC CREDIT UNION	DATA PROCESSING MANUAL 10.1 November 21, 1971	
STANDARD PROCEDURE		
Subject: REQUEST FOR MAILING LABELS		Application No.
PERFORMED BY	ACTION	
User department	1. Complete the "Request for Labels" form (CU-123). Indicate the sequence of account numbers for which output is desired. Forward the form to Data Processing.	
Data processing	2. Keypunch and key verify the "request" cards (CU-010).	
	3. Sort "request" cards on account number, card columns 5-1.	
	4. Process the "request" cards on the computer using program 02-02-087.	
	5. Forward the output to User Department.	
	6. File the "Request for Labels" forms in File Drawer 23A.	
Prepared by	Approved by	Approval date

Figure 4.31. Sample User Instructions: Standard Procedure

R. S. COMPUTATIONS, INC.   DATA PROCESSING
                                  MANUAL 10.1
November 10, 1972   Part II

TRANSACTION CODES

Internal Transactions

	Code to Change Balance Forward Record
Type of Transaction	
1. Establish Due Out for all types of Back Orders	111
2. Increase Due Out for all types of Back Orders	211
3. Decrease Due Out for all types of Back Orders	311
4. Establish Due In	113
5. Increase Due In	213
6. Decrease Due In	313
7. Raise Stock Level	511
8. Decrease Stock Level	531
9. Change Unit of Issue Code	009
10. Physical Inventory Overage	651
11. Physical Inventory Shortage	671

Figure 4.32   Sample User Instructions: Code Listing

unmarked binder. That she simply laid on top of the bookcase until its proper placement could be ascertained. Then the secretary became involved in other responsibilities and forgot about the binder. During the clean-up process, the listing was never replaced. Subsequently, the procedural binder was also misplaced. As fate would have it, the organization had no back-up for the back-up.

6. OPERATING INSTRUCTIONS. The operating instructions are the complete specifications for data processing activities and those external activities involved in the preparation and processing of data on unit-record, peripheral, or computer equipment. They describe the equipment configuration requirements; instructions for setup and teardown; instructions for translation or conversion of inputs and/or source documents; checkpoint, recovery, and restart procedures; all error messages and correction procedures; and console messages and responses. In

addition, wiring diagrams should also be given for unit-record operations that require the use of complex control panels.

The operating instructions may be grouped in four general categories:

a) Setup instructions

b) Instructive output

c) Alternate mode

d) Emergency operations

a) *Setup Instructions.* This group of instructions specifies the operational order of the programs, hardware devices utilized, parameter and/or job control entries, and input and output requirements.

Figures 4.33 and 4.34 illustrate two of the forms included in the setup segment of the operating instructions. Figure 4.33 shows a form for card punching and/or verifying instructions. Figure 4.34 shows a form for the setup of computer hardware.

b) *Instructive Output.* The instructive output segment contains information on the special instructions or signals emitted on the hardware to direct the equipment operator during processing. For computerized operations, the operator is provided with programmed error messages; processing diagnostics indicated by the operating system; checkpoint, recovery, and restart procedures; and query responses and requirements. For unit-record operations, the signals and messages result from machine operations controlled by a wired control panel and a series of edit checks. The console instruction sheet (see Figure 4.29) may be used for documentation of instructive output.

c) *Alternate Mode.* The alternate-mode procedures provide the operations personnel with the detailed contingency plans for functioning under abnormal conditions. The contigency plans are developed only for those systems that have been evaluated and classified as critical.

The actual plans may not be included as part of the system description manual or operator's manual. However, they must be readily available when the conditions for implementation are evident. As had been previously suggested, some notation or evidence of existence must be included in the appropriate manuals. Such precautions do not compromise a company's security or back-up capability.

Each plan must be properly identified for the specific function it is to serve. Following its development, the plan should be tested and debugged. It should also be subjected to periodic audits to determine its operational effectiveness.

CARD PUNCHING AND/OR VERIFYING INSTRUCTIONS					
APPLICATION NAME			APPLICATION NUMBER	EFFECTIVE DATE	

SOURCE DOCUMENTS USED	DATA FIELD	COLUMNS FIRST	COLUMNS LAST	FUNCTION	COMMENTS
CARD FORM NO.					
PROGRAM CARD NO.					

SWITCH SETTINGS

ON	OFF	SWITCH
☐	☐	PROGRAM UNIT
☐	☐	AUTO FEED
☐	☐	AUTO SKIP AUTO DUP.
☐	☐	PRINT
☐	☐	SELF-CHECKING NO.

SPECIAL FEATURES USED

☐ ALTERNATE PROGRAM

☐ AUXILIARY DUPLICATE

☐ HI-SPEED SKIP

☐ SELF-CHECKING NO.

FUNCTION CODES

PUNCH	P
VERIFY	V
PUNCH & VERIFY	PV
DUPLICATE	D
SKIP	S
SELF-CHECKING NO.	NCK
RIGHT JUSTIFY	RJ
LEFT JUSTIFY	LJ
ZERO FILL	ZF
ZERO FILL & RIGHT JUSTIFY	ZFRJ
ZERO FILL & LEFT JUSTIFY	ZFLJ

Figure 4.33. Form for Card Punching and/or Verifying Instructions

MACHINE SET-UP FORM

PAGE _____

APPLICATION NUMBER _____ STEP _____ DATE _____

INPUT DATA CARDS		OUTPUT DATA CARDS	
STACKER NO.	DESCRIPTION	STACKER NO.	DESCRIPTION

DATA NAME NUMBER	I/O	RING IN	OUT	DESCRIPTION	DISPOSITION

DATA NAME NUMBER	I/O	VOLUME SERIAL NO.	DESCRIPTION	DISPOSITION

PRINTER FORM NAME	FORM NO.	NO. OF PARTS	WIDE	NARROW	CARRIAGE CONTROL TAPE	6 L.P.I.	8 L.P.I	ALPHA	NUMERIC

OTHER:

Figure 4.34. Machine Setup Form

d) Emergency Operations. These procedures delineate the action to be taken by an operator in the event of a disruptive event, such as fire, flooding or water damage, vandalism, power failure, or personal accident or illness. The emergency operating procedures are concerned with such factors as the powering down of the hardware, notification of key personnel, demounting and storage of essential records, location of firefighting equipment and fire exits, evacuation of personnel, and storage of programs.

Planning for such contingencies is very important because they can seriously affect both personnel and property. Being prepared can prevent loss of life and property, thereby bringing about considerable monetary savings. Nevertheless, for reasons unknown, many installations fail to include this category of procedures in their standard operating procedures.

These emergency operating procedures are not normally part of the operator's manual, but rather kept separately in what is called the emergency procedures manual. It is maintained on the manager's desk or at the console of the computer. The operations personnel should be trained in the execution of these procedures. Scheduled drills or training sessions should be held periodically to maintain an "emergency readiness" level.

7. PROGRAM LISTING.—A complete listing of each operational computer program must be included in the systems documentation. The program listing should show the coded source program statements of the assembly or compiler language and their machine-language equivalent; when an absolute language is used, the listing must be the tested and debugged version of the operational program. Each listing should be identified with the name of the application or system, program name and number, programmer's name, and effective date. The program listings should be filed in the sequence of operations.

Figure 4.35 illustrates the PL/I source statements for a sample program used to convert inches to feet and yards. As the conversion of the source statements is executed by the compiler, an object code (machine language) and assembler language code from the program may be outputted. This information is included in the documentation package for any subsequent planning, modification, maintenance, or audit. In most organizations, the program listing appears only in the documentation maintained for systems and programming personnel. This practice represents an essential form of management control.

```
      CCS PL/I CCMPILER  360N-PL-464 CL3-2                    BOL

 MCNEY..PRCCECLRE CPTICNS (MAIN),.

    1                  MCNEY..PRLCFCLRE CPTICNS (MAIN),.
    2                  CECLARE(YCS,FT,IN) FIXEC (5),.
    3                  CC YCS=1 BY 1 TC 5C,.
    4                  FT=YCS*3,.
    5                  IN=FT*12,.
    6                  PLT ECIT(YCS,FT,IN) (F(5)),.
    7                  ENC,.
    8                  STCP,.
    9                  ENC MCNEY,.
```

Figure 4.35. PL/I Source Statements for Sample Program Listing

When an organization utilizes a library of subroutines, subprograms, or modules, it should make sure that the applicable listings are included in the system description manual. Each such listing should be attached to the applicable main program. The value of the documentation increases if the listing includes a brief narrative of the purpose and specifies the required implementation procedures. Figure 4.36 illustrates the type of narrative that may be included to explain a subroutine utilized in a main program.

In some organizations, the internal auditors require that a memory dump of each program be included with the program listings. The dumps can be used as an audit trail for periodic audits of the documentation. However, the value of including a memory dump, such as the one illustrated in Figure 4.37, is questionable. To be effective, persons working with that output must be familiar with the object code of the particular hardware and the format of the dump.

For any programs which had been patched, but in which the source deck had not been corrected, patch listings must be included and properly identified. (The subject of patching is discussed more fully in Chapter 6.)

8. GLOSSARY. A glossary is a vital link in the communications process between data processing personnel and nondata-processing personnel in the organization. The semantics problem resulting from the use of specialized terms necessitates the standardization of the vocabulary. Consequently, there are three major vocabulary groups, or glossaries, that systems personnel must develop, maintain, and learn. These glossaries are categorized as:

a) Data processing terms
b) Specialized terms and abbreviations
c) Mnemonic labels

TABLE LOOK-UP

Purpose: In many applications there is the need to search a table for a specific value or record. This subroutine has been designed to provide an efficient means of facilitating such a search.

Calling Name: SERCH

Parameter Number	Description
1	The address of the first record in the table
2	The address of the field being compared to the table
3	The branch to address on an equal condition
4	The branch to address on an unequal condition
5	The address of the increment constant
6	The address of the increment constant, which is equal to one-half of the table storage area
7	The address of the decrement constant, which is the complement of one-half of the table storage area

Programmer: E. F. SZWEDA

Effective Date: November 11, 1971

Figure 4.36 Example of Subroutine Abstract

a) *Data Processing Terms.* The systems group must establish a glossary of the terms most frequently used within the data processing function. It is not necessary to define each of the terms because such defini-

```
DMPX.

P   017643  A0  040000  B0  000000
RA  132100  A1  000001  B1  000001  C(A1)=  0102  2420  0000  0000  0000
FL  040000  A2  014457  B2  000000  C(A2)=  0102  2460  0000  0000  0000
EM  070000  A3  000177  B3  034553  C(A3)=  0000  0000  0000  0000  0000
            A4  000202  B4  000000  C(A4)=  1725  2420  2524  0000  2022
            A5  034553  B5  012233  C(A5)=  2333  0000  0001  0003  4546
            A6  000001  B6  000000  C(A6)=  0102  2420  0000  0000  0000
            A7  010210  B7  000001  C(A7)=  0000  0000  0000  0000  0000
X0  7777  7777  7777  7700  0000
X1  0102  2420  0000  0000  0000
X2  0102  2420  0000  0000  0000
X3  0000  0000  0000  0000  2022
X4  1725  2420  2524  0000  2022
X5  0000  0000  0000  0001  0000
X6  0102  2420  0000  0000  0000
X7  0000  0000  0000  0000  0000
      00000   00000 00000 00000 00000        01022 42000 00000 00000        11162 02524 00000 06146        17252 42025 24000 10170
      00004   00000 00000 00000 00000 00006*17252 42025 24000 00120        00000 00000 00000 00000
      00010   00000 00000 00000 10000        00000 00000 00000 00000 00014*00000 00000 00000 40000        14071 70000 00000 00000
      00016   00000 00000 00000 00000 00021*14071 70000 00000 00047        01030 00000 00100 31033        00000 00000 00000 31060
      00025  *23000 00000 01000 35503        00000 00000 00000 00000 00055*00000 00000 00000 31033        00000 00000 00000 00002
      00057   00000 00000 00000 35277
      00060   00000 00000 00000 00003 00062*00000 00000 00000 00000        00000 00000 00000 40000
      00064   14071 70000 00000 00000        00000 00000 00000 22441        00033 62100 00000 00100        00000 00000 60000 34337
      00070   14071 75700 00000 00000        00000 00000 00000 00000 00076*00000 00000 00000 40000        00000 00000 00000 00000
      00100   00005 55555 55550 00102

      17543   01000 17633 46000 46000
      17544   74630 74140 74050 46000        01000 17633 46000 46000        10622 54661 10633 54661        10644 54661 10655 54661
      17550   51100 17533 20136 63210        02200 00001 46000 46000        04000 17622 00000 00000        51100 17552 20136 76610
      17554   36616 20636 54610 53110        53110 10011 54111 63310        20152 63210 20152 10611        54111 63610 20152 63510
      17560   20152 63410 54111 53210        20152 53010 20152 63710        54111 53510 20152 53410        20152 53310 54111 10211
      17564   54111 10311 54111 10411        54111 10511 63160 46000        04000 17552 46000 46000        00000 00000 00000 17751
      17570   77777 77777 77770 00000        00000 02100 00030 12212        00000 00001 22330 00000        00000 00104 00000 00176
      17574   00000 17700 02020 34553        00000 00000 00000 10170        00000 00000 00000 02022        17252 42025 24000 02022
      17600   00000 00000 00000 10000        04000 14460 00000 00000        74610 51600 17567 76600        51600 17751 01000 17533
      17604   00000 00000 00000 17570        51200 17567 63220 46000        51200 17601 20236 76610        36662 20636 54620 53220
      17610   20222 03220 17655 54220        10622 20623 03260 17614        43622 11662 20622 46000        72666 25470 03060 17623
      17614   63220 76610 20651 15226        01000 17640 46000 46000        54220 20223 03220 17620        01000 17645 46000 46000
      17620   01000 17552 46000 46000        00000 00000 00000 17570        51100 17751 04000 17601        73620 20636 51600 17626
      17624   43652 11262 71600 17626        12262 04000 17614 46000        00000 13175 00000 00001        01000 17752 02000 17633
      17630   11162 60114 11045 52205        21250 52324 55241 75503        20035 55555 55555 55555        04000 17546 00000 00000
      17634   63300 43052 15660 15110        20622 12661 20622 76130        15110 12661 54661 46000        04000 17633 46000 46000
      17640   04000 17616 00000 00000        56110 03110 17641 10622        56610 46000 46000 46000        56110 03110 17643 46000
      17644   04000 17640 46000 46000        04000 17620 00000 00000        56120 20173 03310 17645        71202 20314 20252 46000
      17650   01000 17640 46000 46000        04000 17646 46000 46000        03111 70000 00000 00000        17200 50000 00000 00000
      17654   03141 70000 00000 00000        54320 43206 11223 64720        03120 17710 20321 46000        03230 17660 01000 17722
      17660   54220 43321 11323 20321        03030 17620 72337 77773        03230 17627 62730 17655        43306 20311 11323 46000
      17664   72337 77767 03130 17704        56120 20173 03310 17670        20164 21166 72117 77776        03010 17705 46000 46000
      17670   01000 17722 46000 46000        54220 20271 03320 17675        56120 20167 03310 17620        51320 00002 54431 73331
      17674   04000 17676 46000 46000        51420 00002 54341 46000        73440 73330 37643 46000        51420 00004 03260 17702
      17700   56321 73330 73440 37343        54440 36663 46000 46000        20433 21455 37364 46000        03330 17620 46000 46000
      17704   01000 17712 46000 46000        54220 20223 03220 17620        01000 17722 46000 46000        04000 17620 46000 46000
      17710   01000 17722 46000 46000        04000 17704 46000 46000        00000 00000 00000 00000        54220 43052 76311 12003
      17714   15320 56420 11404 12643        54640 76610 20650 11662        43422 20444 11442 12646        76220 12262 56470 43622
      17720   11646 12226 01000 17640        04000 17712 46000 46000        00000 00000 00000 00000        01000 17645 46000 46000
      17724   20164 43067 15010 46000        03000 17722 56120 10611        51600 17751 56121 20144        21166 72617 77773 46000
      17730   03360 17722 51120 00010        10611 20636 73110 73660        71200 37000 72007 77757        03200 17743 72000 00014
      17734   03300 17741 71200 34000        03110 17744 03060 17722        73160 43672 72000 00004        15606 03060 17722 46000
```

Figure 4.37. Example of Memory Dump

tions may be extracted from the many glossaries available from the various professional societies and vendors. (A sampling of common data processing terms is included in the Glossary.)

b) Specialized Terms and Abbreviations. Each organization and/or industry has its own set of particular terms or jargon, which affect personnel and nondata-processing personnel. Many of the terms are acronyms or abbreviations not readily found in any dictionary or technical text. To facilitate understanding of these terms, a glossary of specialized terms should be published as a standard. A sampling of such terms is included in Figure 4.38.

c) Mnemonic Labels. Many organizations use standardized mnemonic labels in an effort to facilitate the training of personnel and employee understanding of documentation and programs. Such labels are meaningful because they relate more directly to an operation being performed or referenced field; for example, the label PRINT may be used to identify a series of instructions that are executed to output a line of printed data. The use of such terms also simplifies the maintenance of programs, as well as their conversion, modification, and audit.

Figure 4.39 illustrates some suggested mnemonics. It is important to note that the selected mnemonics must have universal understanding— their length is affected by program syntax.

Review Questions: Group 4C

1. What is a system abstract? What information does it contain?
2. What rules are applied to the preparation of a macro-diagram?
3. Why would a manager consider the development of alternate-mode procedures?
4. What is the purpose of an emergency procedures manual? What type of information should it contain?
5. Why are glossaries an important part of a documented data processing system?

Standards for Programming

The standards developed for the programming group are designed to

Word/Term	Abbreviation
Abrasive	ABRSV
Acetate	ACET
Adapter	ADPTR
Adhesive	ADHSV
Air Express	AIREXP
Alignment	ALNMT
Anneal	ANEAL
Aspirin	ASPRN
Audible	AUD
Backplate	BKPLT
Bandage	BNDG
Baseboard	BSBD
Battery	BATRY
Bevel	BEV
Block	BLK
Broadcast	BDCT
Butter	BTR
Capstan	CPSTN
Cellulose	CELOS
Composite	CMPST
Daily	DLY
Diode	DIO
Dummy	DUMY
Elastic	ELAS
Emission	EMISN
Explosive	EXPL
Fabric	FAB
Frequency	FREQ
Furniture	FURN
Gauge	GA
Gland	GLND
Handbook	HNDBK

Figure 4.38 Sample Glossary of Specialized Terms

Data Names	Standardized Program Mnemonic
User Field Name	
Account Number	ACCT
Amount	AMT
Completion Date	COMPDAT
Day	DA
Due Date	DUEDAT
Fee	FEE
Fine	FINE
First Name	FIRNAM
Interest	INT
Last Name	LASNAM
Middle Name	MIDNAM
Month	MO
Monthly Payment	MOPAY
Partial Payment	PARPAY
Payment	PAY
Principal and Interest	PRNINT
Suffix	SFX
Year	YR
Operation Name	
Move Input Record	MVINPT
Move Data Fields	MVDATA
Error Routine 1	ERRTN1
Clear Page	CLRPAG
Test Data Code	TSTCOD
Error Message	ERRMSG
Delimeter Test	DLMTST
Clear Input/Output Areas	CLRIO
End Table Look-up	ENDTLU
Clear Entry	CLRENT

Figure 4.39   Suggested Glossary of Mnemonic Labels

provide a basis for the development, understanding, and maintenance of computer programs.

These programming standards are probably the most difficult standards to enforce. One major reason is that programming personnel tend to resist the application of standards to the programming process. They claim that it limits their creativity and forces them to program less efficiently. Reacting in a practical way, the manager needs to make it clear that no program is finished until the documentation has been completed. The manager, among others, has a vested interest in standards, for he knows the turnover statistics for programmers: it has been estimated that the average length of service for a programmer is 16 months. The manager can minimize the impact of this rate through insistence upon the effective use of documentation.

The application of standards to the programming activity ensures: the design and development of programs that meet the system's objectives; a minimal impact resulting from personnel changes; and a sound basis for subsequent maintenance, conversions, changes, and modifications.

Elements of a Programming Standard

The principal kinds of items included in the programming standard are:
1. The Program abstract
2. The Program flowchart
3. Coding
4. Program listing
5. Layout information
6. Operating instructions
7. Standardized mnemonics

1. THE PROGRAM ABSTRACT. The program abstract is a detailed description of the processing logic and requirements. The logic segment is concerned with the initialization procedures, decisions, and paths; calculations; editing, subprogram, subroutine and/or module references; breakpoints, and data linkages. Requirements are concerned with identification of the inputs, outputs, storage needs, operating system and languages used, interfaces, and hardware configuration. A program abstract form is illustrated in Figure 4.40.

PROGRAM ABSTRACT	APPLICATION NO.	EFFECTIVE DATE ___/___/___	PAGE ___OF___
PROGRAM NAME			PROGRAM NO.

PROGRAM DESCRIPTION

RELATED PROGRAMS

CONFIGURATION REQUIRED	SPECIAL FEATURES UTILIZED
LANGUAGE (S)	STORAGE REQUIREMENTS (PRI. & AUX.)
INPUT DESCRIPTION	OUTPUT DESCRIPTION

PROGRAMMER	APPROVED BY	APPROVAL DATE

Figure 4.40. Program Abstract Form

2. THE PROGRAM FLOWCHART. The program flowchart is used to specify the logic of a computer process symbolically. Consequently, it represents an essential tool in the design, development, implementation, and maintenance of a program. Carefully prepared flowcharts will help to ensure that the program is meeting its stated objectives; to facilitate desk checking; and to furnish an effective communications medium for data processing personnel.

Each program flowchart is maintained at two levels—macro and micro. The macro-flowcharts indicate the major operations and linkage in a program. The micro-flowcharts define the detailed logic necessary for language coding. (The relationship between the two forms is illustrated in Figure 4.18.)

There are sometimes difficulties regarding the level of detail on a micro-flowchart. Many programmers tend to be general in some parts of the flowchart and detailed in others. Such lack of uniformity can cause problems in planning, testing, implementation, and maintenance. Some organizations require several generations of micro-flowchart development. At each descending level in the series, detail is added to provide amplification and clarity. This process continues until the flowchart reaches an appropriate level at which program coding can begin. Whatever the level, it is essential that the degree of detail remains consistent throughout the flowchart.

Many programmers object to detailing their program logic. They prefer a summary-type flowchart, which often is a hybrid of macro and micro principles. However, the value of the summary approach is highly questionable. For example, programmers in the process of designing a payroll program are notorious for gathering all of the federal, state and/ or social security tax calculations into one process symbol labeled as "calculate taxes." This requires amplification because no provision is made for determination of such decision factors as dependents, statutory limitations, taxable earnings, and taxes. The summary approach requires the use of reference data to be found elsewhere in the documentation or included in annotation symbols on the flowchart.

Some programmers prefer to utilize such techniques as decision tables, and program logic narratives. The decision tables (see Figure 4.41) represent an excellent problem-solving technique and, in some instances, they are more concise than program flowcharts in defining program logic. These tables do not enjoy universal usage because some controversy still prevails about their proper usage and application. Also

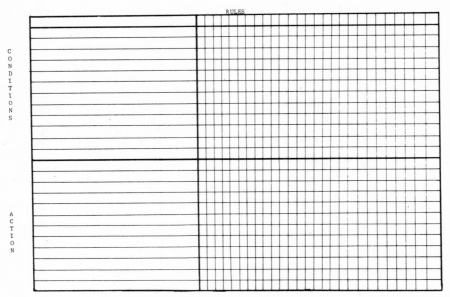

Figure 4.41. Decision Table Form

many programmers find the graphic display of a flowchart more meaningful than a tabular description of the logic.

In some organizations, there is preference toward utilization of one of the types of program logic narrative forms. The program logic narrative form illustrated in Figure 4.42 is a detailed expansion of a program abstract. The programmer writes a concise description of each labeled routine in the program. This generally is an after-the-fact activity that results from copying the comments on the coding sheets or program listing. However, to reach this point, most programmers must use some type of crude or sophisticated logic planning technique. Very few persons are able to plan effectively as they write the language code. To offset these inherent problems, some organizations require that the programmers initially prepare flowcharts and subsequently indicate all modifications and updates on the logic narrative. However, the cross-referencing required when performing program maintenance or modifications raises some question about the effectiveness of this approach.

To provide both a planning and documentation tool, some organizations utilize the type of logic narrative form illustrated in Figure 4.43. Each step in the narrative is equivalent to one or several programming instructions required to accomplish a task. The next sequential step

Program Logic Narrative — Page ______ of ________
Application Number ______ — Date ________________

MAINLINE ROUTINE:

This routine reads the Master Group Life Insurance File and the transactions (Insurance Authorization Cards, Payroll Change Cards, and Cancellation Cards). These are compared by employee number. On a low comparison, due to a new authorization, a branch is made to AUTHINS. When employee numbers are equal, a code check is made. The code 7 cancellation causes a branch to the CANCINS routine. The change cards cause a branch to UPDATE. A high condition on the reading of a transaction card will cause a branch to WRITETAP.

AUTHINS:

This routine creates a new insurance record for writing on tape. It also calculates the annual insurance premium and punches a deduction authorization card for payroll purposes. A branch is back to the Mainline Routine.

CANCINS:

This routine is used to delete a record from the Master Life Insurance File. The record is written on the Inactive Master Insurance File. Also, a deduction cancellation card is punched for the payroll program. A branch is back to the Mainline Routine.

UPDATE:

This routine is used to generate changes to the Master Life Insurance File for an existing record. If a change affects the rate, the annual premium will be recalculated and a new payroll deduction card is punched. A branch is back to the Mainline Routine.

WRITETAP:

This routine copies the Master Group Life Insurance tape. A branch is back to the Mainline Routine.

Figure 4.42 Program Logic Narrative Form: Example A

PROGRAM LOGIC NARRATIVE	PAGE of
APPLICATION NUMBER:	DATE:

STEP NO.	NARRATIVE	GO TO STEP NUMBER IF CONDITION EXISTS				
		+ HI	0 EQ	– LO	UN- COND.	OTHER
1.	Read the YTD tax and earnings record; store the YTD gross, YTD FICA, YTD gross taxable for FICA, YTD FIT, for calculation and output; store name, employee number, and department for output.					
2.	Read and store the current earnings records.					
3.	Multiply hours X rate and half-adjust cents to arrive at current gross.					
4.	Multiply the number of tax exemptions X 13 to arrive at exemption amount.					
5.	Add current gross to the year-to-date gross to develop a new year-to-date gross; add the current gross taxable for FICA to the year-to-date gross taxable for FICA to develop a new year-to-date taxable for FICA.					
6.	Compare the year-to-date taxable for FICA to legal limit; if legal limit is less than the YTD figure, go to step indicated; otherwise calculate the FICA tax amount.			9		
7.	Multiply the current gross taxable for FICA by the current FICA tax rate and half-adjust the cents to arrive at the FICA tax amount.					
8.	Add the FICA tax amount to the YTD FICA; add the gross taxable for FICA to the YTD gross taxable for FICA.					
9	Subtract the exemption amount from the current gross to arrive at the taxable income for FIT. If gross is less than available gross or equal to, go to steps indicated; otherwise calculate FIT.		11	11		

Figure 4.43. Program Logic Narrative Form: Example B

based upon conditional and unconditional branches may also be indicated. A basic disadvantage to this form is the step numbering. For complex problems, the user must write up each modular group of tasks separately and assign a temporary consecutive number to them or use a page-step reference number. Reference numbering changes will occur during the planning, development, and testing process.

As in the case of program flowcharts, the logic narratives must also be revised and their steps renumbered. Some people may consider this simpler than re-drawing the symbol outlines on a program flowchart. However, through careful planning and judicious use of space on the flowcharts, re-drawing or inclusion of steps is only a minor problem.

In the preparation of macro- and micro-flowcharts, there are certain conventions that should be followed. These are:

—The flow of direction must go from top to bottom and from left to right in a logical sequence

—Each micro-step within a macro-block may be assigned a two-digit consecutive number from 01 to 99 to provide a cross-reference between the two diagrams

—The step identification number should appear outside of the symbol block, to the right of the flowline bisector

—The annotation symbol should be used to add clarifying notes to the steps whenever necessary; formulae and any other specialized notes should be written in an annotation block

—A connector symbol must be used to identify the first step on a page and to indicate a flow of continuity; the symbol termed as an inconnector should contain the page number, macro-block and micro-step identification of the last step in the logical flow

—A connector symbol must also be used to identify the flow of continuity from the last symbol on a page; this symbol is termed as the outconnector and contains the page number, macro-block, and micro-step identification of the next step in the logical flow

—A connector symbol must be used from the exit block in order to identify the connectivity between two points on the diagram; the connector should reference the macro-block letter and micro-step number of the entry block

—Multiple flowlines should be connected to one entry flowline per symbol in order to provide clarity

—All exits from a decision symbol must be properly identified

All program flowcharts must be properly updated to reflect all

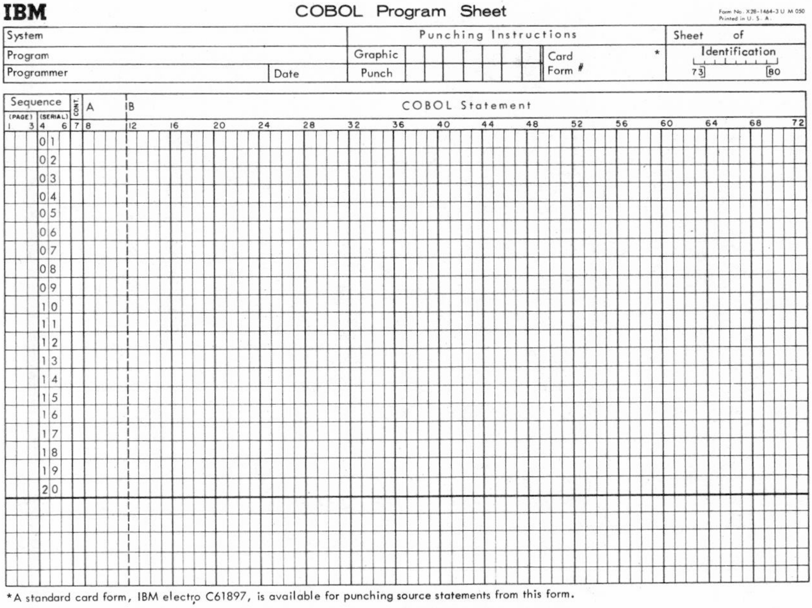

Figure 4.44. COBOL Coding Sheet

changes. Failure to do so reduces the value of the documentation for subsequent maintenance, audit, and modification of the program.

3. CODING. Each programming language has its own type of coding sheet (see Figure 4.44). These sheets may be provided by the vendor or reproduced from a sample and modified to facilitate documentation needs. The coding sheets should carry the name and number of the program, effective date, name of programmer, and page control.

To provide for uniformity in the coding process, a standard should be developed. Such a standard is more effective when applied to a symbolic language than to the absolute or report program generator types. This is because symbolic languages offer greater flexibility in organizing the coding, mnemonics, comments, halts, and work areas.

A coding standard may be organized according to the following classifications:

   a) Coding organization
   b) Comments
   c) Mnemonics
   d) Halts/Interrupts
   a) Coding Organization. In order to reduce or eliminate omissions,

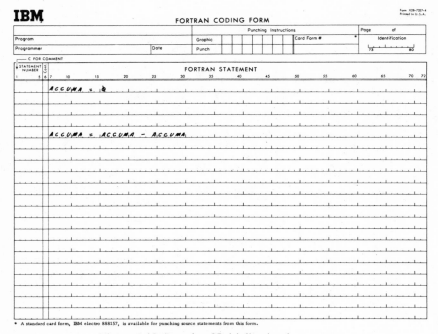

Figure 4.45. Sample of Initialization in FORTRAN

oversights, and inconsistencies that may occur in the coding process, instructions and declaratives should be grouped according to function. This will require that the programmer or coder work with several different coding sheets; however, the entries are made to each respective form as they occur. For example, a programmer working on a COBOL language program would have separate coding sheets for each of the divisions and sections. If he were coding an entry in the procedure division that required the use of an accumulator, a corresponding entry would be made immediately in the working-storage section. This helps to eliminate or reduce such errors as misspelled labels, omissions, or incorrect field length specifications.

A logical sequence for organization of a program would be in the area of: input/output Specifications and Housekeeping/Initialization.

Input/Output Specifications. Before any detailed programming can begin, the input/output specifications must be made known; therefore, these should be coded initially. Also, the necessary operating system requirements should be coded at this time.

Housekeeping/Initialization. It is very dangerous to assume that the

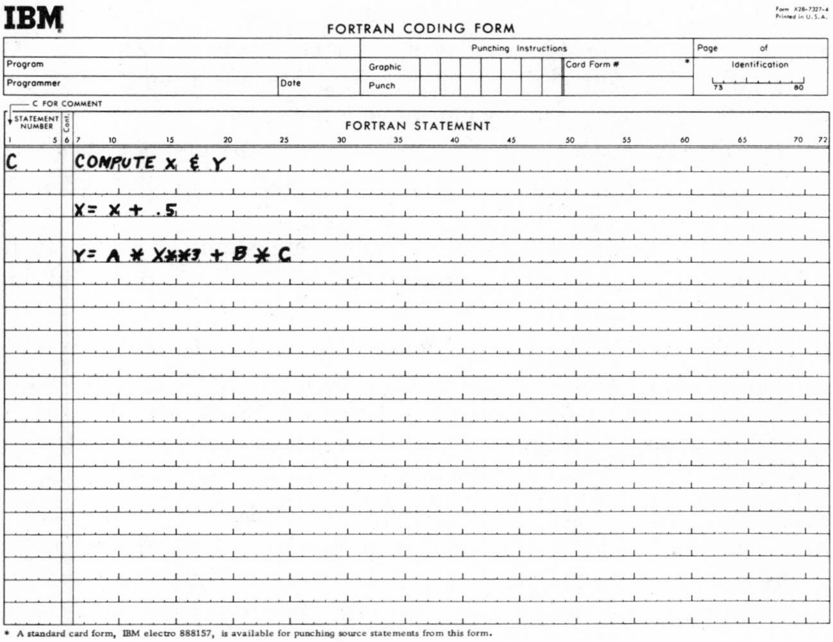

IBM FORTRAN CODING FORM

Form X28-7327-4 Printed in U.S.A.

Program		Punching Instructions		Page of
Programmer	Date	Graphic / Punch	Card Form #	Identification 73 80

C FOR COMMENT

STATEMENT NUMBER	Cont.	FORTRAN STATEMENT
C		COMPUTE X & Y
		X= X + .5
		Y= A * X**3 + B * C

* A standard card form, IBM electro 888157, is available for punching source statements from this form.

Figure 4.46. Example of Comments in FORTRAN

primary memory unit has been reset to a neutral state (blanks or zeros) at the beginning of any program. A programmer must initialize a program by clearing the necessary memory areas to eliminate the presence of any unwanted data that could result in faulty output. In the FORTRAN language, a programmer may perform some housekeeping either by simply initializing an area with a zero value or by subtracting an area from itself, as illustrated in Figure 4.45.

b) *Comments.* Comments are used for identification or clarification of steps, subroutines, and subprograms, as well as for further facilitation of the understanding and documentation of a program. They may appear as a separate line, paragraph, or part of an instruction or declarative statement. The comments do not increase the memory size requirements of a program.

Programming personnel should be encouraged to use comments liberally in a program. The use of comments is illustrated in figures 4.46, 4.47, 4.48, and 4.49. For example, in Figure 4.46, it can be seen that a separate comment statement may be used in the FORTRAN language to identify the action of the succeeding instructions. A paragraph comment as it may appear in a Basic Assembler Language (BAL) program is illustrated in Figure 4.47. Inclusion of a comment as part of a BAL instruction statement is illustrated in Figure 4.48. Identifying a constant area with a comment in BAL is illustrated in Figure 4.49.

c) *Mnemonics.* Occasionally one finds that a programmer has used the names of women, foreign countries, cities, towns, or animals as labels. It can be very difficult to associate any of these with a particular function. That is why it is essential that the mnemonic labels be meaningful to all programming personnel, not just to the author of the program.

The format of an effective labeling method depends on the syntax specifications of the programming language used. One such approach is to utilize an alphabetic prefix of at least two characters with an appended number. The prefix is an acronym constructed by using the first letter of each key word. For example, the letters "EP" can be used to establish an edit word label for printer output. The "E" represents the term edit word and the "P" stands for printer output. By appending the digits 01 to the "EP," the user is able to identify this as the first edit word used in printer output in a given program. A card input area could be designated as "IC."

For field names, it is recommended that a standardized glossary of mnemonics (as illustrated in Figure 4.39) be developed and maintained.

d) *Halts/Interrupts.* The assignment of alphameric codes to halts/ interrupts is much more relevant than is the use of such labels as STOP or END 01. To facilitate the numbering and understanding of halts or interrupts, a scheme should be developed that readily identifies them by type of error or conditions, as illustrated in Figure 4.50.

The standard operations should be grouped and assigned a code. The number code and a brief explanation appear in the console operating instructions. However, an operator reacts more quickly to a halt or interrupt during processing if he is able to identify the condition by number association.

4. PROGRAM LISTING. Listing the currently operational programs is an essential part of the documentation process. A manager must not permit his programming personnel to update an existing program listing simply with pen and/or pencil alterations. This alteration method, erroneously considered to be a time- and labor-saving device, can cause some severe problems for an organization. What happens is that programmers frequently mark up a listing while they are testing, performing

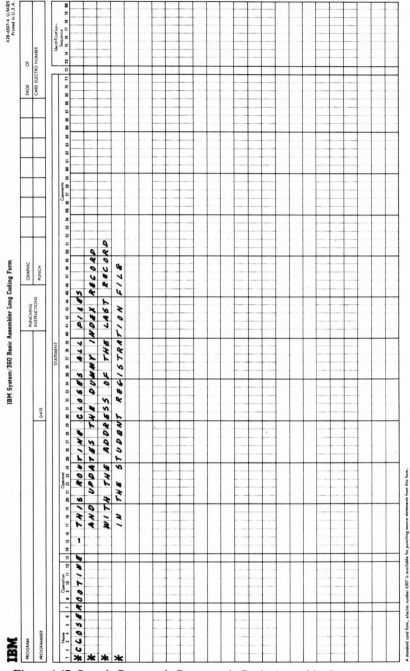

Figure 4.47. Sample Paragraph Comment in Basic Assembler Language (BAL)

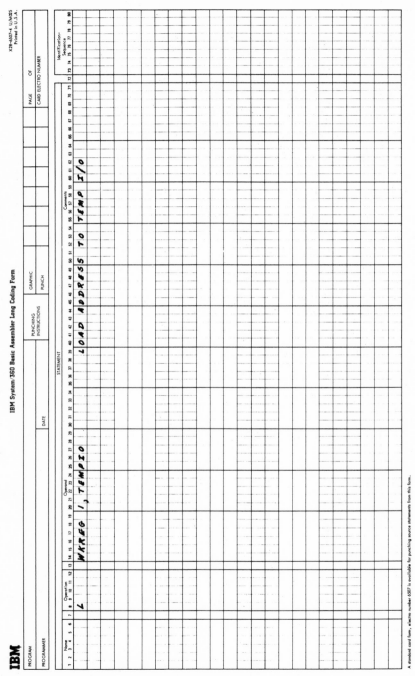

Figure 4.48. Example of Comment Included as Part of BAL Instruction Statement

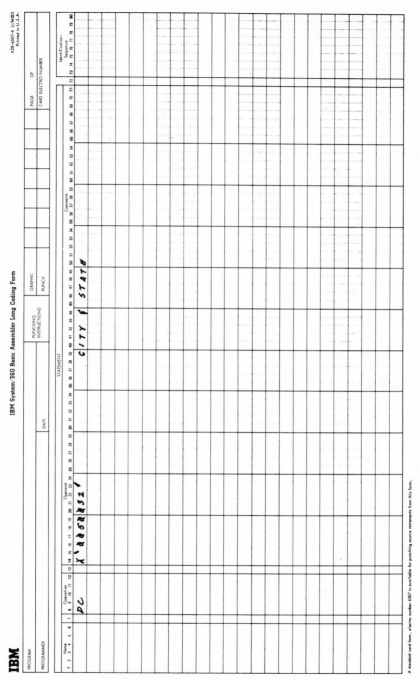

Figure 4.49. Sample Identification of Constants in BAL

Error or Condition	Range
Input Errors	001–099
Sequence Errors	100–199
Control Check Errors	200–299
Tape Read Errors	300–399
Tape Write Errors	400–499
Tape/Disk Label Errors	500–599
Disk Read Errors	600–699
Disk Write Errors	700–799
Operand Data Errors	800-899

Figure 4.50   Suggested Halt/Interrupt Numbering Scheme

maintenance, or implementing modifications. Subsequently, they are so busy that they can and do easily forget to delete these markings, which then, through neglect, become part of the listing. The subsequent use of the listing may well lead the user into making some false assumptions.

Each program listing should be identified with the name of the application or system, program name and number, programmer's name, and the effective date. The listings should be filed in the sequence of operations.

Whenever macros, subroutines, and/or subprograms are used in a program, they must be thoroughly documented in order to provide the following items of information:

—The assigned mnemonic used for program linkage

—A brief description of the purpose

—A listing of the entry and exit parameters

—A halt/interrupt listing, if applicable

—A listing of any restrictions or limitations

—The name of the programmer who developed and tested the macro, subroutine, or subprogram, as well as its effective date

—A listing of any console messages and required responses

—Operator's setup instruction, if applicable

A sample of documentation for a subroutine is illustrated in Figure 4.36.

5. LAYOUT INFORMATION. The program documentation should include the following layout data:

a) Card input/output

b) Printer output
c) Optical scanning and/or MICR document input/output
d) Magnetic and/or paper tape input and output
e) Random access layouts
f) Primary and auxiliary memory layouts
g) Console typewriter/keyboard input and output
h) Visual displays
i) Data base specifications

   a) *Card Input/Output.* The programmer is generally provided with the punched card input/output requirements on a multiple-card layout form (see Figure 4.20). The form does not generally indicate the field content and makes no provision for specification of mnemonics. The record format form (see Figure 4.21) provides additional data to assist the programmer in the initial design and development, and the subsequent maintenance or modification, of a program. The file specification form (see Figure 4.27) furnishes relevant data for preparation of job control and file descriptor entries in a program.

   b) *Printer Output.* A printer spacing chart (see Figure 4.22) indicating the required user format may be provided for the programmer by the systems group. On some occasions, the programmer is given an actual copy, design layout, or sketch of the form. Some organizations provide the programmer with a copy of an output record format form (see Figure 4.21). Submitting a printer spacing chart or an output record format is more desirable for planning and documentation purposes. The spacing chart provides the capability for specifying nonstandard carriage control tape or loop punching.

   To increase documentation value, the programmer may include parenthetically the program mnemonics for the various fields, as illustrated in Figure 4.22. Though the record format form provides for field spacing and mnemonics, most programmers prefer to include a spacing chart with their documentation. The chart affords a quick visual reference to the printer output record.

   c) *Optical Scanning and/or MICR Document Input/Output.* The effectiveness of optical scanning and magnetic ink character recognition systems depends greatly on the reliability of image decoding and translation. The information to be scanned or read must be imprinted in the proper data field, within prescribed tolerances for character or mark location and line spacing. The form layout itself must be compatible with the imprinter and the scanner or reader.

In addition, the programmer must be concerned with the detection and identification of errors that may arise in the conversion or transmission process. Quality-control requirements for data may necessitate the writing of a separate input audit program (see Chapter 7).

A replication of the planning charts (see figures 4.24 and 4.25) and form samples should be included in the documentation.

d) Magnetic and/or Paper Tape Input and Output. The layouts (see Figure 4.26) for these media may be provided by the systems group or developed by the programming staff. An organization may choose to utilize the record format and file specification forms (see Figures 4.21 and 4.27) in lieu of a card or tape layout form (see Figures 4.20 and 4.26). The record format and file specification forms provide documentation data not readily available on the card or tape layout forms. However, it is possible to modify a layout form to include additional documentation data, as illustrated in Figure 4.51.

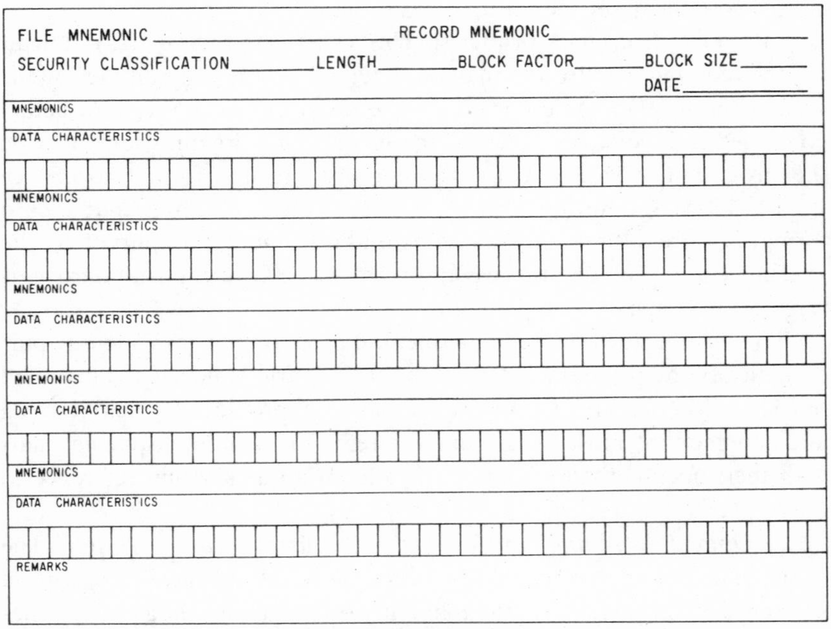
FILE MNEMONIC ______ RECORD MNEMONIC ______
SECURITY CLASSIFICATION ______ LENGTH ______ BLOCK FACTOR ______ BLOCK SIZE ______
DATE ______
MNEMONICS
DATA CHARACTERISTICS
MNEMONICS
DATA CHARACTERISTICS
MNEMONICS
DATA CHARACTERISTICS
MNEMONICS
DATA CHARACTERISTICS
MNEMONICS
DATA CHARACTERISTICS
REMARKS

Figure 4.51. Modified Tape Layout Form

e) Random Access Layouts. The formats of the data stored on random access devices, such as disk, drum, or data cell, may be represented on a record layout worksheet (see Figure 4.28). This information may be supplied to the programmer or it may have to be developed by him during the program design phase.

An organization may choose to utilize both the file specification and record format forms for documentation. These provide data not readily available on the record layout worksheet and simplify the copy reproduction process. Some organizations have chosen to modify the documentation format similar to the form in Figure 4.51.

The documentation should reflect only the information on the device that is relevant to the respective program.

f) Primary and Auxiliary Memory Layouts. Where program logic requires the specific allocation of the primary and/or auxiliary memory units, the format and storage requirements must be documented. The allocations and requirements may be illustrated on a record layout worksheet.

An organization may choose to utilize a record format form for documentation purposes. The form is particularly useful for describing table data.

g) Console Typewriter/Keyboard Input and Output. This segment provides information on query responses and requirements, operational program commands, and error messages. Most of this information is generated by the programmer in the design and development of a program. It is documented on a console instruction sheet (see Figure 4.29) to guide a user and/or console operator.

With the increasing use of time-sharing terminals, a programmer may find it necessary to prepare less technically oriented instruction sheets for user personnel.

h) Visual Displays. The required display formats (see Figure 4.30) may be either provided for the programmer by the systems group or generated as a result of program design. In addition to furnishing a replication of the display, the programmer must prepare user documentation for operation of the device. A sample segment of such information is illustrated in Figure 4.52.

i) Data Base Specifications. This segment of the documentation identifies the necessary data base requirements for executing a given program. It describes the file organizations/structures, contents, linkages, interfaces, and any tables that are part of the data base. The documentation appears on a record layout worksheet (see Figure 4.28) or record format form (see Figure 4.21). The latter may prove to be more

User's Instructions for Display Devices

The following list represents the messages which may appear on the screen and the effective response required for each message.

N.B. Whenever the action "depress the SHIFT and ENTER" keys is directed, depress and hold the SHIFT key, then depress the ENTER key.

List Number	Message Displayed	Response Required
1	"TO START, PRESS THE SHIFT AND ENTER KEYS"	Depress the SHIFT and ENTER keys.
2	"ENTER 3 POSITION DATE"	First, enter one of the appropriate numeric or alphabetic codes listed below: 1—January 2—February 3—March 4—April 5—May 6—June 7—July 8—August 9—September 0—(Numeric) October A—November B—December Then, next to the one position month code, enter two numeric digits for the activity date. Dates 1–9 require a preceding zero.

3   "ENTER SOC. SEC. NO."   Enter the social security number from the New Employee form (Form B-2). When entering the social security number, *do not* separate the digits by dashes, blanks, or special characters.

If no social security number is shown on the form, enter the employee identification number. When entering this data you must precede the employee number with four zeros. The completed entry must be comprised of 9 digits.

Depress SHIFT and ENTER keys.

Figure 4.52   Sample Portion of User Instructions for Displays

advantageous because the data base is generally a series of files. In either case, a catalog should be established to identify the types of records, their groupings, and dependencies.

The documentation should also specify the required programming language interfaces for each file. In addition, information should be included on back-up and restoration capability for each file. This knowledge is particularly important in the development of critical or real-time systems. Restart and recovery procedures affecting any of the files in the data base should also be included.

The programmer must be concerned with the control and integrity of each file or element in the base. Therefore, it is essential that this segment includes information about data entry, availability, retrieval, and controls such as validation, admissibility, and security.

6. OPERATING INSTRUCTIONS. The programming group is responsible for the development of operating instructions relating to computer operations. These operating instructions may be subdefined as follows:

a) Setup instructions
b) Instructive output
c) Alternate mode

a) Setup Instructions. The programming staff must identify the parameters and control characteristics required for operation of a program, the effective operating sequence of the programs, the related storage devices, and the ready and teardown instructions for the hardware. The setup instructions are generally specified on an equipment setup form (see Figure 4.34). The parameter and/or control card information may be indicated on a form like the one illustrated in Figure 4.53.

PARAMETER CARD FORMAT

99999999999999999999999999999999999999999999999999999999999999999999999999999999
1 2 3 4 5 6 7 8 9 10 11 12 13 14 15 16 17 18 19 20 21 22 23 24 25 26 27 28 29 30 31 32 33 34 35 36 37 38 39 40 41 42 43 44 45 46 47 48 49 50 51 52 53 54 55 56 57 58 59 60 61 62 63 64 65 66 67 68 69 70 71 72 73 74 75 76 77 78 79 80

APPLICATION NAME		APPLICATION NUMBER	EFFECTIVE DATE / /
COLUMNS		DATA DESCRIPTION	

Figure 4.53. Sample Format for Parameter Card

b) Instructive Output. This segment contains primarily the error messages and comments emitted by the software, together with checkpoint, recovery, and/or restart instructions. The error messages and comments are documented on a console instruction sheet (see Figure

---

Checkpoint–Restart–Recovery
Procedures

1. Describe the procedures to checkpoint and restart the operation. (If none, indicate unavailability.)
2. Describe the necessary steps required to restart from an unscheduled termination. (If none, indicate unavailability.)
3. Indicate the required job control language to effect action. Identify each procedure by its assigned name. (If none, indicate unavailability.)

Figure 4.54   Format for Checkpoint, Restart, and/or Recovery Procedures

4.29). Checkpoint, recovery, and/or restart procedures may appear in the format illustrated in Figure 4.54.

c) Alternate Mode. The alternate-mode procedures are included only for critical operations. For security reasons, these may not be included in the program specifications manual. Nevertheless, their availability must be noted in the manual.

7. STANDARDIZED MNEMONICS. The standardization of program mnemonics should be accomplished by the programming group. This process should be linked with the standardization of languages. For example, COBOL can be used for business applications; FORTRAN can be used in scientific and technical applications. This reduces the proliferation of languages and simplifies the standardization of activities and documentation.

The construction of the mnemonics is contingent upon the type of programming language and version level available, as well as the type of organization. Working within the syntactical parameters, an organization should develop a meaningful glossary of mnemonics (see Figure 4.39).

The process of maintaining the glossary is not a static one. New terms must be added to the glossary as they are developed. Also, terms no longer relevant must be purged annually from the glossary.

Review Questions: Group 4C

1. Why should a manager advocate the inclusion of a program abstract in the program documentation?

2. What are some of the dangers in permitting pen and/or pencil alterations to program listings?

3. What is the effect of visual displays on a programmer's documentation?

Standard for Users and Operators

The elements contained in this standard are the result of efforts
expended by the systems and programming personnel. The information
is a replication of the relevant forms, charts, listings, etc., from the
system description manual and the program specifications manual.

This standard may be divided into two major parts. They are: the
user's manual and the operator's manual.

1. THE USER'S MANUAL. The user's manual provides the clerical and
control procedures for the user, as well as for the data processing
personnel. The procedures detail the sequence of steps for the preparation of all documents, of the input and output controls, and of a description of the operational flow through the affected departments. The
procedures have to be written clearly and concisely, specifying *who* does
what and *when.*

The user's manual generally includes the following segments:

a) The system flowchart
b) The system abstract
c) Job preparation procedures
d) Glossary
e) Input specifications
f) Output specifications
g) Data base specifications
h) File update procedures

a) *The System Flowchart.* The system flowchart (see Figure 4.55) is
included in the user's manual to describe the general system logic and its
capabilities. It is a copy of the chart included in the system description
manual.

b) *System Abstract.* A copy of the system abstract (see Figures 4.12
and 4.13) is also included in the user's manual. From the abstract, the
user can readily determine the application's characteristics, requirements, and limitations.

c) *Job Preparation Procedures.* Job procedures are an important

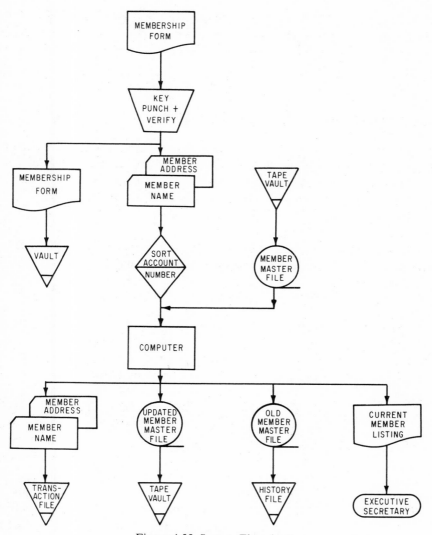

Figure 4.55. System Flowchart

part of the user's manual. They describe input preparation and submission, interrelationships between data elements, priority designations, clerical processing, description of data elements, authorizations required, accuracy and procedural controls, coding structures, and distribution patterns by functional title. For example, a transcription stamp such as the one illustrated in Figure 4.56 may be included in this segment. Other

KEYPUNCH	INVOICE SECTION		BUYER APPROVAL	
REGISTER NO.	DATE RECEIVED		PRICE	
SUPPLIER CODE	TERMS		TERMS	
DUE DATE	F.O.B.	DEST.	F.O.B. POINT	
TAXABLE AMT.	COMM. CODE	INVOICE CLERK	GOVT. CODE	J.E. CODE
NET VALUE	ACCTG. CLASS		STD. COST PER C	

Figure 4.56. Sample Transcription Stamp

types of forms involved in this segment are shown in Figures 4.31, 4.32, and 4.33.

d) Glossary. Inclusion of a glossary defining the terms, acronyms, mnemonics, and abbreviations utilized in the application helps to ease the communications problems. The relevant terms for the glossary in the user's manual are extracted from the glossaries contained in the system description manual and the program specification manual.

e) Input Specifications. This segment defines the input sources, purpose and functions served, contents, element descriptions, references required, editing instructions, samples, and document identification. This material is a copy of the file specifications, record format forms, samples, and layouts that are given in the system description manual.

f) Output Specifications. The output specifications include the medium and mode, element descriptions, formats, query responses and requirements, validity checks, and samples. This material is a replication of that contained in the system description manual.

g) Data Base Specifications. The data base segment describes each file in the application—its purpose, use, content, and data element descriptions. This information is taken from the system description manual and the program specifications manual.

h) File Update Procedures. The file update segment provides a complete description of all expected inputs to be entered or processed against the existing files. It identifies the inputs, formats, sources, and volumes, and the retention, frequency, and error correction procedures affecting the updating process.

2. THE OPERATOR'S MANUAL. The operator's manual contains the detailed information required by the operator to maintain operational effectiveness. The manual defines the equipment configuration, instructions for setup and teardown, recovery and restart procedures, all error messages, responses, and correction procedures.

The operator's manual is a replication of various sections of the program specifications manual and/or system description manual. It should include the following segments: (*a*) setup instructions and (*b*) instructive output.

a) Setup Instructions. Setup instructions specify the hardware devices utilized, the operational order of programs, parameter or job control entries, and input and output requirements. For unit-record operations, this segment is concerned with the control panels utilized, sequence of operations, control card entries, machine switch settings, and input and output requirements. An extract from a sample of such instructions is illustrated in Figure 4.57.

b) Instructive Output. Instructive output contains information on the special instructions and signals emitted by the software and/or hardware during processing. For computerized applications, the operator is furnished with programmed error messages; processing diagnostics; instructions for checkpoint, recovery, and restarts; and query responses and requirements. An excerpt from this segment is illustrated in Figure 4.58.

For unit-record operations, the signals and messages primarily result from machine functions or operations controlled by a wired panel. Additional discrepancy information results from a series of validity, admissibility, and edit checks (see Chapter 7).

The relevant instructive output for a system is generally listed on specially designed forms applicable to the hardware configuration and type of operation.

Review Questions: Group 4D

1. What type of information should be contained in a user's manual?
2. What is the purpose of instructive output in an operator's manual?

List and Summarize

A. List the merged stock balance and transaction cards, using three-part paper, according to Format #3, Appendix A, RS424, Run 1, "Transaction Activity Register." In the process, punch a new stock balance card for each item on Form 109.

1. Process each Plant (Card Column 76) and each Condition (Card Column 28) separately.
2. Wire the 407 control panel to emit and punch date as follows:
   Month—Card Column 77 (1–9 for JAN.–SEP.; ZERO for
   OCT.; J for NOV.; and K for DEC.)
   Day   —Card Columns 78–79
   Year —Card Column 80 (last digit)
3. All Alteration Switches OFF, unless otherwise directed. The switches are wired as follows:
   a. Switch #1—*ON*—turns list off, sets direct entry for accumulators, eliminates control on Class and Part Number (Card Columns 1–19)
   b. Switch #2—*ON*—turns off summary punch switch
   c. Switch #3—*ON*—sets up for Minor Control on Class (Card Columns 1–4)
   d. Switch #4—*ON*—eliminates punching of Description in summary card (Card Columns 20–28)
   e. *All* Switches—*OFF*—causes carriage ejection on a change in the first two positions of Class (Card Columns 1 and 2)
4. Test the Machine and Operation using Master Test Card Set #9 and Summary Card Set #4.
   a. Check printer test output to Master Test Sheet, Format #3 in Appendix B.
   b. Verify the summary card punching by comparing punched card output with Summary Card Set #4.

Figure 4.57 Example of Unit-Record Operations in Setup Instructions

PROGRAMMED HALT AND RESTART PROCEDURES	
APPLICATION NO:	**EFFECTIVE DATE:**
HALT CODE	**REASON — RESTART PROCEDURE**
1111	NO DATE HEADER CARD READ — Keypunch a new date header card. Clear card reader, place date card in front of first input card, and depress start key.
1112	CARDS OUT OF SEQUENCE ON BADGE NUMBER — Clear reader, correct sequence of cards, and depress start key.
1113	WRONG MASTER TAPE ON DRIVE #1 — Remove tape from drive and secure correct master tape from tape librarian. Clear card input, reload, and depress start key.
1114	END OF JOB.

Figure 4.58. Example of Programmed Halt and Restart Procedures in Instructive Output

DOCUMENTATION CONTROL AND RECORD MANAGEMENT

Control of Documentation

To realize the benefits of documentation, the executive committee must develop a control standard. The control is necessary to ensure the accuracy, completeness, and efficiency of the documentation. Failure to attain this documentation status will minimize the effectiveness of the resources employed in the management process.

The effective control of documentation is contingent upon the following:

1. Security
2. Content
3. Identification
4. Communication of Revisions

1. SECURITY. The documentation must be maintained in a fire-resistant vault or cabinet outside of the data processing function. Access should be limited to the systems manager and his assistant. Whenever documentation is withdrawn from the file cabinet or vault, a strict sign-out control must be maintained in order to deny access to unauthorized personnel and to prevent possible loss, destruction, or accidental or deliberate alteration of the material.

The organization should give serious consideration to the feasibility of maintaining an off-premises facility for safeguarding and storing the documentation. (Additional information on the control of documentation is given in Chapter 7, under the subject of peripheral controls.)

2. CONTENT. The documentation must contain the complete informational record on any system, application, or program that is currently operational. Because of its vital effect on the operation of a data processing activity, the documentation should be audited at least once each year by the internal or external audit staff. The audit should be concerned with verifying the accuracy, relevancy, and completeness of the documentation. (Additional information on audits is given in Chapter 7.)

The level of completeness is affected by the contents of the documentation. Therefore, a content standard must be established and maintained. The following stipulations represent the minimum standard necessary to achieve the required completeness:

—All documentation should be maintained in a permanent cover or folder. The maintenance of documentation on a reel of magnetic tape or a disk pack does not negate the need for a hard-copy reference.

—All documentation folders should be clearly identified to simplify location and retrieval. Identification should be on the outside of the folder, preferably on the spine and front of the folder or cover.

—All folders should contain a numeric identification system as part of the label. To facilitate storage and retrieval, the folders should be filed in that sequence.

—Each change or modification to a folder should include a revision page.

—The first page of each documentation folder should be a table of contents, as illustrated in Figure 4.59.

TABLE OF CONTENTS	
Section	Contents
1	System Abstract
2	System Flowchart
3	Program Abstracts
4	Program Flowcharts
5	Program Listings (including Macro, Subroutines, and Subprograms)
6	Layout Information and Samples
7	Operating Instructions
	a. User
	b. Data Processing
8	Glossaries
9	Test Data
	a. Sample Outputs
	b. Test Decks/Data

Figure 4.59 Sample Table of Contents in Documentation Folder

3. IDENTIFICATION. To facilitate the identification, storage, and retrieval of documentation, a numbering system should be developed. The numbering system should be designed primarily to distinguish one system from another. However, the scheme may be expanded to provide additional information about programs within the system.

A suggested basic numbering scheme consists of six digits. It is used to indicate the functional area, processing cycle code, and assigned system number. The number may be expanded to a total of ten digits. The expansion makes provision for data on revisions, operational sequence, and a basic program identification number.

A suggested ten-digit identification scheme is as follows:

$$\underbrace{\underset{a}{XX} \quad \underset{b}{X} \quad \underset{c}{XXX}}_{\text{basic}} \qquad \underbrace{\underset{d}{XX} \quad \underset{e}{X} \quad \underset{f}{X}}_{\text{expanded}}$$

a) Functional area code
b) Processing cycle code
c) Assigned system number
d) Assigned program number
e) Call program identification code
f) Revision code

a) Functional Area Code. The first two digits of the numbering scheme are used to identify the functional area in which the system is operative. This requires a classification grouping of all systems by functional activity. A suggested functional activity classification for a manufacturing type of organization is as follows:

Functional Area	Code No.
Management	00
Payroll	
Hourly	10
Salary	11
Taxes and Earnings	12
Labor Distributions	15
Accounts Payable	20
Accounts Receivable	25
Accounting	
Cost	30
Plant	31

Results	32
Production Control (excluding Bill of Materials and Inventory Control)	35
Bill of Materials and Explosion	40
Inventory Control	45
Purchasing	50
Sales	60
Engineering	65
Personnel	67
Information Retrieval	70
Special Projects	75
Utility and Library	90
Data Processing	99

b) Processing Cycle Code. The third digit indicates the processing frequency. A suggested processing cycle code classification is as follows:

When Processed	Cycle Code
Whenever required	0
Daily	1
Several times per week	2
Weekly	3
Semimonthly	4
Quarterly	6
Semiannually	7
Annually	8
Biennially	9

c) Assigned System Number. The assigned system number is a three-digit control number designated on a consecutive number basis from 001 to 999. The number can be reduced to two digits, although, this does limit the scheme's expansion potential.

d) Assigned Program Number. The assigned program number is a two-digit control number consecutively assigned to the computer programs used in a system. A 00 in these positions of the number scheme indicates that no programs are used.

e) Call Program Identification Code. The ninth digit is used to identify call programs or subprograms linked to a main program. This digit provides the user with the flexibility of specifying a maximum of nine program linkages. The sequence is assigned on the basis of calling order. A zero digit in the position identifies a main program.

f) Revision Code. The tenth digit may be used to indicate the subsequent modifications or revisions to a program. The code may be used to specify a maximum number of nine revisions. A zero digit in the position indicates no revisions to the program.

The functional area code, processing cycle code, and assigned system number should be used as the basic identification on the documentation folder. The relevant segments of the identification number should appear on the various charts and forms included in the documentation. For example, a system abstract would contain only the first six digits of the number; whereas, the program abstract identification would contain the complete ten-digit number.

In addition to providing documentation identification, the scheme may be used for identifying jobs on a production schedule and such input/output media as disk packs and magnetic tapes.

4. COMMUNICATION OF REVISIONS. The distribution of revisions affects all organizational elements that are directly or indirectly involved in the system. Therefore, to ensure a smooth flow of resources, it is necessary for the systems group to communicate the extent of involvement to each affected functional activity by means of conferences and/ or discussions. The revisions should be detailed in a clear and concise manner.

When making a presentation to the user department personnel (including management), the systems personnel must avoid the use of data processing terminology. The jargon tends only to build—or raise higher—a communications barrier.

Communicating the information is particularly important with regard to employees who have been performing their tasks repetitively for such a long period of time that they now perform largely by rote. To avoid confusion, waste, and reruns, it is also necessary to make sure that these persons really do understand the changes.

In addition, the communications process indicates if any additional orientation and/or training of personnel is necessary. And it also indicates whether the documentation is adequate, the stated goals have been met, and any problems remain to be resolved.

Record Management

The use of data processing systems requires the collection, storage, and retrieval of large amounts of data. This requirement has inevitably generated some problems for the data processing operations manager. He is the one involved because it is the operations group that is primarily responsible for retaining the machine-sensible input and transactions used in production of the various reports and output. This necessitates adequate storage space, equipment, management controls, and proper humidity and temperature controls.

To fulfill his delegated responsibility, the operations manager must undertake four specific tasks: classify the data, develop a retention cycle schedule, provide adequate safeguards, and determine a feasible means of storage and reproduction.

The data may be classified as essential, important, beneficial, or nonessential. Data which is irreplacable and/or essential for the continuity of operation should be placed into the essential category. Records that are valuable but reproducible without too much delay should be classed as important. Records useful to an operation but whose loss may cause only a temporary inconvenience would be classified as beneficial. Records that no longer are necessary to an operation go into the nonessential category. The choice of records to be placed in each of these categories varies according to the type of organization performing the classification and the organizational objectives.

The retention cycle schedule for each record is dependent upon such factors as legal requirements, organizational objectives, cost of replication, cost of delayed processing, available hardware and software, and the sophistication of operational systems. Legal requirements rank as one of the primary considerations in the development of the retention cycle schedule.

The safeguards to be provided are primarily affected by the record classifications and the cost of delayed processing. For example, records included in the essential and important categories should be afforded a fire-resistant protective capability of not less than two hours. The best protection, however, is duplication of records and storage of the replicated materials in a separate building. Consideration must also be given to the maintenance of proper temperature and humidity controls. These are necessary to ensure that the records are maintained in usable condition and to avoid possible combustion of materials.

Determining a feasible means of storage and reconstruction requirements is a complex process. The manager must determine how to convert the data in order to reduce the storage space requirements. His decision has to take into consideration the form and format of future requirements. For example, a decision to summarize detail card data to reduce the volume may not be feasible if detail transactions are required for some subsequent applications.

To facilitate records management, the operations manager must establish a file retention standard. The proper application of such a file retention standard will also help to maintain usable materials and to control storage costs. This standard should be developed on the basis of the following:

—A realistic retention period must be established for each document or media. It must be set only after conferring with the affected user, audit, and data processing personnel in order to determine useful record life.

—All stored materials must be properly identified with an external label. The label should specify the system or application name and number, form name and number, retention date, the transaction period represented (month, day, week, year), a period identification (for example: April, or 5/12/72), and the quantity count (for example: Box 1 of 10, or Reel 1 of 5).

—The retention cycle for each document or media must be specified in a file retention standards manual.

—A periodic purge date must be established so that, at a predetermined time, unnecessary materials are removed from the storage area for destruction, scrap, or storage in another area.

Review Questions: Group 4E

1. What are some of the inherent dangers in failing to adequately safeguard the existing documentation?
2. What information can be determined from a processing cycle code that is included in a documentation numbering scheme?
3. Name and briefly describe the data classifications that can be utilized in a record management scheme?

4. What considerations must be made before assigning a retention value to a document?

SUMMARY

Developing effective standards and documentation is a very important part of the management process. They are necessary in the successful execution of the pre-executory and executory phases. Standards and documentation are essential for the determination and maintainance of the overall effectiveness of an operation or organization.

The standards discussed in this chapter are the guides, policies, practices and procedures that must be followed in any organization to ensure compliance with management decisions. These help to maintain a smooth flow of productive resources in accordance with the plan established by the upper echelon. The documentation provides a formal record of the upper echelon's operating decisions.

Standards and documentation have become a communications medium for managers, auditors, users, and data processing personnel. For the manager, this means having a vehicle for defining his specific needs. For the data processor, it means having to design, develop, and implement more relevant and meaningful systems, applications, or programs. For the auditor, it means having the mechanism for ensuring compliance. For the user, it means being given the necessary materials to actuate an operationally effective process.

Each organization must realistically determine how much documentation and standardization is adequate and how best to maintain an effective level. The issues must not be clouded over by the cries of the alarmists who speak of high costs, disruption in employee morale, loss of creativity and efficiency. A quick cost-determination may be made by evaluating the impact of personnel changes and loss of services. How much does it cost to train a new employee? Or, what is the cost in delayed processing to an organization?

CASE STUDIES

Case Study 4.1: The Sevierville Electric Company

The Sevierville Electric Company is a large electric utility serving approximately one million customers in a medium-sized metropolitan area. The company is equipped with second-generation computing and some unit-record equipment. The primary data processing application is calculation of electric- and steam-power utilization and customer billing on a cycle basis. Meter installation and maintenance is also a major application, this being primarily a file update type of processing that occurs almost daily. The next major user is the payroll department; it utilizes the equipment for processing of six different payrolls—hourly, weekly, semimonthly, executive, incentive, and sales commissions. The advertising department makes daily requests for printing of mailing labels and envelopes.

An error in a number of customer bills was discovered by an auditor for the State Public Service Commission. To locate the source of the error, the programming manager was called upon to check the computer programs involved. In attempting to check the first program, he found only a source deck listing. The object deck was in condensed form, thereby preventing the printing of a "quick and dirty" object code listing. Finally, a suitable listing was made available by reassembling the autocoder source deck.

The mainline processing appeared to be logical and correct. Some questions arose over the manner in which a multiplication subroutine was written. However, the logic was assumed to be correct though the technique was not considered to be the best.

The manager then moved to verifying a second program used for calculation of the actual customer bill. Again the mainline processing was assumed to be logical and correct. The same multiplication subroutine was used in the second program.

The decision was then made to key punch some test cards and run a test on the computer. The test data was also calculated on an adding machine to arrive at a planned result. The output from the two computer tests did not match the planned results. The multiplication subroutine was immediately suspect. A check of the programming staff revealed that the person responsible for writing the subroutine was no longer in the employ of the organization.

The programming manager decided to telephone the former employee at his new place of employment. The programmer indicated that he had made a change to the subroutine but could not remember the nature of the change. After gaining some information about the programmer's technique of writing subroutines, the programming manager decided to compare the two subroutines.

In his inspection, he found that the subroutine in the first program had one less instruction statement than that of the second program. The missing card was duplicated and inserted into the first program. The source deck was subsequently reassembled and retested. However, no improvement over the test was evident.

The programming manager than decided to check each step of the subroutine. In the process he found that half-adjust positional alignment was incorrect; this had resulted in a significant error in favor of the company. Upon completing his inspection, he then proceeded to reassemble and retest the first program. This time the outputted result matched the planned result. A change was made to the second program; then it too was reassembled and retested. The actual output matched the expected result.

The programming manager placed the new program listings in his desk. He instructed the secretary to type a new listing of the multiplication subroutine and insert it into the binder containing the various subroutines available to the programmers.

Discussion Questions

1. From your reading of the case study, what major problems, if any, would you say existed in this organization?
2. What solutions would you have applied to the problems detected?
3. Did you agree with the testing procedure? Could it be improved? If so, how? If not, why not?
4. In your opinion, do you feel that the programming manager was correct or incorrect in telephoning the former employee? Why?
5. Would your answer to the previous question be any different if the programming manager had waited until the evening to contact the programmer at home?
6. Would you fault the former employee for failing to remember the change he had actuated? If so, why? If not, why not?
7. Do you agree with the actions taken by the programming manager after he rectified the error condition?
8. What suggestions or recommendations, if any, would you make to the information systems director regarding this aspect of his function?

Case Study 4.2: The Speedeee Wheeels Company

You have been employed by the Speedeee Wheeels Company to evaluate their documentation standards. The company, a fast-growing manufacturer of bicycles, has just installed a new third-generation computer. The major application is a management information system, with primary emphasis on production control, inventory control, and sales forecasting.

Prior to installation of the computer, the company had developed a new documentation standard. However, due to the pressure of conversion, the requirements were relaxed. Following the implementation, the systems manager suggested that the standard be revised because the requirements were much too stringent. Also, they felt that the present documentation was more than adequate for the organization's needs.

At present there is a singular system flowchart for the entire management information system. This chart is drawn on the back of a continuous printer form, about six feet long. It is hung on the wall of the computer center.

The operator's manuals contain a summary-type micro-flowchart, a typewritten set of operating instructions, a copy of the user instructions, and the program listing.

The program specifications manuals contain a micro-flowchart; all input/output layouts for card, tape, and disk units illustrated on multiple card layout forms; the drafts of the operating and user instructions, and listings of any relevant input codes. These manuals are filed in the appropriate programmer's desk.

There are no formal user's manuals. The original and copies of the typewritten instructions are distributed to the affected departments.

The programs are assigned a seven-digit identification number. The first two digits identify the major functional area. The next two digits are used to define the subfunctional area (subsystem). The last three digits are a consecutive number assignment. For example 01-01-047 describes a Bill of Materials explosion in the Production Control segment of the MIS. A listing of these numbers is maintained in a program register. A number may be reassigned if a program has not been operational for at least six months.

The documentation standard that has been developed is to consist of six manuals. Each manual is to be treated as a separate segment of the documentation. The materials are to be filed in the respective manuals by subsystem within major functional area. An index tab will be affixed to the first sheet of each application. The tab will carry the application name. The following represents an outline of the standard:

Manual	*Contents*
1	Description of Application
	a. Objectives
	b. Departments Involved
	c. System Flowchart
2	User Department Procedures
3	Data Processing Procedures
	a. General Internal Procedures
	b. Console Operating Instructions
4	Program Specifications
	a. Program Flowcharts (macro-level)
	b. Layout Information
	c. Console Instructions
	d. Program Abstract
	e. Program Listing
	f. Decision Tables
5	Tape and Disk Files
	a. Layouts
	b. Cross-reference Listing (where files are used)
6	Forms
	a. Samples of all forms
	b. List of all codes used for *each* program

Discussion Questions

1. What advantages or disadvantages are there to maintaining the MIS flowchart on the wall of the computer center?
2. Are the contents of the operator's manuals adequate or inadequate? Would you recommend any changes?
3. Are the contents of the program specifications manuals adequate or inadequate? Would you recommend any changes?
4. Does the lack of formal user's manuals inhibit the operation of effectiveness of Speedeee Wheeels? Why or why not?
5. How would you evaluate the present program identification number scheme?
6. How would you evaluate the existing documentation standard?
7. Would you agree or disagree with the systems manager that the

standard is too restrictive? Would you favor his proposal?

8. What kind of a documentation standard would you recommend for Speedeee Wheeels?

9. How would you comment upon the safeguards applied to the existing documentation? Would there be any need to change the existing arrangements?

5

The Design and Layout of Data Processing Facilities

INTRODUCTION

One of the most important aspects of a data processing operation is the efficient arrangement of the interacting elements in the productive process. This requires the orderly integration of the manpower, equipment, materials, and supporting services to maximize productive capability and output. The effective interaction of these resources is affected by the availability of a favorable working environment—one that will satisfy the functional needs of the personnel and help maintain a high morale level. Optimizing this relationship is not a simple task, because the layout is influenced by the functional activities served by data processing, as well as by factors not under the direct control of either the manager or the organization—factors such as local building codes and geographical location.

The data processing manager becomes involved in the design and development of a facilities layout whenever:

—A new data processing function is established

—Converting to a new equipment configuration

—Expansion occurs resulting from the addition of personnel and/or equipment

—The primary external supporting service or input facility is relocated

—Data communications, data collection, teleprocessing, or time-sharing systems are considered and/or installed

—Flexibility for expansion had not been included in the original design

—Environmental security must be established or improved

—Corporate acquisitions are made

—Organizational consolidations are planned and/or made

—An intensive management information system is being investigated and/or planned

THE OBJECTIVES OF LAYOUT PLANNING

The primary goals in planning a data processing installation layout are to provide for optimal utilization of resources within minimal space requirements at the lowest possible cost. These generalized aims must include the following specific objectives:

1. Efficient utilization of space
2. Minimization of materials handling
3. Elimination or minimization of health hazards
4. Maintenance of high employee morale
5. Efficient utilization of manpower
6. Provision for flexibility needed for changes or expansion
7. Provision for the movement and quality of air
8. Provision for proper color schemes
9. Provision for proper illumination
10. Provision for a safe working environment

Utilization of Space

A good layout represents a fixed expense, so that every effort must be made to maximize the rate of return for each square foot of space being paid for. Due to the emphasis on cost, organizations frequently load an area without considering the actual space requirements for equipment, maintenance, safety, and personnel. This type of attitude can be a major factor in personnel problems and high employee turnover.

The specified space needs for hardware must be secured from the vendor. These specifications indicate precisely the amount of space

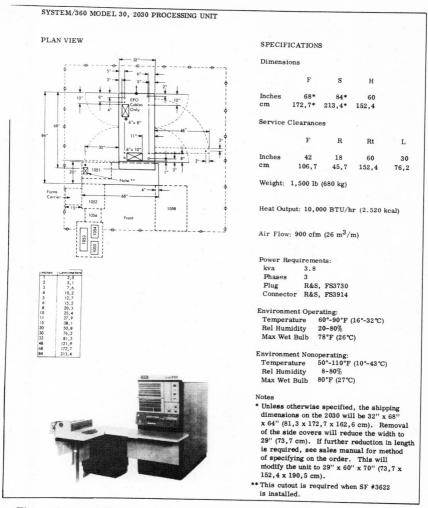

SYSTEM/360 MODEL 30, 2030 PROCESSING UNIT

PLAN VIEW

SPECIFICATIONS

Dimensions

	F	S	H
Inches	68*	84*	60
cm	172,7*	213,4*	152,4

Service Clearances

	F	R	Rt	L
Inches	42	18	60	30
cm	106,7	45,7	152,4	76,2

Weight: 1,500 lb (680 kg)

Heat Output: 10,000 BTU/hr (2.520 kcal)

Air Flow: 900 cfm (26 m^3/m)

Power Requirements:
kva 3.8
Phases 3
Plug R&S, FS3730
Connector R&S, FS3914

Environment Operating:
Temperature 60°-90°F (16°-32°C)
Rel Humidity 20-80%
Max Wet Bulb 78°F (26°C)

Environment Nonoperating:
Temperature 50°-110°F (10°-43°C)
Rel Humidity 8-80%
Max Wet Bulb 80°F (27°C)

Notes

* Unless otherwise specified, the shipping dimensions on the 2030 will be 32" x 68" x 64" (81,3 x 172,7 x 162,6 cm). Removal of the side covers will reduce the width to 29" (73,7 cm). If further reduction in length is required, see sales manual for method of specifying on the order. This will modify the unit to 29" x 60" x 70" (73,7 x 152,4 x 190,5 cm).
** This cutout is required when SF #3622 is installed.

Inches	Centimeters
1	2,5
2	5,1
3	7,6
4	10,2
5	12,7
6	15,2
8	20,3
10	25,4
11	27,9
15	38,1
20	50,8
30	76,2
32	81,3
48	121,9
68	172,7
84	213,4

Figure 5.1. Sample Extract of Planning Specifications. Courtesy IBM Corporation.

needed for each unit—in terms of height, length, width, and maintenance areas. Figure 5.1 is an extract from planning specifications furnished by a vendor.

Consideration must also be given to space for worktables, workbenches, desks, chairs, file and parts cabinets, storage cabinets, temperature and humidity control units, and other supporting equipment. The needs will vary according to the hardware configuration and the objectives of the functional activity.

The width of the aisles must be adequate to permit the flow of materials, machines, and manpower without danger of injury or damage. It is desirable that five-foot and four-foot widths be maintained for traffic and work aisles respectively. Minimum acceptable tolerances for each type is four and three feet.

Very often, organizations fail to provide adequate space between units. This causes traffic and clearance problems, or else interference with operation of other units when preventative or emergency maintenance is being performed. In planning his facility the manager of the data processing operations function must also provide space for operator mobility at and between the machines. These space requirements may or may not be included as part of vendor-supplied specifications included in Figure 5.1. The manager must allow at least three feet behind the printer for the forms rack and forms changes. Depending on the type and size of equipment, four to five feet must be allowed between machines; this figure will also vary due to cabling and maintenance requirements.

In the key punching, verifying, and data recording areas, at least three feet should be left clear between units to allow for operator movement.

Minimizing Materials Handling

The flow of materials can consume a large percentage of available production time if not properly controlled. Every effort must be made to provide for a smooth flow of materials from input to output. This may be somewhat difficult because it is not always possible to provide an ideal productive balance. However, an imbalance may be minimized by positioning supporting equipment, such as control panel racks, near their respective machines: magnetic disk packs, data cells, cartridges, cassettes, and tapes should be near the drives in the computing area; printer output forms should be near printers, and storage racks for punched card stock should be near the key punch machines and punching devices. Figure 5.2 illustrates a portable disk storage device that can be positioned near the disk drives to facilitate the flow of materials.

Figure 5.2. Portable Disk Storage Device. Courtesy Engineered Data Products Inc.

Figure 5.3. Materials-Handling Equipment: Cart and Well-Positioned File Cabinet. Courtesy Wright Line.

Minimizing materials handling makes it necessary to shorten walking distances between materials and equipment, as well as to curtail or eliminate the lifting and carrying of materials. This goal can be achieved by placing supporting cabinets, files, and tables near the equipment or in other convenient locations. It can also be very effective and beneficial to provide carts for the movement of card and form stock, disk packs, card trays, control panels, and reports. Figure 5.3 shows the use of a cart, as well as the convenience of a file cabinet positioned near a card reading device in order to minimize data movement.

Avoiding Health Hazards

The manager must strive to eliminate or minimize all existing and potential health hazards. Failing to deal effectively with such dangers can result in high absenteeism rates, liability suits, and even loss of life—

problems that could be very costly and disruptive to the productive process.

One of the more significant health hazards is noise. Noise is an interference or an undesirable sound resulting from human speech, equipment operations, echoes, and vibration, or from any combination thereof. Prolonged exposure to high auditory levels becomes annoying to employees. What is more, it can reduce their productivity and may also result in injury to their hearing. The level of noise is measured in terms of decibels. It used to be reported by experts that exposure to a level of 100 decibels for a prolonged period of time would reduce productivity and be harmful to employees. However, recent studies conducted by Corliss and Berendt at the National Bureau of Standards have indicated that the exposure level for a full working day should not exceed 85 decibels.

To minimize environmental noise hazards, organizations are now using such sound-absorbing materials as acoustical tile, draperies, carpeting, partitions, and acoustical enclosures.

Acoustical tile on hard walls, ceilings, and floors help to reduce interference caused by the operating equipment, transmission of noise to other areas, vibration, and echoes. The sound-absorbing effectiveness of acoustical tile decreases somewhat as the size of the room increases. But room size can be partially offset by installing a dropped ceiling, as well as acoustical tile.

Drapery material is used for sound absorption in a number of facilities. However, they are reported to be costly and only partially effective. There is also concern about the potential danger from the static electricity levels of fibers used in drapery materials, for the anti-static sprays applied to such fabrics have been only temporarily effective.

Carpeting is also used in many installations. However, careful consideration must be given to selecting a yarn or fiber that will maintain a static electricity level below 2000 static volts, which is the maximum allowable level for the operation of most computer equipment. (The human threshold level is somewhat higher, ranging from 2500 to 3500 volts.) Static electricity affects magnetic recordings and may cause random or intermittant errors in the equipment. The effect on humans is primarily one of petty annoyance, however, because it could be the cause of an accident that would affect the group's productivity. It is important to note that the static voltage levels in fibers, fabrics, and

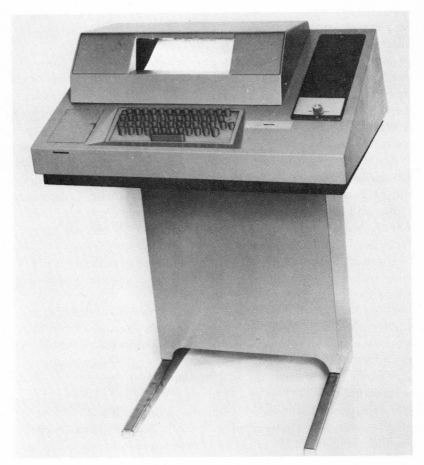

Figure 5.4. Acoustical Cover. Courtesy Novation, Inc.

yarns may increase because of improper humidification of the work area.

Often it is possible to isolate or reduce the noise level by setting up a partial wall between the source of the noise and the employees. Or it may be necessary to totally enclose the source of the interference and install sound-absorbent materials on the inner walls and ceiling; this is more practical than partial walling because it significantly reduces the reverberations.

In open office areas it is advisable to use acoustical covers on the equipment. Such covers can reduce operating noise levels by as much as 50 percent. Also, some of the covers are useful in reducing the operating temperature of the equipment. Figure 5.4 shows a type of acoustical cover used to reduce the operating noise level of the hardware.

Another health hazard in many installations is dust. It may be introduced into the environment through windows, doors, machine operation, materials handling, and the air-conditioning system. For all practical purposes, windows should be opened only in cases of extreme emergency. However, it is best to make alternative arrangements so that the windows can be kept shut, even in an emergency.

Doors in an installation must be properly sealed so as to limit the amount of dust entering the work area. Well-sealed doors also help reduce the transmission of noise to other areas.

Handling of such materials as card and paper stock in machine operations can generate a significant amount of dust in the work area. Part of the daily ritual for many machine operators is to dust out the card reader and punch units. The dust is swept into the air or onto the floor. This serves no genuine purpose at all because it only displaces the dust. It is much more practical to purchase a household or commercial vacuum cleaner (see Figure 5.5) to clean the various devices.

Figure 5.5. Commercial Vacuum Cleaner. Courtesy Armstrong Cork Company.

For security or other reasons, some installations do not allow their housekeeping maintenance staff in the equipment area. Consequently, the areas go uncleaned unless a manager or some of the personnel clean superficially with a dry mop or broom. Nevertheless, it is essential that routine maintenance be performed regularly in order to remove the loose dirt or dust particles.

Improperly installed air-conditioning units can also be responsible for introducing dust, foreign materials, and even corrosive elements into the working environment from either inside or outside the building. Therefore, caution must be exercised by the planners to eliminate the possibility of dust and other contaminants entering through the fresh-air intakes. Without regular inspections and systematic filter changes in the air-conditioned and data processing units, operations can be stopped and personnel and input/output media affected by faulty air-conditioning.

Maintaining High Employee Morale

A favorable work environment can do much to maintain employee morale—an important determinant in high quantitative and qualitative productivity. The manager must provide an adequate work area for each individual, avoiding the establishment of isolation pockets and heavy traffic aisles, which can disrupt the productive process. Visitor chairs should be furnished at those desks where frequent callers stop. Desks and work stations should be positioned so as to avoid having employees working in their own shadows. There should also be an adequate number of telephones and a limit on the number of people sharing one extension line. This is particularly important where incoming and/or outgoing telephone traffic is heavy.

Conference rooms, where provided, should be planned so as to allow about thirty square feet of floor space per person for groups of ten or less. For larger groups, approximately 20 square feet per person should be allocated. Coat storage must also be provided for employees. One six-foot-long coat closet meets the needs of about 24 people, though it would be more desirable to provide individual lockers for everyone.

Efficient Utilization of Manpower

The manager must design the layout for the most efficient utilization of manpower. By positioning the equipment to avoid and/or remove bottlenecks, and by minimizing materials handling, the manager can reduce setup and handling time, as well as personnel idleness—both forced and voluntary.

Despite the fact that a manager has followed the recommended planning practices, he may find it necessary to make some adjustments. To minimize the need for such changes, a manager should solicit the views of his subordinates after he has prepared a preliminary layout design.

In one computer installation observed by this author, the front of the printer was positioned toward the wall. This was done to prevent visitors from viewing any sensitive output on the device. However, this placement also interfered with the operator's normal view of the printer. Consequently, he was forced to make numerous visual checks on the printer to ensure that it was functioning correctly. Obviously this approach fails to consider the proper utilization of the manpower resource. It can also encourage operator dependence upon the console lights for printer problem indication.

Another consideration in optimizing manpower utilization is to place the group leader's or manager's office in a centralized location conveniently accessible to the subordinates. This eliminates the necessity to walk distances whenever a question or problem arises.

Flexibility for Changes or Expansion

A planner must have 20-20 hindsight disguised as foresight when designing the layout. The arrangement must be flexible enough to allow for some future modification or expansion without a major redesign. Providing for the future is just as important as taking care of current needs. The problem is to determine the proper balance. Determining flexibility needs may be projected on the basis of the future objectives of the organization.

The Movement and Quality of Air

The movement and quality of air in an environment is another important consideration. The air already present must be recirculated and fresh air must be introduced. The freshness of the air affects the heat load, relative humidity, filtration, and capacity of the atmosphere inside the building. Therefore, there must be a proper balance between fresh and recirculated air, which in turn, means that the inflow of fresh air must be carefully regulated. The existing air supply should be kept moving to eliminate or reduce stagnancy and odors. It should be filtered to remove dust particles, which affect personnel, equipment, and materials. The quantity and quality of air are best controlled through an air-conditioning system. This process regulates temperature and humidity levels within predefined ranges under a variety of external climatic conditions.

The temperature is measured in terms of degrees Fahrenheit. When the temperature level exceeds 90°, it will induce fatigue in the personnel and ultimately reduce their productivity. Higher temperatures may also adversely alter the materials used in the productive process. For example, some types of magnetic tape have been known to stretch slightly due to increased temperature levels. The electromechanical and electronic equipment may also be affected by high temperature, causing components to act erratically. The vendors have indicated broad temperature limits for the hardware. For example, one vendor recommends a range of 60° to 90°, whereas another specifies limits from 60° to 80°. Such parameters are somewhat deceiving and unrealistic because they fail to consider human comfort. It is much more appropriate to pick a range such as 70° to 72°, which would provide for both computer reliability and personnel comfort. In any event, an organization should pick an optimal temperature point and closely regulate that limit.

The amount of moisture in the air—measured as percentiles of relative humidity—must also be controlled, because it affects the mental alertness of the personnel, the operating efficiency of the equipment, and the texture of such materials as card and forms stock. Furthermore, it increases the heat load in an area as a result of condensation, thus causing a rise in static electricity voltage. Punched card stock, to select one example of moisture effects, is very difficult to process under excessive humidity conditions. The fibers begin to break down, causing jams and misfeeds in the equipment.

The permissible humidity ranges are very broad. The humidity level must be set at a realistic point to prevent condensation on the walls and windows, as well as to reduce the static electricity levels. Most organizations set the humidity level at 50 percent and attempt to control it within a 3 percent range.

Figure 5.6. Specialized Air-Conditioning Unit. Courtesy Floating Floors Inc., a subsidiary of National Lead Company.

There are several different types of air-conditioning systems that can be utilized to control the temperature and humidity ranges. The most popular of these is the underfloor system. This system utilizes the space between the regular building floor and the raised floor. The raised floor, which may also be described as a floating, elevated, or pedestal floor, is an excellent way of supplying air directly to the computer or the room. Also, it reduces the cost of duct work. Figure 5.6 shows two specialized package units designed to provide complete temperature, humidity, and dust control for a computer room. The device controls are shown on the support columns next to the units. The units rest on an elevated floor, which provides a uniform support surface for the computer equipment and simultaneously serves as ducting for the conditioned air. The floor registers shown on the left are used to introduce the conditioned air. Fresh-air ventilation diffusers are hung in the ceiling above, between the illumination panels.

It is also necessary to install temperature and humidity recording instruments. These provide a continuous record of the conditions in the environment. Whenever possible, the instruments should be equipped with visual and/or audible alarms to alert the personnel to possible deviations or problems.

The actual kind and type of equipment selected for an installation varies according to the processing equipment configuration, its usage, and the environment. Due to the complexity of the interactive factors, the author strongly recommends the use of an experienced air-conditioning design engineer, who will be familiar with the distribution systems and mechanical equipment, as well as with the building codes affecting their use.

Proper Color Schemes

Color schemes have a significant psychological effect on personnel and personnel performance. Colors evoke varied reactions from almost all people, so that their effective use can help to establish a satisfying work environment. In addition to providing a stimulus and maintaining employee morale, colors are also used for safety purposes.

Colors can be categorized, in terms of the responses they evoke, as restful, cool, depressing, and warm.

Restful colors, such as beige and light green, are easy on the eyes and reflect light very well, thereby improving the level of illumination in an area. Other colors in pastel shades also offer good reflecting surfaces. Blues and greens have a tendency to induce a cool feeling; yet, when applied judiciously, they can be used for psychological comfort in an environment where heat dissipation may be high. Blacks and grays are depressing colors. Although most of the new data processing equipment now is painted in light shades of gray or green, some older units in black or gray may still be present in an installation. If the equipment is owned, rather than leased, by the organization, it can be painted in a more relaxing color scheme. In contrast to these depressing colors are red, yellow, and orange, which generate a feeling of warmth and excitement. Although such colors can cause fatigue when used monochromatically on large areas, they can be effectively applied to smaller areas, where, for example, they can effectively offset the effect of cool air flowing from the air-conditioning ducts.

File cabinets, desks, and other accessories are available in a variety of colors. Carefully chosen colors can make these items helpful in improving the environment through use of a coordinated color scheme. Furthermore, the supporting equipment currently available within an organization can be repainted in accordance with the general principles and goals of such a scheme.

Color coding is a most useful element of layout design when used to help improve personnel safety. Tops and bottoms of stairways should be painted yellow. Low-clearance areas should be marked with yellow stripes. And all emergency facilities should be painted red. This applies to fire call boxes, fire extinguishers, emergency telephones, and, in some cases, also to first-aid kits.

Proper Illumination

Poor illumination can be either a principal or supplementary cause of mental errors, accidents, and fatigue. The dimmer the illumination, the greater tends to be the number of errors, etc. On the other hand, very bright lighting can also have negative effects. Aside from its direct effect on the eyes, a high level of illumination can raise the heat load in a work area. In addition, it can cause glare when the light is reflected from walls, ceilings, and lighting fixtures.

The illumination requirements are determined by the availability of natural light from nearby windows and skylights, the amount of detail work to be performed, and the different levels of illumination needed at different areas within the environment. A different illumination level is needed, for example, in a display-type data processing installation, where lighting is used to accent a particular area or hardware unit for visitors or sales purposes. However, caution must be exercised to ensure that this highlighting does not interfere with the visibility of indicator lights on the equipment. This same problem can occur if the hardware is in direct sunlight.

Providing proper illumination can also mean providing an emergency lighting system, for there is a trend today toward designing and building windowless environments in order to simplify air-conditioning requirements. The emergency system has to be equipped to automatically turn on battery-operated lights when a power failure occurs. It is equally important that the installation have a sufficient number of these lights and that they are installed and positioned so as to provide suitable emergency lighting.

Illumination for a data processing activity is provided by an incandescent or a fluorescent lighting system. Each system offers significant advantages and disadvantages, which must be evaluated in terms of tangible cost. Figure 5.7 summarizes the comparative merits of the two

	Incandescent	Fluorescent
Installation Cost	Lower	Higher
Operation Cost	Higher	Lower
Maintenance Cost	Higher	Lower
Additional Heat Load Generated	60%	35%
Direction of Light	Downward	Upward and Downward
Highlighting Effectiveness	Good	Poor

Figure 5.7   Comparison of Incandescent and Fluorescent Lighting Systems

systems. The comparison shows that the installation cost of fluorescent fixtures in an existing environment would be higher than that of incandescent fixtures. However, this would be offset by lower operating and maintenance costs. In a totally new environment, though, the incandescent system would lose its advantage of lower installation cost in another way: because of the system's 60 percent heat load (almost double that of the fluorescent system), a more powerful air-conditioning unit would be needed, thereby increasing the overall costs.

Over-illumination can occur with either system, although glaring tends to occur more frequently with the incandescent system. That can be turned to good advantage, though, in instances where a demand for highlighting can be met by using this systems direct-light capability. The fluorescent system, which gives off a more diffused light, is much less effective for highlighting but correspondingly produces much less glare.

Under-illumination is also a problem with either system, but it can be more easily corrected in the fluorescent system, partly because there is less danger of glare. Furthermore, the use of brightly colored paints with a good reflecting surface on walls and ceilings, combined with the fluorescent system's excellent indirect-light capability, can produce an increased level of glareless illumination.

It is recommended by processing equipment vendors that an average minimum illumination of 40 footcandles be maintained throughout the equipment operation area. The amount of light required in the other areas is difficult to determine exactly because of the variety of tasks being performed. Footcandle recommendations for the specific tasks may be obtained by consulting the lighting handbook published by the *Illuminating Engineering Society*.

Proper illumination can also be used to provide an element of safety in the working environment, particularly in the areas in front of and behind the equipment. In some instances, for example, there is insufficient illumination in the rear area, where the field engineers maintaining the equipment must work. Also, the storage areas for data, card, and form stock are deliberately kept dimly lit because they are not used much; this, though, is a false sense of economy. For reasons of safety, as well as efficiency, morale, etc., it is essential that the entire working environment be properly lit.

Another safety factor relating to illumination is the need for the lighting system to be arranged so as to place traffic aisles on separate circuitry from the general working areas. This makes it possible to turn off the lights in various parts of the environment without creating a safety hazard.

A Safe Working Environment

Safety represents both a layout factor and a human attitude. These must be given careful attention in the planning of any facility or operation. But safety does not end with the planning process; rather, it should be a habit planned by the manager and then maintained and enforced by him. Failure to apply safety attitudes and practices continually and effectively will be reflected in employee carelessness, which, in turn, can create serious problems.

The planner must first determine the existing safety codes established and enforced by local governmental agencies, together with those developed by the organization's own safety engineer. These codes have a significant effect on actual design and construction of a data processing facility.

Safety in an environment is concerned with:
1. Emergency aisles and exits
2. Smoking practices
3. Emergency operating procedures
4. Fire detection and prevention
5. Electrical power requirements
6. Good housekeeping

1. EMERGENCY AISLES AND EXITS. Though there are usually company restrictions affecting the use of emergency aisles and exits, many

managers fail to observe them. The author personally observed one instance in which an emergency aisle was used for the storage of supplies, thereby reducing the passageway width to only 30 inches. When this was called to the attention of the manager, he was quick to reply that no one used the passageway, ignoring the fact that this represented an emergency route in the event of fire or other disaster. This happens in many organizations. In fact, even emergency exit doors are allowed to become temporarily blocked. And landings on stairways are used as temporary storage facilities. The manager must enforce practices against the illegal and unwise use of such areas and facilities. He must also ensure that emergency passageways are properly illuminated and that exits are clearly marked.

2. SMOKING PRACTICES. These represent a potential hazard. The chief cause of fire is carelessly discarded cigarettes in storeroom areas or trash containers. What is more, the common and offensive habit of placing lighted cigarettes on the edges of tables, desks, and machines is always a threat to the well-being of both people and property.

To eliminate carelessness with cigarettes, the manager must make sure there are enough ash trays and must prohibit placement of lighted cigarettes on various surfaces or in unauthorized containers. However, it is even safer to ban all smoking in the operations and storage areas. This will greatly reduce the likelihood of fire damaging the equipment, injuring employees, and destroying vital data.

3. EMERGENCY OPERATING PROCEDURES. Every person in the data processing activity must be trained in the implementation of emergency operating procedures. This requires their familiarity with the emergency operating procedures, which should be kept in a binder on the manager's desk and/or the console operator's desk.

4. FIRE DETECTION AND PREVENTION. Devices to detect and prevent fire represent a critical element in the design and operation of a facility. Fire-detection devices are designed to discover a fire at its incipient stages and provide an early warning. In most instances, the types of fire-detection device to be installed will be stipulated by the organization's insurance company. However, if none are specified, the planner should select a device that offers maximum detection capability and that provides for emergency shutoff of the electrical power to the data processing equipment and the air-conditioning plant. A less sophisticated device that may be used is an automatic smoke detector equipped with an audible and/or visual alarm. Such a device is illustrated in Figure 5.8.

Because so many facilities used by the data processing operations group are equipped with sprinkler systems, data processing managers are equipping installations with waterproof equipment covers. The availability of the covers in the installation may help eliminate or minimize water damage. This type of system helps to reduce the water damage somewhat. Many organizations are now equipping their data processing installations with waterproof equipment covers to reduce water damage.

Figure 5.8. Fire Alert Ionization Smoke Detector, FT-200. Courtesy Walter Kidde & Company, Inc.

The prevention of fire cannot always be achieved because of employee carelessness, combustion of stored materials, equipment failure, vandalism, accidents, sabotage, or an act of God. Safety regulations and building codes require that fire-retardant construction materials be used as a preventative safety measure. They also require installation of fire-fighting equipment.

Portable fire extinguishers should be conspicuously and conveniently placed throughout the installation, preferably on wall hangers. They must be recharged and/or examined at least once each year, with some provision for servicing only a few units at a time or obtaining loaners so that the installation is never without protection in the event of emergency.

The employees all need to know how to operate the fire extinguishers. They also need to know which kinds of extinguishers to use in case of an emergency, for using the wrong one can do much more harm than good. Class C fires (fires in live electrical equipment) require the use of carbon-dioxide or dry-chemical extinguishers. Class A fires (fires involving paper, wood, or cloth) should be tackled with extinguishers using soda-acid, foam, water, or antifreeze agent. The Shell Oil Company has recently been experimenting with the use of high-expansion foam as a fire-extinguishing agent for all fire classifications.

5. ELECTRICAL POWER REQUIREMENTS. Electrical power can be an enemy as well as a friend. It is important, therefore, that the personnel know the location of the circuit box and how to turn off the power supply serving the data processing equipment and the air-conditioning unit. It is also useful to arrange for having additional turn-off switches placed near the exits for use in emergency.

Personnel must be warned to turn off the mainline switches on the equipment when they are correcting jams so as to avoid the possibility of electrical shock or of injury caused by moving parts. The manager must periodically spot-check such situations to ensure compliance with such safety rules. One of the severest hazards involves electrical cords and outlets. In some instances where planners fail to provide an adequate number of wall or floor outlets, the employees use extension cords to connect several machines with one outlet. These cords stretched across the floor create a serious tripping hazard. One solution is simply to disconnect equipment when it is not in use. Although this approach may be acceptable in slow productive periods, it is impractical during peak periods. In addition, it endangers the life and serviceability of the electrical cords and plugs. The cords may become worn and frayed, thereby exposing the live wires. Also, when the plugs are disconnected from the outlets, they are left on the floor where they may be stepped on. This can break the contact points or the wire connection to them, thus ultimately endangering the user.

Another problem occurs when floor outlets are left in position after equipment has been moved. In one installation this author observed, the manager simply inverted a large green basket over an outlet in the middle of a traffic aisle until a work order for disconnecting the outlet could be prepared. He rationalized his action by stating that no one would trip over a *green* basket. Another tripping hazard is created by the power and signal cables used to connect the various units. This may be partially overcome by building a bridge over the cables, but a more effective method is to install raised flooring. Figure 5.9 shows the type of

Figure 5.9. Raised Flooring. Courtesy Armstrong Cork Company.

raised flooring available to conceal the cabling beneath the work surface.

6. GOOD HOUSEKEEPING. A clean shop is said to be a safe shop. So the manager should establish and enforce rules for maintaining a clean work environment. Good housekeeping requires that each person coop-

erate and share the responsibility of maintaining a satisfactory environment.

A primary problem is to have files, cartons, and other items returned to their proper storage locations. Frequently, control panels are placed behind or propped up against the machines rather than being returned to the storage racks. Misplaced panels represent a potential slipping and tripping hazard. Placing panels on top of storage or file cabinets is also a very bad practice. Cases and cartons of card stock are frequently left standing in front of a card punch machine or in the key punch area. Only the necessary card stock should be placed near the device; others should be returned to the storeroom or placed in a storage rack. The same problem affects the use of printer forms. Empty cartons must not be left lying on the floor or on top of cabinets, for they constitute both a safety and fire hazard. In installations where cards are retained for scrap salvage, caution must be exercised to reduce the fire hazard potential. Precautions must also be taken in stacking the cartons or cases to prevent them from toppling. Generally, the cartons or cases are not packed tightly, so they are unable to sustain the weight of other cases or cartons. Consequently, a stack may resemble the Leaning Tower of Pisa.

Another frequent housekeeping problem is trash. Card chips strewn about the floor represent a potential slipping hazard, especially on a waxed surface. Trash from the card punches, reproducers, and printers should be placed in large containers. These should be located near the equipment to permit prompt disposal. Small containers should be placed in the key punch area near each machine to collect all scrap and chips. The floors must be cleaned and containers emptied each day to remove all debris from the working area.

Whenever a field engineer completes either preventative or necessary maintenance on the equipment, the area should be checked for any parts that may be left on the floor or on the equipment. Also, any spilled oil or cleaning fluid must be wiped up. When oil continues to drip or leak, the vendor should be notified immediately in order to correct the situation and to eliminate the potential hazard.

Rolling carts can be used very effectively to reduce or eliminate personal injuries caused by lifting or carrying materials. Caution must be exercised not to overload the carts. Sorting racks must be provided where a high volume of card sorting is performed. The racks eliminate the hazardous practice of stacking file trays on the floor around the machine or on top of a worktable.

Proper knives and/or staple-removing devices should be available for opening paper cartons. These implements enable employees to avoid painful paper cuts. In addition, it is important that materials are stacked within safe reaching heights. Where cards and records are stacked on high storage racks, ladders must be furnished to eliminate climbing on the racks.

Review Questions: Group 5A

1. What are some of the conditions or reasons why a data processing manager would have to prepare an installation layout?
2. What are some of the factors that a manager must take into consideration when evaluating his space needs on a layout?
3. Name and discuss some of the health hazards that should be considered in the design of a layout?
4. What would your reaction be if someone suggested painting a large wall surface, faced by the key punch operators, in red?
5. Would it be technically and operationally feasible to maintain the temperature of the computer environment at 66°? Why or why not?
6. A computer room has been equipped with an automatic sprinkler system. However, to minimize water damage, the lines over the equipment have been disconnected. Does this system provide the type of fire protection required in the environment?

SITE EVALUATION AND DETAILED PLANNING

Site Evaluation

The most difficult part of selecting a site is having to choose an optimal location for the operation's function. The selection process is difficult because the operations group is intensely affected by organizational objectives, the human element, external and internal influences, environmental control, and the work flow. These factors are less critical in selecting facilities for such functional activities as systems and programming; the planning for these groups is primarily concerned with work-space allocation and involves little or no productive equipment. (The process of designing the facilities for systems and programming is given later in this chapter.)

Before a new site may be considered or an existing facility evaluated, the manager must be aware of the overall space, structural, power, and air-conditioning needs. These are but guesstimates and will have to be modified when detailed planning is begun. The figures must be reasonable because they are an important part of the preliminary survey. In addition to the generalized space and environmental requirements, the manager must also evaluate the site in terms of efficiency, flexibility, comfort, security, and safety.

The site evaluation or selection is generally limited to choosing from among the following:

—An area within the organization's existing facilities
—An area or building available for lease, rental, or purchase
—A building or area specifically constructed for the purpose
—A special facility such as a mobile trailer or van.

In evaluating each of these possibilities, the primary consideration is space availability. This availability must be compared with the estimated current, proposed, and future needs, which are based on data from the vendors, on survey and/or feasibility studies, and on projections resulting from an analysis of the short-term and long-term goals set by the manager and executive committee. Following the determination of space adequacy, the manager must give consideration to environmental factors, location, communications capability, zoning restrictions, objectives, and costs. These considerations may be grouped within the following categories:

1. Location
2. Floor loading capacity
3. Temperature and moisture control
4. Power

1. LOCATION. Location is an important factor in reducing or eliminating various internal or external hazards within an environment. It is also an important factor in the complicated process of optimizing productivity.

Ideally, the operations facility is housed in a fire-resistant room or building isolated from high temperatures, corrosive substances, water and/or utility pipes, outside walls, windows, and unauthorized personnel.

Most installations are located in an area near or relatively near to the chief supporting activity, or they are centralized for the benefit of all activities in the organization. The practice of locating the data processing operations group near its primary supporting activity was established when unit-record equipment had to be located near the payroll activity. Centralization, on the other hand, occurs when the executive committee believes that this will strengthen the overall effectiveness of the organization. However, neither of these two basic arrangements offers any guarantee of the best security, efficiency, flexibility, safety, or comfort.

In many organizations, the data processing operations activity becomes a public showcase. This decision generally overrides all efficiency, safety, cost, and security considerations. Such an installation is generally glass-enclosed and often placed in the front window. The location leaves the activity vulnerable to vandals, rioters, storms, or even such occurrences as out-of-control motor vehicles. The glass is usually the non-safety type, which can cause lacerating injuries. However, building codes in some areas now require the use of tempered, laminated, or wired glass in modern construction. The glass also poses a blowout possibility during a fire, but this can be minimized by installing an external sprinkler system to provide a blanket of water.

The glass also creates some air-conditioning and humidification problems due to condensation. The moisture caused by condensation, for example, will produce structural damage if not controlled.

Accessibility for delivery of equipment and supplies is another consideration involved in selecting a location. It may be impossible to move equipment into an area without reconstructing a series of doorways, passageways, windows, or outside walls; or without utilizing a crane to lift the equipment to an upper floor or the roof because the freight elevator is inadequate or unavailable. Thus, making an installation accessible can prove to be extremely costly.

The communications capability of each site must be surveyed, particularly if data collection, teleprocessing, or data transmission systems are currently in use, on order, or represent a possible future acquisition. Limitations imposed on signal cable length could affect the location of a facility dependent upon the use of these media for input, and/or output.

Land, construction, and insurance costs are significant factors affecting the selection of any site. The cost of constructing a new facility or remodeling an existing site can result in the modification of the original construction plans or selection of an alternate location. Insurance costs may force selection of an alternate site due to high premiums for fire and liability coverage. Zoning regulations may affect selection because the area may not be available for industrial or business development. Or there may be construction limitations or requirements stipulated in building codes that will affect the layout design.

Location may also present some security problems for a manager. The major problem for most organizations is to limit access to the operations area. In many instances, direct access through a public hallway or an outside door is possible. Access may be limited by stationing a security guard to inspect all employee identification; by installing badge readers or other access control devices on the doors; by limiting entry to key holders; or by installing heavy-gauge, closely woven metal screens on the windows and doors (see Chapter 7). It may be much simpler to locate the activity in an interior area on an upper floor, in that security problems have also arisen where outside air-intake facilities for air-conditioning have been located at ground level.

It may not be entirely practical to locate a facility below ground level or in an area through which heat, gas, and water pipes pass. Below-ground sites may be exposed to the danger of flooding caused by water-main breaks, storms, or sewer backup. Furthermore, service piping is often concealed by the suspended ceiling or raised floor. The potential danger to personnel, equipment, and materials in this type of environment is quite high.

There is also a sociological consideration in selecting the proper location. If a facility is located in a high crime area, it may be difficult to recruit personnel of both sexes for other than normal day-shift schedules. Consequently, some organizations even provide taxi and/or charter bus service for their personnel on the off shifts.

The sites considered should be evaluated in terms of cost and in terms of the advantages and disadvantages of each location. The costs must be allocated between capital and operating expenditures. Capital expenditures, which may be amortized over a period of years, include the cost of construction and the purchase of fixed equipment. Operating expenditures, the recurring expenditures necessary to keep a facility operative, include the costs of utility services, replacing filters in the air-conditioning system, and other necessary items.

2. FLOOR LOADING CAPACITY. After having selected sites that meet the basic space requirements, and provide flexibility for expansion and a potentially optimal location, the planner must investigate the floor loading capacity. Rated floor loadings should be available from the organization's engineering department or the building's manager. If none are available, it may be necessary to arrange for a consulting engineer to make the necessary determinations. The floor must be able to sustain the

weight of the data processing and auxiliary equipment, the furniture, and personnel, and still have some allowance for safety. The requirements should be checked with local building-code provisions to ensure compliance. The overall weight must not place any stress on the walls or the structure that would require reinforcement-type construction, for that would increase installation preparation cost.

One of the major problems in evaluating flooring construction is to determine its ability to sustain a concentrated floor load. A concentrated floor load is one that is applied to a very small area within the entire environment. This condition generally exists where medium- or large-scale computing systems are positioned in a small area to gain optimal productive effectiveness. Rated floor loadings specify the maximum uniform load that may be distributed, but they generally do not indicate a floor's ability to support a single or several concentrated loads in a given area. For most data processing operations, uniform distribution is not feasible if there is also to be an optimal productive flow or balance of operations. Therefore, if objectives are to be achieved, it may be necessary to reinforce the permanent flooring.

Most types of flooring construction, with the exception of tile-arch, do have the capacity to support data processing equipment without reinforcement. Tile-arch, which is generally found in older buildings, requires reinforcement. Materials such as prestressed slab, reinforced concrete, and wood are more desirable, although these too may require structural reinforcement or some load redistribution.

In newer installations, it has become a practice to install raised flooring. This type of flooring is constructed over a permanent base in order to provide an area for power cables, signal cables, air-conditioning ducts, and recessed electrical outlets. In addition, raised floor can be used to redistribute the effect of a concentrated load on a permanent floor, although the raised flooring installed in such a manner must be capable of supporting the maximum weight. Support for the raised flooring is provided either by fire-resistant frame or by stringers that rest on pedestals. The flooring surface (see Figure 5.10) is wood or tile that is installed in sections, which can be easily removed to make the space accessible.

A floor rating of 150 pounds per square foot is desirable but is not commonly found except in warehouses, basements, or first-floor levels of office buildings. An acceptable minimum may be a rated capacity of 100 pounds per square foot.

3. TEMPERATURE AND MOISTURE CONTROL. The movement and qual-

Figure 5.10. Raised Flooring with Pedestal Supports. Courtesy Armstrong Cork Company.

ity of air are very significant factors in site evaluation. Earlier in this chapter we generalized about the effects of air-conditioning on personnel and equipment in the environment. Here we will provide additional information.

Air-conditioning requirements for each site vary according to the physical characteristics of the room or structure, the personnel, the kind and type of processing equipment, the amount and type of illumination, the level of relative humidity, and the supply of fresh air entering the environment. Humidity and temperature requirements vary among vendors, so where an equipment mix of several vendors is used, the parameters will be more difficult to calculate. The heat generated by the hardware is the single most significant factor in determining the heat load imposed on the air-conditioning system. Added to this calculation are the values for the sun's influence, for body heat produced by the employees, for heat from lighting fixtures, and for heat generated in another area but transmitted through the walls or ceilings surrounding the operations activity.

After considering the heat-generating factors, the planner must consider the environment's fresh-air intake. The inputted air may or may not add to the heat load, depending upon the outside temperature and relative humidity. Warm air may have to be cooled and excess moisture removed to maintain a desired humidity level. In the cooler months, larger quantities of fresh air are introduced into the air-conditioning system to assist in the cooling process.

A number of different air-conditioning systems are available and each must be evaluated for a specific application. An organization should not rely upon a building's central air-conditioning system to accommodate the needs of a data processing operation's activity. The air-handling units may be window units or free-standing units, which are successfully used in small- or medium-sized installations. Or they may be built-in units, which have the greater cooling capacity needed to provide satisfactory service for large installations.

The effectiveness of any air-handling unit depends upon the control and recording techniques utilized. It is desirable that the air-conditioning system be equipped with a recording device providing a written record of the environmental conditions for historical and reference purposes. Some of the instrumentation can either electrically or pneumatically activate the control mechanisms in the air-handling units to correct deviations from established environmental standards. Control units of this type are costlier but more effective than maintaining separate unit controls for the humidifier and air-conditioner. Separate controls utilize a separate dry bulb temperature gauge and relative humidity indicator for recording. Consequently, they require manual adjustments that tend to reduce the effectiveness of the air-handling units and to generate personnel problems as a result of the fluctuations in the temperature, humidity, and air flow.

Penetration and condensation of moisture are two problem-causing conditions for a data processing operation. Moisture comes through walls, floors, and ceilings that are made of such porous materials as cinderblocks or concrete. In most instances this can be corrected by applying waterproofing or vapor-sealing materials to the affected surfaces. Where the condition persists it will be necessary to construct a wall within a wall. The inner surface of the inside wall is then vapor-sealed or waterproofed and provision is made to drain off the moisture penetrating the outer wall.

Condensation usually occurs around window areas and causes water accumulations. It is generally corrected by installing a double window or by constructing a wall across the window. The double-window method is much less costly except where thermo-pane or heated glass panels are used. However, this technique is not always satisfactory because there is a tendency for some condensation to form on the metal frames, thereby enabling moisture to collect and cause safety and structural deterioration problems. The wall-across-window method is more desirable because it helps to reduce the heat load. This method is becoming more popular and is the basis of the windowless installations. The most significant disadvantage to this type of construction can be having personnel affected by claustrophobia. It is difficult to screen the data processing personnel for this type of psychological condition. Therefore, the offsetting solution may be to construct false windows in the environment. This is accomplished by placing several panes of translucent plastic or glass in front of warm-light fluorescent fixtures, thereby giving the illusion of daylight coming through a window. Some of the ersatz windows are framed with drapes to create a more authentic illusion and to remove the feeling of a closed-in room.

Condensation that forms on air-conditioning ducts and pipes can be overcome by insulating the surfaces.

4. POWER SUPPLY. The availability and the quality of power at a site must be evaluated for current and future needs. The overall requirements must include the needs of the lighting system, air-conditioning units, and the data processing equipment.

Current transmitted by the utilities or produced by an organization's own power plant should present no power problems because the equipment vendors are able to offer or modify units to operate on the available current supply. To offset voltage fluctuations due to dips and surges, some engineers have recommended the installation of voltage regulators on feeder lines leading into the circuit panels.

The power supply is channeled into the building through the power service entrance from overhead or underground lines. From the distribution panel, the power is relayed to one or more branch circuit panels located in the installation. The panels are equipped with circuit breakers or fuses to take care of any overloads in the current. Circuit breakers—which are more convenient and more commonly used—serve for normal current overloads, whereas fuses are better for protection in severe overload conditions because they have a higher current-interrupting capacity than circuit breakers and will respond much more rapidly to a severe overload condition. After a circuit breaker trips due to an overload condition, it can be quickly reset. Under similar circumstances, fuses are damaged and must be replaced. Another consideration is that the feeder circuit switch must be turned off to deal with a fuse, thereby neutralizing all devices on that branch circuit—which does not occur on branch circuits controlled by circuit breakers. There is a danger that if all power is immediately neutralized, there may be a loss of data or damage to the equipment and its components. In an emergency, power may be turned off selectively for any unit by tripping the assigned breaker. Further, individual breakers provide for an orderly shutdown and greater flexibility in preserving important files being operated.

The circuits for the data processing equipment must be kept independent of those for the air-conditioning units, lighting system, and auxiliary equipment. The branch circuit panels should be divided to separate each element so that an overload in one will not affect or cause a malfunction in any of the others. The circuits in the panels must be properly identified to indicate the facilities controlled by each, for in an emergency there is no time for guesswork. As part of the emergency operating procedure, personnel in the organization must be familiar with safe operation of the control panel.

The availability of electrical power for equipment operating in an online, real-time, or time-sharing environment can be critical or costly. In such situations, provision for standby power to eliminate or limit the interruption to a very brief period of time must be made. Even in less critical environments, it may be necessary to provide auxiliary power where frequent power interruptions or outages occur. The auxiliary power may be supplied by a generator or by a feeder line connected to an alternate substation. However, where auxiliary power service is established, it is necessary to ensure the quality of the power—that is, voltage fluctuations should be controlled. Voltage fluctuations may affect the speeds and accuracy of the equipment; in some instances, they can cause malfunctions.

Detailed Planning

Having selected an optimal site for the data processing operation, the manager must begin the task of detailing the layout in terms of the productive and supporting equipment, as well as the personnel. Physical planning is not difficult but very time-consuming because it requires the development of an operationally effective and satisfactory work environment. To achieve these objectives, the manager finds it necessary to develop several designs before he arrives at the optimal solution. Each layout must include consideration of columns, walls, windows, permanent and temporary partitions, stairwells, elevators, power, air-conditioning, and floor loading requirements. The details of power, air-conditioning, and floor loading should be included in an architectural drawing rather than on the floor layout plan of the installation itself. The floor layout must indicate the location and voltage capacity of the air-handling unit and the electrical outlets. It is not necessary to illustrate either the flow of power lines from the control panels or the ductwork unless they utilize space that will directly affect the layout. Before the manager can physically begin to position the hardware on the layout plan, he needs to analyze the available data about his own installation. The data may be available from such sources as the feasibility study, vendor proposals, system documentation, machine and supplies utilization records, operating schedules, and safety codes. The data may be categorized as follows:

1. Media utilization and movement
2. Hardware characteristics
3. Personnel requirements and characteristics

1. MEDIA UTILIZATION AND MOVEMENT. Initial consideration must be given to the type of input and output media used in the productive process—media such as source documents; punched cards; paper tape; magnetic tape; data cells; disk packs; OCR, OMR, and MICR documents. These media will affect the installation, so the manager must determine the extent and implication of their effects. This may be determined by surveying the volumes and rate of flow of each medium. Volume statistics and the flow schedule may be available from the feasibility study, an existing schedule, and/or a utilization chart. If unavailable, then the manager must survey his users and sample the existing operation to develop reasonable projections. After he has collected data on the type, volume, and rate of flow, the manager determines the movement of these media through the productive process. This pattern is developed by detailing the sequence of operations performed and the movement of materials through these steps. Where timings are available, they can be used to indicate the anticipated workload at each station, identify potential bottlenecks, and help determine the optimal location for supporting equipment.

This information must be coupled with that gathered on manpower and machines before it can all be properly applied. This is very important because one of the specific objectives to be achieved in layout planning is the minimization of materials handling in order to maximize throughput.

2. HARDWARE CHARACTERISTICS. The hardware affects the layout because of its size, power, weight, and air-conditioning requirements. The manager has to consider the number and types of units to be installed, as well as their alignment in a work-flow pattern so as to maintain a productive balance and avoid any bottlenecks.

An optimal equipment alignment may have to be discarded or modified because of floor loading capacity. If the flooring is inadequate, then the equipment must be repositioned to distribute the load over a larger area or over structural beams. To further reduce the load concentration, it is necessary to place card files, paper and card storage racks, and other equipment around the walls—that is, away from the center area or weak floor points.

Noise and interference from the machines may further complicate the layout because the manager may be forced to isolate certain pieces of equipment. This, though, can mean increased materials handling, and it also tends to create a bottleneck in the productive process. Similar problems arise when a computer or high heat producing unit is isolated in a partitioned area. In some instances, such units are positioned near the windows to permit the installation of ductwork over these units for dissipating the extra heat in the outside air. This approach, however, may present some operational and security problems.

The location of electrical connections may have some bearing upon equipment placement, but it may generally be the result of a specific voltage need. The cost of relocating the outlets or installing the necessary voltage power line would be offset by the savings resulting from the efficient use of the equipment.

3. PERSONNEL REQUIREMENTS AND CHARACTERISTICS. People are the most important element in the layout process. They must be provided with favorable working and safety conditions. This requires, among other things, the use of proper color schemes and the need to provide for adequately sized traffic aisles and work stations.

Allocation of less than minimum space parameters creates safety hazards and tends to reduce employee morale. In some installations when a materials cart or portable rack is being moved through the aisle, the machine operators must stop and step aside to permit passage. Frequent occurrences like this disrupt the productive process and annoy the operating personnel. Also, the danger exists that card trays or other materials may be accidentally pulled from worktables or the portable equipment when squeezing through an area. If knocked to the floor, materials such as disk packs, reels of magnetic tape, and control panels may be damaged and rendered ineffectual for continued machine use. Cards dumped on the floor will probably have to be re-sorted. Also, there is the danger that one or several of them may be damaged or may slip beneath a file cabinet or machine and will remain undetected until the report has been processed. This would require a rerun which in turn could force some readjustment of the production schedule.

Concern for the physical characteristics of the employees is a very practical matter in layout design. The manager must determine whether the work stations, handling equipment, and other facilities are the proper height, reach, strength, or range of vision.

Height requirements will vary depending upon whether the activities must be performed while seated or standing. A frequent height problem occurs where the data processing operation's function is divided into a computer and unit-record area. Generally, the floor in the computer room is elevated and the rooms are connected by a ramp. Problems can occur because the planner had failed to consider the height of the door opening, with the result that tall people have to lower their heads in moving to and from the computer area. This type of condition is rectified by raising the door opening height. Painting the striped safety color coding for a low clearance has only limited effectiveness. Another problem related to elevated floors is the slope of the ramp. A person emerging from the room is virtually propelled out, whereas someone entering must strain to move upward. The effect of this hazard becomes very evident when moving a portable materials cart to or from the computer room.

Reaching problems are generally overcome by equipping an installation with safety-type step stools or ladders, and/or by the enforcement of safety standards and practices. The availability of safe climbing equipment will eliminate the dangerous practice of climbing on chairs or cartons to reach materials. In some installations there is a tendency to stack control panel racks to gain greater utilization of space. This is a sound objective, but very often, the racks are stacked too high or are improperly supported, so that the removal of control panels is difficult and even hazardous. There is also the danger that when removing large, fully wired control panels from the upper chutes of the stacked units, an employee may be thrown off balance and be injured. Obviously, materials handling equipment with large capacities will be acquired in such situations and this may present a problem in optimal placement of the equipment.

Strength is a difficult human element to plan for. However, from experience with average individuals, it is known that a manager must control the amount of physical handling, walking, and lifting to reduce or eliminate physical strain and fatigue. Lifting, handling, and walking may be reduced by placing supporting equipment throughout the installation and by positioning equipment for related operations adjacent to each other—for example, placing accounting machines near reproducing or punch devices for summary punching operations.

Range of vision is a significant safety factor that must be implemented in the layout. In most data processing operations, the line of sight creates no problems, as vision is not generally obscured within a room. The problems generally are evident in movement from one room to another—that is, when moving blindly from the computer room through windowless doors or into a passageway. The situation on the doors can be corrected by making cutouts for window inserts, thereby increasing the vision before the door swings open. If an organization has the space available, it may be much more practical to have IN and OUT doors separated by a center rail extending for about 30 to 36 inches inside and outside of the room. Egress into a passageway is generally aided by mounting aligned 45°-mirrors on the wall directly in front of the exit. This will provide a range of vision for the left or right side of the passageway, or both if two mirrors are installed.

Review Questions: Group 5B

1. What initial assessment must a manager make of any site considered as a possible data processing operations facility?
2. Why is floor loading such an important factor in the evaluation and planning of a physical site?
3. Moisture penetration and condensation are two potential problems

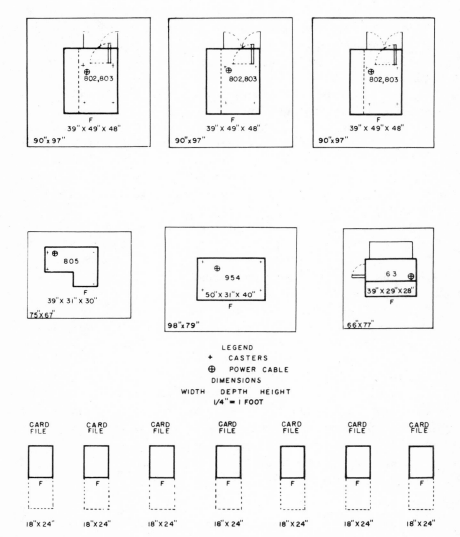

Figure 5.11. Physical Planning Template. Courtesy IBM Corporation.

300

that may affect an operations installation. How may these problems be reduced or eliminated?

4. Why must a manager concern himself with the physical characteristics of his employees in designing a layout?

HOW LAYOUTS ARE MADE

When consideration has been given to all of the interacting factors, the manager is then ready to optimize the layout. This involves using a layout diagram and simulating the manpower, materials, and machine resources in actual production.

The layout diagram is produced by arranging templates, illustrations, or models on grid paper or hardboard to provide a scaled version of an optimal operating facility. The layout development process is concerned with three basic elements:

1. Planning tools
2. Space allocation
3. Optimal equipment placement

Planning Tools

The available planning tools enable a manager to manipulate and hypothesize the physical arrangement of his processing and supporting equipment into an optimal productive layout. The manager is thereby able to evaluate each arrangement before a final architectural drawing is made.

The equipment may be represented on the planning layout by templates, illustrations, and/or models.

Templates are used to illustrate computers, data communications devices, unit-record equipment, desks, tables, chairs, files, furniture, and supporting equipment. They provide two-dimensional outlines of the equipment, specifying the height, depth, width, operating area, and maintenance requirements (see Figure 5.11). The height, depth, and width dimensions are particularly useful in determining the proper setting and angle for battery-operated emergency lights, as well as in evaluating space needs in terms of space availability. For equipment requiring a power supply, the template indicates the location of the

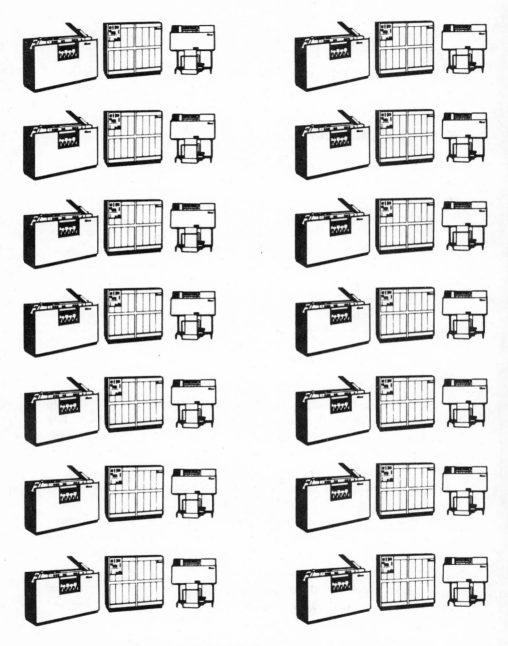

Figure 5.12. Artist's Sketch Models. Courtesy Moore Business Forms, Inc.

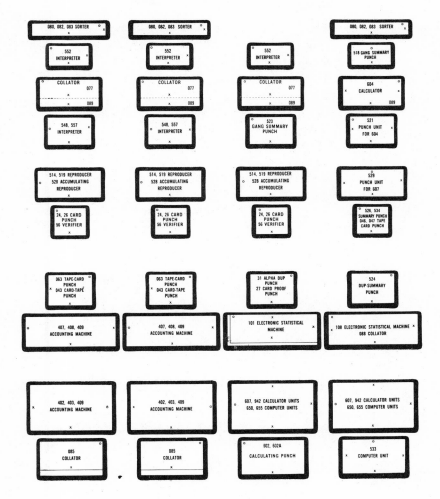

Figure 5.13. Adhesive Block Models

power exit. This enables the manager to determine the necessary placement of a device near an existing or proposed power supply. Templates may be replicated on a copying machine to produce a number of desired units. The copies are then cut up to enable the planner to use each object on the template individually.

The cutouts may be manipulated until the layout has been optimized, at which time they may be affixed to the grid paper or hardboard with paste, glue, or cellophane tape. The layout may then be reproduced on a copying machine, photographed, or prepared as an architectural drawing. Templates are very useful, although some planners criticize them for failing to give the illusion of perspective.

Illustrations are frequently used in the layout planning process. They are generally of two types—the artist's sketch of an object that may be readily reproduced (see Figure 5.12) and the adhesive-backed block (see Figure 5.13). The sketch-type illustrations provide some realism, which may be lacking in the block-type illustrations. Both types can be reproduced or photographed when the layout has been completed. When utilizing illustrations, the planner must indicate the overall space requirements for each object on the grid paper or hardboard. Also, he must make provision for such items as control panel clearances, work area, maintenance requirements, equipment dimensions, and power cable exits. The use of illustrations in layout development tends to increase planning time and effort.

Three-dimensional models (see Figure 5.14), constructed of wood, plastic, or paper, also may be used for physical planning. Paper models are generally flimsy, whereas plastic and wood ones are sturdy. The models are positioned and repositioned on the grid paper or hardboard until a layout plan has been developed. To facilitate reproduction of the layout, the planner must outline the external surfaces of the objects on the grid paper or hardboard, which is a time-consuming chore. Like the illustrations, some models make no provision for location of the power cable exits, clearances for maintenance and control panel housings, or work station requirements. But the models do provide a sense of realism and afford a better perspective than two-dimensional or illustrated objects.

The types of planning tools selected will ultimately depend upon individual preferences. Their use enables a planner to visualize several alternatives and to rework these until he has reached a desirable layout. Though this process is time-consuming, it is less costly than preparing architectural drawings for each possible arrangement.

Some planners have attempted to apply such linear programming techniques as the Graphic, Simplex, and Transportation methods to layout planning. However, the effectiveness of these techniques in the physical planning of a data processing operation installation is questionable. Unlike manufacturing facilities, more consideration must be given to the sequence of operations performed, the time required to perform the steps, the processing schedule, and flow of input and output.

Space Allocation

The manager begins the space allocation segment of physical planning by outlining the external area for the facility on the grid paper or hardboard. After identifying the external parameters, he must specify the internal limiting factors, such as stairwells, elevators, windows, permanent partitions, doors, emergency exits, and columns affecting the room. The air-conditioning unit, radiators, ductwork, and piping or conduit must also be illustrated. Next, the planner must indicate electrical power outlet locations and their respective voltage capacities.

The layout diagram at this point primarily identifies the available floor space and major constraints regarding the machines, materials, and manpower.

Figure 5.14. Three-Dimensional Models. Courtesy "Visual" Industrial Products, Inc.

Optimal Equipment Placement

Utilizing the data collected on the work flow the manager can begin to position his productive equipment. Their placement will be affected by the availability of electrical power outlets, signal cable lengths, and floor loading capacity. If load redistribution is necessary, then the manager must develop alternative arrangements to design an operationally effective environment.

An analysis of the process flow also enables the manager to determine optimal placement for both the portable and stationary materials handling equipment. Portable equipment offers greater placement flexibility in the layout, yet it too must be optimally positioned to achieve maximum utilization and effectiveness. In addition, the placement of stationary equipment may be affected by the floor loading capacity. For example, cabinets for punched card storage may have to be placed against the walls, away from the center areas. This arrangement can increase materials handling, so it may be necessary to position the card cabinets in a sequence that will reduce the walking distances to heavily utilized files. Tables, desks, chairs, and other furniture used in the operation must also be positioned on the diagram at this time.

Next, the manager must give careful consideration to the placement of supervisory stations. A significant factor is their accessibility to the operating personnel in order to allow immediate contact when the need arises. In addition, this will discourage the assumption of nondelegated authority by the subordinates when a decision has to be made and no one in authority is readily available. If an enclosed area is to be constructed for managerial personnel, the space allocation for one such person may range from 100 to 125 square feet.

Having positioned the productive equipment, supervisory stations, and supporting facilities, the manager must then reevaluate his minimal space allocations. He has to consider spaces between machines, in traffic and work aisles, at working stations, and for equipment maintenance. One frequently overlooked factor at this stage is the effect of file cabinets on aisles. Files are repeatedly opened, so that failure to allow adequate clearance in the aisles when the drawers are fully extended, disrupts productivity. Furthermore, people working on the files may have to temporarily stop in order to permit the passage of people and/or materials through the aisles.

Cramped work stations are seldom an inducement for efficiency. Depending upon the size and type of machine, the operator must be provided with adequate space for mobility. In an effort to reduce materials handling and distances, there is a tendency to position tables and other handling equipment too close to the operation, thereby reducing the available work space. Furthermore, the placement of portable handling equipment in the area frequently adds to the congestion. Cramped work stations are found most frequently at the sorters, collators, and reproducers. Reserving space between these machines and others for placement and movement of portable equipment can significantly alleviate this type of congestion.

Having completed his assessment of the space allocations for working stations, work and traffic aisles, and maintenance, the manager turns his attention to environmental safety. He must, for example, verify that his layout has not blocked any emergency exits or limited the size of any emergency passageways. In addition, he should reconsider the placement of fire extinguishers and emergency telephones, for these pieces of equipment *must* be kept accessible. In windowless installations, the manager must reevaluate the placement of battery-operated emergency lights. To prevent interference with the light beams, it will be necessary to ensure that no materials handling or processing equipment gets in the way. The manager must further determine that he has an adequate number of these lights in the installation.

Having completed this preliminary phase, the manager must sample the effectiveness of his design. The process is conducted by simulating the flow of several benchmark applications through the layout to help identify any potential problem or bottlenecks. Modifications can then be made to the layout before it is finalized.

Review Questions: Group 5C

1. Name and describe briefly the tools used in layout planning.
2. What are some of the internal limiting factors a manager must consider in the layout of an operations facility?
3. What is the purpose of simulating the work flow of a benchmark application through the layout design?

LAYOUT OF OFFICE FACILITIES

The office facilities in a data processing organization are used by the personnel involved in programming, systems analysis and design, advanced planning, and training activities. The objectives are concerned primarily with maintaining a flow of communications and with the movement of paper work by the shortest and most direct route. Unlike the operations work area, an office facility is less concerned with productive balance and materials handling. However, environmental considerations such as floor loading, illumination, noise, color, safety, and air-conditioning are relevant for both, although the parameters may be different. Office planning involves the same basic tools and the initial space allocation steps as in the layout of the operations facility. Then the windows, doors, permanent partitions, stairways, columns, ductwork, and any permanent fixtures limiting the available floor space must be marked. The manager then must decide whether the available area will be subdivided into private offices and/or cubicles or left as an open area with only a few office areas for key personnel. If a decision is made to subdivide, more overall space will be required. However, subdivision does afford some degree of privacy and helps reduce or eliminate environmental noise and interference. The space allocation for each employee will be allocated in proportion to the level of importance within the hierarchical structure. A minimum of 70 to 75 square feet should be allocated for each employee. In organizations where an open office area is maintained, the minimum space allocation for a desk and chair combination is, with only minor exceptions, 50 square feet.

There is perhaps a need to give more consideration to traffic aisles and work stations in an open office area. Particular attention must be given to the area behind the desks. The failure to provide adequate space will generally interfere with the smooth flow of employees to and from their work stations. Consequently, this will have a disruptive physical and psychological effect on the other employees in the area. Work stations located near major traffic aisles and elevators must be screened off to reduce and/or eliminate noise and other distractions. The screening may be achieved by installing removable partitions constructed from acoustical materials.

Where file cabinets and desks face each other across an aisle, a minimum of seven feet should be reserved for the combination work and traffic aisle. This allocation of space should provide for both a smooth flow of traffic and minimal distraction to the personnel in the area. This is a consideration most frequently overlooked in the design process.

For both open and enclosed office areas, the minimal space allocations for a traffic aisle width should be five feet for major aisles and between three and four feet for minor or connecting aisles.

Many organizations now include a conference room in an office area. This provides space for meetings with people from other functional activities; enables project leaders to meet with their teams to discuss systems, plans, programs, problems, or progress; facilitates conduct of "sounding" or "brainstorming" sessions; and, to a limited extent, provides a classroom for orientation and training purposes. To facilitate these functions, the room should afford visual and acoustical privacy. The size of a conference room is often determined by the size of the table to be set in the room. For example, a $4' \times 8'$ table seating from six to ten persons (depending upon the type of chairs used) may be placed in a $12' \times 18'$ room. Ideally the chairs in the conference room should be of a pivotal type, with one-foot separations between them. This will permit the audience to face several speakers and to avoid feeling like sardines. A permanent blackboard should also be installed on one of the wall surfaces for use in "chalk-talks" and presentations.

Another special area may be set aside in the office layout for the stenographic pool, plus copying and duplicating equipment. The overall size of this area depends upon the number of personnel to be situated there and the type and number of special devices to be used. However, a minimum allocation of 36 square feet should be included for each secretary. In some organizations, fireproof vaults or cabinets are added for storage of the original copies of documentation and programs. Their sizes vary, so that the specifications should be secured from vendor catalogs.

There is less difficulty in preparing an office layout than an operations one because there will be very little, if any, grouping of major or minor activities· due to the variations in the functional activities. The personnel may be grouped by types of activity, such as programming, systems, or training. Or, instead, the systems, planning, and programming personnel may be grouped into teams of major application areas or projects. The work-flow patterns vary with each application, project, or task.

Review Questions: Group 5D

1. Are there any differences in the planning of an office area as com-

pared with an operations room? If so, what are they?
2. Why should a manager consider the use of cubicle enclosures for his programming and systems personnel?

SUMMARY

In this chapter we have been concerned primarily with the layout of the productive facilities in the data processing function. The primary emphasis was placed on the operations activity, where developing the optimal mix of the manpower, machine, and materials resources is essential. Ideally it would be more advantageous to prepare a layout and construct a building around the design, but the ideal is usually impractical because most facilities must be located within an existing structure. If given the opportunity to select a site, a manager must choose one that will best fit his immediate and future needs. The planner must coordinate the physical and human factors involved into a composite layout that meets both physical and psychological needs. Having given consideration to these factors, he must then prepare the actual layout. With the aid of grid paper or hardboard, plus templates, illustrations, and/or models, the manager develops the layout. To assess the layout, he should simulate the work flow of some representative applications in order to identify potential problems and bottlenecks. When satisfied that the layout will be operationally effective, the manager must then proceed with the construction details, which will be handled by an architect, contractor, or engineer.

After the site has been prepared, it may be necessary to make some changes or modifications, which may be done with little difficulty if flexibility has been included in the original design.

CASE STUDY

Case Study 5.1: The Eric Andrea Cosmetics Company

The Eric Andrea Cosmetics Company has recently completed a feasibility study. As a result of the study, the executive committee has decided to upgrade its existing unit-record equipment to an IBM 360/30 computer configuration with a disk operating system. The organization would like to use the existing area for the data processing operations activity.

The operations room is located in the northwest corner of the building. The two corner walls of the building are filled with large ordinary glass windows. The internal side wall has smaller windows between the two single doors on the wall. The room is not equipped with any air-conditioning or humidification control. On warm days, the back windows are opened to cool the room. The side windows are not opened because they are on the wall most affected by the wind, dust, and dirt—these windows are adjacent to the parking lot and in line with the foundry across the road. The room is equipped with an automatic sprinkler system and two soda-acid fire extinguishers for fire protection.

Tahitian sunset (reddish orange) has been applied to the back-window wall. This color was applied to offset the psychological coldness of the room. Shades of vanilla (greenish yellow) and chocolate (light brown) have been applied to the other wall surfaces.

Illumination is provided by an incandescent lighting system. The footcandle capacity is adequate for current needs. Electrical power for the existing hardware configuration is also adequate. The freestanding electrical outlets are located near the respective equipment.

The desks of the control clerk and the manager and his assistant are located in an open area near the side-window wall. These three people share the one telephone line and extension in the room.

The room is 60 feet long and 25 feet wide. The ceilings are 18 feet high and painted in a shade of vanilla. The floor loading capacity of the room is rated at 100 pounds per square foot.

Discussion Questions

1. After reading this case, what initial observations would you make about the acceptability of the existing physical facility?
2. Does the fact that the area is currently located in the northwest corner of the building have any effect upon the site selection? Why or why not?
3. What effect, if any, do the windows have upon the site?
4. In your opinion are there any undesirable features about the site?
5. Should any recommendations be made to improve the effectiveness of the fire protection in the existing facility? What are they, if any?

6. What comments or suggestions, if any, do you have about the existing color scheme?
7. Without any knowledge of the dimensional requirements of the proposed equipment, what graphic planning can be done at this time?
8. Would you feel it necessary to convert from a fluorescent to an incandescent lighting system? Why or why not?
9. Do you feel that all personnel needs are currently being satisfied? If not, explain why.
10. Are there any safety considerations that should be included in the future plans of the organization?

6

Scheduling and Project Planning

INTRODUCTION

The successful management of a data processing activity is dependent upon scheduling and project planning techniques. Schedules must be developed for and within the various functional activities to reduce and/or eliminate the setting of arbitrary deadline times and dates, as well as to provide a more realistic measure of actual and expected progress. In many organizations, the term "scheduling" is synonymous with "machine loading." Machine loading, however, is but one part of the operations activity and does not encompass the work of the programming, systems, training, or advanced planning groups.

Scheduling involves the allocation of manpower, material, and machine resources to the performance of a task, operation, application, or system within a given time-frame. Each activity, step, or event is allocated a quantum of time estimated or projected as necessary to achieve an objective. The quantum allocation may include time for preparation (setup and handling), as well as actual processing. A schedule may be affected by such factors as priorities, volume, required operations and their sequence, input availability, output requirements, control procedures, personnel proficiency, frequency of reports, etc. The schedule must be both reasonable and realistic, so as to allow for achievement of the desired objective or flow of work; it must also be flexible enough to permit modifications when required.

The concept of project planning is entirely dependent upon the early development of a realistic schedule. The existence of a schedule enables the manager to coordinate, direct, and control the activities and events generated by the executive committee, users, and data processing personnel. A delay of any activity or event may be considered as a deviation from the schedule. The manager should evaluate the effect of the delay on the overall schedule and the project. Based on his analysis, he may then find it necessary to alter the schedule or select and implement an alternative course of action.

The constant flux within an environment or situation requires that the manager apply the principles of dynamic management to his activities; that is, the principles founded on the concept of dynamic management as a constant monitoring of the productive process and its results. This realistic approach must be applied to every plan and schedule developed and implemented in the management process. .

SCHEDULING FACTORS

The scheduling factors vary for each functional group—programming, systems, operations, etc.—in the data processing department. Consequently, each group must develop its own schedule after having carefully considered the internal and external influences directly and indirectly affecting it. For instance, the operations activity is affected by those factors that influence the manipulation of data and production of information and outputs. The schedule of the programming group is affected by a different set of factors, which are inherent in the planning, development, testing, and implementation of a program. The systems group is influenced by those variables concerned with systems analysis, development, and implementation. The training group's schedule depends primarily upon the type and level of training to be provided. The advanced planning group's schedule is affected by the types of projects they are concerned with.

In the development and implementation of a new system, personnel from the data processing functions may be integrated into a project team to accomplish a given task or objective (see Chapter 2). The integrated approach requires only a minor alteration to the scheduling technique. Rather than viewing each activity as mono-functional, the project manager must allow for the interaction of the scheduling variables of the groups in preparation of what should be a multi-functional plan.

To understand scheduling factors and their effects more fully, it is useful to undertake an analysis of the various scheduling factors that must be considered. This is best done by following the basic system of divisionalization in dealing with the five groups in the data processing function (see Chapter 2). These are the operations group, programming group, systems group, training group, and advanced planning and development group.

The Operations Group

The operations group is primarily responsible for the transcription of data and its classification and manipulation to produce outputs and information necessary for operation and management of the overall organization.

The production schedule for this group is generally established on a weekly basis, with provision for daily requirements. It includes the continuous production needs, special and one-time requests, and reruns. Schedules for computer operations must, in addition, allocate time for preventative and emergency maintenance, program assembly and compiling, program testing, and training needs. The basic production schedule is primarily affected by:
1. Priorities
2. Volumes
3. Operations required
4. Input availability
5. Output requirements
6. Reporting frequency
7. Personnel skills
8. Documentation availability

1. PRIORITIES. With a few minor exceptions, priorities in an organization do not remain fixed for any long period of time. This is not an unfavorable condition because it may indicate that new and more important systems are being processed. It may also denote that, based on available utilization statistics, a more effective allocation of resources is

attainable by reshuffling the priorities in the production schedule. A priority status should be allocated to a system only after an assessment of its relative importance to the overall organization has been made. The decision should not be arbitrary but based on fact. Nor should a priority assignment be made on the basis of internal political or social relationships. One criterion to be applied is cost of delay. Systems that may be significantly delayed without affecting the normal operational activities of an organization should be granted a lower priority status. However, applications such as payroll, accounts payable, and accounts receivable are generally exempt from any priority status evaluation. These are regarded as critical or vital to the normal operation of the organization.

When a delay occurs due to a hardware malfunction, loss of power, operator error, or other emergency condition, the manager must determine the delay's effect on the day's schedule. Depending upon the length of delay, the priorities may be dispensed with until normal operations are resumed. The cost of delay would again be used as one of the major criteria in determining which systems will be processed and when.

In most operations groups there is a controversy about the priority status to be allocated to systems and/or programs being developed or modified. Often this type of work is relegated an extremely low priority or "when-time-is-available" status. Consequently, development and implementation schedules slip because of a lack of machine time. There is very little logic in permitting this condition to prevail because the cost of delay can be extremely high to an organization. Sufficient facilities must be made available in order to eliminate the verbal and near-physical personnel conflicts that erupt over importance of activities. However, should an emergency arise, the operations manager may be justified in temporarily limiting available machine time until the crisis has passed or is eased.

2. VOLUMES. Before any time estimates can be developed for each operation, the operations manager must know the work load. Volume statistics must be gathered on the source documents received, cards or records transcribed and processed, and outputs produced. Collecting source-document counts may be a simple or complex problem. If the operations group has developed a document control system, then this will in most cases be a matter of tabulating item, batch, or transmittal counts. For example, volume statistics may be collected from a transmittal document (see form illustrated in Figure 6.1). Document, line item, and record counts are also available from this form.

TRANSMITTAL DOCUMENT				FORM NO. R5-61
SYSTEM/APPLICATION		IDENTIFICATION NUMBER		
ORIGINATOR		LOCATION		
TELEPHONE		DATE		

TYPE OF DATA TRANSMITTED ▶	DOCUMENT	CARD	TAPE	DISK
*REQUIRED ENTRY				
BATCH NUMBER(S)	*	*	*	*
DOCUMENT IDENT.	*			
FILE IDENT.		*		
TAPE IDENT.			*	
DISK IDENT.				*
DOCUMENT COUNT	*			
RECORD COUNT		*	*	*
LINE ITEM COUNT				
HASH TOTAL				
QUANTITY TOTAL				
DOLLAR VALUE TOTAL				
NO. OF BOXES/TAPES/DISKS		*	*	*
SPECIAL INSTRUCTIONS:				

DATA CHECKER	DATE CHECKED / /	KEYING OPERATOR	DATE KEYED / /	VERIFIER OPERATOR	DATE VERIFIED / /	LAST BATCH YES | NO

Figure 6.1. Transmittal Document Form

When such documents are unavailable, the manager must gather data by sampling or physical counts. Sometimes quantitative data may be derived by determining the number of cards punched per document and dividing this into total card volume, as illustrated in Figure 6.2. Whichever technique is applied, it is important that the manager secure quantitative data based on good representative periods. Whenever possible, the minimum and maximum actual or anticipated volumes must be determined to offset work load fluctuations. Failure to analyze volume data may lead to unexpected work loads that could possibly destroy the operational effectiveness of a schedule. Figure 6.3 illustrates use of a chart on which volume stability can be plotted and evaluated.

Statistical data on cards and records must be collected to determine their effect on the input preparation and processing segments of the schedule. As cards are a popular form of input, they will affect all types of unit-record and computing equipment, as well as many manual operations. The statistics may be collected by counting the actual number of cards either as they pass through a sorting device equipped with a counter or by using a tabulator or computer. Counts may also be

METHOD: No. of Source   Estimated Card Volume
             Documents   = ─────────────────────────────────
             Processed   Estimated Average No. of Cards
                                  Punched per Source Document

APPLICATION: No. of Source   62,500
             Documents   = ───────
             Processed   25

RESULT: No. of Source
             Documents   = 2,500
             Processed

Figure 6.2   Example of Method for Estimating Document Volume

derived by analyzing document control records maintained by the control clerk, summary total lines on reports, transmittal or batch control
records (see Figure 6.4), or actual production data. Crude statistics may
also be developed by physically measuring the contents of files and
converting the results by estimating 150 cards per inch; if the cards are
not compressed tightly, then the statistics may be inflated. Another
approximating technique is that of multiplying the estimated average
number of cards punched per document by the number of source documents processed, as illustrated in Figure 6.5. The card volumes will be

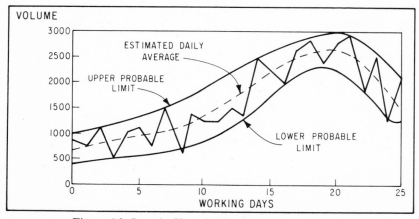

Figure 6.3. Sample Chart for Plotting Volume Trends

RS-64 PAYROLL BATCH CONTROL CARD			
DATE	DEPT.	NO. OF CARDS	BATCH NO.

FIELD DESCRIPTION	TOTAL HOURS	F R A C.	TOTAL AMOUNTS	D E C.
TIME WORKED AND ADJUSTMENTS				
OVERTIME ALLOWANCES AND ADJUSTMENTS				
OTHER ALLOWANCES AND ADJUSTMENTS				
SUB-TOTAL				
NIGHT BONUS AND ADJUSTMENTS				
GROSS				

DOCUMENT CONTROL		
SEQUENCE	OPERATION	INITIALS
1	LOG IN	
2	KEY PUNCH	
3	KEY VERIFY	
4	PROOF	
5	POST-PAYROLL	

Figure 6.4. Sample Form for Batch Control Records

No. of Source Documents Processed	2,500
multiplied by	
Estimated Average No. of Cards Punched Per Document	×25
equals	———
Estimated Punched Card Volume	62,500

Figure 6.5   Example of Method for Estimating Card Volume

used to calculate the processing and preparation time for each operation, and the work loads.

Preparation of records involves the conversion of source data to magnetic tape, drum, or disk by means of a magnetic data recording devise. Unlike cards, these media can only be inputted directly to a computing system or buffered auxiliary device. However, this has a significant impact on the input preparation and processing schedule.

Output statistics are also very significant in schedule development. The output may be a complete report, a calculated result, one element of an application, cards, magnetic tape, or other media. The output requirements significantly affect machine loading. Most of the output is currently generated on tabulators in unit-record operations, and printers in computerized activities. The volumes may be collected by actual count, although this may not be very practical when physically counting printed pages. On some reports, a page number is printed by the equipment at the top or bottom of the form. On some forms, though, consecutive numbers are preprinted by the vendors. These counts may be gathered by the equipment operator, control clerk, or operations manager and posted on a data control form. The statistics may then be tallied to develop quantitative data on output production. Statistics on drafts, checks, or invoices may be secured from the accounting or treasury departments, or by checking beginning and ending control numbers on such forms as the one illustrated in Figure 6.6. Where budget figures are available for chargebacks, these may possibly be used to develop output statistics. If statistics are unavailable, then the manager must apply some sampling techniques to determine the tabulator, printer, and other needs.

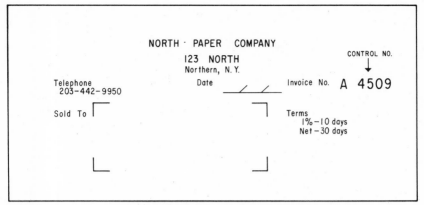

Figure 6.6. Example of a Control Number

Having collected the statistics, the manager evaluates and analyzes the interaction between source document, card, record, and output volumes for each application in the basic production plan. The analyses may be displayed in the form of individual and composite graphs.

3. OPERATIONS REQUIRED. The operations manager must analyze the documentation (see Figure 6.7) to determine the operations and steps required to achieve the desired objectives. This necessitates a detailed breakdown of the manual, semiautomated, and automated operations in the work flow. The automated operations must specify each unit of equipment utilized, as well as the number of passes or runs to be processed on each device. Ultimately, this information should be coupled with the volume data and machine processing speeds to develop the production schedule. Graphs or charts (see Figure 6.8) may again be used to indicate the machine and manual loads.

4. INPUT AVAILABILITY. This element is concerned with the rate of flow and type of input. The rate must be analyzed to determine the peaks and valleys occurring during the day, week, and month. The peaks if not anticipated or expected can generate many problems for the operations manager. Analysis may reveal the need for some alternative action on the rate of flow before a schedule is developed. Input type affects both speed and accuracy. Source documents that are to be transcribed efficiently to card, tape, disk, or drum record formats must be legible, as well as properly designed and colored. Legibility layout and code construction are particularly important in key punching and data recording operations. Ideally, the data to be transcribed should

Abstract of Hourly Payroll Program

Purpose: This system is designed to process the hourly rated employees payroll. It provides for computation of gross pay; social security, federal, state, and city taxes; and the application of deductions for determination of net amount. The system utilizes a single program written in Report Program Generator on an IBM 360 Model 20 computer.

The basic employee information and computations are printed on the Statement of Payroll Account issued to each employee. The program provides for punching of calculated current earnings cards for use in the Labor Distribution System; a year-to-date taxes and earnings record for use in various management reports; and a draft card used in printing the employee payroll draft.

In addition, the program utilizes several subroutines. These provide for: processing of cash advances and adjustments; processing of garnishments and other types of levies; determination of taxable earnings and limits under the social security law; determination of deductions that cannot be applied against the current payroll; and the accumulation of total earnings, taxes, and deductions for preparation of departmental controls.

Method: A set of cards for each employee grouped by card code is read into the computer in employee number sequence. For each employee there is a basic employee information and rate card, a second basic employee information and rate card if an employee carries a dual rate, current earnings cards, cash advances or adjustments, the year-to-date taxes and earnings record, priority deductions (deductions not applied in previous payroll processing), garnishments or levies, and current payroll deductions.

Restrictions: The following represent processing restrictions within the computer program:

1. The cards must be within employee number sequence.
2. The card set for each employee must be in a controlled order sequence, based on card code in card columns 79–80.
3. Each employee card set must contain a tax and earnings card, card code 48 in card columns 79–80.

Storage Requirements: 4000 positions of primary core storage.

Equipment Specifications: 4K, IBM 360 Model 20 computer equipped with a Basic Operating System.

Figure 6.7 Documentation Sample

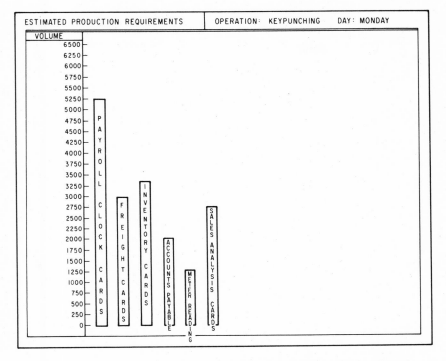

Figure 6.8. Example of Chart for Indicating Estimated Production Requirements

appear on the source document in large, legible, well-spaced characters set on one line reading from left to right in the sequence of the record format. If the documents are unacceptable for transcription purposes, the information will have to be encoded on transcription forms or alignment sheets (see Figure 6.9), or in a rubber stamp block imprinted on a source document (see Figure 6.10). Or an apron may be attached to the form on which the desired information is arranged in transcription sequence, as illustrated in Figure 6.11. The transcription speed is also influenced by the number of card columns or positions to be keyed, duplicated, and skipped per record. Therefore, in order to expedite the input preparation and verification process, repetitive data that can be duplicated should be positioned on the left side of the source document and transcription format. Also, the fields to be recorded should be grouped to eliminate or minimize skipping, in that skipping reduces productivity through interruptions in the keying process. In addition, the

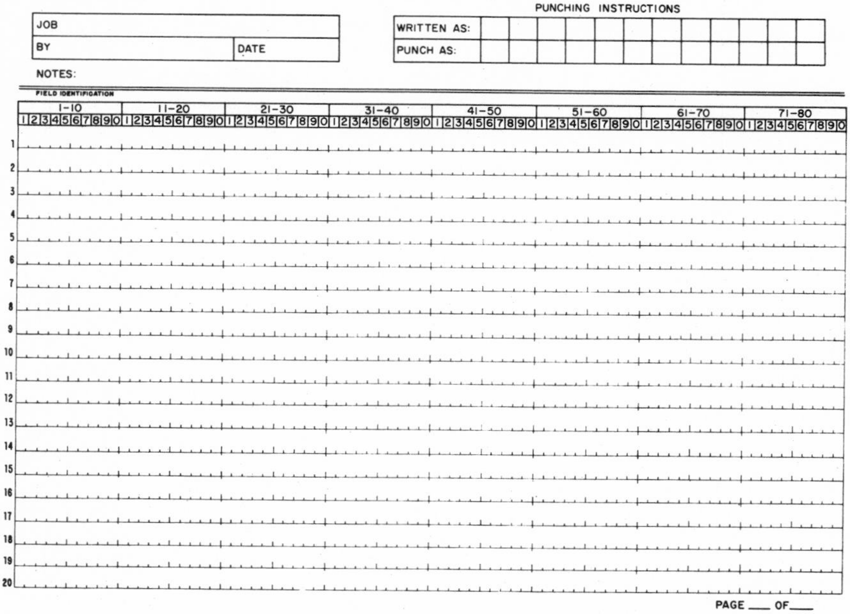
PUNCHING INSTRUCTIONS
JOB
BY
DATE
WRITTEN AS:
PUNCH AS:
NOTES:
FIELD IDENTIFICATION
1–10
11–20
21–30
31–40
41–50
51–60
61–70
71–80
PAGE ___ OF ___

Figure 6.9. Transcription Form

operations manager must determine the amount of numeric, alphabetic, or alphameric data to be transcribed. Due to keyboard design on the input recording devices, numeric data can be entered more rapidly than

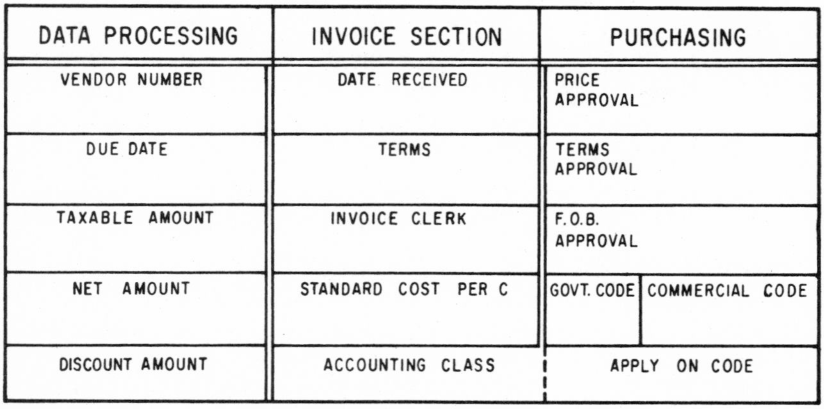
DATA PROCESSING
INVOICE SECTION
PURCHASING
VENDOR NUMBER
DATE RECEIVED
PRICE APPROVAL
DUE DATE
TERMS
TERMS APPROVAL
TAXABLE AMOUNT
INVOICE CLERK
F.O.B. APPROVAL
NET AMOUNT
STANDARD COST PER C
GOVT. CODE
COMMERCIAL CODE
DISCOUNT AMOUNT
ACCOUNTING CLASS
APPLY ON CODE

Figure 6.10. Rubber Stamp Imprint

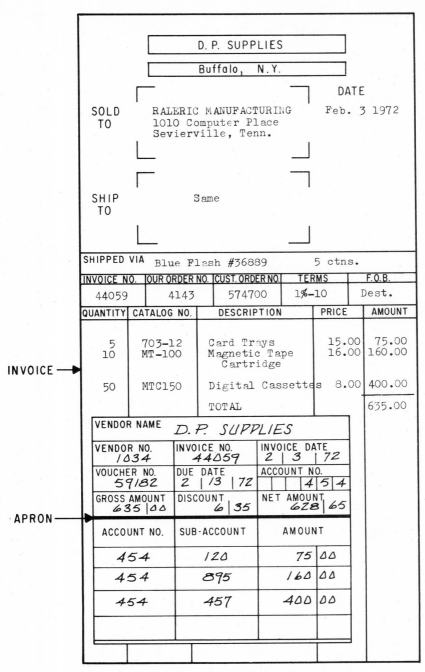

INVOICE →

APRON →

	D. P. SUPPLIES
	Buffalo, N.Y.

SOLD TO RALERIC MANUFACTURING
1010 Computer Place
Sevierville, Tenn.

DATE
Feb. 3 1972

SHIP TO Same

SHIPPED VIA	Blue Flash #36889		5 ctns.	

INVOICE NO.	OUR ORDER NO.	CUST. ORDER NO.	TERMS	F.O.B.
44059	4143	574700	1%-10	Dest.

QUANTITY	CATALOG NO.	DESCRIPTION	PRICE	AMOUNT
5	703-12	Card Trays	15.00	75.00
10	MT-100	Magnetic Tape Cartridge	16.00	160.00
50	MTC150	Digital Cassettes	8.00	400.00
		TOTAL		635.00

VENDOR NAME	D.P. SUPPLIES		
VENDOR NO. 1034	INVOICE NO. 44059	INVOICE DATE 2 | 3 | 72	
VOUCHER NO. 59182	DUE DATE 2 | 13 | 72	ACCOUNT NO. 4 5 4	
GROSS AMOUNT 635 | 00	DISCOUNT 6 | 35	NET AMOUNT 628 | 65	

ACCOUNT NO.	SUB-ACCOUNT	AMOUNT	
454	120	75	00
454	895	160	00
454	457	400	00

Figure 6.11. Apron Attached to Form

alphabetic or alphameric data. The operations manager must also be concerned about the transcription error rate. Experience has shown that an increase in alphabetic and alphameric content on a source document tends to increase the error rate.

5. OUTPUT REQUIREMENTS. To determine output requirements, the operations manager must review and evaluate the documentation, data gathered on required operations (see Figures 6.7 and 6.8), and the printing formats. An analysis of the printer spacing charts will enable the operations manager to determine data type, spacing, and skipping requirements affecting printer and tabulator productivity. In computer printer operations, large volumes of output may be expedited through the use of interchangeable numeric print chains or bars and preferred character features. For example, a printer equipped with a numeric print feature and interchangeable cartridge is capable of achieving a rate of 1285 lines per minute for numeric output. The same printer without the optional items can achieve a rate of only 600 lines per minute. Actual speeds in both cases depend on the operation. Spacing and skipping must be evaluated in conjunction with lines and pages of print to estimate processing time requirements when volumes are known. The other output media, such as cards and magnetic tape, would also have to be evaluated. It is conceivable that if the operations manager found his computer processing capability to be output-bound, he could utilize offline peripheral equipment for output functions.

6. REPORTING FREQUENCY. The reporting cycle must be analyzed to indicate the peaks and valleys in the overall work load. The cycle is graphically plotted for each workday of the month to indicate heavy, normal, and light days, as well as the expected demand upon resources. If the peaks appear to be too radical, the operations manager may initiate a reports audit to determine if priorities may be reassigned or if scheduled due dates or times may be readjusted to correct the imbalance.

7. PERSONNEL SKILLS. The effectiveness of the schedule is very dependent upon personnel availability and proficiency. The two factors are not independent of each other. The operation must be adequately staffed with personnel possessing a reasonable degree of training and experience. Inexperienced and/or poorly trained personnel limit an operations manager's ability to function effectively within the schedule. Therefore, the operations manager must initially assess the capabilities of his personnel. The skills inventory, coupled with knowledge of the work flow,

REPT. NO.	OPERATOR NO.		DATE	SHIFT		BATCH NO.
	KP	VERIFY		KP	VERIFY	
				1 2 3		

MACH.TYPE	MACH.TIME	S	CLERICAL	OTHER CODE	OTHER TIME	CARD VOL.	CARD COLS.	FORM NO.
								ERRORS

Figure 6.12. Unit-Record Production Control Record Form

enable him to determine the individuals to whom specific functions may be assigned. This assessment is also useful in determining assignments for processing in an alternate or emergency mode of operations. As a result, an intensive orientation and training program may have to be conducted to improve the productive capabilities and proficiency levels of the personnel. The productivity and proficiency may be monitored through the use of a production control record as illustrated in Figure 6.12 (this particular form is appropriate for monitoring unit-record operations).

8. DOCUMENTATION AVAILABILITY. An efficient operation depends heavily on the availability of good documentation. The documentation for each system should be the normal and alternate mode procedures contained in the operator's manual (see Chapter 4). The lack of documentation precludes the operations manager from detailing the tasks and developing a preliminary schedule. It also prevents him from determining the training and orientation needs of his personnel. In addition, it hampers his ability to develop the necessary control procedures to ensure uniformity and accuracy of processing.

Preliminary documentation should be made available to the operations manager when the parallel tests are conducted. This will enable him to evaluate each manual and machine operation to be performed and to estimate or compute the required processing time. This data must be compared against the existing schedule to identify overlapping operations, bottlenecks, and problem areas that may cause delays in processing. Very often this evaluation is not made and everyone is optimistic that if any problems occur these may be readily resolved. This is wishful thinking and a most unrealistic attitude. The purpose of scheduling is to ensure concurrency of operations. Failure to achieve this goal increases the operating costs through a misuse of resources.

In computerized operations, it is very important that checkpoint, restart, and recovery procedures be included in the operator's manual. This will help to reduce rerun time scheduling and manipulation of the existing schedule when problems occur.

Integrating these factors into an effective production schedule will require the development and implementation of performance standards for the manpower and machines before time estimates or computations can be made. The end result will be a plan covering all of the operational details contributing to goal attainment. The operations group's schedule must be flexible enough to allow for reruns resulting from contingencies and machine or human errors, and to allow for the processing of special or one-time reports—reports such as payroll data on selected job classifications during contract negotiations. If the basic production schedule is heavy, there will be little time for special or one-time reports, which may then be either processed on an overtime basis or submitted to a service bureau.

Review Questions: Group 6A

1. What is meant by the term "scheduling"?
2. Why must a project manager or leader consider a multi-functional approach to scheduling?
3. Why must volume statistics be evaluated when preparing an operations group's schedule?
4. Why should a systems analyst provide an operations manager with a copy of the preliminary documentation prior to parallel testing?

The Programming Group

The programming group is generally responsible for the preparation of new programs; the writing of programmer's, utility, and conversion programs; and maintenance of existing operational programs. In doing this work, the programmers may analyze system flowcharts, develop macro- and micro-diagrams, code instructions, desk check coding and logic, compile or assemble source programs, test and debug programs, and prepare program documentation. Each of these activities affects the development of a programming activity schedule.

The scheduling factors are qualified by such variables as program size, input/output, complexity, language, programmer efficiency, and testing. The size variable relates to the number of statements, instructions, or storage requirements in a program. Most frequently, program size is expressed as storage requirements or instructions; for example, 32K, 32,000 positions, or 150 instructions. Sometimes, though, program size is simply expressed in number of pages; for example, "12 pages of coding." Input/output refers to the number and types of devices controlled by the program. Certain devices, such as graphic and audio terminals, require more programming interface than a card reader or card punch. (A related factor is that, as additional devices are included in a program, the program's size increases because additional memory positions are required for a work area and controls.) Often the devices are listed in order of interface difficulty from simple to complex. Obviously, more development and test time will be required for more sophisticated i/o devices. Complexity varies according to the length of the program, number of tasks to be performed, and the number of input/output devices used. It may be expressed in levels from simple to very difficult. The language variable refers, obviously, to the programming language in which the problem is to be coded. If several programming languages are generally used in an organization, these must be scaled by levels of difficulty from the absolute to procedure-oriented. Programmer efficiency is a subjective evaluation of a programmer's productivity. Generally, an efficiency factor is assigned on the basis of position and classification level within the programmer's occupational grouping. Consequently, time allocations for senior personnel will be significantly less than those allowed to trainees or juniors. Testing is concerned with testing requirements and the ability of programming personnel to secure adequate machine time to debug a program. Very often a schedule slips considerably because of a lack of adequate machine time for testing and debugging.

In the development of a schedule it is necessary to divide the programming function into the performance categories of (1) new program development and (2) maintenance of existing programs.

New Program Development.

In the development of a new program, the programmer designs the initial logic for solution of a given problem. This process involves the following activities:

1. Program logic development
2. Instruction coding
3. Desk checking
4. Compilation and/or assembly of a program
5. Testing and debugging
6. Program documentation

1. PROGRAM LOGIC DEVELOPMENT. The development of a computer program is a two-phased activity. The first is concerned with understanding the problem and establishing the program requirements. Determining what is to be done requires:

—Interpretation of the system flowchart
—Analysis of the preliminary system's abstract
—Analysis of the macro-flowchart, if provided or available
—Analysis of input, output, and record requirements
—Analysis of required management controls
—Analysis of decision tables, if provided or available
—Analysis of all required functions and formulae.

Having completed an analysis of this data, the programmer prepares a macro-flowchart, logic narrative, or decision table for each program. These media illustrate the conditions or parameters affecting each solution, the required interface between input, output, and data base files, and the linkage to program modules, subroutines, or subprograms. Depending upon both problem complexity and programmer efficiency, the analysis process may require from one-half to ten man-days for each program.

The second phase in logic development is concerned with forming the solution to the problem. This entails the detailed organization and layout of each program. Stating how the problem is to be solved is accomplished by: designing the micro-logic, evaluating and reviewing the logic for conformity with basic objectives, and performing a preliminary desk check.

The programmer will execute the design of his program in the form of micro-flowcharts, which are necessary for program coding. The micro-flowcharts detail the flow of information, processing functions, mathematical operations, module linkages, and special techniques used in the solution. To verify their validity and relevance, the programmer will review the diagrams and compare his design with stated objectives. In addition, a preliminary desk check will be performed to correct any syntactical errors, insert missing labels, and verify linkages to modules, subprograms, and subroutines. Program size, complexity, input/output interfaces, and programmer efficiency all affect the time allocated for program logic development. Up to 22 man-days may have to be allocated for each program designed.

For example, consider the time required to execute program logic development for an accounts payable system. In the system, the vendor file is to be maintained on the disk. The input will be transaction cards generated from the invoices received; the outputs will be remittance advices, plus credit and debit memos. During phase one, the programmer will review the functions of the system; analyze the card input, disk record, and printer layouts; and review the system's flowchart and abstract. This activity could be accomplished by an average programmer in one or one and one-half man-days. In phase two, the programmer will conceptualize his design on a micro-flowchart. Having completed his design, the programmer will then perform a preliminary desk check of the logic. This activity could require approximately two man-days to complete.

2. INSTRUCTION CODING. Instruction coding cannot be performed until the micro-logic for a program has been reviewed, because these functions must not overlap. However, if the logic has been well-designed, the coding process will be greatly expedited. Coding may require from one-half to ten man-days per program to complete.

To facilitate development of a program project schedule and programming performance standard, the programming manager must evaluate the programming languages used. The languages should be listed by coding and implementation difficulty. Degree of coding difficulty can be established on the basis of known experience. For example, an organization utilizing RPG, COBOL, Basic Assembler, and absolute programming languages would list them in that order. RPG is placed at the top of the list because it is the least difficult to code and implement. Coding in absolute language is four to five times as difficult as performing the task in RPG. Although an implementation difficulty rating could be established on the basis of this data processing industry experience, it may not be realistic to do so. The proficiency levels of the organization's programming personnel affect the rating. Therefore, on the basis of personnel performance statistics, an organization must establish its own difficulty rating level.

To return briefly to our example of an accounts payable system, the coding for the program would be in the COBOL language and could require between one and two man-days to complete. Program size and complexity, as well as programmer proficiency, would strongly affect this element of the schedule.

3. DESK CHECKING. This is an element of programming activity that simulates manually the execution of a computer program. Its effectiveness depends upon the preparation of well-designed test data and the availability of planned results. The test data is processed against the program to evaluate each programmed instruction and condition. The effects and the results achieved at each step are recorded on paper or specially prepared desk checking boards. Either during or upon completion of the process, the recorded information is compared with the planned results. Any deviations must be carefully analyzed.

The preparation and implementation of the simulation process can be very time-consuming and somewhat difficult. It is for these reasons that many programmers frown upon desk checking. They prefer to use a computer to locate their clerical and/or logic errors. Experience, however, has shown that if this process is not correctly planned for and controlled, program testing may also be very time-consuming and somewhat difficult. For example, at least two computer runs are required to locate the program errors. The first run is an attempt to produce a valid object program. It is during this pass that the clerical errors are identified. Following correction of these errors, the object deck is then processed with sample test data. The test pass helps to identify the logic errors if the test data has been correctly designed. Sometimes, only a single logic error is located during a test pass and consequently several passes may be required to debug the entire program. The ability to test in this manner is predicated upon the availability of the computer for testing purposes. The lack of adequate machine test time is often one of the primary reasons for schedule slippage in the programming activity.

The test data may subsequently be added to other data and processed through the computer for program testing. It should also be saved for use in maintenance programming. Continuing with our example of the accounts payable program, the programming manager would have to allocate approximately one to one and one-half man-days for desk checking. The time required for desk checking is affected by program size, input/output interface requirements, number of conditions, programming language, and linkages to other subroutines, subprograms, and modules.

4. COMPILATION AND/OR ASSEMBLY OF A PROGRAM. The time required for compilation and assembly of programs is affected by source program size, translator program efficiency, and operating speed of the computer. If a program has been properly designed and desk checked, it is possible to reduce the number of translate runs. Consequently, it will reduce the time required to develop and implement a program. When the computer is available only on a limited schedule for translation and testing, this could cause significant slippage in the overall schedule.

In absolute and low-level programming languages, it is possible to patch the object program to facilitate or expedite testing, without recompiling or reassembling the source statements. Patching, however, is an art that should be attempted only by qualified programmers.

Between one-quarter and one full man-day must be added to the schedule for assembly or compilation of each program. The time element is affected by the amount of desk checking effort expended, as well as by the size of the program.

5. TESTING AND DEBUGGING. The testing element is dependent upon the availability of an object deck, well-constructed test data, a test plan, preliminary documentation, and machine availability. Object deck availability implies that the program contains no clerical errors and is ready for logic and linkage testing. If the testing is to be meaningful and productive, well-constructed test data must be available. Too often, programmers give little or no attention to preparation for testing until coding has been completed. They then select a sampling of actual data or construct some hypothetical cases for testing. Generally, this data is incomplete because it fails to cover all of the conditions or instructions. There is also the danger that the program may be too large to test as one unit. Nevertheless, the programmer decides to proceed as is. Consequently, he may be unable to ensure its reliability. Very often, the problems arising from poor testing do not become evident until some time after the program has been implemented. And when they are discovered, it will be necessary to implement a "quick" solution, which may be only temporary until the unexpected event occurs again. Or it may force the slippage of other project schedules until the problem is

resolved. To offset the effect of these short-term "remedies," many data processing managers and programming managers are enforcing the use of desk checking, together with the development of test plan construction techniques.

A test plan delineates the required hardware interfaces, data requirements, steps for setup and starting, the test operation, termination action, and special instructions. In addition, it must be developed within the stated objectives and limitations for a given program. This is when the author is repeatedly appalled by seeing "good" programmer after "good" programmer approach the testing sessions without a test plan. The lack of a test plan often causes redundancy in testing. Where large programs are segmented into smaller logical units to facilitate testing, a test plan is a definite must. The plan defines the parameters and expected results for each segment. Failure to develop a well-ordered plan may make it very difficult to completely test a segment or to ensure its reliability and relevance.

Many programmers do not prepare their documentation until after the program has been tested, debugged, and implemented. Consequently, they are unable to validate the adequacy and effectiveness of their documentation. In organizations where remote testing is a policy, the lack of good documentation minimizes the effectiveness of the test session. For example, when a program requires operator interaction for the preparation of parameter cards or for responding to console typewriter messages, the instructions must be clear and relevant. If there are any problems, the programmer is able to initiate corrective action before the program is implemented for productive purposes.

The time required for each test shot varies from one to five manhours, although only ten minutes may actually be used on the computer. Most of the time is required to evaluate the results, memory dumps, and program logic, and to make corrections. Though these time requirements may be minimal, they are affected by availability of the equipment for testing.

In a computerized activity, the operations group's schedule should provide a block of time for testing. The block should allocate a minimum of fifteen minutes per programmer. It would also be advisable that a block be available at least twice per day. This would enable a programmer to possibly execute at least two test sessions in a day. The availability of this additional test time may significantly reduce overall project time.

If testing is done on a remote basis, the turnaround times may be better or worse. The effectiveness of remote testing depends on the development of well-formulated test plans and the availability of program documentation. When terminal devices are used for testing, the turnaround times may be improved—providing that the process does not require computer dedication. When a program is tested through a terminal but requires operator interaction for mounting and de-mounting of files, a test plan and good documentation must be available at the computing facility.

A data processing manager and programming manager should not establish different testing procedure policies for different testing environments. Rather they should enforce the development of test plans for each testing environment. This provides the programmer and his manager with direction and control over the testing procedure. The availability of operator documentation will ensure testing of that material too. It may subsequently reduce or eliminate the need for changes uncovered during the parallel test or in the follow-up.

6. PROGRAM DOCUMENTATION. When the programmer has tested his programs and is satisfied that they meet the desired objectives, he must then complete the documentation. The bulk of the documentation will be included in the system description manual and program specifications manual; however, relevant documentation must also be included in the user's manual and operator's manual (see Chapter 4). Approximately one and one-half man-hours are required to prepare each page of documentation.

In order to establish a meaningful schedule for each new programming project, a performance standard must be developed. The standard will result from data collected on programmer activity. This data may be gathered through the use of activity reports, as illustrated in Figure 6.13. This author recommends daily activity feedback because it ensures more reliable information from the programming personnel. Also, it reduces the time lag in detecting project overruns. The information availability is meaningless unless a programming manager plots the results to determine estimated status versus actual status. A simple bar chart, as illustrated in Figure 6.14, may be used to show the achievement level. More sophisticated charting techniques may be used to display progress. Or a programming manager may collect the activity reports, review them, and file them away. This may have limited effectiveness because generally more than one project will be reported on the activity report.

PROGRAMMING ACTIVITY REPORT

	NAME		ENO.	WK. ENDING
	F M LAST			

PROJECT NUMBER	PROGRAM NUMBER	DESCRIPTION	ACTIV. CODE	REG. DAYS*	O.T. DAYS*	EST. CMPLT. DATE	PERCENT COMPLETE

ACTIVITY CODES: FOR MAINTENANCE ACTIVITY, PREFIX CODE WITH "M"

PROBLEM DEFINITION	10	TEST AND DEBUG	40	INSTRUCTOR	70
FLOWCHARTING	20	PREPARE TEST PLAN	45	ATTEND TRAINING SESSION	80
CODING	25	EVALUATE TEST RESULTS	49		
DESK CHECKING	30	DOCUMENTATION	50		
TEST DATA PREPARATION	35	MEETINGS	60	*SHOW TENTHS	

Figure 6.13. Example of Programming Activity Report Form

PROJECT NUMBER_____ NAME _____

EST. START DATE _____ EST. COMPLETION DATE _____ DATE _____

PROGRAM PLAN

MONTH	JAN	FEB	MAR	APR	MAY	JUNE	JULY	AUG
WEEK	1 2 3 4 5	1 2 3 4	1 2 3 4	1 2 3 4 5	1 2 3 4	1 2 3 4	1 2 3 4 5	1 2 3 4
PROBLEM DEFINITION								
FLOWCHARTING								
CODING								
DESK CHECKING								
TEST DATA PREP.								
TEST PLAN PREP.								
TEST AND DEBUG								
EVALUATE TEST								
DOCUMENTATION								
CUTOVER								
	PROGRESS ///// SCHEDULE							

Figure 6.14. Example of Bar Chart Used to Show Status of Programming Activity

Maintenance of Existing Programs

One of the responsibilities of the programming function is to maintain existing operational programs. This requires assignment of one or several programmers to make additions or modifications to existing programs. The alterations may result from such events as changes to the system, new legal or contractual requirements, and poor program performance. The scheduling elements for program maintenance activity must apply only to the addition or modification, not to the entire program. The required time elements are dependent upon the size and complexity of the change, as well as the programming language involved. These factors are significantly affected by the design of the program, incompleteness of the specifications, and coding approach.

Many programmers dread program maintenance assignments. As a result, this responsibility is often relegated to a junior programmer or trainee. For programmers at this level, the experience can be a nightmare. Often the change is relatively minor; however, the programmer must first plod his way through another person's program. The logic may be a maze of exotic coding. If the original programmer had approached the problem in a simple and straightforward manner, the logic review would be less difficult. Also, implementation of the change would be simpler. Consequently, the maintenance process requires a greater expenditure of time, money, and effort.

Many programs require alteration because of production failures based on assumed specifications. Because of schedule pressures, a programmer often makes certain assumptions about the specifications instead of checking with the systems analyst on the project. Sometimes an error or omission of this type can be of the magnitude that it may require redefinition, redesign, and re-implementation of the existing program. The problem may be greater and more costly if other programs are affected by the outputs of the program being altered.

Poor program coding, like exotic coding, can affect program performance. Often exotic programming steps may duplicate software functions normally available in the vendor's package—a redundancy that can add unnecessary steps to a program. However, there is some question about the return on investment gained from removing these extraneous instructions. It may be necessary to remove the odd instructions if the memory requirements become crucial. Routines such as table searches and loops are often poorly coded. As a result, production processing time is increased and unnecessary instructions are added to the program. An experienced programmer can generally modify these routines to reduce processing time and program size.

The tasks in the program maintenance phase are:

1. Review of change specifications
2. Review and definition of program logic
3. Coding of modification or addition
4. Desk checking
5. Assemble or compile
6. Test and debug
7. Program documentation

1. REVIEW OF CHANGE SPECIFICATIONS. Before any change can be made, the programmer must understand the desired objectives. This may require an analysis of the system flowcharts for the system, the macro- and micro-diagrams for the affected program, input and output specifications, and data base layouts. The programmer must understand all of the interacting elements before a change may be effected. Failure to correctly execute a change may set off a chain reaction of unexpected events in the program thereby diminishing its effectiveness and often necessitating a complete rewrite. An analysis of the change may require between one-half and five man-days.

2. REVIEW AND DEFINITION OF PROGRAM LOGIC. The programmer must review the macro- and micro-logic of the existing program. Then, after reviewing the change specifications, he must define the micro-logic for the change and integrate this into the existing program. Caution must be exercised not to delete any necessary instructions and not to alter the effectiveness of others as a result of interjecting a change. Failure to correctly effect the change increases the amount of time needed for program maintenance. The review and definition of the complete logic may require from one-half to five man-days.

3. CODING OF MODIFICATION OR ADDITION. After the programmer has satisfied himself that the change can be correctly effected, he then codes the alteration in the language of the existing program. Coding time depends on program language and varies from one-fourth of a man-day to five man-days.

4. DESK CHECKING. Having completed the coding, the programmer prepares test data. Testing the program logic at the desk enables the programmer to locate most, if not all, of his clerical errors and many of

the logic discrepancies. Desk checking may require from one-fourth of a man-day to two man-days.

5. ASSEMBLE OR COMPILE. Depending upon the programming language used in the existing source program, an assembly or compilation process will be required. Translation may add from one-fourth man-day to one man-day in the schedule.

6. TEST AND DEBUG. Testing requires that the entire program be validated to ensure that the change has not affected the program's operational effectiveness. The programmer should couple the data cards designed to test the change with those used in testing the existing program. This will help to determine the required interaction in the entire program. However, because of the alteration, some of the original test data may have to be purged as it is no longer effective or relevant. The test time requirements vary from one-half to eight man-days; however, as stated previously, this estimate may be significantly affected by hardware availability.

7. PROGRAM DOCUMENTATION. After testing has been concluded, the programmer corrects the documentation. The time allocated for documentation in the program maintenance schedule depends on organization policy. Some organizations require that the documentation be redone for each affected page (see Chapter 4). Naturally, this requires additional man-hours at this point in time; however, it may subsequently save considerable time when changes are required or the program is rewritten. In many cases, only one-half to two man-days is necessary for documentation of the change.

Review Questions: Group 6B

1. What variables affect a programming schedule?
2. Why is program logic development a two-phased activity?
3. Why should a programming manager encourage the use of desk checking techniques?
4. What is the purpose of a test plan?

The Systems Group

The systems group has the responsibility for analysis, design, implementation, and maintenance of manual, unit-record, and computerized systems. The analysis responsibility is concerned with the collection of information on data sources, the processes required to develop and maintain the data, and the output requirements. Design involves the development of a system that will integrate the resources into a goal-attainment pattern. The implementation segment affects conversion of data and records, parallel testing, cutover, and follow-up. The maintenance responsibility is concerned with retaining or improving the relevance and effectiveness of an existing system.

The principal factors affecting the systems group's schedule are:
1. Definition of the objective
2. Data gathering
3. Design and development of the systems
4. System specifications
5. Design of input/output and of file specifications
6. System documentation
7. Implementation
8. System Audit

Each of these functions must be allocated a quantum of time in the development of a schedule. The tasks included in the schedule are governed by system type—that is, manual or computerized. The estimated time element for each task is based on system complexity, number of functions or steps involved, and the number of documents processed or produced. Complexity may be difficult to define in some systems. However, a decision must be made because the scale of complexity bears a direct relationship to the time required for analysis, development, implementation, and subsequent maintenance. The number of functions or steps involved is concerned with an analysis of each manual activity. A study of the documents processed or produced involves an evaluation of existing documents, as well as the design of new ones.

1. DEFINITION OF THE OBJECTIVE. This element involves a multiplicity of activities. Initially, the systems analyst must break down the stated broad objectives into the specific desired goals and tasks. This will identify the problem parameters, requirements, and interrelationships. These affect the elements that become part of the basic system development schedule, as illustrated in Figure 6.15. Having defined his timeframe and approach structure, the systems analyst analyzes the available survey data to gain an understanding of the organizational setting. If

---

Develop Accounts Payable System
1. Review Survey Data
2. Review Feasibility Study
3. Conduct Interviews
    a. Accounts Payable Manager
    b. Accounts Payable Clerks
    c. Auditor
    d. Treasury Department Personnel
4. Analyze Data
    a. Interviews
    b. Functions and Operations
    c. Flow of Work
    d. Quantitative Data
    e. Management Controls
5. Design the Accounts Payable System
    a. Identify Processing
    b. Describe the Major Inputs, Outputs, and Files
    c. Identify Major Decisions
    d. Identify Management Controls
    e. Identify Schedule Constraints
    f. Identify Volumes
6. Prepare System Specifications
    a. Prepare System Flowchart
    b. Prepare I/0 and File Specifications
    c. Prepare Documentation
7. Prepare for Conversion
8. Conduct System Test
9. Conduct Parallel Test
10. Cutover

Figure 6.15   Example of Elements in Basic System Development
Schedule: Developing an Accounts Payable System

this data is not available, the analyst has to conduct a survey to secure such information (see Chapter 8). After analyzing the relevant parts of the survey, he should move on to an evaluation of the feasibility study (see Chapter 8). This study provides the analyst with some generalized data about the resources, inputs, sources of information, and outputs or expected results. Knowledge of this data enables him to conduct more effective interviews in the data gathering segment. These initial tasks in the analysis phase may require from one-half to five days, depending on the complexity of the objective and on the information available.

2. DATA GATHERING. Data gathering begins with interviewing the managers of activities affected by the system. The managers provide the analyst with an overall view of their operation within the organizational structure. Interviewing a manager may require from one-half to two man-hours, based on his activity's involvement with data processing.

After completing the sessions with the managers, the systems analyst interviews the subordinates who are directly involved with development of the source elements, with processing of these elements, and with the equipment used. At least one-half man-hour must be allocated for each interview at this level, although this estimate may have to be increased in instances of large operations and or complex objectives.

Having concluded the interviews, the analyst should be knowledgeable about the functions and operations, flow of work, work load, man-hours required, types of management controls needed and used, inputs, and outputs.

3. DESIGN AND DEVELOPMENT OF THE SYSTEM. From the information gathered earlier, the systems analyst has an understanding of the objectives, data collection, processing, recording, and response requirements. These details must be critically examined to determine if the basic objective is being achieved, as well as to determine the necessity of each operation and whether modifications or improvements can be made to an existing system. Following this determination, the analyst designs and develops a solution to the problem. The solution specifies what processing is to occur; the major inputs, outputs, and files; major decisions; management controls; schedule constraints; and volume estimates. In the development process, the analyst formulates several hypotheses, each of which must be tested through the application of the four tests of feasibility—acceptability, flexibility, ease of operation, and use of resources. Ultimately, an optimal solution is selected and developed for implementation. Scheduling of this design and development segment in the systems group's schedule may require from one-half to thirty man-days to accomplish.

4. SYSTEM SPECIFICATIONS. This task is concerned with graphically illustrating the solution on a system flowchart. The system flowchart illustrates the major entry and exit points, types of media utilized, management controls, major operations, and decisions (see Chapter 4).

Based on the complexity of a proposed system, flowcharting may require from one-fourth to five man-days.

Depending upon the functional organization of the data processing activity, the systems analyst may also be required to develop macro-flowcharts, decision tables, or logic narrative for the programming activity. Preparation of this data may require from one-half to ten man-days per chart.

5. DESIGN OF INPUT/OUTPUT AND FILE SPECIFICATIONS. Having prepared the design of his system, the analyst now has to formalize the input, output, data base, procedural, program logic, and control specifications.

The input specifications describe the purpose, format, sequence, priorities, parameters, and control characteristics of each medium in the system. In specifying the output charcteristics, the analyst prepares the required layouts, particularly for such media as printers, and CRT displays (see Chapter 4); in addition, any tables and files used in the output process must be documented. Detailing the data base specifications may be a large task, for the analyst has to specify file layouts, descriptor tables, formats, coding information, purposes, and priorities. The procedural specifications delineate the process, plus the interactions in it—that is the preliminary user and operations documentation. The program logic specifications, which may be an addition to the data contained on the macro-flowchart, include initialization, editing, logic, calculation, and output functions for each program. Control specifications indicate the parameters, error conditions, breakpoints, and recovery procedures applicable to the system and programs. Between 2 and 22 man-days may be required in the schedule to perform the tasks specified in this segment.

6. SYSTEM DOCUMENTATION. The documentation segment is primarily concerned with preparing the forms previously described (see Chapter 4). Depending upon the organizational requirements, approximately 5 to 15 percent of the scheduled project time must be allocated for this purpose. This may be equal to a period of from one to ten man-days in the overall schedule. Included within this time-frame is the time required for preparation of conversion, parallel testing, and cutover instructions.

7. IMPLEMENTATION. Initially this part of the schedule is concerned with the implementation of a proposed or revised system. Depending upon the approach to implementation and the number of functions and operations involved, this process may require from one-half to 14 man-days.

Within a reasonable period of time after the cutover, the analyst must conduct a follow-up to determine the operational effectiveness of the system. The analyst must evaluate the system, programs, training, documentation, and controls. If any problems are found, these must be rectified. A subsequent follow-up must be conducted to determine the effectiveness of the modification. Where systems are complex or critical, several follow-ups may be conducted to appraise the operational effectiveness.

8. SYSTEM AUDIT. Many organizations now conduct periodic audits to appraise and maintain the operational effectiveness of a system. A system audit is more than a survey. It is meant to identify problems and make specific recommendations, and to maximize a system's performance. It is a vehicle for improvement and control of existing systems and for more effective utilization of resources.

To achieve these specific objectives an organization must evaluate:

—Existing systems
—Input preparation
—Input querying
—Management controls
—User department procedures
—Information processing procedures
—Documentation standards
—Available hardware
—Organizational staffing
—Organizational requirements
—Executive committee interaction

The schedule requirements will be affected primarily by the audit objectives, available documentation, and skill of the auditor-analyst.

The Training Group

The training group in a data processing function is responsible for the dissemination of technical and informational material about information processing. Training is provided for data processing personnel, user organizations, managers at all levels of the organization structure, and other interested persons. Though much of the training is conducted by vendors, many organizations have developed their own education programs and facilities. This approach provides for more intensive concentration of subject matter; reduces travel and lodging costs; and results in less interference with an organization's own operating schedule.

For schedule-planning purposes, the time required for each program must be specified without any consideration as to who will conduct the training. Some travel time considerations may have to be added to the schedule, though these should be minimal. Obviously, the time element is very dependent upon the type of training presented. The principal factors affecting the training group's schedule are (1) orientation sessions and (2) technical training.

1. ORIENTATION SESSIONS. In this category of training, the presentations are designed to provide some degree of familiarization or to answer generalized questions; in no way should they become involved with in-depth specifics or details of an application, software, hardware, or its operation. For example, many organizations offer a survey of data processing program to their personnel (see Figure 6.16). A survey course such as this may require from two to three man-days to present. Though a great deal of information is covered in this type of program, specifics are kept to a minimum.

Orientation sessions may require from one-half to five man-days, contingent upon the amount of data involved in the presentation.

2. TECHNICAL TRAINING. Technical training sessions are detailed presentations designed to familiarize the trainee with the hardware, software utilization, equipment operation, or functional utilization of a system or application. Included within this category are such programs as fundamentals of COBOL programming, basic machine operation, and program evaluation review techniques (PERT). The training period for such sessions may vary from one to twenty days, depending upon the complexity of the subject matter, method of presentation, and experience of the trainees.

The Advanced Planning and Development Group

The unique nature of this functional activity produces some scheduling problems. Some of the performance standards developed for systems personnel may be applicable to the development of a schedule for the advanced planning group.

There are numerous responsibilities delegated to the advanced planning and development group (see Chapter 2); however, three of these

I. Purpose
    To study the technical advances in the manipulation of management
    information
II. Topics Included
    A. Fundamentals of Information Processing
    B. Information Processing Elements and Components
    C. Computer Languages
    D. Programming Concepts
    E. Principles of Systems Analysis
    F. Principles of Systems Design and Implementation
    G. Information Retrieval Methods and Techniques
    H. Features of Second- and Third-Generation Computers
    I. Data Communications Concepts
    J. Computer Orientation

Figure 6.16   Orientation Program Outline for Management Personnel

probably consume most of this group's scheduling efforts. They are:
1. Evaluating data processing effectiveness
2. Evaluating existing systems
3. Evaluating hardware, software, and applications

1. EVALUATING DATA PROCESSING EFFECTIVENESS. One of the major
responsibilities delegated to this group is the evaluation of the overall
effectiveness of the data processing function. Such an undertaking can
be a massive effort requiring the development of controls, reports, and
audits for determining and measuring the progress of an activity. Developing these measures or instruments may require from one to six man-
months, the actual time needed varying according to activity size and
desired degree of detail.

2. EVALUATING EXISTING SYSTEMS. A second major responsibility is
to analyze the effectiveness of existing systems. In many organizations,
this evaluative function may be called a system audit or a reports control
study (see Chapter 7). Also, as stated earlier in this chapter, this responsibility may be delegated to the systems function.

The evaluative process is concerned with determining the costs and
benefits associated with each system. Inherent in the process is an
appraisal of management involvement, stated objectives, effectiveness
and adequacy of resources, and organizational structure. The evaluative
process must include a vehicle for locating problem areas and bottle-

necks, determining the corrective action to be applied, and assessing the effect of corrective action. The development and implementation of an effective feedback procedure (see Chapter 1) may require from three man-days to one man-month of effort, varying according to the complexity of the system.

3. EVALUATING HARDWARE, SOFTWARE, AND APPLICATIONS. As has been previously stated, the evaluation of new hardware, software, and applications is very important to an organization (see Chapter 2). A data processing administrator or manager has to be constantly on the alert for new developments that will increase functional effectiveness and productivity and that will reduce operating costs.

The time span required for the evaluations is dependent upon the evaluator's experience, the availability of information, and the location of installations or facilities where observations may be made. The evaluations may require from two to fifteen man-days per objective.

Review Questions: Group 6C

1. What activities must be considered by a systems manager in the development of a schedule for the systems group?
2. What kind of evaluations may be performed in a system audit?
3. What factors must a data processing manager take into consideration when developing a schedule for the training group?
4. Why might it be more difficult to develop an activity schedule for the advanced planning and development group than for any other functional group in data processing?

PERFORMANCE STANDARDS

A schedule serves to monitor the actual status of available resources within a given time-frame. Therefore, a schedule is essential for the effective application of the five basic management functions in the management process. Developing a schedule can be a very difficult task, but it has to be accomplished, irrespective of difficulty, if a manager is to be in command of an operationally effective activity. The time required for developing a schedule and the level of complexity within the schedule vary according to the size of the project and/or installation.

The development and use of a schedule is affected by the availability and application of realistic performance standards. When applied to a schedule, well-defined and well-documented performance standards can, for example, provide a sound basis for implementation of the feedback concept. This enables a manager to detect, identify, and correct problems that result from interactive application of the resources.

More specifically, the inclusion of performance standards in the schedule provides the manager with the capability to determine the following:

—Operational effectiveness of an activity

—Effective operating schedules

—Realistic due-in times or dates for source documents and data elements

—Realistic due-out times or dates for reports and outputs

—Manpower requirements, plus performance appraisal

—Effectiveness, plus need for personnel training

—Hardware requirements, plus utilization effectiveness

—The proper hardware configuration for an activity

—Procedures for reducing hardware conflicts in the production process

—Efficiency of computer software operating systems

—Effectiveness of computer programs

—Project cost estimates

—Billing charges for processing

—Budget requirements for a functional activity

This type of response capability is possible only if the manager utilizes realistic performance standards and the feedback concept. Because of the number of interacting variables, which affect the group's schedule, the manager must develop and implement performance standards that are realistically based on his group's capabilities. Most data processing departments need effective performance standards for at least three activities: programming, systems analysis, and operations.

Programming

As stated earlier in this chapter, programmer performance is affected by such factors as program complexity, processing functions, and programmer competency. Each of these factors has to be applied and then quantified in order to arrive at an estimate of time needed for program development. The estimate is determined by inserting the quantified variables into a formula for calculation of a reasonable time estimate for project direction and control.

There are a number of available methods for estimating programming, some of which are very sophisticated, others very general. Each programming manager must evaluate his own setting and determine whether a particular method is acceptable as is, needs to be modified, or needs to be abandoned, in favor of developing a new method. For illustrative purposes, the author has selected the estimating technique used in IBM publications. This method is based on the following weighting factors:

1. Input/Output characteristics
2. Major processing functions
3. Programming know-how
4. Job knowledge

1. INPUT/OUTPUT CHARACTERISTICS. The input/output characteristics factor is concerned with the number and types of devices to be controlled by a program. This factor must be coupled with the weight allocated for major processing functions (see below) in order to determine program complexity. The weighting points for input and output are shown in Figure 6.17. These weights are based on consideration of such requirements as data movement, work area definition, and entries for file definition and input/output control.

In examining the table, one realizes that only the disk, tape, and card media are considered. Therefore, this approach may not be entirely satisfactory for installations that utilize other media, such as audio or graphic terminals, for input/output. The programming manager, therefore, may have to develop a satisfactory weighting for other media utilized and include them with the rest of the weighting points in this table. Or else he may have to adapt or develop another estimating method.

2. MAJOR PROCESSING FUNCTIONS. This factor is concerned with the program logic and functions. The IBM method attempts to gauge program complexity in terms of the functions in a program. This is considered to be a more accurate method than attempting to gauge complexity by the number of computer instructions or total storage requirements.

In the determination of weighting points, the programming manager must assess the complexity of each major processing function. This

Characteristic	
Input:	Weighting Points*
Card—single format	1
—multiple formats	2
Each tape per file	1
Each disk per file	1
Output:	
Print per record format (headings plus data)	1
Each tape per file	1
(Note: When tape is completely formatted for slave printing by a lesser machine, assign weightings as though output were print.)	
Card—single format	1
—multiple formats	2
Each disk per file	1

* Included under i/o weightings are such program requirements as DTF entries, DIOCS entries, establishing work areas, and data movement commands.

Figure 6.17   Weighting Points for Input/Output Characteristics

assessment has to take into consideration all of the logic and activity within a functional grouping before any complexity rating can be stated.

The weighting of major processing functions is shown in Figure 6.18. The table includes COBOL and BAL programming languages, but it does not include such others as PL/I, FORTRAN, RPG, or absolute. However, it is useful to realize that the weighting of functions in the PL/I language can be very closely equated with those for COBOL. The same is generally true for FORTRAN and RPG. In the case of the absolute programming language, approximately 50 to 60 percent more processing time may be required than for BAL.

It is also important to note that the scale of complexity in the table is limited to three levels—simple, complex, and very complex. In some of the other estimating methods, the degree of complexity definition is very much higher; not only are their levels more finely structured, but they have subdefinitions of complexity within each level. This requires considerable judgment on the part of the programming manager.

		WEIGHTING POINTS			RANGE	
PROGRAMMING SYSTEM	MAJOR PROCESSING FUNCTION	Simple	Complex	Very Complex	Min.	Max.
S/360 with COBOL	Restructure data	1	3	4		
	Condition checking	1	4	7		
	Data retrieval & presentation	2	5	8		
	Calculate	1	3	5		
	Linkage	1	2	3		
	Total	6	17	27	4	27
S/360 with BAL	Restructure data	4	5	6		
	Condition checking	4	7	9		
	Data retrieval & presentation	4	7	9		
	Calculate	3	5	8		
	Linkage	2	3	5		
	Total	17	27	37	12	37
Utility or package programs (i.e., OPCON, Sort 90, S/360 multi-utility programs)	Control card changes only	1	n/a	n/a		
	Own coding required	2	3	4		
RPG (S/360)		2	8	13		

* Range represents the minimum weighting points that can be developed from the proper use of these tables as applied to a single program.

N/A—not applicable

Figure 6.18   Weighting Points for Processing Functions

The major processing functions can be arranged in the following groupings:

a) Restructure data

b) Data retrieval and presentation

c) Calculate

d) Condition checking

e) Linkage

a) *Restructure Data.* Within this grouping are such functions as combining, condensing, deleting, or rearranging data. Output formatting is excluded from consideration here because it is considered to be an i/o characteristic.

b) *Data Retrieval and Presentation.* This grouping includes such functions as table look-ups, file search, record access techniques, and related index construction.

c) *Calculate.* This grouping is concerned with arithmetic computations.

d) *Condition Checking.* This is primarily concerned with the error-checking functions built into the program to ensure accuracy. (Control checks such as reasonableness, as well as limit checks, are further discussed in Chapter 7.)

e) *Linkage.* This grouping includes such programming activities as checkpoint and restart, overlays, and interfaces with other programming systems, programs, and/or modules.

3. PROGRAMMING KNOW-HOW. As stated earlier in this chapter, programmer competency is a significant factor in program schedule development. Implementing this factor in the calculation requires an assessment of a programmer's skills. Part of this assessment is already known from an analysis of the organization manning chart (see Chapter 3). Also, information is available from the skills inventory and from the job description for a programmer's position. However, if this information is not readily available, the programming manager will have to develop an estimate of group know-how.

The suggested weighting points for programming know-how are given in Figure 6.19.

The table gives only four job titles. As has been stated earlier, job titles are not a valid basis for comparison. Therefore, the programming manager will have to examine the job descriptions to determine which programmer know-how classifications may be applicable. He may also have to examine the skills inventory and the performance appraisal data in order to determine a programmer's competency.

The programming manager may choose to enter additional job titles in the table and assign applicable man-day weighting points for them. Also, depending upon programming staff competency, he may have to somewhat modify the weighting scale parameters.

Note that there are only four job titles.

The four job titles listed in Figure 6.19 are:

a) Senior programmer

b) Programmer

c) Apprentice

d) Trainee

Overall Programming Experience	Man-Days Per Program Weighting Point
Senior Programmer	0.50 to 0.75
Programmer	1.00 to 1.50
Apprentice	2.00 to 3.00
Trainee	3.50 to 4.00

Figure 6.19   Programming Know-How Table

a) *Senior Programmer.* By the description given, a senior programmer is one who is very experienced with a particular hardware configuration and programming system. He also has experience in having written and implemented many programs on different types of hardware. This description is also applicable to the positions of senior systems programmer and senior programmer analyst, as well as to other positions within the specialist skill level.

b) *Programmer.* A programmer is described as a person who has written and implemented programs of various complexities. For purposes of weighting, experience in a particular hardware configuration and programming system is necessary. This broad description applies to persons with a high degree of proficiency at the semiskilled level. Positions such as systems programmer and programmer analyst may also be included in this category. In some organizations, this category may also include the associate programmer positions.

c) *Apprentice.* In the apprentice category are people who have written and implemented several programs. However, their experience with a particular configuration and programming system is limited. This grouping would apply to persons with limited or below-average competency within the semiskilled level. Included in this category are such positions as junior programmer, junior systems programmer, and junior programmer analyst. Depending upon the actual job description, this category may also include the associate programmer, associate systems programmer, and associate programmer analyst positions.

d) *Trainee.* In this category are programming personnel with little or no practical experience. They are at the entry skills level and are being developed for advancement into a junior-level programming position. Positions included in this category can be those of programmer trainee and/or program coder.

Job Knowledge Available	Job-Knowledge Required		
	Much	Some	None
Detailed knowledge of this job	0.75	0.25	0.00
Good general knowledge of this job, with fragmentary detailed knowledge	1.25	0.50	0.00
Fair general knowledge of this job, but little or no detailed knowledge	1.50	0.75	0.00
No job knowledge, but general knowledge of related subjects	1.75	1.00	0.25
No job knowledge, no general knowledge of related subjects	2.00	1.25	0.25

Figure 6.20   Job-Knowledge Table

4. JOB KNOWLEDGE REQUIRED. This factor is concerned with evaluating a programmer's background and subject-matter orientation. The programming manager has to assess the programmer's ability to define a problem and design an optimal solution. In the table shown in Figure 6.20, there are three degrees of job knowledge required. These are compared in matrix form against the programmer's knowledge of a problem. The selected weighting points must be added to the factor selected from the know-how table (see Figure 6.19) to determine the man-day factor.

The required job-knowledge factors are arranged in the following three categories:

a) Much required
b) Some required
c) None required

a) *Much Required.* The "much" factor may consist of one or a combination of the following requirements, the number depending upon the complexity of and processing functions in a program. One requirement is detailed knowledge of difficult-to-understand and complex subject matter. A second requirement is the need for knowledge of complex mathematical or statistical formulae in the development and implementation of a program. A third requirement is the application of special concepts that are not commonly used in the programming process—for example, plotting, teleprocessing, or linear programming.

b) Some Required. In the "some" category, detailed knowledge of the job is required, but the subject matter is more easily understood or less complex than in the "much" category. A second requirement is the use of standard mathematical or statistical formulae. Either one or both of these requirements may be applicable to a given program in this category.

c) None Required. In the "none" category, little or no background is required to understand or execute a program. Simple listing and utility programs, for example, would require only basic information about the input and output for development. Because of the limited job-knowledge requirements, these are the kinds of tasks that would be assigned to junior programmers and programmer trainees.

Application of IBM Estimating Technique

Let us consider how this estimating technique can be applied to a program designed to check the certification requirements of professional and staff employees in a school district (see Figure 6.21). The process also updates the existing professional-staff master tape file. The primary input is data recorded on magnetic tape as a result of optically scanning the professional-staff data collection form. The input is compared against a master certification requirements tape. Certification violations are outputted on the printer. Also, a card is punched for subsequent follow-up processing. Where no violations are detected, the personnel data is processed to produce an updated professional-staff master file.

As the input consists of three different tape files, three weighting points will be required for the input portion of the i/o characteristics factor. The output requires a tape file, a card format, and one print record format. According to the table illustrated in Figure 6.17, therefore, three weighting points for the output are required. So, the sum total for the i/o characteristics is six weighting points.

The programming manager then analyzes the necessary logic and functions required in this program. The program is to be written in the COBOL language for an IBM 360 computer. The structuring of data for this program can be regarded as complex because the scanner output in

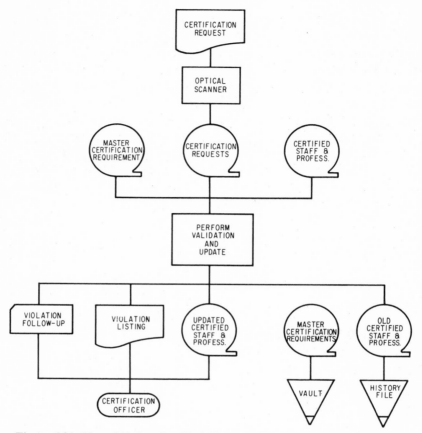

Figure 6.21. Use of Estimating Technique: Validation of Certification Requirements for School District

this case will have to be rearranged and combined for processing purposes. Therefore, three weighting points must be allocated for this processing function. The calculations are relatively simple, so only one weighting point will be allocated. The condition checking and data retrieval functions for this problem can be regarded as complex, so they require an allocation of four and five points respectively for each processing function. Only a simple checkpoint and restart procedure is needed, which means the addition of just one more weighting point. Therefore, a sum total of fourteen weighting points must be allocated for the major processing functions.

The program will be assigned to a competent programmer with good knowledge of the COBOL language and the IBM 360 hardware. A man-day weighting point of 1.0 can be assigned to this person. The programmer has a good general knowledge of the teacher certification process, but detailed knowledge is required for developing the program. Yet the teacher certification subject matter is not complex. A judgment factor must be made about the programmer's knowledge of this job. From an analysis of Figure 6.20 it appears that the "some" category may be most applicable, and a weighting factor of 1.25 should be selected and applied to the calculation.

The effect of these weights is illustrated in Figure 6.22. When the complexity and man-days weighting are determined, they are inserted into the formula for estimating programming time. Use of the formula provides an estimated man-days requirement for a given program. In this particular calculation, the amount of programmers time needed is an estimated 45 man-days. This estimate includes the time requirements for program design, coding, testing, and documentation. The total would have to be revised significantly upward if incomplete or invalid specifications were applied to the design of the program. This revision would occur as a result of the programming manager monitoring the programmer's activity on the project.

The estimated programming time figure is incomplete without the addition of a loss factor and a nonproject time factor. The loss factor is added to the estimated programming time to provide for delays in related processing activities. These delays are not readily predictable, but they do impede progress and consequently require being anticipated. For example, such factors as lack of computer availability; inability to coordinate activities or test results with a user; or improper test execution—any or all of these may occur frequently. Though this much can be expected, the real problem is to determine the proper loading percentage to be applied. A minimum of between 5 and 10 percent should be allocated; for new hardware and programs, a loading factor as high as 20 percent may have to be used.

Programming projects are also affected by such nonproject factors as absenteeism, vacations, holidays, and special assignments. These are not directly related to the project, but they do have a discernable effect on the process. It is possible to control some of these factors in order to minimize the nonproject loading factor. Nevertheless, a range of 20 to 35 percent may have to be allotted for this interference in a project schedule.

Input/Output Characteristics	Weighting Points
Input Characteristics:	
Tape Files (3)	3
Output characteristics:	
Tape File (1)	1
Print Format (1)	1
Single Card Format (1)	1
	—
Total i/o Characteristics	6
Major Processing Functions	
Functions:	
Restructure Data (Complex)	3
Calculate (Simple)	1
Condition Checking (Complex)	4
Data Retrieval & Presentation (Complex)	5
Linkage (Simple)	1
	—
Total Processing Function	14
Total Complexity Points	**20**
	Man-days Weighting
Programming Know How	1.00
Job Knowledge	1.25
	—
Total Man-days Weighting	**2.25**

Est. Programming Time = Complexity × Man-days Weighting
                      = 20×2.25
                      = 45 Man-days

Figure 6.22   Use of Estimating Technique

Therefore, the estimated programming time value of 45 man-days would have to be modified by the loading factors for loss and nonproject time. For illustrative purposes, let us apply a loss factor of 10 percent and a nonproject factor of 25 percent. The calculation is shown in Figure 6.23.

The programming estimating technique is a tool for management decision-making. It forces the programming manager to define a project and establish a performance standard. Through the application of the feedback concept, the programming manager is able to refine the technique for planning and control purposes.

Systems Analysis

The tasks and activities performed within the systems activity are not as clearly defined as in the other functional activities. Therefore the efforts by data processing managers and/or systems group managers to quantify the necessary tasks and activities have been nonexistent or limited. Performance standards for the systems group's function should take into consideration the analysis, design and development, implementation, and follow-up phases. In the analysis phase, the standards should be concerned with data gathering, work flow, management controls, schedules, volumes, and objectives; this data must be carefully evaluated and the system's interaction and effectiveness determined. The design and development phase is affected by such activities as design of a system; development of management controls, programming specifications, and preliminary documentation; and coordination of system design with users and functional activity managers. Implementation is

---

Estimated Programming Time   45 Man-days
Loss Factor Calculation
    Loss Factor Time   = Est. Programming Time×Est. Loss Factor
                            = 45 Man-days×10%
                            = 4.50 Man-days
Nonproject Factor Time Calculation
    Nonproject Factor Time = Est. Programming Time×Est. Nonproject
                                                          Factor
                            = 45×25%
                            = 11.25 Man-days
Optimal Project Time (Man-days)
    Est. Programming Time   45.00 Man-days
    Loss Factor Time   4.50
    Nonproject Factor Time   +11.25

    Total Optimal Project Time   60.75 Man-days

Figure 6.23   Calculation of Loss and Nonproject Values

concerned with such activities as the development of procedures for conversion, training of personnel, system testing, finalizing documentation, and cutover. The follow-up involves such items as considering user problems with a system, implementing additional controls, correcting bugs, and evaluating the cost-benefits picture.

It becomes immediately apparent that it is very difficult to quantify many of these factors. However, an attempt must be made to control the project. A manager must refuse to accept the idea that inevitably there will be an overrun on the project schedule. If indeed there is an overrun, then the manager has either based his projections on invalid assumptions or lacks a feedback control in the project for problem detection. Both of these causes are in turn affected by the use of a systems analyst activity report (see form illustrated in Figure 6.24). The report should be collected on a daily basis and analyzed by the manager for a review of progress and problems. The data should indicate to the manager whether the project is following the stated objectives and whether the resources are being properly utilized; it should also provide a measure of personnel performance. This visibility of progress enables a manager to better direct and control his human resources.

Measurable progress is dependent upon some reasonable quantification of the necessary tasks and activities. The quantification process is affected by the complexity of the system; the number of operations and functions; the number of documents, files, and reports; and the management controls required. Measurable performance standards may be established for tasks within the following three phases:

1. Analysis
2. Design and Development
3. Implementation

1. ANALYSIS. In this phase, the analyst attempts to determine and understand the objectives, organizational setting, policies, practices, and procedures that are affecting the existing system or application. The investigation begins with the function, operation, or document that initiates the sequence of activities. Data on these documents and activities must be collected and charted for subsequent evaluation. In the evaluative process, the analyst determines if the system achieves its objectives efficiently and economically.

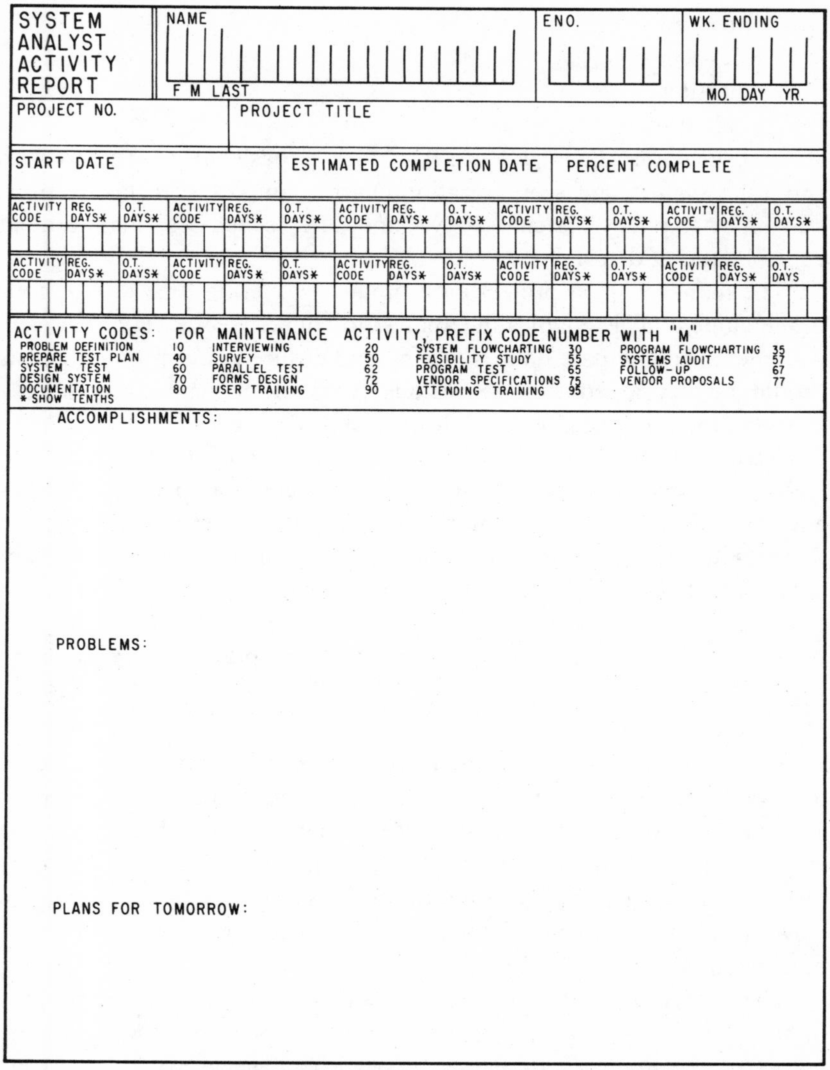

SYSTEM ANALYST ACTIVITY REPORT

NAME — F M LAST

ENO.

WK. ENDING — MO. DAY YR.

PROJECT NO.

PROJECT TITLE

START DATE

ESTIMATED COMPLETION DATE

PERCENT COMPLETE

ACTIVITY CODE	REG. DAYS*	O.T. DAYS*	ACTIVITY CODE	REG. DAYS*	O.T. DAYS*	ACTIVITY CODE	REG. DAYS*	O.T. DAYS*	ACTIVITY CODE	REG. DAYS*	O.T. DAYS*	ACTIVITY CODE	REG. DAYS*	O.T. DAYS*
ACTIVITY CODE	REG. DAYS*	O.T. DAYS*	ACTIVITY CODE	REG. DAYS*	O.T. DAYS*	ACTIVITY CODE	REG. DAYS*	O.T. DAYS*	ACTIVITY CODE	REG. DAYS*	O.T. DAYS*	ACTIVITY CODE	REG. DAYS*	O.T. DAYS

ACTIVITY CODES: FOR MAINTENANCE ACTIVITY, PREFIX CODE NUMBER WITH "M"

PROBLEM DEFINITION	10	INTERVIEWING	20	SYSTEM FLOWCHARTING	30	PROGRAM FLOWCHARTING	35
PREPARE TEST PLAN	40	SURVEY	50	FEASIBILITY STUDY	55	SYSTEMS AUDIT	57
SYSTEM TEST	60	PARALLEL TEST	62	PROGRAM TEST	65	FOLLOW-UP	67
DESIGN SYSTEM	70	FORMS DESIGN	72	VENDOR SPECIFICATIONS	75	VENDOR PROPOSALS	77
DOCUMENTATION	80	USER TRAINING	90	ATTENDING TRAINING	95		

* SHOW TENTHS

ACCOMPLISHMENTS:

PROBLEMS:

PLANS FOR TOMORROW:

Figure 6.24. Systems Analyst Activity Report Form

In the analysis phase, there are five specific tasks that can be quantified. These are the:

a) Collection of documents

b) Interviews
c) File analysis
d) Charting
e) Evaluation of present system

a) Collection of Documents. This task is basically concerned with gathering such items as organization charts; samples of forms, records, and reports; policy statements; volume data; schedules; management control data; and cost data.

The manager must project an estimated gathering time of one hour per document. This enables the analyst to collect basic data about each document. To facilitate data gathering and ensure uniformity, checklists should be developed for the various types of documents. A sample checklist for appraising forms is illustrated in Figure 6.25.

Additional man-days must be allocated to enable the analyst to study the documents, legal requirements, file retention, prepare statistics and narratives. These allocations are primarily determined in accordance with system complexity. For collection of documents, the man-days estimate is as follows:

	Simple	Complex	Very Complex
Man-days	1	2	3-5

b) Interviews. During the interview process, the analyst is interested in learning in detail about the activities at each function or operation. This information enables the analyst to determine the objectives to be met; the work to be performed; the sequence of operations; who performs the tasks; external and internal influences; related costs; volume of work; weaknesses and/or effectiveness of the procedures; and man-hour requirements.

The analyst generally interviews at least the person directly involved in the processing activities of a function or operation. Owing to the nature of the analyst's project, it may also be necessary to interview additional personnel. It is also advisable that the manager of each function or operation be interviewed. This provides the analyst with specific data aboaut present and future objectives. The projected man-hour allocations for basic interviews are as follows:

	Simple	Complex	Very Complex
Man-hours	$\frac{1}{2}-\frac{3}{4}$	$1-1\frac{1}{2}$	$2-2\frac{1}{2}$

1. What is the purpose of the form?
   a) Does the form correlate with that purpose?
   b) Does the form correlate with the system's objectives?
2. Utilization volume?
3. Cost? (Last contract price.)
4. What is the functional relationship of this form to other forms in this and other systems?
5. Is the form temporary or permanent?
6. Is the title descriptive and meaningful?
7. What information is entered at time of origination?
8. What information is added subsequent to origination?
9. Have all the necessary information elements been included on the form?
10. Are there any unnecessary information elements on the form that may be deleted?
11. What use is made of each element of information on the form?
12. What is the volume and significance of errors in origination and processing?
13. What approval signatures are required?
14. What information is transferred to other forms, reports, or records?
15. What is the disposition of each copy?
    a) Does each copy serve a necessary purpose?
    b) Is the distribution adequate?
16. Are there any written procedures governing the preparation and use of the form?

Figure 6.25   Sample Checklist for Form Appraisal

A half hour should be allocated for each additional interview conducted in a function or operation.

c) File Analysis. Files serve as input and output into a system, and are the data base for a management information system. The file requirements increase the number of interfaces and controls in a system. In computerized operations they increase programming requirements.

For file analysis, a checklist as illustrated in Figure 6.26 should be used. Depending upon its complexity, approximately two to four man-hours may be required for analysis and evaluation of each file.

d) Charting. The charting task is primarily involved in the development of a system flowchart for an existing system. However, it is also

---

1. Purpose of the file?
2. Nature, frequency, and volume of references or inquiries?
3. File organization?
4. Storage medium and mode?
5. Header and trailer labels?
6. Information recorded in each position?
7. Source of each data entry?
8. Frequency of file update?
9. Volume of transactions?
10. File maintenance controls?
11. Record volumes?
12. Record sequence and keys?
13. Record format?
14. Data element descriptions?
15. Types of reports prepared from the file?

Figure 6.26   File Checklist

involved with the graphic development of such items as decision-tables, organization charts, work-flow distribution in a function or operation, schedules, and cost-benefit charts. The graphics enable the analyst to gain an understanding of the overall system and its interacting elements.

For preparation of a system flowchart, the manager should allow between a quarter and a half hour per function. The actual time allocation depends on the amount of detail that each organization requires on a flowchart. Whatever the amount of time, it is important to remember that completeness cannot be compromised, for incompleteness can obscure the difficulties and weaknesses in a system. Therefore, additional man-days must be allocated if necessary in order to effect a comprehensive system and illustrate all of the interrelated procedures. The man-days allocation for system flowcharting is primarily determined by the complexity of the system:

	Simple	Complex	Very Complex
Man-days	$\frac{1}{2}$	$1\frac{1}{2}$–2	$3\frac{1}{2}$–4

For preparation of other graphics such as organization charts schedules and so forth, an additional man-days estimate must be made. Though this estimate is based on system complexity, it is also affected by data availability. The estimated man-days allocation may be defined as follows:

Man-days	Simple	Complex	Very Complex
	$1\frac{1}{2}$–3	$2\frac{1}{2}$–4	$3\frac{1}{2}$–6

e) Evaluation of Present System. Up to this point in the process, the systems analyst has been busy describing the system he is studying. Now, though, he has to visualize the flow of data and the process itself in order to pinpoint the strengths, weaknesses, and difficulties in the system.

The evaluation of the system is basically a diagnosis of the steps, machines and equipment, files, forms, reports, and objectives. Initially, the evaluation begins with generalized questions. For example, "Does the system meet current needs and objectives?" Subsequently, the questions become more specific so as to reach into almost every element of the system. To facilitate the evaluation, a series of checklist questions should be developed. One of the specific questions that may be included on the checklist is, "Is each step necessary?"

The man-days allocation for this task in the analysis phase is as follows:

Man-days	Simple	Complex	Very Complex
	$2\frac{1}{2}$–4	5–$7\frac{1}{2}$	$7\frac{1}{2}$–10

The tasks in the analysis phase, together with the respective allocations in man-hours and man-days, are illustrated in tabular form in Figure 6.27.

2. DESIGN AND DEVELOPMENT. In this phase, the analyst designs and develops the solution to the problem. He actually designs several alternative solutions to accomplish the desired goal. Each of the tentative solutions specify the detailed activities to be performed and their sequence. Eventually, an optimal solution is selected.

The principal tasks that may be quantified during this phase are:

a) Development of new flowcharts
b) Development of file specifications
c) Design of new documents
d) Preparation of specifications

a) Development of New Flowcharts. This task involves the development of system flowcharts, decision-tables, and logic narrative descrip-

ACTIVITY	COMPLEXITY LEVEL					
	Simple		Complex		Very Complex	
	Man-hours	Man-days	Man-hours	Man-days	Man-hours	Man-days
Collection of All Documents		1		2		3–5
Each Basic Interview	$\frac{1}{2}$–$\frac{3}{4}$		1–1$\frac{1}{2}$		2–2$\frac{1}{2}$	
Each Additional Interview	$\frac{1}{2}$		$\frac{1}{2}$		$\frac{1}{2}$	
File Analysis	2–3		2–3		2–3	
Charting		$\frac{1}{2}$		1$\frac{1}{2}$–2		3$\frac{1}{2}$–4
Additional Graphics		1$\frac{1}{2}$–3		2$\frac{1}{4}$–4		3$\frac{1}{2}$–6
Evaluation of System		2$\frac{1}{2}$–4		5–7$\frac{1}{2}$		7$\frac{1}{2}$–10

Figure 6.27   Example of Analysis Phase Time Requirements

tions. These media specify the tasks and activities to be performed and their processing sequence.

The projected time element varies according to the number of functions to be performed, the complexity of the system, and the detail-charting requirements of the organization. Furthermore, the time estimate may also have to be significantly increased if macro-flowcharts for programming activity must be prepared.

A manager should project from one-quarter to one-half hour for the description of each logic function. However, an additional man-days allocation must be added to allow for all of the necessary linkages, plus controls in each macro-flowchart. These additional time requirements are as follows:

Man-days	Simple	Complex	Very Complex
	$\frac{1}{2}$–1	$1\frac{1}{2}$–$2\frac{1}{2}$	3–5

b) *Development of File Specifications.* The analyst must prepare the detailed specifications for each file in the system. These specifications indicate such elements as the number, length, and size of files; the record sequence, record types, record sizes, and blocking factor; source of data; and frequency and types of interrogation. As stated earlier in this chapter, a checklist should be developed to ensure uniformity in the preparation of specifications. (See Chapter 4 regarding the documented file formats.)

Approximately two to three man-hours should be projected for preparation of file specifications in this phase.

c) *Design of New Documents.* As a result of either the modification of an existing system or the development of a new one, the design of new documents may be necessary. These new documents must satisfy the system's requirements and objectives. In addition to preparation of these documents, the analyst may also be required to develop new retention policies and filing procedures.

Approximately two to four man-hours may be required to design a new document, depending upon its complexity. To secure user approval and to prepare vendor specifications, it is necessary to add more man-days to the estimate. These additional requirements are as follows:

Man-days	Simple	Complex	Very Complex
	$\frac{1}{2}$–$1\frac{1}{2}$	1–3	$1\frac{1}{2}$–$3\frac{1}{2}$

d) *Preparation of Specifications.* This task in the design and development phase involves documenting the system's requirements. The documentation is necessary to effect the system test, conversion to the new system, training of user and operations personnel, and implementation of management controls. For example, each input is identified by medium, source of origination, and processing requirements. In addition, the schedule and volumes affecting each input are stated.

The time estimate for preparation of these requirements is related to system complexity; the number of inputs, outputs, and files used; and

| ACTIVITY | COMPLEXITY LEVEL | | | | | |
| | Simple | | Complex | | Very Complex | |
	Man-hours	Man-days	Man-hours	Man-days	Man-hours	Man-days
Flowcharting Each Logic Function	$\frac{1}{4}-\frac{1}{2}$		$\frac{1}{4}-\frac{1}{2}$		$\frac{1}{4}-\frac{1}{2}$	
Flowcharting Linkages		$\frac{1}{2}-1$		$1\frac{1}{2}-2\frac{1}{2}$		$3-5$
Develop File Specifications	$2-3$		$2-3$		$2-3$	
Design Each Document	$2-4$		$2-4$		$2-4$	
Coordinate Documents		$\frac{1}{2}-1\frac{1}{2}$		$1-3$		$1\frac{1}{2}-3\frac{1}{2}$
Prepare Specifications		$2\frac{1}{2}-5$		$5-8$		$8-15$

Figure 6.28   Example of Design and Development Phase Time Requirements

the processing requirements and proficiency of the system analyst. The man-day projections for this estimate are as follows:

	Simple	Complex	Very Complex
Man-days	$2\frac{1}{2}-5$	$5-8$	$8-15$

The estimated time projections for the design and development phase are summarized in the table shown in Figure 6.28.

3. IMPLEMENTATION. The effective implementation of a system depends upon careful planning and timing, which, in turn, are based on

the existence of a realistic schedule, good documentation, sound training, and other factors. The schedule must be carefully monitored to provide feedback on project status. Consequently, any problems uncovered must be corrected before cutover takes place.

The tasks that can be reasonably quantified in this phase are:

a) Development of conversion procedures
b) Conversion of data and files
c) Training of personnel
d) System test

(a) *Development of Conversion Procedures.* The conversion procedures must be developed for both user and operating personnel. These procedures include transcription information, controls to be utilized, and code listings. The time estimates are related to the number and types of records and files to be converted, as well as to the degree of coordination required for the various functional activities. The estimated time requirements are as follows:

	Simple	Complex	Very Complex
Man-days	$2\frac{1}{2}$–4	$3\frac{1}{2}$–6	5–10

b) *Conversion of Data and Files.* The conversion of data and files may be either a simple or complex process, depending on the type of media and conversion equipment available. Time requirements are partly dependent upon the capacity and processing speeds of the conversion devices. Furthermore, if in-house resources for conversion are not available, then the organization must use an external capability. This may require the use of additional controls and may prolong the time required for conversion of the media. The estimated man-days projections are:

	Simple	Complex	Very Complex
Man-days	$2\frac{1}{2}$–$7\frac{1}{2}$	5–15	$7\frac{1}{2}$–30

c) *Training of Personnel.* This task is concerned with providing training and orientation for the user and operations personnel. The amount of time required depends upon the objectives of the training program. The estimated time projections for training are:

	Simple	Complex	Very Complex
Man-days	5–15	10–25	15–30

However, this time estimate may have to be revised significantly upward if new hardware or concepts are involved. In such cases, the time requirements will depend largely upon the background and experience of the trainees.

d) System Test. The system test is designed to evaluate all facets of a system. The comprehensive nature of the test requires extensive cooperation between the affected functional activities. It also requires detail checking and verification of the results.

The man-days requirements vary according to test objectives. Some organizations, for example, conduct a parallel test on a sampling basis. This reduces the time requirements significantly. Other organizations choose not to conduct a parallel test, for simple systems. Rather, they prefer to gamble on their ability to react quickly to any problems that develop after cutover.

In addition the time requirements may be extended for systems regarded as critical or important to an organization. This extension results from having to test the system in modules, steps, or phases in order to locate and correct errors.

The time estimates for system testing are difficult to quantify on a standard basis. The manager must evaluate his own setting and use the suggestions listed below simply as guides. These guides for the man-days estimates are as follows:

	Simple	Complex	Very Complex
Man-days	5–7$\frac{1}{2}$	10–30	20–45

The time required by the analyst to finalize all documentation will depend on the accuracy and completeness of the documentation prior to implementation. If the documentation has been prepared and verified as it should be during the various phases of system development, the time requirements for finalizing the material will be minimal. If the documentation has not been prepared adequately prior to implementation, then the analyst faces a difficult task. Ordinarily, between one-half and three man-days may be required if good documentation is available (see Chapter 4). The time for cutover cannot be readily estimated when the project is initiated. However, from one-half to two man-days may be set as an estimate when the project is implemented. Nevertheless, this time could be prolonged if a phased-in implementation of a system is required. The manager of the systems group should be able to prepare a

ACTIVITY	COMPLEXITY LEVEL					
	Simple		Complex		Very Complex	
	Man-hours	Man-days	Man-hours	Man-days	Man-hours	Man-days
Develop Conversion Procedures		$2\frac{1}{2}$–4		$3\frac{1}{2}$–6		5–10
Conversion of Data Files		$2\frac{1}{2}$–$7\frac{1}{2}$		5–15		$7\frac{1}{2}$–30
Training of Personnel		5–15		10–25		15–30
System Test		5–$7\frac{1}{2}$		10–30		20–45
Documentation		1–3		1–3		1–3
Cutover		$\frac{1}{2}$–2		$\frac{1}{2}$–2		$\frac{1}{2}$–2

Figure 6.29   Example of Implementation Phase Time Requirements

rough estimate of the time required for cutover after the system test has been completed.

A summary of the systems activities conducted during the implementation phase is concluded in Figure 6.29.

It is difficult to develop time estimates for systems activities performed during a follow-up phase. The kinds of activities conducted and the length of time required for each is affected by the objectives of the follow-up and the number of personnel performing it. If the system is complex and/or critical to the needs of the organization, the follow-up may be lengthy. For a simple system, however, one man-day or less may be used to conduct interviews with the affected functional activity managers and their subordinates. No attempt may be made to audit the effectiveness of the system, evaluate the training, evaluate the completeness of the documentation, or determine the resulting tangible benefits.

Review Questions: Group 6D

1. What information can a programming manager use in assessing a programmer's skills for assignment of a know-how weighting factor?
2. Why must the loss factor and nonproject time factor be included in programming project time estimates?
3. Of what value are checklists in the development of a schedule for a new system?
4. Some managers argue that it is difficult to quantify the activities of the systems personnel; therefore, no attempt should be made to develop a schedule for the systems function. Do you agree or disagree with this argument? Explain your answer.

Operations

An effective data processing operations activity is dependent upon the development and maintenance of performance standards. These standards represent the basis for formulating and controlling a production schedule for the function. Unlike the performance standards established for the systems and programming activities, these are basically equipment standards. However, they are also utilized to project personnel requirements and to monitor personnel productivity.

The performance standards for the operations group are often referred to as production, or equipment utilization, standards. They may be described as such because of their effect on time allocations for the hardware, personnel, and production.

Any discussion of standards for the operations group must consider two major elements. The first consists of development considerations. The second consists of types of measures.

Development Considerations.

There are a number of factors that influence the formulation of a standard for the operations group. The three most significant factors relating to development are:

1. Machine speeds
2. Setup time
3. Handling time

1. MACHINE SPEEDS. It is difficult to apply universal standards to each equipment category because they vary according to vendor, model within each group, and processing variations. For example, it would be difficult to establish a single machine speed rating for the machines included in the SORTER category. An organization could conceivably have three different sorter models installed—an IBM 082, IBM 083, and IBM 084. The rated machine speeds for these devices vary considerably, from 650 to 2000 cards per minute. The rated machine speeds for each machine may be secured from the equipment operating manual, the vendor's sales staff, or the vendor's equipment proposal.

The basic time requirements for machines may be computed by using a formula, precalculated tables or graphs, or specially prepared machine-load computers. These calculated or extracted time values may require additional adjustment because of time requirements for handling and setup.

The impact of handling time is much more significant on unit-record (EAM) equipment than on computer (EDP) equipment. This results from the number of interruptions that occur in equipment operation. The differing concepts of input, processing, and output in computerized operations and the use of software control systems minimizes handling time needs. Setup time requirements are affected by the handware, required management controls, and available documentation. Therefore, each equipment-related standard must be analyzed to determine if setup and/or handling time requirements must be included.

2. SETUP TIME. Setup time involves readying the equipment initially; performing preliminary machine or control tests; and checking or securing the documented operating procedures. The setup tasks are executed prior to the beginning of an operation. For scheduling purposes, setup time is added to a relevant machine operation as a fixed number of minutes. The figure should remain relatively constant regardless of input/output volume. However, its effect on the processing schedule increases with low volume and decreases with high volume. When five minutes of setup time is required for processing 100,000 records, the

impact is far less than if the same setup time is applied to the processing of 1000 records.

Initially, setup time for each operation is established either as a guesstimate or as an average that is derived from analyzing the equipment utilization records. Subsequently, this time figure can be modified as actual utilization data for a system becomes available. The value must be carefully monitored because it can become unwieldy and consequently have an adverse effect on productivity. Setup time may be reduced by improving the operating procedures, providing additional training for operating personnel, improving the design of the input/ output media; or by positioning the materials or supporting equipment closer to the processing equipment.

3. HANDLING TIME. The need to add a factor for handling time results from the short interruptions that normally occur after an operation has begun. The interruptions are caused by such activities as loading cards in the read hopper; emptying stackers; rewinding and changing tape reels; checking machine halts, interrupts, or console messages; reloading printer or typewriter forms; and checking results. The frequency of interruptions increases with the volume of processing.

Initially, handling time is expressed as an estimate in the schedule. This figure is subsequently adjusted as machine utilization and personnel performance statistics become available. Furthermore, handling time is also affected by operator performance.

To minimize its adverse effect on productivity, handling time must be carefully monitored and controlled. The need to maintain these two requirements may, in turn, be reduced either by redeveloping the operator instructions or by positioning the materials handling equipment near the operation.

Handling time is expressed as a percentage of total time because the longer an operation lasts the greater the handling time. The computation of handling time for scheduling purposes is dependent on the operations manager's definition of percentage of handling. The value may be expressed on the basis of machine time or total time for the job. Two common methods of expressing percentage of handling time are percentage of machine time and percentage of total time.

a) *Percentage of Machine Time.* If the percentage for handling is expressed as a percentage of machine time, the calculated handling time is added to the machine time, too.

For example, assume that the machine time is 3 hours (excluding setup time). The handling time percentage is estimated as 25 percent. The calculation to determine the percentage of machine time is as follows:

Method: Total Time = Machine Time + (Est. Percentage for Handling × Machine Time)

Calculation: Total Time = 3.0 + (.25 × 3.0) = 3.0 + (.75) = 3.75 hours

b) *Percentage of Total Time.* If the percentage of handling is defined as a percentage of total time (except setup) for the job, the calculated result expresses the handling time as a percentage and not time value. In this approach, the handling time is a direct end result of the calculation. The value of handling time is not added to the total time as it is in the method for machine time. Rather, using the same basic data, handling time is calculated as a percentage of total time, as follows:

$$\text{Method: Total Time} = \frac{\text{Machine Time}}{(1.00 - \text{Est. Percentage for Handling})}$$

$$\text{Calculation: Total Time} = \frac{3.00}{(1.00 - .25)} = \frac{3.00}{.75} = 4.0 \text{ hours}$$

Setup time must be added to the total time to determine production time requirements.

This calculation may be simplified by computing an operational effectiveness factor, which then becomes the divisor in the calculation. For example, operational effectiveness = maximum operational effectiveness—estimated handling time percentage.

> 100% Maximum Operational Effectiveness
> −25% Estimated Handling Time Percentage
> ───────
> 75% Operational Effectiveness Factor

$$\text{Total Time} = \frac{\text{Machine Time}}{\text{Operational Effectiveness Factor}}$$

$$\text{Total Time} = \frac{3.0}{.75}$$

Total Time = 4.0 hours

c) Types of Measures. From an analysis of the types of performance measures, it is clear that some types bear directly and others bear indirectly on productivity. Although some of them do reduce time available for production, they are necessary to sustain that capability. The types of performance measures may be arranged according to the following major classifications:

1. Machine measures
2. Testing standards
3. Training standards

1. MACHINE MEASURES. The measures within this classification affect the ability of the operations group to produce a desired output. The standards must be developed before any production schedule can be formulated. They are the basis for allocating and controlling the available machine, material, and manpower resources.

Owing to the number of interacting variables, the machine measures may be subdivided into standards for the following seven categories:

a) Unit-record production
b) Computer production
c) Preventative maintenance
d) Emergency maintenance
e) Rerun Time
f) Idle Time
g) Special Requests

a) Unit-Record Production. The unit-record production standards may also be referred to as either punched card standards or EAM equipment standards. Within this category, separate production standards are developed for such devices as key punches, key verifiers, interpreters, reproducers, etc., in that there are no applicable universal standards for each subcategory of equipment. In the sorter category, for example, an organization may utilize one or several different types. It may be equipped with an IBM 082, 083, and/or 084 sorter, with operating speeds of 650, 1000, and 2000 cards per minute respectively. Therefore, one common standard for the sorting equipment may not be entirely practical. However, the manager must establish a standard for each sorter type.

Consider the following example. A manager must determine the scheduling requirements for sorting 15,000 cards on five columns on an 083 sorter. To determine the production time requirements, he may utilize any one of the following approaches. First, he may use a precalculated graph, such as the one illustrated in Figure 6.30. This graph has been plotted to provide a machine time requirement (lower line) and machine time plus handling time (upper line). As a result of examining the graph, the manager may estimate that 19 minutes will be required to sort each column. This figure must then be multiplied by five—the number of columns to be sorted. Therefore, approximately 95 minutes will be required for the sorting operation. However, some setup time must be added. So the manager estimates that five minutes will be required for setup. Therefore, an estimated 100 minutes will be required in the schedule for this sorting operation.

A second approach may be to utilize the following formula:

$$\text{Machine Time} = \frac{\text{Number of cards} \times \text{number of columns}}{\text{Sorter Speed (cards per minute)}}$$

$$\text{Machine Time} = \frac{15,000 \times 5}{1000}$$

$$\text{Machine Time} = \frac{75,000}{1000}$$

Machine Time = 75 minutes

At this point in the calculation, 75 minutes represents an optimal requirement and does not include handling time. Therefore, the manager must continue with the calculation process. For this example, handling time will be calculated as a percentage of total time, using an operational effectiveness factor.

$$\text{Total Time} = \frac{\text{Machine Time}}{\text{Operational Effectiveness}}$$

$$\text{Total Time} = \frac{75}{.70}$$

Total Time = 107 minutes

This result is incomplete because, realistically, setup time must be added. Initially, a manager may project approximately 5 minutes, which would cover the transporting of the materials to the machine area; the positioning of supporting equipment, such as a portable rack; and the checking of the operating procedure. Therefore, the total machine time plus setup would equal about 112 minutes. This represents a variance of

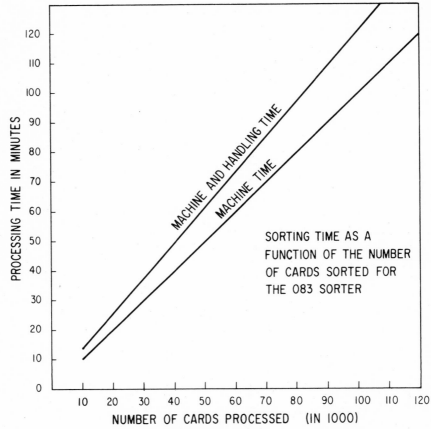

Figure 6.30. Example of Precalculated Sorting Graph

approximately 12 minutes from the data gained by utilizing a precalculated graph. Although the calculations are not as exact, it must be
remembered that both schedule values are approximations that are
subject to modification as the utilization statistics become available.

To shorten the second approach, a manager may establish an effective machine speed. This speed is an average that will apply to all sorting
operations for a given type of device. It is based on the utilization
statistics available to the manager and includes a handling factor of
approximately 20 to 30 percent. The machine speed average is sometimes referred to as net speed. Utilizing the same basic statistics as

previously shown and a net speed of 750 cards per minute, the calculation may be executed as follows:

$$\text{Sorting Time} = \frac{\text{Number of cards} \times \text{number of columns}}{\text{Net Speed}}$$

$$\text{Sorting Time} = \frac{1500 \times 5}{750}$$

$$\text{Sorting Time} = \frac{75,000}{750}$$

$$\text{Sorting Time} = 100 \text{ minutes}$$

Sorting Time	100 minutes
Est. Setup Time	+5 minutes
Est. Sorting Requirements	105 minutes

For large-volume operations, an average net speed may not be satisfactory. In that case, the manager need only modify the sorter speed by the handling factor and use the reduced operating speed as the divisor.

Similar calculations using relevant formulas can be made for scheduling operations on the key punch, key verifier, reproducer, collator, calculator, tabulator (accounting machine), interpreter, and punch machines.

b) *Computer Production.* The computing production standards may be difficult to establish. Program running or elapsed time may be determined by calculating the amount of time required to perform each function in a program. The functional times are then added together to determine total processing time. These timings generally include the i/o media, blocking factors, record sizes, volumes, arm movement, rotational delay, container position, etc. However, they do not include lengthy or excessive operator intervention, or programmer inefficiency. The timings may further be affected by the type and level of operating system and by multi-tasking. For most managers it would be simpler to closely monitor the processing of selected data during the parallel test and extrapolate. Or the manager may use simulation to predict the timings. The simulation may be performed manually or with a computer. Basic data about the program—data such as processing flow, data files, priority, etc.—is inserted into a mathematical model that represents a hardware configuration. As a result of the simulation, all timings and utilization figures will be outputted in a report format for scheduling purposes.

These figures are preliminary and should be used only for planning the initial schedule requirements. However, as utilization figures become available, the values may be modified upward or downward. In a multitasking environment, an average figure may have to be developed because elapsed time will vary each time a program is processed.

c) Preventative Maintenance. The standard for preventative maintenance is established on the basis of information supplied by the equipment manufacturer in his proposal. The proposal states only the time requirement and does not indicate the day or shift for performance of the maintenance. The day and shift are negotiable because of the constraints within which the vendor and the organization must function.

The standard must be included in the schedule and closely monitored because it limits hardware availability for production. Monitoring is also necessary to ensure proper equipment maintenance. If actual maintenance time is significantly below the standard, then either the stated requirement was incorrect or maintenance service may be incomplete. When time requirements exceed the standard, the original specifications may have been understated; or the engineers performing the maintenance may be slow or improperly trained. Also, it may be that either the age of the hardware or heavy utilization requires additional preventative maintenance. If so, then the standard must be modified to reflect this condition.

Very often, early production models require the on-site installation of numerous engineering changes. The maintenance engineer may install some of the devices during the preventative maintenance period. Consequently, he may exceed the scheduled time allocation, thereby incorrectly reflecting a variance in the standard. Before any revision of the standard is made, the situation should be discussed with the vendor's sales and/or maintenance representative. Very often, managers persuade the maintenance engineer to perform only the most important functions and postpone others until the next scheduled period. This enables the manager to return the hardware to production status sooner. Some managers habitually cancel maintenance sessions to retain the computer for productive services. Some may cancel the maintenance session because their production may be lagging. Nevertheless this can be a short-sighted attitude that can subsequently lead to a frequent need for unscheduled maintenance.

d) Emergency Maintenance. Emergency maintenance—sometimes referred to as downtime, or unscheduled, maintenance—requires development of a standard to cover that unit or element of time when the hardware is disabled due to some malfunction. Initially, this type of standard is difficult to establish because of the limited information available to the manager in terms of downtime frequency.

A preliminary standard may be established from the estimated downtime value provided by the vendor. A portion of this value is based on the Mean Time Between Failures (MTBF) statistics resulting from the vendor's equipment-testing program. This provides a failure frequency standard. If the number of failures consistently exceed the standard, then the manager must make some investigative assessment of the quality of preventative maintenance.

The MTBF provides a failure frequency rate but does not indicate the estimated downtime allocation for scheduling purposes. A preliminary value is again supplied by the vendor. This is included as a part of the estimated downtime in the vendor's hardware proposal. It represents the result of downtime statistics collected by the vendors for similar hardware.

To collect data and to determine variances, a log of service calls, elapsed response time, and maintenance time must be kept. This data may subsequently be used for the upward or downward revision of the standard. As the equipment ages and/or utilization increases, emergency maintenance needs may grow. This may necessitate an upward revision of the emergency maintenance standard.

When an organization acquires older equipment, it will be necessary to ascertain the hardware's history, together with the actual or average failure rate. Also, it may be advantageous to learn why the equipment was released by the previous user. This data will enable a manager to establish a more realistic downtime standard for that hardware.

e) Rerun Time. This is a contingency allocation built into the schedule to provide for the reprocessing of a report, output, or operation. The contingency covers the human, machine, program, or data errors occurring in the productive process. Initially it will be very difficult to project the time loss attributable to these conditions. However, as operational statistics become available, they may be used to develop an effective rerun time standard. Also, from this data, a percentage for each error category may be established by utilizing the following formula:

$$\text{Percentage of (Type of) Error} = \frac{\text{Time Lost Due to (Type of) Error}}{\text{Total Productive Time}}$$

Errors reduce operational effectivess and cause a loss of confidence in the data processing department. Therefore, every effort must be made to eliminate, minimize, and control their occurrence. The data errors may be controlled through the use of management controls (see Chapter 7). The machine errors may be due to malfunctions resulting from improper preventative maintenance, component failure, or age of the hardware. To deal with these errors, a manager may find it necessary to implement a series of management controls and/or to closely monitor the hardware failure frequency and preventative maintenance. Operator errors may be reduced or eliminated by providing for more effective direction and control of the personnel, good documentation, and intensive training for operations and user personnel. Errors caused by faulty programs may be resolved through detailed desk checking, preparation of good test plans, construction of complete test data, intensive testing of the object program, and complete verification of test output.

f) Idle Time. An idle-time standard provides a buffer in the schedule for unexpected events. This element is sometimes referred to as slack time—built into the schedule to cover such events as excessive reruns, unscheduled maintenance, special report requests, etc. There is the danger that in maintaining a contingency buffer, a manager may restrict the implementation of a valuable decision-making report simply because time is not available. The operations manager must assess the cost of delay, the value of each report, and its impact on the idle-time standard. The effect of an idle-time standard may be more significant on an organization functioning on a one-shift basis. The organization may have to develop alternate operating procedures. On the other hand, an organization functioning on a two- or three-shift basis in the operations activity has more flexibility because of its ability to overlap production backlog from one shift to another.

g) Special Requests. Specials are one-time or short-term reports or outputs designed for a specific decision-making purpose. Included in this category are such reports as wage and salary data for labor contract negotiations. Often, these requests can be readily absorbed into the normal operating schedule. However, in some organizations, the number of requests for special reports or outputs is quite high. Therefore, the operations manager must examine his production schedule to establish an average time availability for specials. In some organizations, requests for special reports occur on a cyclical basis, such as before, during, and after labor-contract negotiations. From an analysis of the production records, the operations manager will be able to develop an average time requirement. When no data or experience is available, the manager may initially project a one percent time requirement in the schedule for special requests.

The number of requests for special reports can become unwieldy if not controlled. Therefore, it becomes necessary that an administrative procedure be developed and implemented requiring practical and economic justification of such requests (see Appendix VI).

2. TESTING STANDARDS. Testing standards must be developed and included in the schedule to maintain the operational effectiveness of an organization. The standard is developed to meet the functional needs of the programming, systems, operations, advanced planning and development, and audit personnel. The types of standards within this category are:

a) Program assembly and compile
b) Program testing
c) Magnetic tape
d) Forms testing

a) *Program Assembly and Compile.* The projected time standard for assemblies and compiles is affected by the hardware, operating system, language processor, program development, and maintenance requirements. In developing an overall time requirement, the operations manager or programming manager initially determines the estimated program translation time. This can be done by dividing the language processor speed into the estimated number of source program statements or instructions. Or, the operations manager or programming manager may gather data on program sizes to establish an average program size; he then divides this average by the language processor speed to calculate an average translate time.

The number of compiles or assemblies required in a schedule period will depend on the type and number of new programs being developed, and/or existing programs modified. The time standard may be determined by multiplying the average translation speed by the average number of programs requiring translation.

b) Program Testing. A program-testing standard provides for the testing and debugging of new and modified programs. Testing may require from 5 to 25 percent of the available schedule time. As recommended earlier, a minimum of 20 minutes test time should be allocated for each programmer. Failure to provide adequate test time causes slippage in implementation schedules and results in a waste of valuable resources.

c) Magnetic Tape. An organization may choose to develop a norm for testing the quality and condition of its magnetic tape. The test is made by passing each reel through the tape transports twice. The first pass performs a writing function and the second reads back the written data. As a result, it is possible to determine if the tape is worn, stretched, scratched, or damaged.

This testing process may be conducted when a new shipment of magnetic tape is received, to select a source of supply, or to establish a purchasing specification standard. More frequently, the standard is the basis of a tape maintenance and rehabilitation program. The average time for testing a 2400-foot-long reel is approximately five minutes. This value, however, is affected by the number of channels available on the computer and by the manner in which the test program was written. Average time may be increased if the program does not overlap tape rewinding; it may be decreased if more than one channel is available.

It is difficult to establish a norm for magnetic disk pack testing. However, this may be accomplished by developing a load-dump program, which would test reading and writing on the disk. This is a time-consuming process and should be performed only when damage may be suspected. However, some organizations use this technique to test new shipments.

d) Forms Testing. The standard for forms testing is established to evaluate the quality and effectiveness of a form. When a new form is designed, the vendor is asked to submit a paper and/or carbon dummy. The dummies are then processed on the equipment to determine if form objectives are realized. Similar testing may be conducted for the MICR, OCR, and OMR types of forms.

This standard is generally established only in medium- or large-sized data processing organizations. However, many organizations in search of cost reduction cases will frequently have their systems and/or advanced planning personnel evaluating forms construction. As a result, new specifications may be developed that may reduce the form's cost. Forms testing may also be conducted to verify a vendor's compliance with contractual obligations. In this case, an average time standard should be established on the basis of the type of testing to be conducted.

3. TRAINING STANDARDS. To maintain or increase operational effectiveness, training must be provided. Generally, it is limited to systems analysts, programmers, and console operators. However, organizations equipped with online input, output, data communications, and/or data collection terminals must also provide training for users.

The actual schedule requirements depend on the level and extent of training to be provided. As the training plan is evolved, the time requirements for each element or phase should be closely monitored and recorded for subsequent scheduling purposes.

Also, demonstrations may be included in this standard. It is difficult to establish a true time standard because the number of demonstrations conducted will vary. However, the length of such demonstrations can be controlled by providing a standardized routine. Some organizations, in order to minimize disruptions in the productive level, allow demonstrations to be performed only on a fixed schedule basis.

Initially, the data processing manager must project the time available for productive purposes. The approach begins with specifying the base time available and applying the operations standards against this value. Figure 6.31 illustrates the constraints and their effect on a one-shift schedule for a data processing organization. The organization is supported by three programmers. Twenty-eight percent of the schedule is required for application of the various standards. This will consume 11 hours and 20 minutes of the base shift. However, 28 hours and 40 minutes remain, which may be presented as an average of 5 hours and 44 minutes a day.

Review Questions: Group 6E

1. How can basic machine time requirements be determined for a production schedule?
2. How is setup and handling time included in a production schedule?
3. What is the purpose of establishing an idle-time standard?

Schedule Factor	Percentage	Time Requirement
Nonproduction Requirements:		
Maintenance Standards		
Preventative (4 hours per week)	10.0	— 4:00 hrs.
Emergency	.5	— :20 mins.
Reruns		
Machine Error	.5	— :20
Program Error	.5	— :20
Operator Error	.5	— :20
Data Error	.5	— :20
Idle Time	1.0	— :40
Program Development and Maintenance	12.5	— 5:00
Setup Time	2.0	— :80
	28.0%	11 hrs. 20 mins.
Machine Time Available		40:00 hrs.
Nonproduction Requirements		−11:20
Production Time Available		28:40 hrs.

Figure 6.31   Example of Projection of Production Time Availability

4. Why must special requests for one-time reports be controlled?
5. What are the causes of reruns? How may they be minimized?

SCHEDULE DEVELOPMENT AND EVALUATION

Development of a Schedule

With the performance standards established, the data processing manager can develop a project or operation schedule. The primary purpose of the schedule is to achieve a desired objective or to produce a number of outputs within a given time-frame that effectively utilize the available resources. Development and availability of a schedule will enable a manager to:

—Determine and provide for adequate resource requirements
—Establish realistic due-out times for each output

—Reduce machine conflicts resulting from the need for processing of two different outputs or reports simultaneously

—Determine the due-in time for source documents and data elements

Scheduling is a difficult task, but a most important one. Its complexity varies with the size of the installation and/or project. As the size of a project or installation increases, the number of internal and external influences, and their interaction, increase correspondingly. This forces the data processing manager to customize a schedule for each functional activity. He must apply his knowledge, standards, and records to develop a schedule that will fit his needs and desires. The value of an operationally effective schedule will exceed the cost of preparation.

The construction of a schedule begins with identification and analysis of the tasks to be performed. This information is available from procedural documentation, interviews, or activity specification sheets (see Figure 6.32). It must be augmented by due-out and due-in times or dates, as well as by actual or estimated processing time for the required activities.

The schedule that is developed must be flexible in order to provide for some manipulation should problems or delays occur. If buffer or idle time is available, then the difficulties are minimized. However, where no slack exists, the data processing manager will have to adjust the planned schedule.

A number of different schedule formats can be designed and developed, in accordance with individual needs and desires. The documentation is necessary because no data processing manager can hope to retain a schedule in his memory and expect to direct and control effectively. The schedule indicates when his equipment and personnel are busy or idle; what they are being used for; and whether or not he has the capacity to assume new functions.

The tasks or activities, their interrelationships, and the time requirements in a schedule may be illustrated in one of the following ways:

1. Operational flowchart
2. Machine-Load Schedule
3. Gantt chart
4. PERT network

1. OPERATIONAL FLOWCHART. On an operational flowchart, each system or subsystem is broken down into the required clerical and equipment steps and operations. To each step or operation is affixed an

ACTIVITY   SPECIFICATION   SHEET

PROJECT NO.   _____

PROJECT TITLE   _____   DATE | | | | |
                                                          Mo. Day Yr.

EVENT   _____

                   _____

                   _____

                   _____

                   _____

                   _____

                   _____

                   _____

                   _____

                   _____

                   _____

                   _____

                   _____

                   _____

                   _____

                   _____

PRECEDING EVENT   _____

SUCCEEDING EVENT   _____

ESTIMATED TIME
  REQUIREMENTS   _____   _____
                      Man— Days   Man— Hours

ESTIMATED | | | | | |
COMPLETION DATE   Mo.   Day   Yr.

Figure 6.32. Example of Activity Specification Sheet

estimated or standardized time element. The manager may then total the machine and clerical time requirements in order to determine project needs, as illustrated in Figure 6.33. The time elements are also summarized for each type of hardware device. Subsequently the totals are consolidated to produce a daily and weekly machine-load schedule.

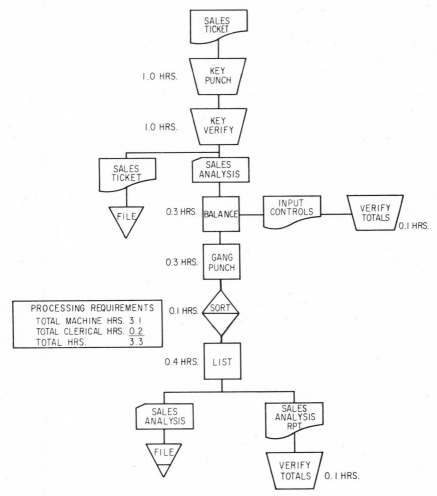

Figure 6.33. Operational Flowchart: Sales Analysis Application Sample

An operational flowchart can be used very effectively in analyzing and determining the resource requirements in a unit-record operation. For totally computerized operations, this type of flowchart is of limited value, for only the auxiliary or offline operations and clerical operations may be specified. The processing within the central processing unit cannot be readily estimated or standardized. It is possible to calculate the processing time requirements by utilizing the instruction, together with input/output timings found in the hardware and programmer reference manuals. But this is not a very simple task and most time-consuming. If the micro-flowchart is sufficiently detailed, the time requirements for each instruction can be calculated to produce an elapsed processing time. In a multi-programming environment, the manually calculated elapsed time figures may be very inaccurate. Under this type of software arrangement, the elapsed time is affected by such factors as program priority; input/output, channel, and controller delays; the amount of multi-tasking; and operator efficiency. Processing time is also affected by equipment features, software capability, input/output volumes, and data set organization.

2. MACHINE-LOAD SCHEDULE. For scheduling of equipment operations, a machine-load schedule may be prepared. However, an individual schedule for each category of equipment must be developed. These schedules identify the machine requirements for a given day and can be expanded to cover a week.

In developing a machine-loading schedule, the data processing manager allocates to each machine the required production activities on the basis of priority and of due-in and due-out requirements. As the allocation is made, the data processing manager becomes aware of any machine conflicts, thus enabling himself to reschedule operations with a lower priority. An example of a machine-load worksheet is illustrated in Figure 6.34.

3. GANTT CHARTS. Gantt charts may also be used to graphically illustrate a schedule. Of the types of documentation formats discussed here, the Gantt charts enjoy universal application. They may be easily applied to machine loading and to project scheduling.

Each of the steps or operations is drawn on the graph in its operational sequence for a given time-frame. The chart is arranged in selected time units and each step, operation, project, or application is plotted in a horizontal line showing the start and stop parameters for each. Figure 6.35 illustrates the use of a Gantt chart to identify the production load for an IBM 026 key punch machine. This chart is established for an eight-hour period and subdivided into ten-minute time elements. Machine 01 has been scheduled for key punching of payroll clock card data. This will utilize approximately seven hours of machine time. The use of a modified Gantt chart for a sales analysis application is illustrated in Figure 6.36. This chart indicates the required machine operations in their sequence of activity and given time-frame. In this example, the key punching and verification functions overlap. However, the succeeding

MACHINE-LOAD SCHEDULE WORKSHEET

APPLICATION NUMBER	OPERATION	OPER. NO.	MACH. FUNCTION	VOLUME	ESTIMATED PROCESSING TIME	DUE IN		DUE OUT		PRIORITY
						DAY	TIME	DAY	TIME	

Figure 6.34. Machine-Load Schedule Worksheet

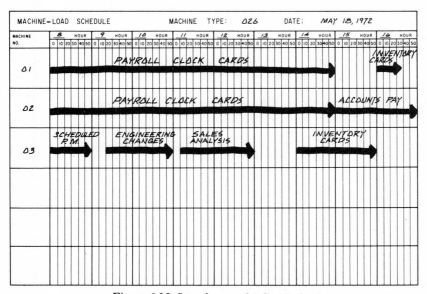

Figure 6.35. Sample use of a Gantt chart

391

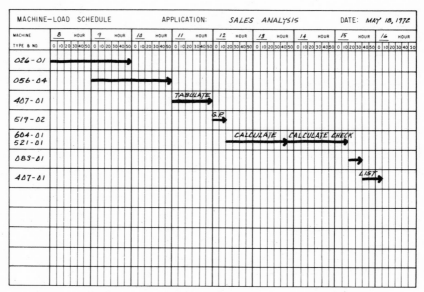

Figure 6.36. Modified Gantt Chart: Sales Analysis Application Sample

operations cannot be overlapped because of their sequential dependence upon each other. The Gantt chart shown in Figure 6.37 illustrates the overlapping of functions in a project to install a computer.

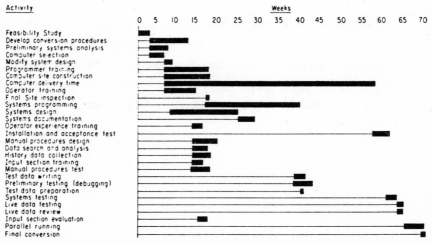

Figure 6.37. Gantt Chart Showing Overlapping of Functions in Computer Installation Project

Though the Gantt chart identifies the tasks and their duration, it does not show their interrelationships. Nor does it show the effect of a delay on the overall project. Also, it may be difficult to work with on a large project involving many tasks.

4. PERT NETWORK. The use of a PERT network in scheduling requires the detailing of activities and allocation of time elements for each activity. This technique requires considerable preparation and planning time and its value for development of a machine-load schedule is questionable. However, it is an excellent tool for development and implementation schedules.

Figure 6.38 illustrates the use of a PERT network for the planning of a computer installation project. This may be compared with the Gantt chart illustrated in Figure 6.37. In the PERT network it can be seen that the relationships of the individual work efforts to each other and the overall project are clearly visible. This definition of work efforts and relationships demands more detailed planning than any of the other scheduling formats. It demands consideration of the resource allocations, unnecessary work efforts, conflicts, waste, and deficiencies. This, however, enables the data processing manager to divide the overall problem into manageable portions. Nevertheless, this approach to planning may be too time-consuming, in that, among other things, the DP manager must not spend more time on the PERT network than on the project itself.

In the development of a network the data processing manager will undoubtedly become aware of alternative approaches to the problem. This is an advantage not readily available in the other scheduling techniques. Also, the network provides a quick means of reporting status, changes, and progress as related to the overall goal. As a result the PERT network is a useful tool in helping to define the problem areas in a project.

Schedule Evaluation

The effectiveness of a manager's schedule is determined by the available feedback. As stated earlier, the need for a feedback reporting mechanism is an integral part of the goal-attainment process. Feedback is particularly important for data processing functions. Once a system is implemented, its activities or the influences affecting it do not remain

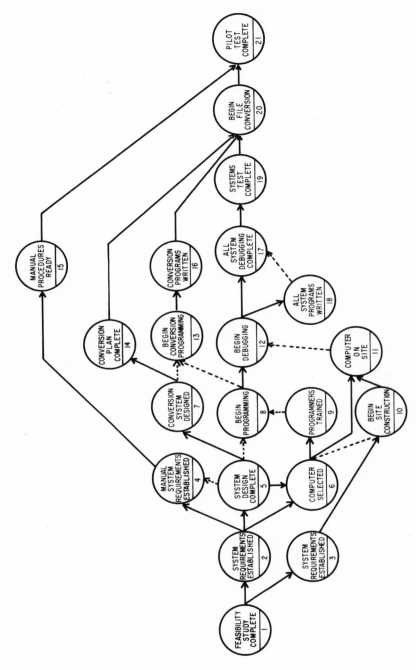

Figure 6.38. PERT Network as Used in Planning Computer Installation Project

static—objectives can change; current objectives may not be met; priorities or requirements change; work loads increase. The effects of these changes or conditions must be quickly detected, identified, and analyzed before any appropriate action can be taken.

The feedback available to the manager may take the form of statistical, oral, or written reports. Most of the feedback on the activities within the systems, programming, advanced planning and development, and training groups may be derived from daily or weekly activity reports. However, in evaluating machine loading, the feedback may be more elaborate. It may be generated from such items as a system measurement instrument, system utilization monitor, computer performance analyzer, or computer performance monitors. The actual names for the devices or packages used in collecting the data may be more exotic. However, their basic function is to monitor or measure personnel and hardware performance and utilization.

The feedback should provide a quick means of reporting status, changes, and progress. A well-designed reporting system can provide a data processing administrator or manager with the following types of information:

—Overall hardware utilization
—The activities accounting for the utilization
—Cost accounting data for chargebacks
—Partition utilization statistics in a multi-tasking environment
—Program efficiency
—Programmer efficiency in testing
—Operator efficiency
—Rerun statistics
—Shift productivity

This type of information may be developed from the data gathered through one of the following methods:

1. Manual recording utilizing a clock
2. Manual recording utilizing an elapsed time recorder
3. Automatic recording utilizing an internal clock
4. Hardware performance monitoring
5. System utilization software

1. MANUAL RECORDING—CLOCK. This technique involves the use of a wall clock or punching clock for data collection. When using a wall

clock, the operator manually logs the start and stop times for an operation based on his clock reading. When a punching clock is used, the start and stop time recording is made on a prescribed form inserted in the device; this form of recording may provide a reading in hours and minutes or in hours and hundreths of hours. In both methods, the operator must enter the application name or number, together with the estimated or actual input/output volume, on the utilization record. The data on the logs or records must subsequently be translated to produce a machine-sensible record. The machine records are then manipulated and summarized to produce the desired management reports. However, owing to the limited amount of feedback collected from this method, only generalized reports may be prepared. For example, although the feedback provides the elapsed processing time for a report or output, it does not actually indicate the status of the CPU, i/o devices, or other hardware features.

2. MANUAL RECORDING—ELAPSED-TIME RECORDER. An elapsed-time recorder provides a readout of the total productive time on a given hardware unit. On the utilization record, the machine operator logs the start and stop readings given by the elapsed-time recorder, the job name or number, i/o volumes, and the wall-clock start and stop time for each operation. The clock start and stop times are used to determine the setup and handling time requirements in an operation.

Elapsed-time recording may also be used to determine the idleness of the personnel. Once the personnel become aware of the fact, they develop ways of ensuring an increased reading on the elapsed-time recorder. Despite the disadvantages, the method is popular with operations managers because the recording devices are available on the computing equipment for rental charge determination. The utilization data is subsequently processed to produce the desired reports. However, the amount of available feedback is again limited under this recording method.

3. AUTOMATED RECORDING—INTERNAL CLOCK. An internal clock may be a hardware or software feature in the form of subroutine or subprogram. The timer can be reset every 24 hours and may be used to output clock and elapsed time on card, tape, disk, or printer media. This recording technique is more accurate and not dependent upon the operator to record hardware utilization. Volumes and job identification

data may also be outputted automatically if incorporated into the software. The output may then be manipulated and summarized to prepare a variety of utilization reports and statistics.

4. HARDWARE PERFORMANCE MONITORS. The hardware performance monitors are portable devices used to measure and record computer activity or utilization. Electrical probes are connected to the wiring to detect and record status signals. These signals study the activity of the central processing unit in relation to data channel and input/output component usage. The signal impulses are connected to counters located in the monitor device. These record the duration of an event or activity or the number of times it occurs. For example, in monitoring the CPU, the device may be wired to collect data on the total available time, supervisor time, wait time, and/or busy time. On the other hand, if connected to a disk drive, it may collect data on seek times and seek counts.

The data from the counters is generally recorded on magnetic tape, which is part of the monitor device. Subsequently, tabular reports, summary reports, and graphs may be prepared from the tape in order to indicate system and device utilization. This information may be used by the advanced planning and development personnel to evaluate the effectiveness of the existing configuration, program coding, and file structures. It may also be used in the survey and feasibility studies to provide quantitative work load data. The availability of this information will enable the systems analyst to determine if and when the hardware can absorb another report. Also, when conducting a feasibility study for hardware acquisition, the systems analyst will have valuable information about the present configuration available.

There is no interference with the operation of the computer, because the monitor is connected only to critical wiring points in the computer circuitry. Also, the device can be connected to the computer within a relatively short period of time.

Though the monitors are capable of determining the time and type of activity during a computer run, they do not specifically check the program. Therefore, they are not capable of indicating undesirable conditions occurring in a program. Also, the purchase price of a monitor is very high. However, a monitor for use with IBM hardware can be acquired on a short-term lease basis.

(A listing of the hardware monitor manufacturers is given in Appendix VII.)

5. SYSTEM UTILIZATION SOFTWARE. Computer system utilization may also be monitored through the use of specially designed software packages. These are installed as part of the operating system software to collect data about the applications in the job stream. The job control card activates the system utilization software and indicates the category of reporting information to be collected. Information on each job is recorded on a tape or disk drive. Subsequently, the information is extracted from the medium by a report generator program. This will permit the processing of management reports on productivity, testing, reruns, billing, cost control, compilation, and/or assembly.

The software requires a minimum amount of core storage and is less costly than a hardware monitor. It requires no operator intervention because the necessary data gathering is activated through the job control cards preceding each job. The software package is also capable of performing a dynamic trace on an instruction being executed. This feature permits the identification of sections of inefficient coding in a program. The collected data may be subsequently processed to indicate activity and utilization. The output must then be carefully analyzed to identify the problem areas and determine the appropriate corrective action.

There is some degradation of the system because the software monitor must make use of the hardware's i/o and processor time for checking utilization and activity. Also, the software package must be tailored to the computer's operating system. If an organization upgrades its software to a new operating system, investment in a new monitor package may be required. However, some vendors provide a trade-in allowance to minimize the loss of investment.

(A listing of the system utilization software package manufacturers is given in Appendix VIII.)

The choice of monitoring technique is dependent upon the data processing manager's needs and objectives—what does he wish to monitor or measure? Cost also becomes a major consideration. A manager must evaluate the start-up, maintenance, machine, and analysis costs. An organization with a small-scale computer or mini-computer may not have very much need for a hardware or software monitor. However, whatever measurement technique is selected, the manager must evaluate the feedback carefully to maintain an effective operation.

Review Questions: Group 6F

1. Why should a manager develop a schedule for his functional activity?
2. Can simulation be effectively applied to the development of a schedule?
3. What is the basic difference between a Gantt chart and modified Gantt chart?
4. Why would someone describe a software monitor as an inefficient way to seek efficiency?
5. How would you defend your decision to acquire a hardware performance monitor for your computer equipment?

SUMMARY

Before a manager can begin to direct and control an activity, he must have a plan and/or schedule to achieve a desired goal. In formulating his plan or schedule, the manager must consider the function's duties and responsibilities, because these have to be converted into events, steps, and operations. Each of them must then be allocated an estimated or standardized time element, each of which may have to be adjusted or modified because of a limited time-frame.

The duties and responsibilities must be converted to performance standards, which become the basis of scheduling and controlling. The performance standards are then available for the detection, identification, and correction of problems resulting from the application of manpower, machine, and material resources.

Graphically, the time elements may be illustrated on a Gantt chart, modified Gantt chart, operational flowchart, or a PERT network. For illustrating machine loads, the Gantt charts are adequate. However, for indicating interrelationships and overlapping activities, a modified Gantt chart or a PERT network is more satisfactory. The modified Gantt chart and the PERT network are also more suitable for scheduling the activities of the systems, programming, training, and the advanced planning and development groups.

When a schedule is implemented, the manager must collect data on the progress or status and compare the feedback with the planned performances. The inclusion of the feedback concept provides the manager with a very important tool for detecting and solving problems—one that enables him to evaluate both personnel and equipment performance. Moreover, it enables him to evaluate the procedures, training, manning requirements, and work load. And it also gives him the opportunity to determine if additional responsibilities or more complex tasks can be assigned to personnel who are performing above-standard. Also, with the schedule and utilization records or activity reports on hand, the manager will be capable of developing a budget control approach, as well as a basis for personnel appraisal and evaluation.

As a result of the many interacting elements in the productive process, the manager may experience some difficulty in establishing a schedule. However, without a schedule he will find it very difficult to optimize the utilization of his manpower, material, machine, and money resources. Through the use of a schedule, the manager may be able to apply 20-20 hindsight as foresight—based on standards and utilization experience.

CASE STUDY

Case Study 6.1: Ruth's Creations

The systems personnel are in the process of parallel testing a new inventory-control application. As the manager of the operations group, you are concerned with the effect of this application on your activity. You are particularly concerned about the key punching, verifying, and sorting effort. There will be approximately 100,000 transaction cards to be key punched and verified at the end of each day. These are punched according to the information given in the accompanying transaction card format. The cards are to be sorted on the stock number before they are written on tape for subsequent processing.

PERFORMANCE STANDARDS

Key Punching

    Key Stroke Requirement Formula:

      Total Key Strokes Required = No. of Cards × Average No. of Columns per Card

Performance Standards

Type of Key Punching	Potential Hourly Key Stroke Rate
Numeric	10,000
Numeric with Some Alphabetic	8,000
Mixed Alphabetic and Numeric	5,000
Alphabetic	4,000

Key Verification

    Standards and formula same as for key verification. However, a factor of 3 percent must be added to allow for stoppages due to error detection.

Sorting

    083 Sorter Speed: 1,000 c.p.m.

      Sorting Time Requirement Formula:

$$\text{Sorting Time} = \frac{\text{No. of Cards} \times \text{No. of Card Columns}}{\text{Sorter Speed}}$$

TRANSACTION CARD FORMAT

Field Description	Cards Columns	Type of Information*
Accounting Class Code	1–4	A/N
Stock Number	5–19	N
Description	20–28	A/N
Status Code	29–30	A/N
Unit of Issue	31–32	A/N
Transaction Code	33	N
Procurement Type	34	A
Quantity	35–40	N

    * A/N = alphameric
      A = alphabetic
      N = numeric

Discussion Questions

1. Given the accompanying information on performance standards, how much time will be required for key punching?
2. How much time will be required for the verification effort?
3. How much time will be required for the sorting effort?
4. Two of the key punching machines are not fully loaded. One of the machines is available for four hours and the second for two hours. Can this be of any benefit to you?
5. Develop an argument to justify a different approach to sorting.
6. What graphic method would you use to illustrate the schedule? Explain your answer.
7. What type of monitoring technique would be most effective in this situation? Explain why.

7

Management Controls for Information Processing

INTRODUCTION

The introduction of automated processing in accounting, reporting, record-keeping, and decision-making activities is forcing changes in organizational operating procedures. The traditional practices of audit and control generally fail to provide adequate protection. Therefore, new policies and practices have to be developed and implemented that will effectively eliminate or minimize the risk of fraud, embezzlement, accidental error, loss of business and/or customers, law violations, sabotage, and embarrassment for an organization. Furthermore, the need to maintain or improve the reliability of information means an increasing emphasis on the development and implementation of procedures for the prevention, detection, and correction of errors. The failure to maintain a basic level of reliability results in the user losing faith in both the system's output and the organization providing that output.

There is a general misconception that hardware reliability can be equated with overall system reliability. This belief stems from the widespread failure to recognize that the basic responsibility for the input preparation, programming, and operation of the computer, as well as the interpretation of its output, rests not with infallible machines but with human beings capable of error. Consequently, it is essential to monitor all of the myriad activities and interactions of men and machines that

403

occur in the realm of data processing. This can be accomplished through the effective use of management controls.

Controls are equally important for both unit-record and computing equipment operations. Therefore, every system that comes into use must include procedures for the detection, identification, correction, and prevention of errors. These procedures should be incorporated into every system during the planning phase and should then be evaluated during the system testing, parallel testing, implementation, and follow-up phases. Controls should never be simply superimposed on a system; rather, they should be built in as an integral part of the operation.

Therefore, each system should be analyzed to determine exactly the type and level of controls required. A control procedure adequate for one phase of a system may not be feasible for another. Consequently, before deciding the type of procedures to be employed, the analyst must first evaluate the system's objectives. In this investigative process, he determines the type of data involved in the system in terms of its characteristics and its relationship to this system and others. The effect of the system's inputs and outputs on other related systems will also be a determining factor in the types and extent of control procedures developed. Next, the analyst identifies the flow of data from source of origination to user output, for this helps in determining the placement of error-detection locations in the system. At each of these points, the analyst must investigate the type of error-checking being conducted, together with its purpose and effectiveness. This will enable him to prepare the procedures best suited to detect and identify the errors in this particular system.

The type of control and its extent of application varies according to the organizational policies, the system, the hardware and software used, and the needs of the user. Also, it is important that the implemented controls provide a proper balance between their cost on the one hand and their value or effectiveness on the other.

MANAGEMENT CONTROL OBJECTIVES

The principal objectives of a program of management control for data processing operations are:

—To ensure that all source data entering into the data processing system are valid

—To ensure that all source data entered into the system are transcribed accurately

—To ensure that all applicable and pertinent data are included as outputs

—To prevent any unauthorized data changes

—To ensure that all erroneous data entries in the system are quickly detected and identified as such, and that authorized corrections are made promptly and accurately

—To ensure that all processing is accomplished accurately

—To prevent the accidental or deliberate alteration of programs, documentation, and files

—To prevent the sabotage or destruction of data processing hardware

—To protect and preserve the organization's assets

The effective implementation of these control objectives will:

—Reduce or eliminate reruns due to errors

—Reduce the need for supplementary processing

—Reduce or eliminate the wasteful use of manpower, machine, material, and money resources

—Enable an organization to continue to transact business despite an accident, disaster, or sabotage

—Reduce or eliminate the possibility of fraud and embezzlement

Review Question: Group 7A

1. What are some of the objectives in a management control program?

TYPES OF MANAGEMENT CONTROLS

Six basic types of controls are appropriate to data processing operations and systems. These are:

1. Equipment controls
2. Input controls
3. Output controls
4. Program controls
5. External controls
6. Peripheral controls

Equipment Controls

The equipment controls are built into the apparatus by the manufacturer to ensure that data is read, processed, transferred, and outputted correctly. Sometimes the controls in this category are referred to as hardware, or system, checks. (The term "system checks" is also used sometimes to describe certain controls in the program control category.)

The kinds of equipment controls available vary from manufacturer to manufacturer. Consideration of the types of controls available must be included in the feasibility study for both new equipment and systems.

Equipment controls are normally operative as a result of internal machine circuitry and are performed automatically. Whenever available in a hardware configuration, they should not be duplicated by other forms of control. Included in the category of equipment controls are the following:

1. Parity check
2. Echo checking
3. Dual Gap Heads
4. Control lights and indicators
5. Dual circuitry
6. File protection
7. Storage protection
8. Diagnostic routines
9. Automatic retransmission
10. Arithmetic overflow detection
11. Cryptographic devices

1. PARITY CHECK. The parity check is the most universal and fundamental control in the equipment category. The technique is used to ensure the validity of data moved within the computer by verifying the binary coding configuration of each code or character. The various characters and codes are handled within the computer as binary bits. The combination of binary "one" bits for each character or code is counted and the sum is then tested for an odd- or even-bit configuration. The sum of bits must match the hardware manufacturer's specification for odd or even data representation. If the hardware is equipped with odd-bit parity circuitry, then all data or instructions moved, added, etc., within the computer must be odd. If the specification is even, the opposite is true. Character or code representation not meeting the hardware specification will cause a parity check error. A corrective action

must then be initiated by the equipment operator.

2. ECHO CHECKING. Echo checking is a technique used to verify the transmission of data between two points. The data impulses transmitted to an output device are returned to the generating source and compared for accuracy. The original information transmitted should be exactly the same as the information outputted. The comparison is generally performed in a buffering device, with any deviation being indicated on the console for operator or program action.

3. DUAL GAP HEADS. The dual gap heads are a hardware feature used on magnetic tape drives. The writing of the data occurs at one gap and the reading at the other. As information is written on a tape record at the write gap, it is immediately read at the read gap to check the accuracy of the transmission. Errors are then signaled on the console for action by the program or operator.

4. CONTROL LIGHTS AND INDICATORS. Control lights and indicators are used to alert the equipment operator about such conditions as arithmetic overflows, parity check errors, system interrupts, attempts to violate storage protection, programmable error conditions, faulty or erroneous data, etc. Responding to the indication provided on the console or components of the computing system, the operator takes the appropriate corrective action.

On data communications devices, the indicators are known as system activity indicators. Most terminals are equipped with a "System Alert" light to indicate a line connection to a distant terminal or computer. On some devices audible sounds are emitted periodically to indicate that the circuit contact is being maintained. Other lights indicate that transmission has been completed or that retransmission is required.

5. DUAL CIRCUITRY. Some hardware is equipped with dual circuitry for arithmetic operations and input/output operations. The arithmetic operations are performed in one of two ways. One way utilizes two separate arithmetic circuits to perform the arithmetic operations and then compare the results. The other way is based on arithmetic complementation, in which dual circuits are used for complementing, adding, recomplementing, and comparing simultaneously. In both methods, the results are compared before data is moved or transferred.

For input/output operations, the card readers and punches are equipped with dual-hole sensing circuitry through which a card is read twice when inputted and twice again when outputted. The comparisons are generally made in the buffering unit, with any deviation being indicated as a reader or punch check. If a bit is dropped, a parity check indicator may be turned on.

6. FILE PROTECTION. File-protection devices are provided on magnetic tape units and magnetic disk drives to prevent accidental erasure of valid data or master records. On a magnetic tape unit, the protection device is a removable plastic ring. Withdrawing the ring inhibits writing on the tape, but allows reading. Inserting the protective ring nullifies the effect of the circuitry and allows both reading and writing on the tape. File protection on a magnetic disk drive is controlled by a control button on the unit. When activated, the button directs the circuitry to inhibit writing on protected records.

7. STORAGE PROTECTION. The storage-protect feature permits the storage or residence of more than one program in the main memory at any one time. It is a hardware feature activated by the executive program to assure correct and continuous operation, with protection against any accidental alteration of the resident programs. This protection is particularly necessary for real-time computing operations.

8. DIAGNOSTIC ROUTINES. Diagnostic routines are stored internally in the system library and utilize the internal circuitry for checking. They are composed of test problems entered into the computer to detect defects in the computer circuitry. The routines may be read into the computer; activated by the field engineer when performing preventative or unscheduled maintenance; or activated by the executive program when a machine interrupt occurs due to a malfunction in the central processor. In some computing systems, the results of the diagnostic routines are stored internally for analysis at a future time, but only if the diagnosed malfunction does not prevent continued computer operations. The form of equipment control involving the use of diagnostic routines is sometimes referred to as circuit testing.

9. AUTOMATIC RETRANSMISSION. Automatic error-detection and retransmission is necessary for data transmitted from an online terminal. Some data communications terminals include provision for the automatic retransmission of characters or messages found to be in error—a technique that also involves automatic error-detection. When a character is found to be in error, retransmission of that character, from a buffering device in the terminal, is requested for a given number of times. If the character cannot be correctly reread, an indicator light is turned on at the console of the terminal to signal the need for operator intervention. The automatic retransmission may take the form of reread-

ing a card, or of backspacing and rereading a tape record.

10. ARITHMETIC OVERFLOW DETECTION. This is a hardware feature used to test the capacity of an arithmetic accumulator. If the result of an arithmetic calculation exceeds the size of the accumulator, the overflow indicator is turned on. This helps to prevent the loss of a significant part of an answer due to the overflow condition. Operator or program action is then required to correct the condition.

11. CRYPTOGRAPHIC DEVICES. These are used to encode and decode sensitive information passing through computers, data communications terminals, and time-sharing terminals. Traditionally, these devices have been used primarily by the military to scramble information. However, many nonmilitary organizations—especially those that are decentralized and those that use public telephone and telegraph lines—are now utilizing such devices to combat the theft or loss of sensitive data.

Review Questions: Group 7B

1. Name the major control categories used in information processing systems.

2. What is the purpose of a parity check?

3. What effect does a cryptographic device have on safeguarding inputs into an information system?

Input Controls

Input controls are primarily well-defined procedures designed to detect the entry or existence of erroneous data in the input preparation process. Their use in the system is intended to insure that:

—All data entering into the system is valid

—Source data are received from all points of origin before processing is initiated

—Source data are properly and accurately converted from human-sensible to machine-readable form

—All original and adjusting entries are made into the system

—All transactions are properly recorded at point of origin

The level and extent of input controls implemented in an information processing cycle will be affected by the type of data collected, the work load, and time available in the processing schedule for their use.

The time constraint may be the most significant factor. If more time is available, then the number and type of input controls implemented will be more intense. However, if time is lacking, either fewer controls will be implemented or fewer documents will be checked.

Some of the more common kinds of input controls are:

1. Document register
2. Batching
3. Transmittal documents and route slips
4. Cancellation and time stamps
5. Document numbering
6. Matching
7. Approvals
8. Verification
9. Self-checking numbers
10. Hash totals
11. Control totals
12. Data checkers
13. Checklists

1. DOCUMENT REGISTER. The document register is one of the oldest forms of input control available. It is primarily used to provide a record of document movement through the information processing cycle. When properly used, it provides an excellent audit trail, although its use may add time to the processing cycle. The individual documents are controlled by maintaining a manual listing of each document as it is processed at the point of origin or received at the point of entry or collection. The register listing generally contains a description of the document and/or control numbers or characteristics that will identify the form. As each document is completely processed, either the identification entry is deleted from the register or an entry is made to indicate disposition. The remaining entries represent those documents in process or missing. In some organizations, dates and times are added to provide more complete identification of the work flow. A sample document register is illustrated in Figure 7.1.

2. BATCHING. A batch is a group or subgroup of transactions affecting a logical file of information. The transactions are ordered or arranged in a manner that gives each group some common identity; for example, a department number or date. The batches are generally limited in size to simplify the error-detecting, -identifying, and -correcting process of errors.

RECORD OF INVOICES							
DATE OF		SUPPLIER'S INVOICE NUMBER	AMOUNT OF INVOICE	OUR P. O. NUMBER	INVOICE		AUDITOR OR CLERK	REMARKS
INVOICE	PAYMENT				NO. OF ITEMS	TOTAL QUANTITY		

Figure 7.1. Sample Document Register

Each batch is preceded by a batch control record (see Figure 7.2). This contains a serially assigned batch control number, the date of origination, a count of the items included, originating source, hash totals of identifying information, and control totals of quantities or amounts. The batches are generally limited in size to simplify the process of detecting, identifying, and correcting errors.

When the documents are translated to a machine-readable form and initially machine processed, the batch or item counts and the hash or

RS-64 PAYROLL BATCH CONTROL CARD

DATE	DEPT.	NO. OF CARDS	BATCH NO.

FIELD DESCRIPTION	TOTAL HOURS	F R A C.	TOTAL AMOUNTS	D E C.
TIME WORKED AND ADJUSTMENTS				
OVERTIME ALLOWANCES AND ADJUSTMENTS				
OTHER ALLOWANCES AND ADJUSTMENTS				
SUB-TOTAL				
NIGHT BONUS AND ADJUSTMENTS				
GROSS				

DOCUMENT CONTROL

SEQUENCE	OPERATION	INITIALS
1	LOG IN	
2	KEY PUNCH	
3	KEY VERIFY	
4	PROOF	
5	POST-PAYROLL	

Figure 7.2. Sample Form for Batch Control Records

control totals are checked against the values posted on the batch control record. Any deviation may be isolated by checking the respective totals. Very often, the machine-readable records are listed on the printer or tabulator to provide an output which can be scanned visually for any discrepancy.

Batches may also be used to reduce key punching effort, thereby minimizing the possibility of error in the transcription process. Repetitive data for a batch can be automatically duplicated by utilizing program control on the key punch machine. For example, a group of work assignment cards with the same department number, hours worked, and work order numbers may be batched and duplicated. The key punch operator would have to punch only the employee number in each card. This type of operation speeds up key punching and reduces the possibility of error.

The above-mentioned operation could also be conducted by key punching only the employee numbers and gangpunching the repetitive data on a reproducer. However, this would result in the need to control the movement of the data elements from the key punch operation.

3. TRANSMITTAL DOCUMENTS AND ROUTE SLIPS. Transmittal documents and route slips (see Figure 7.3) establish control over the movement of documents or batches from one location or another. These forms are used to fix responsibility and accountability for the documents. They are also used to indicate progress or the flow of a document through an operation. In addition to controlling source documents, transmittal documents, as illustrated in Figure 7.3, are used for other machine-readable media, such as cards, paper tape, magnetic tape, etc. Furthermore, they can be used for indicating batch or item counts, hash totals, and control totals generated on the input media.

4. CANCELLATION AND TIME STAMPS. Cancellation and time stamps are used to mark a date and/or time, along with the functional activity name and/or number on a document as it passes through a work station. Cancellation stamps are used to record the same information except for the time of processing. The affixed or imprinted stamp denotes either the document's receipt for processing, or the conclusion of processing at that point. Stamps also provide a record of handling time, which may be compared to a performance standard in order to determine the handling time's effect on the production schedule. This helps to identify not only scheduled processing times but also any delays in processing.

5. DOCUMENT NUMBERING. Assigned-sequence numbers, together

with pre-punched and pre-numbered forms, may be used to control the number of items or records processed. Running a check on the document numbers ensures inclusion of all documents before, during, and after processing. The control numbers may be stamped or imprinted on the documents; punched into, printed on, or interpreted on the cards; or printed on the output processed on a high-speed printer or tabulator.

Serial numbers may be affixed to the batch record control cards or transmittal slips in order to facilitate document movement control. Soft-paper payroll checks and stock certificates contain numbers imprinted by the forms vendors. Pre-punched numbers often appear in punched card drafts or checks to provide an element of document control.

6. MATCHING. In activities where multiple copies of a document are used, it may be necessary to reassemble and match the documents in the forms set before any processing is initiated. This type of control is frequently exercised in the accounts payable section of the accounting department. In this section, the purchase order, receival report, and inspection report are reassembled and matched to verify that the quantity ordered and received is the same as the quantity billed on the vendor's invoice.

Matching may also be performed by checking transaction cards against card files, as well as by checking transaction cards against master magnetic tape files. For example, in surveys where a number of forms are mailed out, the responses are matched against the master cards or magnetic tape for a follow-up on non-responses.

7. APPROVALS. Approvals are used to regulate the entry of data into a system. These require one or several signatures to effect an input change. The approval procedures must be included in the organizational policies and practices, and in the documentation for a system. Approvals may be required for changes to salary or rate fields on payroll records, credit limits in sales records, commission percentages for salesmen, or inventory safety stock or reorder levels.

8. VERIFICATION. To ensure the accurate transcription of the original data into a machine-sensible form, some type of mechanical or manual verification may be required. In some organizations, a manual verification check is made by visually scanning the source documents, machine processable input, or a listing of the transcribed input. The verification may be made for completeness of the data elements recorded on the form. This can be accomplished by checking for missing, incomplete, or inaccurate posting. Or, the verification may be made to determine

TRANSMITTAL DOCUMENT		FORM NO. R5-61
SYSTEM/APPLICATION	IDENTIFICATION NUMBER	
ORIGINATOR	LOCATION	
TELEPHONE	DATE	

TYPE OF DATA TRANSMITTED ▶	DOCUMENT	CARD	TAPE	DISK
* REQUIRED ENTRY				
BATCH NUMBER(S)	*	*	*	*
DOCUMENT IDENT.	*			
FILE IDENT.		*		
TAPE IDENT.			*	
DISK IDENT.				*
DOCUMENT COUNT	*			
RECORD COUNT		*	*	*
LINE ITEM COUNT				
HASH TOTAL				
QUANTITY TOTAL				
DOLLAR VALUE TOTAL				
NO. OF BOXES/TAPES/DISKS		*	*	*
SPECIAL INSTRUCTIONS:				

DATA CHECKER	DATE CHECKED / /	KEYING OPERATOR	DATE KEYED / /	VERIFIER OPERATOR	DATE VERIFIED / /	LAST BATCH YES	NO

Figure 7.3. Transmittal Document Form

whether the correct form or proper code was used to initiate a desired action. In some instances, only selected fields are scanned on the form. For example, in an accounts payable application, depending on the user's procedure, a clerk may verify the calculations on gross, discount, and net amounts before submitting an invoice for transcription.

Data recorded on magnetic tape or disk may be either listed for visual verification or mechanically verified on a keystroke to tape or disk device before inclusion in the process. Traditionally, punched cards are key verified with the original source documents to ensure proper transcription. However, some studies have shown this to be an ineffective method of error detection. Audit tests are performed periodically on data collection and data transmission equipment to verify the performance of the hardware and personnel. To verify a successful transmission, control totals or dummy transactions may be included in the sending process for prompt detection of incorrect or missing data. Peripheral equipment such as collators and sorters may be used to perform a data admissability check on blank fields, card codes, double punching, etc., which may affect input validity.

9. SELF-CHECKING NUMBERS. The self-checking number control is

used to prevent or detect the incorrect transcription or unauthorized entry of identification numbers, such as account or employee numbers, on data input. The identification numbers are calculated according to a predetermined formula to generate a check digit. The check digit may be subsequently verified within the hardware to ensure that the inputted number is valid. If there is a change in the construction of the identification number, then a change will be reflected in the check-digit value.

There are a number of different check-digit formulae in existence. However, for illustrative purposes, this discussion will be limited to the use of the Modulus 11, because this is a popular system.

The check digit is generated as follows:

Step 1: Assign to each digit in the identification number, beginning with the least significant position, a weighting factor ranging from 2 to 7.

Step 2: Multiply each digit in the identification number by the assigned weighting factor.

Step 3: Add together all of the products.

Step 4: Divide the sum of the products by 11.

Step 5: Subtract the remainder, from the division in the previous step, from the modulus value of 11.

Step 6: Append the result of the subtraction, which is the check digit, to the identification number.

For example, let us calculate the check digit for the account number 411 42 9285:

Account Number:	4 1 1 4 2 9 2 8 5
Weighting Factors:	4 3 2 7 6 5 4 3 2
Products:	16 3 2 28 12 45 8 24 10
Add the Products:	$16+3+2+28+12+45+8+24+10 = 148$
Divide Total by 11:	$148 \div 11 = 13$, Remainder 5
Subtract Remainder:	$11 - 5 = 6$
Check Digit:	6
Account Number with Appended Check Digit:	411429285<u>6</u>

Alphabetic codes may also be checked by generating the check digit from the numeric characters in each position.

The use of check digits in records obviously increases the size of the record or necessitates restructuring of the record. To some degree, it also increases the possibility of data error. Nevertheless, it is very effective in detecting transcription, transposition, and transmission errors.

The check digit may be calculated manually and appended to the identification numbers on the source document before they are submitted for transcription. Or the check digit may be generated on the specially equipped online or interim data recording devices.

10. HASH TOTALS. A hash total is a sum that results from adding together the contents of a particular data field in all the records in a batch or file. The fields used for hash totals are not normally summed, such as account numbers, invoice numbers, and patient numbers. The totals are generated before processing is initiated and subsequently checked during processing. A missing record may be found by subtracting the current total from the beginning hash total.

Hash totals may be posted on a batch control record, transmittal slip, or route slip in order to provide for document control. Totals may also be developed for alphabetic fields by summing the numeric portion of each character.

11. CONTROL TOTALS. Control totals are sums generated as a result of accumulating quantity or amount fields in a group of records. As the records are again processed, the fields are accumulated and then compared with the beginning totals as proof that all records have been included.

The beginning totals may be posted on batch control records, transmittal documents route slips, or control logs. For example, a control total may be generated on the number of standard and overtime hours for employees in a given department. These totals will be checked during the processing cycle to detect any possible errors.

To simplify the detection, identification, and correction of errors, the control totals are established by convenient or appropriate organizational groups, such as departments, plants, or branch offices.

12. DATA CHECKERS. Data checkers are the people who validate the source documents and/or input before they are transcribed or processed. The checker manipulates the documents or records according to the procedures developed by the systems analyst. The procedures are established to verify the completeness of a form; the accuracy of calculations; the fact that survey forms have been returned by canvassers; etc. Or, the data checkers may be responsible for performing visual verification checks on the source documents and input.

13. CHECKLISTS. Checklists are prepared by the systems analyst to assist in the preparation of inputs, and to check documents and inputs for completeness and accuracy. The checklists are included in the sys-

tem's documentation. An example of a checklist procedure is shown in Figure 7.4. The list in this example is used to validate the completeness of an inventory transaction record before it is submitted for key punching.

Review Questions: Group 7C

1. Why should a data processing manager advocate the use of input controls in an information processing system?
2. How can a self-checking number be used as a form of input control?
3. How can a checklist be an effective form of input control?
4. What input control or controls would you recommend for a system surveying the needs of a day-care center?

Output Controls

Output controls in the information processing cycle are primarily procedural checks. They are more difficult to establish because they are affected by the intermediate processes performed between input and output. For example, an organization may establish calculated payroll tax deductions as one of the output control totals. Initially, this is an unknown value because the only relevant input control total would be the number of tax exemptions. This value becomes the basis for verifying the accuracy of the federal, and possibly the state and local, income tax calculations. The verification is made by subtracting the exemption

---

The stockroom clerk will edit the Stock Transaction Form (RAS-33A) for completeness and accuracy. Check:

    (a) Department Number
    (b) Inventory Class
    (c) Status
    (d) Unit of Issue
    (e) Piece Part Number
    (f) Quantity
    (g) Requisition Number

Figure 7.4   Example of Checklist Procedure

dollar value from the calculated gross and then applying the respective tax formulae. The payroll clerk performs this calculation for each department to minimize the error-detection problem.

Output controls are developed and implemented to ensure that:
—Reports and outputs are accurate
—No unauthorized entries to the system have been made
—Detected errors and exceptions have been corrected
—Outputs and reports are in proper format
—Reports appear in human-sensible language
—Proper disposition is made of all outputs and reports

These objectives may be attained through the use of the following techniques:
1. Totals
2. Checkpoints and Restart Procedures
3. Setup Procedures
4. Sampling
5. Reports Control
6. Console Operating Procedures
7. Distribution Instructions

1. TOTALS. The output total control is determined primarily by the available input control totals. However, as has been stated earlier, the totals generated at the initiation of the information processing cycle may not be identical with those outputted. In a file update process, the input master file record count differs from the updated master file record count because of the inputted add/delete transactions. Therefore, for balancing purposes, separate add/delete item counts and totals have to be generated. These would be intermediate totals used for balancing purposes. For example:

Master File Record Count	4938
Transaction File	
New Records Count	+200
Delete Records Count	−150
Updated Master File Record Count	4988

In the design phase, the systems analyst must develop the necessary output-verification procedures for operations and user personnel. For batch processing, he should establish a procedure to identify each batch, to count the transactions included, and to accumulate the relevant hash and control fields. Management reports may be balanced by crossfooting the horizontal row and/or vertical columns of totals. In a payroll report, the sum total of the various deduction amounts, plus the net pay, must equal the gross pay amount. For disk and tape master file maintenance operations, the analyst should provide for hash totals, input/output record and add/delete counts, and control totals. To maintain program-to-program compatibility, particularly on tape and disk operations, record accountability should be developed and maintained.

If a discrepancy is found in a report, the report should not be released until the cause of the deviation is known. Provision is then made for either correcting the report or producing a supplementary report. In instances where the output becomes input for another program or system, the problem may be more difficult to cope with. Unavailability of time can impose a severe limitation on the problem-correction process. With the advent of more sophisticated management information systems, there is a greater need for maintaining informational validity and control. Failure to support accurate data can only result in faulty and ineffectual decision-making.

2. CHECKPOINTS AND RESTART PROCEDURES. Checkpoints are included in a system to determine if processing has been accurately performed up to a given point. The checkpoints have the effect of breaking down a large system into workable and controllable segments. As each segment is correctly processed, the results are recorded on an output medium. Any errors that are detected and identified can be corrected at each checkpoint. The processing is then reiterated from the last checkpoint.

The restart procedures indicate the required corrective action, and the steps to reinitiate processing in the system. These procedures must be included in the user and operations documentation for a given system.

The availability of checkpoints and restart procedures helps to reduce the number of reruns, particularly on long runs. Also, they help to minimize the effects that problems and errors can have on the production schedule.

3. SETUP PROCEDURES. The setup procedures are designed to ensure the output of user reports in a proper and meaningful format. The procedures are included as part of the operations documentation.

The operator's manual must include information that enables the operator to setup the hardware for output of the desired report. In addition, a sample of the form is included. This sample should indicate the proper alignment and the fields that are to be outputted. This information enables the operator to verify the reasonableness of the output before continuing processing. To reinforce this observational method, many organizations prepare test data, which precedes the actual data in the output process. The sample included in the documentation should be identical with the initial output. In addition to verifying the alignment and format, the test decks provide a check on processing accuracy.

4. SAMPLING. Statistical sampling techniques may be used to check the reasonableness and accuracy of output. A random number generator may be used to select the sample sizes required and the records or output to be checked.

5. REPORTS CONTROL. A reports control system should be established to bring about the optimal use of resources. This system must be established to ensure the propriety, relevance, clarity, and timeliness of the reports.

Each report should be evaluated according to the checklist shown in Figure 7.5. Reports that do not produce a favorable response to the checklist questions must be further evaluated. Then, if necessary, they must be either redesigned to meet management objectives or deleted from the production schedule to conserve valuable resources.

6. CONSOLE OPERATING PROCEDURES. The console operating procedures for a given system obviously need to provide the necessary operator instructions. This means that operator responses must be carefully tested prior to system implementation and then be monitored during the follow-up. Of particular importance is the instructive output. This segment contains the error messages, operator instructions for checkpoints and restarts, and processing diagnostics. The failure to react properly to these conditions or instructions may result in faulty or inaccurate processing and outputs. A sample of a suggested form for instructive output is given in Figure 7.6.

7. DISTRIBUTION INSTRUCTIONS. Data processing has become an invaluable tool in the decision-making process. Consequently, when an output or report is produced, it must be promptly dispatched to the next operation or user after its accuracy has been validated. Dispatching the output that is scheduled to be input to another operation or system is generally less of a problem. Part of this problem is handled by effective

documentation. Also, the use of a tape/disk librarian helps to overcome some of the difficulties that may arise.

The system documentation should include instructions for processing the report and for then distributing it. A sample distribution form is given in Figure 7.7. Distribution to a user may be made by special messenger, intra- or inter-plant mail, regular mail, or pickup by functional area. The pickup may be arranged because the distribution schedule does not fit the user's schedule. Distribution by special messenger,

---

Each report must be evaluated on the basis of the following criteria:

1. Is the report necessary?
2. Does the report contain unnecessary data, which detracts from its clarity?
3. Does the report contain all the necessary data useful for decision-making?
4. Is the report issued when needed?
5. Should the report be condensed?
6. Can the report be combined with another to increase their effectiveness?
7. Does the report contribute to the overall effectiveness of the organization?
8. Is the sequence of the outputted data elements satisfactory?
9. Are those data items most frequently referenced in the proper locations?

Figure 7.5 Checklist for Reports Control System

though somewhat expensive, may be the most effective method. Intra- or inter-plant mail is frequently the least effective method of distribution, principally because only two pickups and deliveries are possible—one in the morning and the other in the afternoon.

The method of distribution selected for each system should be tested prior to implementation and should be monitored in the follow-up phase.

Some of the output controls may overlap or be supplemented by the control techniques in the program, external, and peripheral categories. Furthermore, the output controls may be affected by the output medium, work load, cost, and time. It is the time factor that may have the most significant influence on the level and extent of controls developed and implemented in this category.

```
┌─────────────────────────────────────────────────────────────┐
│              COMPUTER  CONSOLE  MESSAGES                      │
│                                                              │
│  PROGRAM NO:              PROGRAM TITLE:                      │
│                                                              │
│        DATE:                        PAGE____of____           │
├──────┬──────────────────────────┬───────────────────────────┤
│ OPER.│                          │                           │
│ NO.  │        MESSAGES          │     OPERATOR  ACTION       │
├──────┼──────────────────────────┼───────────────────────────┤
│      │                          │                           │
│      │                          │                           │
│      │                          │                           │
│      │                          │                           │
│      │                          │                           │
│      │                          │                           │
│      │                          │                           │
│      │                          │                           │
│      │                          │                           │
│      │                          │                           │
│      │                          │                           │
│      │                          │                           │
│      │                          │                           │
│      │                          │                           │
│      │                          │                           │
│      │                          │                           │
│      │                          │                           │
│      │                          │                           │
└──────┴──────────────────────────┴───────────────────────────┘
```

Figure 7.6. Sample Form for Console Operating Procedures—Instructive Output

	DISTRIBUTION PROCEDURE				DATE:		PAGE ___ OF ___					

PROGRAM NO: PROGRAM TITLE:

FORM NO: FORM TITLE:

STEP NO: DUE OUT:

                                       (TIME)   (DATE)

PART NO.	PROCESSING					TO	LOCATION	DISTRIBUTE VIA					
	DECOL	BURST	BIND	TRIM	CFP			SPECIAL MESSEN-GER	INTER-PLANT MAIL	INTRA-PLANT MAIL	U.S. MAIL (REG)	U.S. MAIL (AIR)	PICK UP

SPECIAL INSTRUCTIONS

Figure 7.7. Sample Form for Distribution Procedure

Review Questions: Group 7D

1. What are the objectives of an output control program?
2. Why would a data processing manager require the development and implementation of checkpoint and restart procedures in a system?
3. How are console operating procedures used as an output control?
4. What approaches might a manager consider to facilitate distribution of the outputs?

Program Controls

The program controls are an integral part of a computer program or machine operation. Sound planning and effective implementation of these checks provide the user with a series of sophisticated control tools. The checks and their associated procedures enable the user to detect and identify an error condition; they also indicate the necessary remedial action and facilitate reprocessing or prompt error recovery. Also, with some of the techniques, it is possible to develop an audit record of the actions occurring and exercised.

Program controls—sometimes referred to as programming, or processing, checks—are designed principally to ensure that:

—All transactions are properly posted
—Any lost or non-processed data is promptly detected
—All codes and conditions are verified prior to processing
—The arithmetic and logic checks are performed accurately
—All data has been processed through each program

Failure to achieve these objectives may result in invalid or inaccurate outputs, which, in turn, would invalidate any decisions based on these outputs.

The most common forms of program controls are:

1. Crossfooting
2. Edit checks
3. Zero balancing
4. Existence checks
5. Negative balance test
6. Self-checking number
7. Sequence checks
8. Completeness checks

9. Reasonableness checks
10. Combination checks
11. Range checks
12. Limit checks
13. Date checks
14. Totals
15. Housekeeping checks
16. Labels
17. Passwords
18. Transaction logs

1. CROSSFOOTING. Crossfooting is a technique that utilizes addition and/or subtraction of a horizontal row or vertical column of factors or elements in order to prove processing and posting accuracy. In some crossfooting operations, the factors are added together; then they are recalculated by subtracting each factor and adding the sum of the previous addition to the negative amount, which should result in a zero balance. Crossfooting is used frequently in accounting operations, such as payroll. Here the net pay amounts and individual deductions are accumulated for final totals and then added horizontally to determine if they equal the total gross earnings (see Figure 7.8). In posting operations, a record is updated in a working storage area and proved with a crossfoot check before being moved to permanent storage on tape, data cell, or disk replacing the original record.

2. EDIT CHECKS. Editing is a common data processing practice utilizing computing or unit-record equipment to test the input or output data against predetermined codes, conditions, or standards. Edit checks are used to ensure data compatibility, not data accuracy. Accuracy must be determined by other means. It is intended that the edit checks performed in the program detect any errors in the process. Subsequently, procedures have to be executed to correct the exceptions or conditions before either processing is continued or output distribution is made.

Editing is normally performed for evaluating data item size, mode, and construction. As a result, an edit check is sometimes referred to as a formatting check. The field size is generally fixed and a check is made to determine if a predetermined number of positions have been filled. On a variable length field there will also be a known parameter for acceptable minimums and maximums; however, it may be more difficult to check size. Mode and construction of an item are almost synonymous. In mode evaluation, a field is examined to determine if the area or contents are to be blank, numeric, alphabetic, or alphameric. Most of the checking in programs is accomplished on this basis. In a test for blanks, a card column, memory position, record position, or field must be tested for the presence or absence of blank characters. Often an area that is blank is selected for insertion of zeros or other desired data, whereas, in other situations, a field must be left blank for subsequent operations where data resulting from the process will be inserted in the tested positions. Testing for numerics is generally performed to determine if a field is free of any zone bits other than sign bits, which may indicate the presence of an alphabetic or special character. The presence of such characters in a test position may indicate a data recording or coding error. Alphabetic fields are not tested as frequently as blank or numeric fields, except for essential data items. For example, in payroll operations, the name field is tested because it is required for check-writing operations.

Construction of an item may incorporate some of the testing for mode. However, it is more generally concerned with the overall composition of a field. Items are checked for such conditions as the left- or right-justification of a field; the presence or absence of preceding zeros; and checking the makeup of a code—that is, alphabetic-numeric-alphabetic.

3. ZERO BALANCING. Zero balancing is a technique in which the accumulation of a given quantity or amount field is subtracted from a predetermined beginning balance so as to arrive at a zero balance. Any balance other than a zero will indicate an error condition. The beginning balances are extracted from a batch control record, transmittal slip, or control log. The value must be transcribed to a machine-readable form for entry into the system. These totals will either precede or follow the data. If the totals precede the data, then the method is called the header balancing method; if they follow the data, then this is referred to as the trailer balancing method.

4. EXISTENCE CHECKS. Existence checks are a form of validity check to determine if a tested code is active, acceptable, or valid. The input may be compared with a deck of master cards, master tape, or reference table to determine its admissability. All unmatched items must then be investigated for cause of the deviation. For example, occupation codes may be compared mechanically with an authorized occupations code card file or magnetic tape in order to resolve any input errors in the codes prior to processing a manning and authorization listing.

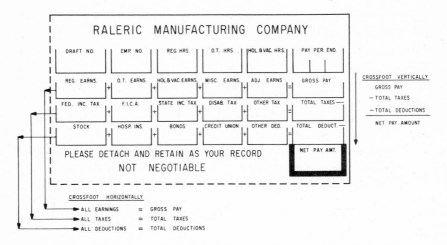

Figure 7.8. Example of Crossfooting: Payroll Application

5. NEGATIVE BALANCE TEST. This is a technique used to test the result of an arithmetic operation for a negative balance. In payroll operations, the negative balance test is used to determine if the amount of deductions has exceeded gross pay earnings. In computerized operations, an internal procedure can be initiated to resolve the negative balance. In unit-record, accounting machine operations, a negative balance condition can be signaled by the printing of a CR (credit) or minus sign (−) on the print-out.

6. SELF-CHECKING NUMBER. As a program control, the self-checking number is used to validate the identification code for a possible transposition or transcription error. Each time that the equipment processes the identification number, a check digit is computed. The newly calculated digit is then compared with the appended digit in the identification number. If the two digits are not the same, an error-condition signal on the console or other output medium indicates the need for operator or user action.

Another popular self-checking number technique is the Modulus-10 method. The Modulus-10 formula is calculated as follows:

Step 1: Multiply the units position and every alternate digit in the identification number by 2.

Step 2: Crossfoot the digits in the product and those digits in the identification number not multiplied by 2.

Step 3: Subtract the crossfooted total from the next higher number ending in zero.

Step 4: The remainder is the check digit.

Step 5: Append the check digit to the identification number.

Example of Modulus-10:

Identification number	1 2 3 4 5
Alternate digits	1 3 5
Multiply alternate digits by 2	×2
	_____
Product	2 7 0
Crossfoot the product (270) and those digits not included in the multiplication (2, 4)	2+7+0+2+4=15
Subtract total from the next higher number ending in zero	20 −15
	_____
	5
Check digit	5
Append check digit	123455̲

As a program control, the self-checking number will help to detect transcription, transposition, and accidental or deliberate alteration errors.

7. SEQUENCE CHECK. Sequence checks are made to ensure that the data is arranged or ordered in an ascending or descending sequence prior to processing. The checks are a very important part of the file update process when the file is organized in a sequential or serial mode. Failure to input the transactions in a predetermined sequence will cause unnecessary delays in processing. Reports are also outputted in a user-desired sequence to facilitate their use. For example, in a labor distribution report, the work order numbers are ordered within each department worked. This enables the accountant to extract the totals for each work order and subsequently to allocate these charges properly in other reports.

The sequence check may also be used to select duplicate records from a master or reference file or to assemble data for processing.

8. COMPLETENESS CHECK. A completeness check is made to ensure either that the desired information is included in all of the data fields in a record or that all input is included and in sequence. For example, in an inventory control application, a back-order release record may be

checked to determine if it contains a part number, requisition number, and a notation regarding quantity to be released. If the needed information is missing, the record must be identified as incomplete and procedures must then be executed to process this exception.

A simple example of the completeness check occurs in payroll processing, when the input transactions are compared with the employee payroll master file; the failure to locate a matching master record causes the transactions to be identified for exception processing. A completeness check may also be used for a punched card payroll application utilizing a fixed sequence input. In this case, a check is made to ensure that each input data set contains at least an employee master card that includes name, pay rate, and other vital information; a tax-and-earnings card used to check the social security tax limits and update year-to-date earnings and taxes; and a multiple deduction card for authorized deductions. These three cards would be required for each employee, including new hires, in a predetermined sequence. Processing would not be performed for an employee in any of whose cards a deviation was found.

9. REASONABLENESS CHECK. A reasonableness check is a test made on a field to determine if it has exceeded a predetermined parameter. If it has not exceeded the parameter, then the field is regarded or treated as a normal condition. The check does not ensure that the data is valid, but only that it has not exceeded a stated parameter. Reasonableness checks are used quite frequently in payroll operations, where a parameter has been established on the gross pay figure. Or they may be used to ensure that a customer has not exceeded a credit limitation on an order.

Sometimes a reasonableness check may be modified by an allowable deviation factor. The deviation factor allows for a positive or negative deviation from the stated parameter. For example, on purchase order receivals, an organization may consider an order complete if the quantity falls within a five percent deviation. Therefore, in a 1000-unit order, it would consider as complete an overshipment of 1050 units or an undershipment of 950 units. The percentage of allowable deviation on the stated parameters is determined by the system or by the item being processed.

The reasonableness check is frequently utilized as part of an exception reporting system. This eliminates unnecessary details from reports and indicates only deviations, thereby providing more meaningful data in the decision-making process. An effective reporting system provides the manager only with those situations that cannot be corrected at lower levels in the organizational structure.

10. COMBINATION CHECKS. Combination checks are performed on a record or on several input items to determine their logical relationship and to remove any erroneous combinations of data. Some auditors refer to combination checks as relationship checks.

Combination checks may be made on medical input, for example, to ensure that a diagnosis code for a pregnancy may be found only in a female patient's record. Or, that a medication dosage does not exceed the allowable tolerances for a given age. Also, the checks may be used to ensure that a requisition for a given stock item can be issued to the requesting unit and in the quantity requested.

11. RANGE CHECK. The range check is a basic validity or admissability test applied to a code or data item to determine if it compares to a given set of parameters. The parameters may be included in a table to facilitate a table look-up in memory, or as master or cross-reference files. The check may be simple or complex, depending upon the procedures required, as well as the data element or set relationships. The steps required to develop and implement this type of check may require more sophisticated skills and resources than an organization has available. Also, the dynamic nature of the tables and files necessitates constant updating and control. The cost of implementing this check may have to be evaluated in terms of what price the users are willing to pay for accurate data. This evaluation will be required when an organization is equipped with online remote terminals to a central processing unit, for a significant amount of error detection will have to be made by the computer. To minimize the cost of disruption, prompt and effective correction procedures will also have to be available.

12. LIMIT CHECK. In a limit check, input and output data are compared with a predefined set of minimum and maximum parameters. The check is made to ensure that the data or record lies within a set of predefined values. The parameters may be a single set of minimum or maximum parameters, or several sets. For example, a check on a series of code numbers between 1000 and 1999 may be made. This series may be extended to check the codes between 1000 and 1999 and between 2500 and 3999. Consequently, codes between 2000 and 2499 and above 3999 may be detected as errors.

The limit check can also be used as a data admissibility check. In this usage, the check is made only to ensure that a code lies between a lower and upper parameter.

13. DATE CHECK. Input records may be checked to determine if they are acceptable on a given date. Date checks can be used to select

transactions due for payment in an accounts payable application; to select the effective date of salary increases for employees; to select employees eligible for a merit rating or promotion; or to select inputted items coded with an entry prior to a given date.

14. TOTALS. Totals may be used to control the number of records processed and the accuracy of processing. The type and level of control established in this category is affected by the input, output, and procedural requirements. The total controls may take the form of batch counts, record counts, hash totals, or control totals. Identification fields are frequently accumulated to produce hash totals on records inputted and outputted. The number of transactions processed in a batch may be counted for a batch count on input items. Record counts are used as a control over the number of records in the information processing cycle. In updating operations, the input record count must be adjusted to reflect the additions and deletions in the process. For output or report preparation, the records are counted to ensure processing accuracy. The failure to balance at a control point indicates a missing or lost record. In updating operations on tape, disk, and disk pack, record counts are developed and often incorporated into the internal header and trailer labels.

Control totals may be established to verify the input, output, and processing accuracy on quantity and amount fields. To increase their effectiveness in detecting and identifying errors, the control totals should be established for appropriately sized groupings or for some common units, such as department, plant, wing, etc. This reduces the time required to locate any errors occurring in the process.

15. HOUSEKEEPING CHECKS. The housekeeping checks should be part of standard operating procedure in every data processing organization. The housekeeping functions should be performed at the beginning of each computer program to clear buffers, clear registers, reset program switches and bit masks, initialize areas, etc. The checks may be performed independently or in conjunction with an IOCS package.

16. LABELS. A label is an internal identification affixed to a data file on tape or disk to check the file's validity before processing is initiated. The label checking performed in a program ensures that the desired file is actually mounted on a desired unit. For example, a payroll master tape is checked to ensure that it is the current updated file. If it is, then payroll processing is initiated; if it is not, an error indication is signaled to the operator.

The checking is generally performed by the software, such as IOCS, based on parameters stipulated by the programmers. This arrangement simplifies the error-checking process for volume, header, and trailer labels.

17. PASSWORDS. The password is a preestablished key used to identify a user and his right to access a given file. The passwords consist of numbers, letters, and symbols, which identify an authorized user and his terminal location. An authorized user may be given the right to process on the hardware; to enter data changes; or to access data or request a print-out. In some organizations, several passwords may be required to effect an operation.

Passwords may have to be changed often to maintain security. Also, procedures must be developed in order to determine a "need-to-know" basis. This step is necessary to limit file access only to authorized users.

18. TRANSACTION LOGS. Transaction logs represent a sophisticated technique for recording events that occur on a computer. The logs may be used to record the users' identification, the files they accessed, and type of inquiry. Subsequently, this information is processed to detect any attempts by unauthorized users to violate file security.

The technique may be further expanded to include a copy of the change transaction, so as to provide an audit trail for the accidental or deliberate entry of erroneous data. This method can be particularly useful for recording data entries from online remote terminals.

The program controls that are implemented may have to be evaluated on a cost-effectiveness basis. It is evident that the implementation of some of the checks, such as transaction logs, may be expensive. The cost is not prohibitive; however, one must determine the worth of the information obtained for this outlay. Also, an organization may not have the personnel resources available to develop and implement some of the checks. Or, the hardware may not have the capacity or the features to implement some of the checks.

Review Questions: Group 7E

1. What type of program control would be used in an inventory control system to ensure numeric data in the part number field of a transaction record?

2. Why would it be advantageous for a manager to advocate the use of a negative balance test in an accounts payable system?

3. How can a self-checking number be used as a form of program control?
4. If the organization was developing a management information system utilizing terminals, what specific program controls should be considered for application to user personnel?

External Controls

External controls are primarily concerned with providing protection against the entry of unauthorized data into the system—that is, preventing erroneous data from entering the system and unauthorized data from filtering in. These controls are designed to supplement and/or reinforce the controls available in the other categories. As a result, they may overlap, to a limited degree, some of the other controls implemented in a information processing cycle. However, they are a necessary part of the interacting network of controls needed to maintain system reliability.

The external controls are primarily procedural and manual, except for those included in the computer auditing category. Among the more common forms of external control are:
1. Data control
2. Exception processing
3. Sampling
4. Administrative procedures
5. Computer audits

1. DATA CONTROL. Data control involves the use of data checkers to validate input and output. The procedures for the controls must be developed by the systems analyst in conjunction with the internal and/ or external auditors.

The input validation should be concerned with receipt of inputs, error detection, and data quality. The receipt of inputs must be governed by procedures delineating the schedule, the accountability for and method of movement, and the types and level of control totals. The error-detection and data quality procedures should include such items as checklists to facilitate data preparation and conversion by the data originator or the data transcriber. Also, these two procedures should include methods or steps for reconciling the errors in data or coding, or for investigating questionable items.

The output validation procedures are primarily concerned with accuracy, format, and distribution requirements. The specific requirements for each output or report should result from an assessment of user, auditor, and data processing needs. Most organizations consider accuracy to be the prime requirement for evaluating each output or report. The procedures are primarily concerned with balancing the report. These same procedures often do not include any information on how to resolve discrepancies in totals.

Many organizations rely on the equipment operator to determine whether the output appears to be reasonable. Consequently, incomplete reports may be issued. Very often, an improper switch setting, erroneous coding of a parameter card, or an incorrect response on the console typewriter may result in one or more fields being deleted from a report. This situation goes undetected until the report is received by the user.

To add clarity to each report, provisions should be made for self-explanatory columnar headings. Many organizations have established a standardized glossary of terms for use in report and form captions. For example, the letters R. M. would always be used to designate the words *raw materials.* Or, EMP may be used to identify the word *employee.* The captions should be imprinted on a form either by the vendor or as part of the machine or program operation. If the latter is not feasible, an overlay heading can be used.

The distribution requirements should include the report handling and notification procedures as well. These would include the due-out schedule; special instructions, such as decollation, bursting, or binding; and provision for notifying the user when the report either is complete or has been delayed.

Data control procedures are a must for an organization using an outside service bureau for its processing.

2. EXCEPTION PROCESSING. A procedure must be established to ensure that exceptions and limit violations identified during processing are promptly investigated and corrected. This procedure should include a feedback control mechanism to evaluate the effectiveness of the correction.

Exception-processing procedures are often neglected in the design and implementation of a system. Consequently, satisfactory answers cannot be provided for discrepancies in reported inventories; complaints or questions from customers regarding their billings, orders, or subscriptions; and inquiries from managers.

3. SAMPLING. Sampling may be used to verify the reasonableness and accuracy of inputs, outputs, and processing. The technique may be used to identify deviation trends, acceptable variations, or error probabilities.

Collecting data to establish a basic criterion and selection of a sample can be very difficult and time-consuming. However, to establish deviation trends and error probabilities, data must first be collected to work out normal limits and historical averages. For example, to establish acceptable limits on collected data, it is necessary to develop a historical base for some period of time. This enables the analyst to calculate an arithmetic average (mean) and the variance for the data elements. A decision must then be made to determine what value (plus or minus) constitutes an acceptable limit. Subsequently, a probability may be calculated to provide a distribution based on different assumptions. Again, a decision must be made on the acceptable limits to be applied in testing for undesirable deviations. The limits and decision rules must be monitored periodically to determine their accuracy and relevancy. It is quite possible that when a new system is implemented, frequent revision of the limits and rules may be necessary until the system stabilizes itself.

Norms are frequently set on the amount of transaction activity generated from a terminal. Any unusual activity can be used to immediately trigger an exception or limit violation warning. Action must then be taken to determine the cause of the condition. If the increased activity is regarded as an acceptable condition, then the limits will have to be revised. However, it may also reflect the presence of a new or inadequately trained operator at the terminal.

Selecting sample transactions or items for validation purposes may be accomplished manually or through the use of data processing equipment. The selection may be made on the basis of a random sample, a specific criterion, or a combination of various criteria. Manual methods for selection of random items or transactions can be very time-consuming and costly. Furthermore, some bias may be introduced into the selection process. A computer can be used to generate the random numbers, select the desired sample sizes, and print a listing of the items selected. Based on his design plan, the analyst or auditor may then proceed to make conclusions about the statistical universe being sampled.

The sampling techniques may also be used in conjunction with predetermined comparison criteria and multiple files. Several related files are randomly sampled. The selected items are then processed against predetermined criteria. For example, a file of back-ordered items may be compared with a master inventory file to verify the quantity fields.

4. ADMINISTRATIVE PROCEDURES. Administrative procedures are concerned with maintaining system accuracy, efficiency, and reliability. Among the primary concerns here are the procedures for distribution, maintenance, and periodic auditing of documentation that affects existing systems. Also, the administrative procedures must be concerned with delineating the personnel authorized to effect a data change as well as the extent of their authority to do so. Inherent in these procedures are the steps and forms to be followed in executing a change transaction. This will help to provide a documented audit trail of the events and activities.

Administrative procedures may also be concerned with the data retention policies and practices. In some organizations, this responsibility may be delegated to the data processing administrator or manager. However, most either leave this responsibility with the internal auditor or follow the guidelines stipulated by the external auditors. A part of this segment should be the procedures governing use of magnetic tape in lieu of Internal Revenue Service forms, such as W2, 1099. Consideration should also be given to policies for the retention of data that may subsequently be used in a legal action. At present, though, there is some legal dispute regarding the admissibility of computer records as legal evidence.

The administrative procedures may also delineate the methods for disposal of sensitive data. This would cover disposing of such items as the contents of wastebaskets, carbons removed from outputs, and reports or records no longer required for retention. The procedures may also govern the practices for deleting sensitive data from such media as magnetic tape, drum, disk, or data cell. Many organizations utilize a technique known as write-over. For example, before a magnetic tape containing sensitive data is returned to "scratch" status, a stream of random digits is written several times over the records. This same procedure may be followed on a random access unit where a record has been either deleted or expanded and rewritten in an overflow area. It is intended that this practice will make it difficult to retrieve data from deleted or unused areas.

The procedures may also govern the safeguards to be followed for online terminal devices at remote locations. For example, the practice may require the removal of a ribbon from a teletypewriter or printer following the processing of sensitive data.

5. COMPUTER AUDITS. Computer audits—computer-assisted auditing techniques as they are sometimes called—are an effective way of extending audit capability. It is intended that these techniques should reduce the effort required to select and verify the input, output, and processing transactions in a system. These techniques are also intended to determine the effectiveness of the management controls utilized in the system. The audit techniques can be performed with unit-record or computing equipment, although the EAM devices are less flexible.

There are several different computer-auditing techniques, but each of them utilizes the same basic approach. This approach to auditing may be described as:

—Identifying the inputs into the system
—Identifying the outputs of the system
—Determining how the inputs are processed
—Testing the efficiency and effect of the system's controls

Among the more common computer auditing techniques are:

a) Detailed testing
b) Sampling
c) Graphic displays
d) Graphic displays
e) Specialized analysis
f) Automated flowcharting

a) *Detailed Testing.* In this technique, the auditor prepares the necessary programs and/or control panels to assist him in evaluating the system. He will use actual or hypothetical data that is representative of the system's inputs. Included will be various types of error transactions to evaluate the system's error detection and identification capabilities. This will enable the auditor to evaluate the performance of a program, its related subroutines, total controls, and file maintenance procedures.

The detailed testing technique is also used to verify the computational capabilities of a system. If any deviations are found, the auditor will be able to concentrate his attention in that area. The hardware may also be used to simulate the complete processing of a segment of the system. Both of these methods enable the auditor to process a large volume of data in a shorter time span and with only limited clerical effort.

b) Sampling. The computer may be used to generate the random numbers, select the sample size within a desired level of confidence, and provide an output of the selected records and/or transactions. The auditor may then follow the processing cycle from input to output in each of the selected items. The processing and outputs may be verified either by utilizing existing print-outs and controls or by preparing a series of predetermined results.

The auditor may possibly take the selected items and process them through only a predetermined portion of the system. Very often, the area that is selected either is one that has a high error rate or is one of the key activities in the system.

Sometimes, however, an auditor will select some cases and supervise their manipulation, manually and mechanically, through the processing cycle.

c) Exception Analysis. Exception analysis is probably the most comprehensive method of auditing because the auditor evaluates an entire file or group of files. The auditor establishes desired exception criteria and applies these to all of the records in the file. Within a relatively short period of time the auditor may select from a merchandise inventory file, for example, those items that have an unusual cost/price relationship. The exception items may be outputted on a printer for a detailed follow-up. Or, the auditor may take two files and compare items in the records for discrepancies. For example, a cost bulletin file may be compared with the engineering material and layout file concerning standard cost or quantities. Any discrepancies found may be outputted on a printer for reconciliation purposes. This same approach is frequently followed when comparing physical inventory quantities with the on-hand balances in the master inventory file.

d) Graphic Displays. Graphic displays are used to evaluate certain aspects of a single file or multiple files. Generally a printer or plotter is used. However, it is also feasible and practical to use a cathode-ray tube terminal for this purpose.

The auditor determines the sets of criteria and applies these against a single- or multiple-file application. For example, this technique may be used very effectively in displaying a comparison of current and prior year expense accounts.

e) Specialized Analysis. Specialized analysis is an auditing technique that requires the use of special-purpose computer programs. The programs may be written by the auditor or extracted from a program library. Specialized analysis programs may be used for such purposes as cash-flow analysis, portfolio analysis, projected interest income, and evaluation of depreciation schedules. The application of these programs to a large file can significantly reduce the time required for such an analysis.

f) Automated Flowcharting. Automated flowcharting is a technique designed to audit an organization's computer programs. The software will automatically block-diagram the instructions in a given program. However, it does not validate program performance.

This technique may be used when an organization's existing documentation is obsolete or unavailable. It is also used to highlight the controls written in the program being evaluated. Furthermore, it is frequently used in comparison with existing documentation to determine its accuracy and relevance. Sometimes, it is used to conduct a surprise audit on an existing operational program to determine if any deliberate alterations had been made.

A sample of an automated flowchart is illustrated in Figure 7.9.

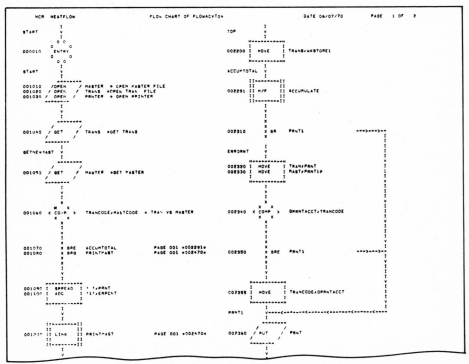

Figure 7.9. Example of Automated Flowchart. Courtesy NCR.

Review Questions: Group 7F

1. Why must a data processing manager be concerned with the implementation of external controls within the organization?
2. A frequent complaint of magazine subscribers is that they are unable to secure a satisfactory response to their questions about renewals. How can this problem be overcome within the data processing factor?
3. What are some of the different policies and practices that should be incorporated into administrative procedures?
4. If you were asked to select a form of computer auditing for the organization, which technique would you choose? Why?

Peripheral Controls

Peripheral controls, also called supplementary checks, may be described as a series of procedures directly affecting the data processing organization. They are used to direct and control the activities and functions of the data processing personnel, environment, programs, documentation, and files. Unlike the other control categories, peripheral controls are somewhat more general in their context and application.

The peripheral controls are principally concerned with:

a) Environmental security
b) Personnel practices
c) Tape and disk file control

Environmental Security

Environmental security is concerned with safeguarding the data processing organization and its information. The latter includes the sensitive data files, programs, and documentation.

The safeguards must be tailored to the needs and desires of the organization. However, the measures developed and implemented must minimize the probability or opportunity for the theft or destruction of data files, programs, documentation, or equipment. Unfortunately the problems become more complex for the organization, and the data processing executives. Prevention and contingency plans established must be in order to cope with a variety of hazards resulting from poor data processing management, accidents, disasters, and sabotage. These plans must include provisions for protecting the data processing personnel from environmental hazards and sabotage.

The environmental safeguards may be grouped into the following classifications:

1) Equipment protection
2) Standard operating procedures
3) Information protection

1. EQUIPMENT PROTECTION. Equipment protection actually entails securing both the data processing area and its equipment. The selected measures must comply with local building and fire protection codes. However, the data processing requirements may have to exceed the stipulated local regulations (see Chapter 5). In multistoried buildings, for example, the floor above the data processing operations area should be reasonably watertight so as to protect the hardware, files, and materials from water damage. Also, the structural floor that supports the raised flooring must provide for good drainage in case of flooding or coolant leakage. These are items not generally covered in local building codes, but they are of considerable significance to the data processing function. In one installation, for instance, the failure to provide for a watertight facility resulted in severe damage to the equipment. A fire on an upper floor caused water seepage through the ceilings, which subsequently affected the hardware. The lack of floor drainage in another installation caused major damage to the cabling and wiring when flooding resulted from an undetected water-pipe break beneath the raised floor surface. In this case, the damage could certainly have been lessened by the installation of water detection alarms.

Environmental protection also requires limiting entry access to authorized personnel. The measures can be as simple as not listing the location of the processing center in the building directory, and eliminating wall directional signs. Visitor access must also be severely limited. There is very little purpose in parading visitors through the data processing center to view the equipment. Visitors have been known to pick up cards out of files for samples, push buttons on the hardware, remove protection rings from magnetic tape files, and drop tape reels or disk packs accidentally. Situations such as these have caused delays in processing.

Access into the environment may be controlled through many different methods. Some are highly sophisticated and others are quite simple. One of the simplest methods requires recognition of the person seeking admittance by the operating personnel or a security guard. The identity check may depend upon personal recognition, the presence of an authorization certificate in a card file, an admittance pass, or an identification badge. Identity checks are often supplemented by a sign-in procedure to provide a documented access record. It must be pointed out, though, that these access control methods have not proven entirely successful in every environment.

Some organizations are implementing more sophisticated access controls. One such method involves the use of a specially encoded plastic card that can unlock the door when inserted into a reading device. To extend the security capability of such controls, some of these devices require knowledge and manual entry of a predetermined ID code through an attached keyboard (see Figure 7.10). The manually entered

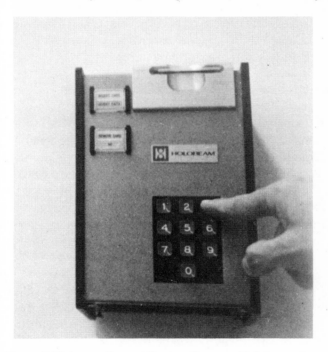

Figure 7.10 Access Control Device. Courtesy Holobeam, Inc.

code must agree with that encoded in the card or stored in a computer memory bank before the person is allowed to enter. One important advantage of these devices is that they generally permit the manager to alter the entry codes so that invalid, lost, or stolen cards are ineffective. Often these same devices can activate an automatic reaction to an unauthorized user. This may consist of sounding buzzers or horns, turning on a closed-circuit television camera, alerting the security patrol, etc. In addition, a machine-processable record of output of the user identification and time entry may be made. Some of the devices also are capable of storing information on entry privileges. These not only control access to an area, but can also limit entry by time of day and day of week.

Blackouts, brownouts, and fluctuations in the voltage and frequency of the incoming power supply pose a threat to the equipment and data. These conditions may cause a computer malfunction, unexplained data errors, reruns, disruptions in the normal operating schedule, and financial losses.

To a limited extent some of the power problems can be countered by the use of checkpoint and restart procedures, redistribution of the work load to the night shift, proper ventilation of the power panel area, cleaning of contact points on the circuit breakers, and effecting changes on transformer taps.

However, these solutions may not be entirely practical or applicable in all instances. For example, it may not be feasible to insert the checkpoints in a program on short production runs. And shifting the work load to a night shift may not coincide with the operational needs of an organization. Therefore, it may be more practical to control the incoming power supply itself. For blackouts, it may be necessary for an organization to acquire an auxiliary generator to produce the needed power. This however, can be an expensive item that may not be economically justifiable. The effects of brownouts, temporary blackouts, and voltage problems can be minimized through the use of an uninterruptible power system (UPS). The device is generally installed between the computer and the incoming power supply to remove any variations from the power signal. Also, such a device is capable of providing standby power should the incoming power supply fail. It draws on a bank of batteries until the power supply is restored. Another major power problem involves power-supply fluctuations that are not necessarily caused by brownouts but by such conditions as power surges, overloads, and low voltage. The effects of these fluctuations can be minimized through the use of a voltage regulator, filter capacitator, or isolation transformer. These devices are less expensive than auxiliary generators or uninterruptible power-supply devices. However, they may not provide all of the protection needed by an organization. A device should be acquired only after monitoring the power supply and proving practical and economic justification through a feasibility study.

2. STANDARD OPERATING PROCEDURES. The standard operating procedures must be used to augment the environmental safeguards and to facilitate continued operation. They require preplanning and testing prior to implementation, as well as subsequent evaluation to determine their effectiveness.

Included in this category are the following types of procedures:

a) Back-up
b) Damage control
c) Fire emergency
d) Training

a) *Back-up.* The back-up, or alternate-mode, procedures are developed to facilitate a continuity of operations under other than normal operating conditions. Each such procedure must be evaluated to determine the cost of delayed processing to an organization (see Chapter 6).

The back-up procedures should include the processing documentation; provisions for the transportation of data, personnel, programs, documentation, and supplies; and the agreements for utilization of the alternate facilities. Depending upon organizational security requirements, these procedures may be either included as part of the system's documentation or controlled by the manager.

b) *Damage Control.* To minimize the loss or destruction of the equipment and/or information, damage-control procedures must be established. An important part of these procedures is a determination of record values and the safeguards to be applied to each. The type of damage control to be applied will be affected by the record storage medium. Whenever damage-control equipment is required, its location and application must be documented in the procedures.

One of the items that should be given serious consideration is the use of waterproof covers on the equipment, files, and materials. Such covers are very effective in minimizing the effects of water, smoke, dust, residue, and steam damage.

c) *Fire Emergency.* A written fire-emergency plan must be prepared and documented as part of the standard operating procedures. The installation's personnel should be very familiar with the plan because it delineates their specific responsibilities and actions. The fire-emergency plan must include the location and method for disconnecting the power supply for the data processing equipment and the air-conditioning system. Also, the plan must stipulate the procedures for notifying the internal and/or external firefighting authorities; evacuating personnel; and safeguarding the records. It must also make clear the extent of personnel participation in firefighting and damage control.

d) *Training.* The training procedures are essential to maintaining an emergency readiness status. The personnel must know the location and proper operation or application of firefighting and damage-control equipment. Their awareness must extend beyond knowledge of the fact that instructions are included in the standard operating procedures. This necessitates the periodic training and testing of the personnel in a simulated emergency operating condition. They should also be trained in the proper use of fire extinguishers in a controlled firefighting environment.

Also, the personnel must be trained in the proper power-disconnect techniques for the data processing and air-conditioning equipment.

3. INFORMATION PROTECTION. The measures designed to safeguard the information also provide some element of protection for the environment as well. The procedures within this catogory may be placed into the following classifications:

a) Record classification
b) Material storage
c) Insurance

a) *Record Classification.* A value classification must be applied to the information for record management and protection purposes. As stated in Chapter 4, the information may be assigned one of four value groupings—essential, important, beneficial, and nonessential. The amount of protection afforded is directly proportional to the record-value classification.

Records in the "essential" and "important" classifications need to be afforded the highest level of protection. To minimize the chances of loss or destruction, only those records directly required in the productive operations should be temporarily stored in the processing area. Other records in this same classification should be stored in a fire-resistant storage room in noncombustible containers. The area should have a fire-resistant capability of two hours. If the records are to be stored in some other types of containers, an automatic sprinkler system should be available.

To provide greater security, many organizations are storing duplicated key programs, documentation, and master or sensitive data files at a remote (off-premises) location. Although this procedure may be somewhat more costly, it does provide an organization with a processing capability if its data processing center and entire contents are destroyed.

Only those records in the "beneficial" category currently needed for productive processing should be stored in the operations area. The others should be removed from the operations area and either assigned a scratch status, destroyed, or temporarily held in the storage area for salvage purposes.

Diligence must be exercised in removing all unnecessary combustible substances from a storage area in order to minimize the risk of fire.

b) Material Storage. A policy should be established to govern the storage of supporting materials and records. Only minimum quantities of cards, forms, and other supporting materials should be kept in the processing area. The presence of these materials increases the fire risk. Very often, this policy is not enforced, and consequently the materials are scattered throughout the area, thereby creating both a potential fire and safety hazard.

One or more storage areas should be available for the paper and magnetic based media. The areas should be surrounded by fire-resistant walls. It is suggested that magnetic based media be maintained in a separate room. Maximum fire protection must be afforded to these media. Many organizations have equipped these storage areas with automatic carbon-dioxide actuation systems to minimize the damage potential. Also, it is recommended that a storage area for such media be limited to 10,000 cubic feet, and that the media be stored in noncombustible containers. Where combustible storage containers are used, the area should be limited to 5,000 cubic feet. In addition to having an automatic firefighting capability, the storage area should be equipped with portable fire extinguishers.

The storage area for paper records and materials can be significantly larger because much more is known about the resistance of these media to fire. It is recommended that the storage area for paper be limited to 50,000 cubic feet. This area must be periodically inventoried to remove records that are no longer useful. Also, where the retention schedule requires continued preservation of paper records, an alternative should be considered—for example, microfilm or magnetic tape storage.

c) Insurance. Insurance has become a means of protecting an organization's investment in data processing. It may be acquired to provide coverage for the damage or destruction of equipment and records. Or it may be acquired to provide compensation for expenses resulting from the inability to use the available equipment and/or records.

In the former category there are three standard types of coverage and two that are specifically related to data processing. The standard fire contents, office contents, and valuable papers and records forms provide good coverage for the equipment. However, the media coverage is somewhat limited. Owing to the number of exclusions and limitations in these forms, specialized policies for equipment and records have been developed. However, the equipment and records must be covered in separate policies. The equipment policy may help to cover a lessee's liability for the hardware. The records policy covers the cost of reproduction of the media under emergency conditions and includes some extra expense allowances. The coverage for software systems may be very limited or nonexistent. This is due to the fact that they may be very costly to reproduce.

To cover the loss of equipment and/or records utilization, a data processing extra expense policy should be considered. This policy helps to minimize the expenses resulting from the replacement of equipment and records. Care must be taken to determine what extra expenses will be incurred. This determination will not be a very simple task, but an organization should attempt to come reasonably close.

Personnel Practices

Safeguards must also be applied to the personnel within the data processing activity. The measures must be designed to minimize the effectiveness of unscrupulous, careless, or incompetent personnel. Indirectly, these practices may also be used to reduce the disruptive effects of employee turnover and to avoid heavy reliance on any one individual.

The personnel safeguards may include the following practices:
1. Code of ethics
2. Nondisclosure agreements
3. Buddy system
4. Rotation
5. Vacations
6. Access control
7. Insurance
8. Authorizations
9. Separation of duties

1. CODE OF ETHICS. A code of ethics is a set of formal or informal rules stipulating a required pattern of conduct. The code is applicable to data processing personnel because they are involved in manipulating sensitive data for various functional activities in the organization. The information they are dealing with should not be divulged, either internally or externally. A copy of the code is usually given to employees when they are hired by the organization. Included in the code is a statement that the accidental or deliberate disclosure of sensitive data may result in termination of employment. Many organizations require that employees acknowledge receipt of the code by having them sign the form. The carbon copy is then included as a part of the employees' personnel record. The code of ethics should also be applied to service-bureau personnel who are responsible for processing data for a number of different clients.

The code of ethics may also be applied to those personnel responsible for influencing an order or contract. For example, the code may prohibit the personnel from accepting any gifts from vendors. Or it may be more comprehensive, requiring the personnel to indicate their financial interests or relationships with vendors of data processing equipment, forms, and supplies in an annual report.

2. NONDISCLOSURE AGREEMENTS. Nondisclosure agreements are legal contracts prohibiting personnel from disclosing information about an organization's systems, programs, simulation models, or other sensitive data to a competitor or other organization. In essence, the agreements state that any techniques developed by employees during the course of employment become property of the organization.

Nondisclosure agreements should also be required of service bureaus and/or consultants performing services for the organization. The agreements may also be utilized when programs are loaned to another organization.

3. BUDDY SYSTEM. The buddy system is a practice requiring the presence of two or more persons in the processing center, particularly on off-shifts, weekends, and holidays. The practice is intended to minimize the opportunity for the deliberate alteration of programs, documentation, and/or data. Many organizations limit this practice to the programming staff. However, some are not extending the practice to the systems and operations personnel. In addition to providing an audit safeguard, the practice increases environmental security and personnel safety.

4. ROTATION. The basic rotation practice is to reassign the personnel periodically to processing different applications. This eliminates the possibility of placing too heavy a reliance upon any one individual for performance of certain jobs. Also, it reduces the opportunities for an unscrupulous employee to deliberately alter programs and/or data.

Many organizations frown upon the rotation practice because it requires better training of the personnel and effective documentation. However, the lack of flexibility in an organization becomes very apparent when a so-called operations specialist is absent, ill, or on vacation. Processing almost grinds to a halt because no other member of the activity is able to maintain a continuity of processing.

This author once viewed the crisis that may occur in an organization when a "key" employee is absent. The person who normally processed the payroll and all related reports was absent. The operations manager and another operator attempted to correctly assemble all of the input data. Neither one was overly successful because, to complicate matters further, the available documentation was obsolete. Though the payroll was written on schedule, there were a number of errors that were resolved only after the "key" operator returned to her duties.

Some organizations extend the basic rotation practice to alternating the processing of applications on different shifts. This practice may not be entirely practical for an organization because the schedule may not permit such flexibility. Other organizations attempt to rotate the schedule rather than the personnel. Wherever practical they attempt to process sensitive data on an abnormal schedule basis. The same approach may be followed in the transmission of sensitive data via communication lines. Alternating operating schedules is a further attempt to minimize the possibility of any theft, fraud, or destructive action.

5. VACATIONS. Vacations are regarded as a fringe benefit for data processing employees. Few persons would give much consideration to employee vacations as a control technique. However, an organization that can ill afford to have its employees take a vacation can hardly be considered well-managed. This type of situation indicates that a problem exists in the documentation, training methods, personnel, or the manner of assigning and delegating authority and responsibility.

6. ACCESS CONTROL. The limited access practice restricts the use or availability of equipment or information to qualified personnel. This status is allocated to personnel on the basis of "need-to-know." This minimizes the opportunity for the theft or destruction of documentation,

programs, sensitive data, or equipment. An additional measure of security is implemented when all accesses are recorded in a log. The log should be audited frequently to detect any unusual activity. For example, access to documentation for a given system should be limited to the systems analyst or programmer assigned to a project. When the documentation is removed from the vault or file, a sign-out record must be completed to maintain accountability for the information.

To ensure that the security is maintained, many organizations are limiting access to documentation storage areas to managerial personnel. In one organization, a disgruntled programmer who had been given his termination notice entered the storage area and pulled several instruction cards from each of the source and object program decks. This act of sabotage would not have been noticed immediately if the employee had selected a different place to discard the punched cards. He had placed them in a wastebasket next to his desk. Fortunately for the organization, the unusual number of cards was detected before the waste materials had been collected. However, a considerable expenditure of time and money was required to reconstruct the program decks. Personnel who are terminated should be given severance pay in lieu of notice. This will prevent unscrupulous persons from committing some form of sabotage.

7. INSURANCE. The insurance safeguards are intended to minimize the losses occurring from the activities of data processing personnel. One of the measures is the bonding of employees by a national insurance company. A second form of insurance is to cover liability for errors and omissions incurred while processing data for other organizations. Also, organizations engaged in data processing services for others may carry liability insurance to protect them from law suits arising from alleged violations of contract or code of ethics.

8. AUTHORIZATIONS. Documented authorizations should be required to effect any changes to the programs and/or systems. The authorizations then become part of the documentation package to provide an audit trail and change history. This practice keeps a manager aware of changes being made, and it will provide a control over the personnel executing the changes.

To minimize the occurrence of accidental or deliberate errors, the changes should be audited by the manager.

9. SEPARATION OF DUTIES. This practice is concerned with separating the duties of the console operator, programmer, and systems analyst in productive processing. The console operator must not be permitted to

modify or change any program or system. A programmer or systems analyst should not function as an operator for any program written by them. Frequently the latter situation occurs because either the operator has not been trained or the documentation has not been completed. Neither of these reasons is acceptable. The training and documentation must be completed prior to implementation of the program or system.

Very often the practice of separating duties is ignored by many organizations. The managers permit their console operators to modify programs and consider this an essential part of their training. However, this may be an invitation for an unscrupulous operator to commit fraud very freely.

Tape and Disk File Control

In tape and disk oriented hardware systems there is a need for a file-protection procedure not common to unit-record equipment systems. The digitized information on the tapes and disks is erasable; consequently, valuable information is in danger of accidental and/or deliberate alteration. Therefore, a management control procedure providing maximum protection and utilization of the existing tapes and disks must be developed and maintained.

To provide a measure of protection it is necessary that a media library be established with an effective record-keeping system. The library system should provide and maintain the following data:

—A means of locating any disk or tape in the library files or vault

—A record indicating the borrower's name, plus the date and time of issue and return

—A means of identifying scratch tapes and disks

—A means of identifying tape availability when retention expires

—A quality control record indicating the number of read and write errors, length of tape, and date of media test or certification

—Available areas on disk for data and/or program storage

—A retention control to prevent accidental or deliberate destruction of data and programs

Tape files are much easier to control than those maintained on removable disks. The disks generally, because of their large storage capacity, contain several files. Therefore, availability areas must be carefully controlled to prevent the accidental destruction of data and programs, despite their protection by read only bits, or header and trailer labels. Another problem is that because of their size, disks in many installations are placed on racks or trees near the disk drives or spindles in the computer room. This eliminates some of the physical control which a librarian can exercise over the disks.

The tape and disk file control is composed of the following elements:
1) Library organization
2) Numbering scheme
3) Recording system

1. LIBRARY ORGANIZATION. The organization of the tape and disk file library should actually be incorporated into a documented methods standard. The standard should delineate the organizational structure for the library function; relevant job descriptions; security arrangements; the emergency operating procedures for protecting the tapes and disks; library processing methods; and testing procedures.

The library processing methods will detail the requirements for recording new acquisitions, media assignment and retention, and label specifications. The testing procedure will indicate the testing methods, cycle, and results reporting.

To simplify understanding of the procedure, a glossary of tape and disk related terms should be included in the library organization standard. This is useful for auditors and for training the library clerks who are generally not oriented toward data processing.

2. NUMBERING SCHEME. Part of the physical control of tape and disks may be facilitated through the use of an external numbering scheme. The suggested numbering scheme can be composed of a modified documentation control number (see Chapter 4), a file number, and a disposition code. This will help identify the functional area, processing cycle, assigned system number, assigned program number, file number, and disposition code.

The suggested identification scheme would appear as follows:

$$\underbrace{XX}_{a} \quad \underbrace{X}_{b} \quad \underbrace{XXX}_{c} \quad \underbrace{XX}_{d} \quad \underbrace{X}_{e} \quad \underbrace{XX}_{f}$$

(*a*) Functional area
(*b*) Processing cycle code
(*c*) Assigned system number
(*d*) Assigned program number
(*e*) File number
(*f*) Disposition code

a) Functional Area. The first two digits of the numbering scheme identify the functional area in which the program or data is used. This necessitates grouping all of the systems within their major functional activities. A suggested functional activity scheme is as follows:

Functional Area	Application Code
Management	00
Payroll	
Hourly	10
Salary	11
Taxes and Earnings	12
Labor Distributions	15
Accounts Payable	20
Accounts Receivable	25
Accounting	
Cost	30
Plant	31
Results	32
Production Control	35
(excluding Bill of Materials and Inventory Control)	
Bill of Materials and Explosion	40
Inventory Control	45
Purchasing	50
Sales	60
Engineering	65
Personnel	67
Information Retrieval	70
Special Projects	75
Utility and Library	90
Data Processing	99

b) Processing Cycle Code. The third digit in the numbering scheme identifies the processing frequency. A suggested scheme is as follows:

When Processed	Cycle Code
Whenever required	0
Daily	1
Several times per week	2
Weekly	3
Semimonthly	4

Monthly	5
Quarterly	6
Semiannually	7
Annually	8
Biennially	9

c) Assigned System Number. The assigned system number is a three-digit control number designated on a consecutive number basis from 001 to 999, within the functional area. The number can be reduced to two digits, but this limits expansion capability.

d) Assigned Program Number. This is a two-digit number that is assigned to the programs within a system on a consecutive basis from 01 to 99.

e) File Number. The ninth digit identifies the number of files used by the system and/or program. The consecutive digits from 1 to 9 identify each file in the sequence outputted. It is conceivable that all nine digits may be utilized for magnetic tape files, whereas, only a few digits may be used for disks. The code assists the librarian and operator in handling the multiple tape and disk files.

f) Disposition Code. The last two digits in the numbering scheme identify the purpose of the output. These digits are optional in the identification scheme. A suggested disposition code scheme is illustrated in Figure 7.11.

For magnetic tape units the identification number and other relevant data is entered on an external label and affixed to the reel. If a change is made, a new label may be affixed over the existing label. Some sample labels are illustrated in Figure 7.12.

The idea of adhering an external label with an identification number and other data to a disk is not entirely practical. It is much simpler to carry a serial number identification label on the disk and maintain information regarding the files on an availability table record maintained by the librarian.

3. RECORDING SYSTEM. The standard established for the tape and disk library should delineate the record-keeping procedure for controlling the utilization and disposition of the media. An integral part of the procedure consists of four basic forms. These are:

a) Media identification
b) Media history
c) File history

Dispositon of Output	Disposition Code
Social security data for Social Security Administration (applicable to tax only)	00
For use by Headquarters Organization	01
Records retention only	05
Input to the same operation at a later time	10
Card and printer output and input to the same operation at a later time	11
Card output and input to the same operation at a later time	12
Printer output and input to the same operation at a later time	13
Input to another operation	20
Card and printer output and input to another operation	21
Card output and input to another operation	22
Printer output and input to another operation	23
Input to another program in the same system	30
Input to the same operation at a later time and to another system	40
Card and printer output only	51
Card output only	52
Printer output only	53
Teletype output	54
Output for offline conversion	55
Output for data communications only	56
Exception output	99

Figure 7.11   Example of Tape and Disk File Disposition Code

d) Media availability

a) *Media Identification.* The librarian is personally, or in conjunction with the operations manager, responsible for identification of each tape or disk. The primary control involves the use of an identification number and a consecutively assigned serial number. In addition, a ten-character name or mnemonic file label is used to identify the contents of the file. The file label may be used as part of the internal label in the input/output control software. That label is developed by the programmer and communicated to the librarian through the documentation.

A suggested serial number assignment form is illustrated in Figure 7.13.

TITLE			GENERATE DATE			DENSITY
OUTPUT FROM:			INPUT TO:			
RELEASE DATE		REEL		DRIVE		
		OF				

DESCRIPTION				GENERATE DATE		
PROGRAM NO.	PHYS. UNIT		FILE NO.	SCRATCH DATE		
REEL	DENSITY					
OF	200		556	800		1600

GENERATION DATE	RETENTION DATE	
FILE SYMBOL		
TOTAL RECORDS	NO. PER BLOCK	DENSITY

DESCRIPTION				FILE SYMBOL
DATE WRITTEN	EFFECTIVE DATE	RELEASE DATE		DEVICE
DENSITY	NO. CHANNELS	FOOTAGE	SERIAL NO.	

Figure 7.12. Samples of External Tape Labels

SERIAL NUMBER ASSIGNMENT MEDIUM:									
DATE: PAGE ____ OF ____									
SERIAL NUMBER (MEDIUM)	FILE NUMBER	FILE IDENTIFICATION	ASSIGNMENT DATE			SCRATCH DATE			
			MO.	DAY	YR.	MO.	DAY	YR.	

Figure 7.13. Sample Form for Serial Number Assignment—Tape and Disk Media

b) *Media History.* In the library it is essential to maintain a historical record of the programs or data files stored on the tape or disk. It is conceivable that more than one file may be stored on a reel of magnetic tape. If this is a common practice in an operations activity, then the data files must be listed on the historical record (see Figure 7.14), in the sequence stored and the approximate allocated footage for each. Due to the disk's storage capacity, more than one file will be stored on the medium. The files should be listed in their sequence on the disk and the specific record allocation addresses occupied. In some organizations, a

FILE	REEL	DATE WRITTEN			ERRORS		REMARKS
NO.	OF	MO.	DAY	YR.	READ	WRITE	

MEDIA HISTORY

PAGE ____ OF ____

MEDIUM SERIAL NO: DENSITY: LENGTH:

VENDOR: TYPE: DATE RCVD.:

Figure 7.14. Sample Form for Media Historical Record

disk pack availability table is maintained to indicate current allocations on the medium. This enables a manager, programmer, or systems analyst to readily determine area availability for expansion of existing file space or insertion of new information on the pack. The availability record will have to be updated periodically when the disk files are reorganized to optimize space utilization.

In addition to indicating the space availability status the media history form also provides some indication of effectiveness status. Such a determination is made by either commercially or in-house conducting tests on the media. The number and types of errors indicated by the testing must be recorded on the medium's history. As a result of either of these operations, it may become necessary to cut and discard part of the tape, or to restrict the use of certain address locations on the disk. The restriction must be noted on the availability table or history. When the magnetic tape must be shortened, the information must be recorded to reflect the new available storage length. This practice is not uncommon because as utilization of a given tape increases, the possibility of stretching, damage, or cinching also increases. To reduce the amount of time spent on tape rehabilitation, many organizations are purchasing smaller reels for use with programs or small files. The normal 2400-foot lengths are used for larger applications.

The historical information provides the manager with utilization data for efficient management of these resources.

c) File History. The file history represents a continuous record (see form in Figure 7.15) of the information appearing on a tape or disk. The history indicates the application number; the written, effective, and scratch dates; and the retention cycle or period.

In some organizations, the file history is adapted in a slightly different manner. A separate file history form is established for each application, as illustrated in Figure 7.16. This form lists the application name and number and the reel or pack serial number on which the related file is stored. In addition, the generation, effective, and scratch dates are shown. The scratch date must be adequate to prevent the premature destruction of valuable information.

In establishing the retention period or cycle, the manager must consider the file updating frequency, back-up requirements, and file reconstruction capability. The concept of back-up retention applies readily to magnetic tape processing. However, this approach to back-up is not practical for systems using disk pack media. In tape processing,

FILE HISTORY												PAGE _____ OF _____		

MEDIUM SERIAL NO: DENSITY: LENGTH:

FILE NO.	FILE NAME	GENERATION			EFFECTIVE			SCRATCH			RET.	ERROR	
		MO.	DAY	YR.	MO.	DAY	YR.	MO.	DAY	YR.		R	W

Figure 7.15. Sample Form for File History

SERIAL NO.	REEL OF	GENERATION			GENERATED ON PROGRAM NO.	EFFECTIVE			SCRATCH			RELEASED			ISSUED TO:			RETURNED		
		MO.	DAY	YR.		MO.	DAY	YR.	MO.	DAY	YR.	MO.	DAY	YR.	DATE MO. DAY		INIT.	DATE MO. DAY		INIT.

FILE HISTORY · DATE: · PAGE ____ OF ____

APPLICATION NUMBER: · APPLICATION TITLE: · RETENTION CYCLE:

Figure 7.16. Sample of Modified Form for File History

there is a popular retention scheme known as the grandfather-father-son storage scheme (see Figure 7.17). It provides an element of control for reconstruction of file data. The grandfather is the original or first-generation tape. When the transactions are applied against the grandfather tape in an update process, a tape called the "father" is generated. Subsequently, transactions are applied against the father tape with the new end result being identified as the "son." For back-up control purposes the grandfather tape is still available along with the transaction activities. Should some question or problem arise during the generation of the son tape, the original is still available as back-up. Ultimately, the grandfather tape is released as a scratch tape, with the father tape moving up the hierarchical structure as the new grandfather tape, just as the previous son now becomes the father and a new son is generated in the most recent update.

The strict application of the grandfather-father-son scheme to disks is not economically justifiable owing to the cost differential involved. A reel of tape may be purchased for a fraction of the cost of a disk. Also, the scheme does not provide for optimal utilization of the storage capacity on the medium. However, the same control and file restoration

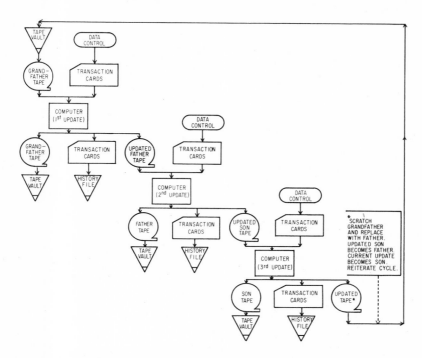

Figure 7.17. Grandfather-Father-Son Storage Scheme

capability may be utilized by dumping the contents of the disk file on to magnetic tape. This data file, along with the transactions, can be used to generate the equivalent of a father tape. In some organizations, the information stored on the disk for a given file is dumped as printer or typewriter output. However, file reconstruction would require re-translation to machine-sensible code.

d) Media Availability. To gain maximum utilization from the tapes and disks, some organizations maintain a date of availability control. A separate form (see Figure 7.18) is established, which lists the serial numbers of the media available for productive purposes. In actual practice, a separate availability form is maintained for disks and another for tapes. The disk availability form also indicates the number of tracks or records available and their location.

When a disk or tape is returned to service, the entry is deleted from the availability form. In the case of disk entries, if only a part of the available area is needed, the pack entry is not deleted but modified. Deleting entries from the media availability form is simpler than remov-

SERIAL	MEDIUM		FOOTAGE	REISSUED TO APPLICATION		DATE		
NO.	TAPE	DISK	TRACKS	NUMBER	TITLE	MO.	DAY	YR.

MEDIA AVAILABILITY   DATE: PAGE ____ OF ____

Figure 7.18. Sample Form for Media Availability

ing the selected tapes or disks from a "scratch area." If a library organizes and maintains its tapes and disks on an in-use versus scratch basis, the librarian must search two separate areas for available media. This places an added burden on the librarian to prevent a misfiling of the media in a wrong area of the library.

DETERMINATION OF COST-BENEFIT

In this chapter we have discussed a number of different procedures for the prevention, detection, and correction of errors. Some are very simple and require few resources for actuation. Others are complex and require a greater expenditure of resources in their implementation and use. Therefore, it becomes necessary to determine what price a user should pay for accurate data. Or, what price is a user willing to pay for obtaining accurate data? The greater the need or desire for accuracy, the more costly will be the system because of increased resource needs.

In developing or modifying a system, the data processing personnel must determine the cost of supplying a required or desired qualitative level. The cost may be negligible or minimal because the user's requirements can be absorbed within the existing resource structure. It is also possible that the costs may be minimized if greater effectiveness can be achieved from an existing system. However, an additional expenditure may be required if the system's requirements necessitate an increased resource capacity. The user must then determine if the requirements are justified in light of the additional cost. The data processing personnel should not make the final decision regarding the design and implementation of a management control for a user. They should provide the user with the various alternatives and costs. The user must be the final decision maker because he is aware of the internal and external constraints which are affecting his needs.

Unfortunately no blanket policy can be applied to evaluating cost-benefit relationships, because the requirements vary among users and because each data element has a different value.

Review Questions: Group 7G

1. What type of protection can be afforded to the data processing equipment?

2. At the weekly staff luncheon, the president has expressed his concern about the safeguards applied to the organization's accounting records. What suggestions, if any, would you make?
3. What is the value of the buddy system as a personnel safeguard?
4. Why is it necessary to establish a formal record-keeping system in a tape and disk library?
5. What are the two primary factors in evaluating a user's request for the design and implementation of a particular management control?

SUMMARY

In the management of a data processing organization, it becomes essential to install a series of controls concerned with the protection and production of data in the information processing cycle. These controls are sometimes referred to as audit controls, but they may exceed those normally required by the auditor. Despite the many categories and types of management controls, they are primarily responsible for the quality of the input and output in an organization. In a sense, it may be more practical to regard these as quality controls.

An organization does not operate in a vacuum. In the dynamic environment there are a number of interacting influences that may be constant or variable and that have a direct or indirect bearing on the operating procedures of a data processing activity. Therefore, it is essential to the very life of the organization that a series of management controls to maximize the operational effectiveness of the available resources be established and maintained. The optimization of the resources requires that the data be valid, applicable, processed accurately, and quickly. This requires the development and application of equipment, input, output, program, external, and peripheral controls. Some of these controls may be applied simply and quickly, but others may require additional time, effort, and expense.

The degree to which controls are applied varies with the system and depends on the equipment, procedures used, cost, and benefits. Good controls must be built into every system during the analysis and design phases of systems planning; they must never be superimposed.

CASE STUDIES

Case Study 7.1:The Raleric Manufacturing Company

The Raleric Manufacturing Company is located in an industrial park on the outskirts of a large metropolitan area. Adjacent to the manufacturing facility is a three-storied building housing the corporate offices. The Computer Center is in the northwest corner of the building. The systems and programming staff are located on the second floor in the southwest corner of the building. The advanced planning and development group is housed on the third floor in the center of the building.

The Computing Center is on the left side of a main traffic aisle. It houses the key punch and peripheral equipment operations, in addition to the computer hardware. Also, numerous file cabinets for master files and program data are located in the area. Master tapes, payroll checks, and accounts payable drafts are kept in a vault near the door. The other active and scratch tapes are maintained in a large rack adjacent to the tape drives. Due to a company safety practice restricting weight handling, a considerable quantity of card and forms stock is kept in the processing area.

There is a large storage area adjacent to the Computer Center and to the right of the traffic aisle. This area is used to store all history records except magnetic tape. The records are stored in their original shipping cartons. Also, the card and form stock necessary to support the activity are stored here. The electrical power-supply disconnects for the computer, air-conditioning, and peripheral equipment are located near the door of the storage area.

Access to the Computer Center is not limited because the inputs are delivered there by the various clerks and outputs are picked up from the rack located near the door. The storage area also remains unlocked to facilitate easy access to the supplies by the operations personnel. Portable carbon-dioxide extinguishers are located in the Computer Center, and water extinguishers are located in the storage area. An automatic water sprinkler system is located in the Computer Center. However, to minimize water damage to the computer, the water line passing directly over that equipment had been removed.

The company is proud of its Computer Center, so it permits the personnel to bring visitors through the center during the prime shift. Arrangements can also be made for tours during the off-shift hours.

The personnel in the Computer Center like the setting because it is next to a beautiful flower garden. They also like its nearness to an emergency fire-door, which gives them a quick jump on the line heading for the cafeteria at the lunch hour. The off-shift personnel are also pleased, because the center is located near the parking lot. In the summer, the operators use the windows to reach the garden or parking lot. Though this method of exit and entry is frowned upon, it has never been formally discouraged by the chief administrator.

Discussion Questions

1. In your opinion, should the company, which is located in an industrial park, be concerned with environmental safeguards?
2. How would you evaluate the safeguards in effect for the sensitive data and programs in the computer center?
3. Do you feel that the organization's weight handling safety policy is entirely practical?
4. Should some alternate arrangement be provided for the power-supply disconnect? Or is it acceptable in its present form?
5. Do you feel any changes are needed in the existing entry access policy for users and visitors?
6. Does it appear that the organization has an effective firefighting and damage-control procedure?
7. Should the personnel's informal entry and exit practices continue to be condoned by the chief administrator? What changes, if any, would you recommend to him?
8. What overall plan of safeguards would you recommend for the data processing activity of this organization?

Case Study 7.2: Eric-Andrea Ice Cream Delights

Your staff is in the process of readying a presentation for management acceptance of a proposed new system. The primary purpose of the system is to reflect employee eligibility and participation in a new group life insurance plan.

The payroll master tape will be used to determine those employees eligible for participation. In the process of determining employee eligibility, the system will compute the amount of coverage an employee qualifies for. It will also compute the monthly premium and prepare a payroll authorization form. The authorization then becomes input for generating records on the group life insurance master tape and the payroll deduction tape. Also, the system must provide for automatic increases in coverage and premiums when an employee's salary increases. Furthermore, the system must provide for cancellation or reduction of coverage and premiums based on employee election for a change.

Provision must also be made to reflect changes in eligibility status when employees are deleted from the master payroll tape due to terminations, leaves of absence, maternity leaves, etc.

As the group life insurance master tape is updated each week, a listing of the coverage will be prepared for the insurance clerk. Also, she would like the following outputs:
—Authorizations executed
—Authorizations not executed
—Cancellations and changes
—Additions
—Deduction changes
—Deduction additions
—Deduction deletions

Discussion Questions

1. *What general categories of control must be considered in the implementation of the proposed system?*
2. *What input controls, if any, should be considered for implementation?*
3. *What program checks would be most appropriate for this system?*
4. *What controls, if any, would be relevant to safeguarding the outputs?*
5. *Prepare an argument for or against utilizing a computer audit on this system after it has been implemented.*

8

The Survey and Feasibility Studies

INTRODUCTION

Because he is constantly involved in some form of decision-making, the manager must have access to accurate, relevant, and timely information. Much of this data is gathered during the pre-executory phase, through the use of survey and feasibility studies. These tools help the manager to define an objective; evaluate the organizational setting; consider possible courses of action; select an optimal course of action; and determine operational effectiveness.

The survey provides preliminary and general information about the overall organization; its data processing function; the data processing equipment, applications and software; and, possibly, additional information about any interacting satellite activities. The survey information, therefore, provides a basic orientation about the setting in which a goal is to be attained.

The feasibility studies evaluate the technical, economic, and operational feasibility of existing or proposed systems, resource allocations, schedules, hardware devices, or standards.

470

THE SURVEY

A preliminary step to the formulation of any plan is an understanding of the setting in which it is to be accomplished. The manager must, therefore, determine the organization's influences and constraints on his objectives, plans, and activities. He must ascertain how each of these elements affects the operation or function. He must also ascertain the extent and value of the contribution made by these elements. Making these evaluations requires the availability of preliminary information about the organization and its data processing attitudes, needs, and capabilities. This information becomes available to the data processing manager and his personnel through the performance of a survey or analysis of survey data.

The concept of a survey is subject to many pros and cons. This author recommends that an in-depth survey be performed initially, on a one-time basis, to gather data about the overall organization and the role of information processing within that organization. It is not intended that the survey be performed on a when-needed basis, because this generally means a survey that is limited in scope, depth, and time. This, in turn, can mean that the information gathered may turn out to be incomplete and/or inaccurate.

The survey must be documented for form a data base or catalog of information. This data will enable the data processing manager or administrator to answer queries raised by the executive committee regarding the information processing function. Also, it can be used to help evaluate the validity of requests for information processing services (see Appendix VI), and to provide comparative data for cost-benefit analysis in feasibility studies. In addition, it is extremely useful in planning the approach for a feasibility study and/or systems analysis, and formulating the questions to be raised by an interviewer in either of those fact-gathering techniques.

In the context defined by this author, then, the survey is not a substitute for a feasibility study, for a feasibility study culminates in a recommendation to the executive committee calling for the expenditure of funds and allocation of resources. Nor is the survey intended to be used as an analysis of an existing system to give managers a list of areas requiring improvement. Also, the survey is not to be used as a systems audit or reports control study designed to evaluate the effectiveness and documentation of existing operational systems. But much rather it is an updated document providing selective background information about the organization. Much of the information contained in the survey can be used to explain current needs and attitudes and, to a limited degree, future trends. The survey may also help to identify the source of any problems or significant constraints. For data processing personnel, the survey provides information that will help them to better understand the overall organization and the functional activities affected by the project.

The major categories of information gathered in a survey are:

1. General organization information
2. Data processing equipment currently installed
3. The data processing organization
4. Data processing equipment installed at a satellite organization
5. The data processing function at the satellite
6. Information processing systems
7. Data processing equipment on order

General Organization Information

To gain an understanding about an organization it may be necessary to study its:

1. History
2. Size
3. Structure
4. Type
5. Product or service

1. HISTORY. Historical data is gathered or analyzed in order to provide an understanding about the organization's evolvement. The history may explain the executive committee's involvement in information processing functions and activities; executive committee preference for certain projects; the organization's policies, practices, and philosophies; the constraints affecting the organization; organizational strengths and weaknessess; and the source of problems. Some of the historical information may be gathered from materials provided to new employees. However, to achieve a fuller background, it may be necessary to research the annual reports, organizational publications, industry reports, a stock prospectus, stock analyst reports, etc.

2. SIZE. The size provides some preliminary information, which is used in conjunction with data on equipment, and systems. This informa-

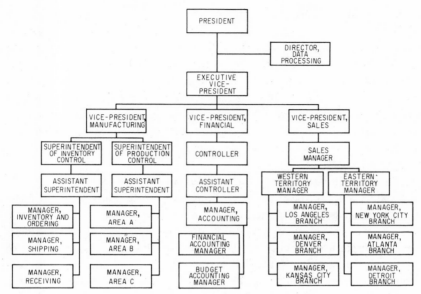

Figure 8.1. Example of Overall Organization Chart

tion enables the manager to determine the type of hardware an organization is capable of supporting, as well as to arrive at judgment about the sophistication of the currently operational systems and those under development or proposed.

3. STRUCTURE. The structure delineates the responsibilities and lines of authority within the organization. Information on the structure is generally secured from the organization chart (see Figure 8.1), job descriptions, and functional activity managers. This information is particularly useful when determining the functional activities affected in the analysis, design, implementation, maintenance, and audit of a system. Also, it provides relevant and necessary data for the formulation of questions to be used in the interviewing of personnel. The structural information can also be very useful in estimating the time requirements for interviews, flowcharting, data analyses, etc., in a project schedule.

4. TYPE. Type identifies the primary activity of an organization. It indicates if an organization is involved in manufacturing, business, medical, commercial, educational, research, governmental, religious, utility, or service activities. Organization type will significantly affect the type of data processing equipment selected, and the systems developed and implemented. For example, in a manufacturing organization, the

primary emphasis may be on inventory and production control systems. In a hospital, on the other hand, the emphasis may be placed on the medical record or accounts receivable systems.

5. PRODUCT OR SERVICE. The product line or services offered by an organization may also affect equipment selection and systems development. For example, an organization engaged primarily in scientific research will be interested in equipment with fast internal computational capability and slower input/output speeds. The applications in this example would be mathematically oriented.

The organizational information provides the manager with some preliminary information about the environmental setting. However, this information must be supplemented with other interacting data gathered in the survey. In some organizations, the history, size, product line or service, organization charts, and listing of managerial personnel are maintained in a policy standards manual. Very often, information on the structure and manning can be secured from the internal telephone directory. The manual and directory may be used very effectively in a survey which has to be done with minimal research time and effort.

Data Processing Equipment Currently Installed

This segment of the survey provides a detailed census of the existing information processing capability in the central organization. The following types of information may be gathered in this segment:
1. Unit-record equipment
2. Computing equipment
3. Software availability
4. Peripheral equipment
5. Utilization statistics

1. UNIT-RECORD EQUIPMENT. The manager must determine the number and types of devices available for input preparation and processing, as well as their rated processing speeds. This list should also include information on the special features installed on a given device. For example, a key punch machine may be equipped with such features as alternate program control and self-checking number generator. The listing should also indicate the costs of the devices, whether they are being rented, leased, or purchased. The cost data should include a separate category for maintenance charges for each device.

This information will enable a manager to evaluate the unit-record processing capability of the organization. The cost data would be available for any comparative cost analysis.

2. COMPUTING EQUIPMENT. The inventory of computing equipment is more detailed because of the number of features and supporting devices required in a configuration. Figure 8.2 illustrates an inventory listing for an IBM 360/30 equipped with compatibility for a second-generation 1401 computer.

As for unit-record equipment, the rental, lease, or purchase costs and maintenance charges should be included. In addition, information about real-time and time-sharing capability should be included as part of the inventory.

Additional technical data for such items as densities, transfer rates, storage capacities, etc., should be included as part of the computing equipment census. The technical data is not always readily available or known in an organization. Frequently the vendor's representative must be contacted to secure information regarding a particular device. Therefore, the technical information should be a part of the basic equipment survey.

3. SOFTWARE AVAILABILITY. This segment of the survey should identify the capability of the operating system, identify the programming languages, and include narrative descriptions of the special software packages, such as cash-flow analysis. Programming languages provide an indicator of the types of applications processed and their level of sophistication. It may also provide some measure of programming capability in an organization. However, one must be careful to identify subsets of higher level languages in use. The subset is generally less powerful than the complete language. It lacks certain processing capabilities associated with larger primary storage needs. In addition, it may require additional coding to effect the same result.

4. PERIPHERAL EQUIPMENT. An inventory of the supporting peripheral equipment must also be made to provide a more complete picture of productive potential. The availability of such devices as data communications equipment may indicate somewhat more sophisticated applications and the need for additional management controls. The full impact of these devices cannot be assessed until the currently operational systems are evaluated.

5. UTILIZATION STATISTICS. The utilization statistics are an important part of the survey because they indicate whether or not the hard-

Description	Quantity	Machine Number	Model or Feature
Processing Unit—16K (Bytes)	1	2030	D
Decimal Arithmetic	1		3237
1051 Attachment	1		7915
Basic 1401 Compatibility	1		4456
Magnetic Tape Compatibility	1		4467
1402/1403 Attachment	1		4463
Programmed Mode Switch	1		5856
Card Read Punch	1	2540	1
Punch Feed Read	1		5890
Control Unit	1	1051	N1
CPU Attachment	1		3130
1st Punch Attachment	1		4410
1st Reader Attachment	1		4411
Printer-Keyboard	1	1052	8
Control Unit	1	2821	1
Punch Feed Read Control	1		5895
1100 LPM Printer Adaptor	1		3615
Printer 1100 LPM	1	1403	N1
Interchangeable Train Cartridge	1	1416	1
Tape Control Unit	1	2803	1
7-Track Compatibility	1		7125
Data Conversion	1		3228
Magnetic Tape Unit	5	2401	2

Figure 8.2   IBM 360/30 Configuration Inventory

ware is being used to its fullest capacity. A powerful computer that is only partially utilized leaves time available for the development of additional systems. The utilization statistics may be extracted from the operator or machine records, or from the output from hardware or software monitors. Wherever possible, fluctuations in the processing cycle should also be recorded.

The information collected identifies the available productive capacity of an organization. Some of the data for this segment of the survey may be extracted from an equipment status report detailing all of the equipment currently installed and related costs.

The Data Processing Organization

Though the manager has familiarized himself with the general organizational setting and the available productive power of the hardware,
he must also study the functional organization responsible for maintaining that capability. A survey of this segment requires an evaluation of (1)
organization and manning, and (2) standards.

1. ORGANIZATION AND MANNING. The survey of this element begins
with an analysis and documentation of the organization chart. In addition to delineating the lines of authority and responsibility, the chart
should indicate the manning strength for each position. This data provides the manager with an assessment of the manpower resource capability. This data may also be extracted from an internal telephone
directory.

Some organizations maintain confidential or semi-confidential personnel authorization and manning reports, which classify the positions
within data processing by functional activity. These reports may include
the person's salary or salary range for that position, plus a job description. Many of the organizations provide a copy of the overall organization and manning report to the data processing administrator for use by
the systems manager and the advanced planning and development manager. The reports can be very useful in the performance of feasibility
studies.

2. STANDARDS. In this segment the manager is concerned with determining the methods and performance standards utilized by the organization. The documentation segment of the methods standard is particularly important. If good documentation is available, the analysis of
existing and proposed systems will be simplified and also more effective.

The performance standards are used primarily for schedule preparation. However, if the performance standards are realistic, they will also
serve as an excellent indicator of personnel experience and know-how.

Satellite Data Processing Equipment

The hardware installed at a satellite function will vary from a data
communications terminal to a medium-sized, and in some groups, a
large-sized computing system. The available productive capacity must
be evaluated because of its actual or potential influence on the opera-

tional effectiveness of the central data processing organization. Often the outputs from the centralized data processing activity are transmitted to the satellite group for production of a final report or desired output. For example, payroll data may be processed at the central location and a portion of the output is transmitted to the satellite for preparation of the payroll drafts and statements.

Evaluation of the hardware should be conducted in the same manner as that for the centralized data processing organization. Often, the necessary information for this segment may be extracted from the equipment status report.

The Satellite Data Processing Function

One of the survey aims is to achieve a better understanding of the environment. This understanding should include an evaluation of the information processing capability at the satellite organization. Of primary concern is the degree and level of interaction between the satellite and central data processing functions. The patterns of interaction vary from organization to organization. Even within an organization, the interacting relationships may vary. This condition may be the result of organization growth, development of subsidiaries, acquisitions, consolidations, or takeovers.

These relationships must be understood and the information documented to facilitate future planning and development. For the data processing manager and his personnel, it becomes necessary to evaluate the impact of the satellite function on any system being studied, developed, or modified. This will ensure more effective planning, development, and implementation.

In some organizations, the data processing manager of the central function is able to utilize the available resources at a satellite function. For example, organizations frequently utilize programming and system personnel from a satellite activity to supplement the staff of the central activity. Also, in some organizations, the contingency plans call for the utilization of a satellite activity to minimize the effect of a crisis.

Information Processing Systems

This survey segment may be very time-consuming if adequate documentation of existing and proposed systems is not available. The collected data may be grouped into two classifications: (1) System narratives and (2) Quantitative data.

1. SYSTEM NARRATIVES. The desired information must indicate the primary inputs/outputs and the processing performed. This data is available from a system abstract form as illustrated in Figure 8.3. In addition to listing the currently operative applications, the manager must also include those proposed for immediate conversion and future development. Some of this data should be available in the form of preliminary documentation for those applications scheduled for immediate conversion or currently under development. Data on future conversions should be available from the applicable feasibility studies. The manager should also consider those applications related to the activities of the satellite organization.

2. QUANTITATIVE DATA. In an analyses of the current systems, the manager needs to secure input and output volume statistics, and actual or estimated processing times. For those systems in the process of conversion, under development, or proposed for future development, the manager should secure estimated processing times. The schedule data will enable the manager to determine the amount of productive time available and required for current and future purposes. Separate statistics should be collected on the involvement of the satellite group in the total process.

Data Processing Equipment on Order

This segment involves developing an inventory of future equipment acquisitions. The listing should include equipment under contract and that for which a letter of intent has been executed. Though the latter category is subject to change, it does represent a potential acquisition for planning purposes.

The equipment on order has a direct bearing on the planning and organizing functions, therefore, the manager must secure the specific details of what is scheduled for delivery. The information may be grouped into the following categories:

1. Peripheral devices
2. Unit-record equipment
3. Computing equipment

SYSTEM ABSTRACT	APPLICATION NO.	EFFECTIVE DATE __ / __ / __	PAGE __ OF __
SYSTEM TITLE			

SYSTEM DESCRIPTION

EQUIPMENT CONFIGURATION	RELATED SYSTEMS
STORAGE REQUIREMENTS (PRI. & AUX.)	PROGRAMMING LANGUAGE(S)
INPUT DESCRIPTION	OUTPUT DESCRIPTION
APPROVED BY	APPROVAL DATE

Figure 8.3. System Abstract Form

480

1. PERIPHERAL DEVICES. The equipment in this category is designed to support the existing or proposed operational capability. The inventory must indicate the type and quantity on order, proposed application, expected delivery date, special features, and costs. The description should be as complete as possible in order to indicate the device capability. For example, the description of a data communications device would include: operating speed, transmission mode, error detection, error correction, transmission code, input/output media, and devices transmitted or received from.

2. UNIT-RECORD EQUIPMENT. The inventory for unit-record equipment is similar to that for peripheral equipment. It may be somewhat simpler because fewer types of devices are involved. The inventory must list the model numbers, quantities on order, special features, proposed use, expected delivery date, and costs.

3. COMPUTING EQUIPMENT. Of the three equipment categories this one is perhaps the most complicated, because the hardware descriptions are very detailed. It is suggested that the inventory be presented by component. For example, the central processing unit, input, output, etc., would each be described individually.

In addition to the hardware listing, the manager must stipulate the operating system, programming languages, and special application packages available.

It may be possible to secure some of this information from the equipment status report.

Value of the Survey

The survey in this context provides the data processing administrator and manager with meaningful decision-making data. The data gathered should be studied by the data processing manager and his personnel prior to initiating any new development or modification project. This information will help them to define and understand the stated objectives; to establish the checklists used in information gathering; and to help establish a basic rapport when conducting interviews during feasibility studies and systems analysis projects. Also it eliminates the redundant effort in the collection of this information. Much of this same information is repetitively gathered by systems personnel when preparing for interviews, analyzing or modifying an existing system, or developing a new system. The data is used to help determine whether the objectives are being accomplished or whether the optimal approach is to be developed within an existing or projected environment.

The value of a survey may be quickly lost, however, if an organization is unwilling to update the information to maintain its currency, relevancy, and accuracy. Maintaining its operational effectiveness will enhance its value in formulating relevant and meaningful approaches, and the effective allocation of resources.

Consulting services and management advisory services will generally perform a survey prior to submitting a proposal or after acceptance of a contract. This survey is a preliminary review to familiarize the consultant with the client's organization. These surveys generally focus on the setting of the information processing activity within the overall organization, and its interaction with other functional activities. Depending upon the nature of the proposal or contract, detailed studies of the existing or proposed systems may subsequently be performed.

Review Questions: Group 8A

1. What is the purpose of a survey?
2. Why is it important to gather general information about the organization during the survey process?
3. It has been suggested that, in order to facilitate data gathering you should extract the organization charts from an employee publication printed last year. What would be your reaction to this suggestion?
4. The equipment status report lists on a single-line entry an IBM 360/40 computer, under the heading of computing equipment. Would this information be adequate for your needs in a survey? Why or why not?
5. What is the value of a system narrative?
6. Why should it be necessary to maintain an inventory of data processing equipment which is on order?

FEASIBILITY STUDIES

A feasibility study can be described as a logical, systematic, and well-documented approach to solving a problem or analyzing a proposal. More aptly, it may be defined as a critical investigation conducted to establish the practical or economic justification, or both, of an idea, standard, technique, software, or hardware. The concept is not new, it has been applied to different problems in varying degrees for many years. Properly executed it becomes a critical examination for determining an organization's needs, and the cost-benefit relationships of existing and proposed approaches. The end result is a proposal to the executive committee recommending a particular solution or approach. In some organizations, a feasibility study is referred to as a justification study.

The feasibility study can be used to answer the following types of questions and considerations for an organization:

—Whether or not the organization really needs an automated data processing capability

—Is an approach technically and/or operationally feasible?

—What functions can be automated effectively?

—How much and what level of automation can be applied?

—What type of hardware to acquire?

—What would be the most economical method of acquiring hardware?

—Should information processing be performed in-house or at a service bureau?

—Should an organization acquire proprietary software products?

—What is the most advantageous method of acquiring proprietary software?

—How long can an existing hardware configuration continue to meet the needs of an organization?

In analyzing these and many other situations, the feasibility study is basically concerned with an evaluation of the present and future objectives, current operations, and any actual or hypothetical conditions or problems.

To better understand the concept of feasibility studies, it is useful to examine the following categories:

1. Tests of feasibility
2. Who conducts the study?
3. Objectives of the study
4. The study phases

Tests of Feasibility

There are four tests of feasibility which must be uniformly applied to the evaluation of each problem or proposal. These tests are applied to determine the best approach to achieve a given objective. It is not intended that a different approach be implemented merely to substitute for a traditional approach or to achieve marginal benefits.

Inherent in these tests is an evaluation of the technical, economic, and operational feasibility of a current and/or proposed approach. When applying the feasibility tests to a system, it may help to ensure that a manual mess may not become an automated mess. For purposes of discussion, we shall apply the feasibility tests to a system. The four tests are:

1. Acceptability
2. Flexibility
3. Use of resources
4. Ease of operation

1. ACCEPTABILITY. Both the current and any proposed system must interact with a number of internal and external influences or constraints affecting its operational effectiveness. The primary acceptance will come if it has been determined that the system meets the stated objectives. The system may also have to conform to relevant local, state, and/or federal regulations. An organization may be affected by various wage and hour laws; city, county, state, and federal income taxes; corporate franchise taxes; drug regulations, etc. Any infringement or violation of the laws must be avoided.

Contractual requirements may also place certain parameters and constraints upon a system. A payroll system may be affected by the contract negotiated between the organization and its employees. A purchase order system may also be affected by any quantity purchase agreements negotiated with the suppliers.

The system must also respond to the management controls stipulated by the internal or external auditors. The management controls must provide a clearly defined audit trail that relates the source documents to the outputs (see Chapter 7). The user must also accept the system. If the system is difficult to use or manage, the executive committee, employees, members, or customers will seek an alternate method to secure their response needs. A very frequent complaint among users is that it is impossible to secure a rapid response to a simple question when the information is stored on data processing records. Users also complain that they must forego necessary data from reports or outputs, or are harnessed with difficult procedures in order to secure "improved" information. Very often the personnel responsible for designing and developing a system become overly concerned with technical considerations at the expense of the user. Consequently, the outputs may not contain all of the necessary data. Or, the report formats may not be in a desired sequence or human-sensible format. The user may also have to access two different reports to secure the necessary information.

The mark of a good system is its ability to provide the necessary interaction from the required resources within the stated constraints. This ability will enhance the utility and efficiency of a system. As a result, the cost of development and implementation may be significantly reduced and the break-even point reached earlier.

2. FLEXIBILITY. Every system must be flexible, because it may be affected by the passage of time, changes in legal requirements, adverse conditions, and a variety of other problems or variations. Any system, for example, that becomes too rigid and cannot respond to change will lose its effectiveness. Therefore, within every system there must be some provision for flexibility to provide growth for the organization of tomorrow. Every system must be evaluated for its current and long-term usefulness. A manager must also determine how easily changes and modifications may be effected. In the evaluation of a system, these determinations help to increase the system's utility and life span.

Flexibility must be deliberately designed into a system. This can only be accomplished after an analysis of the requirements. This is done by trying to apply hindsight to the planning process ahead of time.

3. USE OF RESOURCES. In applying this test of feasibility, the manager evaluates the effect or impact of an existing or proposed system upon the available resources in an organization. This may require consideration of functional responsibility realignment; recruitment, selection, and training of data processing personnel; reassignment, or retraining, of other personnel; consideration of the adequacy of available resources; elimination of duplicate operations, reporting requirements, or records; integration of machine functions to maximize throughput; and economies in operating costs. Also, the manager must be certain that the user is ready or in a position to utilize the outputs, or prepare the necessary inputs.

The success of any approach is dependent upon the optimal utilization of the available resources.

4. EASE OF OPERATION. When an approach is tested for ease of operation it is evaluated for its responsiveness to current and projected

needs. A system, for example, must be user-oriented. It must be able to perform the normal and exceptional processing requirements. This capability will add to the efficiency of the system, and increase its utility and life span.

The ease of operation is also concerned with the ease of system maintenance, and expandability. The original design must facilitate the implementation of changes and modifications as they become necessary.

The effective application of this test will help to reduce or minimize development, implementation, and maintenance costs.

The application of the four tests shouldn't be limited to feasibility studies. The tests must also be applied to the major phases of system and programming activity—analysis, design, implementation, and follow-up.

Who Conducts the Study?

A feasibility study may be conducted by:
1. Equipment vendors
2. Management consultants
3. Data processing personnel
4. Study team

1. EQUIPMENT VENDORS. Vendors will often conduct a generalized feasibility study to determine the equipment and system needs of an organization. The final report may or may not include an equipment or services proposal. However, the proposal will recommend only the vendor's own equipment or services. It will make no mention of the competition and may tend to "oversell" the product. On occasion they tend to "undersell" in order to gain the account. Subsequently, they work to upgrade the account with additional hardware placement or services. To offset this natural bias, many organizations solicit studies from several vendors. Someone within the organization will then have to evaluate each proposal to determine its feasibility.

This service is provided by the equipment vendors free of charge. If an organization lacks qualified personnel to perform the study, this could be an advantage. As a result of the study, the vendor may recommend equipment or services that will reasonably satisfy the organization's needs. The obvious disadvantage is that the equipment vendor is interested in installing his own hardware or selling his own services. Consequently a recommendation may be based only upon marginal justification. This procedure is not to be confused with vendor requests for proposals based on previously prepared specifications (see Chapter 9).

2. MANAGEMENT CONSULTANTS. Management consultants may be used to augment an organization's own staff in conducting a feasibility study. Or, they may provide the expertise to do a job within a narrow time-frame.

Management consultants will generally provide an impartial, objective study because they are not connected with a particular equipment vendor. A disadvantage may be expense. Consultant rates may range from 2.5 to 3.5 times as much as that paid to an organization's own information processing personnel. However, the consultants provide personnel with the necessary expertise for the limited time required. This is less costly than realigning an organization's own staff to perform the study. Some organizations are fearful of utilizing consultants for specialized projects because they do not wish to have any sensitive data divulged to their competitors. In such situations, it is recommended that the organization prepare and execute a nondisclosure agreement with the consultants.

3. DATA PROCESSING PERSONNEL. An organization may utilize its own information processing specialists to conduct the study. Generally the organization will attempt to assign personnel to the project who are familiar with the functional area under consideration. This approach may require a realignment of the staff for the term of the project. Some organizations utilize the advanced planning and development personnel to conduct the necessary studies. In some medium- and large-sized organizations, it is possible to temporarily borrow personnel from a satellite function to participate in the feasibility study.

An organization's own personnel are familiar with the organization and its policies and practices, personnel, and systems. As a result, many of the preliminaries for information gathering may be unnecessary. That information would be gained by reviewing the available survey and systems documentation. However, the in-house staff may not have the necessary expertise to perform a successful evaluation of a problem or approach. For example, a staff that is oriented toward batch processing may not be capable of analyzing online, interactive applications or hardware.

4. STUDY TEAM. The study team approach brings together a group with varied skills and knowlege, as well as interest in the organization.

The team is sometimes referred to as a task force or project group (see Chapter 2).

The functional area representatives on the study team serve as liaison between the information processing specialists and the activity under consideration. This approach will help to significantly reduce development and implementation costs, and ensure achievement of desired objectives. However, the complexity of the systems under consideration may require that the team devote their full time to the feasibility study. For some organizations, this approach may not be very practical because they are unable to commit the key personnel to the project for any length of time.

The effectiveness of the study-team approach depends entirely on the use of key personnel to conduct the feasibility study. Subsequently, these same people are utilized in the design, development, and implementation of the recommended approach. Ultimately, the key personnel are reassigned to their functional areas to direct and control the new or modified approach.

There are certain characteristics or qualities desirable of team members participating in a feasibility study:

—They should be familiar with the philosophies and objectives of the organization.

—The group must have knowledge of accounting and operating methods, as well as legal and audit requirements.

—The personnel should be willing to work with details.

—They should be imaginative, creative, objective thinkers.

—They must consider only the overall needs of the organization.

Obviously, it will be difficult to locate personnel who will meet all of the desired traits or characteristics. However, the executive committee must select persons for this task who will make objective recommendations. The executive committee should also recognize that there may be some need to train the personnel within the study group. This may be necessary because of their lack of familiarity with feasibility study techniques and with the design and operation of data systems.

The composition of the study group and the approach selected will obviously depend upon the scope and objectives of the study; the time available; the type of personnel available; and the budget allocation. An outside source may very often be more objective than an in-house group. However, sometimes these persons too may be pressured into reaching certain conclusions.

Objectives of the Study

The scope and objectives of the feasibility study are generally conveyed to the data processing administrator or manager by letter or memorandum. These objectives provide both a sense of direction for conducting the study and a basis for reviewing progress. As in all management planning, the general objectives must be defined into specific goals. When the definition process has been completed, the specific objectives should be discussed with the executive committee to ensure that the desired goals are being considered. As a result of this discussion the objectives may have to be altered or modified before the actual study is initiated. Sometimes during the study itself it becomes evident that the objectives must be realigned, altered, or modified. This information should be conveyed to the executive committee, along with the practical importance for changing the objectives. A manager should never allow himself to become bound by the objectives when it is evident that some change is necessary. Nevertheless, he needs to be in a position to offer a constructive suggestion when recommending a change. Failure to apply the proper direction in the feasibility study may produce an end result which may be ineffective or of limited value. Among the more typical general objectives may be to:

—Reduce clerical cost through reduction of clerical work force
—Permit more timely decisions by managers
—Reduce high clerical costs by improving the methods of data acquisition and processing
—Reduce or eliminate repetitive operations
—Evaluate the effectiveness of existing manual and mechanized operations
—Reduce or eliminate processing backlogs
—Provide new approaches to complex or repetitive computational problems
—Review and improve schedules
—Measure the performance of a system
—Evaluate a software package acquisition
—Evaluate the alternatives for acquiring hardware

The list by no means exhaust the realm of possibilities. The general objectives must be defined in order to answer the what, why, how, who, when, and where (see Chapter 1). These answers must be further broken down into the tasks and operations needed to form the structural frame-work for the feasibility study.

For example, a memorandum is sent from the executive committee to the data processing manager instructing him to, "Develop and imple-ment an interactive billing and collection system." To define the scope of this objective the data processing manager must raise the following questions:

—Why is this request being made?
—Is this a new development or modification of an existing system?
—Is this system a subsystem?
—What is the expected life of the system?
—What functional areas are to be affected?
—What are the performance requirements?
—What is the required user response time?
—What resource limitations have been placed on the system?
—What time-frame has been allocated for the project?

The responses to these questions will enable the manager to establish the structural framework for the collection of data in the study. The structural framework will specify the tasks and operations for such activities as:

—Identifying the necessary functions to be carried out
—Description and analysis of the existing system
—Determination of required inputs, outputs, and files
—Evaluation of alternative approaches

These tasks and operations are not generalized headings because during the definition process the manager will have made certain rele-vant determinations. For example, in the billing and collection system, some of the required functions may include the following:

—An accounting for the charges, allowances, credits, and adjust-ments
—The capability of preparing a follow-up on overdue accounts
—The ability to retrieve open accounts
—The ability to prepare various management reports, such as a daily trial balance, aging of accounts by stated periods, etc.

This represents but a partial listing of the required functions in a simple billing and collection system. However, as a result of these predeterminations, the study personnel are able to prepare themselves for the required fact gathering and evaluations.

The Study Phases

When the specific objectives have been defined and detailed the feasibility study may be initiated. A basic feasibility study may be composed of six phases:
1. Analysis of existing system or approach
2. Determination of current costs
3. Development of an alternative approach
4. Determination of the proposed costs
5. Advantages and disadvantages
6. Report of findings and recommendations

Analysis of Existing System or Approach

The foundation of the feasibility study is an analysis of the present system or approach to a given problem. This phase can be termed as the fact finding or fact gathering phase. It is during this initial phase that the personnel study the current objectives, organizational structure, policies, practices, documentation, schedules, machine utilization, quality of outputs, files, volumes, qualitative controls, work flow, performance requirements, system constraints, internal and external influences, and procedures. The information gathered becomes the basis of comparison for subsequent phases in the feasibility study.

In analyzing the existing system, the analyst must determine in detail what is being performed, when it is being done, who performs the work, the complexity of the process, and why the work is being performed. This process results in an in-depth analysis of each function and a determination of its relationship to the total system. In addition to analyzing the operations the analyst also gathers data on the volumes, frequencies, and man-hour requirements. Also, the management controls employed in the system must be identified and evaluated.

The information is collected by interviewing the managers and the personnel of the affected functional activities. However, prior to initiat-

1. What data files are currently in existence?
2. What is the purpose of each data file?
3. What media forms are used for the existing files?
4. What is the record arrangement in each file?
5. What information is recorded in each file?
6. What is the sequence of each file?
7. What data validation methods are required?
8. What file or data conversion is required?
9. What data is redundant in each file?
10. Do the files interface with any other files?
11. What are the file maintenance requirements?
12. Who is responsible for the file maintenance?
13. What is the frequency of file updating?
14. What is the volume of transactions in the update?
15. Where are the data files located?
16. Is there any back-up provision or security requirement for the existing data files?
17. What management controls are used in the file update process?
18. What is the frequency of references or inquiries to each data file?
19. What reports or outputs are prepared from the data files?
20. What systems utilize these data files?
21. What programs utilize these data files?
22. What is the file retention period?
23. What header and trailer labels are used in each file?
24. What is the file mnemonic?
25. What are the record mnemonics?

Figure 8.4   Standardized Checklist for Data Gathering Files

ing the necessary interviews, the analyst must review the available survey data. This will provide the interviewer with background information for defining the problem, and planning his interview approach and questions. This information helps the analyst to establish a basic rapport for the interview because he will have a preliminary understanding of the functional area.

The information in the interviews should be gathered through the use of standardized checklists (see Figure 8.4) developed for such items as inputs, outputs, data sets, etc. The collected information must then be documented in detail for a subsequent evaluation in this phase. This information enables the analyst to determine input, output, performance and reporting requirements, the external and internal influences and constraints affecting the system, current operating costs, and what is currently being accomplished.

The documented data must be collated and correlated to provide the basis for analyses and decisions in this and succeeding phases of the feasibility study. In concluding this phase the analyst will be in a position to answer several important questions about the existing operation. These are:

—Are current needs and objectives achieved?

—Should new or modified objectives be developed?

—What types and volumes of input, output, and reference data are being used?

—What is the effect of the current system on the user and operating personnel?

—What is the efficiency of the existing system or approach?

—What is the processing sequence of the applications and their input/output requirements?

—What is the adequacy and timeliness of user and operating instructions?

—What is the productivity for each application?

—What is the quality of the user reports?

—What is the competence level of the user and operating personnel?

—What is the output distribution?

—What control procedures are used and their effectiveness?

—What is the effectiveness of the system's testing and maintenance procedures?

A critical evaluation of the system may disclose that it is no longer responsive to the user's needs. Therefore, new or modified objectives may have to be developed. Or, the existing system will have to be modified or redesigned. The redesign, however, may not necessarily require an automated system.

Information on input, output, and reference data types and volumes will enable the analyst to calculate the costs for phase two, as well as potential applications in phase three of the study. In subsequent phases, it may be necessary to translate these requirements into equipment specifications. At this point, the analyst must also resolve the effect of the present system on the user and operating personnel. The operating personnel are responsible for the functional effectiveness of the system and, therefore, it is necessary to determine its ease of operation and flexibility. The effect on the users must be analyzed to determine if the system discourages or deters their use of information processing techniques. Or are there possibilities for future development or expansion of the system?

Determination of Current Costs

In evaluating any system, it is necessary to ascertain the present operating costs. Subsequently these will be compared with those in the proposed system to determine which are reduced, eliminated, or increased. The amount of cost data required may vary from one organization to another; therefore, this specification should be made by the executive committee prior to the start of the feasibility study. The cost data should reflect not only the operating costs of data processing but also those of the functions or activities affected by the system. In addition, the amortized one-time costs must be included. A complete cost picture will provide a realistic comparative cost base against any proposed system. There is little justification for applying new or additional resources to a system if only marginal benefits are to be achieved.

Accurate cost data must be gathered by the analyst. This data may be secured from available accounting records or from average cost rates for each element in the system. The average cost method is frequently used for comparative cost data. Figure 8.5 illustrates how composite average rates may be developed for the key punch operator and peripheral equipment operator job classifications. The average does not include any allowance for overtime—a figure that is dependent upon organizational policies regarding overtime pay. Therefore, if utilization of personnel on an overtime basis is required, the values must be reflected in the system's costs.

In addition this phase must include relevant equipment costs, including special features; supplies; amortized one-time costs; operation and maintenance costs for processing, electrical power, and air conditioning equipment; insurance; space costs; and supporting equipment, such as files, desks, etc.

The current costs will be compared with those in phase four of the study. Also, the costs are a necessary part of the benefit and recommendation data included in phases five and six.

| Department | Job Classification | Grade | Number | HOURLY RATE | | | Average Rate |
				Base	@111.3%	Total	
105	Key Punch Operator	205	1	2.50	2.78	2.78	
		203	6	2.06	2.29	13.74	
			7			16.52	2.3600
105	Peripheral Equipment	209	2	3.29	3.66	7.32	
	Operator	207	3	2.92	3.25	9.75	
		205	2	2.50	2.78	5.56	
			7			22.63	3.2328
105	Control Clerk	206	1	2.73	3.04	3.04	
			1			3.04	
110	Key Punch Operator	205	1	2.50	2.78	2.78	
		203	4	2.06	2.29	9.16	
			5			11.94	2.3880
110	Peripheral Equipment	207	1	2.92	3.25	3.25	
	Operator	204	1	2.28	2.54	2.54	
			2			5.79	2.8950

@ Includes Loading Rate for Overhead Costs

Figure 8.5 Examples of Composite Average Rates of Hourly Wages for Specific Job Classifications

Development of an Alternative Approach

The development of an alternative approach may be a complex and time-consuming process because it is concerned with planning for the future. The alternative identifies with considerable clarity the approach to be followed. One method of developing an alternative approach may be through the use of simulation techniques. These techniques facilitate the study of an operation or process without direct analysis of the activity. The analysis is performed by constructing a mathematical model to study a real-life situation. The known factors, the characteristics of the unknown factors, and their relationships are processed through the model to produce some probable outcomes and alternatives. These ouputs do not provide a solution in themselves but will help the manager in selecting an optimal approach. The simulation outputs generally take the form of plotted graphs, a listing of numerical values, or narrative descriptions. These differ from the detailed descriptions of a system as described in Chapter 4. For data processing purposes, it is possible to simulate the management and operational processes, resource requirements, and schedules within the parameters for a given environment. The technique is frequently used when evaluating the need and placement of data communications facilities.

Many alternative recommendations do not require the use of the simulation techniques. These recommendations may be for systems that require the compilation of data, file maintenance, record keeping, or some computations. They must be described in sufficient detail to enable the executive committee and other information processing personnel to understand the proposal. The proposal must identify the objectives; impact upon the existing organization; content and format of all records, files, and outputs; estimates of equipment utilization; and preliminary time estimates for development and implementation.

A suggested outline of the data to be included is as follows:

—A broad narrative of the scope of the system and the primary reason or reasons for its development and implementation

—A system flowchart illustrating the flow of information through the proposed system

—System flowcharts of the subsystems, and macro- and micro-flowcharts for programming solutions

—A system abstract (see Figure 8.3) for the system and each subsystem to identify, in layman's terminology, their aims, functions, and equipment requirements

—The inputs, outputs, data elements, records, and files should be described in detail. This segment should also include specimen forms and/or illustrations

—In addition, the media types, their source and distribution, and actual or estimated volumes must be specified

—The suggested management controls and their importance should also be specified

—The estimated development, implementation, equipment utilization, and productivity statistics should also be included; this data will subsequently be used to evaluate the system's impact on the schedule, personnel resources, and costs

—The security and back-up requirements for the system should also be specified

—Conversion needs and problems should also be specified

—A program abstract (see Figure 8.6) for each program in the system. For an existing program, the form will actually record only its current description. However, for a proposed program it will be a generalization of what is desired. Subsequently, this information must be completed to reflect actual status of the program

—Any other constraints or requirements such as training needs, special installation arrangements, or compatibility with existing systems should be identified

Some of the information included may have to be modified or revised prior to or during the design and implementation of the system. However, at this point of the study this information serves to indicate "what" is, and "why" it is necessary. Subsequently it will be used to identify the relative advantages or disadvantages, or both, of the existing and proposed systems. Also, the information may be used to develop the necessary equipment requirements.

To increase the usefulness of this phase, the systems should be listed and identified as initial, new, or future development. Systems in the initial category are developed and implemented first because they are the simplest, or provide the fastest rate of return on investment, or are the ones most important to the organization. In the new category are those systems that may not have been previously developed and implemented due to cost, marginal benefit, lack of resources, or the lack of readiness or inability of the user organization to effectively utilize the outputs. Future systems are those desired or needed, but not currently as important, or are dependent upon the development and implementation of another system.

Due to a lack of necessary expertise, time, or adequate staff, it may be most beneficial to utilize a consultant for this phase of the feasibility study. For an organization initially entering into automated information processing or substantially enlarging that capability, it may be very beneficial to utilize an outside source for this phase. This may help to ensure that only cost justified systems are recommended.

Determination of the Proposed Costs

Upon completion of phase three, the analyst must define the new, reduced, increased, or eliminated costs under the proposed alternative. This may be difficult, because the analyst may not have access to all of the necessary cost data. Costs for such items as site preparation, special equipment, transportation charges, or hardware may not be immediately

PROGRAM ABSTRACT	APPLICATION NO.	EFFECTIVE DATE ___/___/___	PAGE ___ of ___

PROGRAM NAME	PROGRAM NO.

PROGRAM DESCRIPTION

RELATED PROGRAMS

CONFIGURATION REQUIRED	SPECIAL FEATURES UTILIZED
LANGUAGE(S)	STORAGE REQUIREMENTS (PRI. & AUX.)
INPUT DESCRIPTION	OUTPUT DESCRIPTION

PROGRAMMER	APPROVED BY	APPROVAL DATE

Figure 8.6. Program Abstract

498

available. However, it is possible to obtain a fairly accurate and detailed cost analysis through the following methods:

—By visiting the facilities of other organizations, particularly those with similar systems, problems, or hardware; information can be gained through discussions with the user, operations and executive committee personnel

—By conducting preliminary discussions with representatives of various equipment and software vendors.

—By attending demonstrations sponsored by the equipment and software vendors

—By visiting the public or organization library and researching handbooks prepared by one of the published data processing services, such as Auerbach Info, Inc.

—By conducting preliminary discussions with a consulting construction engineer or contractor.

The costs in this phase of the feasibility study may be classified as (1) Pre-installation costs or (2) Continuing costs.

1. PRE-INSTALLATION COSTS. Those costs incurred prior to the implementation of a system or application, or installation of hardware are included in this category. Sometimes these costs are called conversion, start-up, one-time costs, or initialization expenses. The last term is rather new and many people mistakenly tend to apply it to program development. The major costs in this category are:

a) Site preparation
b) Special equipment
c) Transportation charges
d) Personnel
e) Training
f) Travel
g) Program, file, and data conversion
h) Initial supplies
i) Equipment installation

a) *Site Preparation.* These costs are concerned with readying a facility, or modifying an existing site. Included are such items as electrical power supply and all wiring; air conditioning and humidity control; sound conditioning; painting; carpeting; draperies; false flooring; environmental security provisions; fire, water, and smoke detection and control; and emergency lighting.

b) *Special Equipment.* This category includes any special equipment needed to support the data processing equipment. Included are such items as electrical power generators and voltage regulators.

c) *Transportation Charges.* The cost of delivering equipment to a site must also be listed. Included are any insurance expenses involved in transporting the equipment to the site.

d) *Personnel.* These costs are incurred as a result of employing additional and temporary personnel for systems analysis and development, programming, operations, and training. A significant cost is recruitment and selection—an expensive process (see Chapter 3). In addition, the cost of conducting the feasibility study should be included in this segment.

e) *Training.* This can be a major cost item if a massive systems and programming effort is underway, or if a totally new information processing concept is being introduced into the organization. Included may be the cost of a training instructor. However, some organizations prefer to include this expense under the personnel cost category.

If training is not provided on-site this cost category should include the fees, lodging expenses, and personnel transportation costs.

f) *Travel.* This category includes costs incurred in traveling to system- and program-testing sessions, hardware or software demonstrations, or visits to other installations. If specific accountability of all costs is required, it may be necessary to include travel costs for off-site training sessions.

g) *Program, File, and Data Conversion.* This segment includes costs incurred in converting or modifying the existing programs, and the data and files from one medium to another. An organization may utilize software vendors, a service bureau, or another data processing facility to perform the conversions and modifications. Extensive coding and translation of files may also be necessary, which may require the employment of some temporary clerical personnel and key-driven machine operators.

In addition to the machine and personnel requirements, control procedures must be developed and tested to ensure conversion accuracy. This includes input audit programs to check the data elements and record formats. The control costs must be included in this cost category.

The costs of parallel or dual operations should also be included. The overlapping of operations may result in additional equipment, personnel, and supplies costs for the required period of time. In converting to online, or online real-time systems, this item could represent a substantial expenditure.

h) *Initial Supplies.* This category includes the purchase of furniture, magnetic tapes, magnetic disks, storage cabinets, punch cards, and forms supplies, and other materials necessary to effect implementation of a system or installation of hardware.

i) Equipment Installation. These are costs that may be incurred in the installation of equipment. Included are such items as utilizing a crane to lift a computer or vault to an upper building location and the removal of windows to facilitate entry of the hardware. This cost category is often overlooked in the determination of proposed costs.

2. CONTINUING COSTS. Continuing costs are often called recurring or supporting costs because they represent a repetitive expenditure of funds to maintain utility and operation of the system, application, or hardware. The costs may be classified as:

a) Equipment costs
b) Equipment maintenance
c) Personnel
d) Supplies
e) Utilities
f) Space
g) Insurance
h) Transportation

a) Equipment Costs. This category includes the expenses incurred in acquiring and utilizing the unit-record, computing, online and offline peripheral, and auxiliary equipment. These costs may have to be identified and listed by projected installation dates. For example, on a long-term project certain pieces of hardware are initially installed. Subsequently, additional components or devices are added as the necessary systems or programs are ready. Therefore, only the actual equipment cost for each phase of the project should be shown.

b) Equipment Maintenance. This cost item includes the service charges for preventative and emergency maintenance performed on the information processing and special equipment used to support the operations function. The costs in this category are the fixed annual contract prices negotiated to provide maintenance for leased and purchased equipment.

c) Personnel. These are the salary and fringe benefit costs for the managers, systems analysts, programmers, and operations personnel required to provide continued support for the systems and hardware. Where personnel outside of the data processing function are required to support a system, they too should be included in this expense category. For example, a data entry clerk may be employed by a hospital in each ward or floor wing to insure greater input accuracy at a data entry terminal. Though this clerk assists the medical personnel, her primary function is to ensure accurate record-keeping. Her salary and fringe benefits must be included as a system cost.

d) Supplies. The supplies in this category are those required to maintain the operating efficiency of a system or hardware. They include such items as printer forms, punch cards, magnetic tape, magnetic disks, microfilm, and magnetic cards. The supply needs may be calculated from the input, output, and reference data volumes shown in the study.

e) Utilities. When the utility expenses can be identified, these should be included to present a more realistic cost-benefit picture. The cost of telephone, telegraph, coaxial cable, leased wire, microwave, or satellite service in a data communications or time-sharing system should be included in this category.

f) Space. The determination of a floor or area space cost may be more relevant to the installation of hardware than a system. However, if the implementation of a system requires the specific allocation or acquisition of space, this cost should be reflected here.

When an organization establishes off-site record storage facilities on a lease or rental basis, the cost should be included in this category. If a facility is specially constructed or acquired for that function, the cost may be shown as a one-time cost under site preparation or a more specific category.

g) Insurance. The expenses incurred to provide such insurance protection as fidelity bonds, and equipment or records policies, must be included in this segment. However, it should not include equipment transportation insurance.

h) Transportation. Transportation expenditures may result from the implementation of a system or installation of hardware. Expenses may be incurred for such essential activities as transporting records and documentation to an off-site storage area; transporting inputs and outputs to and from a processing center such as a service bureau; transporting personnel, inputs, outputs, and supplies to and from an off-premises processing facility; to expedite the disposition of outputs and reports to a user; or to expedite inputs for processing.

Advantages and Disadvantages

At this point, the analyst must objectively identify the relative advantages and/or disadvantages of the present approach and those expected from the proposed approach. He should detail specifically how the advantages provide for an effective goal-attainment process. The impact of the disadvantages must also be made clear.

The following represents an extract from the advantages listed in an actual feasibility study:

The proposed Production Control system will improve the competitive position of the organization by:

Reducing clerical effort.

Reducing the number and frequency of errors generated by manual processing.

Significantly reducing the work force.

Maintaining a realistic economic inventory level.

Increasing stock status reliability.

Effecting more efficient manufacturing operations.

Enabling management to obtain reports on a regular and timely basis.

The advantages listed imply a great many accomplishments. However, they do not specify how these advantages will contribute to the more effective accomplishment of the production control objectives. For example, it fails to indicate how more efficient manufacturing operations will occur. In this particular organization, more efficient and economical operations may result from reducing the number of machine setups which will ultimately reduce scrap losses. Improved stock status reliability and economical ordering depend on computerized determination of raw material requirements, automated preparation of purchase requisitions, and more frequent updating of inventory records.

The study listed no advantages for the present system and no disadvantages for the proposed. The following, however, were listed as disadvantages of the existing system:

"A large clerical work force is required.

Sophisticated inventory control methods are lacking.

System is a production reporting system."

The disadvantages do not include any specifics to identify the problems. The large clerical work force is the result of the system's excessive paper handling requirements. The statement regarding the lack of sophistication in inventory control is unclear. The present system utilizes economical ordering (EOQ) models in the inventory control procedures except for a bill of materials explosion. This, however, is due to the lack of a larger computing configuration.

The comparative advantages of a proposed system must adequately justify the application of new or additional resources. The benefits must significantly exceed the costs involved. The actual commitment of resources is a decision by the executive committee. However, the information processing specialists will be responsible for identifying the impact on the organization; applications or systems suitable for immediate or future development; optimal equipment; adequacy of available resources; expected economies; and probable procedures.

Report of Findings and Recommendations

Basically, the report is a written proposal, based on conclusions reached by the study participants. This proposal should be clear and accurate so that the executive committee can effectively evaluate current and future operations and objectives. The final report should be factual, concise, and direct, including adequate supporting documentation. It should emphasize the strengths and weaknesses of the proposed system or approach to allow adequate consideration by the executive committee. The report should also include the signatures of those persons who conducted the feasibility study, together with a comment that the group has been impartial.

The report should contain the following information:
1. Definition of task
2. Objectives
3. Summary of current system
4. Description of proposed system
5. Estimated work load
6. Equipment configuration and specifications
7. Costs and benefits
8. Personnel
9. Timetable
10. Summary of findings

1. DEFINITION OF TASK. This is a broad narrative description of the task. It is a general statement indicating the extent of the study, the approach, and the functional activities affected. The following for example, represents an extract from a feasibility study:

"The purpose of this study was to analyze the existing Billing and Collection system; correct the associated problems; and evaluate the need for electronic data processing support. The first step involved an in-depth analysis of the system, its associated functions, tasks, and methods. The collected information was analyzed to locate the problem areas. Subsequently the problems were identified as to their nature and effect on the total system. The use of electronic data processing was also evaluated as an alternative approach.

Affected by the study were the Bookkeeping, Billing, Credit, Legal, and Audit Departments."

2. OBJECTIVES. A description of the general scope and specific objectives of the feasibility study should follow the introduction. This identifies the basis from which the study was initiated and the direction of development for a proposed system or approach. The definition of the objectives should agree to that originally stated by executive committee. To facilitate understanding, the general and specific objectives are listed separately.

3. SUMMARY OF CURRENT SYSTEM. A summary of the current system or approach and its objectives is also necessary. A critical evaluation of the existing system or approach may reveal that it is no longer responsive to the user's current or projected needs. The specific deficiencies and their impact on the organization must be identified. This information will enable the analyst to recommend a modification of objectives and/or the system, or a total redesign of the existing system or approach. The recommendation for redesign or modification of the system or approach does not necessarily require an automated technique. This information can be used by the executive committee to determine whether an alternate approach will improve or correct a condition with limited or no expenditure of funds required for new equipment or systems design.

4. DESCRIPTION OF PROPOSED SYSTEM. Also to be included is a detailed description of the proposed system or approach indicating how it will correct or supplant present or future deficiencies. The description should indicate what would be done, when would it be done, who would do the work, how would the work be done, where would it be done, and why would it be done. This detail is necessary to provide the executive committee with an understanding of the proposal. Also, the details are necessary for the complete development of a system when project approval is granted by the executive committee.

The description should be fully documented (see Chapter 4). These documents may subsequently be used for determination of equipment specifications.

5. ESTIMATED WORK LOAD. An estimate of the work load for each system, application, or approach must be included. The estimates should include proposed man-hour and schedule requirements and volume data.

6. EQUIPMENT CONFIGURATION AND SPECIFICATIONS. A description of the equipment configuration and specifications required should also be included. However, unless an equipment vendor or consultant has been involved in the feasibility study, this segment may be a very rough generalization. The proposed configuration is determined on the basis of input and output types, storage requirements, processing sequences, and work load volume. A processing estimate may be made for each system by utilizing estimated computer speeds. Rerun, handling, and setup time must also be added to the processing time estimates.

Generally these time estimates tend to underestimate the actual requirements because of inadequate speed formulae and incomplete system development. However, the estimates provide fairly accurate data on operation's personnel requirements, equipment costs, projected total work load, and adequacy of the proposed equipment configuration.

7. COSTS AND BENEFITS. A comparative cost-benefit chart of the present and proposed system is an essential element of the final report. The chart should identify the current costs; those to be eliminated, reduced, or increased; and new costs generated by the proposed system. The chart should include the costs and benefits of the data processing activity, and that of the function affected by the system.

The chart should show specifics, not broad statements. The dollar value attributed to the costs must be reasonable and valid. The same rule should apply to the benefits indicated. There generally is no problem with tangible benefits because a dollar value may be attributed to them. Often the tangible benefits are subdefined into direct and indirect benefits. The former represent the savings derived from such items as the elimination of manpower, reduction of equipment costs, or a decrease in supplies expenses. The indirect benefits are generally more difficult to identify. However, diverting the use of office or warehouse space, or furniture, for other needs may be described as an indirect benefit.

The intangible benefits are those that should be subjected to the most scrutiny. The benefits are often listed in the cost-benefit charts as improvements in the management of a function or organization. However, the listings make no attempt to apply a quantitative value to these improvements or an estimated probability of attainment. This lack of quantification is unrealistic because the intangible benefits have some effect upon the organization. For example, it is frequently stated that increased costs will be avoided through the installation of information processing equipment. This statement is much too broad and has very little merit. The analyst must identify what costs would increase and the value of the cost avoidance.

After evaluating the comparative data, the executive committee should be able to determine if the benefits to be derived outweigh the costs and disadvantages.

8. PERSONNEL. The personnel segment of the final report is often very closely scrutinized by the executive committee. Primarily the group is concerned with the impact of the proposal upon the organization. The executive committee will be concerned with knowing:

—If there are any proposed changes to the basic organization structure

—If the changes require a realignment of functional responsibilities

—If there will be any displacement of personnel

—If the displaced personnel can be retrained and/or reassigned to other positions

—If additional information processing specialists must be recruited

—If additional training must be provided for the existing information processing and user personnel

—If the user is willing and ready to interact in the system or approach

With this information, the executive committee will be able to determine what plans or actions are necessary to minimize any adverse reactions and to ensure the success of the proposal.

A summary of the personnel requirements under the proposed system or approach and brief job descriptions should be included. Salary structures for each position, and recruitment, selection, and training costs should also be indicated in order to facilitate cost analyses.

9. TIMETABLE. A proposed timetable indicating when a system, application, or approach will be operational should be enclosed. This schedule should indicate the approximate dates for complete development of a system, application, or approach; installation of equipment; and implementation of the proposal. The schedule should be graphically

illustrated by utilizing a GANTT chart, PERT network, or a listing of tasks and events. In addition, the time requirements for file and data conversion, parallel operations, and site preparation should be included.

10. SUMMARY OF FINDINGS. The summary represents the recommendations to the executive committee by the study participants. It should represent the best method for accomplishing a desired objective, not just an alternative merely for the sake of change.

In preparing this segment, the analyst should determine if the proposal does in fact meet the four tests of feasibility. He should also gauge whether the proposal will be able to effectively accomplish a given goal.

The feasibility or justification study is an in-depth analysis and evaluation of an existing or proposed approach. The data is collected through interviews, observations, and study of existing documentation, policies, and practices. The data collected will provide information on the scope and objectives of the approach, performance requirements, the internal and external influences, constraints, required interfaces, and current method. When the information has been assembled the study participants must evaluate it to identify and locate any operational problems. Subsequently the study participants must determine if it will be necessary to develop and evaluate an alternative concept. In the process they will also develop comparative cost and benefit data. Ultimately, the study participants will make recommendations to the executive committee for the committee's evaluation and approval. The recommendations do not contain the detailed design or implementation procedures. After approval is granted, the detailed development, design, and implementation of the approved concept must be performed.

Review Questions: Group 8B

1. Define the term "feasibility study."
2. Name and describe the four tests of feasibility.
3. Why must feasibility-study participants be creative and objective thinkers?
4. Why is the study of the present system such an important part of the feasibility study?
5. It is frequently argued that intangible benefits should not be in the cost-benefit charts. Do you agree or disagree with this attitude? Why?
6. How much detail should be included in a feasibility study which is

recommending the development and implementation of a new system?

7. What information should the final report of a feasibility study contain?

EXECUTIVE DECISION AND RECOMMENDATION DEVELOPMENT

Executive Committee Decision

When the feasibility study has been completed and presented to the executive committee, a decision must be made by the committee to accept, modify, or reject the recommendations. Despite the recommendations made, the ultimate decision must be made by the executive committee. It is only this group that can direct the allocation and application of resources based on need and priorities. Very little justification exists for applying new or additional resources to a system or approach that is functioning satisfactorily, unless a significant cost-benefit advantage can be achieved.

The decision may be based on the following considerations:

1. Equipment utilization
2. Expansion potential
3. Personnel requirements
4. Systems or applications
5. Overall cost or benefit

1. EQUIPMENT UTILIZATION. If hardware is recommended, the two prime considerations are need and capacity. A critical evaluation of equipment need must be made by the executive committee. They must determine why the equipment is necessary, and if such an acquisition is in the best interests of the organization.

Where there is no prior experience with equipment the evaluation will be more difficult. The committee must determine if the functions to be automated require the size, type, and cost of equipment proposed. A careful analysis of the proposed information processing systems must be made.

Where additional equipment acquisition or replacement is recommended, the evaluation may be somewhat less difficult but no less important. The committee must determine if the proposal is due to the presence of "fill jobs." Very often these filler systems are not cost or benefit justified, or they have not been approved by the executive committee. The fill jobs tend to find their way to the hardware because of the pressure to show high equipment utilization and justify the budget. Also, systems with marginal cost or benefit justification are automated because the information processing personnel are interested in cultivating new users. They regard these as minor investments with the optimistic view that they will get the big jobs later. However, these fill jobs may also consume productive time in the operating schedule. Consequently they inhibit implementation of more important systems due to a lack of available machine time.

The proposed size, type, and capacity must also be carefully scrutinized to determine if this hardware will adequately support the needs of the organization. The judgment may be difficult to make because the proposed configuration is subject to change. However, the preliminary design information included in the feasibility study will provide a reasonable approximation of basic hardware needs.

The committee should question the adequacy of storage and processing capacity. These items may affect the data handling, and output capability of the hardware. Very often, study participants will recommend unrealistically smaller or less powerful equipment to gain approval. This argument represents very often short-sighted thinking, in that subsequent upgrading to a more desirable level may generate unnecessary costs and problems. For example, in an organization viewed by this author, the study participants recommended a card-oriented computer rather than the tape-oriented configuration that was both necessary and justified. Consequently, all of the information processing systems were less effective than desired because of the resultant lack of storage and processing capability. After two years of ineffective operation, the organization added the tape processing capability to their existing configuration. Virtually all of the programs had to be rewritten to take advantage of the tape concepts. If the tape-oriented computer had been recommended and approved initially, expenditures for programming, system design, documentation, training, etc., could have been minimized.

2. EXPANSION POTENTIAL. The executive committee must resolve whether the new system or approach will adequately meet present and future needs. This is not a simple task. The system or approach selected must provide for growth in the organization of tomorrow. This growth may be the result of organizational expansion, or increases in the ser-

vices or product lines offered. The most direct and immediate impact of such an occurrence may be an increase in the volume of work. The organization's growth may also require the development of additional subsystems, or more sophistication in the systems and hardware currently used. The executive committee is in the best position to determine flexibility needs because they have an overall view of the organization, its needs and objectives.

If a proposed solution is found to have limited expansion potential then the executive committee must determine its durability. How long will the proposed concept support the needs of an organization? If the value justifies the cost of implementation an interim system or approach may be acceptable. The same critical evaluation must be applied when appraising a proposed hardware configuration. How long will it support the needs of the organization? The same critical evaluation must be applied when appraising proposed hardware.

3. PERSONNEL REQUIREMENTS. The personnel requirements for the proposed alternative must also be analyzed. The analysis must consider the cost-benefit factors, and impact upon the organization. Both of these considerations are interrelated. Any changes to the organization will affect the cost-benefit picture. The costs may result from structural changes to the organization, realignment of responsibilities, recruitment and selection, training and retraining, and displacement of personnel. The impact of these changes may be very pronounced upon an organization. Displacement and/or reassignment of personnel, for example, are potential problems. Therefore, the executive committee must consider what measures are necessary to minimize or limit the negative or adverse effects of any changes.

The staffing requirements may change as a result of the completed design. However, the executive committee cannot afford to wait until such time before considering or developing plans to anticipate any contingencies which may arise.

Very often, only the cost-benefit picture is evaluated. What is more, this evaluation is limited to the ratio's effect on the data processing activity. However, this is but one part of the report and it fails to provide a complete cost-benefit or impact analysis.

4. SYSTEMS OR APPLICATIONS. The executive group must carefully study the system, application, or approach involved. Initially, the evaluation is concerned with a study of the system documentation or approach narrative. This documentation will indicate such data as:

—A layman's description of the system or approach

—Identification of the inputs, outputs, their sources and destinations

—Identification of the management control, software, and equipment requirements

The flowchart should also be analyzed to evaluate the work flow, media utilized, processing activity, and control points. The graphics will provide for a faster understanding of the proposal. This understanding is reinforced by the abstracts.

Where a number of systems or approaches are involved, the executive committee must evaluate the proposed items. Are those which affect current, immediate, and future needs included? Are the proposals properly classified? Which are most urgent? Which have been problems in the past?

The information on the system or approach should be used to help evaluate the proposed equipment and the expansion potential.

5. OVERALL COST OR BENEFIT. All of the factors previously discussed affect the overall cost-benefit evaluation. The executive committee must determine if a satisfactory cost-benefit relationship will result from adoption of a recommended proposal. The costs associated with the system or approach must not exceed the benefits to be derived. The benefits in most instances are actually negative costs—reductions in hardware rentals, personnel salaries, and supplies. In most organizations, the emphasis is on tangible or actual costs and savings. This is not an unrealistic position. Too frequently, new systems are developed or hardware acquired on the basis of intangible savings—savings or benefits that, for the most part, are generalizations but not quantified. The costs and benefits must be quantified in order to facilitate effective decision-making. However, the values attributed to these factors must be valid and reasonable. The costs of the feasibility study, and those of the design, development, and implementation of the approach or system, must be offset by the benefits or annual savings. The executive committee needs to determine if the cost of the proposal can be absorbed from operating revenues within a reasonable period of time. The committee will not be willing to dip into the capital surplus to support a proposal.

Following an analysis of the feasibility study, the executive committee must either reject, modify, or approve the proposal. If it votes for rejection, then either the project is terminated only to be discarded or held in abeyance for subsequent approval. Should the committee elect to modify the proposal, then parts of it may not be accepted or the committee will recommend a different timetable and implementation approach; this will frequently happen when a proposal involves a massive system, such as a management information system. The modifications may be required because the proposal does not blend with the long-term objectives; new performance requirements or constraints are introduced; or limited monetary resources are available. To facilitate development and implementation the modified proposal may be divided into phases.

If the proposal is approved, then the planning for development and implementation of the system, or approach must be initiated. If hardware acquisition is part of the approved proposal, the development of equipment specifications for the vendors must then be undertaken. Ultimately, the vendor proposals must be investigated by the systems personnel and/or advanced planning and development personnel before a contract for equipment acquisition is executed.

Developing the Approved Recommendation

Following the recommendations of the executive committee, the requirements of their proposal must be finalized. The finalization of requirements is not to be misconstrued as an applications analysis. The form of the new system or approach has already been determined during the third phase of the feasibility study—development of an alternative approach. During that phase the required goals, functions, performance requirements, constraints, interfaces, processing modes, and input-outputs for a new system or modified approach had been determined. The development and evaluation of an alternative concept must be accomplished at that time in order to prepare a realistic cost-benefit picture for the executive committee. After the proposal has been approved these design requirements are briefly verified before any final design is initiated. This process is often described as completion of system analysis or completion of system requirements. The verification step or process is necessary because of the length of time required to conduct a feasibility study and secure a decision from the executive committee. During this time lag, changes may occur within the environment that may impose new requirements or constraints upon the proposed system or approach.

The verification also enables the analyst to secure a sign-off on the project requirements for a functional activity. The sign-off is necessary to ensure that the requirements remain static and not fluid. Too frequently, project schedules are overrun because the requirements remain in a constant state of flux. The verification process also helps to maintain a channel of communications between the information processing personnel and functional activity. Very often after interviews are completed, the functional activity is unaware of the status of the project until system testing or conversion is initiated.

After the final requirements have been established, the project development and implementation schedule will also be finalized. This schedule will facilitate the completion of the design specifications; establishment of the user procedures; development of conversion procedures; preparation of vendor specifications; preparation of the necessary computer programs; training of personnel; system testing; data and file conversion; parallel testing; and project implementation.

(Implementation planning and preparation, plus the preparation of vendor specifications, are discussed in Chapter 9. Additional data on systems, programming, and training tasks; time requirements; and documentation is given in Chapters 3, 4, 5, 6, and 7. Site planning is covered in Chapter 5.)

Review Questions: Group 8C

1. What factors are utilized by the executive committee to evaluate a final report and feasibility study?
2. Why must special consideration be given to the personnel impact on the organization?
3. What is the value of providing documented data for the executive committee concerning a proposed system?
4. Why must the final requirements be determined before detailed design planning is initiated?
5. What is the effect of the final requirements on the implementation schedule developed earlier in the feasibility study?

SUMMARY

This chapter has been devoted to suggesting how an organization should determine whether, to what extent, and how or how not to utilize a proposed system, application, hardware device, idea, or standard. There are many considerations that must be resolved before any decision is made. Therefore, a uniform method for investigation and documentation of each proposal should be followed.

The survey described in this chapter is not synonymous with the feasibility study. The survey is an updated document intended to provide preliminary information about the organization and its setting. It is the source of background information for fact-gathering interviews conducted during a feasibility study and systems analysis. This data enables the analyst to better understand the functional activity affected and to develop the topics or questions for the interviews.

A feasibility study is a logical, systematic, and well-documented approach to solving a problem or analyzing a proposal. Properly executed, it becomes a critical examination for determining an organization's needs, and the cost-benefit relationships of existing and proposed approaches.

The feasibility study begins with an analysis of what is currently being done. This indicates what type of information is being processed; where it comes from; where it goes; who uses it; why the processing is done; and how the information is processed. This process is then evaluated to determine its responsiveness to current and future needs, and objectives. If any deficiencies are found, these must be identified and evaluated to determine if a correction or new design must be developed and implemented.

If an alternative approach is necessary, it should be detailed for proper review and development. The detailed documentation should include flowcharts, abstracts, record layouts, and work-load statistics.

The analysis needs to include a cost-benefit comparison. It must be determined if the benefits to be derived from the proposal surpass the costs involved. Ultimately, the advantages and/or disadvantages of the present and proposed systems have to be objectively identified. The advantages of the proposed system must indicate how they will improve the present goal-attainment process.

The culmination of the study is a recommendation to the executive committee. This group then evaluates how well the proposal suits the needs and objectives of the organization. The committee's task will then be to approve, reject, or modify the recommendation. Approval will mean the preparation of equipment specifications and/or the development and implementation of the completed design.

CASE STUDIES

Case Study 8.1: The Blalock-Watson Wood Products Corporation

The following is a feasibility study conducted by the senior systems analyst for the Blalock-Watson Wood Products, Corporation.

STUDY

I   Introduction

The purpose of this feasibility study was to:
1. Review the existing punched card equipment operations.
2. Determine the economic justification of acquiring a computer to:
    a) Increase the productive capability of data processing
    b) Increase scheduling flexibility
    c) Replace the existing punched card equipment
    d) Provide additional computer capability
    e) Implement additional applications

II   Current Status

At present the organization is utilizing two IBM 1401 computers for 16 hours each day. For two Saturdays each month the computer is scheduled for a 16-hour operation. During the peak periods the computers are utilized approximately 24 hours per day.

The punched card operations are primarily used for input conversion, validation, and balancing. However, due to special requirements for an early closing of the books, approximately 8 hours of overtime is required for processing of accounting reports each month.

III   Findings

The acquisition of a computer is economically justified.

IV   Final Report

The following punched card equipment can be released:

Two 407 Accounting Machines

Two 514 Reproducers

One 083 Sorter

One 077 Collator

It is recommended that the computer be purchased and amortized over a seven-year period. It is estimated that a 10% salvage value will be available at the end of that period. The purchase price of the system is $465,000. The average annual cost is $75,000.

Other economies include the following:

Released Punched Card Equipment	$35,750
Overtime Salaries	5,850
Reduction of 1 Equipment Operator	10,800
Total Direct	$52,400

Indirect economies may include the following:

Reduction of 1 Equipment Operator	$12,500
Reduction of 1 Accounting Clerk	8,500
Reduction of 1 Billing Clerk	8,500
Total Indirect	$29,500

These costs and benefits may be summarized as follows:

Direct and Indirect Economies	$81,900
Cost of Computer	− 75,000
Net Annual savings	6,900

Discussion Questions

1. What are the general and specific objectives of the study?
2. What are the advantages of the current system?
3. What are the disadvantages of the current system?
4. How effective is the cost-benefit data included in the study?
5. What is the impact of the proposed system on the organization?
6. What information was included about potential applications?
7. What is the estimated work load for the new hardware?
8. If you were a member of the executive committee, how would you evaluate the final report section?
9. Is the information included in the findings section supported by the data included in the final report section?
10. How would the executive committee evaluate the contents of the feasibility study?
11. Could this feasibility study be improved upon? If so, how? If not, why not?

Case Study 8.2: Raleric Wire Products

The following is a feasibility study conducted for the company by a project team composed of an information processing specialist, a member of the production control department, and a senior merchandise control specialist.

PROPOSAL FOR DEVELOPMENT OF A COMPUTERIZED PRODUCTION AND MERCHANDISE CONTROL SYSTEM

1. Introduction

We believe that progress, which resulted in computers, is a direct result of computer utilization.

We believe that the vast amount of potential savings available can be tapped only through computer utilization.

We have developed our feasibility study based on two applications interacting as one system.

2. Current System

The present system was developed and implemented early in 1962. It utilizes a large clerical work force to handle the clerical needs of the system. To meet the customer requirements, a four-week inventory is maintained. This approach is not very economical.

The current production control system produces weekly reports to indicate the outputs for the current week. However, the cutoff for inputs into the system is Friday A.M. Therefore, there is a slight time lag in reporting actual weekly productive status.

3. Management Information System

Our concept is to be designed as a management information system. This simply means that all information related to the system is contained in the computer for service inquiries and operating decisions. All orders, changes, etc., become inputs to the computer for editing and analysis.

If no errors or exceptions are found, the computer will check the stock levels for the requested item. If available, a select and pack document will be issued. If the item is out of stock, a production request will be issued. When the order is selected and shipped, the information is fed back into the computer. If no shipping notification is received, an exception report is issued.

The information is then available for a variety of analysis reports.

4. Savings

We have estimated the following annual savings to offset the cost of development and to pay for future operation of the system.

Personnel Reduction	$195,000
Office Supplies Reduction	1,500
Scrap Loss Reduction	100,000
Reduction of Inventory Charges	8,000
	$304,500

5. Analysis of Costs and Savings

Data Processing Operating Costs

Present	$213,700
Proposed	− 315,000
Additional Costs	$101,300

Estimated Savings New System

Estimated Savings	$304,500
Less Additional Operating Costs	− 101,300
Estimated Annual Savings	$203,200

6. Proposed Future Applications

The following represent applications to be developed upon completion of the proposed system:

General Ledger
Movement of Personnel
Quality Control Statistics
Industrial Engineering Layouts

7. Implementation Timetable

We anticipate that the system would be operational two years from initiation of the project.

8. Recommendations

—That the proposed system be approved in its entirety. We do *not* recommend partial development because of potential planning, programming, and coordination problems.

—That a computer be placed on order immediately to ensure delivery.

Discussion Questions

1. What are the objectives of the proposed system?
2. What are the advantages and disadvantages of the present system?
3. What information is available about the proposed application? Is it complete or incomplete? If incomplete, what else is necessary?

4. How effective is the comparative cost analysis in sections four and five?
5. What is the impact of the proposed system on the organization?
6. What is the effect of the proposed future applications on the production and merchandise control system, and on the organization?
7. What is the estimated equipment utilization?
8. In your opinion, how will the executive committee evaluate this study?
9. On the basis of this study, would you recommend approval of the project? Why or why not?
10. Could this feasibility study be improved upon? If so, how? If not, why not?

9

Vendor Specifications, Proposals, and Implementation

INTRODUCTION

Following approval of the feasibility study recommendations, the executive committee must determine the best source of acquisition, supply, or development. This is not a simple task. For example, there are at least two dozen manufacturers of data processing computing equipment that produce hardware suitable for most organizations Each manufacturer offers a variety of models, and each model has a variety of units. The problem may be even more complex when an organization has to choose the source of supply for a desired data processing service. Consequently, the number of interacting variables and suppliers may increase significantly.

The complexity of the selection process requires that the customer, *not* the vendor or manufacturer, establish the basis of comparison. The basis of comparison is written specifications submitted to the vendors and manufacturers by the organization.

SELECTING VENDORS

Prior to solicitation of proposals the manager must make certain that equal opportunity and appropriate consideration is given to all qualified vendors and manufacturers. It is not in an organization's best interest to

521

forego the solicitation of proposals. Frequently, a manager will favor a certain vendor or manufacturer because of personal friendship or because of possible personal gain, previous business exposure, lack of personal expertise, or a belief in the vendor's or manufacturer's technical ability. Consequently, the manager will never know whether the feasibility study recommendations can be achieved more economically or efficiently, or both.

The selection process begins with the manager evaluating the prospective firms from whom he expects to solicit a proposal. The manager must select out those firms which will be unable to submit a realistic proposal. In addition to identifying the qualified firms, the evaluation process helps to indicate the "most qualified." Selecting the most qualified firms will limit the number of responses and ensure a more realistic analysis of each. The limitation will also make the appraisal process more manageable, expedite the results, and reduce its costs.

The criteria for selection of the most qualified firms are as follows:
1. Type of organization
2. Financial position
3. Experience
4. Personnel proposed
5. Current contracts

1. TYPE OF ORGANIZATION. A manager must be concerned with the stability of the vendor or manufacturer. An organization cannot afford to execute a contract with a firm which will be unable to meet its commitments. In his evaluation, the manager must determine how long a firm has been in business, the number of its employees, and its experience.

It must be noted that though a firm may be relatively new or small, its capabilities may be strong and effective.

2. FINANCIAL POSITION. The financial stability of an organization is very important. If the firm is in a questionnable financial position, it may be unable to complete a contract. Some customers have had to help contracting firms remain solvent in order to complete a project.

Financial data may be secured from annual reports, banks, credit bureaus, and rating organizations such as Dun & Bradstreet.

3. EXPERIENCE. The manager must determine if a potential contractor has had previous experience in developing or implementing a particular project. The evaluation may help to identify the limitations and capabilities of a particular firm.

The firm's capabilities in a given project can be ascertained by verifying the references provided to the organization. When verifying the references, the data processing manager should contact the person for whom the contract was performed. This check will enable the manager to secure a description of the project; number of people involved; the approximate man-hours, man-months, or man-years required; and the starting and completion dates for the project.

4. PERSONNEL PROPOSED. This criterion may be used to identify the current limitations and capabilities of a firm. The vendor or manufacturer should provide résumés for the personnel to be involved in the project.

If a firm is new or has not performed on a particular project, the résumés may indicate if the personnel proposed have the necessary experience. These people may have performed on a related project while in the employ of another company. To verify these capabilities, the manager should consult previous employers.

5. CURRENT CONTRACTS. During the evaluation process, the manager should request a listing of the contractor's current clients. Armed with this information, a manager should attempt to assess a contractor's current performance and technical capabilities. The assessment is actually made by contacting the various client organizations and soliciting information—the same basic information given above in connection with the experience criterion. The responses will enable a manager to determine if the level of performance and capabilities have remained the same, improved, or regressed. The last situation may occur if a contractor has tried to grow too rapidly or has assumed too many commitments.

The current contracts evaluation offers a manager an excellent opportunity to appraise the abilities of a new organization.

Preliminary Evaluation of Vendors

The manager may evaluate the firms semiannually or annually in order to develop a selected but small "favored suppliers" listing. The listing is generally limited to about 10 or 12 firms in each contract type of category—that is, key punching, software, time-sharing, and so forth. This approach, however, may not be very advantageous because all of the firms on the listing may not be capable of responding to a particular set of specifications. Therefore, it may be more beneficial to retain a somewhat larger listing of firms in each category and then to reevaluate their technical competence prior to each project. To facilitate the reevaluation, the manager supplies the firms with an outline of the task to be performed. This information will enable the firms to respond more specifically to the manager's inquiry.

In either evaluation approach, the manager must ultimately submit the necessary specifications to the selected vendors or manufacturers. This often is referred to as the request for proposal, or RFP, process. The number of firms selected for solicitation will depend upon the manager. Many experts feel that from three to ten firms should be approached. Six has been the number cited by many as an optimal figure.

PREPARATION OF SPECIFICATIONS

The requests for proposal, or RFPs, must be standardized for each contract category to ensure uniform responses from the potential vendors or manufacturers. The formats for hardware, software, systems, or services will vary somewhat. However, each of these categories is very similar in the following informational areas:
1. General instructions
2. Customer requirements
3. Proposal presentation

General Instructions

The general instructions stipulate the ground rules to be followed in dealing with each and every prospective vendor or manufacturer. The guidelines must be used in order to provide equal opportunity and consideration to all contractors.
   a. General objectives
   b. Technical coordinator
   c. Timetables
   d. Benchmarks
   e. Method of submission
   f. Method of presentation
   g. Level of effort expected
   h. Required contractual provisions

i. Type of cost proposal desired

1. GENERAL OBJECTIVES. This is a brief statement specifying the desired general objectives of the proposal request. It may also contain a brief description of the task. However, the task will be detailed in the customer requirements segment of the RFP.

2. TECHNICAL COORDINATOR. The manager should select one person to whom all inquiries regarding the request are to be directed. This person shall be identified in this segment of the RFP.

Due to the complexity and scope of the task, the ground rules may stipulate that all questions must be submitted in writing and properly referenced to the request. Depending upon the nature of the inquiry and the response, copies may be submitted to all other potential contractors. Also, a final date for inquiries may be stipulated here or in the timetable.

3. TIMETABLES. The timetables indicate the dates and times of relevant actions in the request and selection process. This will include dates for briefings, closing date for inquiries, period for benchmark demonstrations, dates for submission of proposals, contractor presentation dates, award date, and desired implementation or installation date.

4. BENCHMARKS. Benchmarks are used to evaluate the ability of a system, software, service, or hardware to perform predefined tasks. When benchmark problems are chosen for evaluation they must be representative of the organization's needs. Generally they are used to validate any timings or results specified by the contractor. For example, when applied to equipment evaluation, they may measure and analyze the processing capability (e.g., logic, computation); timing needs (e.g., input/output, execution); or equipment requirements (e.g., memory, channels). The benchmark problem or problem mix, and sample or live data, will be submitted to the contractor through the technical coordinator.

The RFP may include a request that a presentation be made to demonstrate the capabilities of the hardware, system, software, or service. The timetable will indicate the allowable time period for such presentations. Also, a disclaimer should be included specifying that costs incurred in the preparation and presentation of benchmarks will be borne by the potential vendor or manufacturer.

A representative job mix can be established as a benchmark to evaluate the cost of processing using a time-sharing service. The output would provide the average processing cost per minute. The organization may choose to be more specific and establish separate problems for the business-oriented and scientific programs. The programs could be fur-

Section I

General Instructions

A. Purpose

The purpose of this RFP is to solicit proposals for the design and development of an automated Customer Billing and Collection System.

B. Project Coordinator

All inquiries concerning this RFP are to be directed to:

Ralph A. Szweda

Computer Systems Coordinator

All questions should be submitted in writing, referencing the specific paragraph.

C. Project Timetable

1. Availability of RFP	August 11, 1972
2. Contractors Briefing	August 25, 1972
3. Closing date for inquiries	October 11, 1972
4. Benchmark Presentations	October 2-10, 1972
5. Contractor Proposals Due	November 1, 1972
6. Contractor Presentations	November 6-10, 1972
7. Contract Award	November 22, 1972
8. Desired Installation Date	January 5, 1973

D. Presentations

Dates for benchmark presentations will be arranged with the Project Coordinator.

The bidders are encouraged to make an oral presentation to supplement the written proposal. The dates for such presentations must be arranged with the coordinator.

E. Method of Submission

The written proposal must be submitted in three bound copies to the Project Coordinator's office before 5 P.M. on November 1, 1972. All supporting graphics and documentation must be included with the proposal.

Figure 9.1. Sample Extract of Request for Proposal (RFP) General Instructions

ther subdivided into the input/output bound versus compute bound applications.

5. METHOD OF SUBMISSION. The method of submission specifies the number of proposal copies to be submitted and to whom they must be directed. Also, this segment indicates the final date and time for acceptance of proposals. It may also include the statement that no late proposals will be considered.

6. METHOD OF PRESENTATION. Potential contractors are generally invited to make oral presentations. This enables the vendor or manufacturer to point out the significant features of his proposal. Also, it provides the manager with an opportunity to raise any clarifying questions. Presentation dates are stipulated in the timetable.

7. LEVEL OF EFFORT EXPECTED. A brief statement of the level of effort expected can be included in the general instructions. The level can be expressed in terms of man-days, man-months, or dollar value.

8. REQUIRED CONTRACTUAL PROVISIONS. A brief statement of the required contractual provisions may be indicated in the general instructions. These should be elaborated upon in the proposed presentation segment. The general instructions may identify the type of provision, such as penalty clauses for late delivery or for non-delivery.

9. TYPE OF COST PROPOSAL DESIRED. The type of cost proposal desired should be stipulated in the general instructions to facilitate a contractor's proposed planning. This information may or may not be elaborated upon in the customer requirements segment. The general instructions should stipulate if the proposal should provide for time and expense, fixed price, lease, purchase, etc.

An extract of the general instructions that could be included in an RFP is illustrated in Figure 9.1.

Review Questions: Group 9A

1. Why should the data processing manager be concerned about the financial stability of a potential contractor?
2. What selection criteria would be most applicable to a newly organized software development firm?
3. Who must establish the basis of comparison for vendor proposals?
4. Why is it necessary to formalize the request for proposal?

5. Why should a technical coordinator be named for RFP data dissemination?

Customer Requirements

This section of the RFP provides a statement of the problem; description of the task; or equipment requirements. The actual requirements stipulated will vary depending upon the type of proposal solicited. For example, Figure 9.2 illustrates the relevant equipment specifications which may be included in this section of the request for proposal. These specifications are for the acquisition of a complete computer configuration. The specifications may not be as comprehensive for acquisition of individual units such as magnetic disk, data cell, or online terminals.

The requirements in this section of the RFP specify the mandatory and desirable features or characteristics in a proposal. The manager must be certain that what he establishes as a mandatory need is in fact a priority item. There is the danger that by imposing such limitations or constraints one minimizes the probability of soliciting a desired proposal. The vendor or manufacturer must provide for these limitations or constraints in his proposal in order to merit consideration. For example, an organization may stipulate the requirement for an ANSI COBOL capability. If an equipment vendor or manufacturer could not comply with this software requirement, he would be eliminated from the selection process. The imposition of a cost ceiling often inhibits vendors or manufacturers from submitting optimally effective proposals.

Desirable features or characteristics are limitations to a degree. The requirements in this category represent items which would simplify implementation and utilization of the system, software, service, or hardware. Failure by the vendor or manufacturer to include a response for a desirable item may or may not result in a penalty. None will result if the potential contractor is able to present an alternative which may better serve the needs of an organization.

The customer requirements section of the RFP may contain the following:
1. Statement of the task or problem
2. Technical requirements
3. Required cost proposal
4. Compatibility
5. Delivery
6. Customer assistance
7. Reliability

GENERAL

These specifications are divided into three parts:

I Equipment Specifications

II Software Specifications

III Customer Assistance Specifications

I. Equipment Specifications

All responses must be in writing. Supporting technical data and manuals should also be included.

A. *Basic Desired Configuration*
1. Central Processor: minimum memory size 16K.
2. Printer: 132 alpha/numeric print positions. Minimum printing speed 950 lines per minutes in alphabetic mode.
3. Card Reader: minimum input speed 800 cards per minute.
4. Card Punch: minimum output speed 250 cards per minute.
5. Magnetic Tape Drives: 4 drives are desired; minimum density 800 BPI, and a transfer rate of 60KC.

B. *Optional Equipment*
Furnish descriptions, technical and cost (rental, lease, purchase, maintenance) data for this equipment grouping. This equipment is desirable but not necessary to the basic configuration.
1. Console typewriter.
2. Additional memory units.
3. Random access units.
4. Teleprocessing devices.

C. *Advanced Programming Features*
Fully describe each available feature and its costs.

D. *Time-Sharing Features*
1. Describe the techniques available.
2. Equipment configuration required.
3. Cost data for each technique.
4. Response time for each technique.
5. Error detection and correction features.

E. *Cost Data*
1. Describe the rental, lease, or purchase cost for each unit.
2. Describe the billing method.
3. Specify the number of base hours on rental.

    4. Define shift.

    5. Define shift differential.

    6. Define overtime and charges.

    7. Describe any special allowances available.

F. *Equipment Maintenance Provisions*

    1. Cost to the user.

    2. Where are the maintenance personnel based?

    3. How many maintenance personnel will be supplied?

    4. If maintenance personnel are assigned on a full-time basis, where do they reside?

    5. What is the estimated downtime per unit for scheduled maintenance? On which shift is maintenance performed?

    6. Specify estimated downtime per unit for unscheduled maintenance.

    7. Specify the maximum elapsed time between request for maintenance service and arrival of maintenance personnel on both prime shifts and off-shifts.

    8. If the recommended equipment complement includes peripheral equipment not manufactured by the contractor, the recipient of the contract will be responsible for maintenance and performance.

    9. What credits are given for downtime?

G. *Expandability*

    1. Describe the necessary steps to be taken to install the equipment identified as "optional."

    2. What is the estimated downtime for installing each unit?

    3. What costs will be incurred for the installation of each unit?

    4. Will reprogramming be necessary?

H. *Site Engineering*

    1. Specify the necessary space, power, communications wiring, fire-protection, floor-loading, air-conditioning, and air-humidification requirements for each unit in the basic and optional equipment categories.

    2. What are the estimated costs for site preparation?

    3. What site engineering assistance will be provided by the manufacturer to plan for, and install, the equipment?

I. *Other Costs*
   1. Indicate and identify the personnel costs to be incurred.
   2. Indicate and identify the supplies costs to be incurred.
   3. Indicate and identify the projected conversion costs.
   4. Specify the required insurance coverage for the equipment configuration.
   5. Indicate the transportation and installation costs for the basic configuration.

J. *Emergency Back-Up*
   1. What effort will be made by the manufacturer to assist the organization in securing compatible equipment to meet such emergencies as fire, major equipment breakdown, floods, etc.?
   2. Specify the location where back-up equipment is available.
   3. What is the cost for the use of the equipment?
   4. What is the accessibility of the equipment?

K. *Controls*
   1. What error-detection features are available on the basic configuration?
   2. What error-correction features are available on the basic configuration?

L. *Installation and Delivery Dates*
   1. When can the basic configuration be made available?
   2. How many days prior to the installation date must the site be ready?
   3. How much time is required by the manufacturer to install the equipment?

II. Software Specifications

All responses must be in writing. Supporting technical data and manuals should be included. Include data only on the packages which are currently available and fully operative. The software must be delivered prior to hardware installation.

A. *Operating System*
   1. Describe its functional characteristics.
   2. What level of programming languages will it support?
   3. What input/output devices will it support?
   4. What library functions does it perform?

   5. What data management concepts can it support?
   6. What is the required primary storage overhead?
   7. What is the required system residence overhead?
   8. What special features are available?
   9. What is its cost?

B. *Programming Languages*
   1. What assemblers, compilers, generators, utility programs, and debugging routines are available?
   2. What are the functional characteristics of each package?
   3. What are the overhead requirements for each package?
   4. What are the costs? How are the charges determined?
   5. What data management capabilities does it contain?
   6. What is the language compatibility?
   7. What teleprocessing capability is available in each language?
   8. What are the training requirements for each package?
   9. What self-documenting features are available in each package?

C. *Application Packages*
   (Detailed documentation will be required for each selected package.)
   1. What application packages are available?
   2. What is their cost? How are the charges determined?
   3. What are the ownership rights to each package?
   4. Are there any limitations to the use of the package?
   5. What documentation is available?
   6. Who is responsible for updating or modifying the package?
   7. Who is responsible for updating or modifying the documentation?

D. *Libraries*
   1. List the sources or locations of libraries where user programs are available.

III. Customer Assistance Specifications

All responses must be in writing. Training programs should be adequately described. Résumés of support personnel may be requested.

A. *Personnel Training*
  1. What training programs are available?
  2. Who may receive training?
  3. What preliminary training is required by the participants in the training courses?
  4. What is the duration of the training classes?
  5. Where are the courses given?
  6. When are the training courses given, such as pre-installation, during testing, after implementation, or when modifications are made?
  7. What costs are involved?

B. *Program Testing Time*
  1. How much time is made available to the organization for program testing, compiling, file conversion, and data purification?
  2. What is the cost for additional time required to perform program testing, compiling, file conversion, or data purification?
  3. Where are the facilities for performing the pre-installation activities located?

C. *Systems and Programming Support*
  1. Specify the number, types, and level of personnel to be available for assistance.
  2. What are the responsibilities of the manufacturer's personnel for conversion, testing, and installation?
  3. Are the personnel resident or on call?
  4. What is the duration of their assistance?
  5. What is the availability of the supporting personnel for post-installation assistance?
  6. What are the responsibilities of the supporting personnel for post-installation problems?

Figure 9.2 Equipment Specifications for Computer Acquisition

1. STATEMENT OF THE TASK OR PROBLEM. This segment describes the task to be accomplished or the problem to be solved. The manager will have no difficulty in completing this segment for current problems or tasks. However, preparing a statement affecting a future situation may

present a more formidable challenge for the manager due to the many uncertainties. The manager must state the task or problem as accurately as possible to ensure the receipt of a proposal which will meet the user's needs efficiently and economically.

2. TECHNICAL REQUIREMENTS. This segment goes beyond the generalized statement of the task or problem. Here the manager delineates the mandatory and desirable characteristics or features to be included in a proposal. Figure 9.2 illustrates the type of information which may be sought in an equipment RFP. The vendor's or manufacturer's responses should indicate the technical characteristics of the hardware; the available software support in the form of operating systems, utility programs, and programming languages; and assistance in the form of maintenance, training, documentation, etc. The response data becomes an important part of the subsequent cost-performance evaluation.

3. REQUIRED COST PROPOSAL. Preliminary data about the required cost proposal should be included in the ground rules in the general instructions section. This segment will indicate the desired detailed cost breakdown for cost-performance analyses.

4. COMPATIBILITY. Compatibility requirements for hardware, software, or performance may be included in the RFP to ensure interaction with an existing environment. The requirements are an attempt to improve the cost-effectiveness of the potential contractor's proposal. Also their inclusion may minimize the impact of any change and the time needed to implement the selected proposal. Traditionally, hardware compatibility has been required when acquiring peripherals or upgrading within a given vendor's equipment line. This is somewhat unrealistic because the customer could be certain of securing electronic compatibility and to some degree logical compatibility. The latter could be readily achieved with some additional programming effort. However, the traditional requirements are not entirely valid for plug-to-plug peripherals. The data processing manager must stipulate the necessary hardware, software, and performance compatibility with the existing hardware configuration. The requirements are necessary to secure both electronic and logical compatibility and avoid degradation of the operating characteristics. Hopefully, the manager will secure better performance as a result of faster response times, and improved device reliability at a lower cost.

Software compatibility is often stipulated in order to avoid reprogramming. Within a vendor's line of computers, the general requirement is for upward compatibility. This mode of compatibility will generally ensure continued use of existing programs without modification. However, this approach may result in under-utilization of the proposed hardware. On some occasions a downward compatibility is sought. This capability will ensure that the existing programs are also processable on the smaller units. The operational flexibility desired actually imposes some severe constraints upon the organization. Downward compatibility can be effective only if the programs can be accommodated within the memory capacity of the smaller machines without modification. Software compatibility may also be desired when considering conversion from one vendor's equipment to that of another. The manager may indicate the specific requirement for a given language such as COBOL or FORTRAN.

Performance requirements may be included in the RFP to indicate that a particular level of operation is desired or that no degradation from an existing level occurs. Compatibility may be stated for such factors as storage capacity, cycle time, recording densities, access time, cost, transfer rates, or reliability. The responses to these requirements may be more difficult to evaluate. However, the cost-effectiveness ratio may prove more beneficial for the organization.

Compatibility should be sought as a means of reducing costs. However, a manager must carefully assess the compatibility requirements. There is the danger that these limitations may hamper an organization from securing an optimally effective approach.

5. DELIVERY. Stipulating a desired delivery date or timetable can be a tricky thing. A manager must forecast when the organization will be ready to accept and utilize the desired hardware, system, software, or service. Where dates are essential, these must be identified as mandatory. The mandatory dates may also be stipulated in one of the required contractual clauses.

6. CUSTOMER ASSISTANCE. Customer assistance is the support provided by the vendor or manufacturer. The assistance may take the form of hardware or software maintenance, user training, or documentation. During the evaluation process the manager will attempt to place a value on each of these characteristics or features. If a contractor's proposal indicates only limited training for uses, then the manager must determine the impact upon the organization. What costs would be incurred in

providing additional training for users? Or, what costs may result from
limited training for users? If the manager is willing to accept the contractor's proposal, then he must consider an alternative approach to
minimize the negative effects.

7. RELIABILITY. Reliability is a desirable quality control characteristic or feature; it is a requirement that will be critically evaluated in the
selection process. For example, in an online real-time application, hardware reliability is essential. Reliability may also be a significant factor
when evaluating plug-to-plug peripherals.

Proposal Presentation

This section of the RFP delineates the manner in which a contractor's
proposal is to be presented. The prescribed format is designed to ensure
uniformity in the presentation and evaluation of information.

The following items may be included:
1. Proposal summary
2. Response to requirements
3. Proposed concept
4. Benchmark results
5. Cost data
6. Facility requirements
7. Supporting documentation

1. PROPOSAL SUMMARY. In this segment the contractor is requested
to prepare a summary of his proposal and to list the general recommendations and conclusions. This information serves as an introduction to
the contractor's proposal and indicates whether or not the contents are a
valid response to the RFP.

2. RESPONSE TO REQUIREMENTS. This segment should contain the
vendor's or manufacturer's responses to the mandatory or desirable
requirements stipulated in the specifications. This approach helps to
highlight the response data and simplifies the selection process.

3. PROPOSED CONCEPT. The proposed concept should be a detailed
response by the vendor or manufacturer to the submitted specifications
(see Figure 9.2). The concept should also indicate any variations from
the RFP proposed by the potential contractor. The variation must be
explained to facilitate understanding and to indicate how it will improve
upon the original specifications.

The concept may be described as follows:
a) Concept description
b) Technical data
c) Timing data

a) Concept Description. The description of the concept represents the recommended approach or solution to a problem or task. In addition to detailing the contractor's proposal, the description should identify the concept's advantages and salient attributes. Also, the degree or level, and type of compatibility to the existing environment, should be stipulated. The description may also indicate the expandability of the proposal to the future needs of the organization.

The vendor or manufacturer may be requested to specify where a similar approach has been developed and implemented.

b) Technical Data. This segment should provide complete technical details to support the proposal previously described. In addition to listing the various operating characteristics, the data should also include summaries derived from the timings to indicate the work load capability. A contractor's hardware proposal will list the operating characteristics of a configuration, the hardware controls, software availability, work load estimates, expandability, and reliability. A software proposal may specify such items as the primary programming language, restart and error procedures, algorithms utilized, data base organization, etc.

The technical responses will be critically evaluated in the selection process.

c) Timing Tables. Timing tables requested in the general instructions should be included in this segment of the contractor's proposal. The tables are approximations for an estimated work load. They represent attempts by the vendor or manufacturer to prove that their proposal can meet the customer's requirements efficiently and economically.

Timing for equipment specifications are requested to identify the estimated hours of utilization in relation to available hours. For new hardware acquisition an organization is particularly concerned if the projected work load will exceed the number of available base hours. Any excess requirements above the base may increase the production costs for an organization. Software timings may be requested in order to determine function speeds for such operations as transfer, logic, arithmetic, conversion, etc. The data included in the timing tables may be the result of hand timing, simulation, or benchmark problems.

4. BENCHMARK RESULTS. The data in this segment may contain an

outline of the benchmark problems and a report of the test results. Prior to receipt of the contractor's proposal, the manager should have viewed the "live" benchmark demonstrations.

5. COST DATA. The cost information is generally submitted in tabular form in accordance with the specifications included in the general instructions. The cost data may be itemized as follows:

a) One-time
b) Approach cost
c) Customer assistance
d) Supplies
e) Conversion

a) One-Time. The one-time costs are those incurred by the customer prior to implementation of the proposal. For example, in an equipment proposal the contractor would primarily list the related transportation, insurance, and equipment installation costs.

b) Approach Cost. The data in this segment must closely abide to the ground rules. These costs will identify the lease, rental, or purchase arrangements, or, other cost arrangements such as fixed price, cost plus fixed fee, time and expense, etc. In addition, any maintenance charges involved must be specified.

c) Customer Assistance. These costs represent those incurred as a result of securing contractor support. They include expenses for such items as training, testing, conversion, documentation, reproduction, etc.

d) Supplies. The supplies costs represent those items initially required to develop and implement the proposed concept. Included are such items as magnetic tape, magnetic disks, special forms, etc.

e) Conversion. These costs are incurred in converting from one mode of operation to another. They may include such items as key punching, program recoding, data coding, parallel testing, etc.

6. FACILITY REQUIREMENTS. Whenever special facilities, such as air-conditioning, power, etc., are required to support the proposal these should be identified in this segment. Also the specifics such as dimensions, required voltages, temperatures, etc., must be indicated.

7. SUPPORTING DOCUMENTATION. The supporting documentation segment should include relevant technical manuals, configuration drawings, program listings, installation layouts, etc. Generally, these items are necessary to facilitate understanding of the proposed concept and technical data.

The specifications are designed to make the selection and evaluation process competitive and objective. This is necessary because of the multiplicity of designs, approaches, and configurations available to the information processor. Also, the specifications form a realistic base for the cost-benefit, cost-effectiveness, and trade-off analyses.

THE VENDOR AND THE RFP

Upon receipt of the request for proposal, the vendor or manufacturer must begin to develop an optimal response to meet the customer's needs. The potential contractor must be concerned with proposing an effective solution or approach within an economical cost range. As a result, he must perform a series of cost-performance trade-offs to recommend an efficient and economical proposal.

Depending upon the type of RFP submitted by the organization, the contractor may choose to simulate the problem or task. A model of the desired approach and its environment must be generated. The problem parameters or constraints are applied against the model and the results are analyzed. The experimentation is continued until an optimal approach is determined.

Equipment vendors have developed configurators to determine the optimal hardware/software mix to meet a user's needs. These configurators select the optimal hardware/software mix only from their own product line. However, this enables a potential contractor to submit a tangible proposal based on fact and not merely rhetoric.

Review Questions: Group 9B

1. What requirements should a customer include in the RFP to ensure that no degradation in system performance will result from implementation of a new approach?
2. Why is it necessary to specify the format for a potential contractor's responses?
3. How are timing tables developed?
4. Why would a contractor use simulation to prepare a response to an RFP?

VALIDATING THE PROPOSALS

The validation process is one of evaluating and ranking the submitted proposals against the requirements stipulated in the RFP. This process can be difficult and complicated, and often very time-consuming. However, it is necessary if an organization is to determine a proposal's capability to fulfill its needs within a reasonable overall cost constraint. Also, it is essential if an organization is to free itself of the single-vendor procurement concept.

The diversity of designs and approaches to information processing requires consideration of various vendors and manufacturers for the procurement of hardware, software, systems, or services. In the equipment area, for example, there is a significant trend toward mixing the components in a configuration. This has resulted from the growing number of suppliers offering a variety of freestanding or plug-to-plug peripherals. Experience by a number of organizations has shown that hardware mixing can significantly improve the price-performance ratio in a facility.

This discussion of the validation process will consider the following:
1. Criteria
2. Methods
3. Personnel

Criteria

The proposals submitted by the contractors must be evaluated against a predetermined set of criteria. The criteria are necessary to objectively evaluate a proposal's ability to meet the organization's needs.

The criteria are categorized by mandatory, and desirable, characteristics. If a proposal fails to include a mandatory requirement, then for all practical purposes it is considered to be non-responsive. The desirable characteristics may be somewhat more difficult to evaluate because the contractor may choose to ignore them, recommend an alternative, or submit as requested. Very often a proposal will contain a large list of alternative suggestions. The alternatives are included with the hope that the customer will acquire some of the features because their worth may exceed the cost of procurement.

Instead of classifying the criteria, they may be listed in a ranking

order. For example, an organization may choose to rank its criteria as follows:
—Software performance
—Hardware performance
—Support availability
—Compatibility
—Expansion capability
—Delivery
—Cost

The criteria listed above are too general, however, and each requires subdefinition to identify its relevant desirable characteristics or features. For example, the hardware performance criterion would have to be subdivided into the specific devices (i.e. central processor, input, output, data transmission), and their relevant characteristics. Therefore, the characteristics desired in an input device may include the following:
—Medium capacity
—Recording rates
—Buffering: number, location, operation, restrictions
—Channels: number, operation, restrictions
—Conversion form and rates
—Online/Offline operation switching
—Checking features

An analysis of these criteria will help to validate each input device. Subsequently the same process is repeated for each component or feature according to the relevant criteria. Ultimately the individual evaluations are combined to produce an overall appraisal for the proposed hardware configuration. The criteria for the overall appraisal may include such characteristics as compatibility, reliability, expandability, delivery, throughput capability, etc. These same criteria are then applied against each proposed configuration.

The criteria for evaluating a service such as time-sharing would be quite different. For example, one organization used the following ranking:
—System availability
—Reliability
—Programming languages available
—Costs (connect, CPU, storage, minimum, terminal, excess charges, initiation)
—Response time

—Maximum program size
—Maximum storage space
—Ease of use
—File security
—Editing
—Formatting
—Program library
—Programming assistance
—Documentation

This listing may not be complete or properly ranked for another firm. Each organization must establish its own criteria based on its own needs and desires.

Methods

The selection criteria must be incorporated into a proposed validation method. The method will provide the framework for determining the effectiveness of the vendor's or manufacturer's recommendations, and the related costs.

The validation approach selected may be simple or highly sophisticated. Also, it may be subjective or objective. The level of sophistication and degree of objectivity tend to correlate with the size of the organization. For example, large information processing organizations tend to utilize the more sophisticated and objective approaches. This may be due to their technical competence, or an increased awareness or consciousness of cost-performance. The organization-type may also influence the selection of a validation method. Governmental organizations, for example, attempt to utilize the more sophisticated and objective approaches to proposal validation. This may be due to public scrutiny of their actions.

An organization may choose any one of the following validation methods or combinations thereof:

1. Checklists
2. Criteria tables
3. Published evaluation reports
4. Benchmark problems
5. Test problem
6. Simulation
7. Cost-Value analysis

1. What are the costs?
2. How will data conversion be handled?
3. What types of input controls will be provided?
4. What types of output controls will be provided?
5. How will data be protected?
6. What is the expected turnaround time?
7. What emergency back-up is available?
8. What type of training will be provided to user personnel?
9. What special reports can be prepared?
10. What documentation will be made available?

Figure 9.3   Example of Validation Checklist used for Service Bureau Proposals

1. CHECKLISTS. The checklist approach is relatively simple and very subjective. The criteria are incorporated into a checklist to be compared against the contractor's responses. Due to the subjective nature of this method, the vendor or manufacturer with the best marketing rhetoric in his proposal will probably secure the contract. This negates the proposition that the user should consider the advantages and disadvantages of each response and determine the cost-benefit relationship of each item in the proposal.

Figure 9.3 illustrates a checklist used by one organization for evaluation of service bureau proposals. The questions are very general and do not clearly define acceptable or desirable characteristics. As a result, the defendability of the final selection is somewhat questionable.

The checklist technique is most effective when the criteria are more detailed and when applied to minor proposals. The detailing of the criteria adds credibility to the selection process. Figure 9.4 illustrates a detailed checklist, developed by an organization for evaluation of proprietary software packages. It provides preliminary data that is subsequently combined with that gathered during the benchmark testing process to produce an overall appraisal.

2. CRITERIA TABLES. The criteria tables use a tabular approach to proposal validation. A table is established for each segment of the proposal and the responses are noted therein. A criteria table for a basic system comparison is illustrated in Table 9.1. The responses within this table must be technically evaluated to determine their effectiveness. Some organizations will take the table as illustrated in Table 9.1 and rank each response. Table 9.2 illustrates how the criteria table would appear with the numerical ranking. The ranking is assigned on the basis

1. What is the package designed to do?
2. Who developed the software package?
3. How is the package organized?
4. Is the package operable?
5. Can the package operate on our hardware configuration?
6. Will the package require modification?
7. Who will modify the package?
8. Can package be modified if necessary?
9. What are the overall costs?
10. Is thorough and comprehensive documentation available?
11. Who will maintain the package?
12. How long will package maintenance be available?
13. What are the package constraints?
14. Where is the package currently utilized?
15. What is the primary language?
16. What i/o techniques are utilized?
17. What are the required i/o formats?
18. How must the input be organized?
19. What controls are included?
20. What user training is provided?

Figure 9.4   Example of Software Validation Checklist

of 1 to 10. The lower numeric ranking is assigned to the more desirable responses. Subsequently, these rankings are accumulated for a total score. The vendor with the lowest total score is assumed to have submitted the best response for that segment. There is a danger that the responses may be superficially evaluated without an analysis of the technical data; hence the ranking may be incorrect. In examining Table 9.2, it will be noted that under the column labeled "core size," both IBM and GE have been ranked with a numeric value of 1. This ranking may not be accurate if it has been assigned merely on the basis of 32K. The 32K in GE terminology could mean either word or character capacity. If the 32K represents word capacity, then the effective character rate would be 132K–100K larger than IBM's proposal of 32K. In addition to capacity, the central processor should also be evaluated for transfer, logic, arithmetic, and conversion operation speeds; address structures; buffering, etc.

The results from the separate tables are then combined into an overall comparison summary. Again a ranking ranging from 1 to 10 is

Table 9.1 Example of Criteria Table for a Basic System Comparison

Vendor and Model No.	Core Size	Tape Speed	Printer Speed Range	Card Read Range	Card Punch Range
Burroughs-3500	16K	72KC	1040 LPM	800 CPM	300 CPM
GE-415	32K	60KC	1200 LPM	900 CPM	300 CPM
Honeywell-200	16K	66KC (B)	950 LPM	800 CPM	300 CPM
IBM 360/30	32K	60KC (B)	1100 LPM	1000 CPM	300 CPM
NCR-315	20K	83KC	1000 LPM	2000 CPM	250 CPM
RCA-70/25	16K	66KC (B)	1250 LPM	1435 CPM	300 CPM

(B) Backward read feature

applied. The ranking range could be readily increased if more than ten vendors or manufacturers were asked to participate in the selection process. An extract of an overall comparison summary is illustrated in Table 9.3. The vendor with the lowest overall score would be the prime contendor for the equipment contract.

A somewhat more sophisticated approach to criteria tables is through the assignment of numerical values to the desirable characteris-

Table 9.2 Example of Criteria Table, with Numerical Ranking, for a Basic System Comparison

Vendor and Model No.	Core Size	Tape Speed	Printer Speed Range	Card Read Range	Card Punch Range	Total Score
Burroughs-3500	16K	72KC	1040 LPM	800 CPM	300 CPM	
Ranking	3	2	4	5	1	15
GE-415	32K	60KC	1200 LPM	900 CPM	300 CPM	
Ranking	1	4	2	4	1	11
Honeywell-200	16K	66KC (B)	950 LPM	800 CPM	300 CPM	
Ranking	3	3	6	5	1	18
IBM 360/30	32K	60KC (B)	1100 LPM	1000 CPM	300 CPM	
Ranking	1	4	3	3	1	12
NCR-315	20K	83KC	1000 LPM	2000 CPM	250 CPM	
Ranking	2	1	5	1	2	10
RCA-70/25	16K	66KC (B)	1250 LPM	1435 CPM	300 CPM	
Ranking	3	3	1	2	1	10

(B) Backward read feature

Table 9.3   Sample Extract of Overall Comparison Summary

Characteristic	Burroughs	GE	IBM	Honeywell	NCR	RCA
Rental Cost	4	5	6	1	3	2
Delivery	4	3	2	1	4	1
Software						
Performance	X	3	2	1	3	4
Expandability	X	3	2	2	4	1

tics within criteria groupings. This, therefore, forces a manager to rank his groupings, (hardware performance, software performance, vendor support, etc.) by relative importance. He then assigns a numerical value to each grouping. The sum total of values for all groups does not normally exceed 100. The manager must then appraise the desirable characteristics in each grouping and assign them a value. The sum total of values in each group shall not exceed the total allocated to it initially. As the proposals are evaluated the responses to the desired characteristics are assigned a value ranging from 1 to 10. This response value is multiplied by the characteristic value to determine a vendor score for that characteristic. The vendor scores are then summed to produce a group total and ultimately an overall total for the proposal. For illustrative purposes, the software grouping has been extracted from one orga-

Table 9.4   Sample Extract of Criteria Table, with Weighted Values, for a Software Comparison

Desirable Characteristics	Criteria Value	Vendor A		Vendor B	
		Response Value	Response Score	Response Value	Response Score
Availability	5	5	25	10	50
Cost	4	6	24	3	12
Reliability	3	6	18	6	18
Documentation	3	5	15	8	24
Maintenance	3	7	21	4	12
Training	2	7	14	5	10
Data Management	5	8	40	5	25
Total	25		157		151

nization's criteria table (see Table 9.4). The software category has been allocated an overall numerical value of 25. Note that software availability and a data management capability were two very important factors in the evaluation. The software group total indicates a very close score between the two competing vendors. However, the final outcome will be affected by the scores of the other criteria groupings.

3. PUBLISHED EVALUATION REPORTS. Published evaluation reports on hardware and software performance are also used for proposal validation. This approach is often frowned upon because it is regarded as too subjective and not very sophisticated. Yet many organizations use the published reports in conjunction with other methods to validate the proposals. The Auerbach reports for example are used frequently for evaluation of hardware devices, and software packages.

A published evaluation report may not be available for a particular hardware configuration, software package, or specific application. Therefore, the organization would be forced to seek an alternative proposal validation method. Also, performance reports are not generally available for appraising facilities, management proposals, time-sharing services, or service bureau agencies.

However, the reports are an excellent source of information particularly where the information processing staff lacks detailed knowledge of a proposed device or package.

4. BENCHMARK PROBLEMS. Benchmark problems are regarded as one of the more effective ways to validate a proposal. The selected problems are designed to provide the user with a realistic assessment of stated performance. Therefore, the manager must select benchmark problems which are truly representative of the expected workload and the criteria. The application of these problems against the proposed hardware, system, service, or software will provide the manager with a tangible basis for comparing all contractor proposals. The tests should enable the organization to effectively evaluate time requirements, equipment requirements, and/or processing capability. For example, when benchmarks are applied to a hardware proposal they may be used to identify the throughput capability of the equipment and its ability to deal with specific applications.

The decision to utilize benchmark problems for validation purposes must be made prior to dissemination of the RFPs. The benchmark documentation should be available to the prospective contractors at the time the RFP specifications are distributed. Prior to preparing the benchmark problems a manager must determine the expected results. This resolution is necessary in order to minimize the evaluation of unnecessary outputs, and facilitate construction of test data. The benchmark documentation will include information about the test data and the specific results required. However, this information should not identify the contents of the actual test data.

This approach to proposal validation requires the existence of operational hardware, software, services, or systems—an obvious disadvantage. However, this could be an advantage because it will ensure that the recommended proposal is functional, not merely marketing rhetoric. Another possible disadvantage is time. Time will affect the length or number of problems tested. Therefore, the manager must establish workable sizes for each problem and extrapolate from the test results. Establishing the problem sizes and mix requires intensive planning to produce a representative performance evaluation.

Despite the planning and preparation problems and apparent disadvantages the benchmark approach is very popular.

5. TEST PROBLEMS. The test problems are intended to evaluate the functional effectiveness of a segment of the contractor's proposal. This enables a manager to evaluate the various capabilities of the hardware, software, service, or system without necessarily processing a complete application. Test problems also help to evaluate the truly important capabilities, which are so often overlooked, inadequately measured or evaluated in the benchmark problems.

Test problems may be developed to evaluate the time required to translate source code into object code; response time for two or more jobs in a multi-programming environment; overhead requirements of the operating system for CPU and channel time in executing a user program; component overlap; length of time required to execute an instruction; etc. The results can be used for cost-performance trade-off judgments. However, the factors or functions tested or measured must be relevant to the proposal's objectives.

The test problems are frequently used to supplement the benchmark evaluations or any other proposal validating method. Often they are used to give the systems and programming personnel experience in utilizing the hardware, software, service, or system. The testing will provide limited information about the ease of operation and learning.

6. SIMULATION. Simulation is the most sophisticated technique for proposal validation. Properly utilized, this technique can provide mean-

ingful decision-making data to facilitate the optimal selection of a contractor proposal. However, the technique is still not used very much, owing to the costs and efforts required for its implementation. The higher costs result from the construction of one or several mathematical models, development of a data base for the variables, computer utilization, and the number of alternatives desired.

Developing the necessary model or models for proposal validation requires considerable effort (see Figure 9.5). The manager must formulate the primary and secondary objectives, as well as determine the controllable and uncontrollable variables affecting the model. When the model has been developed it must then be tested and debugged. This process may result in changes to the model and some of its parameters.

The tested model is then manipulated and the results analyzed. The variables may then be altered and the model remanipulated to produce another alternative. There is no limitation to the number of iterations that may be performed on a model. However, most users of this validation method prefer to keep the number of iterations to a minimum because of the cost and effort required.

An organization may utilize one of the simulation languages, such as GPSS (General Purpose Systems Simulator), Simscript, or CSS (Computer Systems Simulator), for proposal validation purposes. The manipulation of the model or models can be performed in a batch or online mode. The online mode is more desirable because the fast turnaround facilitates monitoring, evaluation, and modification of the model and results.

An organization may choose to develop a configurator to simulate the best hardware/software mix to meet the organization's needs. The configurator initially translates the user's requirements into one or more models. These models are then processed against the data base containing the hardware/software performance information to produce a number of calculations. These calculations are subsequently outputted in a variety of desired reports.

To construct such a configurator requires a significant investment in time and resources. Therefore, it may be more advantageous for an organization to utilize one of the proprietary packages, such as SCERT, which has been developed by COMRESS, Inc. of Rockville, Maryland.

The SCERT simulator works in five phases. The first is a detailed description of the present or planned work load and setting, which is written out on the special data collection forms. This information is then used to generate a methematical model of the current and projected

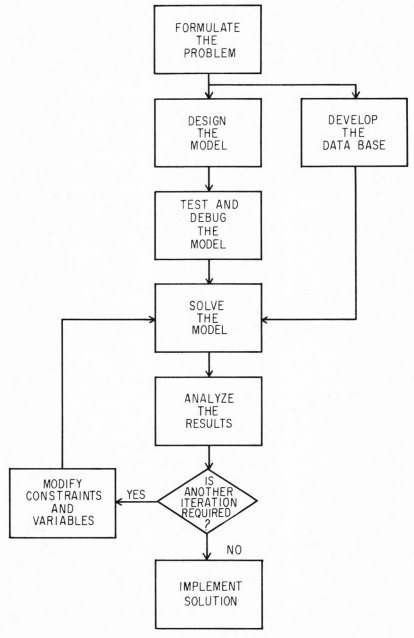

Figure 9.5. Approach to Simulation

work load. The second phase involves using the component data base to develop a mathematical model of the hardware and software configuration under consideration. The third phase involves a merger of the work load model and the hardware/software model in order to perform some necessary computations, such as internal processing and memory requirements, file structuring, overhead requirements, etc. This data indicates what happens or what is required for each task or function simulated. The fourth phase is the heart of the SCERT program. All of the data and models developed in the previous phases are integrated into a full simulation process. This enables the simulator to fully explode each program or random event to produce the net throughput timing. The last phase is the production of various output reports indicating the simulated configuration, CPU utilization, programming requirements, computer capability, cost summary, etc.

The configurators are still actually in development. In the future, though, they will undoubtedly be less costly to process and more flexible in operation. They will have the capability to identify optimal hardware/software configurations from the various competitive components.

7. COST-VALUE ANALYSIS. The cost-value technique is used primarily for the evaluation of equipment proposals. The technique may also be referred to as cost-effectiveness analysis. In this method the responses to the mandatory requirements in the RFP are only validated. The premise is that these requirements do not have to be evaluated. The cost-value technique is more concerned with evaluating the worth of a desired feature proposed by the potential contractor.

For example, an organization expresses a desire for an April delivery but a contractor indicates a possible January date. What is the value of the earlier delivery? Or, what would be the value of a delivery in July? The manager must determine if the earlier delivery date would enable him to begin profit-oriented operations sooner. Or, would the later delivery date cause him to seek an alternative processing method, which would increase operating costs? The value or worth in either situation must be determined. Subsequently, the positive or negative worth is subtracted from the total cost of the proposed configuration. The difference represents the total cost required to meet the RFP needs. This is but a calculation and does not lower the actual cost paid to the contractor.

Many organizations argue that the values assigned to the desirable features are very arbitrary and subjective. Consequently, the value attributed may or may not offer a realistic appraisal of actual worth. A counterargument is offered that the assigned values provide the executive committee with some tangible data in assessing a feature's worth to an organization. As a result, there is increased confidence in the proposal finally selected.

The cost-value analysis may also be very helpful in appraising the value of expansion features included in the proposal. The expansion capability may be assessed to determine either the ability of the equipment to assume a larger work load or the ability to interface additional features with the basic configuration. To some degree, the validation technique can also evaluate upgrading within a family of equipment.

The proposal validation method selected will be affected by the time and resources that a manager wishes to expend. It also depends upon whether a manager wishes to be objective or subjective in the selection process. The failure to apply an objective method may only help to increase operating costs needlessly.

Personnel

Prior to submitting the RFPs to the vendors or manufacturers, an organization must also determine who will validate and evaluate the submitted proposals. The selection will depend upon the type of hardward, software, system, or services desired; time available; in-house expertise; and funds availability. The RFPs may be issued for such activities as:
—Hardware acquisition
—Time-sharing services
—Packaged software
—Programming assistance
—Facilities management
—System studies
—Analysis and design services
—Service bureau support
—Training and education services
—Data conversion and preparation services
This variety of activities will force a manager to determine if outside assistance is necessary to validate a contractor's proposal. If a decision is

made to use outside assistance, the manager must determine the source of that service. Assistance may be secured from the following:

—Independent consultants specializing in data processing

—Management consultants offering related services in information processing

—Management consultants specializing in information processing services

—Accounting firms offering related information processing services

—Service bureau organizations offering a variety of services

—Computer-related service organizations offering a variety of services and subject matter expertise

—Colleges and universities—that is, from research groups and individual faculty members with expertise in information processing services

—Computer manufacturers and vendors

Governmental organizations tend to utilize outside assistance for proposal validation particularly for hardware selection. Many large organizations secure outside assistance either to verify their findings or to perform the evaluation and validation process. Still others prefer to utilize their own in-house expertise. This is particularly true of organizations with their own advanced planning and development groups. Many small- and medium-sized organizations tend to favor outside assistance. This is particularly true when an organization is initially becoming involved in automated information processing.

If outside assistance is deemed necessary, a manager should provide the advisory group with the following:

—A very specific definition of the objectives

—A schedule with checkpoints at which progress reports are due

—A description of the interaction required with in-house personnel

Though outside assistance is used in proposal validation, the final responsibility for selection remains with the data processing manager or administrator, and with the organization.

NEGOTIATING THE CONTRACT

Upon completion of the validation process, the manager must select the one proposal that best fulfills the organization's present and future needs. This proposal and the RFP specifications must then be converted to contractual terminology. Obviously, the data processing manager or administrator, or both, are not responsible for this legalistic conversion. However, they are responsible for preparing a checklist for the organization's legal advisors of the items that are to be included in the contract. The organization must act as an equal party in the contracting process.

Site Preparation

1. Time requirements for site preparation must be clearly stated. Sufficient time must be included to provide for construction, if necessary.
2. The site requirements for the following must be specified:
   a) Floor loading needs
   b) Fire detection and protection
   c) Power supply and lighting needs, both regular and emergency
   d) Air-conditioning and air humidification, both regular and emergency
   e) Physical and maintenance space for and around each unit
   f) Service and storage areas for maintenance personnel
3. The space requirements for the following must be specified, if relevant:
   a) Power generator
   b) Air-control equipment
   c) Power rooms
   d) Office space for managers, plus operations, programming, systems, and user personnel
   e) Service and record storage areas

Figure 9.6   Checklist for Contract Preparation

Through the checklist process, the manager ensures that the necessary specifications are included in the legal document. Figure 9.6, for example, illustrates some of the details that may appear on the checklist for ultimate inclusion in the contract. In this example, the information would be incorporated into the contractual clauses under the heading of site preparation.

Contract negotiation and preparation cannot be taken lightly. The vendors or manufacturers will undoubtedly move to protect themselves contractually. The organization must move equally as adroitly to have a well-defined contract prepared—one that will prevent shifting the burden of responsibility to the customer. Items such as standards of performance, delivery dates, acceptance standards, back-up requirements, termination, etc., must be carefully stipulated by the organization in order to minimize the possibility of subsequent litigation for breach of contract, negligence, fraud, misrepresentation, etc.

The termination clause is the most frequently overlooked clause in contracts relating to data processing services. Consequently, there may be no provision for notice of termination, right of access to a customer's property, documentation, control of back-up files, etc.

If the legal staff or advisors are not very familiar with matters related to information processing contracts, then it may be advisable to call their attention to the American Bar Association's publication entitled "Computers and the Law." Research on reported cases, and articles appearing in the ABA's journal, will also assist them with contractual questions related to information processing.

IMPLEMENTATION PLANNING AND PREPARATION

Following the execution of the contract, the data processing manager must prepare the organization for implementation of the proposal. The planning and readiness process affects the entire organization, not only the information processing activity. It requires involvement by the executive committee, user personnel, and information processing personnel. This interaction of the concerned parties will help to ensure: a progressive phasing-in of the project; readiness by the users to participate in the inputs and outputs; and adjustments by the organization to facilitate success of the new approach. Both the preliminary and final planning to ensure success of implementation and subsequent operation depend on the information gathered during the feasibility study (see Chapter 8). The reader will note that the impact upon the organization must have been previously evaluated. As a result, plans now have to be developed and implemented to minimize or eliminate any possible negative effects.

In the planning and preparation for implementation of the project, the manager must consider the following:
1. The conversion approach
2. Planning factors
3. Readiness status

Conversion Approach

The conversion approach to be selected is primarily determined by the project's objectives and the difficulty of integrating this task into the existing framework. The decision may also be influenced by the technical expertise possessed by an organization, as well as factors relating to available resources, time, and cost.

The approach to project implementation may be:

1. Gradual
2. Immediate
3. Overlapping

1. GRADUAL. The gradual approach extends or prolongs the time period allocated to the overall project. It is hoped that by extending the time-frame, an organization can carefully and completely develop and test the new concept before any changes are made. Alternatively, this approach is used in an attempt to minimize or eliminate any negative impact resulting from the transition.

The gradual approach is favored by small organizations that have little or no practical experience in information processing techniques and/or low-volume activities. This approach enables these organizations to wade into the new concept without becoming quickly submerged in a quagmire of problems. The approach is also favored by large organizations for the progressive phasing-in of complex projects. In this case, the segments are modularized and carefully implemented to ensure user readiness and ultimate success of the new project. The approach may also be favored when converting from a manual to automated method of processing. To a limited degree, it is also favored by organizations converting from unit-record to computerized equipment. This mode of operation helps to ensure that the existing systems are designed to take advantage of the new equipment.

The gradual approach is rarely used for computer-to-computer conversions, owing to the resulting overlapping equipment costs.

Before deciding on the gradual approach, the organization must carefully determine the cost-benefit relationship. In some situations, this approach helps to minimize costs because it does not require an immediate investment in a larger staff or more equipment. In other situations, though, costs may be incurred for travel and lodging at test centers, equipment rental, overtime work, data conversion etc.—all because of the lack of an in-house processing capability.

2. IMMEDIATE. The immediate approach implies a relatively instantaneous implementation capability. This presupposes that all of the necessary development, testing, debugging, training, conversion, and documentation has been completed prior to the targeted cutover date. This state of readiness enables an organization to virtually remove one computer from the area and replace it immediately with another machine. The approach may also be applied successfully when upgrading within a family of computers.

For most organizations, the immediate approach to conversion and implementation is too radical. It requires the availability of a well-developed and well-coordinated schedule. Generally, the time allocations in the project schedule provide for very little room for error, limited flexibility for developing alternatives, and only brief orientation and training sessions. Consequently, this tight scheduling tends to increase personnel problems. In addition, it may encourage faulty design and poor testing by the employees working under pressure in order to meet a schedule. Furthermore, parallel testing may be discouraged due to the limited amount of time availability.

The immediate approach is often forced upon the data processing manager by the executive committee in order to reduce or eliminate overlapping equipment or operating costs. However, if the costs are carefully assessed, it will be evident that, in the immediate approach, the support costs are significantly higher than the equipment or operating costs. A data processing manager wishing to impress the upper echelon may also recommend an immediate approach. Through the effective use of rhetoric and cost data, the manager should be able to readily substantiate his short-term position. However, it is highly unlikely that he will be ultimately successful unless adequate lead-time preceded delivery and acceptance of the hardware, software, or system, or unless the manager has a large staff available, with adequate resources for conversion and implementation.

A data processing manager or administrator may recommend the use of emulation or simulation to facilitate an immediate implementation of hardware. The emulator is a hardware feature that causes the central processor to react like the replaced machine when executing the program. Consequently it achieves the same results as were previously attainable. However, the emulation process does not utilize the full capabilities of the new hardware.

Simulation is accomplished through the use of a software package that is resident in the primary memory unit. This software translates the instructions of the "foreign" program into the hardware's "required" language. Following the translation, the simulated program can then be processed. However, it can only utilize the device types originally specified in the program. This often results in a significant loss of processing power.

In both emulation and simulation, there is a significant under-utilization of the replacement hardware. However, the emulation and simulation techniques facilitate conversion from one hardware configuration to another without overlapping equipment costs. It also permits an organization to gradually reprogram its existing systems and applications. However, there is no assurance that the reprogramming effort will be conducted. This author is personally aware of a number of data processing activities that are still emulating IBM 1401, 1440, and 1620 programs on their IBM 360s. Two of these installations were among the first to accept delivery on the new 360s. Each of these two organizations is a high-volume operation with several high-priority systems affecting the overall organization. In each of these activities, it is very questionable whether the savings on equipment costs can offset the losses incurred from under-utilization of the more powerful computer.

3. OVERLAPPING. The overlapping approach provides a buffer period to facilitate the transition from one method to another. This time interval provides an organization with the ability to conduct additional parallel tests to ensure success of the new approach. The length of the buffer period will vary with the complexity of the project, the time and resources available, the organization size, and the costs. For most organizations, the buffer period ranges from one to six months. In one organization viewed by this author, the overlap period had been projected for a period of one year. This interval was deemed necessary to convert to a more sophisticated inventory/production control system utilizing new hardware and software. The system was modularized and allowed for a progressive phasing-in of the completed segments. However, in another organization due to convert to a different hardware vendor and software language, the data processing manager decided upon an open-ended overlap period. He decided to overlap for as long as would be necessary, although the projected period was not to have exceeded nine months. As a result of inaccurate training projections, faulty or inadequate preliminary design data from the feasibility study, poor testing procedures, and poor documentation, the overlap period

extended to nearly 22 months beyond the equipment delivery date. This overrun proved to be very costly to the overall organization and damaging to the data processing activity.

In conversion from manual to automated processes, overlapping machine costs will not be a factor. However, personnel and supplies costs can be significant. Conversions from unit-record to computing equipment are affected by some level of machine costs, as well as personnel and supplies expenses. In converting from one type of computer to another, the machine costs could be very significant. Even when implementing a software, service, or systems package, the equipment, personnel, and supplies costs can be significant.

For most organizations, the overlapping approach provides the smoothest and most effective transition. An organization selecting this approach should allow for as much overlap as it can afford. This will help to ensure more effective systems and applications, better communications and organizational interaction, and more effective documentation. However, the time interval selected should not be open-ended; a time limit must be established for planning, directing, and controlling purposes.

Which Approach?

In actual operation, many organizations utilize a combination of these approaches to conversion and implementation. The implementation approach selected should be determined only after a cost-benefit analysis has been completed. This analysis must not be restricted to machine, software, service, or system costs. Rather, it must also take into consideration the following factors: time, manpower and materials resource availability, impact upon the organization, and user readiness. When the approach has been selected, the manager may then proceed to develop his plan of action.

Planning Factors

After the approach to conversion and implementation has been determined by the executive committee, data processing administrator, data processing manager, and users, the structural framework for its execution must be developed. This framework must be evolved prior to the implementation of the new hardware, software, system, or service. The tasks and activities within the framework constitute the project's implementation plan and schedule. The detailing of the tasks and activities is necessary for direction and control purposes, and subsequently for the readiness status evaluation. A generalized overview of the implementation objectives and related activities is illustrated in Figure 9.7.

The entire implementation plan should be prepared only after a review of the feasibility study, RFP, accepted vendor's or manufacturer's proposal, and negotiated contract. This review brings into focus all of the necessary tasks, contraints, and parameters affecting project implementation and the schedule. The plan is also affected by the type of project being implemented—hardware, software, system, or service.

The implementation plan and schedule may include the following general factors:

1. Site requirements
2. Communications requirements
3. Organizational manning
4. Information processing personnel requirements
5. System development
6. Program development
7. Data and file conversion
8. Parallel operations
9. Implementation

1. SITE REQUIREMENTS. The site requirements have to be determined in order to facilitate preparation of a safe working environment (see Chapter 5). The manager must make certain that he adheres to the requirements stipulated in the negotiated contract, local building codes, and organizational policies. Sufficient advanced planning and preparation must be executed to ensure a state of readiness for delivery. This may be a very critical factor where facility construction or renovation is required.

The specific factors that may be included in the consideration of site requirements involve determination or evaluation of:

—Overall space requirements
—Equipment layout and space requirements for operations and maintenance
—Floor loading capacity
—Power and lighting requirements, both regular and emergency

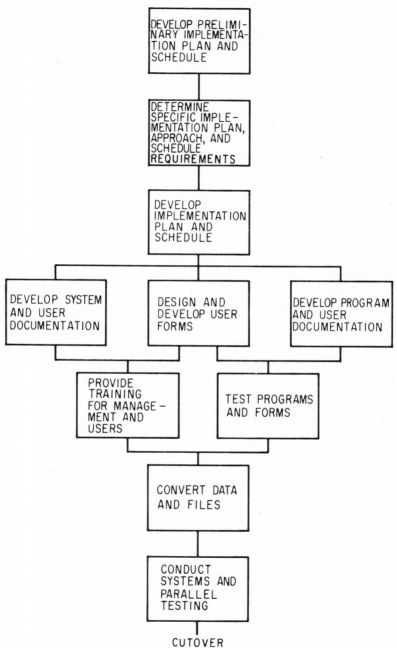

Figure 9.7. Generalized Overview of Implementation Objectives

—Air-conditioning and humidification control requirements, both regular and emergency

—Raised flooring for cabling and wiring

—Smoke-detection and alarm systems

—Fire-detection, alarm, and protection systems

—Water-detection and damage-control systems

—Service and storage areas

—Tape and disk library

—Environmental security and protection against vandalism or sabotage, or both

—Office, work area, and conference room space

—Space and positional requirements for materials handling equipment

—Scheduled completion dates

—Vendor or manufacturer site-acceptance requirements stipulated in the contract

2. COMMUNICATIONS REQUIREMENTS. These factors are relevant to the planning process only if the project involves teleprocessing or data communications equipment, or a time-sharing service.

Factors to be considered are:

—Equipment layout and space requirements for operation and maintenance

—Wiring requirements and limitations

—Type of circuit required

—Encryption device requirements

—Scheduled installation date

—Environmental security

—Development of user documentation

—Training of user personnel

—Development of management controls

3. ORGANIZATIONAL MANNING. During the feasibility study, an evaluation of the proposal's impact upon the organization had to be determined. With the approval of the executive committee, the data processing administrator and manager must now finalize both the organizational structure and manning requirements for the new approach. In all likelihood, the proposed costs and savings are based on changes to the organization chart or manning strengths, or both (see Chapters 2 and 3).

Factors to be considered are:

—Development of a new organization chart
—Development of new job descriptions
—Orientation and training of user personnel
—Reassignment and retraining of personnel
—Scheduled release of personnel
—Coordination required with interrelating activities.

4. INFORMATION PROCESSING PERSONNEL REQUIREMENTS. The factors involved in this segment will vary significantly, depending upon the type of information processing organization currently in existence. If none exists, then the executive committee must establish such an organization by either appointing a temporary administrator or recruiting an executive to head up the activity (see Chapters 2 and 3).

The factors to be considered are:

—Review skills inventory for background and experience of personnel
—Determine required manning strength prior to installation of the new project
—Determine recruitment and selection requirements
—Recruit and select personnel
—Determine and provide the necessary level of orientation, training. and retraining

5. SYSTEM DEVELOPMENT. This is one of the most difficult parts of the implementation plan and very time-consuming in the schedule. The actual effort and length of time required for the activities in this part of the plan will depend upon the amount of detail previously developed and upon priorities established by the executive committee. The planning for this phase can begin only after the requirements have been finalized (see Chapter 8). The requirements must then be correlated with the detailed design information from the feasibility study. The final design process and the interrelated activities can then be initiated (see Chapters 3, 4, 6, and 7 regarding the relevant systems development tasks).

The factors that may be included for each system are:

—Review of source documents and/or input
—Analysis of input, output, working file, and reference data needs
—Determination of output and reporting requirements
—Analysis of the system flowcharts, logic charts, or decision tables
—Development of methods and performance standards

—Preparation of complete documentation for each system and application

—Development and establishment of the necessary management controls

—Coordination of system and parallel testing

—Determination of the estimated dates of completion

—Development of an overall project schedule

6. PROGRAM DEVELOPMENT. As in the case of systems development, this phase of the implementation plan and schedule is an extension of the development work performed in the feasibility study. The preliminary design data developed in the feasibility study is subject to change or modification. The design again is affected by the finalized system's requirements. As a result, some redefinition of the initial design data may be necessary before final design of a program can be initiated (see Chapters 3, 4, 6, and 7 regarding the relevant program development tasks).

The factors that may be included in this segment are:

—Development or redevelopment of the macro- and micro-flow-charts

—Analysis of the program specifications

—Instruction coding

—Desk checking of source programs

—Assembly and compilation of source programs

—Preparation of test data and test plan

—Testing and debugging of the object programs

—Preparation of complete program documentation

7. DATA AND FILE CONVERSION. The conversion and purification of data and files may be performed prior to, during, and after implementation. The amount and type of data and files converted and checked prior to implementation will depend upon the priority schedule established for system and program development. This phase of the implementation plan requires a significant amount of control and coordination. One of the problems encountered by the manager during this phase is to secure complete data and files for purification and conversion. As a result, he has to develop and implement numerous management controls (see Chapter 7). The availability of the information for conversion is also a problem that requires careful scheduling and coordination.

The factors that may be included in this segment are:

—Development of management controls to ensure qualitative conversion

—Development of the necessary administrative procedures to ensure correction or validation of exceptions

—Coordination of the conversions with the interrelated activities

—Development of the necessary procedures for manual transcription of the information to coding sheets

—Development of the necessary transcription forms

—Provision for orientation and training on the proper use of transcription codes

8. PARALLEL OPERATIONS. This is one of the most important events in the conversion and implementation cycle. Parallel processing is the simultaneous production of output and reports using the current and proposed approach. This period of dual-system operation enables an organization to test and prove the mathematical and procedural accuracy of the new approach. It also represents an evaluation of the approach's ability to meet the desired objectives.

The parallel-processing phase must not be taken lightly, because it entails a complete system's test. This testing requires an effective interaction between the responsible functional activities and the information processing organization. The coordination is required in order to evaluate the source documents, inputs, documentation, management controls, effectiveness of training and orientation, procedures, reports and outputs, and programs. Too frequently this evaluation is not taken seriously enough; consequently, major problems arise when the new approach is implemented. In one organization, for example, the payroll group considered itself too busy to evaluate the proposed payroll system and its outputs. When the new system was implemented, the users were very unhappy. Despite its earlier agreements and acceptance of the preliminary test outputs, the payroll group suddenly decided it couldn't "live" with the system. As a result, the organization scrapped its new approach and simply computerized the existing unit-record payroll approach. This meant reverting back to processing the payroll and its by-products over a period of four and one-half days instead of one eight-hour shift. This regression resulted in a significant waste of manpower, money, materials, and machine resources, as well as of time. Perhaps it could have been prevented by initial executive committee involvement in the project. Alternatively, perhaps more effective coordination by the data processing manager during the feasibility study and subsequent development of the system would have prevented this problem.

The factors that may be included in this segment are:

—Coordination of conversion and purification of the necessary data and files

—Coordination of the machine loading for conversion, purification, and testing

—Coordination of the checkout of the outputs and reports

—Coordination of the preparation and availability of user and processing documentation

—Provision for the necessary orientation and training

—Development of the plan and schedule for dual operations

9. IMPLEMENTATION. The implementation phase is concerned with effecting the full operational status of the new project. This may be the culmination of a complete project or the accomplishment of one of a series of goals. The planning within this phase is concerned with determining if the new project can be made fully operational on the desired date. The scheduling is primarily concerned with the actual cutover and, to some degree, with the final details to ensure a successful phasing-in.

The factors in this segment may include:

—A readiness review of the affected activities

—Conducting of orientation seminars on cutover

—Conducting of a management presentation for final acceptance

Each of the factors in the implementation plan must be allocated a time element for scheduling purposes. Both the scheduled activities and the time elements should then be translated to a GANTT chart (see Figure 9.8) or PERT network (see Figure 9.9). The schedule will facilitate the execution of the management functions of planning, organizing, coordinating, directing, and controlling.

Readiness Status

The readiness status evaluation is a formal review of the progress in an implementation plan and schedule. It indicates an organization's preparedness to generate and utilize the project's information products. The review's feedback will enable the manager to develop and initiate appropriate corrective measures, or to implement an alternative course of action when necessary.

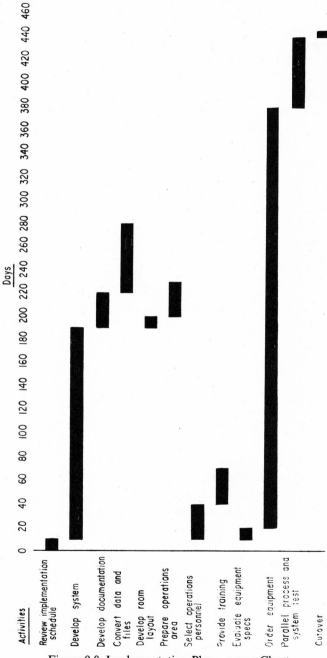

Figure 9.8. Implementation Plan—GANTT Chart

The target date for a readiness review is generally dependent upon the type of project. The date needs to allow adequate lead time to facilitate implementation of other measures to ensure a reasonable state of readiness, or rescheduling of the project cutover. The corrective action should be decided upon only after an analysis of the contractual provisions for delivery and acceptance, and/or review of the implementation plan. A contract for hardware acquisition may require that the

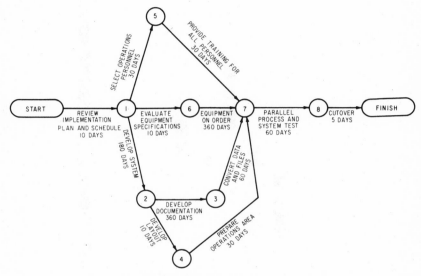

Figure 9.9. Implementation Plan—PERT Network

necessary environmental facilities be ready at least 30 days prior to project cutover. Alternatively, the implementation plan may require that at least 50 percent of the necessary effort be completed in order to facilitate a significant productive cutover.

The readiness review may utilize an existing GANTT chart or PERT network for status evaluation. Or, instead, a detailed checklist including all of the essential and interacting tasks and steps may be prepared. The status of each key activity is evaluated to determine if any slippage has occurred. Where slippage has occurred, it may be necessary to increase the resources to correct the problem. However, any proposed changes must be evaluated to determine their effect on the overall project.

THE FOLLOW-UP

After the project has been implemented, a follow-up procedure should be initiated to evaluate its effectiveness. This post-implementation evaluation may be a one-time review or it may be continued for as long a period as is deemed necessary. The follow-up may be conducted to determine the following:

—Have desired objectives been achieved?

—Must the originally stated objectives be modified?

—Have the savings outlined in the feasibility study actually been achieved, surpassed, or negated by increased operating costs?

—Is the phase-out time table being adhered to?

—What is the effectiveness of the documentation in the systems, programming, operations, and user organizations?

—Are the recommended changes to the organization structure realistic?

—Are the personnel duties and responsibilities properly defined and assigned?

—Are the management controls effective for capturing, processing, and reporting data?

—Has the training been adequate?

—Have all of the data and files been converted properly and accurately?

—What is the estimated versus actual machine loading?

—What are the "before and after" costs for personnel, supplies, and machines?

—Does the operations area provide for a safe, secure, and productive working environment?

—What is the actual versus authorized personnel strength?

If the results of the follow-up are unsatisfactory, it may be necessary to modify or re-plan the entire project. The follow-up may be conducted by the systems or advanced planning and development personnel. The latter group may be somewhat more impartial in judging the effectiveness of the hardware, software, system, application, service, etc.

The post-implementation evaluation should subsequently be supplemented by an annual systems audit program based on the follow-up principle. The audit may be conducted by the internal or external auditors, advanced planning and development personnel, systems personnel, or management consultants (see Chapter 7).

Review Questions: Group 9C

1. How may the proposal validation process be made more objective?
2. What are some of the arguments for and against the use of benchmark problems in proposal validation?
3. Why would it be beneficial for a small organization to utilize a simulator for proposal validation?
4. Why should a data processing manager or administrator participate in contract negotiations for the acquisition of data processing services?
5. If an organization was developing a massive management information system, would it be practical for it to utilize a gradual approach to conversion and implementation? Why or why not?
6. If an organization was to utilize an outside optical-scanning service for data conversion, what events would be included in the implementation plan?
7. Why is a readiness review necessary?
8. What factors might be included in a system's follow-up?

SUMMARY

After the need for a new or modified approach to information processing has been justified, the manager must develop the specifications for the request for proposal (RFP). The RFP delineates the organization's required and desired characteristics in the new or modified approach. However, before the specifications can be released, the manager must select the vendors capable of submitting a realistic response. This will require an evaluation of the prospective bidder's organization, financial position, experience, personnel, and technical capability. The manager may perform the contractor evaluations annually, semiannually, or prior to release of the RFPs.

The request for proposal will indicate to the prospective bidder the organization's needs and desires. It is a formal document designed to ensure uniform distribution of the specifications, a more uniform response format, and competitive bidding. The RFPs are generally divided into three parts: general instructions, customer requirements, and proposal presentation. The general instructions specify the ground rules for the bidder's response; the customer requirements delineate the problem; and the proposal presentation delineates the required responses to the problem.

In order to respond to the RFP, the bidder may perform a series of cost-performance analyses. These may be accomplished by utilizing simulation models or configurators. This process will enable the bidder to submit a meaningful proposal based on fact, rather than marketing rhetoric.

The contractor responses must then be evaluated and ranked by the organization. Though this may be difficult and time-consuming, it is necessary in order to evaluate each proposal's capability. The proposals should initially be compared with the criteria developed by the manager. These criteria are incorporated into a singular or combinatorial validating method. The validating methods include such approaches as checklists, criteria tables, evaluation reports, benchmark problems, test problems, cost-value analysis, and simulation.

The proposals may be validated by the organization's own personnel and/or by an external group of information processing specialists. If an organization chooses to utilize an external group, it must clearly define the objectives of the validation, require progress reports, and require interaction with in-house personnel.

When a vendor has been selected, a contract must be negotiated. The manager must work closely with the legal staff to ensure that all of the necessary items are included in the agreement. After the terms have been agreed upon, the manager develops an implementation plan and schedule. Both the plan and schedule are affected by the conversion approach selected by the manager and the executive committee. The conversion approach may be gradual, overlapping, or immediate. Following selection of an approach, the manager formulates the actual implementation plan and schedule. An integral part of the plan is a readiness review. This review is necessary to ensure that the organization is capable of generating and utilizing the products of the new information processing approach. When the new approach has been implemented, a follow-up must be initiated to evaluate its effectiveness. The follow-up may be conducted once or it may be continued for as long as is deemed necessary. A follow-up of the implemented system may be performed in order to determine that the desired goals have been achieved, the projected tangible savings have been realized, the phase-out timetable is being adhered to, the user and operation's documentation is effective, and so on. If the results of the follow-up are unsatisfactory, it may be necessary to modify and replan the implemented approach.

CASE STUDY

Case Study 9.1: Cogency, Consistency, and Clarity College

The director of academic data processing for the college has determined that there exists a need for a new hardware configuration on campus. This new configuration is intended primarily to provide "hands-on" training for students in the data processing curriculum. Some consideration may also be given to utilizing the new configuration as a terminal to an existing in-house IBM 360/40 system.

The director contacted his marketing representative and informed him verbally of his desires. The marketing representative responded with a letter indicating four possible configurations. Each configuration was outlined by machine and model number. In addition, some advantages were listed. Two of the four configurations were recommended as better choices for the colleges.

In his closing paragraph, the representative extended an invitation to discuss the contents of his letter.

Discussion Questions

1. Is adequate justification for acquiring a new configuration indicated?
2. Should the director have conducted a feasibility study to provide proper justification?
3. Is the single vendor contact justified in this instance?
4. What kind of request for proposal could be developed for the college?
5. How effective is the vendor's response for validation and planning purposes?
6. What validation approach or approaches might conceivably be applied to this response?
7. Did the director execute his responsibilities as a manager correctly?

Appendix I: Occupations in a Data Processing Installation

The dynamic nature of the information processing industry has resulted in a proliferation of position titles. Titles may be confusing; therefore, each position must be evaluated by the stated responsibilities and requirements.

This Appendix includes the occupational descriptions of the positions found most frequently in a data processing installation. The descriptions have been extracted from among those published by the Employment Service of the United States Department of Labor.

PRIMARY AND ALTERNATE TITLES

To facilitate understanding of the titles, the descriptions include primary titles and their corresponding alternate titles for selected occupations. The titles are:

PRIMARY TITLE	ALTERNATE TITLES
Data Processing Manager*	Director of Data Processing
	Information Systems Director
	Management Information Director
	Computer Services Manager
	Director of Management Services
	Data Processing Coordinator
	Manager of Data Processing

* The title may be related to single functional activities, such as Manager of Systems Analysis, Manager of Programming, Manager of Computer Operations, Manager of Unit-Record Equipment, Manager of Applications Programming, Systems Manager, Programming Manager, etc.

573

	Manager of Information Systems
	Director of Information Systems
	Vice-President, Data Processing
	Vice-President, Information Processing
	Director of Information
	Manager, Management Information Systems
Project Director	Project Manager
	Project Planner
	Project Coordinator
	Project Leader
	Project Administrator
	Project Consultant
	Senior Analyst
	Senior Systems Engineer
	Lead Analyst
	Lead Programmer
	Data Processing Coordinator
Systems Analyst	Systems and Procedures Analyst
	Information Processing Analyst
	Systems Engineer
	Data-Methods Analyst
	Information Systems Planner
	Systems Consultant
	Information Systems Analyst
	Computer Systems Specialist
	Applied-Systems Analyst
Operations Research Analyst	
	Operations Analyst
	Management Science Analyst
	Management-Operations Analyst
Programmer	Applications Programmer
	Programmer Analyst
	Programming Engineer
	Systems Programmer
	Software Programmer
	Commercial Programmer
	Business Programmer
	Technical Programmer
	Scientific Programmer
	Computer Programmer
	Business Applications Programmer

Scientific Applications Programmer
Business Systems Programmer
Software Systems Programmer
Simulation Programmer
Operating Systems Programmer

OCCUPATIONAL DESCRIPTIONS

The selected occupational descriptions include the following titles:

1. Manager, Data Processing
2. Project Director, Data Processing
3. Systems Analyst, Data Processing
4. Operations Research Analyst
5. Programmer, Business
6. Programmer, Engineering and Scientific
7. Computer Operator
8. Computer-Peripheral-Equipment Operator
9. Key Punch Operator

Manager, Data Processing

Occupational Definition

Directs and coordinates planning and production activities of electronic data-processing division. Consults with management to define boundaries and priorities of tentative projects, discuss equipment acquisitions, determine specific information requirements of management, scientists, or engineers, and allocate operating time of computer systems. Confers with department heads involved with proposed projects to ensure cooperation and further define nature of project. Consults with SYSTEMS ENGINEER, ELECTRONIC DATA PROCESSING to define equipment needs. Reviews project feasibility studies. Establishes work standards. Assigns, schedules, and reviews work. Interprets policies, purposes, and goals of organization to subordinates. Prepares progress reports to inform management of project development and deviation from predicted goals. Contracts with management specialists or technical personnel to solve problems. Revises computer operating schedule to introduce new program testing and operating runs. Reviews reports of computer and peripheral equipment production, malfunction, and maintenance to ascertain costs and plan operating changes within his department. Analyzes data requirements and flow to recommend reorganization or departmental realignment within the company. Participates in decisions concerning personnel staffing and promotions within electronic data processing departments. Directs training of subordinates. Prepares proposals and solicits purchases of analysis, programming, and computer services from outside firms.

Education, Training, and Experience

Two years of formal post-high school training in data processing with courses in business administration and accounting or engineering, or equivalent practical experience, is necessary for small computer installations. College graduation with major in one or more of the above fields is preferred for large installations. Experience in systems analysis, programming, and computer operations is desirable. In installations offering more sophisticated services, such as operations research and engineering simulation, a college mathematics major coupled with experience listed above is desirable.

Special Characteristics

APTITUDES. Verbal ability to translate technical terminology into terms understandable to management and department heads.

Numerical ability to apply knowledge of linear or differential equations in evaluating work of department, preparing reports and proposals for management, and selling services to outside users.

Spatial ability to read engineering drawings, charts, and diagrams; to understand presentations, proposed solutions, and progress reports of business or engineering problems.

Form perception to see pertinent detail in drawing charts, diagrams, and other presentations.

Clerical perception to detect and avoid errors in reading and preparing reports.

INTERESTS. An interest in scientific and technical subjects to cope with wide range of technical and scientific problems processed through computer.

A preference for business contacts with people in directing activities of computer department and to sell ideas or services.

TEMPERAMENT. Must be able to direct, control, and plan the operations of the division, bringing together knowledge of operations and information needs of departments, such as accounting, purchasing, engineering, sales, and inventory control.

Required to deal with people such as management, department heads, and manufacturers' representatives to exchange information and ideas, discuss equipment and their uses, elicit information from departments, and to answer inquiries from department heads.

Ability to influence management and department heads to enlist their support for acceptance, expansion, and sophistication of computer systems; and ability to sell excess computer time and services to outside clients.

Required to make judgmental decisions concerning equipment needs, scope of assignments, allocation of computer time, and organization of departments.

Required to make decisions based on factual data to evaluate progress or success of computerized projects.

PHYSICAL ACTIVITIES AND ENVIRONMENT. Work is sedentary.

Occasionally walks to various departments and offices; stands during conferences and discussions with management, department heads, and supervisor of computer operations.

Talking and hearing required in conferences and during exchanges of information.

Near visual acuity and accommodation required for reading reports and charts.

Work is performed inside.

Project Director, Data Processing

Occupational Definition

Plans, directs, and reviews business electronic data-processing projects, coordinates planning, testing, and operating phases to complete project with maximum balance of planning and equipment time, man-hours, and new equipment expenditures. Prepares project feasibility and progress reports. Confers with department heads who provide input and use output data to define content and format. Schedules and assigns duties to OPERATIONS RESEARCH ANALYSTS based on evaluation of their knowledge of specific disciplines. Coordinates activities of workers performing successive phases of problem analysis, solution outlining, solution detailing, program coding, testing, and debugging (error elimination). Reviews output data and related reports, applying knowledge of systems, procedures, methods, and data requirements of management and other output users to ensure adherence to predetermined standards and devise techniques for improved performance on similar future projects. Directs revision of continuous control project to adapt it to new data requirements or improve operations by using new techniques or equipment.

Education, Training, and Experience

A bachelor's or master's degree in business administration, with extensive course content in accounting and mathematics or statistics often required. Employers frequently waive academic training requirements for currently employed workers with extensive systems analysis, design, and follow-up responsibility in electronic data processing, and supervisory experience in tabulating-machine departments. Employers frequently require a degree or equivalent experience either in industrial engineering, or the engineering discipline most directly related to their manufacturing processes, when expanding business data processing to an integrated system that includes production forecasting, planning, and control.

Background knowledge and experience usually include a minimum of one to three years' experience in systems analysis and concurrent familiarization with structure, work flow requirements, and standards of the employing organization.

Current trend is toward greater mathematical sophistication than previously expected from workers at this level. The need for advanced mathematics becomes more urgent as computer applications become involved not only with normal business data processing, but also with the involved problems of operations research.

Special Characteristics

APTITUDES. Verbal ability to elicit information and discuss project intentions, problems, and progress, and to prepare reports.

Numerical ability to analyze problems and develop systems statements in form capable of being programmed. Mathematics varies from arithmetic and algebra for simple, single-purpose systems design to differential equations and mathematical statistics for complex systems involving optimization, simulation, or forecasting.

Spatial ability to develop, interpret, or integrate operational work flow diagrams and charts.

Clerical perception to recognize pertinent detail and avoid perceptual errors when working with verbal material, which often is in highly contracted and conventionalized form.

INTERESTS. A preference for prestige-type activities, and for business contact with others to participate in conferences with management, advise and inform others regarding the potentialities, limitations, and alternative methods of data processing, supervise analysts and coordinate their activities.

A preference for activities that are technical in nature, to read and keep informed of computer development and new or more refined systems and procedures techniques.

TEMPERAMENT. Ability to perform a variety of duties involving frequent change, ranging from direct involvement in problem analysis to coordination of subsequent work processes until each project is operational.

Must be able to direct and plan an entire area of work activity, assigning subordinates on the basis of knowledge of individual specializations and abilities, and control activities through personal contact and reports.

Must be able to deal with people in nonsupervisory situations requiring considerable tact, to secure cooperation from management and all personnel affected by project.

Required to make decisions on a judgmental basis when supervising others and developing approaches to problems on basis of past experience. Evaluates fixed cost, time, manpower allocation, and output specifications to judge efficiency or project development and operation.

Required to make decisions based on factual data, as in planning proposed system around capabilities and limitations of a specific computer system.

PHYSICAL ACTIVITIES AND ENVIRONMENT. Work is sedentary, with occasional standing and walking required.

Occasionally lifts and carries books, charts, diagrams, and other records seldom exceeding 10 pounds.

Talking and hearing to discuss problems and progress.

Near visual acuity to work with reports, charts, and diagrams and other printed or written records.

Work is performed inside.

Systems Analyst, Data Processing

Occupational Definition

Analyzes business problems, such as development of integrated production, inventory control, and cost analysis, to refine its formulation and convert it to programmable form for application to electronic data-processing system. Confers with PROJECT DIRECTOR, BUSINESS DATA PROCESSING and department heads of units involved to ascertain specific output requirements, such as types of breakouts, degree of data summarization, and format for management reports. Confers with personnel of operating units to devise plans for obtaining and standardizing input data. Studies current, or develops new systems and procedures, to devise work flow sequence. Analyzes alternative means of deriving input data to select most feasible and economical method. Develops process flow charts or diagrams in outlined and then in detailed form for programming, indicating external verification points, such as audit trial printouts. May work as member of team, applying specialized knowledge to one phase of project development. May coordinate activities of team members. May direct preparation of programs.

Education, Training, and Experience

College graduation with courses in business administration and accounting usually is required for entrants without prior experience in data processing. Some employers, while requiring a college degree, do not require a specific major or course content. A successful college record is regarded as proof of ability to reason logically which is considered more important for successful performance than knowledge of techniques acquired in any specific area. Many employers waive the formal education requirements for those workers employed in their establishments who have had several years' manual and machine systems experience prior to computer conversion. Business programmers without a college degree can, through experience, acquire a background in business systems and procedures and may thereby advance into systems analysis. Currently, the trend is to require a knowledge of advanced mathematics because of the rapidly increasing sophistication of business systems. Continuing education, through specialized courses, self-study, and participation in activities of professional associations, is the rule rather than the exception in this occupation, as in all higher level occupations related to the computer.

Special Characteristics

APTITUDES. Verbal ability to discuss problems and progress, prepare reports, and make annotations for graphic representations of work.

Numerical ability to select from alternatives to develop optimum system, procedures, and methods. Mathematical investigation of such factors as variation in volume of input data, and frequency of appearance of exceptions of normal workflow in processing, is often necessary. Level of mathematics varies from business arithmetic and algebra to differential equations.

Spatial ability to visualize, prepare, and review two-dimensional graphic representations of workflow.

Form perception to identify nonverbal symbols on records such as block diagrams and flow charts.

Clerical perception to avoid perceptual errors and recognize pertinent detail in the recording and identifying of letters and numbers that often occur in abbreviated or acronymic combinations.

INTERESTS. A preference for activities that are technical and analytical, and those that are abstract and creative in nature, to devise new or to modify standardized computer-oriented systems to meet the specific needs of an organization.

TEMPERAMENT. Ability to confer with personnel from other departments, develop flow charts, devise workflow sequence, and prepare reports.

Required to deal with people in conference and interview situations.

Required to make judgmental decisions to select from alternatives when devising optimal system.

Required to make decisions on basis of factual data to design system within machine capability.

PHYSICAL ACTIVITIES AND ENVIRONMENT. Work is sedentary, with occasional standing and walking. Occasional handling of source documents, books, charts, and other records that seldom exceed 10 pounds.

Talking and hearing to discuss and confer with management and technical personnel.

Near visual acuity to prepare and review workflow charts and diagrams.

Work is performed inside.

OPERATIONS RESEARCH ANALYST

Occupational Definition

Formulates mathematical model of management problems by application of advanced mathematics and research methods to provide quantitative basis for planning, forecasting, and making decisions. Analyzes problems in terms of management information requirements. Studies problem, such as selecting from competitive proposals a plan that affords maximum probability of profit or effectiveness in relation to cost or risk. Prepares mathematical model of problem area in form of one or several equations that relate constants and variables, restrictions, alternatives, conflicting objectives, and their numerical parameters. Gathers, relates, and identifies data with variables in model by applying personal judgment and mathematical tests. Specifies manipulative and computational methods to be applied to formulations and refers to data processing division for solving equations, programming, and processing. Reviews operations and testing of model to ensure adequacy or determine need for reformulation. Prepares written, nontechnical reports to management, indicating problem solution or range of possible alternatives in rank of desirability and probability of success when there is no single solution. Writes follow-up reports, evaluating effectiveness of research implementation. May specialize in research and preparation of contract proposals specifying the competence of an organization to perform research, development, or production work. May develop and apply time and cost networks, such as Program Evaluation and Review Technique (PERT), to plan and control large-scale business projects. May work in areas associated with engineering, as when analyzing and evaluating alternative physical systems, such as production processes, in terms of effectiveness and cost. May work alone or as member of a team.

Education, Training, and Experience

College degree with emphasis on advanced mathematics and statistics is usually the minimum educational requirement. A combination of advanced degrees in mathematics and business administration is especially desirable. A doctorate in mathematics is frequently required. Specific training in operations research at the graduate level is rapidly becoming a standardized requirement, as more schools offer courses in this interdisciplinary occupational area. Many workers have acquired the necessary background in mathematics through education and experience in engineering and the physical sciences, and knowledge of specialized techniques through self-study and participation in activities of professional organizations.

Special Characteristics

APTITUDES. Verbal ability to understand technical languages of various professional disciplines such as engineering and accounting, to give oral reports and to prepare written reports on results of research in lay terminology to management.

Numerical ability to understand and work with such mathematical specializations as game, queuing, and probability theory, and statistical inference, to prepare formulations, specify manipulative methods and evaluate effectiveness.

Spatial ability to prepare and interpret charts, diagrams, graphs, and maps.

Clerical perception to recognize pertinent detail in compilation and analysis of statistical data, and to avoid perceptual errors in working with higher forms of mathematics.

INTERESTS. A preference for activities that are technical in nature to apply analytical, experimental, and quantitative techniques in the solution of management problems such as long-range forecasting, planning, and control.

Interests in devising mathematical equations, analyzing the methods used for their manipulation, and evaluating their practical effectiveness.

TEMPERAMENT. Requires ability to perform a variety of tasks related to the solution of various problems on all departmental levels. This involves conversing in several professional disciplines with personnel at all operating levels to gather and relate data and opinions relevant to problem under study.

Must possess ability to make judgmental decisions such as probability of continuity or change in conditions, and assign arbitrary weights and values to problem factors when conventional statistical methods are not applicable.

Must possess ability to make decisions based on verifiable data, such as tabular records of previous organizational experience.

PHYSICAL ACTIVITIES AND ENVIRONMENT. Work is sedentary, and occasionally involves lifting and carrying books, ledgers, and statistical tabulations seldom exceeding 10 pounds.

Talking and hearing to discuss organization goals and priorities with management and acquire data pertinent to the problem from other organizational personnel.

Near visual acuity to read and work with a variety of data from many sources, and to refer to texts and technical papers.

Work is performed inside.

Programmer, Business

Occupational Definition

Converts symbolic statement of business problems to detailed logical flow charts for coding into computer language. Analyzes all or part of workflow chart or diagram representing business problem by applying knowledge of computer capabilities, subject matter, algebra, and symbolic logic to develop sequence of program steps. Confers with supervisor and representatives of departments concerned with program, to resolve questions of program intent, output requirements, input data acquisition, extent of automatic programming and coding use and modification, and inclusion of internal checks and controls. Writes detailed, logical flow chart in symbolic form to represent work order of data to be processed by the computer system, and describes input, output, arithmetic, and logical operations involved. Converts detailed, logical flow chart to language processable by computer (PROGRAMMER, DETAIL). Devises sample input data to provide test of program adequacy. Prepares block diagrams to specify equipment configuration. Observes or operates computer to test coded program, using actual or sample input data. Corrects program error by such methods as altering program steps and sequence. Prepares written instructions (run book) to guide operating personnel during production runs. Analyzes, reviews, and rewrites programs to increase operating efficiency or adapt to new requirements. Compiles documentation of program development and subsequent revisions. May specialize in writing programs for one make and type of computer.

Education, Training, and Experience

Minimum requirements are high school graduation with six months to two years of technical training in computer operations and in general principles of programming and coding, or equivalent job experience in these areas. Current trend is to hire college graduates for promotional potential with training in accounting, business administration, and mathematics, and provide them with a year of on-the-job training to qualify them for programming. In installations concerned with the application of the computer to more complex areas such as market research and statistical forecasting, a college degree in mathematics is preferred.

Special Characteristics

APTITUDES. Must possess verbal ability to understand and analyze oral or written statements concerning a variety of business problems and to discuss them with others.

Must possess numerical ability to interpret workflow charts, program problems, and understand machine logic. Level of mathematics varies from arithmetic and algebra for simple business data-processing problems to differential equations and mathematical statistics for involved problems such as forecasting or optimization.

Must possess form perception to see pertinent detail in symbols when reading, interpreting, or preparing charts, diagrams, and code sheets.

Clerical perception to detect errors in letters, words, and numbers recorded on charts, diagrams, and code sheets.

INTERESTS. An interest in activities technical in nature to effectively analyze problems, and to design logical flow charts and block diagrams.

An interest in activities that are carried out in relation to processes, techniques, and machines, to plan sequence steps, to prepare instructions, and to test programs.

TEMPERAMENT. Required to make judgmental decisions to plan logical sequence of steps and prepare logical flow chart for a project, keeping in mind capacities and limitations of computer and integrated machine units.

Must be able to conform to accepted standards and techniques in developing and testing programs and writing instructions for computer operators to follow.

PHYSICAL ACTIVITIES AND ENVIRONMENT. Work is sedentary, requiring occasional lifting and carrying of such items as source materials, run books, and documentations seldom exceeding 10 pounds.

Talking and hearing to communicate with systems, program coding, and operating personnel.

Near visual acuity and accommodation required to review statistical data and interpret charts and diagrams.

Work is performed inside.

Programmer, Engineering and Scientific

Occupational Definition

Converts scientific, engineering, and other technical problem formulations to format processable by computer. Resolves symbolic formulations, prepares logical flow charts and block diagrams, and encodes resolvent equations for processing by applying knowledge of advanced mathematics, such as differential equations and numerical analysis, and understanding of computer capabilities and limitations. Confers with engineering and other technical personnel to resolve problems of intent, inaccuracy, or feasibility of computer processing. Observes or operates computer during testing or processing runs to analyze and correct programming and coding errors. Reviews results of computer runs with interested technical personnel to determine necessity for modifications and rerun. Develops new subroutines for a specific area of application, or expands on applicability of current general programs, such as FORTRAN, to simplify statement, programming, or coding of future problems. May supervise other programming personnel. May specialize in single area of application, such as numerical control, to develop processors that permit programming for contour-controlled machine tools in source-oriented language.

Education, Training, and Experience

College degree with major in mathematics or engineering is usually the minimum educational requirement. A master's degree or doctorate in mathematics or engineering is a common requirement where analysis or programming is extremely complex or where work duties involve basic research in mathematics or programming. From two to four years of on-the-job training, with gradually decreasing amounts of supervision and with increasingly complex work assignments, are regarded as necessary for the worker to become familiar with at least one class of computer, programming language, and applications area. Short (one to four weeks) training sessions are given by employers and computer manufacturers to provide basic training and (later) specialized training. Current trends toward simplification of programming languages and greater applicability of generalized programs, and requirement of basic computer orientation and programming courses for college degree in physical sciences or engineering, will reduce on-the-job training time.

Special Characteristics

APTITUDES. Verbal ability to discuss problems and equipment requirements with other technical personnel, to prepare computer flow charts, written records, reports, and recommendations and to read technical publications.

Numerical ability to interpret mathematical formulation, to select from alternative computational methods, to frame program within limitations of the computer to be used, prepare logical flow charts and diagrams, to convert program steps to coded computer instructions, and to review work. Level of mathematics may vary from arithmetic and algebra to advanced differential equations in the course of writing a single program, and may also include applications of numerical analysis.

Spatial ability to prepare logical flow charts specifying sequences of operating instructions and flow of data through computer system, to design input and output forms, and to interpret detailed drawings, diagrams, and other graphic data.

Form perception to see pertinent detail in charts, diagrams, and drawings, and distinguish symbols in subject matter areas such as physics and electrical engineering.

Clerical perception to avoid perceptual errors in recording of alphanumeric and special symbologies.

Motor coordination to operate calculator or computer.

INTERESTS. A preference for activities technical in nature, to use mathematics to reduce formulations to computer-processable form.

TEMPERAMENT. Required to make decisions on a judgmental basis, using past experience and knowledge to select best method of programming and coding a problem and thereby avoiding costly, time-consuming analyses of alternate techniques.

Required to make factual decisions, such as evaluation of program accuracy by computer acceptance, presence of error messages or obvious output distortions.

Must be able to conform to accepted standards and techniques in developing and testing programs, and in writing instructions for digital-computer operator.

PHYSICAL ACTIVITIES AND ENVIRONMENT. Work is sedentary, requiring occasional lifting and carrying of source data, books, charts, and diagrams seldom exceeding 10 pounds.

Talking and hearing to confer and collaborate with other technical personnel.

Near visual acuity to prepare logical flow charts from lengthy mathematical statements of problem, and to convert program steps to coded computer instructions.

Work is performed inside.

Computer Operator

Occupational Definition

Monitors and controls electronic digital computer to process business, scientific, engineering, or other data, according to operating instructions. Sets control switches on computer and peripheral equipment, such as external memory, data communicating, synchronizing, input, and output recording or display devices, to integrate and operate equipment according to program, routines, subroutines, and data requirements specified in written operating instructions. Selects and loads input and output units with materials, such as tapes or punchcards and printout forms, for operating runs, or oversees operators of peripheral equipment who perform these functions. Moves switches to clear system and start operation of equipment. Observes machines and control panel on computer console for error lights, verification printouts, and error messages, and machine stoppage or faulty output. Types alternate commands into computer console, according to predetermined instructions, to correct error or failure and resume operations. Notifies supervisor of errors or equipment stoppage. Clears unit at end of operating run and reviews schedule to determine next assignment. Records operating and down-time. Wires control panels of peripheral equipment. May control computer to provide input or output service for another computer under instructions from operator of that unit.

Education, Training, and Experience

A high school education meets the minimum educational requirements of some employers, but an increasing number of employers are demanding an additional several months to two years of technical school training in data processing. This training usually includes such courses as data-processing mathematics, accounting, business practices, elementary programming, and operation of computers, peripheral equipment, and tabulating machines.

The employer or computer manufacturer usually provides one to three weeks of formal instruction for the specific computer system the worker will operate. Length of subsequent on-the-job training and experience required to achieve adequate performance ranges from a few months to one year because computer systems and equipment vary in complexity and need for operator intervention. Except in small units, a minimum of three to six months prior experience in operation of peripheral equipment frequently is required.

Special Characteristics

APTITUDES. Verbal ability to comprehend technical language of operating instructions and equipment manuals and to explain clearly any operating problems and difficulties in interpreting program intent.

Numerical ability at level of arithmetic to prepare operating records, time computer runs, and adhere to fixed operating schedule. While not always an operator requirement, an understanding of data-processing mathematics (the number systems used, algebra, and logic) is almost essential to discuss operating difficulties with programming personnel, and to progress from routine production runs to the testing of new programs.

Spatial perception to wire control panels for peripheral equipment.

Form perception to identify flaws in input and output materials.

Clerical perception to avoid perceptual errors in preparing operating records, and to recognize alphabetic, numeric, and mnemonic symbols.

Motor coordination, to set up machines rapidly and move keys and switches to correct errors or stoppages quickly.

INTERESTS. A preference for working with machines and processes to continuously operate and monitor the equipment that makes up the computer system.

Interest in activities of concrete and organized nature to operate machines according to specific and detailed instructions.

TEMPERAMENT. Work situation requires ability to perform a variety of work tasks subject to frequent change in the simultaneous operation of a console and a variety of peripheral equipment, the integration of which varies from program to program, or even during a single operating run, and which demands rapid transfer of attention from one piece of equipment to another.

Accuracy required to operate system effectively and minimize down-time and rescheduling of runs. Carelessness in following written and oral instructions can cause extensive rebuilding of program or input data, or even lead to irrecoverable loss of data.

PHYSICAL ACTIVITIES AND ENVIRONMENT. Work is light. Lifts, carries, and positions tape reels, punchcard decks, output forms, and control panels seldom exceeding 20 pounds.

Stands and walks frequently when loading and monitoring machines.

Reaches for and fingers switches and keys on console and peripheral machines. Wires control panels, loads and removes input and output materials.

Talking and hearing to frequently exchange information concerning program and system requirements with other workers and to receive or give instructions.

Near visual acuity and accommodation to follow detailed operating log, monitor computer and peripheral machines for signs of malfunction, and analyze console messages or high-speed printer output for cause of error or stoppage.

Color vision to distinguish between colored wires when wiring control panels, to identify color-coded cards or forms and to monitor colored display lights if used.

Work is performed inside.

Computer–Peripheral–Equipment Operator

Occupational Definition

Operates on-line or off-line peripheral machines, according to instructions, to transfer data from one form to another, print output, and read data into and out of digital computer. Mounts and positions materials, such as reels of magnetic or paper tape onto spindles, décks of cards in hoppers, bank checks in magnetic ink reader-sorter, notices in optical scanner, or output forms and carriage tape in printing devices. Sets guides, keys, and switches according to oral instructions or run book to prepare equipment for operation. Selects specified wired control panels or wires panels according to diagrams and inserts them into machines. Presses switches to start off-line machines, such as card-tape converters, or to inter-connect on-line equipment, such as tape or card computer input and output devices, and high-speed printer or other output recorder. Observes materials for creases, tears, or printing defects and watches machines and error lights to detect machine malfunction. Removes faulty materials and notifies supervisor of machine stoppage or error. Unloads and labels card or tape input and output and places them in storage or routes them to library. Separates and sorts printed output forms, using decollator, to prepare them for distribution. May operate tabulating machines, such as sorters and collators.

Education, Training, and Experience

High school graduate. Post-high school training in operation of electronic or electromechanical data-processing equipment is desirable. Employers frequently regard worker as understudy to computer operators and apply same education and aptitude standards to them.

Special Characteristics

APTITUDES. Verbal ability to read written instructions and handbooks and to communicate with supervisor about operating functions.

Spatial ability to follow diagrams to wire control panels, position and thread tapes onto spindles, or position decks of cards in hoppers.

Clerical perception to identify and record, without error, data such as dates, program numbers, departments, and routings on forms.

Motor coordination and finger and manual dexterity to load and unload machines quickly and minimize down-time, to thread ribbons of tape over guides and through rollers, and to handle cards and tapes deftly without bending, tearing, or otherwise damaging them.

INTERESTS. An interest in activities concerned with machines, processes, and techniques to operate various machines. Preference for activities of a routine and organized nature to follow well-defined instructions for any of several different machines.

TEMPERAMENT. Worker must be adept at performing a variety of tasks requiring frequent change to operate a number of machines in varying combinations and sequences.

When operating peripheral equipment, must adhere to established standards for accuracy, such as observing printer output forms for defects in alignment, spacing, margin, and overprinting. Immediate response to indication of error in operation of peripheral equipment is vital.

PHYSICAL ACTIVITIES AND ENVIRONMENT. Work is light, involving frequent standing and walking when operating machines and lifting and carrying tapes, cards, and forms not exceeding 20 pounds.

Reaches, handles, and fingers to mount tapes onto spindles, position decks of cards in hoppers, and thread tape through guides and rollers of peripheral units or wire control panels.

Near visual acuity to read labels on reels, to wire plug boards from diagrams, to scan printout for error, and to read operating instructions and handbooks.

Color vision to distinguish between various colors of wires to ensure correct wiring of control panels.

Work is performed inside.

---

*The title may be related to single functional activities, such as Manager of Systems Analysis, Manager of Programming, Manager of Computer Operations, Manager of Unit-Record Equipment, Manager of Applications Programming, Systems Manager, Programming Manager.

Key Punch Operator

Occupational Definition

Operates alphabetic and numeric key punch machine, similar in operation to electric typewriter, to transcribe data from source material onto punchcards and to reproduce prepunched data. Attaches skip bar to machine and previously punched program card around machine drum to control duplication and spacing of constant data. Loads machine with decks of punchcards. Moves switches and depresses keys to select automatic or manual duplication and spacing, selects alphabetic or numeric punching, and transfers cards through machine stations. Depresses keys to transcribe new data in prescribed sequence from source material into perforations on card. Inserts previously punched card into card gauge to verify registration of punches. Observes machine to detect faulty feeding, positioning, ejecting, duplicating, skipping, punching, or other mechanical malfunctions and notifies supervisor. Removes jammed cards, using prying knife. May tend machines that automatically sort, merge, or match punchcards into specified groups. May key punch numerical data only and be designated KEY PUNCH OPERATOR, NUMERIC.

Education, Training, and Experience

High school graduate preferred with demonstrated proficiency in typing on standard or electric typewriter. High school or business school training in key punch operation is desirable. Frequently, one week of training is provided by employer or manufacturer of equipment.

Special Characteristics

APTITUDES. Verbal ability to understand oral and written instructions, such as manufacturers' operating manuals, and to learn operation of machine.

Clerical perception to perceive pertinent detail in tabular material consisting of combinations of letters and numbers, and avoid perceptual error in transferring this data to punchcards.

Motor coordination to read work sheets and simultaneously operate keyboard of approximately 40 keys to punch data on cards.

Finger dexterity to move switches on machine.

INTERESTS. Preference for organized and routine activities to transfer data onto punchcards.

TEMPERAMENT. Must be able to perform repetitive duties of operating key punch machine.

Ability to follow specific instructions and set procedures to transfer data onto punchcards.

Required to work to precise and established standards of accuracy to key punch data at high rate of speed.

PHYSICAL ACTIVITIES AND ENVIRONMENT. Work is sedentary with infrequent lifting of decks of cards when loading machine.

Reaches for and handles code sheets, business records, and decks of cards; fingers switches and keys to operate machine.

Near visual acuity to read copy when key punching.

Work is performed inside.

Appendix II: Psychological Tests

The following is a list of the tests that may be included in a test battery administered during the personnel selection process.

GENERAL INTELLIGENCE TESTS

California Test of Mental Maturity. Published by the California Test Bureau. Used to test memory, spatial relationships, logical reasoning, numerical reasoning, and vocabulary.

SRA—Primary Mental Abilities Test. Published by Science Research Associates, Inc. Used to test verbal ability, space perception, arithmetic ability, and word reasoning.

APTITUDE TESTS

Aptitude Assessment Battery—Programming. Published by Brandon/Systems Press. Used to measure a person's protracted concentration and accuracy in working with symbols, instructions, and arithmetic operations. Regarded as a bold approach to evaluating programming trainees.

RPAT—Revised Programmers Aptitude Test. Published by Psychological Corporation for use by the IBM Corporation and its customers. Used to measure abstract reasoning, numerical reasoning, and arithmetic ability.

Data Processing Machine Operators Aptitude Test. Published by Psychological Corporation for use by the IBM Corporation and its customers. Used to measure skills or abilities required for a peripheral equipment operator.

Card Punch Operator Aptitude Test. Published by the Psychological Corporation for IBM Corporation and its customers. Used to measure the abilities and skills required for key punching and key verification operations.

592

PROFICIENCY TESTS

NCR—Electronic Data Processing Tests. Published by National Cash Register Corporation for use by the NCR Corporation and its customers. Used to measure a person's flowcharting and simulated programming ability.

INTEREST TESTS

Kuder Preference Record-Vocational. Published by Science Research Associates.
Kuder Preference Record-Personal. Published by Science Research Associates.
Strong Vocational Interest Blank. Published by Stanford University Press.
Thurstone Interest Schedule. Published by the Psychological Corporation.

PERSONALITY AND TEMPERAMENT TESTS

Guilford-Zimmerman Temperament Survey. Published by Sheridan Supply Company. Used for describing a normal personality. Regarded as one of the best in this category.
Heston Personal Adjustment Inventory. Published by World Book Company. Used to study sociality, confidence, and personal relations. Considered to be a good rough-screening device.
Minnesota Multiphasic Personality Inventory. Published by the Psychological Corporation. Used to determine abnormal rather than normal traits. It is a lengthy test and requires interpretation by a clinical psychologist.

Appendix III: Standardized Charting Symbols

This appendix identifies the various symbols used to represent the functions of an information processing system. They are used in the preparation of system flowcharts, marco-flowcharts, and micro-flowcharts. The charts are used to analyze a problem; to design and implement a solution; and to provide documentation for training, user, operating, and audit personnel.

There are four major symbol-utilization categories. These are:

1. Basic symbols
2. Specialized process symbols
3. Specialized media symbols
4. Additional symbols

BASIC SYMBOLS

The basic symbols are general-purpose symbols established for given functions and are always used to represent that function. They may be used to represent any function in an information processing system. Included in this category are the:

1. Input/Output symbol
2. Process symbol
3. Flowline symbol
4. Annotation symbol

1. INPUT/OUTPUT SYMBOL. This symbol represents an input/output (i/o) function. It is used to represent all data or information available for processing (input); or the recording of processed information (output).

2. Process Symbol. This symbol is used to represent any processing function. It may be used to illustrate a single or group of operations; a computer instruction; EAM or EDP equipment, etc.

3. Flowline Symbol. This symbol represents the function of linking symbols. It indicates the sequence of available information and executable operations. The flow direction is represented by lines drawn between the symbols. The normal flow of direction is from left to right and top to bottom. Open arrowheads can be placed on the flowlines to ensure understanding of the flow of direction on the chart.

When the flow of direction does not follow the normal direction (left to right and top to bottom), then open arrowheads must be used.

Flowlines may cross when they have no logical interrelation.

Two or more incoming flowlines may join with one outgoing flowline.

Open arrowheads should be placed near the junction points to illustrate flowlines entering and leaving a point.

4. Annotation Symbol. This symbol is used to add descriptive comments or explanatory notes to a chart. The annotation symbol is connected to any symbol by a broken line at the point where the comment is most meaningful.

SPECIALIZED PROCESS SYMBOL

The specialized process symbols are used to provide greater clarity to a flowchart by identifying a specific type of processing operation. These symbols are used in lieu of the basic process symbol. Included in this category are the:

1. Decision symbol
2. Pre-defined process symbol
3. Preparation symbol
4. Auxiliary operation symbol
5. Manual operation symbol

6. Merge symbol
7. Extract symbol
8. Sort symbol
9. Collate symbol

1. Decision Symbol. This symbol is used in switching-type and decision operations to determine which alternative or logical path should be followed. The entry into the decision symbol should be from the top. Exits may be made from the bottom point (normal) or either side.

Multiple exits may be made from the bottom or sides of the decision symbol.

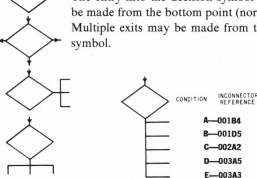

CONDITION	INCONNECTOR REFERENCE
A	001B4
B	001D5
C	002A2
D	003A5
E	003A3

To identify the alternative paths, some standardized method of identification should be used. A suggested scheme is:

Path Identification			Condition
or	Yes		Condition satisfied
or	No		Condition not satisfied
or	EQ		Equal
or	UN or	NE	Unequal
			Positive
			Negative
or	GR		Greater than
or	GR/E or	GE	Greater than or equal to
or	L		Less than
or	LE		Less than or equal to
Hi			High
Lo			Low
0 or	Z		Zero

2. PRE-DEFINED PROCESS SYMBOL. This symbol is used to indicate linkage to a subroutine, subprogram, logical unit, or process. The activity represented by the symbol is not normally represented on this flowchart.

3. PREPARATION SYMBOL. This symbol is used to represent a modification of an instruction or series of instructions, which alter the effect of a program. The modifications include such activities as subroutine initialization; setting an internal switch; initializing, incrementing, or decrementing an index register, etc.

4. AUXILIARY OPERATION SYMBOL. This symbol represents operations performed on equipment that is not under the direct control of the central processing unit. It is normally used to describe equipment which operates at its own speed and is not affected by the speed of its human operator. The symbol may be used to represent such operations as punched card sorting, or punched card collating performed on unit-record equipment.

5. MANUAL OPERATION SYMBOL. This symbol is used to represent any offline input or output producing process geared to the speed of a human being. The symbol may be used to represent such offline keying operations as key punching, key-to-magnetic tape, and key-to-magnetic disk. Alternatively, it may be used to represent such functions as checking control totals, or logging batch control entries.

6. MERGE SYMBOL. This symbol may be used to represent online or offline operations that generate one set of items from two or more sets—in the same sequence.

7. EXTRACT SYMBOL. This symbol is used for online or offline operations in which two or more sets of items are generated from one set.

8. Sᴏʀᴛ Sʏᴍʙᴏʟ. This symbol may be used to represent the online or offline sorting operations.

9. Cᴏʟʟᴀᴛᴇ Sʏᴍʙᴏʟ. This symbol represents a combination of the merge and extract operations. Two or more sets of items may be generated from two or more other sets. The collate symbol may be used for online or offline operations.

SPECIALIZED MEDIA SYMBOLS

The specialized media symbols are used to specifically identify the media on which the information is recorded for input or output, or both. Included in this category are the following:

1. Punched card symbol
2. Magnetic tape symbol
3. Punched tape symbol
4. Document symbol
5. Online storage symbol
6. Offline storage symbol
7. Display symbol
8. Communication link symbol
9. Manual input symbol
10. Magnetic drum symbol
11. Magnetic disk symbol
12. Core symbol

1. Pᴜɴᴄʜᴇᴅ Cᴀʀᴅ Sʏᴍʙᴏʟ. Any form of input or output requiring the use of punched cards is represented by this symbol. The symbol is used to represent data in any size or shape of punched card. This includes mark scan cards, mark sense cards, stub cards, partial cards, etc.

This symbol may also be used to represent a deck of cards or file of cards. However, there are also specialized symbols to represent both of these functions.

A collection of punched cards may be illustrated utilizing the specialized deck of cards symbols.

A file of related punched cards may be illustrated utilizing the specialized file of cards symbol.

2. Mᴀɢɴᴇᴛɪᴄ Tᴀᴘᴇ Sʏᴍʙᴏʟ. This symbol is used to represent the use of magnetic tape as an input/output medium. The symbol applies to magnetic tape regardless of type, width, length, or information content.

3. Pᴜɴᴄʜᴇᴅ Tᴀᴘᴇ Sʏᴍʙᴏʟ. This symbol is used to represent all forms of punched tape used as an input or output medium. The symbol is not limited to punched paper tape; it also applies to such media as punched plastic tape, punched metal tape, etc.

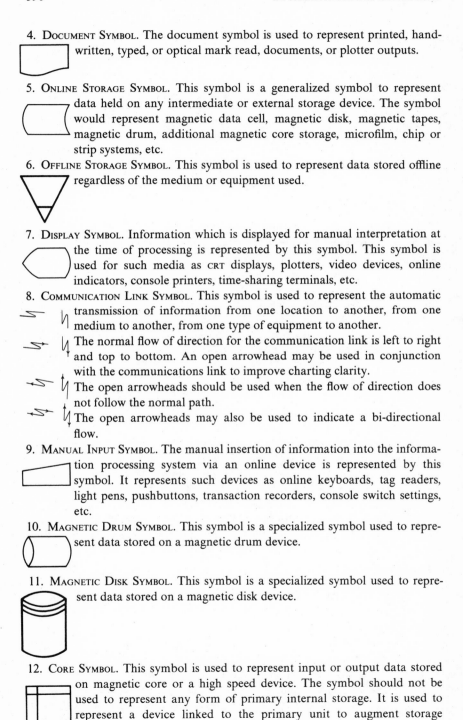

4. DOCUMENT SYMBOL. The document symbol is used to represent printed, hand-written, typed, or optical mark read, documents, or plotter outputs.

5. ONLINE STORAGE SYMBOL. This symbol is a generalized symbol to represent data held on any intermediate or external storage device. The symbol would represent magnetic data cell, magnetic disk, magnetic tapes, magnetic drum, additional magnetic core storage, microfilm, chip or strip systems, etc.

6. OFFLINE STORAGE SYMBOL. This symbol is used to represent data stored offline regardless of the medium or equipment used.

7. DISPLAY SYMBOL. Information which is displayed for manual interpretation at the time of processing is represented by this symbol. This symbol is used for such media as CRT displays, plotters, video devices, online indicators, console printers, time-sharing terminals, etc.

8. COMMUNICATION LINK SYMBOL. This symbol is used to represent the automatic transmission of information from one location to another, from one medium to another, from one type of equipment to another.

The normal flow of direction for the communication link is left to right and top to bottom. An open arrowhead may be used in conjunction with the communications link to improve charting clarity.

The open arrowheads should be used when the flow of direction does not follow the normal path.

The open arrowheads may also be used to indicate a bi-directional flow.

9. MANUAL INPUT SYMBOL. The manual insertion of information into the information processing system via an online device is represented by this symbol. It represents such devices as online keyboards, tag readers, light pens, pushbuttons, transaction recorders, console switch settings, etc.

10. MAGNETIC DRUM SYMBOL. This symbol is a specialized symbol used to represent data stored on a magnetic drum device.

11. MAGNETIC DISK SYMBOL. This symbol is a specialized symbol used to represent data stored on a magnetic disk device.

12. CORE SYMBOL. This symbol is used to represent input or output data stored on magnetic core or a high speed device. The symbol should not be used to represent any form of primary internal storage. It is used to represent a device linked to the primary unit to augment storage capability.

ADDITIONAL SYMBOLS

These symbols are primarily used on a chart to display continuity of functions or operations, and to identify entry and termination points. Included in this category of symbols are the following:

1. Connector
2. Terminal
3. Parallel mode

1. CONNECTOR. The connector symbol is used to maintain a flow of continuity on the flowchart. It may be used to illustrate either a physical break due to paper limitation or an awkward line requirement.

OUTCONNECTOR INCONNECTOR The connectors usually appear in pairs. The inconnector or entry connector has a flowline leaving from it. the outconnector or exit connector has only a flowline entering it.

2. TERMINAL. The terminal or interrupt symbol may be used to illustrate initial starting points, exits from a logical path, interrupts, delay, halts, and returns from an interrupted process.

3. PARALLEL MODE. The parallel mode symbol is used to represent the beginning or end of two or more simultaneous operations.

The symbols in this appendix may be drawn by using a flowcharting template.

Appendix IV: Professional Associations

Administrative Management Society, Willow Grove, Pa. 19090

American Bankers' Association, 90 Park Avenue New York, N.Y. 10016

American Documentation Institute, 2000 P Street, N.W. Washington, D.C. 20036

American Federation of Information Processing Societies, 210 Summit Avenue, Montvale, N.J. 07645

American Institute of Industrial Engineers, 345 East 47th Street, New York, N.Y. 10017

American Management Association, 135 West 50th Street, New York, N.Y. 10020

American Records Management Association, 7201 South Leamington, Chicago, Ill. 60638

American Society for Information Science, 2011 Eye Street, N.W., Washington, D.C. 20006

American Society of Mechanical Engineers, 345 East 47th Street, New York, N.Y. 10017

Armed Forces Management Association, 1025 Connecticut Avenue, N.W., Washington, D.C. 20036

Association for Computing Machinery, 1133 Avenue of the Americas, New York, N.Y. 10036

Association of Consulting Management Engineers, 347 Madison Avenue, New York, N.Y. 10017

Association for Educational Data Systems, 610 Jefferson Building, Iowa City, Iowa 52240

Association for Systems Management, 24587 Bagley Road, Cleveland, Ohio 44138

Association for Data Processing Service Organizations, Inc., 551 Fifth Avenue, Suite 425, New York, N.Y. 10017

Business Equipment Manufacturers Association, 1828 L Street, N.W., Washington, D.C. 20036

Data Processing Management Association, 505 Busse Highway, Park Ridge, Ill. 60068

Electronic Computing—Hospital Oriented, c/o Mr. William Isaacs, Post Office Box 452, Skokie, Ill. 60076

Federal Government Accountants Association, 1523 L Street, N.W., Washington, D.C. 20005

Financial Executives' Institute, 50 West 44th Street, New York, N.Y. 10036

Industrial Management Society, 330 South Wells Street, Chicago, Ill. 60606

Institute of Electrical & Electronics Engineers, 345 East 47th Street, New York, N.Y. 10017

Institute of Management Sciences, 250 North, White Plains, N.Y. 10605

Life Office Management Association, 757 Third Avenue, New York, N.Y. 10017

National Association of Accountants, 505 Park Avenue, New York, N.Y. 10022

National Association of Credit Management, 44 East 23rd Street, New York, N.Y. 10010

National Association of Manufacturers, 2 East 48th Street, New York, N.Y. 10017

National Business Forms Association, 300 North Lee Street, Alexandria, Va. 22314

National Microfilm Association, 250 Prince George Street, Annapolis, Md. 21404

National Retail Merchants' Association, 100 West 31st Street, New York, N.Y. 10001

Numerical Control Society, 44 Nassau Street, Princeton, N.J. 08540

Operations Research Society of America, 428 East Preston Street, Baltimore, Md. 21202

Railway Systems and Management Association, 163 East Walton Street, Chicago, Ill. 60611

Society for Advancement of Management, 16 West 40th Street, New York, N.Y. 10018

Society of Data Educators, c/o Enoch J. Haga, Executive Director, 247 Edythe Street, Livermore, Ca. 94550

Society for Information Display, 654 North Sepulveda Blvd., Suite 5, Los Angeles, Ca. 90049

Simulation Councils, Inc., Post Office Box 2228, La Jolla, Ca. 92038

Appendix V: Professional Education Services

AMR International Inc., Advanced Management Research, 280 Park Avenue, New York, N.Y. 10017

Auerbach Institute, 121 North Broad Street, Philadelphia, Pa. 19107

Automation Training Center, 1930 Isaac Newton Square, East Reston, Va. 22070

Barnett Data Systems, 1010 Rockville Pike, Rockville, Md. 20852

Berkley Enterprises, Inc., 815 Washington Street, Newtonville, Mass. 02160

Brandon Systems Institute, 30 East 42nd Street, New York, N.Y. 10017

CGA Computer Associates, 715 Park Avenue, East Orange, N.J. 07017

Computer Applications Incorporated, 555 Madison Avenue, New York, N.Y. 10022

Computer Environments Corporation, 3 Lebanon Street, Hanover, N.H. 03755

Computer Methods Corporation, 470 Mamaroneck Avenue, White Plains, N.Y. 10605

Computer Seminar Associates, 1530 Locust Street, Philadelphia, Pa. 19102

Computer Usage Company, Inc., 51 Weaver Street, Greenwich, Ct. 06830

Electronics, Inc., 2790 Harbor Blvd., Costa Mesa, Ca. 92626

IBM Systems Research Institute, 78 United Nations Plaza, New York, N.Y. 10017

Institute for Advanced Technology, C-E-I-R Inc., 5272 River Road, Washington, D.C. 20016

Institute for Automation Research, Inc., Tavern Square, 110 North Royal Street, Alexandria, Va. 22314

Institute for Professional Education, University Computing Company, 1949 Stemmons Freeway, Dallas, Tex. 75207

Lutter and Helmstrom, Inc., 20 North Wacker Drive, Chicago, Ill. 60606
Programming Sciences Corporation, 90 Park Avenue, New York, N.Y. 10016
Seminars for Management Corporation, 320 Fifth Avenue, New York, N.Y. 10001
Service Bureau Corporation, 1350 Avenue of the Americas, New York, N. Y. 10019
Stanford Research Institute, 333 Ravenswood Avenue, Menlo Park, Ca. 94025
Strategic Systems Inc., 605 Third Avenue, New York, N.Y. 10016
Systemation, Inc., Box 730, Colorado Springs, Col. 80901

Appendix VI: Suggested Standard for Processing Requests for Data Processing Services

R. S. Computations, Inc.

Data Processing Manual 10.1
February 3, 1972

Justification for Data Processing Services

1. GENERAL

1.1 This instruction prescribes the procedure for handling of requests for the services of the Data Processing Organization.

1.2 Form RS 1819, "Request For Data Processing Services," shall be issued when the services of the Systems, Programming, or Operations Group is required.

2. REQUESTING ORGANIZATION

2.1 The organization requesting information processing services shall:

(a) issue Form RS 1819 in duplicate, retaining one copy and forwarding the original to the Data Processing Administrator.

(b) provide concise, accurate details, and an analysis of costs to manually produce the data required.

3. DATA PROCESSING ORGANIZATION

3.1 The Data Processing organization shall:
  (a) immediately acknowledge receipt of Form RS 1819.
  (b) determine the scope and objective of the request.
  (c) review the available information and determine if the request
      is unacceptable, requires additional investigation, or is acceptable.

> (1) if unacceptable, an immediate response must be made to the requesting organization.
> (2) if additional investigation is required, the requesting organization must be notified to supply additional details.
> (3) if acceptable, a case number will be assigned to the request and the Data Processing Administrator will allocate the necessary resources.

Appendix VII: Hardware Performance Monitor Manufacturers

Allied Computer Technology, 3112 Pennsylvania Avenue, Santa Monica, Ca. 90404
Computer Synectics, Inc., 328 Martin Avenue, Santa Clara, Ca. 95050
COMRESS, 2 Research Court, Rockville, Md. 20850
IBM Corporation, 112 East Post Road, White Plains, N.Y. 10601

Appendix VIII: System Utilization Software Package Manufacturers

Appendix VIII: System Utilization Software Package Manufacturers

Boole and Babbage, Incorporated, 1121 San Antonio Road, Palo Alto, Ca. 94303

Boothe Resources International, 3435 Wilshire Boulevard, Los Angeles, Ca. 90005

Computing Efficiency, Incorporated, 35 Orville Drive, Islip, N.Y. 11716

IBM Corporation, 112 East Post Road, White Plains, N.Y. 10601

Webster Computer Corporation, 1 Padanaram Road, Danbury, Ct. 06810

Glossary

This glossary is not intended to serve as a dictionary of data processing terms per se. Rather, it is an example of what an organization may develop for its own personnel.

ACCESS METHOD: A data management technique available to the user for transferring data between an input/output device and the primary storage unit

ACCESS TIME: Time required to locate data or an instruction in the storage unit and transfer it to the arithmetic unit for processing; or the time required to return the result from the arithmetic unit to the storage device

ADDRESS: A designation which identifies a register, memory location, a device, or destination of a communications message

ADDRESS MODIFICATION: The process of changing the address part of a machine language instruction by means of coded instructions, under the control of stored program instructions

ALGOL: Algebraic Oriented Language; a procedural oriented algebraic language used for the solution of technical and scientific problems

ALGORITHM: A fixed, detailed calculating procedure for solving a problem

ALPHAMERIC (or ALPHANUMERIC):   Characters that may be letters of the alphabet, numbers, or special symbols

ANALOG COMPUTER: A computer that operates on data by performing physical processes on that data

ANNOTATION: An added descriptive comment or explanatory note used on a flowchart or in a program

ARITHMETIC UNIT: That part of the central processing unit in which arithmetic and logic operations are performed

ASCII: American Standard Code for Information Interchange; this is the proposed standard for character code used in digital communications over telephone lines

ASSOCIATIVE MEMORY: A memory unit in which the storage locations are identified by their contents rather than their addresses, names, or positions

AUDIT TRAIL: A means for identifying the actions performed on data as it moves through an information processing cycle from source document to output or report; or tracing the output to its source of derivation

BACKGROUND PROGRAM: A program that can be executed in a multi-programming environment whenever the facilities of the computer are not required by a program with a higher priority

BASIC: A symbolic programming language designed primarily for giving a user an interactive computing capability

BATCH PROCESSING: An approach to processing in which data and/or programs are collected for execution in a serial manner

BOOLEAN ALGEBRA: A form of algebra named after English mathematician George Boole; it is a process of reasoning using symbolic logic and dealing with classes, propositions, and yes/no criteria; it includes such operations as AND, OR, NOT, EXCEPT, IF, THEN, etc

BOS: Basic Operating System

BTAM: Basic Telecommunications Access Method

BUFFER: A temporary storage device used during data transfers

BUG: An error or malfunction

CALL: Transfer control to a specified closed subroutine

CENTRAL PROCESSOR: That component of the computing system that contains an arithmetic, control, and storage unit

CHECKPOINT: A place in a routine where a check or a recording of data for restart purposes is performed

CLEAR: Replace information in the memory with a blank or zero

COBOL: Common Business Oriented Language; a large-file business processing language

COM: A microfilm printer (Computer Output Microfilm) that can take output directly from a computer; this process is a substitute for line printer or magnetic tape output

COMPUTER NETWORK: A complex consisting of two or more interconnected computing units

COMPUTER UTILITY: A service providing computational capability through the use of data communications; synonymous with time-shared

CONFIGURATION: A group of machines which interact or are programmed to operate as a system

CONVERTER: A device to convert the representation of information from one mode to another

CONVERSATION MODE: The process of communicating with a computer via a terminal device and securing a response on the terminal

CPU: Central Processing Unit

CRT: Cathode-Ray Tube; An electronic tube on which information may be stored by a beam of electrons emitted for a thermionic storage device

DASD: Direct Access Storage Device

DATA: The basic elements of information represented by numeric, alphabetic, or special characters, which are processed on the equipment

DATA BASE MANAGEMENT: A software technique for the storage, updating, and retrieval of information stored in a common data bank

DATA COLLECTION: The process of gathering data from one or several points to a central location via a terminal

DATA COMMUNICATIONS: The transmission of encoded information via telephone and telegraph lines

DATA PHONE: Data sets manufactured and supplied by the Bell System for transmission of data over a telephone network

DEBUGGING: The process of determining the accuracy of a program, application, or system

DECISION TABLE: A table of all contingencies that are to be considered in the description of a problem, together with the actions to be taken

DIAGNOSTIC ROUTINE: A test program used to detect and locate any errors in the hardware or a computer program

DOUBLE PRECISION: A data word requiring two computer words for storage; synonymous with double length

DOS: Disk Operating System

DUMP: A computer program that outputs the contents of the memory onto a listing, punched cards, magnetic or paper tape; synonymous with memory dump, storage dump, and core dump

EAM: Electrical Accounting Machine; pertains to electromechanical processing equipment, such as key punches, collators, tabulators, etc

EBCDIC: Extended Binary Coded Decimal Interchange Code; an eight-bit code used to represent data in many computer systems

EBR: Electron Beam Recorder; A type of COM designed to generate images, via an electron beam, directly onto EBR microfilm

EMULATE: To imitate one system with another to achieve the same results as the imitated system

EXECUTIVE ROUTINE: A program that controls processing and execution of other routines and programs; the routine is considered to be part of the machine itself; synonymous with monitor, supervisor routine, supervisor program, operating system, or executive control

FIELD: A unit of information is a record

FILE: A collection of records directed toward the same purpose

FILE MAINTENANCE: Process of updating a master file with the changes which had occurred

FIRMWARE: Software that is fixed within the computer system, usually in a read-only memory unit

FOREGROUND PROGRAM: A program in a multi-programming environment that has a high priority over other programs in the computer system

FORMAT: A predetermined arrangement of characters in a file, record, or listing

FORTRAN: Formula Translator; an algebraic procedure-oriented language used for technical and scientific problems

GENERAL PURPOSE COMPUTER: A computer that is designed to handle a wide variety of problems

HARD COPY: A form of computer output which is printed on a printer or typewriter

HARDWARE: The physical equipment or devices that constitute the computer and/or peripheral equipment complement

HEURISTIC: A trial-and-error method for solution of a problem

HOLLERITH: A particular type of code or punched card utilizing 12 rows per column and usually 80 columns per card

HOUSEKEEPING: A routine that does not effect the solution of the problem, but is necessary for operation of the computer

HYBRID COMPUTER: A computer using both analog representation and discrete representation of data

IDP: Integrated Data Processing; a form of processing in which data acquisition and data processing are coordinated into a coherent system

INDEX REGISTER: A hardware component that is used to hold a quantity that may be used to modify an address

INFORMATION RETRIEVAL: A method of locating data or information from a collection of records or documents

INPUT JOB STREAM: A sequence of job control statements entering the computer system; the sequence may also include input data

I/O: Input/Output; input or output, or both

INTERFACE: The concept of connecting two different hardware units with different functions

IOCS: Input/Output Control System; a set of routines designed to control the input and output operations required in a user's program

IPL: Initial Program Loader; a procedure that causes the initial part of an operating system or other program to be loaded into main storage

JOB CONTROL STATEMENT: A statement that is used to identify a job and its requirements to the operating system

KEY: One or more characters in a data item that is used to identify the item or control its use

LDX: Long Distance Xerography; a name used by the Xerox Corporation to identify its high-speed facsimile system utilizing terminal equipment and a wide-band data communications channel

LSI: Large-Scale Integration; the accumulation of a large number of circuits on a single chip of semiconductor

MACHINE LANGUAGE: A language that is used directly by a machine

MACRO INSTRUCTION: An instruction in a source language that is equivalent to a specified sequence of machine instructions

MACRO-PROGRAMMING: Programming with macro instructions

MANAGEMENT INFORMATION SYSTEMS: Management performed with the aid of automatic data processing

MICR: Magnetic Ink Character Recognition; automated recognition or printing of characters with magnetic ink

MICRO INSTRUCTION: A basic or elementary machine instruction; or a set of basic commands or pseudo-commands built into the computer and translated by the hardware into machine commands

MICRO-PROGRAMMING: Programming with micro instructions

MICROSECOND: One-millionth of a second

MILLISECOND: One-thousandth of a second

MODEM: A device that modulates and demodulates signals transmitted over communications facilities

MONITOR: A hardware device or software package that can be used to measure either the performance of a computer system or the utilization of specific devices

MULTIPLEXING: The division of a transmission facility into two or more channels

MULTIPROCESSING: The operation of more than one processing unit within a single system

MULTI-PROGRAMMING: A technique for handling numerous routines and programs by overlapping their functions in a single computer

NANOSECOND: One-billionth of a second

OBJECT PROGRAM: A compiled or assembled program that is ready to be loaded into a computer

OCR: Optical Character Recognition; the automatic recognition of printed or written characters on inputs through photoelectric techniques

OFFLINE SYSTEM: A system in which the devices are not under the direction and control of a central processing unit

ONLINE SYSTEM: A system in which the devices are connected directly to the central processing unit

OPERATING SYSTEM: Software that controls the execution of computer programs

OVERFLOW: The generation of a quantity beyond the capacity of a register or location as a result of an arithmetic operation

PARTITION: An area of main storage allocated for one program and the data on which it operates

PATCH: A single instruction or section of coding that may be used to correct or alter a program

PRIORITY: Designated order of importance

QTAM: Queued Telecommunications Access Method

READ-ONLY STORAGE (ROS):   A memory unit that cannot be altered during normal program execution; the unit may contain micro-programs or firmware

RECORD: A collection of fields

REDUNDANCY: A segment or portion of a message that can be eliminated without loss of essential information

REMOTE BATCH PROCESSING: A batch processing system that can be executed from remote terminals

REMOTE TERMINAL COMPUTING: The use of a terminal device connected to a central computer, from a remote location, for online or remote batch processing

RESPONSE TIME: The amount of time that elapses between an inquiry on a terminal and a response at that same terminal

SEGMENTED PROGRAM: A self-contained program held in the auxiliary or secondary storage unit required in the main memory; or a program divided into functional parts for operation or testing

SIGN: A symbol, bit, or indicator that distinguishes positive from negative numbers or values

SIMPLEX CHANNEL: A one-way channel

SNAPSHOT: A dynamic dump of the contents of selected storage locations and registers; the dump occurs at specified points in a machine run

SOFTWARE: A collection of programming language, mainline programs, and utility and library programs used in the solution of a computer problem

SOURCE DOCUMENT: A document from which basic data elements are secured

STATEMENT: An expression or instruction of a computer program

SUBPROGRAM: A part of a larger computer program; this program can be translated into machine language independently of the main program

SUBROUTINE: A series of computer instructions written to perform a given task for a number of different programs

SUPERVISOR: A primary control program in the operating system for altering or interrupting the flow of operation through the CPU

SYMBOL TABLE: A table of labels and their numeric values

SYNTAX: The structure of a statement, expression, or instruction in a programming language

TELECOMMUNICATIONS: The transmission of signals over long distances

TELEPROCESSING: A form of information handling in which a computing system utilizes communications facilities

TIE LINE: A private-line communication channel provided by a communications carrier for linking two or more points

TRACE: A routine written to record the events that result from the step-by-step execution of a program

USER: Anyone utilizing the services of a computing system

UTILITY ROUTINE: A standardized routine developed to assist in the operation of a computer

VIRTUAL MEMORY: A technique that permits the user to utilize secondary storage as an extension of core memory; this gives the user the appearance of a large core memory

VOLATILE DISPLAY: A nonpermanent image appearing on the screen of a visual display device

Bibliography

Abraham, Alfred B. "Coding a Customer's Information System for EDP Use," *The New York Certified Public Accountant*, October 1969, pp. 762-763, 766-769.

Albers, Henry H. *Organized Executive Action*. New York: John Wiley & Sons, Inc., 1961.

Allen, Brandt. "Danger Ahead! Safeguard Your Computer," *Harvard Business Review*, November-December 1968, pp. 97-101.

Amato, Vincent V. "Computer Feasibility Studies: The Do-It-Yourself Approach," *Management Review*, February 1970, pp. 2-9.

Anshen, Melvin. "The Manager and the Black Box," *Harvard Business Review*, November-December 1960, pp. 85-92.

Avots, Ivars. "The Management Side of PERT," *California Management Review*, Winter 1962, pp. 16-27.

Barnett, John H. "Information System Danger Signals," *Management Services*, January-February 1971, pp. 27-30.

Batten, J. D. *Tough Minded Management*. New York: American Management Association, 1963.

Becker, R. T. "Executives Use Computer to Develop EDP Skills," *Administrative Management*, February 1971, pp. 28-29.

Beehler, Paul J. "EDP: Stimulating Systematic Corporate Planning," *Journal of Systems Management*, November 1969, pp. 26-31.

Bellin, Eugene. "Facilities Management, an Approach to Successful Data Processing Management," *Journal of Systems Management*, January 1971, pp. 18-20.

Bellotto, Sam, Jr. "Documentation: EDP's Neglected Necessity," *Administrative Management*, January, 1971, pp. 24-26.

Biesser, James. "Management by Objectives or Appraisal," *Data Management*, April 1970, pp. 24-25.

Bigelow, Robert P. "Contract Caveats," *Datamation*, September 15, 1970, pp. 41-44.

Bittel, Lester R. *What Every Supervisor Should Know*. New York: McGraw-Hill Book Company, 1959.

Bodenstab, Charles J. "10 Tips for Successful Implementation of Computer Systems," *Financial Executive*, November 1970, pp. 64-66, 68, 70.

Boulden, James B., and Elwood S. Buffa. "Corporate Models: On-Line, Real-Time Systems," *Harvard Business Review*, July-August 1970, pp. 65-83.

Brandon, Dick H. *Management Standards for Data Processing*. Princeton, N.J.: D. Van Nostrand Company, Inc., 1963.

Bride, Edward J. "DP Center 'Invaded,' " *Computerworld*, July 15, 1970, pp. 1, 4.

Bromberg, Howard. "Software Buying," *Datamation*, September 15, 1970, pp. 35-40.

Brown, David S. *Delegating and Sharing Work*. Washington, D.C.: Leadership Resources, Inc., 1966.

Burck, Gilbert. *The Computer Age and Its Potential for Management*. New York: Harper & Row, Publishers, 1965.

Burck, Gilbert, *et al. The Computer Age*. New York: Harper & Row, Publishers, 1965.

Bursk, Edward C., and John F. Chapman (eds.). *New Decision-Making Tools for Managers*. Cambridge, Mass.: Harvard University Press, 1963.

Carr, Peter F. "Poor Security Leaves DP Facilities Ripe for Sabotage," *Computerworld*, June 17, 1970, pp. 1, 4.

Cassimus, Perry. "Design Considerations for Real/Time Systems," *Journal of Systems Management*, December 1969, pp. 23-28.

Chapin, Ned. "Flow Chart Packages," *Data Management*, October 1970, pp. 16-17.

―――. "Program Documentation―The Valuable Burden," *Software Age*, May 1968, pp. 24-30.

―――. "Running Time Analysis for Flow Charters," *Software Age*, February/March 1971, pp. 13-15, 30.

Charles, P. L. *The Management of Computer Programming Projects*. New York: American Management Association, 1967.

Chesebrough, Wilfred C. "Decision Tables as a Systems Technique," *Honeywell Computer Journal*, Fall 1970, pp. 18-25.

Cleff, Samuel H., and Robert M. Hecht. "Computer Man-Job Match," *The Personnel Administrator*, September-October 1970, pp. 3-4, 7-8, 11-12.

Chu, Albert L. C. "Computer Security: Achilles Heel," *Business Automation*, February 1971, pp. 32-38.

Cleland, David I. "Why Project Management?" *Business Horizons*, Winter 1964, pp. 81-88.

Clifton, Harold D. *Systems Analysis for Business Data Processing*. Princeton, N.J.: Auerbach Publishers, Inc., 1970.

Connally, Gerald E. "Personnel Administration and the Computer," *Personnel Journal*, August 1969, pp. 605-611, 642.

Connolly, James J. "Case Study of a Computer Audit Program," *The Price Waterhouse Review*, Summer 1966, pp. 34-45.

Corsiglia, Jack. "Matching Computers to the Job—First Step Towards Selection," *Data Processing Magazine*, December 1970, pp. 23-27.

Coughlan, Joseph D., and William K. Strand. "Decision-Making and Fallibility," *The Price Waterhouse Review*, Summer 1969, pp. 54-60.

Davidson, Timothy A. "Design Guidelines to Minimize Computer Input Errors," *The Office*, November 1969, pp. 55-58.

Davis, Earl F., and James L. Blose. "Tax Treatment of Software Costs," *Business Automation*, February 1971, pp. 42-45.

Dean, Neal J., and James W. Taylor. "Managing to Manage the Computer," *Harvard Business Review*, September-October 1966, pp. 98-100.

"Developments in System Analyst Training," *EDP Analyzer*, September 1970, pp. 1-14.

DeVitt, Robert G. "Cut Expenses by Taking Care of Your Tape," *Computer Decisions*, October 1970, pp. 42-45.

Diebold, John. "Bad Decisions on Computer Use," *Harvard Business Review*, January-February 1969, pp. 14-16, 27-28, 176.

Dippl, Gene, and William C. House. *Information Systems*. Glenview, Ill.: Scott, Foresman, & Company, 1969.

Doney, Lloyd D., and Walter H. Houghton. "Effective Use of Consultants in Operational Areas," *Data Management*, January 1971, pp. 29-31.

Dorn, Philip H. "Standards Now!" *Journal of Systems Management*, October 1969, pp. 11-13.

Dratler, Louise H. "Facilities Management—Boon or Bane?" *Management Services*, September-October 1970, pp. 41-45.

Drucker, Peter F. *The Practice of Management*. New York: Harper and Brothers, Publishers, 1954.

Ehlers, Marvin W. "Management's Blunder Buffer," *Business Automation*, March 1966, pp. 38-41.

Enger, N. L. *Putting MIS to Work*. New York: American Management Association, 1969.

Estes, Neil. "Step-by-Step Costing of Information Systems," *Journal of Systems Management*, October 1969, pp. 20-28.

Ettorre, Anthony F. "Meaningful EDP Appraisal," *The Personnel Administrator*, January-February 1971, pp. 40-41.

Evans, Marshall K., and Lou R. Hague. "Master Plan for Information Systems," *Harvard Business Review*, January-February 1962, pp. 92-103.

Ewell, James M. "The Total Systems Concept and How to Organize for It," *Computers and Automation*, September 1961, pp. 9-13.

"Facilities Management: Cure-All for DP Headaches?" *Business Automation*, March 1971, pp. 26-31, 34.

Farmer, Jerome. "Auditing and The Computer—A Suggested Program," *Journal of Accountancy*, July 1970, pp. 53-56.

Federoff, Andrea M. "Minicomputers Are Used for This," *Computer Decisions*, August 1970, pp. 17-22.

Fisch, Gerald G. "Line-Staff Is Obsolete," *Harvard Business Review*, September-October 1961, pp. 67-79.

Flannagan, John C., and Robert Miller. *Performance Record Handbook for Supervisors*. Chicago: Science Research Associates, Inc., 1955.

Flippo, Edwin B. *Principles of Personnel Management*. New York: McGraw-Hill Book Company, 1961.

Frazier, Dwight M. "Systems Test," *Computers and Automation*, September 1970, pp. 22-24.

Fried, Louis. "Shopping for Commercial Software," *Data Processing Magazine*, August 1970, pp. 37-39.

Gaddis, Paul O. "The Project Manager," *Harvard Business Review*, May-June 1959, pp. 89-97.

Gallagher, James D. *Management Information Systems and the Computer*. New York: American Management Association, 1961.

Giguere, M. A. "Finding Forms Analysts," *Business Automation*, March 1, 1971, pp. 52.

Goetz, Billy E. *Management Planning and Control*. New York: McGraw-Hill Book Company, 1949.

Golgart, Carl W. "Changing Times in Management," *Advanced Management Journal*, January 1970, pp. 33-38.

Gottfried, Ira S. "Motivation of Data Processors—Why and How," *Data Management*, September 1970, pp. 104-106.

Gray, Max, and Herbert B. Lassiter. "Project Control for Data Processing," *Datamation*, February 1968, pp. 33-38.

Hallinan, Arthur J., and Gilbert A. Mehling. "Internal Audit of a Computer Disaster Plan," *The Internal Auditor*, November-December 1970, pp. 12-16.

Hare, VanCourt, Jr. *Systems Analysis: A Diagnostic Approach*. New York: Harcourt, Brace & World, Inc., 1967.

Harrison, William L. "Program Testing," *Data Management*, December 1969, pp. 30-33.

Head, Robert V. *Real-Time Business Systems.* New York: Holt, Rinehart & Winston, Inc., 1965.

Heeschen, Paul E. "Auditing Data Processing Administratives—Operational Auditing Applied to EDP," *The Internal Auditor,* November-December, 1970, pp. 55-62.

Hirsch, Rudolph E. "The Value of Information," *The Price Waterhouse Review,* Spring 1968, pp. 22-27.

Hollinger, C. Robert. "Managing the Computer for Competitive Advantage," *Business Horizons,* December 1970, pp. 17-28.

Horwitz, Geoffrey B. "EDP Auditing—The Coming of Age," *Journal of Accountancy,* August 1970, pp. 48-56.

Howes, Paul R. "EDP Security: Is Your Guard Up?" *The Price Waterhouse Review,* Spring 1971, pp. 46-53.

Jasinski, Frank J. "Adapting Organization to New Technology," *Harvard Business Review,* January-February 1959, pp. 79-86.

Johansen, H., and A. B. Robertson. *Management Glossary.* Edited by E. F. L. Brech. New York: American Elsevier Publishing Co., Inc., 1968.

John, Richard C., and Thomas J. Nissen. "Evaluating Internal Control in EDP Audits," *Journal of Accountancy,* February 1970, pp. 31-38.

Johnson, Richard A., Fremont E. Kast, and James E. Rosenzweig. *The Theory and Management of Systems.* 2d edition. New York: McGraw-Hill Book Company, 1967.

Joslin, Edward O. "Techniques of Selecting EDP Equipment," *Data Management,* February 1970, pp. 28-30.

Kapur, Gopal K. "Sharpen Your EDP Staff Through In-House Training," *Computer Decisions,* March 1971, pp. 36-37.

Karp, William. "Management in the Computer Age," *Data Management,* November 1970, pp. 23-25.

Karush, Arnold D. "Evaluating Timesharing Systems Using the Benchmark Method," *Data Processing Magazine,* May 1970, pp. 42-44.

Kaufman, Felix. "Data Systems that Cross Company Boundaries," *Harvard Business Review,* January-February 1966, pp. 141-155.

———. *Electronic Data Processing and Auditing.* New York: The Ronald Press Company, 1961.

Keller, Arnold E. "A Look at the Programming Environment," *Business Automation,* December 1969, pp. 40-45.

Kelly, Joseph F. *Computerized Management Information Systems.* New York: The Macmillan Company, 1970.

Kelly, William F. *Management Through Systems and Procedures.* New York: John Wiley & Sons, Inc., 1969.

Kibbee, Joel M., Clifford J. Craft, and Burt Nanus. *Management Games.* New York: Reinhold Publishing Corporation, 1962.

Klasson, Charles R., and Kenneth W. Olm. "Managerial Implications of Integrated Business Operations," *California Management Review*, Fall 1965, pp. 21-31.

Knight, J. B. "A Practical Approach to the Systems Audit," *Journal of Systems Management*, November 1970, pp. 17-18.

Kolence, Kenneth W. "A Software View of Measurement Tools," *Datamation*, January 1, 1971, pp. 32-38.

Kovalcik, Eugene J. "Understanding Systems Engineering," *Journal of Systems Management*, September 1970, pp. 15-21.

Laden, H. N., and T. R. Gildersleeve. *System Design for Computer Applications*. New York: John Wiley & Sons, Inc., 1963.

Laska, Richard M. "Should a Consultant Be Your Guide Through EDP Country?," *Computer Decisions*, January 1971, pp. 26-31.

Leavitt, Harold J. *Managerial Psychology*. Chicago: University of Chicago Press, 1964.

Leufert, Werner W. "Project Management Games," *Datamation*, September 15, 1970, pp. 24-34.

Lewis, Ralph H. "Operations Research Without Tears," *The Arthur Young Journal*, Winter-Spring 1970, pp. 3-13.

Likert, Renis. *New Patterns of Management*. New York: McGraw-Hill Book Company, 1961.

Lindsay, William F. "Software and the General Manager," *Management Services*, July-August 1970, pp. 48-58.

Lipsett, Laurance, Frank P. Rodgers, and Harold M. Kentner. *Personnel Selection and Recruitment*. Boston: Allyn & Bacon, Inc., 1964.

"Management & the Computer," Wall Street Journal Study, 1969.

"Managing the Programming Effort," *EDP Analyzer*, June 1968.

"Managing the Systems Effort," *EDP Analyzer*, July 1968.

Manne, Alan S. *Economic Analysis for Business Decisions*. New York: McGraw-Hill Book Company, 1961.

Martino, R. L. *Project Management and Control*. Vols. 1-3. New York: American Management Association, 1964.

————. "A Total Management System," *Data Processing for Management*, April 1963, pp. 31-37.

Maynard, Jeff. "Objectives of Program Design," *Software Age*, August-September 1970, pp. 13-15.

McFarland, Dalton E. *Management: Principles and Practices*. New York: The Macmillan Company, 1964.

McInnis, John W. "An Approach to the Control of Programming Projects," *Computer Services*, March-April 1970, pp. 46-50.

McKinsey & Company, Inc. *Unlocking the Computer's Profit Potential*. 1968.

McNairn, William N. "Objectives," *The Price Waterhouse Review*, Spring 1970, pp. 34-41.

Meehan, Joseph. "The Computer Finks," *Forum 70*, February 1970, pp. 27-30.

Melitz, Peter W. "Impact of Electronic Data Processing on Managers," *Advanced Management*, April 1961, pp. 4-6.

Menkhaus, Edward J. "EDP: What's It Worth?" *Business Automation*, November 1969, pp. 48-54.

Miller, Robert W. "How to Plan and Control with PERT," *Harvard Business Review*, March-April 1962, pp. 93-104.

Moore, Michael R. "EDP AUDITS: A Systems Approach," *The Arthur Young Journal*, Winter 1968, pp. 5-15.

Morse, Robert V. "Control Systems for Better Project Management," *Computer Decisions*, July 1971, pp. 28-31.

Murdick, Robert G., and Joel E. Ross: "Education for Systems: III, Management-Information Systems: Training for Businessmen," *Journal of Systems Management*, October 1969, pp. 36-39.

————. *Information Systems for Modern Management*. Englewood Cliffs, N.J.: Prentice-Hall, Inc., 1971.

National Bureau of Standards. "Hazardous Noise Levels in Computer Labs," *NBS Technical News Bulletin*, September 1970, p. 204.

Nelson, E. A. *Management Handbook for the Estimation of Computer Programming Costs*. Commerce Clearinghouse, Springfield, Va., 1967.

Neuschel, Richard F. *Management by System*. New York: McGraw-Hill Book Company, 1960.

Newman, Maurice S. "Imaginative Use of the Computer," *Financial Executive*, September 1970, pp. 28-35.

Newman, William H., and Charles E. Summer, Jr. *The Process of Management*, Englewood Cliffs, N.J.: Prentice-Hall, Inc., 1961.

Nixon, John W. "Must Data Processing Be Mismanaged," *Data Management*, November 1970, pp. 33-37.

"Now It's More of a Science," *Business Week*, December 28, 1963, pp. 44, 46, 51.

Optner, Stanford L. *Systems Analysis for Business and Industrial Problem Solving*. Englewood Cliffs, N.J.: Prentice-Hall, Inc., 1965.

"Overall Guidance of Data Processing," *EDP Analyzer*, August 1968.

Parets, Lawrence. "How to Select a Data Processing Consultant," *Financial Executive*, September 1970, pp. 36-38, 40, 42.

Parnell, Douglass M., Jr. "EDP Facilities Management: Abdication or Salvation?" *Computers and Automation*, October 1970, pp. 23-27.

Paul, Robert. "What to Expect from a Project Leader," *Computers and Data Processing*, February 1964, pp. 17-20.

Perham, John. "The Computer: A Target," *Dun's Review*, January 1971, pp. 34-36.

Pfiffner, John M., and Frank P. Sherwood. *Administrative Organization*. Englewood Cliffs, N.J.: Prentice-Hall, Inc., 1964.

"Planning for Your New Computer," *Computer Decisions,* December 1970, pp. 10–13.

Porter, W. Thomas, Jr. *Auditing Electronic Systems.* Belmont, Calif.: Wadsworth Publishing Co., Inc., 1966.

"Proprietary Software Is Beginning to Grow Up," *Computer Decisions,* February 1971, pp. 30–33.

Redfield, Charles E. *Communication in Management.* Chicago: University of Chicago Press, 1958.

Rosen, Saul (ed.). *Programming Systems and Languages.* New York: McGraw-Hill Book Company, 1967.

Roy, Herbert J. H. "Using Computer-Based Control Systems for Decision-Making," *Advanced Management Journal,* January 1971, pp. 57–62.

Sampson, Robert C. *Managing the Managers.* New York: McGraw-Hill Book Company, 1965.

Schoderbek, Peter P., and James D. Babcock. "At Last—Management More Active in EDP," *Business Horizons,* December 1969, pp. 53–58.

Schultz, George P., and Thomas L. Whisler (eds.). *Management Organization and the Computer.* Glencoe, Ill.: The Free Press, 1960.

Schwab, Bernhard. "The Economics of Sharing Computers," *Harvard Business Review,* September–October 1968, pp. 61–70.

Scotese, Peter G. "What Top Management Expects of EDP, and Vice Versa," *Business Automation,* February 1971, pp. 48–53.

Scott, William G. *Human Relations in Management.* Homewood, Ill.: Richard D. Irwin, Inc., 1962.

Sharpe, William F. *The Economics of Computers.* New York: Columbia University Press, 1969.

Simpson, Sanford C. "An Automated Data Processing Documentation Control System," *Journal of Systems Management,* November 1970, pp. 12–16.

"Skills Inventory Pool Produces 'Man for the Job,'" *Administrative Management,* April 1970, pp. 58–60.

Smith, Paul T. *Computers, Systems, and Profits.* New York: American Management Association, 1969.

Spett, Milton C. "Standards for Evaluating Data Processing Management," *Datamation,* December 1969, pp. 171, 174–178.

Statland, Norman. "The Economics of Computer Replacement," *Systems Management,* March 1963, pp. 11–13, 59.

Stearns, M. I. "Education and Practice," *The Internal Auditor,* January–February 1970, pp. 68–74.

Stewart, John M. "Making Project Management Work," *Business Horizons,* Fall 1965, pp. 54–68.

Strasser, Charles. "What Management Can Do for EDP," *Advanced Management Journal,* January 1970, pp. 39–43.

Stuart, Senter. "Optimization—It *Can* Pay Off," *Business Automation*, March 1966, pp. 46–49.

Szweda, Ralph A. "An Approach to EDP Documentation," *The Credit Union Executive*, Spring 1970, pp. 11–14.

———. "Audit Controls for Data Processing Operations," *The Credit Union Executive*, Fall 1966, pp. 2–7.

———. "Choosing the Right Computer for Your Credit Union," *The Credit Union Executive*, Fall 1967, pp. 17–25.

———. "Documenting the EDP System," *The Credit Union Executive*, Summer 1970, pp. 18–32.

———. "Studying Proposals from Computer Vendors," *The Credit Union Executive*, Winter 1967, pp. 19–29.

Tagen, Warren B. "Educating the Internal Auditor in EDP," *The Internal Auditor*, January–February 1970, pp. 48–61.

Taylor, James W., and Neal J. Dean. "Managing to Manage the Computer," *Harvard Business Review*, September–October 1966.

"The Configurator: Today and Tomorrow," *Computer Decisions*, February 1971, pp. 38–43.

"The Corporate Data File," *EDP Analyzer*, November 1969.

This, Leslie. *Communicating Within the Organization*. Washington, D.C.: Leadership Resources, Inc., 1966.

Thompson, John M. "Why Is Everyone Leaving?" Data Management, November 1969, pp. 25–27.

Thorne, Jack F. "Internal Control of Real-Time Systems," *Data Management*, January 1971, pp. 34–37.

Tilles, Seymour. "The Manager's Job—A Systems Approach," *Harvard Business Review*, January–February 1963, pp. 73–81.

Toan, Arthur B., Jr. "Management Information Systems," *The Price Waterhouse Review*, Spring 1970, pp. 42–53.

Totaro, J. Burt. "How to Get Your Money's Worth with Consultants," *Data Processing Magazine*, April 1970, pp. 18–21, 24.

Van Tassel, Dennie. "Information Security in a Computer Environment," *Computers and Automation*, July 1969, pp. 24–28.

Warner, C. Dudley. "Monitoring: A Key to Cost Efficiency," *Datamation*, January 1971, pp. 40–49.

Warren, Joseph B. "People Problems," *Business Automation*, October 1970, pp. 46–51.

Wasserman, Joseph J. "Plugging the Leaks in Computer Security," *Harvard Business Review*, September–October 1969, pp. 119–129.

Webb, Richard. *"Audassist," The Journal of Accountancy*, November 1970, pp. 53–58.

Weihrich, W. Fred. "Computer Selection," *Data Management*, February 1970, pp. 31–33.

Weindling, Ralph. *A Management Guide to Computer Feasibility.* Detroit: American Data Processing, Inc., 1962.

Welke, Larry A. "How to Buy Proprietary Software," *Computer Decisions,* February 1971, pp. 14-16.

Wessel, Milton R. "Computer Services and the Law," *Business Automation,* November 1970, pp. 48-50.

Whisler, F. L., and S. F. Harper (eds.). *Performance Appraisal Research and Practice.* New York: Holt, Rinehart & Winston, Inc., 1962.

Wolaver, John. "Information Retrieval: Three Alternatives," *Honeywell Computer Journal,* Fall 1970, pp. 13-17.

Vergin, Roger C., and Andrew J. Grimes. "Management Myths and EDP," *California Management Review,* Fall 1964, pp. 59-70.

Young, Douglas K. "Profit Potential in Small and Growing Businesses," *The Price Waterhouse Review,* Summer 1969, pp. 23-29.

Young, Stanley. *Management: A Systems Analysis.* Glenview, Ill.: Scott, Foresman & Company, 1966.

Index